Fundamentals of Criminal Law

Fundamentals of Criminal Law

Responsibility, Culpability, and Wrongdoing

A P SIMESTER

OXFORD
UNIVERSITY PRESS

OXFORD
UNIVERSITY PRESS

Great Clarendon Street, Oxford, OX2 6DP,
United Kingdom

Oxford University Press is a department of the University of Oxford.
It furthers the University's objective of excellence in research, scholarship,
and education by publishing worldwide. Oxford is a registered trade mark of
Oxford University Press in the UK and in certain other countries

First Edition published in 2021

Impression: 3

Published in the United States of America by Oxford University Press
198 Madison Avenue, New York, NY 10016, United States of America

British Library Cataloguing in Publication Data

Data available

Library of Congress Control Number: 2020942240

ISBN 978–0–19–885314–5

DOI: 10.1093/oso/9780198853145.001.0001

Printed and bound in the UK by
TJ Books Limited

Preface

It's a bit like getting married. The day itself goes smoothly. Or not. But how it goes is not a function of the moment. It is a function of the weeks, the months, even the years that went before. It is a function of what went into it.

When I stood up that evening, we were in Singapore. It was a hot August night, some fourteen years ago now. Bob Sullivan and Tony Smith were there, two of my oldest friends. I had written the speech earlier that evening. By then, though, that was the only thing left undone. The details had been sweated. I told a story, and I said thank you.

The story was about Sir Francis Drake. Had Drake not seen off the Spanish Armada, I might have been making that speech in Spanish. My main point, however, was one that had been told to me by James Crawford. When we think of the raid at Cádiz, we think of Drake making orders to a helmsman, someone holding the wheel and steering the *Elizabeth Bonaventure* through the thin and thick of cannon fire. Yet there was no helm. There was a tiller, below decks. Men pulled the tiller in response to shouted commands from above. But in the noise, the smoke, the fire, the confusion, things could go awry. Perhaps what happened was not ordered at all. Instead of hither, the boat might go thither. At best, it was partially disciplined chaos.

Life can be like that. I didn't foresee the course that led to Singapore in 2006. Neither did I have any idea that I would become an academic criminal lawyer. *Some* of the blame for that lies with Jim Evans, my first teacher at Auckland. Jim believed in ideas, and he encouraged me to do so too. At that time, Auckland had no jurisprudence class, but in our second year Jim wrote and delivered *two* single-semester modules, on Legal Theory and Law and Action. In his office. For just three students (Diane Stephenson, Paul Key, now QC, and me). *And for no teaching credit*. Nobody would do that now. But it made all the difference. It set me, and I think Paul, on the path to Oxbridge doctorates.

At which point Joseph Raz took over. 'You see that sentence?' Yes, Joseph. 'The next sentence doesn't follow.' Ah. It turns out that thinking is a science as well as an art. So far as I can tell, the range and sheer quality of Joseph's supervision record is without parallel in English-speaking Law Faculties. Joseph had never worked in the areas I was writing on, but that made no difference. He could interrogate, terrify, and inspire just by the rigour of his intellect.

Arguments were good or bad, whatever the area. Joseph's stamp is upon all his students. We cannot be Joseph, but we can aspire to make him proud.

And so, just as it was in 2006, now is the time to say thank you. Not only to Jim and Joseph, but to all the friends who have contributed to this book, directly and indirectly. Across the years, there are too many to name here. While preparing the manuscript, I was blessed with comments on various individual chapters from Alexander Greenberg, Alon Harel, Doug Husak, Henry Mares, Massimo Renzo, Ian Simester, John Stanton-Ife, and Bob Sullivan. Early drafts of the entire book were read by John Child, James Edwards, Miri Gur-Arye, Andrew Halpin, and Findlay Stark. James was especially helpful in making suggestions regarding the book's structure and, as I was closing in on the final manuscript, Andrew was a constantly available last-minute consultant and point of reference. I was also very fortunate to benefit from a work-in-progress conference organized at King's by Massimo, where commentaries were given on selected chapters by Antje du Bois-Pedain, Jeremy Horder, Niki Lacey, Grant Lamond, and Matt Matravers. No academic works in a vacuum. It has been a privilege to share in a tradition of great legal thinkers, prior and current. Like that day in 2006, the outcome is shaped by what went before. It is the product not of one person but of all of us.

To one of those thinkers, this is also a chance to say goodbye. I first met John Gardner in 1990, when we were both DPhil students. We made a friendship founded partly in criminal law, but especially in the mutual sympathy that arose naturally between Raztafarians. Walking around Christ Church Meadow, we would exchange Joseph stories. Whether it was some fundamental insight into analytical method that had been dropped into a conversation, or Joseph's acting out a hypothetical in his rooms—clambering over a chair or the couch, usually in order to shoot someone—there was always something to fuel his students' conversations. Not that John needed fuel. He was already faster than anyone else in a room. Not always right, of course (who could be that?), but most certainly quicker. John saw directions, and made connections, that galvanized the rest of us. Yet that was only part of it. Most of all, I remember how much he was alive.

Like Drake's, my voyages have not been made alone. The history of these chapters is bound up with the history of my family. Ultimately, these are the people to whom this book belongs. To Winnie and Michelle, to Ian, Caitlin, and Elliot: this book is of, and because of, you all.

A P S
National Day, 2020

Acknowledgements

In writing this book, I have drawn directly or indirectly from a number of existing articles and book chapters, some of which were co-authored. I am grateful both to my co-authors and to the many colleagues and friends who commented on drafts of those papers. They include:

'A Disintegrated Theory of Culpability' in D Baker and J Horder (eds), *The Sanctity of Life and the Criminal Law: The Legacy of Glanville Williams* (CUP 2013) 178.

'Accessory Liability and Common Unlawful Purposes' (2017) 133 LQR 73.

'Agency' (1996) 15 Law and Phil 159.

'Can Negligence be Culpable?' in J Horder (ed), *Oxford Essays in Jurisprudence* (4th Series, OUP 2000) 85.

'Causation in (Criminal) Law' (2017) 133 LQR 416.

'Crime, Blameworthiness, and Outcomes' (2019) 39 OJLS 50 (J R Edwards and A P Simester).

'Duress, Necessity: How Many Defences?' (2005) 16 King's College LJ 121 (W Chan and A P Simester).

'Four Functions of Mens Rea' (2011) 70 CLJ 381 (W Chan and A P Simester).

'Is Strict Liability Always Wrong?' in A P Simester (ed), *Appraising Strict Liability* (OUP 2005) 21.

'Mistakes in Defence' (1992) 12 OJLS 295.

'Moral Certainty, and the Boundaries of Intention' (1996) 16 OJLS 445.

'Necessity, Torture and the Rule of Law' in V Ramraj (ed), *Emergencies and the Limits of Legality* (CUP 2008) 289.

'On Justifications and Excuses' in L Zedner and J Roberts (eds), *Principles and Values in Criminal Law and Criminal Justice: Essays in Honour of Andrew Ashworth* (OUP 2012) 95.

'On the So-called Requirement for Voluntary Action' (1998) 1 Buffalo Crim LR 403.

'Paradigm Intention' (1992) 11 Law and Phil 235.

'The Mental Element in Complicity' (2006) 122 LQR 578.
'Why Distinguish Intention from Foresight?' in A P Simester and A T H Smith (eds), *Harm and Culpability* (OUP 1996) 71.
'Why Omissions are Special' (1995) 1 Legal Theory 311.
'Wrongs and Reasons' (2009) 72 MLR 648.

Table of Contents

Table of Cases

EUROPEAN COURT OF HUMAN RIGHTS

NATIONAL COURTS

Australia

Canada

Germany

Hong Kong

India

Malaysia

New Zealand

Singapore

United Kingdom

United States

List of Abbreviations

The following abbreviations for oft-cited books and articles are used in the text and footnotes:

Appraising Strict Liability	A P Simester (ed), *Appraising Strict Liability* (OUP 2005).
Bennett, *Tanner*	J Bennett, 'Morality and Consequences' in S McMurrin (ed), *The Tanner Lectures on Human Values* (University of Utah Press 1980) 45.
Bennett, *The Act Itself*	J Bennett, *The Act Itself* (Clarendon 1995).
Crimes, Harms, and Wrongs	A P Simester and A von Hirsch, *Crimes, Harm, and Wrongs: On the Principles of Criminalisation* (Hart 2011).
Davidson, *EAE*	D Davidson, *Essays on Actions and Events* (OUP 1980).
Duff, *IACL*	R A Duff, *Intention, Agency and Practical Reason* (Basil Blackwell 1990).
Fletcher, *Rethinking*	G Fletcher, *Rethinking Criminal Law* (Brown 1978).
Frankfurt, *Importance*	H G Frankfurt, *The Importance of what We Care about* (CUP 1988).
Gardner, *Offences and Defences*	J Gardner, *Offences and Defences: Selected Essays in the Philosophy of Criminal Law* (OUP 2007).
Harm and Culpability	A P Simester and A T H Smith (eds.), *Harm and Culpability* (OUP 1996).
Hart, *Punishment and Responsibility*	H L A Hart, *Punishment and Responsibility* (OUP 1968).
Hart and Honoré	H L A Hart and A M Honoré, *Causation in the Law* (2nd edn, OUP 1985).
Mackie, *Ethics*	J L Mackie, *Ethics: Inventing Right and Wrong* (Penguin 1977).

Moore, *Act and Crime*	M S Moore, *Act and Crime: The Theory of Action and its Implications for Criminal Law* (Clarendon 1993).
Moore, *Causation and Responsibility*	M S Moore, *Causation and Responsibility: An Essay in Law, Morals, and Metaphysics* (OUP 2009).
Moore, *Placing Blame*	M S Moore, *Placing Blame: A Theory of the Criminal Law* (Clarendon 1997).
Nagel, *Mortal Questions*	T Nagel, *Mortal Questions* (CUP 1979).
Raz, *Practical Reason and Norms*	J Raz, *Practical Reason and Norms* (2nd edn, OUP 1990).
Simester and Sullivan	A P Simester et al, *Simester and Sullivan's Criminal Law: Theory and Doctrine* (7th edn, Hart 2019). Williams, *CLGP* G Williams, *Criminal Law: The General Part* (2nd edn, Stevens 1961).
Williams, *TBCL*	G Williams, *Textbook of Criminal Law* (2nd edn, Stevens 1983).

The following abbreviations for standard textbooks and statutory materials are used in the text and footnotes.

Case Reports

AC	Appeal Cases
All ER	All England Law Reports
C & P	Carrington and Payne's Reports
CA	Court of Appeal
CJ	Chief Justice
CLR	Commonwealth Law Reports
Cox CC	Cox's Criminal Cases
Cr App R	Criminal Appeal Reports
Crim	Criminal
Crim LR	Criminal Law Reports
CSC	Supreme Court of Canada
DLR	Dominion Law Reports
DPP	Director of Public Prosecutions
EHRR	European Human Rights Reports
ER	English Reports

EWCA	Court of Appeal of England & Wales
HC	High Court
HCA	High Court of Australia
HCJAC	High Court of Justiciary, Appeal Court
HL	House of Lords
HMSO	Her Majesty's Stationery Office
KB	King's Bench
Ky	Kentucky
LTR	Law Times Reports
MLJ	Malaysian Law Journal
Mood & R	Moody & Robinson reports
MR	Master of the Rolls
NI	Northern Ireland
NZ	New Zealand
PC	Privy Council
QB	Queen's Bench
QBD	Queen's Bench Division
R	Reports
RTR	Road Traffic Reports
SASR	South Australian State Reports
SC	Supreme Court
SGCA	Singapore Court of Appeal
TLR	Times Law Reports
UKHL	United Kingdom House of Lourds
UKSC	United Kingdom Supreme Court
US	United States
WLR	Weekly Law Reports

Books, Journals, and Publishers

Am Crim LR	American Criminal Law Review
Am Phil Q	American Philosophical Quarterly
CLJ	Cambridge Law Journal
Crim	Criminal
CUP	Cambridge University Press
J	Journal
J App Phil	Journal of Applied Philosophy
L	Law or Legal
LJ	Law Journal
LQR	Law Quarterly Review
LR	Law Review
MLR	Modern Law Review
OJLS	Oxford Journal of Legal Studies

OUP	Oxford University Press
Ox Rev	Oxford Review
Phil	Philosophy, Philosophical
Proc Arist Soc	Proceedings of the Aristotelian Society
Psych	Psychology
Soc	Social
UP	University Press

PART I
GROUNDWORK

1

Crime, Responsibility, Culpability, and Wrongdoing

The criminal law is a multi-function tool. Among other things, it operates to prevent certain kinds of wrongs, and to punish them when they occur. Those functions are compatible.[1] But they are often thought to be in tension. Understandably, many writers seek to explain the criminal law in terms of a single, dominant function. So, for example, it may be claimed that *the* purpose, or at least the primary purpose, of enacting criminal laws is to grease the wheels of retributive justice.[2] On this account, the (primary) reason for criminalizing actions is not to deter those actions. Rather, it is to legitimate their punishment by the state. Enacting offences remains important: but it is important for rule of law reasons, including the need to give people advance notice that they may be punished by the state when they do wrong. We should criminalize, one might say, in order to comply with legality constraints. Thus its role is subsidiary.

Reductive visions of this kind are, I think, too narrow. From a retributive perspective, a society in which nobody violated its laws would be lacking a successful criminal law, since nobody would have been punished. Admittedly, its criminal law would not have miscarried, in as much as nobody failed to receive their just deserts either. But the picture that results is artificial. Gratuitously so. It is gratuitous because there is no reason why the criminal legal system must have one exclusive or even primary function.[3] The *ex ante* role of

[1] See J R Edwards and A P Simester, 'Prevention with a Moral Voice' in A P Simester, A du Bois-Pedain, and U Neumann (eds), *Liberal Criminal Theory: Essays for Andreas von Hirsch* (Hart 2014) 43.

[2] Moore, *Placing Blame*, 186–87. Compare D N Husak, *Overcriminalization: The Limits of the Criminal Law* (OUP 2008) ch 1, suggesting that excessive criminalization is wrong because it generates too much punishment. Conversely, it may be claimed that *the* purpose is to prevent wrongdoing: see, e.g., Hart, *Punishment and Responsibility*, 35ff. Although the point is not important here, Moore claims exclusivity as well as primacy (*Placing Blame*, 78–79): 'Of the possible functions for criminal law, only the achievement of retributive justice is its actual function.'

[3] A similar worry arises for Antony Duff's suggestion that the primary purpose of the criminal law, and the main reason for enacting crimes, is in order to be able *to put people on trial* and thereby call them to account for their alleged wrongs: 'Relational Reasons and the Criminal Law' in L Green and B Leiter (eds), *Oxford Studies in Philosophy of Law: Volume 2* (OUP 2013) 175, 196: 'the substantive dimension of the criminal law must be understood and rationalized in terms of the procedural dimension that it exists to serve.' On that view, if there are no allegations of wrongdoing, the system has not fulfilled its purpose. Duff is himself hostile to 'grand' unifying theories (see 'Theorizing Criminal Law: a

Fundamentals of Criminal Law. A P Simester, Oxford University Press (2021). © A P Simester.
DOI: 10.1093/oso/9780198853145.003.0001

criminalization need not be subordinated to the criminal law's *ex post* role of punishing miscreants. The preventive aims of criminalization can share the stage with the retributive aims of sentencing.[4] Prevention can be done with a moral voice.

There is nothing wrong with conceiving of the criminal law in terms of punishment. Up to a point. The error is to move from thinking that because it is a punishing institution, that's all it is. The error, in other words, is to fetishize just one function of the criminal law. The criminal law has multiple functions, including preventive, interrogatory, and punitive. No single function need predominate.

Forego the error, then. It is surely not a mistake to hold that the criminal law is bound up with matters of moral censure and retributive hard treatment. Tort and contract law sometimes impose punitive sanctions. In the criminal law, though, it is a core function. Neither is that moral tone adopted only when sentencing. It is part of criminalization too. Other parts of the law can create duties not to act: criminal laws buttress them with expressions of condemnation. 'Don't φ,' they say: 'it's *wrong*.' Whether in preventive or punitive mode, the criminal law speaks with a moral voice.

The transition from prohibition to punishment does, however, involve a narrowing of focus, a move from the general to the particular. Acts of criminalization speak to φing as an act-type, at least pro tanto.[5] Judicial acts of sentencing, on the other hand, focus moral condemnation upon particular instances of φing. Those of us who are retributivists tend to think that sentences ought to express censure by imposing *deserved* hard treatment. But it is important to notice that official condemnation of a defendant is not dependent upon the formal imposition of punishment. It crystallizes prior to sentencing. State punishment may be a characteristic function of the criminal law, yet its occurrence is neither necessary nor sufficient. Punitive damages can be found in tort;[6] a conviction may be accompanied by discharge.[7] It is the *conviction*, not the

25th Anniversary Essay' (2005) 25 OJLS 353, 355–59), and appears to strike a more pluralist tone in *The Realm of Criminal Law* (OUP 2018).

[4] I do not claim that prevention, whether direct (by deterrence) or indirect (via social influence), is the only legitimate goal of criminalization. The aim of helping to legitimate state trials and punishments has been mentioned already. For some other reasons to criminalize, see *Crimes, Harms, and Wrongs*, § 11.2(e).

[5] 'Pro tanto' is used throughout this book in its philosophical rather than ordinary legal sense. To say that φing is a pro tanto wrong, or a pro tanto crime, indicates that the judgement of wrongness is provisional; specifically, that it is subject to possible justifications.

[6] Albeit rarely in common-law jurisdictions outside the US. The point here is conceptual.

[7] Indeed, as well as allowing a discharge without sentence following conviction, some jurisdictions explicitly distinguish between that and a discharge *without conviction* (i.e., where the finding of guilt is not recorded). See, e.g., ss 106 and 108 of the Sentencing Act 2002 (NZ).

punishment, that labels the defendant a criminal. A conviction makes a public, denunciatory statement about the defendant. It literally pronounces that she is 'guilty'.

For the most part, tort law merely has a verdict. It pins a breach of duty upon the defendant, without reflecting officially upon her moral condition.[8] To that extent, the tort verdict is transparent, lacking extra-legal content.[9] It is a conduit to damages. Unsuccessful tort defendants do not acquire a 'tort record'. The adverse verdict is made for the plaintiff's benefit and entails no formal public censure.[10] Characteristically, tort law mixes prevention with compensation, not punishment. This is why it does not acknowledge excusatory defences like duress.[11] It also helps to explain why tort liability can readily be vicarious and, indeed, defrayed by insurance: because it serves primarily to move money around. Applicants for a visa, or for admission to the Law Society, need not disclose a history of tortfeasance.

By contrast, convictions articulate judgements about the defendant personally. Someone with a criminal conviction suffers, as Lord Reid once put it, 'the disgrace of criminality'.[12] The adverse verdict itself damages her relationship with the community, damage that can be tangible as well as symbolic. It is no surprise that offending rates are more responsive to increases in the probability of being caught and convicted than to increases in the expected sentence.[13] For many 'convicted criminals', the greatest detriment will not be fines or imprisonment but being marked as a criminal and subjected to the collateral consequences of being so marked. Such consequences can include deprivation of civil rights; loss of public benefits; ineligibility for employment, licenses, and permits.[14] Sentencing just makes it worse.

[8] The underlying distinction I have in mind here, between objects of moral evaluation, is explored in chapters 11 and 14.

[9] Admittedly, some tort verdicts have a vindicatory aspect, most notably in the context of defamation. However, their expressive power mainly resides in what they say about the *plaintiff*—in their acknowledgement that the plaintiff was wronged.

[10] Which is not to deny that tort verdicts can have stigmatizing *effects*, especially where they lead to an award of punitive damages. For discussion of cases where, because of inadequacies in the Scots law of evidence, crowd-funded tort claims were deployed to bypass the criminal law's process requirements, see F Stark, 'Tort Law, Expression, and Duplicative Wrongs' in J Oberdiek and P Miller (eds), *Civil Wrongs and Justice in Private Law* (OUP forthcoming). Needless to say, bypassing such protections can be problematic where the verdict is effectively stigmatizing. Similar concerns inform the reluctance to embrace punitive damages outside the US.

[11] See, e.g., J Goldberg, 'Inexcusable Wrongs' (2015) 103 California LR 470; J Goudkamp, *Tort Law Defences* (Hart 2013) § 4.3.2.5. On the rare occasions (outside the US, at least) where tort law might contemplate punitive damages, the existence of an excuse ought to foreclose that possibility.

[12] *Warner v Metropolitan Police Comr* [1969] 2 AC 256, 272.

[13] See, e.g., A von Hirsch et al, *Criminal Deterrence and Sentencing Severity: An Analysis of Recent Research* (Hart 1999) § 10.2.

[14] See, e.g., G J Chin, 'Collateral Consequences of Criminal Conviction' (2017) 18(3) Criminology, Crim Justice, Law & Soc 1; Z Hoskins, 'Collateral Restrictions' in C Flanders and Z Hoskins (eds), *The*

Much of the underlying difference between the criminal and civil law therefore lies in the distinctive social significance of the criminal law—especially, of the conviction. Both kinds of law can be effective as regulatory tools. But as regulatory tools go, the criminal law is a sledgehammer. It makes habitually loaded utterances that the civil law does not, and its judgments of the accused have a symbolic significance that civil judgments lack. They condemn not merely the defendant's φing, but *the defendant for φing*.

1.1 Restricting the domain of analysis

Whether preventive, interrogative, or punitive, all parts of the criminal justice system need justification, including the multifarious powers that officials require to make everything work. Being caught up in the criminal law is not glamorous, or noble. It is not a fine thing to be called to account for one's alleged wrong. It is sordid and nasty, and it wrecks people's lives. Merely being arrested has the potential to ruin a career. At the same time, the needs of actual and potential defendants must be balanced against the interests of others in the community, notably actual and potential victims as well as other participants in the criminal justice process. Criminalization involves familiar trade-offs of this kind. But so does the rest of the criminal justice system. No single book can cover all of the issues at stake, not even one restricted to fundamentals. Amongst other things, this book is not about *which* activities the state should criminalize. (On that subject, see *Crimes, Harms, and Wrongs*, which can in many ways be thought of as a first volume to the present work.) Neither is it concerned with the 'special part' doctrines,[15] policing, or evidence. Nor is it about punishment. Our primary concern is to investigate the substantive general part doctrines that underpin criminal convictions, and to ask what contributions they make toward fleshing out criminal prohibitions and supporting the condemnatory judgements that convictions articulate. As such, the territory for evaluation mainly concerns crimes for which even a bare conviction is a significant setback to the convicted person's interests. The book explores the minimum doctrinal conditions for a polity—a polity that respects its

New Philosophy of Criminal Law (Rowman Littlefield 2016) 249; Z Hoskins, 'Ex-Offender Restrictions' (2014) 31 J App Phil 33; G J Chin, 'Race, the War on Drugs, and the Collateral Consequences of Criminal Conviction' (2002) 6 J Gender, Race & Justice 255; K M Olivares, V S Burton, and F T Cullen, 'The Collateral Consequences of a Felony Conviction: A National Study of State Legal Codes 10 Years Later' (1996) 60(3) Federal Probation 10.

[15] That is, with the part of criminal law that defines specific offences. See, e.g., R A Duff and S Green (eds), *Defining Crimes: Essays on The Special Part of the Criminal Law* (OUP 2005).

citizens—to subject persons to official moral condemnation. It addresses, that is to say, state regulation and censure of serious wrongs.

1.1.1 Regulatory offences

Sometimes, prevention is genuinely in tension with condemnation. It is a lamentable truth that the common law[16] makes no categorical division between serious and so-called 'regulatory' offences. Parking violations are technically part of English criminal law even though they lack the sort of moral condemnation associated with more serious wrongs. Neither are they rare. In sheer statistical terms, the number of regulatory offences, typically enforceable by agencies other than the police, comfortably exceeds the number of stigmatic imprisonable crimes.

The existence of such offences reflects the fact that the criminal law of advanced economies often has other fish to fry besides holding agents to account for serious wrongs. In practice, it is extensively influenced by instrumental considerations—not least of which is funding. Most criminal justice systems require the vast majority of defendants to plead guilty if they are to avoid catastrophic overload. Indeed, regulatory wrongs characteristically do not lead to convictions. They are typically disposed of without going to court at all. Regulatory agencies tend to rely on the prospect of criminal prosecution as a negotiating tool. Trips to the courtroom are reserved for only the most serious cases.[17]

At an everyday level, too, most people distinguish informally between minor, regulatory offences and 'true' crimes. The familiar questions concerning one's criminal liability that we all face when completing employment applications, applying to join the Law Society, and the like, are not meant to elicit disclosure of parking infringements. In turn, to the extent that English law restricts 'strict' liability to minor offences,[18] its use need not be so objectionable as when it is found in serious crimes.[19] In much of Part III of this book, therefore,

[16] In this book, I take the 'common law' to refer primarily to the common law of England and the Commonwealth of Nations. US interpretations of the common law began to diverge relatively early and are, to that extent, less well aligned with the common law of the Commonwealth.

[17] See § 13.2.2(iii).

[18] We should also distinguish the more troubling form of strict liability found, say, in England from the standard form of strict liability found in jurisdictions like Canada and New Zealand, where fault is presumed but can be rebutted by means of a generic 'due diligence' defence. In those jurisdictions, the essential difference between strict liability and negligence is the burden of proof. See *Simester and Sullivan*, § 6.4.

[19] Moreover, there are certain instrumental arguments that favour it. See § 13.2.

discussion of the foundations of blaming judgements will address regulatory offences only tangentially.[20] Perhaps we should, as English law does, accept that regulatory offences are an important part of our criminal law. It may even be that they deserve recognition as a second, 'quasi-criminal' paradigm. Be that as it may, trials for serious wrongs and their associated appeals retain a central place in the criminal law. The jurisprudence arising from those cases produces ongoing controversies of a normative and conceptual nature, a state of affairs that is growing rather than diminishing. It is sufficient to warrant a book of this sort that there is a substantial body of the criminal law that generates stigmatic convictions, convictions which are understood by participants, and the public in general, as conveying moral censure.

Arguably, even that concedes too much. There is a great deal to be said for exiling so-called 'regulatory offences' formally from the criminal law.[21] In the long term, strict liability risks undermining the distinctive nature, and value, of criminal law as a governance tool.[22] More immediately, the moral significance of convictions for serious offences inevitably informs the idea of a 'criminal conviction' even for regulatory wrongs. That is part of the lesson to be learned from the story of Sir Peter Berger, a brave man who retired as Bursar of Selwyn College, Cambridge, rather than risk being convicted of strict liability health-and-safety offences.[23] If regulatory offences are no more than 'quasi-criminal', they retain by that very token something of the criminal character. The symbolic social meaning of a quasi-criminal conviction may be diluted, but it is not vacated. This is why Sir Peter Berger's decision was rational and no mere mistake: because the condemnation associated with serious criminal convictions leeches into regulatory offences too. And to that extent, strict liability in regulatory offences *is* defective. In response to its undoubted existence in jurisdictions like England, we might say, 'So much the worse for those jurisdictions, which have been abusing their regulatory resources.' The convenient attachment of criminal liability to regulatory rules is no more than bad—and lazy—work by the legislature. It is lazy work abetted by judicial decisions: not

[20] But see §§ 13.2–3. Moreover, the discussion of responsibility in Part II remains relevant to such offences.

[21] Compare P H Robinson, 'The Criminal–Civil Distinction and the Utility of Desert' (1996) 76 Boston ULR 201, 214: 'Serious deterrent sanctions can and ought to be imposed [for regulatory violations] but they can as easily and effectively be imposed under an administrative system distinct from criminal law that carries a noncriminal label, such as "'violation"'. See also F H Mann's proposal in 'Punitive Civil Sanctions: The Middle Ground Between Criminal and Civil Law' (1992) 101 Yale LJ 1795.

[22] See § 13.3.3; P H Robinson, 'Strict Liability's Criminogenic Effect' (2018) 12 Crim L and Phil 411.

[23] *Appraising Strict Liability*, vii.

the ones, like *Sweet v Parsley*,[24] which required mens rea but the ones, like *Woodrow*,[25] that did not.

1.1.2 Normativity

Were we analysing the fundamentals of criminal law through the lens of a jurisdiction like France, we might have little to say concerning the use of strict liability. French law's relatively clear-cut distinction between crimes and administrative wrongs ('*Contraventions*') facilitates a stronger commitment in that jurisdiction to mens rea requirements within the criminal law. In this book, however, the substantive criminal-law doctrines under investigation are Anglophone. They derive primarily from the common law, crystallized variously by codes and judicial rulings. While reference will be made to civilian legal traditions, it is impractical to analyse two such divergent traditions together. The concepts deployed may look similar, but they operate within the context of different liability structures. Consequently, the translation is not clean.

Still, there remains much to say to non-Anglophone jurisdictions. The deeper problems that arise at common law arise elsewhere too. To what extent should a criminal legal system penalize failures to prevent harm to others? Should it treat such failures as if the harm was authored by a positive act? Questions of this type can be asked in any jurisdiction. Our responses may be affected by institutional features of a particular legal system, and by a community's particular value system, but the underlying disputes are shared. Whether negligence can be culpable is not a problem restricted to the common law. Neither is the inquiry whether, and when, necessity should be available as a defence to serious crimes. The discussion in this book is relevant to those issues wherever they are faced.

It is relevant because the main genre of discourse is ethical, and sited firmly in the deontological tradition. I do not search here for the blaming practices of the criminal law that would do most societal good, or for those practices that can be conducted most effectively and at least cost. Rather, the fundamental

[24] [1970] AC 132 (HL).

[25] (1846) 15 M & W 404, 153 ER 907. D, a tobacco supplier, was found to be guilty of possessing adulterated tobacco under the Adulteration Act 1842 even though he had no reasonable ground to suspect that the tobacco was adulterated. The Court of Exchequer Chamber overruled an earlier decision by the King's Bench in *Dixon* (1814) 3 M & S 11 that defendants could not be convicted of selling impure foods unless they knew of the impurities.

concern is to identify when conviction for a serious crime will meet those normative standards that license public censure. As we shall see, one central constraint is the need, when condemning someone morally for φing, to tell the truth. But the law must respect other values too, values such as fairness and freedom. Hence the analysis combines argument from moral and political philosophy, and the philosophy of action, with an awareness of the instrumental constraints that a legal system must observe. The criminal law may have a distinctive moral voice: but its justification requires more than abstract moral argument.

This cannot be an exercise in first-order theory. The discussion addresses the broad structure of existing institutional practices, not a blank slate. One aim of a normative theory of criminal culpability must be to show how the elements of a crime reflect, or might be revised to reflect, moral culpability on the part of a defendant. But it must also square those elements with the rule of law, the pragmatic needs of evidence and procedure, and indeed the preventive function of criminal law.[26] Inevitably, there are compromises in all of this. *Legal* analysis must attend to the law's practical history and to the social and institutional constraints that shackle it. Displacing the fundamentals of our existing system would involve prohibitive transactional costs. So we cannot usefully answer our theoretical questions in a legal vacuum.

Similar trade-offs arise for what might be called the analytical jurisprudence of the criminal law. One ground for interrogating mens rea concepts is that mishandling them risks direct injustice. But that isn't the only consideration. The law needs to be intelligible to its subjects in order to guide them. When it says, 'Do not intentionally kill anyone,' we should be entitled to assume that by this it means, do not intentionally kill anyone. More or less. There are instrumental reasons why legal concepts may become technical at the margins, for example to facilitate guidance to citizens and juries, or to negotiate problems of evidence. The general part of the criminal law itself imposes a significant degree of regimentation, in as much as the moral evaluation of a person's conduct may admit of far greater nuance than it is practical for criminal offences to reflect. Not all moral distinctions should be reflected in the law.

Even among the distinctions that ought to be legally salient, moreover, we shall cover only a subset. Given the sheer scale of the criminal law, this book cannot explore all of its elements, especially those specific to particular forms of wrongdoing.[27] The focus here is restricted to general part doctrines, ranging

[26] On the relations between mens rea and, respectively, the rule of law and prevention, see esp. § 3.3.
[27] Such as dishonesty.

from actus reus requirements such as causation and voluntariness, across mens rea categories like intention and negligence, to a panoply of capacity-based, rationale-based, and other kinds of defence.[28] That spectrum is itself non-exhaustive.[29] Our concern is with the core doctrines, and with the broad *structure* of responsibility, culpability, and wrongdoing in the criminal law. The omitted doctrines are not unimportant. But they tend to be narrower, or secondary in character, or in some other way less central. We can acknowledge the book's incompleteness in this dimension without apology. Faced with a canvas of this kind, the best a legal philosopher can do is to sketch shape and structure; to show how things work in broad terms, not in every detail.

1.2 Two master questions; two wrong answers

That shape and structure is informed by a core moral thread. Defendants should not be convicted of a stigmatic criminal offence unless they are culpable for the wrong of which they are being convicted.[30] Let us call this (a version of) the *culpability principle*. Given the social significance of the criminal conviction, and its role as a gateway to punishment, it is imperative that convictions, at least for serious offences, should be deserved. It is imperative that convictions should speak the truth.

Imperative but not inevitable. In practice, conviction of the blameless happens for all sorts of reasons. Sometimes the failure is epistemic. A court might reasonably conclude that D is guilty of an offence when, in truth, D did not commit it.[31] Moreover, even if the trial verdict is impeccable in its own terms, fault may lie elsewhere. Perhaps there were procedural failures by officials, or inadequate legal representation, causing available evidence to be overlooked.[32] In this book, we focus on a different source of blameless convictions: the substantive law itself. Even when all the relevant evidence is available and correctly

[28] For an overview of the shape and structure of those doctrines within common-law systems, see chapter 2.

[29] Omissions include, e.g., intoxication and transferred mens rea. (See, respectively, A P Simester, 'Intoxication is Never a Defence' [2009] Crim LR 3; *Simester and Sullivan*, § 5.7.) For reasons of space, the focus is also upon individual human agents: in general, we shall not be concerned with the accountability of states, corporations, or other forms of collective agents.

[30] In this book, I take culpability to be a moral rather than legal concept. See chapter 11. On the point that a defendant's culpability must relate to the particular crime of which she is convicted, see § 13.1.

[31] Aligned with conventions in many criminal-law treatises, D refers to a person (the defendant).

[32] Or perhaps the D entered into a plea bargain despite being innocent. For a pointed critique of the coercive nature of plea bargaining, see J H Langbein, 'Torture and Plea Bargaining' (1978) 46 U Chicago LR 3.

evaluated, conviction of the blameless may be comprehended by the very terms of the crime and the criminal-law doctrines that surround it. That state of affairs can sometimes be justified.[33] But it is always problematic.[34] So far as practicable, we should aim to craft our general part doctrines so as to avoid convicting those who are not culpable for their alleged crime.

Consider, then, two master questions for this book:

(I) Under what conditions do the criminal law's substantive, general part doctrines justify its convicting defendants?
(II) What role(s) do different doctrines play in that justification?

The demand that we convict only the culpable cannot be met unless our substantive legal doctrines are working as they ought. So we should not try to answer these master questions without reference to culpability. But it does not follow that conviction is justified *whenever* the defendant is culpable. Even more to the point, it does not follow that our criminal law doctrines are working as they ought *in virtue of* ensuring that the convicted are culpable. Suppose that one were to offer the following answers to our master questions:

(I) When the defendant is culpable.
(II) Establishing culpability.

I take those answers to be wrong.

The answers are wrong because, as we said at the outset, culpability is only a part of what the criminal law is about. The multiplicity of the criminal law's functions carries over to its substantive doctrines too. Many doctrines—including those of causation, omissions, complicity, and indeed some mens rea requirements—are concerned with culpability only indirectly or tangentially. Moreover, even when culpability *is* at the heart of criminal-law doctrines, and directly informing their content, it does not imply what it is often thought to imply. It does not, for example, imply that there should be no elements of negligence or strict liability in the criminal law. Neither does it imply that liability should be unaffected by outcomes. Culpability alone does not shape the general part.

[33] Exceptionally. We have pointed already to the possibility of marginalia. A more extreme possibility is noted in § 13 n 1.

[34] These claims are defended at greater length in chapter 13, when we come to discuss strict liability. For the argument that justifications of necessity still leave a wrong, see § 18.3.

At least one aspect of these claims is uncontroversial. Even legal moralists generally concede that persons should not be convicted for acting culpably unless their conduct falls within an existing criminal prohibition. Moreover, not all such prohibitions are justified. Telling lies may be blameworthy[35] when done without justification or excuse, but it does not follow that it ought to be criminalized. Some wrongs, especially less serious ones, do not warrant coercive state intervention.[36] Hence establishing culpability is not enough to justify a conviction.

It is tempting to set this line of thought to one side. Let us accept a background principle of *legitimate enactment*: which holds that enacting an offence of φing must be justified, and that this can only be so where (i) the offence is formulated in accordance with the rule of law;[37] and (ii) the offence meets standard criminalization constraints such as the harm principle. The legitimate enactment principle was very much at the heart of *Crimes, Harms, and Wrongs*.[38] However, since the present book is not directly concerned with justifying acts of criminalization,[39] we can assume for the purposes of question (I) that the relevant crime involves a legitimately-enacted prohibition.[40] Hence, it may seem, we need only a minor tweak to our original answers:

(I) Assuming the prohibition is legitimately enacted, when the defendant is culpable.
(II) Establishing culpability.

But this revision will not do either. It will not do because what is required of legislative enactments is a justified act of *generic* prohibition. In order to focus that prohibition upon particular cases, the law must appeal to general part doctrines. And many of those doctrines are not, or are not directly, concerned with establishing culpability.

[35] I take 'blameworthy' and 'culpable' to be synonymous in this book. For discussion, see chapter 11. I prefer these terms to the language of 'fault', which is ambiguous in as much as it is also associated with aretaic appraisals. In tort, conduct may be said to be 'faulty' when it falls short of an expected standard of conduct, without its necessarily being culpable.

[36] Cp. the 'Standard Harms Analysis' in criminalization theory: *Crimes, Harms, and Wrongs*, § 4.2.

[37] See, e.g., *Simester and Sullivan*, §§ 2.1–4. For the avoidance of doubt, I treat *fair labelling* (ibid, § 2.4) as falling within the rule of law.

[38] For present purposes, I need not take a view about the validity of the harm principle (as opposed, say, to paternalism or legal moralism). The point is that debates about these matters are for the most part debates about what *kinds* of crimes the legislature ought to enact.

[39] Albeit see § 1.5.

[40] Some deny that criminalization involves acts of prohibition: see R A Duff and S E Marshall, '"Remote Harms" and the Two Harm Principles' in A P Simester, A du Bois-Pedain, and U Neumann (eds), *Liberal Criminal Theory: Essays in Honour of Andreas von Hirsch* (Hart 2014) 205, 220–21. Nothing turns on that debate here.

How so? Part of the explanation is that there are multiple foundational principles informing the general part doctrines. Alongside culpability and legitimate enactment are further principles, to be defined in later chapters, of *moral responsibility*, *wrongdoing*, and *ascriptive responsibility*. I do not claim that these five principles are the only foundational principles for criminal law. From the perspective of the general part doctrines, however, these are the most important ones. As will be seen in the next two sections, culpability is served by moral responsibility, and it is entwined with wrongdoing: but the latter principles, and the doctrines they govern, are independently significant. The principle of ascriptive responsibility, on the other hand, is related more closely to wrongdoing and legitimate enactment than to culpability per se. Its primary function is to moderate the state's generic prohibition by identifying those defendants who fall within its scope. As such, it is a criminalization principle.

Not exclusively. The criminal law's ascriptive responsibility doctrines are themselves responsive to matters of culpability. But perhaps the more interesting point is that the converse holds too. Whether D's conviction is justified is, in part, a question of scope: a question whether the relevant prohibition should (and sufficiently clearly does) extend to a case like D's. And *that* question depends, *inter alia*, upon the content of the general part as a whole. When paving the road from prohibition to conviction, even culpability-related doctrines are criminalization doctrines too.

More on all this across the rest of the book. Let me sketch the further principles in turn.

1.3 Moral responsibility

The principle of moral responsibility holds that defendants ought not to be convicted of a stigmatic offence unless they are morally responsible for the wrong of which they are being convicted. Some writers use 'morally responsible' as a synonym for 'blameworthy' but, whatever the language, there is an important distinction to be drawn here. In order to be culpable for a wrong, the defendant must also be morally responsible for it. However, it does not follow that we should assimilate the two. In the terminology of this book, to be 'morally responsible' for an event is to be *eligible* for evaluations of praise or blame in respect of that event.[41] Despite being morally responsible for φing, an actor may not be culpable when, for example, her φing was a non-negligent accident,

[41] See § 4.1.

or justified, or excused—possibilities to be explored in Part III. Yet we cannot evaluate the extent to which D actually is praise- or blame-worthy for that event unless, as a prior matter, D is morally responsible for it. So understood, moral responsibility is a prerequisite of culpability. It is foundational in criminal law because it is foundational to culpability.

The criminal law engages directly with moral responsibility through a variety of doctrines. Some (infancy; insanity) function as irresponsibility defences, and can themselves have independent significance.[42] By contrast, the voluntariness requirement typically sits alongside the actus reus elements. Structurally speaking, the doctrines operate very differently,[43] notwithstanding their common rationale. On the one hand, children and the insane *can* act voluntarily and, indeed, with intention. They are blameless, not because their conduct is accidental, but because they are unsuitable candidates for praise or blame. They are not, or they are not yet, sufficiently *moral* agents.[44] On the other hand, D can *be* a moral agent even while behaving involuntarily: as when D suffers a muscle spasm, or is knocked off balance in a crowd. Either way, a criminal conviction is foreclosed, and this is not simply because the defendant lacks culpability.[45] Something more fundamental is missing. What is missing is moral responsibility.

Infancy and insanity are relatively specialist topics, which this book cannot treat in depth.[46] Of wider interest in the criminal law is the alleged requirement for voluntary action. The literature here is problematic. Many writers hold that agents are morally responsible only for the effects of their own actions, so that a threshold condition of moral evaluation is (causative) *agency*. Agency, in turn, is typically understood in terms of bodily movements that are intentional under at least one description—such movements are 'voluntary' in the sense that they are *volitional*.[47] One of the main themes of Part II is that both of those thoughts contain error. A better account of moral responsibility combines the criteria of agency and (what I term[48]) non-involuntariness—but does not require both. Either is sufficient.[49] The payoff of this point, for the criminal law, is

[42] Notably, a finding of insanity typically leads to a special verdict that differs from outright acquittal.
[43] See the sketch in chapter 2.
[44] At least in respect of their alleged wrongdoing. I do not claim that insanity is a status defence, although some versions of infancy certainly are. See §§ 2.2, 17.5.
[45] Or mens rea: one might, for example, involuntarily possess something 'knowingly'.
[46] See § 17.5.
[47] A classic discussion is Moore, *Act and Crime*.
[48] In § 8.2.1.
[49] See also § 4.3, making the point that D's behavior might not be involuntary, because avoidable, even when it does not occur as an instance of D's agency. A fuller exploration of the relationship between voluntariness, agency, and moral responsibility is in chapters 8–9.

that one can be morally responsible for events that were not brought about by one's own action.

Voluntariness and agency are explored in chapters 8 and 9. More generally, moral responsibility doctrines differ from culpability doctrines in three important ways. For one thing, the former are *capacity*-related. They focus upon the abilities we have to control our behaviour, and to govern it by moral reasoning. Like culpability itself, such capacities can come in degrees. An injury may leave one with reduced control over one's physical movements; one's awareness may be clouded when in a dissociative state; depending on her age, a child may have some ability to reason morally about her actions. Moral responsibility is thus a threshold condition. Unless D has sufficient capacities to subordinate her conduct to moral reasons, we cannot embark on an assessment of D's criminal liability. We do not cross the threshold.

It follows that moral responsibility doctrines operate negatively. If behaviour is involuntary or a child is under-age, moral responsibility—and in turn culpability—is negated. But establishing moral responsibility makes no positive contribution to establishing either culpability or praiseworthiness. Once moral responsibility is made out, its existence is neutral about whether D actually deserves blame or praise.[50] A finding of moral responsibility does no more than get us through a gateway to evaluating whether an agent is culpable for what she did.[51] Once through the gateway, we enter the realm of reasons. Now it matters *why* the defendant φed, and whether her doing so reflects badly on her by disclosing a moral vice on her part.[52] To assess culpability, we must investigate the quality of D's practical reasoning, and how D engaged with the reasons she had not to φ. But if D was not morally responsible for φing, we never get that far.

Relatedly, by the time we get to the culpability evaluation, the inquiry is no longer context-free. Now it also matters *what* was done and in what circumstances. Moral responsibility is insensitive to such considerations. If D is, say, automatic or paralysed, D's moral responsibility for φing is undermined regardless of the seriousness of φing itself. This is a key part of the distinction between exemptions for involuntariness and rationale-based excuses like duress, and why it is a mistake to align the two. Automatism goes to capacity and moral

[50] Grant Lamond has observed to me that, for this reason, the moral responsibility requirement is better characterized in terms of a constraint than a principle. Nothing here turns on that (valid) point.

[51] This is not to claim that, once the moral responsibility threshold is crossed, capacity limitations are irrelevant to blameworthiness. There are controversial issues in this area: see the discussions in § 12.3.5 (negligence) and § 19.1 (hybrid defences).

[52] See especially the account of culpability developed in chapters 11–12.

responsibility. Duress goes to culpability—it is *not* a denial of D's responsibility for her actions. George Fletcher was mistaken when he suggested that 'claims of excuse concede that the act was wrongful, but seek to avoid the attribution of the act to the actor.'[53] Both automatism and duress can exonerate, but they do so in ways that are structurally unalike. By contrast with negations of moral responsibility, the culpability-denying power of a duress claim always depends on the gravity or what was done and the seriousness of the threat that prompted it.[54]

1.4 Wrongdoing

The general part doctrines are also guided by a principle that D's φing should be an instance of wrongdoing: that is, an *unjustified moral wrong*. Wrongdoing is both foundational to culpability and distinct from it. Culpability requires an object as well as a subject: there must be something that D is to blame *for*. And that thing—that instance of φing—must have been something morally problematic.[55] We cannot blame a person for doing the right thing.[56] Thus a conclusion that D is culpable for some wrong implies that the wrong occurred. However, the converse does not hold. D may act wrongly, and without justification, without being to blame for doing so. Perhaps D's φing was accidental and without negligence, or was done under duress. Blameworthiness arises not from doing the wrong thing, but from how D *engages* with the reasons why she ought not to have done it.

Outside the law, not everyone agrees that culpability requires a wrong. Some think that one can be blameworthy simply for acting against a first-order reason, where that reason is not a matter of duty. Others have suggested that one can be blamed simply for having certain characteristics or thoughts—indeed, 'thoughtcrimes' are not unknown to the statute books.[57] There are difficult issues here, some of which are canvassed in § 11.1. Those issues are not, however, central in the criminal law. Consider the following timeline:

[53] *Rethinking*, 759; see esp. 798ff. So too was J L Austin, 'A Plea for Excuses' (1956) 57 Proc Arist Soc 1, 3. John Gardner makes this point powerfully in *Offences and Defences* ch 6. See § 17.5 below.

[54] See, further, § 17.2.

[55] The language of wrongdoing is naturally ambiguous. For clarification of the usages in this book, see § 2.1.

[56] This is not to deny that we may validly blame a person *when* she does something good, e.g. for doing a wrong that has unexpectedly good side-effects. Such possibilities require us (and the law) to be careful about which action we are judging D *for*. See §§ 11.1–2, 14.2.

[57] e.g. Treason Act 1351 (UK); Penal Code (Singapore), s 121A.

t_1: The state criminalizes φing.
t_2: D φs.
t_3: D is tried and (perhaps after appeals) convicted of φing.
t_4: D is sentenced.

By the time the general part doctrines are deployed in court, φing has already been declared to be a legal wrong (at t_1).[58] So there is something in place for the evaluation of culpability, and indeed the conviction, to grip on. This is not to accept (or deny) that thoughtcrimes may be wrongs. But thoughtcrimes are not, or at least not primarily, a problem for the wrongdoing principle. They are primarily a problem for the state's act of criminalization at t_1. According to the principle of legitimate enactment, the proscription of φing should itself be morally justified—both in terms of the restrictions it places on freedom and in terms of its compliance with the rule of law. And the criminalization of thoughts is not legitimate.

One might also doubt whether, having been criminalized, it follows that φing is a *moral* wrong. But that too is a challenge for the principle of legitimate enactment, a challenge that ought to be met at t_1.[59] *If* the proscription of φing is itself morally justified, D has a pro tanto moral obligation not to φ.[60] In terms of the criminal law's general part, however, the wrongdoing principle operates on the footing that the demands of legitimate enactment have been met. It assumes, post-t_1, that φing is a pro tanto moral wrong.

For criminal law doctrine, the distinctive implications of the wrongdoing principle lie elsewhere. They lie in relating proscriptions to the particular case of D's φing. One of those implications is a matter of communication. Like any blaming judgement, the conviction must state *what* the blame is for. The wrongdoing principle requires us to identify the (prohibited) wrong that the defendant actually did. As we shall see, doctrines of ascriptive responsibility play a key role in that task. They both convey and, in their normative aspects, regulate the impact of *outcome luck*.[61] Killing is a distinct wrong from

[58] Or at least it should have been: *pace* decisions such as *Shaw v DPP* [1962] AC 220, in which the House of Lords asserted a residual power vested in the courts to criminalize the defendant's conduct (a power since disavowed in *Knuller (Publishing, Printing and Promotions) Ltd v DPP* [1973] AC 435 (HL). See *Simester and Sullivan*, § 2.2. For the purposes of this book, I take it that *Shaw* was an instance of illegitimate enactment.

[59] Note that this is not merely dependent on the terms of the relevant enactment. As we observed in § 1.2, the scope of a prohibition also depends on relevant general part doctrines. Back to this point in § 1.5.

[60] A claim made in *Crimes, Harms, and Wrongs*, § 2.3. See in particular § 2.3(b); also § 11.1.1.

[61] By way of example (to which we return in § 4.2), suppose that I am staying at my friend's house. I go out one day, negligently leaving the door unlocked. Foreseeably, vandals enter and damage the property. I may cause the damage in tort. I may also be blameworthy for its occurrence. But I do not *cause* the damage for the purposes of the criminal law: § 5.3.4.

attempted killing, and it is appropriate for the law to recognize that by labelling them with different convictions. Luck can also be accommodated by constructive liability offences.[62] Provided the consequence is a matter of *intrinsic* luck,[63] we may be culpable for it. But that doesn't mean someone who kills is, other things equal, *more* culpable than one who tries to kill. Because the grounds of an agent's culpability are determined at the point of her raw behaviour, not by its subsequent effects, those effects leave untouched her degree of culpability for bringing them about.[64] Outcome luck changes D's wrong. It changes what D is culpable *for*. But it does not change the degree of his culpability.[65]

Something that can eliminate D's culpability, on the other hand, is a justification. And it is the wrongdoing requirement, not culpability, that gives justifications their distinctive importance. The difference between justification and excuse has no importance for modern criminal law verdicts,[66] and rightly so: both should lead to acquittals because, whether justified or (sufficiently) excused, D's action is not (sufficiently) culpable to warrant conviction. This is partly why we should be untroubled that many formal legal defences, like self-defence and duress, both overlap and cut across the justification–excuse distinction. So why do lawyers and criminal theorists worry about it? The answer is that wrongdoing has independent legal, as well as moral,[67] significance. It tracks a distinction between *lawful* and *unlawful* conduct, a distinction that resounds across other legal domains including both tort and public law. Justifications make the difference between that which is lawful and that which is, at best, excused—and which is inexcusable for officials.[68]

A cautionary point. Doctrinal overlaps are deeply embedded in the criminal law, which tends to obscure the underlying principles identified here. I have just noted that the distinction between wrongdoing and culpability finds no sharp parallel in criminal law doctrines of justification and excuse. The same applies to justification and mens rea. If a person commits a pro tanto offence without, all things considered, acting wrongfully, that person acts with justification. But whether she acts wrongfully depends on why she does it. One of the

62 See § 13.5.

63 See § 13.5–13.5.1.

64 Neither, it will be argued, are they altered by constitutive luck: § 14.4.1. Given the increasing sophistication of genetics and neuroscience, it is plausible that our everyday assumptions of free will come increasingly into question. But our blaming practices will survive, in as much as culpability judgements do not press such questions: see also §§ 11.4.2–11.5.

65 See chapter 14.

66 At least since the abolition of forfeiture laws by the Forfeiture Act 1870 (UK). Even prior to that, forfeiture was only partially aligned with the justification–excuse distinction. For interesting discussion, see N D Hurnard, *The King's Pardon for Homicide before AD 1307* (OUP 1969).

67 On the moral priority of justifications, see § 17.2.1.

68 On the unavailability of excuses to officials, see § 17.4.

central points to be fleshed out in Part III of this book is that many of the most important differences between intended, advertent, and inadvertent actions lie within the domain of wrongdoing. They lie, most prominently,[69] in the structure of an action's justification. D's mental state very often affects the range of considerations that D may invoke to justify a pro tanto wrong. I will argue later, for example, that unintended side-effects generally cannot be invoked to justify an intended action—an argument that goes primarily to wrongdoing, and to culpability only indirectly.[70] This helps to explain why Constable Dadson was unjustified.[71] Like Tony Blair.[72]

1.5 Legitimate enactment and the general part

Let's go back to our timeline:

t_1: The state criminalizes φing (let us assume, legitimately).
t_2: D φs.
t_3: D is tried and (perhaps after appeals) convicted of φing.
t_4: D is sentenced.

Any theory of the general part must attend to the point that whether D has committed a crime depends not just on the terms of the original proscription but also on whether the general part doctrines extend that proscription to a case like D's. Because the scope of those doctrines tends to be adjudicated at t_3—that is, during the trial stage and any related appeals—it is natural for the courts, and academics, to focus on whether they track D's culpability. Something has gone wrong, perhaps the very kind of thing that motivated the state at t_1. But was D to blame for that?

As was said already, the courts should certainly ask that question. The criminal law's condemnatory aspect is what makes the culpability principle a foundational principle for its general part doctrines, and the one that is most distinctive from tort and other areas of private law. The culpability principle is

[69] Though not exclusively. Mens rea elements can also play a constitutive role in making D's action the kind of wrong it is: see § 3.2.

[70] See chapter 16.

[71] *Dadson* (1850) 2 Den 35, 169 ER 407 (CCR). (D shot and wounded a thief. Unbeknown to D, the thief was a felon, and D would have been justified in shooting to prevent the escape of a felon.) See § 16.3.

[72] R Cryer and A P Simester, 'Iraq and the Use of Force: Do the Side-effects Justify the Means?' (2005) 7 Theoretical Inquiries in Law 9.

at the heart of worries about strict liability crimes in Anglo-American criminal law. It mandates both that the criminal law should contain mens rea requirements and that it should recognize excuses. Yet the importance of the culpability principle is frequently overstated. Doling out convictions is a distinctive function of the criminal law, but it isn't the only one. We should not lose sight of the criminal law's regulatory role: a role in which it resembles rather than differs from tort.

One might think that doubts about the appropriate scope of coercive regulation, whether through criminal or tort law, should all have been resolved at t_1. Provided the state's act of prohibiting φing is (and continues to be) justified, and is done in terms that comply with the rule of law, it seems natural to conclude that convicting a defendant who φs is justified, provided only that the culpability principle is satisfied. That conclusion would be too hasty. We noted in § 1.2 that acts of criminalization are generic in nature. They depend for their application upon the doctrines of the general part. To the extent that those doctrines qualify the prohibition itself, they are, we observed, criminalization doctrines too. We can say this even of doctrines that primarily serve principles relating to culpability. But many general part doctrines modify the scope of prohibitions without doing so for culpability-based reasons. These doctrines may *also* serve culpability-related principles. But that is not their primary function. And they come into their own when they deny that the criminal law should extend to culpable instances of φing.

Suppose, then, that a statute creates an offence of recklessly damaging another's property, and that its doing so meets standard criminalization constraints. None the less, application of the offence at t_3 necessarily raises further questions for the general part. What, for instance, if D did not personally harm the property, but had deliberately allowed the harm to occur; or had created the opportunity for someone else to damage it? Who, we might ask, should be caught up in that legitimately enacted net of 'damaging another's property'? Never mind D's culpability: in negotiating these questions about the scope of the prohibition, the general part doctrines are primarily concerned with matters of *ascriptive responsibility*. Moral responsibility is not the only kind of responsibility that we need.

1.5.1 Ascriptive responsibility

The principle of ascriptive responsibility requires that D must be properly accountable for the event constituting the crime with which she is charged.[73] And

[73] For reasons to be explained later, ascriptive responsibility has a family resemblance—and no more than that—to the idea of accountability developed in Gary Watson's work. See § 4.2.

it is not a culpability principle. We can be ascriptively responsible for an event without being culpable for its occurrence. Conversely, we can be blameworthy for an event, yet not accountable for it within the terms of the criminal law. Not everything that goes wrong is our concern. When something does go wrong, ascriptive responsibility norms help to identify the suitable defendants. They speak to the conditions under which an event belongs to an agent such that the agent can legitimately be called to account for it. Those conditions differ between morality and law, and even between crime and tort: a possibility illustrated by vicarious liability. Unlike in the criminal law, it may be legitimate to hold defendants tortiously liable for harmful events, on a vicarious basis, even in the absence of moral responsibility.

Within the criminal law, ascriptive responsibility is managed primarily by the actus reus doctrines of causation, omissions, and complicity. Paradigmatically, we are accountable for the causal effects of our own actions. The typical defendant in a criminal damage trial is someone who inflicted the harm personally. Only rarely should we be accountable for harms that we, as individuals, do not ourselves bring about. Yet rarely does not mean never. An adequate theory of the general part must therefore include an explanation not only of causation, but of liability for omissions and for complicity. Parents are often ascribed with legal responsibility for ills that befall their own children whereas strangers are not. Rightly so. Perhaps D ought to intervene: it does not follow that the state should coerce her to do so—let alone via the threat of conviction and punishment. Sometimes, though, the state ought to hold people accountable for things they do not prevent. Including the actions of others.

In exploring these problems, we cannot evade questions of prevention.[74] Even someone who denies that prevention is a legitimate aim of the criminal law must take account of its deterrent effects. Inevitably, therefore, the ascriptive responsibility principle is bound up with issues of criminalization. Our theory of criminal causation, omissions, and complicity must, somewhere along the way, ask: how much should the state require of us? As will be seen in chapters 5 through 7, that question is at the heart of debates about the scope of those doctrines. The ascriptive responsibility principle requires us to consider the implications of general part doctrines for individual liberty—for

[74] The demands of prevention can be taken too far. Recent fears about terrorism have given rise to profoundly inchoate offences carrying long terms of imprisonment. For many such offences, it may be doubted whether there is any wrongdoing at their core: rather, they are driven by worries about future possible wrongs. Offences of that kind can ask too much of us. See, e.g., A P Simester, 'Prophylactic Crimes' in G R Sullivan and I Dennis (eds), *Seeking Security: Pre-empting Criminal Harms* (Hart 2012) 59. But the literature is voluminous.

the effective scope of the law's original prohibition at t_1. If I am liable only for harms caused by my own actions, that preserves to me a greater range of freedoms than if I am also liable for harms that I fail to prevent. In the latter case, I am more likely to have to give up whatever I am doing in order to comply with the law. The extent to which I am justifiably required to do so depends, ultimately, on questions about the appropriate reach of state coercion into the lives of citizens. Thus a commitment to the ideal that convictions must be justified requires more than a commitment to the culpability principle. It also requires a commitment to the principle of ascriptive responsibility.

The principle has a distinctive role because of its legal context. If we were thinking purely in terms of a moral system, ascriptive responsibility would serve the wrongdoing principle. Suppose that something *goes* wrong. Suddenly, Bill's arm is broken. Bill, we can agree, has a right to physical integrity. What turns this incursion upon Bill's rights into a (pro tanto) moral wrong by Dave is, typically, that Dave caused the breakage by his voluntary conduct. Morally speaking, there is a constitutive relationship between ascriptive responsibility and wrongdoing, one in which agency and causation are paradigm. An analogous relationship holds in criminal law. But the waters are muddier. Criminal-law doctrines such as causation and omissions must observe wider criminalization and rule of law constraints. They must observe, that is to say, the principle of legitimate enactment. It may be a moral wrong for James to stand by while Bill is being attacked, but it may not be a criminal wrong—and for good reason. Or so I shall argue in chapter 6.

1.5.2 Mens rea

There are other ways in which the general part doctrines can modify a prohibition. Consider again our *exemplum* crime of recklessly damaging another's property. What counts as recklessness? The answer we give to that question directly affects the scope of the offence. This is because the pro tanto crime is not the actus reus by itself—not the causing of damage to another's property—but the actus reus when done with its specified mens rea.[75] Just as changing the actus reus modifies our freedom, so too does changing the mens rea.

To illustrate, consider the notorious case of *Caldwell*,[76] now overruled. In that case, the House of Lords held that a defendant acts 'recklessly' in English

[75] See, on this point, §§ 2.1 and 3.4.1.

[76] *Metropolitan Police Commissioner v Caldwell* [1982] AC 341.

law when she fails to foresee an obvious and serious risk of causing the relevant harm. Since recklessness is a staple mens rea element in stigmatic offences, the controversy ignited by the decision became, in effect, a battleground for rival theories about the minimum standards of culpability required for a criminal conviction. As we see in Part III, those who explain culpability in terms of an agent's *choice* to act wrongfully will tend to oppose the reasoning in *Caldwell*, since inadvertent actors do not choose to take the risk of causing harm. On the other hand, those who think, with me,[77] that inadvertent negligence can be culpable may be more sympathetic to the decision.

But we need not be.

We need not be, because there are non-culpability-based grounds for restricting the scope of recklessness in the criminal law; grounds that engage the principle of legitimate enactment. One of those grounds derives from the rule of law. If there is widespread exposure to state interference for inadvertent wrongdoing, it becomes much harder for citizens to plan and get on with their lives, without fearing the unforeseen disruption that a criminal charges entails.[78] That consideration counts against predicating liability on 'inadvertent recklessness', of the kind contemplated in *Caldwell*. So too do the implications for freedom. To prohibit inadvertent-but-reckless damage to another's property widens the scope of the proscription itself. Prior to the decision in *Caldwell*, English law permitted its citizens to be careless with the property of others, but it prohibited them from deliberately taking unreasonable risks with that property.[79] The difference is not merely a matter of culpability. It is also a difference of liberty.[80] Restricting 'recklessness' to cases of advertent property damage means that the prospect of criminal liability has fewer implications for the lives of law-abiding individuals: because those individuals are required to refrain from acting riskily on fewer occasions—that is, only when they advert to the risk that their actions may damage another's property. By narrowing the mens rea definition, we trade off the invasiveness of the prohibition against the protection of property rights. It follows that mens rea elements, too, can play a key role in negotiating the scope of a prohibition. Even if we accept that '*Caldwell* recklessness' can be culpable, we should deny that the offence that resulted from *Caldwell* was legitimate.

[77] See chapters 11–12.
[78] This point is explored in § 3.3.
[79] This, pre-*Caldwell* position was eventually restored in *G* [2003] UKHL 50.
[80] See, more fully, § 3.3.1. For a similar argument in the context of complicity liability, see § 7.4.

1.6 Two better answers

The connection between ascription doctrines and criminalization may be obvious. But the point generalizes. Perhaps the key insight when thinking about the general part doctrines is that their operation is bi-directional. It is no accident that the doctrines explored in this book are called doctrines *of the general part*. They are not specific to D's case, or even specific to φing. They apply to future cases and to other prohibitions too. The scope of any prohibition enacted at t_1 turns, in significant part, on the range of cases brought within that prohibition by the general part doctrines. When the courts modify doctrines of mens rea or justification, for example, they also modify the prohibition and its deterrent effects. So it does not suffice to justify a conviction that our substantive doctrines capture those who culpable when an instance of φing occurs. Whether D's culpable conduct should amount to a crime is, at the same time, a question whether the relevant prohibition should extend in future to a case *like* D's, and whether it is right that others like D should be deterred from acting as they do. The question to ask is not, simply, is *this* defendant deserving of conviction? It is also: what would the world look like if the criminal law's doctrines were to make this person, and others like him, liable? That is a question we should ask of any regulatory system.

A better response, then, to our master questions might be as follows:

(I) Under what conditions do the criminal law's substantive doctrines justify its convicting defendants?
Answer: Assuming the prohibition is legitimately enacted, when the defendant is culpable *and* ascriptively responsible.

(II) What role do different doctrines play in that justification?
Answer: Establishing moral responsibility, ascriptive responsibility, wrongdoing, and culpability; and helping to ensure that the prohibition satisfies the principle of legitimate enactment.

These are better answers, not comprehensive ones. The general part doctrines sometimes make other contributions, for example to principles of evidence.[81] Neither do these answers yield a clean-cut analysis. Frequently the doctrines serve more than one foundational principle, requiring mediation and compromise. Exploring how they do so will occupy the rest of this book.

[81] See, e.g., § 13.2.2(ii) (strict liability, reverse burdens, and corporations) and § 12.4 (the distinction between ordinary and gross negligence).

2
Structure and Nomenclature

This and the next chapter are groundwork. I claimed in the opening chapter that the general part doctrines play a variety of roles in justifying convictions. Before substantiating that claim in Parts II and III, we should first say something about what those doctrines are and how they interrelate. The taxonomy is laid out here as a matter of interpretive exegesis, not argument. It can be thought of as a possible—if fairly conventional—overview of the criminal law, one that is yet to be defended and which emerges from the rest of the book. One payoff of these two chapters is therefore heuristic. Especially for those who are not common lawyers, the taxonomy is intended to help readers make better sense of the problems explored in the rest of the book. But there is an analytical payoff too. Across Parts II and III, I will defend this taxonomy in terms of the principles identified in chapter 1. Albeit not without refinement, our general part doctrines are broadly justified. And, shorn of existing obscurities and misunderstandings, the structure within which they sit is robust.

In terms of the basic framework, it is conventional these days for common lawyers to divide up the law of crimes into three rather broad groupings: actus reus (the so-called 'external' or 'physical' elements of the crime); mens rea (the defendant's mental state or, sometimes, the lack of it); and defences. The master question for criminal liability then becomes one of concurrence—is there a moment in time at which the actus reus and mens rea requirements of the offence are simultaneously satisfied, and there are no defences available?[1] However, this threefold division is not clean, and the contents of each part are not independent of one another. A rough structural sketch of the criminal law, at least in the modern common-law era, might look something like the following:

[1] The concurrence requirement is not without qualification. See, e.g., *Simester and Sullivan*, § 5.8; also below, § 14.2.4.

Fundamentals of Criminal Law. A P Simester, Oxford University Press (2021). © A P Simester.
DOI: 10.1093/oso/9780198853145.003.0002

Main offence components

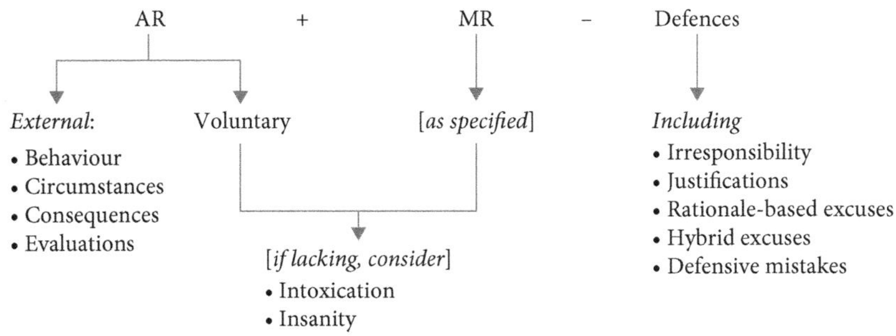

The picture is a complex one. (And that's without mentioning complicity.) Suppose that D lacks mens rea or her behaviour is involuntary. Outright acquittal may not follow if the explanation for that lies in D's insanity or her intoxication. In such cases, the relevant criminal law doctrines work against the interests of the defendant, in as much as they operate to deprive her of the acquittal to which she would otherwise be entitled.[2] On other occasions, though, insanity can be a substantive legal *defence*, relieving D of liability when she does have mens rea.[3] There is also crossover between the defendant's mental state and the availability of justificatory and excusatory defences.[4] Even within the realm of defences, some legal categories (such as duress) may cut across underlying moral categories such as justification and excuse, while the so-called defence of automatism is in law a claim of insanity or a denial of voluntariness—and not a defence at all.[5] *Et cetera.*

The reasons for this complexity are in part institutional. Frequently, the gist of an offence (or *crime*[6]) is straightforward. The wrongness of murder, for example, was a matter of public comment before the writing of the Old Testament.[7] And most of us know where we aren't allowed to park. Once we get down to details, however, the law's inner workings become unavoidably technical. It will not do to enact an undefined crime of 'murder' and leave it

[2] For explanation of this point in the context of the common-law doctrines of intoxication, see A P Simester, 'Intoxication is Never a Defence' [2009] Crim LR 3. Lack of mens rea due to a condition satisfying the insanity definition will lead to a special verdict rather than outright acquittal.

[3] Exceptionally, so too can certain very narrow intoxication defences. For an example, see A P Simester, 'Getting Drunk in Singapore and Malaysia' [2012] Singapore JLS 76, §§ VII–VIII.

[4] See esp. chapter 16; also chapters 17 and 18.

[5] Cf., for example, D Ormerod and K Laird, *Smith and Hogan's Criminal Law* (14th edn, OUP 2015) § 11.3; S Yeo, N Morgan, and Chan W C, *Criminal Law in Malaysia and Singapore* (2nd edn, LexisNexis 2012) ch 26.

[6] In this book, I use 'crime' and 'offence' interchangeably. While the latter term is generally associated with less serious crimes (notably, of the regulatory variety discussed in chapter 13), both involve breaches of the criminal law.

[7] An early (pre-2000 BC) example is found in the Sumerian Code of Ur-Nammu.

to juries to determine whether D has committed one. Definitions need to be formalized and doctrines need to be articulated. Rules and standards for identifying what counts as culpable wrongdoing need to be incorporated so as to generate predictable, fair, and consistent law, law constrained by the rights of those the system governs—notably the rights of potential and actual defendants. Inevitably, this results in a loss of nuance. Generality and the rule of law must be traded off against the desirability of case-by-case moral precision.

Some nuance can—must—legitimately be left to sentencing. Proof of mens rea, for example, does relatively little to pin down the degree of a defendant's culpability. A person who *recklessly* injures another without justification or excuse may deserve blame, but for liability purposes recklessness is a binary variable. It is either present or absent. In order to know more precisely how much punishment is deserved, we need to know more about the degree of recklessness shown by that person, what dispositions and attitudes he evinced by his conduct, what mitigations he may have, and so on. These considerations may inform the sentencing decision even where they are too fine-grained to inform the conviction. The norms governing sentencing are not the same as those governing convictions. At issue in sentencing is not the possibility of punishing the innocent but, rather, the question of how much to punish the guilty. Given the social significance that a criminal conviction has for citizens, and the starkness of that all-or-nothing verdict, there is a strong case for structuring the criminal law—including its evidential and procedural rules—so as to minimize the risk of mistaken convictions,[8] by restricting convictions for serious offences to cases where proof of the offence requirements clearly establishes that the defendant is a culpable wrongdoer. By contrast, the sentencing decision involves selection from a continuum of options after the defendant has been convicted. (Matters relating to sentencing may also go beyond the instant offence, as when a court takes into account the defendant's previous convictions.) It follows that finer-grained evaluations can be made, with less compelling reasons to err presumptively in favour of the defendant.

At the same time, the substantive criminal law cannot become purely technical. It cannot cut itself adrift of moral norms, and it cannot remainder all the moral texture to sentencing. Its doctrines must reliably track a defendant's responsibility, and culpability, for the wrong of which she is convicted. Much has been written about both responsibility and culpability. However, for the

[8] In so far as practicable. Inevitably, the goal of reducing false positives (convictions of the innocent) must be reconciled with the basic needs of a working criminal justice system, and with the goal of reducing false negatives (acquittals of the guilty). I cannot explore those issues here.

most part the criminal law does not reference those concepts explicitly.[9] One challenge for this and the next chapter is therefore translational. Laying out the criminal law's structure and working doctrines offers the chance to make some preliminary remarks about how the major legal doctrines relate to the principles identified in chapter 1. It is also an opportunity to introduce certain definitions that will be used throughout the book.

2.1 Wrongdoing

To what extent are the criminal law's organizing distinctions meaningful? Here's one red herring. It is sometimes suggested that the actus reus of a crime articulates the harm that the law is concerned to prevent or punish, while mens rea is concerned with the defendant's culpability for causing that harm. As so often, there is a grain of truth in this. Mens rea in some form is a necessary condition of culpability,[10] and proving the actus reus plays an indispensable role in establishing what the defendant is culpable for. But it is not the case that D's wrong can always be defined in terms of actus reus components, let alone in terms of causing harm. (Throughout this book, a 'wrong' refers to a breach of duty.[11]) Many activities become wrongs only because of the agent's motivations:[12] we can usefully call these *motivational wrongs*. Theft, for example, involves a dishonest appropriation of another person's property with intention permanently to deprive.[13] Without that (ulterior) intention,[14] D's conduct does not count as 'theft'. Perhaps it is a moral wrong;[15] it may be a tortious conversion or a trespass to goods. However, it is not *the criminal-law wrong of theft*. In offences such as these, D's mens rea is a wrong-making feature of his conduct, not merely a supplier of culpability.

More on that in chapter 3. What we can say here is that the combination of actus reus and mens rea marks out the criminal law's (pro tanto) wrong.[16]

9 Cf. diminished responsibility in some jurisdictions, including England (Homicide Act 1957, s 2).

10 See chapter 11.

11 More specifically, a moral or legal wrong refers to a breach of moral or legal duty, as the case may be. Judith Thomson helpfully distinguishes between using 'wrong' as a verb or noun (as in the text here), on the one hand, and adverbial or adjectival usages of 'wrong'—cognate with 'ought'—on the other. As noted later in this subsection, I use 'wrongful' in relation to the latter sense. See J J Thomson, *The Realm of Rights* (Harvard UP 1990) 122.

12 See § 3.2.

13 At least in English law: Theft Act 1968 (UK), s 1.

14 J Horder, 'Crimes of Ulterior Intent' in *Harm and Culpability* 153. See below, § 3.4.1.

15 Moral duties, I take it, can be strict: see also § 2.2.

16 As noted in chapter 1, to say that φing is a 'pro tanto' wrong indicates that the judgement of wrongness is provisional. Typically, justified φing is not a wrong: see chapter 18.

Let us call one such actus reus–mens rea combination φing. By criminalizing φing, the state establishes a duty not to φ. That duty, in turn, excludes from consideration any countervailing reasons that may weigh in favour of φing, apart from those justifications and condonations recognized as defences within the criminal law.[17]

The generalization operates at more than one level. Φing may be pro tanto *unlawful* (and a civil-law wrong); it may be a pro tanto *crime* (or criminal wrong); and it may be a pro tanto moral wrong. Criminalization speaks to all three. If φing is not already unlawful, criminalization makes it so.[18] And if φing is not already *mala in se*, justified criminalization can help to make it a moral wrong.[19]

Suppose, however, that φing is already pro tanto unlawful and *mala in se*. Even then, criminalization can modify what the law counts as wrongdoing. To see this, notice first that D need not commit 'the wrong of φing' whenever she φs. Imagine that V attacks D. D shoots V, injuring him, in proportionate self-defence. D has committed the pro tanto wrong of injuring V. But she has not wronged him *simpliciter*.[20] Neither has she acted *wrongfully*. (For the purposes of this book, I take an action to be 'wrongful' when it is done without justification.[21] An unjustified wrong is no longer a pro tanto wrong but a wrong *simpliciter*.[22] And a person who does an unjustified wrong is a *wrongdoer*.) In declaring that φing is a pro tanto crime, lawmakers make it the case that φing is a pro tanto wrong and, if done without justification, wrongful. But that's not all they do. They also speak to what kinds of reasons *for* φing are allowed. Justifications are, of course, available in morality, at civil law, and in criminal law. But *criminal* prohibitions rule out in advance some of those reasons that

[17] By 'condonations' I have in mind defences that speak to the legal but not moral permissibility of φing: see § 17.2. Unless the context indicates otherwise, in this book I generally assimilate condonations with justifications.

[18] This is not to deny that an act of φing can have civil-law effects: even a thief acquires a possessory title to what she steals. Whether φing becomes actionable at civil law will depend on additional considerations, such as standing and damage.

[19] For discussion, see *Crimes, Harms, and Wrongs*, 24–29; also below, § 11.1.1. For the most part, I assume in this book that φing is something the state has good reason to criminalize: a working assumption shared by the criminal law's substantive doctrines.

[20] As will be argued in chapter 18.

[21] The terminology is stipulative. One might reasonably object that φing should only be described as 'wrongful' when it is culpable for D to φ. There is an important thought here about the grounds of culpability which we discuss in §§ 11.6 and 14.2.2–3. According to that thought, the guiding reasons pertaining to D's action sometimes diverge from the reasons by which D ought to be guided. (I follow Raz in distinguishing between 'guiding' and 'explanatory' reasons: *Practical Reason and Norms*, 16–20.) One might then prefer to deny that D had 'chosen wrongfully' even if the action D chose to do was, in the sense used in this book, a 'wrongful' action. My own usage is stipulated primarily to avoid ambiguity.

[22] This is not to deny that justified φing can be a wrong. The special case of necessity will be explored in chapter 18.

could otherwise be available to D.[23] One reason for this is systemic. Because civil and criminal duties serve distinct functions and attract different normative constraints, it follows that even if φing is a pro tanto wrong in both systems, the range of actionable instances of φing need not be the same. Consent, for example, may be a civil-law defence notwithstanding that it fails to defeat criminal liability.[24]

Lawmakers may also confine justificatory defences for rule of law reasons. Sometimes, doing so can improve guidance to citizens and officials.[25] On other occasions, confinement may be done for the sake of withholding decision-making power from courts and citizens.[26] Just as courts ordinarily should defer to considered legislative adjudications upon morally controversial issues in other spheres,[27] so should they here. The same applies to citizens, for whom asserting a justification, even one legally recognized, is generally permissible only when matters are urgent and recourse to the state is unavailable.[28]

2.1.1 From pro tanto wrong to wrongdoing

The foregoing gives us three groupings that form a coherent whole. In marking out the pro tanto wrong, the actus reus–mens rea combination captures one side of the so-called 'offence–defence' divide. That divide is a familiar one, but it is also misleading. By itself, the actus reus–mens rea combination is merely a *pro tanto offence*. The *offence* proper is committed not merely by D's satisfying the actus reus and mens rea requirements: D must concurrently lack any defence. Thus, the offence is the complete package. Its ingredients and their structuring are the main concern of this book. Finally, what is prohibited—*unlawful*—lies

[23] Cp. J Raz, *The Morality of Freedom* (Clarendon 1986) 77: 'the law demands the right to define the permissible exceptions.'

[24] As in the well-known case of *Brown* [1994] 1 AC 212 (which is not to defend the decision itself). The tort doctrine is known as *volenti non fit iniuria*. Another defeater of tort liability unavailable in crime is the doctrine of *ex turpi causa non oritur action*, which forecloses civil—but not criminal—liability arising out of the plaintiff's illegal enterprise: see, e.g., *Wacker* [2002] EWCA Crim 1944. These civil-law defences do not make the conduct lawful, but they defeat the plaintiff's claim.

[25] See, e.g., F Schauer, *Playing by the Rules* (Clarendon 1991) § 7.4; Gardner, *Offences and Defences*, 106.

[26] e.g. *Quayle* [2005] EWCA Crim 1415 (self-help pain relief using controlled drugs); also protests against Government action such as *Jones* [2005] QB 259. In *Jones*, vandalism at an RAF airbase was defended as an attempt to prevent the UK from invading Iraq and thereby committing an international-law crime of aggression. The claim was ruled incapable of constituting a justification under UK law.

[27] At least in the UK. Expectations of judicial deference vary with the constitutional arrangements of particular jurisdictions.

[28] See § 18.4.

between the pro tanto offence and the offence proper. It is the impermissible wrong, the pro tanto offence when done without justification.[29]

The legal and social significance of unlawfulness and criminality are readily appreciated. Assuming the prohibition is justified, conduct that is unlawful is also conduct that ought not to be done.[30] It may be resisted by others,[31] for example, and discountenanced by equitable doctrines that intercept benefits flowing from it.[32] It becomes criminal, however, only when *all* the elements are satisfied, including negative elements such as excuses and the other non-justificatory defences. So it is a mistake to aver that 'a justified action is not criminal, whereas an excused defendant has committed a crime but is not punishable.'[33] Apart from anything else, that misunderstands the centrality of the conviction. The unjustified-but-excused defendant's action may be wrongful, indeed unlawful. But it is not a crime.[34] Neither is the defendant a criminal. What the law criminalizes, and what the criminal law condemns, is not wrongdoing per se; but *culpable* wrongdoing.[35]

What roles does that leave for the pro tanto offence? Primarily, communicative ones. In marking out the pro tanto offence, we advance the rule of law. The actus reus–mens rea combination defines the outer boundaries of our criminal-law duty—of what we must, or must not, do. In so doing, it gives legal recognition to the interests (and rights, where applicable) being protected. Admittedly, that duty is subject to justified exceptions. But it is not cancelled by them.[36] Justifications allow that the reasons against doing the relevant action, which are also the reasons why it is a pro tanto offence, may be defeated even though they continue to militate against D's action. In such cases, the point of the duty is still engaged, albeit D is permitted to set back the interests that the

[29] Some ambiguity lurks here. Φing may be 'permissible' in the sense of being justifi*able*—when guiding reasons exist such that, all things considered, one *may* φ. (Cp. T M Scanlon, *Moral Dimensions: Permissibility, Meaning, Blame* (Harvard UP 2008).) At the same time, D's φing may be *im*permissible in the sense of being unjustifi*ed*—typically, I argue in Part III, where D did not act for the guiding reasons otherwise capable of justifying her φing. For the most part, my concern in this book is with whether D's φing is (un)justified.

[30] See *Crimes, Harms, and Wrongs*, 24–29.

[31] Depending upon their motivations: see § 17.3.2.

[32] 'Let the hand receiving be ever so chaste': Bridgeman v Green (1757) Wilm 58, 65.

[33] M Berman, 'Justification and Excuse, Law and Morality' (2003) 53 Duke LJ 1, 4 (emphases omitted).

[34] Ibid, 18ff.

[35] Assuming that the criminal law conforms to the culpability principle. Strict liability crimes would, of course, be an exception. An illegitimate one: § 13.3.

[36] See, further, § 17.6.2–4. A duty that is cancelled ceases to exist. As Raz writes in *Practical Reason and Norms*, 27, 'The need to take an injured man to hospital at the time I promised to meet a friend at Carfax is a reason for not keeping the appointment which overrides the promise which is a reason for keeping it. The fact that my friend has released me from my promise is a reason for nothing at all and yet it cancels the reason to go to Carfax created by the promise.'

duty protects. There remains, in other words, something for us (and the law) to regret; something that called for explanation—indeed, the very thing that motivated the criminal law's intervention.[37] Alas that, on this occasion, the defendant had undefeated reasons to do it.

I defend this analysis in § 17.6. One of its implications is that justifications are secondary markers of the relevant wrong. The actus reus–mens rea combination gives the pro tanto crime its primary specification. It articulates what wrong is in play. Justifications may qualify that wrong, but they do not modify its basic character.[38] At most, they carve out exceptions which reduce the normative space the wrong occupies.[39]

Neither is there any reason to acknowledge D's lack of justification in the offence label. The impermissibility of D's wrongdoing is implicit in the conviction itself. Moreover, that impermissibility is justification-unspecific.[40] What is lacking is not any particular defence but all of them. A full statement of D's wrong would list all the missing justifications, and there is simply no need for that. Justifications make no contribution to identifying what *kind* of wrong was done. As such, the offence label is rightly tied to the pro tanto offence rather than to the defences. This is especially important to third parties. Even persons uninvolved in the crime or the trial may have an interest in its findings.[41] Those findings are articulated by means of the criminal conviction. Despite her conviction of careless driving,[42] a school may be content to employ D as a teacher; but not as its bus driver. It matters, therefore, that the public record should capture the gist of D's wrong. How well it does so depends, in turn, upon how well it captures the gist of the pro tanto offence.

Setting out the pro tanto offence also guides potential defendants. As we have noted, to claim that one acted in self-defence when injuring V is not to deny that the interests being protected by the relevant offence were set back. It is not to claim that the duty not to injure V was cancelled. Rather, it is to claim that there were supplementary reasons why doing so was, on that occasion, permissible. In an important sense, however, those reasons do not themselves directly engage the law. It is not prohibited to protect oneself. What brings the criminal law into play is that, in doing so, *one injures another*.

[37] Gardner, *Offences and Defences*, 96–97.

[38] Indeed, justifications are themselves responsive to the pro tanto wrong. The availability of a justification varies according to the pro tanto wrong it is invoked to exculpate. See § 18.2.

[39] And necessity doesn't even do that. See, further on these claims, §§ 17.6 and 18.3.

[40] This is part of the reason why defendants should bear at least an evidential burden to raise defences such as self-defence. It would be unduly onerous to expect the prosecution in every case to prove systematically the absence of every possible defence, whether or not alleged by the defendant.

[41] See also §§ 13.3.1, 14.3.

[42] Compare s 3 of the Road Traffic Act 1988 (UK).

This supplementary character of justifications alters their role in terms of the guidance they offer to the public. As John Gardner puts it,[43]

> 'Legal justifications are not there to be directly followed by potential offenders. They merely permit one to follow reasons which would otherwise have been pre-emptively defeated. So there is no need for them to aspire to standards which apply to legal rules when they *are* there to be directly followed. It means that justifications can introduce an element of flexibility into the law which often cannot be accommodated, compatibly with the exacting demands of the rule of law, in the very definition of the offence.'

One reason why defence definitions require less precision is that they present modified demands of fair warning.[44] The actus reus–mens rea combination delineates the *outer* boundaries of the criminal law's regulatory interest. Citizens need clear advice that, provided they steer around those boundaries, they can live their lives without fearing the disaster of criminal liability. Sometimes, though, especially in emergencies,[45] they may transgress those very boundaries. Then, of course, they are still in need of guidance about what the law allows. But their need is different. The need is not one of *alerting* defendants to the potential for criminal wrongdoing. That bridge has been crossed.[46]

More than crossed. Justifications allow us to turn off the highway for the minor roads. Rarely if ever do we have absolute duties that admit of no derogation.[47] Ordinarily, the interests they protect admit of trade-offs. When our

[43] Gardner, *Offences and Defences*, 117.

[44] See, also, § 3.3. In 'Decisions Rules and Conduct Rules: On Acoustic Separation in Criminal Law' (1984) 97 Harvard LR 625, 638, Meir Dan-Cohen proposes a different reason for discounting the guidance function of justifications. He suggests that sometimes justifications should play no role in guiding the defendant. At least where the source of the justification is the actor's self-interest, they should operate purely as decision rules for courts. 'The test of necessity,' he says, 'should be the actor's willingness to face, as an alternative to the ill consequences of abiding by the law, the threat of criminal punishment unmitigated by the prospect of legal reprieve.' (The passage contemplates necessity, but the logic extends to self-defence.) Dan-Cohen is worried about the incentives here: if we suppress the guidance, 'The willingness of the individual to pay the price of his transgression lends credence to the claim of necessity by helping to assure the judge that the evil averted by the transgression was compelling.' While I agree with Dan-Cohen that *excuses* are decision rules and not conduct rules (see § 17.4), I don't think his argument works for justifications. First, the law does not encourage justified actions: it merely permits them. Secondly, the argument effectively calls for deceptive manipulation. Rather than pretending that D's contemplated action is impermissible, and creating unjust incentives to allow oneself to be harmed, the law should tell the truth about the lawfulness of D's response. In this respect, I concur with Paul Robinson's inclusion of justifications but not excuses within his Code of Conduct for the public: *Structure and Function in Criminal Law* (OUP 1997). However, Robinson goes awry when he also excludes mens rea from his Code of Conduct. The reasons for this are given in § 3.3.1.

[45] See § 18.4.

[46] This point is taken up in § 19.4.2–3.

[47] Perhaps torture is an exception: see §§ 18.2.

legitimate interests (in, say, bodily integrity) come into conflict, my interests must sometimes accommodate yours—but not always. Justifications allow the law to make those accommodations, and to do so without denying that any interest worthy of protection is being infringed; which is why they do not alter the kind of wrong that the pro tanto offence addresses. Rather, they acknowledge the *mutuality* of our co-existence in a community, and the give-and-take that our co-existence requires.[48]

Trade-offs of this kind demand a nuanced evaluation of the interests, rights, and duties at stake in a particular case. For that reason, justifications involve an element of proportionality that cannot be pre-determined: they are sensitive to the localized circumstances in which a pro tanto wrong is committed. At issue is no longer the boundary of the law's generic proscription, but the more ad hoc question of how far the circumstances support an *exeat*. Once the latter question is on the table, a degree of precision must be sacrificed when specifying in advance what is permissible. It must be sacrificed for the sake of flexibility: in order to allow courts to adjudicate particular cases according to their merits. It must be sacrificed, that is to say, for the sake of justice.

2.1.2 Justification or offence modifier?

Admittedly, some of the distinctions involved in this argument are controversial,[49] and I return to them in § 17.6. For now, let us take the offence–defence division to be a broadly meaningful one. In the context of injurious self-defence, for example, we can say the defendant's duty not to cause non-consensual injury is *engaged*, in as much that the interests protected by that duty are indeed set back. This suggests that self-defence is a justification.[50] The grounds for criminalizing actions that cause bodily harm originate in our concern to prevent such injuries.[51] Those grounds continue to apply even though the defendant's conduct is, when done in self-defence, permitted.

Contrast what are sometimes called *offence modifiers*,[52] which narrow the pro tanto crime itself. One historical example is the restriction in Coke's 1628

[48] More on this in § 18.3.3.
[49] Notably, the infringement–violation distinction. See § 17.6.1.
[50] *Mistaken* self-defence, on the other hand, is not: see § 19.3.
[51] Compare s 47 of the Offences Against the Person Act 1861 (UK). A parallel story can be told under a retributive theory of criminalization, in as much as the wrongfulness of such actions derives from their harmfulness.
[52] P H Robinson, 'Criminal Law Defences: A Systematic Analysis' (1982) 82 Columbia LR 199, 220: 'But there is a critical conceptual distinction between [offence modifier and justification]: one consists of a criminalization decision, the other provides an exculpation for conduct that remains generally

formulation of common-law murder to killing a person 'under the king's peace'.[53] According to this restriction, which is probably no longer part of the law,[54] the law of murder simply did not recognize a duty interdicting the killing of an enemy alien in the course of war, because enemy aliens were not under the monarch's peace. The restriction was part of the actus reus, not a defence element.

Classifying specific elements as modifier or justification can be a debatable matter.[55] Not always: it would be bizarre to characterize the absence of death as a defence element in murder, or the age of the victim as a defence element in statutory rape. But often enough. One might, for example, argue that V's being an enemy soldier *should* be a matter of justification rather than an offence modifier. Embedded in that argument is the thought that there is something problematic about killing any human being, and that protecting the interest we all have in life is—or at least, should be—the point of our pro tanto duty not to kill. Coke's definition of murder rested upon deep distinctions in the historical common law between classes of persons. The *common* law was not concerned with the interests of enemy aliens. Unsurprisingly, the Model Penal Code omits the restriction.[56] Rightly so. The pro tanto offence signals the character of the wrong with which the criminal law is concerned. And one reason why Coke's formulation is nowadays problematic is that it sends the wrong signals concerning what we care about.

The argument against that historical definition trades upon the thought that there can be more (and less) appropriate classifications of elements as modifier or justification. Frequently, however, things are less straightforward. At least where there are multiple justifications for criminalizing some activity, lawmakers might legitimately choose between them, and that choice may have implications for the offence–justification divide. Suppose that D, charged with an offence of causing bodily harm, points out that V consented fully and freely to its infliction. Whether consent in that context is properly seen as a defence

criminalized. Where conduct is covered by an offence modification, it is not in fact a legally recognized harm. Such conduct is always tolerated by the criminal law. Justified conduct, on the other hand, causes a legally recognized harm or evil. The conduct remains generally condemned and prohibited. It is tolerated only when, by the infliction of the intermediate harm or evil, a greater societal harm is avoided or benefit gained.'

[53] 3 Co Inst 47. Judicial execution is another example.

[54] It is nowadays treated as a jurisdictional element: *Adebolajo* [2014] EWCA Crim 2779, [33]. The point was not even considered in *Blackman* [2017] EWCA Crim 190. Neither is it discussed by Lord Mustill in *Attorney General's Reference (No 3 of 1994)* [1997] UKHL 31, whose judgment contains the most helpful modern statement of the common-law crime of murder.

[55] This holds particularly when the element is one of *circumstance*. See § 2.3.1.

[56] Model Penal Code, § 210.

rendering the conduct lawful,[57] or as denying the pro tanto offence, turns in part on the rationale for enacting the crime itself.[58] One might consider that, in the presence of consent, there is no wrong in such cases, nothing for the state to regulate.[59] On that autonomy-driven approach, non-consent would be an actus reus element and not a matter of defence. Where reasonable disagreement is possible, there may be no clear answer to the question whether a particular factor should be treated as going to offence or defence.

Either way, the classification has a number of practical implications. A familiar one is the burden of proof. In calling defendants to account for, say, causing actual bodily harm, one might reasonably expect those defendants to offer an explanation of *why* they chose to do so.[60] To be sure, they need offer no such explanation until the prosecution has proved the pro tanto offence beyond reasonable doubt.[61] Once that is done, however, the defendant should incur at least an evidential burden to raise evidence suggesting the possible availability of a defence; the absence of any such defence may be presumed by the court unless D discharges that burden. The point is, of course, that the actus reus–mens rea combination establishes *something to answer for*,[62] an event warranting the criminal law's regulatory intervention: something we can legitimately ask D to explain.

The offence–defence distinction can also have substantive legal implications. One implication is the common-law rule,[63] defended in chapter 16, that a defendant may not rely for exoneration upon justificatory facts of which she was unaware. By contrast, an offence simply cannot be committed if one of its actus reus elements is missing, even if the defendant was unaware of that.[64] A second

[57] See, e.g., s 87 of the Singapore Penal Code.

[58] A similar debate exists in the context of criminalizing sexual penetration. See, especially, M Madden Dempsey and J Herring, 'Why Sexual Penetration Requires Justification' (2007) 27 OJLS 467; J Wall, 'Sexual Offences and General Reasons Not to Have Sex' (2015) 35 OJLS 777.

[59] P Roberts, 'The Philosophical Foundations of Consent in the Criminal Law' (1997) 17 OJLS 389. The issues here are famously complex. For some discussion, see *Crimes, Harms, and Wrongs*, chs 9–10.

[60] As will be noted in chapter 17, justifications and rationale-based excuses are tied to intentional action.

[61] Moreover, in many jurisdictions, once such an explanation is on the table the prosecution may be required to rebut it beyond reasonable doubt, as at common law: *Woolmington v DPP* [1935] AC 462. Contrast, e.g., s 107 of the Evidence Act 1997 (Singapore), which places the burden of proving defences upon the defendant, to the balance of probabilities. English law nowadays imposes a similar burden regarding statutory (not common-law) defences: see *Simester and Sullivan*, § 3.2(i)(a).

[62] Compare Gardner, *Offences and Defences*, 82: 'More to the point, so far as criminal lawyers are concerned, the acquisition of a moral duty to offer some justification for what one did is *itself* a normative consequence of doing it.'

[63] *Dadson* (1850) 4 Cox CC 358; *Thain* [1985] NI 457.

[64] Notoriously exemplified by *Deller* (1952) 36 Cr App R 184. D sold a car, stating as he did so that title was free of encumbrances notwithstanding that he had previously mortgaged it to a finance company. D was charged with obtaining the proceeds of the car sale under false pretences. Unknown to D, however, the mortgage was invalid for lack of registration. By chance, therefore, D's pretence was not false. He could not be convicted of the offence charged because the actus reus was not satisfied. (Of course,

implication is the rule, still found in some jurisdictions but now abandoned in England, that mistakes going to justifications (and to other rationale-based defences[65]) must be *reasonable*.[66] By contrast, even unreasonable mistakes going to the presence of actus reus elements have the potential to exonerate the defendant by negating her mens rea.[67] We explore these substantive implications in Part III of this book. For now, we should note their practical worth. Especially where there is no prior reason why a particular element should be allocated to offence or defence, the potential to choose gives flexibility to the lawmaker. Other things being equal, there is no reason why lawmakers should foreclose these possibilities when determining what form a crime should take.

2.2 From wrongdoing to culpability: Other defences

The case for distinguishing offence components from justifications does not, of course, establish that the other defences are coherently grouped together. Indeed, there is at least one defence—outright infancy[68]—that could be treated as floating free of the tripartite organization with which we began this chapter. In practice (albeit not in principle), infancy resembles procedural defences like diplomatic immunity, in that it applies independently of any of the relevant offence elements. In this sense, infancy is unique in the common law:[69] it is a substantive irresponsibility defence that functions like a procedural bar. Whatever an infant does, regardless of his state of mind, cannot be a crime. The only criterion of this absolute bar to liability is the defendant's age. Infants are deemed to be insufficiently developed qua moral agents *generally* for official judgements to be appropriate—regardless of what they do or why.

alternative charges—with different actus reus requirements—may be available. Nowadays, Deller could be convicted of at least one such, namely attempted fraud by false representation.)

[65] See §§ 17.1–2.

[66] See § 19.2.

[67] At least for offences requiring advertence to the relevant actus reus elements. For discussion of negligence and constructive liability, see chapters 12 and 13 respectively.

[68] *Simester and Sullivan*, § 19.4. By 'outright', I mean only to distinguish infancy from what might be called 'presumptive' infancy defences, where it is a contestable matter whether the defendant understood the wrongness of his actions: *C* [1996] AC 1. In England and Wales, outright infancy applies to anyone under the age of 10 years (contrast, e.g., France (13); Germany (14); and Spain (16)). The presumptive infancy defence, which at common law applied to anyone below 14 years of age, was abolished in the UK by s 34 of the Crime and Disorder Act 1998.

[69] Though not everywhere: insanity, for example, operates as a status defence in Norway. For a fascinating discussion, see M Moore, 'The Quest for a Responsible Responsibility Test: Norwegian Insanity Law after Breivik' (2015) 9 Crim L and Phil 645. *Unfitness to plead* is, of course, a procedural bar to trial—but, as noted in § 4.1, it is not a substantive defence, and it should not be confused with the insanity defence.

However, no other substantive defence in the common law is like that, and we are not concerned in this book with procedural defences. Even the rest of the irresponsibility defences require that D's irresponsibility must *relate* to the actus reus and/or mens rea of the offence charged.[70] Indeed, all of the defences, including infancy and the justifications, are compatible with proof of the pro tanto offence—and most of them specifically assume it.[71] It is natural, therefore, to separate them as a third group, distinct from the actus reus and mens rea.

That does not resolve the matter. In the structural organization set out earlier, we noted that justifications sit alongside the pro tanto offence in marking out what is *unlawful*. In that respect, they are decoupled from the other defences, which do not depend on guiding reasons that render D's action permissible. One might ask whether a similar link can be made between pro tanto offence elements and other kinds of defence. In particular, a parallel might be drawn between the rationale-based excuses[72] and mens rea. Both address the defendant's culpability. Organizationally, then, why not classify them together?

One answer to this question is pragmatic.[73] As with justifications, there is increased nuance and flexibility to be had from a legal system that does *not* merge rationale-based excuses with the pro tanto offence elements. We can fairly ask defendants who chose to perpetrate a pro tanto wrong to explain themselves, and to bear at least an evidential burden in doing so. Moreover, where their excuse rests upon a mistake, it is legitimate to expect that mistake to be a reasonable one (just as it should be for justifications). It will be argued in chapter 17 that the case for distinguishing pro tanto wrongs from their justification rests, in part, on the thought that justifications do not merely cancel the underlying duty. By that very token, however, the case for segregating excuses is even stronger. It is stronger because, once unjustified, a pro tanto wrongdoer is a wrongdoer *simpliciter*. She does a wrong, and an unlawful one at that,[74] whether or not she is excused.

Yet that leaves a puzzle about the underlying merits. A pro tanto offence done without justification is an unlawful act and a wrong *simpliciter*. Its lack

[70] So a schizophrenic might, on occasion, rightly be held responsible for her act of driving in excess of the speed limit. (Compare *Kay* [2017] EWCA Crim 647, [16]–[20].) A similar constraint applied to the presumptive infancy defence mentioned above in n 68. On the irresponsibility defences generally, see § 17.5.

[71] This sometimes affects disposal outcomes. The insanity verdict, for instance, is not available unless D is shown to have satisfied the external elements of the actus reus. Absent that, D is entitled to a simple acquittal.

[72] Notably duress: see §§ 17.1–2.

[73] For another pragmatic reason, see § 17.6.4.

[74] See §§ 17.2–4.

of justification directly affects questions concerning whether others, including officials, may intervene to prevent the defendant's conduct. Such conduct does not constitute an offence, however, if an excuse is available, wherefore the defendant may be insufficiently culpable to warrant conviction for her wrong. Suppose we accept this. Suppose, in other words, that we accept that excuses are rightly placed on the 'defence' side of the offence–defence line. One might then naturally ask, why is mens rea on the *offence* side? If an absence of mens rea exculpates because (like excuses) it denies culpability, why is it too not a defence matter?

Questions of this sort are raised by criminal codes such as the Griffith Code in Queensland, and to a lesser extent the Macaulay Code in India, which define numerous serious offences without any mens rea provision at all; and remainder the exculpatory power of no-fault claims to *defences* of accident and non-negligent mistake. In effect, such offences are ones of negligence with—since the denial of negligence is a defence—a modified onus of proof.

There is no reason why particular offences cannot be structured in this way. Indeed, that is the point of a generic accident or 'due diligence' defence, which comes into its own in the context of so-called *strict liability* offences.[75] But there are multiple reasons why, in terms of the criminal law's basic organizing distinctions, mens rea belongs with the pro tanto offence. One reason lies in the sheer onerousness of being called to account. The criminal law doesn't simply offer a forum for the accused to explain herself. It *requires* that there be an explanation, or at least a reasonably possible explanation, once a pro tanto criminal wrong is proved; on pain of the official condemnation that a conviction embodies. As we observed in chapter 1, the threatened conviction represents a personalized, blaming judgement by the state; not merely a public judgement that something went wrong. Explaining oneself in such circumstances can be traumatic, expensive, and damaging. In turn, the state should not demand such an explanation unless the prima facie case has been established of a *culpable* wrong—not merely an actus reus.

One might address that first worry by reallocating burdens of proof. However, there are also substantive differences. While mens rea requirements are *also* culpability elements, culpability isn't all they address. We have noted already that mens rea can play a role in making D's conduct the wrong it is.[76] The mens rea specification also has an important function in offering

[75] See chapter 13. Some Commonwealth jurisdictions allow the defendant to prove absence of fault as a defence to such offences. See, e.g., *R v City of Sault Ste Marie* [1978] 2 SCR 1299; *Millar v MOT* [1986] 1 NZLR 660 (CA).

[76] Above, § 2.1; see also § 3.2.

guidance to potential defendants. It delimits the scope of the defendant's pro tanto criminal-law duty. In so doing, it moderates the defendant's freedom.[77] This makes mens rea requirements fundamentally unlike rationale-based excuses, which do not have a role to play in guiding the behaviour of potential offenders.[78] Suppose that the state enacts an offence of criminal damage for which (advertent[79]) recklessness is the minimum mens rea requirement. That means, in turn, that D has a (pro tanto) criminal-law duty to 'not damage another's property *recklessly*'. D does *not* have a criminal-law duty to 'not damage another's property'. Should D be unaware of the risk, the crime does not speak to her. If it is unlawful to damage V's property inadvertently—and permitted for others to prevent D from doing so—that would not be because of the criminal law. Such a prohibition—and permission—would have to be added by the civil law.[80]

2.3 Between responsibility and wrong: The actus reus

So far, we have identified three significant distinctions that help to structure the criminal law. First is the pro tanto crime (the actus reus–mens rea combination), which specifies the criminal wrong and substantiates the offence label. Second is the combination of actus reus, mens rea, and lack of justification: which marks out the prohibited wrong. Finally, in the absence of other defences, we have the crime itself.

What kinds of contribution do various actus reus elements make to specifying the (pro tanto) wrong? Outside the law, whether a person's conduct constitutes φing is typically resolved by asking whether there is something done by that conduct that falls within our ordinary-language concept of φing. Unfortunately, concepts have a knack of being both subtle and fluid. Debbie may *stab* or *poison* Victor. Either way, if her doing so causes his death, she *kills* Victor; yet on those same facts, she does not *murder* him. Which of these wrongs do criminal lawyers care about? In one sense, only murder. By whatever causal means. Yet there is a strict sense in which we might reply: none of them. Of course, we care about wrongs. The criminal law should be driven by

[77] This argument is developed in § 3.3.1.

[78] See § 17.4.

[79] Unless the context makes clear an alternative meaning, I use 'reckless' throughout this book to refer to what is sometimes called 'subjective' or 'advertent' recklessness, requiring foresight of an unreasonable risk on D's part. For general discussion, see *Simester and Sullivan*, § 5.2.

[80] Which is one reason why 'prevention of crime' does not swallow entirely other defences such as self-defence and defence of property. See *Simester and Sullivan*, §§ 21.2, 21.5.

them. We also care about the kinds of wrongs perpetrated by each defendant. The various crimes identified within a legal system ought to engage meaningful distinctions in the public mind. But the law's building blocks are necessarily formalized.[81] They require us to distil our pro tanto wrongs into certain types of actus reus and mens rea elements, elements about which we can make a range of doctrinal generalizations and which interact in a reasonably predictable manner. And so what we regulate is a schematic approximation of the wrong. This is one price of institutionalizing a blaming system: the loss of moral nuance. Infinite hues of wrongdoing are remaindered to a palette, all for the sake of a system that reliably tracks constraints of responsibility, culpability, and legitimate enactment. Manageable lumps of concrete must stand in for sculpture.

Our two most basic lumps are the actus reus elements of *behaviour* and *consequence*. Many descriptions of conduct can be broken down into a behavioural process or a bringing about of some consequence. Or both: 'I walked to the dairy' entails both that I was at the dairy and that I got there by walking. Crimes may involve multiple behaviour or consequence elements, perhaps as alternatives.[82] But there is a wide variety. Some crimes do not require proof of a consequence element.[83] And some forms of behaviour may involve conduct that is described not just in terms of movement, or the absence thereof, but in terms of a bodily arrangement. Sitting still and standing still, for example, each involves an absence of movement and the maintenance of different poses. It is only a small stretch of language to say that D's sitting still can be an action: a thing done,[84] constituted by D's conduct. In criminal-law terms, the thing done by D is a behaviour element.

One reason why behaviour elements are basic is that, in describing D's behaviour, they tie the criminal wrong to D. They help to ensure that D is ascriptively responsible, and as such answerable, for the event constituting the actus reus. Something similar can be said for consequence elements. Typically, it is the fact that Debbie's conduct *causes* Victor's death that turns Debbie's action into a homicide for which she in particular is answerable. Conversely, suppose that David adds poison to his mother's glass of milk. She drinks the milk but, before the poison can take effect, dies of an unrelated heart attack.[85] David has not

[81] A classic study is P H Robinson and J A Grall, 'Element Analysis in Defining Criminal Liability: The Model Penal Code and Beyond' (1983) 35 Stanford LR 681.

[82] See, e.g., s 32 of the Offences Against the Person Act 1861 (UK): 'putting' or 'throwing' a stone (etc.) upon a railway.

[83] Below, § 2.3.1.

[84] Rather than not done, on the whole: see § 6.1.2. On the terminology of action and things done, see § 2.4.

[85] Loosely based on the facts of *White* [1910] 2 KB 124.

murdered his mother. Despite satisfying all other elements of that crime, his conduct did not cause her death.

A second role for behaviour elements makes them even more basic than consequences—and explains why the former are at least implicitly present in all offences that comply with the culpability principle.[86] Behaviour elements are also central to *moral* responsibility. Indeed, one way in which the law marks the distinction between behaviour and consequence is by demanding that behaviour elements must be *voluntary*; whereas consequence elements need only stand in a causal relationship to that behaviour.[87] If D's hand strikes and injures V during an epileptic seizure, there is causation of that injury but D's behaviour is involuntary and, on these facts, no crime occurs. V is ascriptively but not morally responsible for the injury. Contrast a case where D causes an outcome that would have happened anyway. D may be morally (and ascriptively) responsible for the occurrence of a consequence element even if that consequence was unavoidable; provided it was caused by D's voluntary behaviour.[88]

Notice that there is already a gap here between law and language. Conceptually, we might hold, or at least think it arguable, that 'D injured V' during the epileptic fit. But from the criminal law's perspective, this is not even a borderline case. It is a straightforward case of non-liability.[89] The difference reflects something of a tension in modern Anglo-American criminal law, between the plain language of many statutes and the lure of a 'principled' criminal law:[90] a law that regulates wrongs against a more sophisticated awareness of what conclusions about responsibility and culpability require. This is not to lose sight of the structure of wrongdoing, which remains at the heart of the criminal law's concern. But it is to place it within a more regimented framework.

Regimentation still leaves ample space for variety. Many of the more serious wrongs in the criminal law are consequence-based. Section 18 of English law's Offences Against the Person Act (OAPA) 1861, for example, prohibits intentionally 'causing grievous bodily harm' to another person. Wrongs of this kind involve an implicit behaviour element, the character of which is unspecified. *Any* causative act (or omission) will do. But wrongs can arise in other ways too. Some are dependent upon the *kind* of behaviour by which an agent brings

[86] See esp. § 8.4.2–3.

[87] In general, the consequence must be *caused*. It is open to the lawmaker to substitute a different kind of causal relationship in specific contexts (e.g. an 'inducing' or 'procuring' of something: especially important in some forms of complicity liability). However, causation is—rightly—the central kind of causal relation in criminal law, at least for principal offenders. See chapter 5.

[88] A thesis of chapters 8–9.

[89] Albeit, under English law, this would be classified as a case of insanity: *Sullivan* [1984] AC 156. For critical discussion, see *Simester and Sullivan*, § 19.1(ii)(d).

[90] See, e.g., Andrew Ashworth's elegant treatise, *Principles of Criminal Law* (OUP 1991).

about a consequence. Stealing something is not the same wrong, for example, as obtaining it by threats of violence. Both forms of obtaining may be dishonest, but the use of threats significantly changes the character of the wrong, sufficiently so to warrant its separate criminalization.[91] Still other wrongs depend upon the motivation with which one acts, as when an offer becomes blackmail only if communicated for certain kinds of reasons.[92] Or there may be a mix of types. Recklessly causing grievous bodily harm, for example, also contravenes section 18 of the OAPA 1861 when done with intent to resist arrest—a wrong dependent upon both consequence and motivation.

Unsurprisingly, reducing such wrongs to workable elements tends to generate an imperfect conceptual fit. The richly textured language of wrongdoing is not always a sound basis for delineating mainstream offences. Consider section 20 of the OAPA 1861, which proscribes the reckless 'infliction' of grievous bodily harm. As Gardner has emphasized, this is not the same wrong as *causing* such harm. It is the wrong of causing such harm *by inflicting it*.[93] But that distinction is not endorsed by the courts,[94] and rightly so.[95] It is too fine. In law, we must concede, 'inflicting' does not mean inflicting. The crime is consequence-based.

2.3.1 Other wrong-defining elements

Contrast the English crime of theft. According to section 1(1) of the Theft Act 1968, 'A person is guilty of theft if he dishonestly appropriates property belonging to another with the intention of permanently depriving the other of it.' One might naturally think of theft as a deprivation-based wrong. Yet there is no consequence element at all in this offence definition. A thief may 'appropriate' property, for example, by touching or moving it, but there is no particular state of affairs that her appropriation must bring about.[96] Of course, the

[91] For general discussion, see A P Simester and G R Sullivan, 'On the Nature and Rationale of Property Offences' in R A Duff and S P Green (eds), *Defining Crimes: Essays on the Criminal Law's Special Part* (OUP 2005) 168.

[92] G Lamond, 'Coercion, Threats, and the Puzzle of Blackmail' in *Harm and Culpability* 215.

[93] *Offences and Defences*, 34ff.

[94] *Burstow* [1998] AC 147 (HL).

[95] For Gardner, what counts is that the harm is caused by violence. Consider, though, the facts of *DPP v K* [1990] 1 All ER 331, in which D secreted acid in a hair dryer, causing V to be burned when he used it. Was the harm 'inflicted'? (What if the acid merely dripped or oozed onto V?) It seems undesirable for such a serious conviction to turn on this question in what is, fundamentally, a harm-based wrong. But questions about the extent to which fine-grained offence definitions are desirable lie outside the scope of this book. For some discussion of these issues, see *Crimes, Harms, and Wrongs*, § 11.4.

[96] It need not, for example, end up in a different place.

world is different once the property is touched—it is now a world in which that touching has happened. At least from the perspective of the criminal law, however, that difference is not a distinct actus reus element. In the hands of the 1968 Act, theft is become a motivational wrong: a wrong constituted not by the effects of one's conduct but, primarily, by its mens rea elements.[97]

Theft may be an unlikely specimen, but numerous wrongs are not consequence-based. Rape, for example, is a profound wrong independently of any harm that it undoubtedly, even typically, causes. Neither, however, is it a mere behavioural crime. What turns sexual intercourse into rape is the incorporation of additional *circumstances* accompanying D's conduct. It is one thing to say that Sam had sexual intercourse with Alex; quite another to say that Sam did so without Alex's consent.

Broadly speaking, circumstance elements in crimes are events or states of affairs that accompany but need not be caused by the agent's behaviour. Perhaps they *are* caused by the agent. Imagine that there is a crime of selling 'stripped' books—that is, books from which the front cover has been removed and returned to the publisher for refund.[98] When James sells Karen a stripped book, it may be James himself who has removed the cover. The fact that the book is stripped is, none the less, a circumstance element because that James made it so does not matter.[99]

Beneath that unifying roof, though, circumstances are a *very* mixed bag.[100] Sometimes, they can play a role in establishing D's ascriptive responsibility for an event. (When my dog bites a passer-by, the criminal law focuses its attention on me because the dog is mine.[101]) Or they may take in certain kinds of legal status.[102] (Including the ownership of dogs.) On other occasions, they involve triggering events over which D may have no control. Perhaps a lifeguard fails to sound the alarm when a shark enters the bay: from the lifeguard's perspective, the shark's entry is a circumstance. Alternatively, they may be simple facts about the world. Suppose that I am rude to someone in the elevator. It turns out

[97] See chapter 3. For discussion of the difficulties surrounding theft, see *Simester and Sullivan*, ch 13.

[98] Typically, for paperbacks, only the cover need be returned by the bookseller in order to claim a refund of the book price. The stripped book itself should then be pulped. However, 'some street merchants in many major cities obtain (almost certainly illegally) and sell stripped books, for a fraction of the suggested retail price': A N Greco, *The Economics of the Publishing and Information Industries: The Search for Yield in a Disintermediated World* (Routledge 2015) 204.

[99] On the relationship between circumstances and moral luck, see § 14.4.

[100] Some may be what the Model Penal Code defines as non-material: § 1.13(10). I disregard such elements here (see § 15.4.1).

[101] See § 8.4.2.

[102] See, e.g., *Smith (David)* [1974] QB 354 (CA): in the context of criminal damage, the property must 'belong to another'; something about which the defendant must be at least reckless. See *Simester and Sullivan*, § 14.5(v).

that person is my girlfriend's father. Now we have two actions, one intended and the other mortifying. In this case, the additional circumstance discloses an identity of reference but not of meaning; the things done are not the same. Preventing a stranger from entering my home may be lawful, but if she happens to be a police officer with a search warrant it becomes the actus reus of a crime.

Again, there is ample space for nuance. As a rule, when a piece of conduct can be described in various non-equivalent ways, there has been a variety of actions. Despite that, we often think of referential identity cases as involving the same 'thing done', in the sense that the additional information does not change our expectations about the actor's underlying conduct. It is intelligible to say that my insulting the gentleman in the elevator *is*, in that sense, my insulting my girlfriend's father (in the elevator). The latter description seems no more than a partial elaboration upon the former—incorporating the same behaviour and consequence elements (if any), and merely varying the accompanying circumstances.[103] But that is not a general feature of circumstance elements. In other cases, the way we think about such additional information may be more complex. Suppose that we say, 'Sam had sexual intercourse with Alex,' and complete the sentence, 'without Alex's concurrence.' The additional circumstance offers more than simple elaboration. Unlike, say, 'Sam had adulterous sexual intercourse with Alex,' it is likely to alter our expectations about the piece of conduct itself.

2.3.2 Evaluative terms

En passant, it is worth drawing attention to another type of offence element, one that is often parasitic upon our familiar trio of behaviour, consequence, and circumstance. Imagine that lawmakers enact an offence of 'reckless driving'.[104] Typically, recklessness here is not a mens rea term. In adjudicating such an offence, we should not ask ourselves, 'Was the defendant aware that she may be driving a car?' We should inquire instead into the *manner* of her driving—into whether it was dangerous. 'Reckless', in this context, qualifies the behaviour

[103] Another class of referential identity cases depend upon identity of semantic reference rather than upon further circumstances. To take a navigational sight from the Evening Star *is* (without more) to take a sight from the Morning Star; but these descriptions are logically distinct, and one enjoined to avoid sighting by the Evening Star might unintentionally do so by using the Morning Star 'instead'. I take these to be different things done.

[104] See, e.g., Road Traffic Act (Singapore), s 64; Road Traffic Act 1972 (UK), s 2 (now repealed). US states take a wider range of approaches to such offences.

element in the offence. Hence, it is an actus reus term. One might, for example, drive in a reckless manner (the *actus*) deliberately (the *mens*).[105]

Happily in the UK, reckless driving has been substituted by an offence of 'dangerous' driving,[106] thus removing at least one source of confusion. But if 'dangerous' is more patently an actus reus element, what kind of element is it? One might naturally look to categorize it as part of a compound behaviour element—that of 'dangerous driving'. Or one might think of it as a kind of shorthand circumstance element—a reference to the circumstances accompanying the driving. But either resolution would be to miss something important about such elements: that they are evaluative in nature. As will be suggested in § 15.4.2, what is interesting about evaluative elements is that they need not attract corresponding mens rea requirements.[107] Depending how the offence is set up, the prosecution may well have to prove that D intended to drive in the fashion that she did: but it is ordinarily a question for the court whether the manner of that driving was dangerous. And it does not matter whether D herself thought it was.[108]

Qua wrong-making features, evaluative elements are not restricted to qualifying D's behaviour.[109] (Or indeed to qualifying actus reus elements.[110]) Unlike the example of dangerous driving, their relation to D's behaviour may be indirect. Suppose that a crime is enacted of 'intentionally exhibiting an obscene sculpture'. On standard canons of interpretation, D can only be guilty of such a crime if he intentionally exhibits a sculpture; but he need not know or intend that the sculpture he intends to exhibit is obscene. Whether the sculpture is obscene is an evaluative question. It involves a legal assessment of the facts that may be contrary to D's own understanding of his actions. Unsurprisingly, evaluative elements of this type tend to generate rule of law problems—indeed, the test for obscenity in English law is so nebulous as to be unworkable.[111] In

[105] WJ Winslade, 'Brady on Recklessness' (1972) 33 Analysis 31.

[106] See s 2 of the Road Traffic Act 1988 (UK).

[107] Which is not to deny that they *may*. A notable example used to be the requirement of dishonesty in the English law of theft, as interpreted by *Ghosh* [1982] QB 1053 (CA); which effectively allowed an ignorance-of-morality answer to liability. In *Ghosh* (at 1064), the Court of Appeal set out a two-part test to determine dishonesty, where satisfaction of both parts was required: (i) Was what was done dishonest according to the ordinary standards of reasonable and honest people? (ii) Did the defendant realize that reasonable and honest people would regard what he did as dishonest? (See, e.g., *Simester and Sullivan*, § 13.8(iv), and accompanying references.) Part (ii) was later excised from the law by the Supreme Court in *Ivey v Genting Casinos* [2017] UKSC 67.

[108] Compare the Model Penal Code, § 2.02(9).

[109] Whether an instance of bodily harm counts as 'grievous', for example, is an evaluative question: Offences Against the Person Act 1861 (UK), ss 18, 20.

[110] Cp. 'reasonable' force in self-defence.

[111] For discussion, see *Simester and Sullivan*, § 2.3(i); compare too *Simester and Sullivan*, § 12.2 ('sexual').

general, evaluative elements are more welcome in the context of defence elements.[112] Provided they are used with care, however, they can add flexibility to prohibitions without sacrificing the law's power to guide. As the European Court of Human Rights once observed, 'The need to avoid excessive rigidity and to keep pace with changing circumstances means that many laws are inevitably couched in terms which, to a greater or lesser extent, are vague.'[113] An evil, perhaps, but a necessary one.

2.4 From the prohibition to the particular: Nomenclature

Recall our timeline from chapter 1:

> t_1: The state criminalizes φing.
> t_2: D φs.
> t_3: D is tried and (perhaps after appeals) convicted of φing.
> t_4: D is sentenced.

We said in chapter 1 that the transition from pro tanto offence to crime is a shift from generic to particular. That is true in more than one sense. We have pointed already to the first sense. In the form in which they are enacted at t_1, criminal-law prohibitions are inevitably provisional. The question whether a particular instance of φing constitutes a crime turns, ultimately, on whether φing is done on that occasion without defence. Lawmakers help to manage that transition by regulating how the various defences are to be assessed. But the assessment itself is delegated to the courts at t_3. Such an arrangement is unavoidable not merely because the court acts as fact-finder, but because its adjudication typically involves an element of discretion, especially in the context of defences.[114] Φing might be done in a myriad of possible circumstances and contexts, and it is impracticable to specify disposals in advance for every combination of them. (Even were it possible, doing so would require laws so convoluted that their capacity to guide courts and citizens would be significantly impaired.) This doesn't mean the courts get a free hand in deciding what to do with defendants who claim, say, a rationale-based excuse for their φing. But it does require lawmakers to embed evaluative standards within the rules they

[112] Above, § 2.1.1.
[113] *Kokkinakis v Greece* (1994) 17 EHRR 397, [40].
[114] Although not exclusively in that context: see § 2.3.2.

create: and then leave it to the courts. Whether D's φing constitutes a criminal offence depends, in the end, on the details.

One reason why prohibitions are incompletely specified, therefore, is to facilitate a division of labour. But adjudication also involves a second kind of transition. A criminal-law prohibition of φing proscribes a *type*, whereas criminal convictions are for tokens thereof. 'Do not murder' enjoins an activity rather than a particular instance of murdering. Indeed, it would be intelligible to deny outright that 'murder' is a crime. One might prefer to say that it is only particular instances of murder that are crimes.[115] Nothing much turns on whether we accept this, save that it is perfectly natural to think of acts of criminalization as speaking in terms of types, and to talk about 'the wrong (or crime) of φing'. What matters is to avoid confusing the usages.

To that end, I distinguish in this book between a *deed*, or an *action*, which is tied to a particular description, and the underlying *conduct*, or *behaviour*,[116] that it describes.[117] The same piece of conduct constitutes as many actions as there are different (valid) descriptions of it; and it may be intended, foreseen, unforeseen, *et cetera*, under some of those descriptions and not others. For example, when I kill Hamish my conduct might constitute the actions of moving my finger, pulling the trigger, shooting Hamish, and killing him. Some of those actions may be intended (including, say, moving my finger and pulling the trigger) and others inadvertent (including shooting Hamish and killing him). Some descriptions may contain embedded mental states—as when I murder Hamish. To the extent that each description of my conduct differs, it identifies a distinct *thing done*, or not done, through that piece of conduct. In general, it is things done or not done—φings[118]—that criminal-law proscriptions specify.

Things done are not particulars. As Jennifer Hornsby notes, '"I did the same thing to you" and "He did the same thing today as he did yesterday" do not record identities between particular events.'[119] A *piece of conduct*, by contrast, refers to a particular. Thus we specify a deed or action (that is, a piece of conduct under a description) by specifying (i) a piece of conduct, and (ii) a thing done.

[115] I owe this thought to Nils Jareborg. The same ambiguity applies to the language of wrongs.

[116] I use 'conduct' and 'behaviour' interchangeably in this book.

[117] A similar distinction is drawn by J L Mackie between 'act' and 'action' in 'The Grounds of Responsibility' in P M S Hacker and J Raz (eds), *Law, Morality and Society: Essays in Honour of H.L.A. Hart* (Clarendon 1977) 175, 176. In my usage, however, conduct does not presuppose agency.

[118] Unless the context makes it clear otherwise, my usage of φings includes both doings and not-doings. (On the account here, not-doings are a species of deed, in that they too are tied to descriptions of conduct. See § 6.1.1–2.) Sometimes, of course, the distinction becomes important: we return to it in chapters 5 and 6.

[119] J Hornsby, *Actions* (Routledge and Kegan Paul, 1980) 16. In what follows, I sometimes use 'piece of conduct', in order to emphasize that it refers to a particular event.

So when we ask, 'did she do this dreadful action?', we are asking whether there was a piece of conduct by her that constituted doing this dreadful thing. And when we ask whether she committed the crime of φing, we are asking whether her conduct can be described in terms of the actus reus and mens rea elements of φing, and not described in terms of any relevant defence.

The language of 'action' is ambiguous. Usually this is unproblematic, and the meaning is clarified by the context. Sometimes, however, we need to refer to action in a narrower sense: for example, in contradistinction to *inaction*, or to signal that D's behaviour is an instance of D's *agency*, or as one side of an action/*omission* dichotomy. Because of these possibilities, I will occasionally need a more specific term, especially in Part II. To allow for that, I shall take an 'action' to be a deed in respect of which D is an agent (that is, an 'action' rather than a mere event).[120] A deed, by contrast, describes D's behaviour without making any commitment regarding D's agency: it may or may not be an action. And where the contrast is with omissions, I will use 'act' rather than 'action' to point to that. Actions, acts, and omissions are all subcategories of deeds, which is the true generic term here: but the language of action is so familiar that it seems best not to abandon it. All four are tied to descriptions of D's conduct; the designations 'action', 'act', and 'omission' simply categorize various aspects of those descriptions.

Conduct itself is a kind of *event*: an event marked out by its involving a bodily movement or non-movement. For the purposes of the criminal law, we may conveniently restrict the scope of conduct to those bodily movements and non-movements by the defendant that are externally manifested, in as much as they are observable without looking below the surface of the body. (Doubtless such observation need not be visual and might be assisted by amplifying instruments—although not, say, by an X-ray machine.) Thus, breathing out, blinking, and moving one's finger count as bodily movements; thinking, deciding, and instances of internal neurological activity are not. This is not to contest that various 'internal' activities—notoriously, 'compassing the death of the king'[121]—are things done. However, the definition adopted here effectively segregates purely mental events from conduct, which means that they cannot constitute actions *within the scope of this book*. That is not a conceptual matter. In principle, we could have 'thoughtcrimes'.[122] But we shouldn't. And so I offer no account of them here.

[120] On this distinction, see especially chapter 9. More precisely, therefore, we specify an *action* (as opposed to a deed) by D by specifying (i) a piece of conduct *in respect of which D is an agent*, and (ii) a thing done.

[121] Treason Act 1351 (UK). The provision is still in force.

[122] G Orwell, *Nineteen Eighty-Fours* (Secker & Warburg, 1949).

3

Five Functions, and Two Kinds, of Mens Rea

How do our mens rea doctrines relate to the foundational principles identified in chapter 1? One answer is fairly uncontroversial.[1] Most people agree that mens rea is relevant to *culpability*. The maxim *actus non fit reus nisi mens sit rea* has been around for centuries.[2] Causing harm to another person may be undesirable. It may be a moral or a civil wrong. According to the culpability principle,[3] however, that should not be enough to support a conviction. The moral turpitude associated with a criminal conviction demands some element of blameworthiness. And to show that, we need mens rea. The House of Lords recognized this candidly in *Sweet v Parsley*, when holding that mens rea is a presumed element of all criminal offences:[4]

> 'there has for centuries been a presumption that Parliament did not intend to make criminals of persons who were in no way blameworthy in what they did. This means that, whenever a section is silent as to mens rea there is a presumption that, in order to give effect to the will of Parliament, we must read in words appropriate to require mens rea.'

In the more sordid litigation of everyday criminal law, the presumption is often rebutted, even for some very serious crimes.[5] Yet the very existence of the mens rea presumption reflects an underlying idea that, unless the wrong is done advertently, or at least negligently,[6] a criminal conviction is inappropriate.

[1] Although cf. Hart, who argued for a rule of law-based account of mens rea: below, § 3.3.

[2] See, e.g., Coke, *Third Institute* (1641) 6, 107; *Fowler v Padget* 7 Term Rep 514 (Lord Kenyon). Compare C S Kenny, *Outlines of Criminal Law* (2nd edn, CUP 1904) 39: 'no external conduct, however serious or even fatal its consequences may have been, is ever punished unless it is produced by some form of *mens rea.*'

[3] See § 1.2; also chapter 13.

[4] [1970] AC 132, 148 (Lord Reid); see also at 153 (Lord Morris) and 162–63 (Lord Diplock); *B v DPP* [2000] 2 AC 428.

[5] Notably in under-age sexual offences: e.g. the Sexual Offences Act 2003 (UK), ss 5–8.

[6] Nothing turns here on the vexed but semantic question whether negligence is truly a form of 'mens rea', in as much as it does not involve any particular state of mind. For convenience of expression, I assume that it is.

Fundamentals of Criminal Law. A P Simester, Oxford University Press (2021). © A P Simester.
DOI: 10.1093/oso/9780198853145.003.0003

So far so good. Mens rea has a direct relation to culpability, which we explore in Part III. Some common law writers, however, see a tighter connection. They characterize mens rea as *the* culpability element,[7] suggesting not only that mens rea helps to establish blameworthiness but, much more strongly, that this is its essential function.

There is an element of hyperbole in this. Certainly, mens rea in some form is a necessary component of culpability findings. But no one seriously suggests that it is sufficient. Showing mens rea requires only that the prosecutor establish that the defendant had, at the time of doing the actus reus, the specified mental state towards that actus reus which is required for the crime. It does not follow that the defendant did a culpable wrong. In particular, she may avail herself of a variety of defences, thereby negating the attribution of culpability despite the presence of mens rea.[8] Even a finding of insanity is compatible with that conclusion;[9] all the more so for the rationale-based defences, such as self-defence and duress, where the defendant concedes mens rea and goes on to offer further and exculpating reasons why she chose to do the actus reus.[10] Mens rea is not *the* culpability element. It is not whole of the culpability story.

Moreover, in Part III it will be argued that there are limits upon the extent to which mens rea is even necessary. *Some* element of mens rea will be required before a defendant can properly be treated as blameworthy for an action. But it does not follow that every actus reus element should be accompanied by a mens rea requirement. Sometimes, as we see in chapter 13, *constructive liability* may be justified. In an offence of dangerous driving causing death,[11] say, there is no need to show mens rea in respect of the occurrence of death. Death is a strict liability element: none the less, culpability may lie in respect of the entire offence. One who causes death by driving dangerously is normally culpable in respect of that death—because it is precisely such risks that make it wrong to drive dangerously in the first place.

[7] For example, in S Yeo, N Morgan, and Chan W C, *Criminal Law in Malaysia and Singapore* (2nd edn, LexisNexis 2012), the very term 'mens rea' is eschewed in favour of 'the fault element'.

[8] Admittedly, this holds primarily for forms of mens rea like intention or knowledge. The presence of a justification may block findings of certain partially evaluative mens rea elements, such as recklessness. See further chapter 16.

[9] At least where D's condition is such that he lacks understanding of the wrongness of his act: cp. *M'Naghten* (1843) 10 C & F 200, 8 ER 718.

[10] As Andrew Ashworth points out in the context of medical necessity, it is unhelpful to conceal the complexity of such cases by concluding that the doctor lacks a 'criminal intention': 'Criminal Liability in a Medical Context: the Treatment of Good Intentions' in *Harm and Culpability* 173. Neither should we accept the suggestion in *Williams (Gladstone)* (1983) [1987] 3 All ER 411 (CA) and *Beckford v R* [1988] 1 AC 130 (PC) that one who acts in self-defence lacks an intention 'to act unlawfully': see §§ 19.2.1–19.3.

[11] See, e.g., s 1 of the Road Traffic Act 1988 (UK); below, § 13.5.

3.1 Beyond culpability

So we may quibble about the close—too close—identification that is sometimes made between mens rea and culpability. Admittedly, mens rea is indispensable to culpability, in that we need more than a bare actus reus to conclude that a defendant deserves the official sanctions of the criminal law. Yet the contribution made by mens rea does not suffice for that purpose; and its role in establishing culpability is not a simple one.

More importantly, however, we should question the conventional association between mens rea and culpability at a deeper level. Mens rea is relevant to culpability, yes. But it serves other purposes too, purposes that are quite distinct and just as important. The existence of these other functions is sometimes overlooked, and is liable to be concealed by depicting mens rea as the culpability element.

To summarize what follows, mens rea serves at least five different functions, which we can group into two broad categories. Within the first category, it helps to establish the moral guilt of the defendant's conduct. It helps, in other words, to establish that D's φing was an instance of *culpable wrongdoing*. We have pointed already to one way in which it does this: by contributing to findings of culpability. Sometimes, however, mens rea constitutes the morally wrongful character of D's behaviour in a more fundamental way. It discharges this second role by helping to identify what kind of action D is performing. In these cases, the finding of mens rea is integral to the moral wrongness of the action for which D is being held responsible. Thirdly, mens rea affects the availability of justifications. Whether D's pro tanto wrong was, all things considered, wrongful—unjustified—and an instance of wrongdoing depends on the reasons why D did it. We outline the second and third functions in the next section, and will explore all three more fully in Part III.

The other category was flagged up in § 1.5.2. It concerns the principle of legitimate enactment. Mens rea has important roles to play in articulating, and notifying, the limits of citizens' freedom. More specifically, a fourth function of mens rea is to secure fair warning to defendants, ensuring they have sufficient advance notice that, by their conduct, they risk violating the criminal law. Finally, mens rea plays a key mediating role in criminalization, being part of the trade-off between the protection of potential victims and the preservation of liberties for potential defendants. These further roles often demand more stringent mens rea standards for liability than is needed to establish culpability. They help to explain why negligence, and sometimes even recklessness, is excluded in certain contexts of the criminal law, notwithstanding that one so acting might be culpable. We turn to them in § 3.3.

3.2 Mens rea and wrongdoing

In the criminal law, we don't convict people for doing permitted things. We convict them only for doing things that are (prohibited) wrongs. But what makes φing a wrong? Let us start by thinking about the actus reus in isolation. Often the answer is straightforward. What makes D's behaviour problematic, and a candidate for potential blaming judgments, is some observable harm that it causes. If D stabs V, or sets fire to his property, the conduct is pro tanto undesirable—the *actus* is *reus*—just in virtue of its external elements, and independently of D's mens rea. In these kinds of cases, bringing about the harmful consequence is the very source of the wrong. Correspondingly, the criminal law's interest in preventing such conduct arises out of the nature of the *actus* itself. These are the classic types of cases likely to influence us towards thinking of mens rea as a culpability element. The actus reus articulates the harm; and we can move directly to the second stage, of establishing blameworthiness.

On other occasions, however, the *actus* is not inherently *reus*. The external elements of D's conduct may not by themselves disclose anything undesirable. Suppose that D stalks towards V with fist drawn back.[12] What is the moral character of D's conduct? It depends. Perhaps D intends to strike V. Or perhaps D is a criminal law professor, acting out a scenario in order to demonstrate the moral ambiguity of such cases to his students. Whether D's conduct is a wrong of attempted assault depends on D's intentions.[13] It is only if he means to strike that D's otherwise lawful conduct becomes the wrong it then is. The same is true of theft. Picking up a glass of beer from the bar counter is not the stuff of theft, although it is the actus reus of theft. It lacks the nature of theft, unless and until it is done dishonestly with intent to deprive. In motivational wrongs like these, D's mental state is integral to the moral character of her action. Without

[12] See also § 7.4.

[13] T M Scanlon disagrees: *Moral Dimensions: Permissibility, Meaning, Blame* (Harvard UP 2008), esp. 41–46. Scanlon allows that D's intention may make his action an instance of attempt, but denies that it is D's intention as such that makes that (or any other) action wrong. For a critique in the context of inchoate wrongs, see V Tadros, *Wrongs and Crimes* (OUP 2016) ch 16. More generally, as Douglas Husak has pointed out, Scanlon's denial, that intentions are non-derivatively relevant to permissibility, is incompatible with the existing structure and content of Anglo-American criminal law: D Husak, 'The Costs to Criminal Theory of Supposing that Intentions are Irrelevant to Permissibility' (2009) 3 Crim L and Phil 51.

it, there is no reason to think of her conduct as constituting the kind of action that warrants condemnation by the state.

Mens rea can also *change* the type of moral wrong that D's commits. In *Court*,[14] for example, D placed a twelve-year-old girl, fully clothed, across his knees and beat her on the buttocks. The House of Lords ruled that such conduct, if a disciplinary measure, was a mere assault; but if done for sexual gratification, it was an indecent assault.[15] The judgment allows that some actions are not, by their external elements, inherently problematic, but are capable of being made so when done for certain kinds of reasons. Court's ulterior motivation was not a culpability constituent. Rather, it made his conduct the kind of wrong it was.

All of these cases turn on the general point that the nature of an action cannot always be determined by reference to its external, actus reus features alone. As Glanville Williams put it, 'the act constituting a crime may in some circumstances be objectively innocent, and take its criminal colouring entirely from the intent with which it is done.'[16] Where that is so, the law may have no regulatory interest in D's conduct unless it is motivated in certain ways. For these varieties of crime, mens rea does far more than simply establish a connection between harm and culpability—because, in itself, the actus reus does not identify anything we shouldn't be doing.[17]

Our modern criminal law contains some very important classes of offences that involve mens-rea-dependent wrongs, especially (though not exclusively) in *ulterior intent* crimes.[18] These include most economic wrongs, such as exploitation and predatory behaviour; and indeed blackmail, where the distinction between a threat and a warning depends on the defendant's motivation.[19] To some extent the dependence of economic wrongs on mens rea is an inevitable feature of marketplace transactions, where the actions of an economic actor are always likely to affect the interests of others. D may know that, by pricing her goods lower, she will take business away from V, and perhaps even force V out of business. Yet D does no wrong unless she prices her goods accordingly *in order* to drive V out of business. Here, the distinction between a side-effect of economic activity and an intended effect is central to our

[14] [1989] AC 28.

[15] Contrary to s 14 of the Sexual Offences Act 1956 (now replaced by s 3 of the Sexual Offences Act 2003).

[16] *CLGP*, 22.

[17] Mens-rea-dependent wrongs of this kind also constitute one of the two major classes of *specific intent* crimes for the purposes of intoxication doctrine: A P Simester, 'Intoxication is Never a Defence' [2009] Crim LR 3, § IV.

[18] Below, § 3.4–3.4.1.

[19] G Lamond, 'Coercion, Threats, and the Puzzle of Blackmail' in *Harm and Culpability* 215.

assessment of the wrongfulness of D's conduct. V's economic interests are by their nature exposed to the adverse effects of others' economic activity: there is no general duty to avoid injury to economic interests, and the mere fact that those interests are harmed cannot establish that D's act wrongs the victim. Hence it is only the intention with which D acts that makes her conduct properly described as a (wrongful) attack on V. In a broadly free market, persons are normally left alone to pursue their own interests, even if their self-advancing conduct has deleterious side-effects for others. Those side-effects are a natural feature of competitive interaction. However, where they are deliberately sought, D is no longer pursuing her own interests but, instead, attacking the interests of others. That is a moral wrong; and it is a wrong even if she attacks those interests merely in order to advance her own position (a characteristic of wrongs such as dumping).

Another significant class of intention-dependent wrongs comprises pre-emptive crimes. Pre-emptive crimes seek to prohibit conduct that is not in itself harmful, but which becomes problematic when perpetrated for nefarious ends. There is nothing wrong with buying fertilizer; but if done with intent to make a bomb, an offence is committed against section 5 of the Terrorism Act 2006 (UK).[20] Pre-emptive offences often involve a trade-off between actus reus and mens rea elements. Sometimes, it will be better to criminalize via a more specific actus reus, such as possession of an automatic firearm. The more precisely defined offence offers better, more detailed guidance to citizens about their freedoms and obligations, letting them know where the law stands by marking out what counts as wrongful conduct clearly in advance. But as the inchoate law of attempts itself demonstrates, sometimes this precision about the actus reus is not available. In such cases, we depend on the defendant's intention to help mark out those inchoate acts that are criminal wrongs, and which constitute a criminal attempt, or a crime against the Terrorism Act 2006, or some other preparatory offence. Moreover such intention-rich offences, despite their intangible actus reus, will frequently be more accurate in labelling D's criminality, because they more clearly identity the moral character of D's behaviour.[21] A conviction of some (hypothetical) offence of buying controlled

[20] Section 5 creates an offence of preparation of terrorist acts. According to subsection (1), 'a person commits an offence if, with the intention of (a) committing acts of terrorism, or (b) assisting another to commit such acts, he engages in any conduct in preparation for giving effect to his intention.' There are criminalization worries here: see, e.g., A P Simester, 'Prophylactic Crimes' in G R Sullivan and I Dennis (eds), *Seeking Security: Pre-empting Criminal Harms* (Hart 2012) 59.

[21] On the principle of fair labelling, see A Ashworth, 'The Elasticity of Mens Rea' in C Tapper (ed), *Crime, Proof and Punishment: Essays in Memory of Sir Rupert Cross* (Butterworth 1981) 45, 53–56; G Williams, 'Convictions and Fair Labelling' [1983] CLJ 85; *Simester and Sullivan*, § 2.4.

fertilizer may not adequately describe D's wrongdoing in a case where D's intention was to manufacture a bomb. In such cases, mens rea requirements facilitate more flexible prohibitions while still controlling the risk of attaching liability to morally innocent conduct.

3.2.1 Mediating justifications

Consider now the third function. According to the wrongdoing principle, justified φing should not beget a criminal sanction. But whether φing is justified depends, in various ways, upon D's mens rea. Sometimes, rather than making φing wrong, mens rea helps to make it right. Or at least okay.

How it does so will be explored in Part III of this book, and can only be summarized here. Suppose that D's φing, a pro tanto crime, is intended. Two things follow. First, D may claim a justification in law only if his reasons for φing fit within a legally-recognized justification such as self-defence, prevention of crime, or the like. There is no open-ended justification of 'moral reasonableness'. Partly, this is a rule of law matter.[22] But it also holds outside the law. D's claim to moral justification cannot be grounded in the mere existence of undefeated reasons to φ. It must be grounded in the reasons why D *chose* to φ. Those reasons must be sufficient to make φing permissible. Which means, in turn, that English law is right to hold that D cannot appeal to ancillary, unintended benefits to justify his φing.[23]

The same analysis helps to explain why a mens rea standard of intention differs from those mens rea states, like recklessness and negligence, that contain an inherently evaluative component. Consider E, who μs advertently without intending to do so. Imposing recklessness as a condition of liability recognizes, implicitly, that E's μing is an instance of wrongdoing only if the risk of μing is unreasonable, *taking into account other foreseen side-effects*. Similarly, F's inadvertent ρing is negligent only if that risk is unreasonable, taking into account other *foreseeable* side-effects. The explanation of why someone does something, in other words, has a direct impact upon the range of reasons that are available to justify her doing it. And this, in turn, has an elegant payoff for our understanding of the mens rea 'hierarchy' of intention, recklessness, and

22 See § 2.1.

23 Here I am taking sides in the old debate between Robinson, Fletcher, and others: see chapter 16. Cp. *Dadson* (1850) 2 Den 35, 169 ER 407 (CCR), where the benefit was unforeseen; *Thain* [1985] NI 457, where the benefit was foreseen but unintended. These cases are discussed in § 16.3.

negligence. The difference between them need not be a question of degrees of culpability. It is (also) a matter of wrongdoing.

These claims will be developed principally in chapter 16. One implication of the argument there is that we should distinguish the claim that 'D's φing is justifiable' from the claim that 'D's φing is justified'. Albeit the latter implies the former, typically it is the latter that counts for criminal law. In chapter 18, however, I will suggest that whether φing is justifiable can itself depend on why one does it. In cases of lesser-evils necessity, it may be fatal to D's case that φing is intended. Justifiability turns, in part, on the kind of justification being claimed. And at least sometimes, reasons of necessity are excluded from the justification of intending φing.[24]

3.3 Mens rea and legitimate enactment

The fourth and fifth mens rea functions concern the protection of citizens from state intervention. One form of protection is via what scholars often call the 'fair warning' principle. This is not quite the same as the overlapping principle that the liability of citizens should be ascertained by determinate legal rules, and we need to begin by getting that distinction clear. Both involve rule of law values. The latter, which is sometimes known as the principle of legality, requires that no one should be convicted of any offence unless a law exists that designates her conduct a crime: *nullum crimen sine lege*, no crime without law. It also requires that the law should be prospective, not retrospective. Often, as in the US, it is a constitutional matter. While the common law contains a presumption against retrospective crimes, that presumption is nowadays buttressed by Article 7 of the European Convention on Human Rights, which plainly interdicts retroactive criminal laws. The law, especially the criminal law, should be fixed and definite, not alterable. The potential for criminal liability of a would-be actor should exist before she acts, not originate in the subsequent discretion of others.

The legality principle requires that liability should be determined by the rule of *law*, not the rule of officials. By contrast, concern for fair warning brings out a slightly different dimension of the rule of law: that its rules should offer advance guidance to the persons who are subject to them. An unpublished law may be constitutionally valid, for instance, but it is defective as part of a system of rules designed to guide society's behaviour—like the doomsday device in *Dr*

[24] See esp. §§ 18.2.1, 18.5.2.

Strangelove, it fails as a deterrent. The distinction is helpfully brought out by Lord Bingham in *Rimmington and Goldstein*:[25]

> 'There are two guiding principles: no one should be punished under a law unless it is sufficiently clear and certain to enable him to know what conduct is forbidden before he does it; and no one should be punished for any act which was not clearly and ascertainably punishable when the act was done.'

Bingham's second principle is the basic constitutional one: that if something is not illegal, no liability can follow even if it ought to be illegal, and indeed even if most people thought it was. His first principle, on the other hand, concerns predictability and fair warning. Individuals need to be able to predict the legal implications of their actions in advance, so that they have fair warning that their contemplated actions will risk incurring a criminal sanction; so that they know where they stand and can properly decide what to do in light of the law's guidance. With secure, reliable law, citizens are enabled to steer clear of criminal liability by choice, to navigate their way through life without unexpected legal consequences befalling them. Absent such law, the ability to plan one's life is undermined.

There is a growing tendency internationally to constitutionalize this principle too.[26] Fair warning ordinarily requires not only that criminal laws exist prospectively, but also that they be stated clearly and in a reasonably precise fashion. Extending the Article 7 jurisprudence, the European Court has emphasized the aim that 'the individual can know from the wording of the relevant provision and, if need be, with the assistance of the courts' interpretation of it, what acts and omissions will make him liable.'[27] That ambition seems hard to contest. None the less, caution is appropriate here. The goal of fair warning is not to ensure textual certainty for its own sake. What really counts is whether D can anticipate liability in the case at hand—whether criminal liability comes as a surprise, as something contrary to *ex ante* expectations.[28] A focus on

[25] [2005] UKHL 63, [33].

[26] American jurisprudence in this area is well developed. See, e.g., *Papachristou v City of Jacksonville* 405 US 156, 162 (1972) (vagrancy ordinance void for vagueness); *Conally v General Construction Company* 269 US 385, 391 (1926) ('A statute which either forbids or requires the doing of an act in terms so vague that men of common intelligence must necessarily guess at its meaning and differ as to its application, violates the first essential of due process of law').

[27] *Kokkinakas v Greece* (1994) 17 EHRR 397, 423. See *G v Federal Republic of Germany* (1989) 60 DR 252, 262; *Misra and Srivastava* [2004] EWCA Crim 2375, [29]–[34].

[28] Compare John Gardner's introduction to H L A Hart's *Punishment and Responsibility* (2nd edn, OUP 2008) xxxvi: 'the law must be such that those subject to it can reliably be guided by it, either to avoid violating it or to build *the legal consequences* of having violated it into their thinking about what future actions may be open to them.' (Emphasis added.)

predictable liability rather than legislative clarity leaves space for what Andrew Ashworth calls a 'Thin Ice' principle:[29]

> 'A rounded view of the doctrine of criminal law must, however, look further than the cluster of three legality principles. If one of the aims of the criminal law is to convict those who culpably cause harm, this constitutes a policy goal which should form part of the doctrine of criminal law and which may properly enter into decisions on interpretation. The claim here is not that criminal laws should be extended retrospectively to citizens' conduct, but rather that people who knowingly "sail close to the wind" should not be surprised if the law is interpreted so as to include their conduct. This may be termed the "thin ice" principle, after the dictum of Lord Morris that "those who skate on thin ice can hardly expect to find a sign which will denote the precise spot where he [*sic*] will fall in."[30] Surely this argument might properly militate against a restrictive construction: the essence of the non-retroactivity principle is that the courts should not frustrate justified expectations, and these should not exist in controversial or manifestly doubtful cases.'

To be sure, obscure or discretionary (or retroactive) laws are likely to be insufficiently predictable, likely to offer inadequate *ex ante* guidance to citizens. But, if the objection is one of fair warning rather than the constitutional one of retroactive criminalisation, disappointing the *ex ante* expectations of a defendant may carry less weight when those expectations are unjustified. And expectations may be unjustified because of the kind of conduct the defendant contemplates, not just because of clearly-drafted proscriptions. One illustration of this is the well-known decision in *R. v R*,[31] where the House of Lords rejected spousal immunity in the common law crime of rape, thereby upholding the defendant's conviction of attempting to rape his wife. The decision is defensible on a thin-ice basis: when interpreting the current law of rape, R's anticipation of a legal immunity generated no reason for the courts to find one. It should have made no difference had R obtained an opinion from a lawyer, immediately prior to making his wife submit to intercourse, that in legal terms he would not be committing rape. His conduct was profoundly wrong, the very wrong of rape. This is not to say that courts may invent law retroactively in order to catch husbands who rape their wives. (That *would* violate the

[29] A Ashworth, 'Interpreting Criminal Statutes: A Crisis of Legality?' (1991) 107 LQR 419, 443.
[30] *Knuller v DPP* [1973] AC 435, 463. The official report is corrected to 'they'.
[31] [1992] 1 AC 599.

constraint of legality.[32]) But it is to say that, in considering what the current law is, the fact that R thought it was different should not count for much in circumstances like these, where the defendant's act breached in the most fundamental way his wife's right to bodily integrity. For R, the demands of fair warning were sufficiently met.

Understood in this wider sense, of liability's being anticipatable and not surprising, fair warning is also supported by mens rea requirements. H L A Hart saw this clearly.[33] Indeed, for Hart, warning rather than culpability is *the* basic function of mens rea. By proving intention or recklessness, the prosecution establishes that D chose to perpetrate the actus reus; this, in turn, serves to ensure that D had (and rejected) the opportunity to avoid wrongdoing, and so to evade the attentions of the criminal law.[34] Perhaps Hart exaggerated. Certainly, he underestimated the distinctive importance of culpability in the criminal law.[35] But he was right to observe that, by ensuring that the defendant has notice of his actions, mens rea requirements foster the rule of law.

The fair warning role of mens rea is especially important in the contexts of consequence-based crimes and omissions liability. Crimes of these sorts often involve no particular form of conduct, no conduct of a kind that might put the defendant on notice that—lo!—a conviction is at hand. Consequence-based crimes such as manslaughter, or criminal damage, require only that death, damage, *et cetera*, be caused by *any* piece of behaviour by the defendant. If I walk into a new building and switch on the light, I may have no idea that, because of some fault in the wiring system, an explosion will result, perhaps causing fatalities. And there is nothing distinctive about switching on a light to alert me to the potential for danger.

The same holds for omission-based liability, which is by its nature activity-unspecific. We do not complain of what the defendant does, but of what she does not. Yet as we observe in § 6.1.2, there are so many ways in which one can fail to rescue another person, so many things one may be doing instead.

[32] Strictly speaking, *R. v R* did not do that. Formally, the House of Lords held that, by the time of R's actions, the historical immunity for spouses had ceased to be part of the law: thus their Lordships did not abolish the immunity but merely acknowledged that it was gone. This (controversial) reasoning enabled the decision to survive a challenge under Article 7 of the European Convention of Human Rights before the European Court of Human Rights in *SW v UK* (1995) 21 EHRR 363. The careful analysis in *R* may be contrasted with the subsequent decision in *C* [2004] EWCA Crim 392, where C appealed his conviction in 2002 of raping his wife *in 1970*. Relying on the decision in *R. v R*, the Court of Appeal simply pronounced (at [22]) that 'the stark fact is that R was convicted. . . . The decision [by their Lordships] applied to events that had already taken place, as well as those in the future.' For discussion, see *Simester and Sullivan*, § 2.2.

[33] See, e.g., Hart, *Punishment and Responsibility*, 181–82.

[34] Subject, of course, to the possibility of defences: ibid, ch 2.

[35] A point made by J Gardner, 'Wrongs and Faults' in *Appraising Strict Liability* 51, 71.

Perhaps I am talking on the 'phone, or walking to work, or eating my lunch, and romancing a new friend, or writing an article . . . . Any of these things may be engaging my attention while, *at the same time*, I am failing to rescue the victim. Easy to see, then, how liability might come as a shock.

Considerations of fair warning supply one ground why we tend to restrict omissions liability to specialist actors, such as parents and doctors. Part of the reason for our willingness to impose positive legal duties on such actors is that we can expect them, in virtue of their roles, to be on notice of the need to act; to look out for the interests of those to whom they owe such duties. Even then, though, positive obligations have the potential to surprise. There are so many things that a parent has to do each day, some involving her children and many not, that we cannot reasonably expect any parent constantly to be alert to the possibility that something may be amiss, constantly to be thinking about her charges to the exclusion of the rest of her life.

Mens rea requirements address such problems by helping to make sure that the consequence, or the omission, comes not out of the blue. For those types of crime in particular, there is especial reason why stigmatic criminal liability should normally be confined to reckless or intentional wrongdoing. Otherwise, liability for inadvertent harms can make it too difficult for citizens, even citizens owing specific legal duties, to pursue their own lives without fear of unexpected criminal charges. If whatever activity they are engaged in does not, of itself, give them notice of disaster, we must rely on mens rea to ensure they have it.

John Gardner, however, would go even further. Advancing what he describes as 'the mens rea principle', he argues that 'criminal wrongs should be such that one does not commit them unless one intends or is aware of at least one wrong-making feature of what one is about to do, such that (assuming one knows the law) one is also alerted to the fact that what one is about to do will be of interest to the criminal law.'[36] Thus Gardner requires awareness rather than notice. The rationale for his principle is also rooted in fair warning arguments, along the lines advanced originally by Hart:[37]

> 'According to the ideal known as the rule of law, those of us about to commit a criminal wrong should be put on stark notice that that is what we are about to do. The criminal law should not ambush us unexpectedly. Of course, to avoid unexpected ambushes we all need to know what the law requires of us.

[36] Ibid, 70.
[37] Ibid, 69–70.

> For that reason, criminal laws should be clear, open, consistent, stable, and prospective. They should also forbid specific actions (not courses of action, activities, ways of life, etc.). Even all this, however, is not enough to ensure that those of us about to violate the criminal law are put on stark notice that we are about to violate it. For we may know the law and yet have no grasp that what we are about to do might constitute a violation of it. That is because often we have no idea which actions we are about to perform. I make a light-hearted remark and (surprise!) I offend one of my guests. I turn on my oven and (surprise!) I blow all the fuses. The mens rea principle is the principle according to which such actions—the self-surprising ones—should not be criminal wrongs.'

There is much to admire in this analysis, including its rule-of-law commitment to protect subject-citizens from oppressive and unexpected use of the state's power. But Gardner's conclusion now strikes me as too strong. For two reasons. First, to the extent that the rule of law enjoins unpredictable interference by the State, liability for negligence is reasonably predictable. Moreover, unless negligence liability be no deterrent, the argument prima facie deprives victims of protection from similarly unlooked-for intrusions by other citizens. The demand that notice be 'stark' seems unduly weighted in favour of defendants. At least where the interest at stake is sufficiently important, as in manslaughter, a mens rea standard of gross negligence may be defensible.[38]

Secondly, and perhaps more importantly, Gardner's requirement that a criminal wrongdoer must intend or be aware of at least one wrong-making feature of the action neglects the gateway role of some activity-specific prohibitions. Perhaps the best example of this is rape. There is nothing wrong, or wrong-making, about sexual intercourse per se. But one reason why it is acceptable to criminalize negligence with respect to non-consensual sex, as many jurisdictions have, is that matters of consent are so closely bound up with the very nature of sexual intercourse that those engaging in sex are, implicitly, on notice that questions of consent are in play. The context is so intimate that alertness to the will of one's partner can be expected of every responsible actor, and a failure to exhibit such alertness is itself ground for condemnation. It isn't like carelessly tossing a stone aside, only—lo!—to hear the sound of breaking glass. To make criminal damage an offence of negligence would be unfair

[38] This claim assumes that an adequately formulated and sufficiently robust (gross) negligence standard can take account of considerations such as the defendant's intellectual limitations. For related discussion, see § 12.3.4.

because there is not always reason to inquire about the circumstances of one's conduct. Sometimes the unexpected happens. But sex is a specific activity, and not like behaviour that happens to cause property damage. It is distinctive in a manner that generates an immediate and obvious duty to consider whether one's partner consents.

Gardner's principle is absolute. That's a mistake. Fair warning constraints admit of a trade-off, a trade-off in which mens rea plays a part. Notice of impending criminal liability must be adequate rather than stark. Some activities are more obviously dangerous than others, some interests more in need of protection. The same holds for omission-based duties, some of which are more specific than others. The anaesthetist may be surprised to find that a tube is detached,[39] just as the railway gatekeeper may be startled to discover the gate left open.[40] Neither can complain, however, that these events were unlooked-for. In other cases, by contrast, it may only be the presence of mens rea, and in particular of intention or advertence, that guarantees sufficient warning of imminent liability.

3.3.1 Negotiating the parameters of criminalization

The fifth role of mens rea is perhaps the least familiar. It too concerns the relationship of citizens with the state. As well as helping to secure fair warning, the so-called 'fault' requirements in offences can also play an important role in mediating the scope of the prohibitions themselves, especially for those offences where the mental element is not required to identify a wrong.

It is common, indeed too common, for criminal lawyers to think of the criminal law in *ex post* terms, where the defendant has already acted; and our task is to decide whether she satisfies the criteria of an offence, including all of its actus reus and mens rea components. At this *ex post* stage, the temptation is to focus on the particular defendant, the character and circumstances of her conduct, and on whether she deserves punishment for what she has done. From an *ex* post viewpoint, it is easy to conceive of the offence specification as setting the criteria of punishment. But, as we said in chapter 1, that conception is incomplete. The offence should exist even before φing is done. This is because the primary role of an offence, *ex ante*, is to articulate a prohibition. Do

[39] *Adomako* [1995] AC 171: see § 12.4.
[40] *Pittwood* (1902) 19 TLR 37: see § 5.4.

not do φ *in future*, the prohibition says, and it backs that up with the prospect of punishment.

This *ex ante* role is central to the operation of any offence as a guide to citizens. It is the prospect of conviction and punishment, not the infliction of punishment itself, that supplies incentives to would-be wrongdoers.[41] The question of punishment only arises, in a sense, once the guiding function of a prohibition has failed. So we should begin by considering offences from an *ex ante* perspective: as measures of criminalization. And, when interpreting offences alongside our general part doctrines, we should be less tempted to respond to backward-looking considerations about the culpability of the particular defendant, and influenced rather more by the implications of a given interpretation for the scope of activity the offence prohibits.

Seen from that perspective, the important point here is that the content of the prohibition *includes* the mens rea specification,[42] and that the nature of its mens rea requirement directly affects the guidance given by the proscription. Which blows a hole in the speakers of some acoustic separationists. Paul Robinson, for instance, argues that we should eliminate culpability elements from an ideal Code of Conduct and remainder them to a Code of Adjudication. Doing so, he contends, would enhance the law's communicative potential.[43] To the extent that liability elements are *exclusively* concerned with culpability, that's fair enough. As will be noted in § 17.4, rationale-based excuses are adjudicatory rather than guiding. When they function as *ex post* culpability elements, the same applies to mens rea: it too is adjudicatory rather than guiding. *But not exclusively*. The mens rea specification is also part of the *ex ante* guidance to citizens. It helps to tell them about the extent of their criminal-law obligations. So it cannot be remaindered to a Code of Adjudication.

By way of example, let us start with a putative crime where the actus reus comprises sexual intercourse with a person under the age of 16 years. Consider, next, *what this offence leaves us free to do*. The answer depends on its mens rea requirement. If, to commit the offence, D must intend or know that her partner is aged under 16, D is left with considerable freedom of action. She must refrain from sex only when she knows or purposes that her partner be underage.

[41] This point is key to reconciling deterrent and retributive functions in the criminal law. See J R Edwards and A P Simester, 'Prevention with a Moral Voice' in A P Simester, A du Bois-Pedain, and U Neumann (eds), *Liberal Criminal Theory: Essays for Andreas von Hirsch* (Hart 2014) 43, 45ff.

[42] See §§ 2.1–2.

[43] P H Robinson, *Structure and Function in Criminal Law* (OUP 1997) 185; P H Robinson, 'Rules of Conduct and Principles of Adjudication' (1990) 57 U Chicago LR 729, 736–39.

Contrast a mens rea element of (subjective) recklessness. If recklessness suffices for a conviction, it follows that D must refrain from sex whenever she suspects that her partner may be underage. By contrast with the knowledge-based offence, the scope of the prohibition is become larger: the former version permits her to proceed despite realizing her partner may be underage; the latter does not.

All the more so when, as in many jurisdictions, the mens rea element is negligence. Now D is not at liberty to have sex unless she *takes care* that her partner is of age. This is not to suggest that a prohibition of negligent underage sex is inappropriate. The point is simply that it is broader, more intrusive, and that its wider scope needs to be justified. Broader still would be the extreme case of strict liability,[44] in which case D might only be sure of avoiding liability by refraining from sex altogether.

Similar implications arise for consequence-based crimes, such as causing damage to another's property. Suppose that my friends and I have a cricket bat, and a ball, and want to play a game on the street. But there are windows nearby. Can we play? It depends. If the mens rea requirement of a criminal damage offence is intention, we only need to cease and desist when we are targeting the windows.[45] A standard of recklessness could mean we have to forego the cricket even if we are not targeting the windows—but only if we know the windows are there and realize we may break them.[46] Negligence, on the other hand, might require our game to be preceded by a thorough health-and-safety check. Strict liability would rule it out altogether. Play at your own risk.

As it happens, current English criminal law leaves people with the latitude to be careless with the property of others, but not the freedom deliberately to take risks.[47] The difference may look like one of culpability; but it is also, perhaps even primarily, a difference of liberty.[48] When contemplating whether to prohibit conduct, one should not only consider the magnitude and seriousness of the harms involved. One should also consider the value of the conduct to be prohibited and the impact of its proscription upon the freedom of citizens. Mens rea elements can help to negotiate these considerations. They help to balance the invasiveness of a prohibition against the interests of those whom the law seeks to protect. Setting a more stringent mens rea requirement

[44] e.g. Sexual Offences Act 2003 (UK), ss 5–8 (offences against children under 13).

[45] Or, perhaps, virtually certain to break them: see §§ 15.2–3.

[46] Provided, that is, that the foreseen risk is an unreasonable one. (For discussion of the English law, see *Simester and Sullivan*, § 5.2.)

[47] Criminal Damage Act 1971 (UK), s 1; *G* [2003] UKHL 50.

[48] For an argument along these lines in the context of complicity liability, see § 7.4.

means that the prospect of liability will have less impact on the day-to-day lives of law-abiding individuals. Simply put, persons will be required to alter their behaviour on fewer occasions—only when they know, or suspect, or ought to know (as the case may be) about the risk. By pitching the standard of mens rea higher, we make it easier for citizens to comply with the law, and we reduce the range of activities they have to sacrifice in order to avoid the risk of a criminal conviction.

The criminal law is designed to safeguard us from threats of harm. But criminal prohibitions are themselves threatening, in so far as they coercively restrict our freedom. Ordinary citizens must not only be shielded from the predations of others; they need also to be shielded from the state, which should not intrude upon their everyday, innocent activities. Quite apart from its other roles, the requirement of a mental element has an important function to play in keeping citizens outside the scope of criminal prohibitions. Mens rea, that is to say, protects freedom.

3.4 Two kinds of mens rea element

Before concluding, we should add some more taxonomy. Perhaps the most familiar types of mens rea element are *corresponding*, or dependent, mens rea elements. Standardized elements of this type are said to include purpose, intention, knowledge, recklessness, and negligence, although the variety is considerable.[49] In § 2.2, we noted that these mens rea requirements form part of the pro tanto criminal wrong. They can also change the character of D's moral wrong, a possibility contemplated in § 3.2. Many people hold, for example, that murder is a different wrong from manslaughter, and not merely a more culpable one. Assuming that is right, the criminal law has reason to label them separately. Plausibly too, it is only the infliction of *intended* pain, and not the advertent causing of pain, that can constitute torture. Causing pain recklessly, on that view, should not be criminalized as torture—because it is not the *wrong* of torture.

Even when the normative character of a crime is derived primarily from its actus reus elements, we saw in § 3.3 that mens rea requirements play an indispensable role in delineating its boundaries. They safeguard liberty as well as

[49] An interesting example is the definition of 'heedlessly' once proposed by the Law Commission for England and Wales in s 22 of its Draft Criminal Code: LC143, *Codification of the Criminal Law* (HMSO 1985).

guilt. But corresponding mens rea elements do not do this independently. Our typology of actus reus elements from § 2.3 has certain payoffs here. An evaluative element, we noted, generally has no corresponding mens rea requirement. Circumstance elements are also distinctive. An instructive example is *Pace and Rogers*,[50] in which D was charged with attempting to convert 'criminal property'. He purchased second-hand metal that he suspected was stolen. Had it indeed been stolen, he could have been convicted under the Proceeds of Crime Act 2002, liability for which requires only that an offender *suspects* the property is stolen. However, the metal was not in fact stolen. (It was transacted as part of a police 'sting' operation.) What state of mind, then, sufficed for the attempt?

According to section 1(1) of the Criminal Attempts Act 1981 (UK), a criminal attempt must be done 'with intent to commit an offence'. Since D merely suspected the property was stolen, the Court of Appeal quite properly quashed his conviction. As it did so, however, the Court remarked that 'as a matter of ordinary language and in accordance with principle, an "intent to commit an offence" connotes an intent to commit all the elements of the offence.'[51] Not so. Since circumstance elements are characteristically uncaused by D (indeed, are typically outside D's control), D cannot sensibly be required to have an intention to 'commit' them; nor even an intention that they be present. When applied to circumstance elements within an actus reus, common law translates the mens rea requirement of 'intention' to require a cognitive equivalent: belief that the circumstance exists.[52] Of course, D might want to buy the metal *only if* it is stolen. In this case, it is true in a narrower sense that D intends to {convert property that is stolen}, in that the fact that the property is stolen forms part of his motivation for acting; it is internal to what D is aiming to achieve.[53] But that is an abnormal case, bordering on pathological. In the standard case, D is aware that the metal is stolen, yet neither intends nor hopes, indeed does not care, that it is. D none the less intends to {convert stolen property} because he intends to {convert property} *believing* that the property is stolen.[54]

[50] [2014] EWCA Crim 186.

[51] [2014] EWCA Crim 186, [62].

[52] See § 15.1.3. For helpful discussion of belief elements in the criminal law, see S C Shute, 'Knowledge and Belief in the Criminal Law' and G R Sullivan, 'Knowledge, Belief and Culpability' in S C Shute and A P Simester (eds), *Criminal Law Theory: Doctrines of the General Part* (OUP 2002) 184 and 207 respectively. My comments on this issue are necessarily brief. For much fuller exploration of the difficulties raised, see G Yaffe, *Attempts: In the Philosophy of Action and the Criminal Law* (OUP 2010) esp. ch 5 and R A Duff, *Criminal Attempts* (OUP 1997) ch 1.

[53] As Antony Duff would put it, in that narrower kind of case (and unlike the standard case), D would regard himself as having failed should the property turn out not be stolen: *IACL*, 61–63; Duff, *Criminal Attempts* (n 52) ch 1; below, § 15.1.1.

[54] Parallel complexities arise for recklessness and circumstances. See, e.g., *Simester and Sullivan*, § 5.2(iii).

3.4.1 Ulterior mens rea elements

Not all mens rea elements, however, 'correspond' to an actus reus element. Sometimes the intentional doing of an actus reus becomes a pro tanto crime only when done for some *further* reason. D may legitimately carry a crowbar in her bag; but if she is carrying the crowbar with intent to use it in a burglary, she commits the crime of 'going equipped'.[55] Crimes of this sort are said to require an 'ulterior' intent,[56] in that they involve an intention that is ulterior to the actus reus. The actus reus of going equipped is simple possession of the crowbar—it does not matter whether or how it is actually used.[57] But it does matter how it is intended to be used.

Often, the gap between corresponding and ulterior intentions admits of a gap between present and future, in terms of when the intention is to be acted upon. The English law of theft illustrates this nicely. According to section 1(1) of the Theft Act 1968, theft is committed if the defendant 'dishonestly appropriates property belonging to another with the intention of permanently depriving the other of it.' If James dishonestly appropriates property belonging to another, to become guilty of theft he need not intend to deprive permanently *by that act of appropriation*; it is enough that his action is accompanied by a future intention to deprive.[58]

On other occasions, a temporal gap may foreclose liability. In this context, it can be especially important not to confuse corresponding with ulterior forms of mens rea.[59] Consider the following example:[60]

> D is an assassin who has been hired to kill V. One evening she drives over to V's house in order to shoot him when he comes home. On the way, however, she is involved in an accident when she collides with a cyclist who has suddenly cut in front of her car. Upon getting out of the car, D recognizes that the cyclist is V, who is dead as a result of the accident.

Perhaps D is guilty of a homicide offence, but she has not murdered V. She causes his death by driving into him, and at that time she has an intention to kill

[55] Contrary to the Theft Act 1968 (UK), s 25.
[56] J Horder, 'Crimes of Ulterior Intent' in *Harm and Culpability* 153.
[57] *Rodley* (1913) 9 Cr App R 69, 76.
[58] *Morris* [1984] AC 320; *Gomez* [1993] AC 442 (HL). For criticism, see *Simester and Sullivan*, § 13.6(ii).
[59] As is sometimes done when it is denied that one can intend to act (in the future) unintentionally. The current intention is typically ulterior. For insightful discussion, see Yaffe, *Attempts* (n 52) 181ff.
[60] Adopted from *Simester and Sullivan*, § 5.8.

him. Yet her driving is not accompanied by a present intention (thereby) to kill or cause grievous injury. Some writers take this kind of example to put pressure on the concurrence requirement, by showing that D's mens rea must 'actuate' rather than accompany her conduct;[61] but that seems doubtful.[62] Suppose that D is in a hurry, because late to get into position, and it is her speed that causes the accident. In this case we can say that D's intention to assassinate V 'actuates' the behaviour that causes death. None the less, the case is not one of murder. It is not murder because D's intention is of the wrong kind. It is ulterior to her causative action, not corresponding. D does not intend by behaving as she does to cause V's death.[63]

Fine distinctions like this are typical of the kinds of motivational wrongs that we discussed in § 3.2. However, it is worth emphasizing that ulterior mens rea elements need not involve an intention—and this possibility can make them very complex indeed. Consider the English crime of aggravated criminal damage, enacted by section 1(2) of the Criminal Damage Act 1971:

> A person who without lawful excuse destroys or damages any property, whether belonging to himself or another—
> (a) intending to destroy or damage any property or being reckless as to whether any property would be destroyed or damaged; and
> (b) [i] intending by the destruction or damage to endanger the life of another or [ii] *being reckless as to whether the life of another would be thereby endangered*;
> shall be guilty of an offence. [Emphasis added.]

Like element (b)[i], element (b)[ii] is an ulterior mens rea element, albeit one that constitutes a different wrong. Without one of them, the subsection specifies no crime at all, since it is not unlawful to destroy or damage one's own property. It follows that the two cannot be collapsed, say, for the purposes of ascertaining the corresponding inchoate wrongs in attempts liability. Trying {to cause damage to property intending that life is thereby endangered} is not the

[61] See, e.g., A F Sarch, 'Knowledge, Recklessness and the Connection Requirement Between Actus Reus and Mens Rea' (2015) 120 Penn St LR 1.

[62] Proponents of an actuation requirement also face difficulties in explaining why, in cases of recklessness, foresight of a risk is *actuating*—when it is normally something *despite which* the defendant acts. The concurrence requirement is, in short, not a causal requirement.

[63] Notice that this view leaves open the possibility that the preparation/attempt line in inchoate liability does not track the distinction between present and future intentions. Since crimes of attempt are motivational wrongs, it is plausible that the latter suffices for liability. Suppose that D enters V's house and draws her pistol in order to shoot him; whereupon V dies of shock. In principle, this could be a case of murder, on the basis that D has crossed the preparation threshold and commenced her attempt.

same thing done as trying {to cause damage to property being reckless whether life is thereby endangered}. In principle, only the former inchoate wrong ought to require that one is trying to endanger life as well as property. In turn, however, this means that such elements cannot be assimilated with, say, circumstances for the purposes of attempts liability.[64] Were there a distinct wrong of trying {to cause damage to property belonging to another, intending that life is thereby endangered}, it would ordinarily suffice that the inchoate wrongdoer *believes* the property is someone else's.

This disanalogy with circumstance elements in the context of inchoate wrongs is accompanied by a disanalogy with corresponding mens rea elements. Ulterior mens rea elements tend to play a distinctive role in structuring criminal wrongs, and this shows up in their inchoate counterparts. We saw earlier that, while stolen property can be converted on the back of a suspicion, trying to convert stolen property requires a belief that the property is stolen. In effect, the corresponding mens rea element in the substantive offence drops out when it comes to the dependent, attempt-based offence. That does not happen in the two aggravated criminal damage offences above. And that is because, in the latter offences, the ulterior mens rea requirements are playing a different kind of role in constituting D's wrong.

3.5 Conclusion

Still, it is no aim of this book to develop a taxonomy of wrongs, even inchoate ones. Later chapters will be concerned mainly with corresponding forms of mens rea. Our sketch of actus reus and mens rea elements in §§ 2.3 and 3.4 was just that: a sketch. Many of the issues raised are controversial and worthy of books in themselves. But we have a long way to go. Armed with some basic distinctions, it is time to move on. Our set-up work is done.

Conventionally, mens rea is thought of as a culpability requirement. Helping to establish culpability is certainly one of its roles, and an important one at that. However, it has other roles too. Mens rea elements can perform at least five different sorts of function in an offence, and those other effects need also to be considered when discussing what mens rea standard ought to be set for a given offence.

[64] Cf. G R Sullivan, 'Bad Thoughts and Bad Acts' [1990] Crim LR 559. An insightful discussion is J Child, 'The Structure, Coherence and Limits of Inchoate Liability: The New Ulterior Element' (2014) 34 Legal Studies 537.

Indeed, it is those other functions, and not culpability, that supply the main explanations why negligence should be used so rarely in serious offences. Against claims by some writers to the contrary, I argue in this book that inadvertent negligence *can* be blameworthy.[65] That isn't what prevents negligence from being used more commonly. Rather, in some crimes there is no place for negligence liability because D's intention or awareness contributes to making the conduct a wrong. And more generally, limiting the use of negligence helps to constrain state power, both by reducing the risk of unexpected liability and by restricting the deterrent scope of the law's prohibitions. Choice-based mens rea standards can assist to secure fair warning for potential defendants and, at the same time, help negotiate the fraught line between preventing wrongs and preserving freedom. To appreciate these last two functions, though, we have to stop focusing on the criminal law as a punishing institution, and be willing to think about it from a forward-looking perspective, as a body of *ex ante* proscriptions.

Some of the propositions advanced in this chapter are familiar. The purpose of the chapter is, in a sense, to draw them together. Seen alongside, they reveal that mens rea is *not*, uniquely or even predominantly, about culpability. *Actus non fit reus nisi mens sit rea* may be a beginning. But it is far from the end.

[65] See chapters 11–12.

PART II
RESPONSIBILITY

4

Moral and Ascriptive Responsibilities

Imagine the following scenario. One fine September morning, Jim is discovered dead in his home. His skull has been crushed by a blow inflicted with a heavy object. The police are called. Upon further investigation, they establish that he was murdered by his daughter, Alice, who killed him in order to receive her inheritance under his will.

Intuitively, most criminal lawyers would regard this as a straightforward example of criminal wrongdoing. A combination of features marks it out:

(i) Alice intends her behaviour to cause Jim's death.
(ii) Her behaviour does cause his death.
(iii) She is an agent with respect to her behaviour; the behaviour is her own voluntary action, not an involuntary bodily movement.
(iv) Alice's behaviour constitutes a positive act causing Jim's death, rather than an omission.
(v) Alice acts while in a normal state of mind.
(vi) Her action in killing Jim is unjustified.

This is a clear—even paradigm—case for the imposition of criminal liability, combining as it does such features as intentional rather than advertent or inadvertent action, successful action rather than mere attempt, and voluntary agency rather than mere event. In the following chapters, we will explore the importance of many of these component features. Yet few would doubt that their presence together makes this a central case, not only for state punishment but for blame generally.

Equally, though, few would suggest that the criminal law should concern itself only with paradigm cases, and that criminal liability should never be inflicted, for example, upon wrongdoers who do not intend their crimes. Harder cases await. What if, although Alice had not realized it, Jim was about to attack her? Or the blow was inflicted not by Alice, but by a vase falling accidentally from the bookshelf, and she had deliberately failed to summon an ambulance to save him? Or that the vase had caused death instantly, but had fallen because

Fundamentals of Criminal Law. A P Simester, Oxford University Press (2021). © A P Simester.
DOI: 10.1093/oso/9780198853145.003.0004

Alice negligently dislodged it? *Et cetera*. As we stretch the criminal net beyond the paradigm cases, we confront questions about how far we may legitimately extend its reach. Are there boundaries beyond which we should not venture?

There are. The culpability principle supplies one such. It ring-fences the possibility of criminal convictions around those defendants who are blameworthy for Jim's death. Indeed, in our September scenario, that principle is likely to exclude virtually everyone in the jurisdiction except Alice. Ultimately, however, it needs supplementation. Suppose that Keith—a mutual friend—had suspected Alice might try to murder Jim that week, and had done nothing to warn him? Keith may deserve reproach, but ought we to convict him of a crime? Ordinarily not of a homicide offence, at any rate. Similarly, the stranger who deliberately fails to save a child from drowning may be morally culpable for allowing the child to die, but normally lies outwith the law of murder.[1] Additional principles, of *responsibility*, are needed to identify who should be criminally liable for such harms.

In order to develop those principles, we need to say something more about a distinction introduced in chapter 1. *Ascriptive responsibility* norms differ in kind from norms of *moral responsibility*, and both should be further distinguished from blameworthiness or culpability.[2] As Hart observed, there are different senses in which one can be said to be 'responsible' for something,[3] including causation ('the storm was responsible for the loss of the ship'), duty ('the captain was responsible for the safety of the ship'), reliability or dutifulness ('Anna is a responsible sort of person'), and even legal liability ('the court held the captain responsible for the disaster'). Some of these usages, especially those connected with causation and duty, are directly relevant to responsibility criteria in the criminal law. But none of them names the two categories with which the law must start.

4.1 Moral responsibility

Let us begin with moral responsibility. Philosophers generally tie moral responsibility to culpability. But they do so with varying degrees of tightness. Most commonly, it is said that to be morally responsible for an event is to be

[1] An interesting discussion is A Norrie, 'Legal and Social Murder: What's the Difference?' [2018] Crim LR 531.

[2] As noted in chapter 1, I treat 'blameworthiness' and 'culpability' as synonymous. See further chapter 11.

[3] See Hart, *Punishment and Responsibility*, 210.

worthy of blame (or praise, as the case may be[4]) in respect of that event. In some ways, however, that connection is too tight. It tends to obscure some important differences in the ingredients of a culpability evaluation. Crudely put for the moment, we should distinguish (i) questions about D's actual capacities with respect to an event from (ii) questions about how D *exercised* those capacities. The former are different in kind from the latter.

For the purposes of this book, therefore, 'moral responsibility' designates an agent's *eligibility* for evaluations of moral praise- or blame-worthiness in respect of some event.[5] The extent to which D is praise- or blame-worthy for an event is a question we don't get to explore unless, first, D is morally responsible for it.[6] On this view, finding moral responsibility is no more than a gateway on the road to finding culpability. It is a condition of blaming judgements in the criminal law because it is a condition of (correct) blaming judgements *simpliciter*. More than that: it is strictly a precondition. Once moral responsibility is established, its existence is neutral about whether D is in fact blameworthy, praiseworthy, or neither.

Moral responsibility is a form of capacity responsibility: one might term it, more fully, *moral-agent-capacity* responsibility. Its existence depends upon various more specific capacities on the part of the agent. At perhaps the rawest level, an agent must have *physical* capacity in respect of an event, a requirement that depends on whether the event's occurrence lies within the agent's physical control. The criminal law accommodates this demand through a general requirement of voluntariness, including the related 'defence' of impossibility: we consider these further in chapter 8. Like moral responsibility, moreover, the scope of voluntariness extends beyond the physical level. Both require that the defendant also has *deliberative* capacity in respect of an event; a requirement that is satisfied when the event's occurrence is within an agent's deliberative control: deliberative capacity thus imports, and implies, physical

[4] *Pace* R J Wallace, *Responsibility and the Moral Sentiments* (Harvard UP 1994) 12. Wallace ties moral responsibility to judgements of blame *rather than* praise. Compare, too, D Husak, 'Gardner on the Philosophy of Criminal Law' (2009) 29 OJLS 169, 173: 'a philosophical analysis of responsibility should begin . . . with an accusation of wrongdoing.'

[5] For analogous usages, see, e.g., T M Scanlon, *What We Owe to Each Other* (Harvard UP 1998) 248; A M Smith, 'Responsibility for Attitudes: Activity and Passivity in Mental Life' (2005) 115 Ethics 236, 238. The language of 'events' is meant (for now) to be ecumenical. As we noted in chapter 2, liability in criminal law can range over a variety of actus reus elements. In § 4.3, I suggest that D's moral responsibility for outcomes or states of affairs comes through the relationship of those outcomes or states of affairs to events that involve behaviour by D. (See further § 8.4.) In general, therefore, one can substitute 'behaviour' for 'event' in what follows, and I do so later. However, it needs to be borne in mind that such behaviour need not be an instance of D's agency. Complications also arise regarding D's moral responsibility for *the behaviour of another*: see chapter 7.

[6] For linguistic variation, I sometimes use 'for' rather than 'in respect of'. Nothing of substance is intended by this.

capacity.[7] Finally, the agent must also be a *moral* agent in respect of the event, in the sense that she is capable of recognizing and acting for salient moral reasons. Insane persons, for example, may sometimes act for reasons and intend the harm they inflict—they may possess deliberative capacity in respect of their conduct—but they may lack the capacity to recognize that their actions are morally wrong. Agents of this kind, too, are not morally responsible for their actions, even if those actions are voluntary. At this point, though, voluntariness doctrines run out. The criminal law must exculpate such actions by supplementary means: specifically, by means of the irresponsibility defences.[8]

What unites these types of capacity responsibility is that they all concern the agent's ability to be guided by moral reasons concerning her behaviour. D is morally responsible for her φing if she has the capacity to recognize, evaluate, and, ultimately, respond to reasons for and against φing. (Moral responsibility is, thus, relational.[9]) And she lacks moral responsibility when she lacks one or more of those capacities. People often fail to act for the reasons by which they should have been guided. When they fail because they were incapable of responding to those reasons, they lack moral responsibility. That incapacity to respond may be physical, as when D is paralysed; or it may be psychological, as when D suffers from insane delusions. The upshot is the same. D lacks the ability to govern her behaviour by moral reasoning.

Or, we might say, she lacks *sufficient* ability. Like the underlying capacities that it rests upon, moral responsibility for an event can come in degrees. An injury may leave one with reduced control over one's physical movements; one's awareness may be clouded when in a hypoglycaemic state; depending on her age, a child may have *some* ability to reason morally about her actions. Moral responsibility is thus a threshold condition. Unless the threshold is satisfied—unless D has sufficient capacities to subordinate her conduct to

[7] Within the common law, a state of deliberative incapacity is often said to invoke the defence of automatism. As will be explained in chapter 8, that 'defence' is properly folded into the voluntariness requirement. See esp. § 8.5.

[8] See § 17.5.

[9] The discussion here is in many ways sympathetic to Antony Duff's account of reason-responsiveness in *Answering for Crime: Responsibility and Liability in the Criminal Law* (Hart 2007) 38ff, albeit Duff does not there consider the possibility of physical incapacity. At points, though, Duff seems to think of capacity-based responsibility as a non-relational property of the agent. (Cp. Moore's characterization of insanity as a status defence: 'The Quest for a Responsible Responsibility Test: The Norwegian Insanity Law after Breivik' (2015) 9 Crim L and Phil 645.) While the matter is not of central importance here, it seems to me plausible that an agent might lack moral reasoning capacities in respect of some but not all of her actions. That possibility is allowed for in the *M'Naghten* Rules, which regulate insanity under English criminal law, and was endorsed in *Kay* [2017] EWCA Crim 647. Cp. Law Commission No. 177, *A Criminal Code for England and Wales* (HMSO 1989) para. 11.16; also the partial defence of diminished responsibility in English law (Homicide Act 1957, s 2; as reformulated in 2009), which requires that D's abnormality of mental functioning must *explain* D's conduct.

moral reasons—we cannot embark on an assessment of D's culpability. We simply don't get that far. This, in turn, is why the criminal law's irresponsibility defences, like the requirement of voluntariness, operate separately from the culpability elements and the rationale-based defences. They do not speak to the *quality* of D's practical reasoning, but to her capacity for it. They speak, in other words, to D's moral responsibility for the event constituting her alleged offence, without which no defendant should suffer a conviction.[10]

Culpability, then, implies moral responsibility. The converse does not hold. D may be a full moral agent whose voluntarily behaviour satisfies the actus reus of an offence, but whose doing so was neither intentional nor negligent: as when a doctor administers appropriate medical treatment which causes an unexpected reaction that kills the patient. The example illustrates, in part, why we have distinguished between moral responsibility and culpability in the first place. We need both, but they operate in quite different ways. Whereas mens rea, justification, and excuse elements are interdependent,[11] the voluntariness requirement and the irresponsibility defences are fundamentally separate.

All of this remains, of course, to be fleshed out in later chapters.[12] It is worth emphasizing, though, that moral responsibility is concerned with the preconditions of praise- or blame-*worthiness* in respect of an event; not with the preconditions of praising or blaming. Blaming someone is itself an action, and its justification is not established simply by showing that the person being blamed for φing is actually blameworthy for φing. Amongst other things, we should reach that conclusion for undefeated reasons. (In the criminal law, moreover, we should do so while observing appropriate procedural and evidential constraints.) Even then, perhaps we should refrain from expressing our blaming judgement if we know that extreme consequences, even suicide, might follow.[13]

[10] Even when that threshold is crossed, and moral responsibility is established, limitations of capacity can make a difference to the agent's culpability. This possibility is contemplated by criminal law's hybrid defences, discussed in § 19.1; it would also be relevant to sentencing.

[11] As will be seen in Part III. On the distinction between irresponsibility defences and excuses, see § 17.5.

[12] Neither have I addressed here the debate over determinism, which might be thought to undermine the claim that we can be responsible agents at all. Partly, this is because the possibility of determinism does not seem to undermine the particular concepts of responsibility, and culpability, that are the subject of this book and which inform the criminal law. But more on this in §§ 11.4–5, 14.4.1.

[13] This last consideration is especially poignant in the criminal law, where (as we noted in chapter 1) the mere conviction can, and frequently does, damage the defendant's life. This is why many jurisdictions have a disposal option of *discharge without conviction*, to complement one of conviction and discharge (i.e. without further punishment). See, e.g., ss 106–109 of the Sentencing Act 2002 (NZ): according to the guidance found in s 107 of that Act, 'The court must not discharge an offender without conviction unless the court is satisfied that the direct and indirect consequences of a conviction would be out of all proportion to the gravity of the offence.'

Or perhaps we have no *standing* to express blame. This last possibility invokes an important distinction between moral and ascriptive responsibility. Many forms of responsibility are relational. Relational to what, though? It depends on what kind of responsibility we are talking about. Indeed, one might intelligibly describe D as a 'morally responsible agent', as if moral responsibility were a status and not relational at all. However, such a usage is apt to confuse, and adds little to characterizing D as a 'moral agent'. Moral responsibility, in the sense used in this book, *is* relational: D is morally responsible *for* something, such as the occurrence of an actus reus. Suppose that Dorothy observes Edgar in difficulties in the swimming pool. Being paralysed from the waist down, she is unable to rescue him so uses her cell-phone to call for help. Dorothy is morally responsible for the latter deed (calling for help) but not the former (failing to rescue). As the example suggests, criminal lawyers should certainly ask, 'Who is morally responsible for what?'

But they should not ask, 'Who is morally responsible for what *to whom*?' Like capacity responsibility more generally,[14] moral responsibility for an event is not relative to an audience.[15] Rather, it is tied to the agent and event that are candidates for evaluation. The 'to whom' predicate is a matter of ascriptive responsibility.

In this aspect, moral responsibility is kindred to what John Gardner calls 'basic responsibility',[16] which is similarly capacity-based and audience-independent. Kindred, but not twin. In Gardner's account, one is only basically responsible for φing if one has the ability to *explain* why one φed. This connects responsibility to the explanation as well as to the φing. As such, D might be morally responsible for φing without her being basically responsible for it, for example when D is insane or unable to communicate at the point of giving an explanation. The criminal law occasionally reflects this difference when it distinguishes between insanity and 'unfitness to plead': the latter is tied to the time of the trial, the former to D's φing. Conversely, at the point of trial, one may be basically responsible for φing without having been morally responsible at the earlier time. When asked why she did not rescue Edgar, Dorothy can fully explain herself: because I was paralysed.[17]

[14] To be clear: the *kind* (and degree) of capacity responsibility that is appropriately required within a legal system will be system-dependent. Tort law, for instance, may not demand moral responsibility in respect of a liability-generating event, whereas the higher standard should be required for criminal law. See, e.g., J Goudkamp, *Tort Law Defences* (Hart 2013) 50–52.

[15] *Ex abundante cautela*, this is not to suggest that the content of morality is society-independent. (It is possible, too, that a society may have a distinct conception of culpability. I am not concerned with that here.)

[16] *Offences and Defences*, ch 12.

[17] Admittedly, this explanation is different in kind from the explanation offered by a rationale-based excuse or justification (see §§ 17.1–2). But either kind of explanation suffices for the criminal law.

For the purposes of the criminal law, these differences are relatively unimportant. If D lacks basic responsibility at the time of her φing, normally she will also lack moral responsibility. Even where D *is* morally responsible for φing, a criminal conviction should not ensue if she lacks the ability to explain herself by the time the state calls her to account. But that conclusion arises for different reasons. We may have to hand unequivocal proof that D φed intentionally and without defence. None the less, the trial should not proceed.

4.2 Ascriptive responsibility

Ascriptive responsibility, by contrast, *is* audience-relative. Amongst other things, it is concerned with accountability to that audience. When we are ascriptively responsible for an event, we may be eligible for (social, criminal, *et cetera*, as the case may be) evaluations in respect of that event. But whether we are so responsible depends upon the kind of evaluation being made. If I lie to my partner about whom I met for lunch today, I may owe her an explanation. At least on these facts, however, I owe no such explanation to the state—and the criminal law is appropriately addressed only to those actions for which D is ascriptively responsible *to the state*.

As understood in this book, ascriptive responsibility has a family resemblance to what Gary Watson has called the second 'face' of responsibility—accountability—which, like ascriptive responsibility, is concerned with the conditions under which D can be blamed or praised by a particular audience.[18] Philosophers following Watson have tended to distinguish between responsibility-as-attributability and responsibility-as-accountability. While not everyone draws the distinction in precisely the same way, roughly speaking conduct is said to be attributable to an agent when it reflects upon the agent herself—when it manifests her virtues and vices—in such a way that the agent is eligible for moral appraisal in respect of that conduct.[19] Responsibility-as-*accountability* builds upon that. It assumes that the conduct is attributable, and asks whether a blaming or praising judgement by the relevant audience would be justified. John Martin Fischer and Neal Tognazzini summarize the distinction neatly:[20]

[18] The *locus classicus* is G Watson, 'Two Faces of Responsibility' (1996) 24 Philosophical Topics 227.

[19] On Watson's own division, responsibility-as-attributability requires only that the agent be an appropriate object for *aretaic* appraisal.

[20] J M Fischer and N Tognazzini, 'The Physiognomy of Responsibility' (2011) 82 Phil and Phenomenological Research 381.

> '[M]oral responsibility has two faces: attributability and accountability. It is one thing to talk about the connection the agent has with her action; it is quite another to talk about the potential interaction the agent might have with her moral community.'

Attribution is dyadic: D is responsible *for* φing. Accountability is triadic: D is responsible for φing *to* a certain audience. Moving from the former to the latter, according to Fischer and Tognazzini, requires us to discuss additional matters, such as justification, excuse, and standing.

Antony Duff also explains 'criminal responsibility' in triadic terms.[21] For Duff, we are criminally responsible *for* φing *to* our fellow citizens. Whether we are accountable in a criminal court for φing depends, in turn, on the kind of wrong that φing is. It depends, Duff argues, on whether φing is (pro tanto) a public moral wrong. The public aspect of my wrong is what gives my fellow citizens standing to call me to account for it.

If we grant that the state represents the citizenry in criminal proceedings, the shape of Duff's analysis looks, at first glance, rather like what I have called ascriptive responsibility. But there are important reasons why a lawyer should not carve up responsibility in the manner contemplated by Watson and Duff. One such reason is that it makes findings of causation look like they speak to attributability and, hence, that they are prior to accountability. Fischer and Tognazzini implicitly embrace this thought. For them, the first question to ask, when considering whether to hold Sam attributably-responsible for some moral wrong, A, is the following:[22]

> 'Did Sam do A?'

For the lawyer, however, that starting point is more complicated than it may seem.[23] Whether Sam 'did' A depends on the context in which we are asking the question. The answer differs—and it should differ—across morality, tort, and criminal law. Suppose that A is 'an action causing Jim's death'. In law, whether Sam did A is *not* a pre-legal question. Many doctrines of causation are not prior to accountability: they depend upon the nature of the audience and

[21] R A Duff, *Answering for Crime* (Hart 2007) 23ff *et passim*.

[22] 'The Physiognomy of Responsibility' (n 20) 382.

[23] There is also the concern that the authors' approach is likely to influence how one thinks about moral luck—as it does for Gardner (see § 14.2.2). Granted, we need to know whether Sam did A in order to know what, if anything, Sam is culpable *for*. However, as will be argued in chapter 14, the *degree* of Sam's culpability for doing A does not depend on whether A is actually done.

the purpose for which the agent is being evaluated.[24] They are, in my terms, doctrines of ascriptive responsibility: which is no less foundational than, and does not presuppose, moral responsibility.[25]

Imagine that I am staying at my friend's house. I go out one day, negligently leaving the door unlocked. Foreseeably, vandals enter and damage the property. I may be liable for causing the damage in tort. I may also be blameworthy for its occurrence. But I do not cause the damage for the purposes of the criminal law.[26] In this sense, causation, like ascriptive responsibility doctrines more generally, is about the reference point of any (potential) assessment of culpability: about what we are to blame *for*. In our September scenario, there is no point in prosecuting Keith for a homicide offence, however culpable we may think him, if Jim's death cannot be ascribed to him.

We can approach this thought from another angle. Watson's division is oriented toward *ex post*, retrospective evaluations of events that have already occurred. Both attribution and accountability contemplate Sam's responsibility *for having done* A. Fair enough, one might say. That seems a natural way to think about responsibility judgements. When it comes to a trial, lawyers tend to have an *ex post* focus too. But they err when they adopt that perspective exclusively. Unlike moral responsibility, findings of ascriptive responsibility are intertwined with norms about the appropriate scope of our obligations. And the scope of our obligations is an *ex ante* matter. The prohibition comes first. Whether an event should constitute a crime is not the same question as whether it should be made a tort; and whether it constitutes a pro tanto moral wrong is a different question again. Norms of ascriptive responsibility are intimately bound up with those questions. They cannot be remaindered to the last stage of the process.

Seen in this light, it is not just that the *range* of wrongs for which a person is accountable varies with the context. Admittedly, that point is very important. Duff acknowledges it when he asserts that D should not be accountable in a criminal court for φing unless φing is a 'public' wrong. As it happens, I don't

24 I do not make this claim for *direct* causation (see §§ 5.1–2). But I do make it for indirect causation (in § 5.3).

25 The conceptual importance of this last point is more readily apparent in tort, where moral responsibility is not always required: it is possible, for example, to have child tortfeasors. Perhaps more interestingly, tort law (sometimes legitimately) includes vicarious liability among its doctrines of ascription. D may be vicariously accountable in tort for events without having any moral responsibility for them. In moral and criminal-law contexts, the centrality of moral responsibility means that we can neglect vicarious liability. But an analogous challenge arises for criminal complicity: see §§ 7.1–2. Even outside the legal system, it strikes me that we can sometimes be accountable—say, to our partners—for involuntary acts of betrayal: as in the climax of Orwell's *1984*, discussed in § 17.5.

26 Rightly so: see, in particular, § 5.3.4–5.

think publicness is a very helpful test.[27] But set that aside. What matters for present purposes is that Duff treats his inquiry as an *input* into the criminalization decision; as something that bears on whether φing should be criminalized. For Duff, whether D is criminally responsible for φing is a question prior to criminal law. It is a property of φing's pre-legal, or at least pre-criminal, (public) wrongness.

I think that's a mistake. What *counts* as φing is, in part, an upshot of considerations that bear on criminalization, such as the costs in liberty that would result if prohibitions extended to the case in hand. Unlike Duff's analysis, therefore, whether φing is rightly ascribed to D in the criminal law itself depends on criminalization norms. Those norms help to determine what events we should be accountable for: and one of the ways in which they do that is through the general part's ascriptive responsibility doctrines.

4.2.1 Grounds of ascription

How so? Criminal law knows three major, overlapping paths to ascription. The most important path runs through causative action. Imagine that Wendy stabs Steve, wounding him fatally. While he is dying, David arrives on the scene and shoots Steve through the heart so that he dies instantly. We might blame (and convict) Wendy for attempted murder. But she is not responsible for Steve's death because she did not cause it. David did.

Part of the very idea of ascriptive responsibility is that it involves some sort of relationship between the defendant and an event or state of affairs. The paradigm way of establishing such a relationship is by showing that D caused the event through her own act—more specifically, through an active intervention in the world. This claim, to be elaborated in §§ 5.1–2, should come as no surprise. Causation is deeply embedded in our self-understanding as agents. It may overstate the matter to say that 'We are what we do.' But we are, in part, what we do. Our identity is not just an internal matter, a thing merely *revealed* by how we behave. Rather, it is bound up with, and partly constituted by, our interactions with the world around us. Ascriptive responsibility tracks those interactions for which we are accountable. And causation by positive agency is at the heart of that.

[27] For criticism of Duff on this score, see J R Edwards and A P Simester, 'What's Public about Crime?' (2017) 37 OJLS 105.

At the heart, but circumnavigable. A defendant may be ascriptively responsible for the consequences of an omission, for example, if she is under a duty to intervene. Sarah is not free to stand by and watch her own child drown, even if she may do so were the victim a stranger.

The criminal law is sometimes justified in regulating failures to intervene, although chapter 6 will contend that such cases should be relatively rare. Prohibiting an omission is not like prohibiting an act. When the law prevents Ian from punching Bob, it leaves him with plenty of options and rules out only one. Ian is free to choose what to do and not do instead. By contrast, when the law proscribes an omission, it tells him exactly what to do. If her child is drowning, Sarah *must* rescue him—she is not free to choose what to do instead. One option is *required*, and all the other options are ruled out. As such, liability for omissions is more likely to impinge upon individual freedom.

The arguments in chapter 6 offer a powerful example of how the burdens of criminalization bear upon our doctrines of ascriptive responsibility. On a liberal approach, the law should respect the individuality of its citizens by judging them primarily according to their own positive acts. The process of shaping and controlling a person's life ordinarily should be left to that person; it tends to be undermined if she is constantly forced to assume responsibility for events she does not bring about.[28] So far as practicable, therefore, the state should leave its citizens free to live their own lives, and pursue their own goals, without having legal duties to intervene constantly besetting them. This is why there is no general duty to prevent crime[29]—and why principles of ascription are so important.

Implicit in this reasoning, however, is that omissions are special not because they deny moral responsibility, but because of the implications of their proscription for individual autonomy. Thus they are not ruled out *tout court*.[30] There is more than one ground of ascription. We have already noted one exception to the need for a positive act: where the victim was Sarah's own child. Often, these exceptional duties to intervene arise from some special role the defendant occupies.[31] (Regulatory law often uses omissions liability in this way, with duties falling, say, upon a factory owner.) But even that kind of connection

[28] As *Hart and Honoré* puts it (at lxxx–xi), 'respect for ourselves and others as distinct persons would be much weakened, if not dissolved, if we could not think of ourselves as the separate authors of the changes we make in the world.' See § 5.2.1.

[29] Cp. *Clarkson* [1971] 1 WLR 1402; and why, as Lord Esher MR put it, 'A man is entitled to be as negligent as he pleases towards the whole world if he owes no duty to them [*sic*].' *Le Lievre v Gould* [1893] 1 QB 491, 497.

[30] We return to this point in § 4.3.2 and, later, in § 8.4.

[31] As with legislation addressing dog owners (§ 8.4.2); cp. too the doctrine in *Miller* [1983] 2 AC 161 (§ 5.3.1).

may not be needed. Autonomy-based reasons cut both ways, and sometimes the reasons for a stranger to get involved may justify an extension of responsibility. Suppose that Ian, a passer-by, sees a child drowning in a paddling pool. He can rescue the child at no risk to himself. In this situation, for Ian not to intervene would be monstrous. Although English criminal law does not at the moment criminalize such cases, it might well do so.[32]

The third major path to ascription is via complicity. In certain situations, the defendant may be ascribed with responsibility for an event without having caused it by either act or omission. Liability doctrines of this type are sometimes said to impose 'secondary' liability. They extend the reach of the criminal law to encompass persons who do not themselves perpetrate a crime, but who are nevertheless parties to its commission.

Suppose that David plans to kill Tony. Knowing this, Rebecca lends David her gun. Rebecca is a participant in Tony's murder, and his death may be ascribed to her as a secondary party. Rebecca does not cause Tony's death.[33] Yet she is not like a mere bystander, who can claim that David's action has nothing to do with her; that it is none of her business. Instead, she has involved herself in the murder, and *made* it her business. Thus, although it is David who kills Tony, Rebecca shares in the ascriptive responsibility for his death.

Like liability for omissions, secondary liability involves an extension of the criminal law beyond the paradigm form of wrongdoing with which we began this chapter—in particular, beyond the core element of personal causation. As such, it involves a greater intrusion upon citizens' freedom of action: not only must D not strike V, she must refrain from doing anything to help someone else strike V—a much greater limitation upon what she is left free to do. This raises difficult questions of public policy. If Rebecca is a shopkeeper, for example, should she refuse to sell a gun to David if she thinks he has an illicit purpose? Complicity law squarely raises problems of autonomy once more,[34] problems that lack easy solution. Reasonable disagreement abounds. Yet, once again, ascription is not ruled out *tout court*.

[32] See, e.g., A Cadoppi, 'Failure to Rescue and the Continental Criminal Law' in M A Menlowe and R A McCall Smith (eds), *The Duty to Rescue: The Jurisprudence of Aid* (Aldershot 1993) 93; A Ashworth and E Steiner, 'Criminal omissions and public duties: the French experience' (1990) 10 Legal Studies 153.

[33] This claim will be defended in §§ 5.3.4 and 7.2.

[34] This can be especially in point when complicity liability is itself predicated upon an omission, which sometimes occurs when the secondary party has some form of control over the wrongdoer. Compare *Du Cros v Lambourne* [1907] 1 KB 40, in which the passenger in a car was convicted of being party to dangerous driving, on the basis that he owned the car and failed to exercise his right of control over the driver's actions.

We turn to ascriptive responsibility across the next three chapters. Chapters 5, 6, and 7 respectively will discuss causation, omissions, and complicity liability in more detail. For now, the important thing is to emphasize that whereas findings of moral responsibility are relative to particular events, and so are naturally evaluated *ex post*, ascription also has *ex ante* dimensions. What we are accountable for constrains our freedom. By contrast with moral responsibility, ascriptive responsibility norms are responsive to considerations of political morality and the appropriate reach of the state. Doctrines of ascription are, at one and the same time, doctrines of criminalization. Like all such doctrines, therefore, they allow for trade-offs.[35] Sometimes, they are appropriately displaced by more specific, prophylactic crimes.[36] They are unlike moral responsibility and the requirement of voluntariness, in that there is no unifying minimum.

4.3 An unfortunate commixture: The so-called voluntary act requirement

The rest of Part II investigates the major doctrines of ascriptive and moral responsibilities in criminal law. Before that, however, the distinction elaborated in §§ 4.1–2 can help us to debunk a familiar myth. Criminal lawyers sometimes claim that there ought to be proof of a *voluntary act* by the defendant if she is to be convicted of any offence.[37] This claim reflects the—valid—insights that one is eligible for blame in respect of some outcome only when one is morally responsible for that outcome, and that one cannot be morally responsible for bringing anything about unless it is brought about voluntarily. Unfortunately, the claim extends those insights in a problematic fashion. As Andrew Ashworth once put it,[38]

> 'To proceed to conviction without proof of a voluntary act would be to fail, in the most fundamental way, to show respect for individuals as rational, choosing beings. More generally, if people were liable to conviction despite

[35] It also bears noting that ascriptive responsibility doctrines can be negotiable against each other—the scope for complicity rules, for example, will depend in part on the scope of ascriptive rules of causation (see § 7.2).

[36] See, e.g., § 7.1, in the context of complicity.

[37] A noble tradition: see, e.g., R Cross and P A Jones, *Introduction to Criminal Law* (3rd edn, Butterworths 1953) 32; J W C Turner, *Kenny's Outlines of Criminal Law* (17th edn, CUP 1958) 26–27; J F Stephen, *History of the Criminal Law of England* vol II (Macmillan 1883) 97.

[38] A Ashworth, *Principles of Criminal Law* (2nd edn, OUP 1995) 95.

> doing nothing, or if something had been done *to* them, this would fail to respect their autonomy and would certainly not give them fair warning of the criminal sanction, unless reasonable duties had been made plain to them.'

But we need to be cautious here. The requirement that D's behaviour constitutes an 'act' is different from the requirement that it be voluntary. One of those requirements—voluntariness—should indeed be pervasive in the criminal law.[39] But the same is not true for the act requirement.

Michael Moore disagrees. For Moore, the criminal law both does and should require a voluntary act by D before he may be convicted of any crime, and that 'the best interpretation of that doctrine is to require what metaphysically is an act (on my theory, a volitionally caused bodily movement).'[40] The gist of Moore's claim is that positive agency, which in his account is inherently volitional,[41] is central to moral responsibility and thus to criminal liability. This position is not novel. Various writers have suggested that the key to moral responsibility is, rather than voluntariness, an account of agency—that is, of the action–event distinction, between bodily movements we make as agents and movements that merely happen to occur. John Bishop articulates the idea nicely:[42]

> 'We hold an agent morally responsible for a given outcome only if it came about or persisted *through that person's own action*. Thus, even if an agent's *behaviour* contributed to a certain outcome, the agent would not be morally responsible for it unless the behaviour involved the agent's own action.'

I think this is mistaken. Admittedly, there are reasons why action is part of the paradigm of criminal wrongdoing, and why it ordinarily should be required; for action is at the heart of a number of forms of *ascriptive* responsibility. Without such responsibility, mere culpability does not warrant a conviction. Yet no single element of our opening paradigm in § 4 is a necessary component of ascriptive responsibility. (Indeed, neither is culpability.) Although it must be established that the occurrence of the actus reus can be ascribed to D before he may be convicted, no particular feature—not even action—is the *sine qua non* of that step.

[39] See chapter 8.
[40] Moore, *Act and Crime*, 350.
[41] For an alternative approach, see chapter 9.
[42] J Bishop, *Natural Agency* (CUP 1989) 13 (emphasis in original). See too J L Austin, 'A Plea for Excuses' in *Philosophical Papers* (3rd edn, OUP 1979) 175, 178.

Neither is action indispensable to *moral* responsibility. Chapter 8 will argue that we can be morally responsible for our *non-involuntary* behaviour,[43] even in the absence of agency. A person lacks moral responsibility for her behaviour only if it is neither non-involuntary nor an instance of her agency.

There are two aspects of the claim that positive agency is necessary for moral responsibility with which we should take issue here. These are that a defendant should only be criminally liable for behaviour that constitutes (i) an 'action' as opposed to an omission; and (ii) an 'action' as opposed to an event. Neither is an essential feature of moral, or indeed ascriptive, responsibility. Even without them, the defendant may sometimes properly be held responsible for an actus reus.

4.3.1 Moral responsibility for events without agency

Start with the second possibility, of moral responsibility without agency. This possibility depends upon the existence of deeds that are neither action nor involuntary. Suppose a stranger jogs my arm, leading me to loosen my grip on a plate I am holding. I am talking to someone, and do not notice the incident, nor the fact that the plate is slowly slipping from my grasp until, alas! it drops to the floor and shatters. My dropping the plate was not involuntary, since it was preventable. I could, perhaps should, have noticed what was happening and grasped the plate more firmly. That being so, it is open for us to assess my blameworthiness, and perhaps hold me negligent, for dropping the plate. I am morally responsible for dropping the plate even though my doing so was not an instance of my agency.[44]

There is a considerable variety of behaviour that is not willed in any way, yet which may—and sometimes ought to be—inhibited or suppressed, perhaps with an effort. Examples are sneezing, unintentional yawning, belching, and that even greater social sin, voiding wind. Suppose D 'commits' such a faux pas at a dinner party. This would not normally be an instance of agency. Yet it seems implausible that D should *therefore* be exempt from censure for failing to control his body. I am not suggesting that such behaviour is *always* eligible for censure. Sometimes, no doubt, it is unavoidable or beyond D's control. But defence of the voluntary act thesis requires that all such behaviour is unavoidable

[43] See § 8.2.1.

[44] Another example might be my forgetting to hold my breath (perhaps during a medical examination).

unless it is action (indeed, for Moore, unless it occurs volitionally). A better account concludes that D can be morally responsible for her behaviour and its consequences if she has the deliberative capacity to behave differently, *whether or not* her behaviour is action. It is simply a mistake to hold that agency is necessary for moral responsibility.

Admittedly, the mistake is an alluring one. We can see its attraction when we look at the language of 'control', something that many writers take to be a condition of moral responsibility.[45] Thomas Nagel has put the idea as follows:[46]

> 'People cannot be morally assessed for what is not their fault, or for what is due to factors beyond their control. . . . the appropriateness of moral assessment is easily undermined by the discovery that the act or attribute, no matter how good or bad, is not under the person's control.'

It seems intuitive to interpret this control condition in terms of agency. In Bishop's account, for example, an action is a 'controlled exercise of the agent's power', an 'exercise of the agent's control'.[47] But an outcome might be within (that is, not beyond) D's control without its being produced by an exercise of D's control qua agent. This possibility occurs when the outcome is avoidable by D.

4.3.2 Moral responsibility without positive acts

More on those claims in chapters 8 and 9. One may also be morally responsible for the consequences of an omission. Consider a question asked by *Smith and Hogan*:[48]

> 'Suppose D is sitting at the corner of a corridor with his legs stretched across it. He hears V running down the corridor and deliberately remains still with the intention that V, on turning the corner, shall fall over his legs. Why should this not be a battery? It would be if D had put out his legs with the intention of tripping up V.'

45 See especially D Husak, 'Does Criminal Liability Require an Act?' in *The Philosophy of Criminal Law: Selected Essays* (OUP 2010) ch 1. Husak argues for a control condition in criminal law rather than an act requirement.

46 T Nagel, 'Moral Luck' in *Mortal Questions* (CUP 1979) 24, 25. (See also chapter 14 below.) Nagel himself connects control to agency.

47 Bishop, *Natural Agency* (n 42) 23, 25.

48 D Ormerod and K Laird, *Smith and Hogan's Criminal Law* (14th edn, OUP 2015) 713.

In general, of course, this is not an assault. But that is for reasons of ascription, not moral responsibility. Clearly, as *Smith and Hogan* contemplates, D is morally responsible for not moving his leg, and for the consequence that P falls over.

One reason why Moore denies moral responsibility for omissions lies in the way he conceptualizes them:[49]

> '[O]missions are simply absent actions. An omission to save life is not some kind of ghostly act of saving life, and certainly not some ghostly kind of killing. It is literally nothing at all. An omission to save X at some time t is just the absence of any instantiation of the type of action "saving X".'

Punishment for omissions, on that view, is no better than punishment for mere states of affairs. In neither case is D in any sense an author of the relevant event or state, and in neither case should she be held morally responsible or criminally liable for it.

Yet the definition is misleading. An omission is not the same thing as an absence of action;[50] because the class of non-movements of bodies is not the same as the class of things which are not bodily movements. The latter includes events and states of affairs *simpliciter*, while the former does not. Hence there is a salient difference between omissions and states of affairs.

This point merits elaboration.[51] The familiar distinction between positive acts and omissions operates at the level of *descriptions* of behaviour rather than at the level of the raw behaviour itself.[52] As many writers have observed, a particular piece of behaviour may simultaneously be described in different ways: as when I move my finger, pull a trigger, and fire a gun. Some such descriptions identify omissions—perhaps I also fail to shoot Victor. These various acts and omissions all describe the same piece of behaviour, which itself comprises movement and/or non-movement. Like acts, omissions therefore tell us *something* (albeit, often, little) about the agent's behaviour: that it did not involve whatever was omitted. As such, the class of omissions differs from the

[49] Moore, *Act and Crime*, 28; Moore, *Causation and Responsibility*, 53.

[50] Neither is it the same as an instance of inaction. Part of the difficulty here is that Moore works with a unified conception of 'action' as opposed to event, omission, and inaction. But the act/omission distinction cuts across both the action/event *and* the bodily movement/bodily non-movement distinctions. One may omit by either bodily movement or bodily non-movement, and whether or not we characterize an instance of behaviour as an action or an omission has no necessary implications for whether we should take that behaviour (which is, as such, independent of description) to involve a positive movement. See, further. § 6.1.1.

[51] See also § 6.1.

[52] On the distinction drawn in this book between behaviour and its descriptions, see § 2.4.

class of event-descriptions that are not acts. The latter includes descriptions of natural events not involving an agent at all. Sunsets are not acts, but they are not omissions either. It follows that omissions are not simply 'absent actions', and they are not 'literally nothing at all'. They are instantiations of an agent's behaviour under certain kinds of description.

4.3.3 Moral responsibility for situations?

More on omissions in chapter 6. There is another worry for the analysis here. If we abandon the 'act' requirement in order to accommodate omissions, might that leave open the possibility that one may be held responsible for an actus reus that specifies only a state of affairs and no behavioural element?

It is certainly true that crimes such as murder, rape, and assault—with which ordinary citizens are most familiar, and which have the greatest moral resonance—are crimes that require wrong*doing*, and which necessarily involve some act or omission by the defendant. But many less well-known crimes prima facie involve no behavioural element. These offences penalize a defendant on the basis of the situation in which she finds herself. Sometimes known as crimes of 'situational liability',[53] they are crimes where the actus reus is simply an event or circumstance that is in some way connected to the defendant. An example may be seen in the notorious English case of *Larsonneur*.[54] In that case, D was convicted of being found in the United Kingdom when permission for her to enter the country had previously been refused. It was, however, undisputed that the only reason for her being back on UK soil was that she had been forcibly returned there by the police. In convicting her of a situational liability offence, the law picked out D solely because it was she to whom the actus reus happened, and not because of anything she did.

[53] P R Glazebrook, 'Situational Liability' in Glazebrook (ed), *Reshaping the Criminal Law: Essays in Honour of Glanville Williams* (Stevens 1978) 108; M D Cohen, 'The "Actus Reus" and Offenses of "Situation"' (1972) 7 Israel LR 186. Crimes of this sort are sometimes ruled unconstitutional in the United States: *Robinson v California* 370 US 660 (1962) (being addicted to narcotics); *Papachristou v City of Jacksonville* 405 US 156 (1972) (being a vagrant).

[54] *Larsonneur* (1933) 149 LTR 542. For the purposes of this discussion, I take the defendant's entry into the UK to have been physically involuntary (as opposed to being under duress, regarding which see § 17.2). Doubtless, as some writers have observed, the defendant actually walked off the boat onto the dock; but she was already in the UK when the boat docked. (Neither did the statute require that she 'land'.) In any event, nothing need turn on this—as may be seen in *Winzar v Chief Constable of Kent* The Times, 28 March 1983, where the defendant was convicted of being found drunk on a highway, having been carried there by the police.

What challenge do these crimes present to the need for moral responsibility? *Larsonneur* has been widely criticized, and rightly so.[55] One might, for example, worry that the language used in the offence does not appear to require any mens rea element on the part of the defendant. This is an important, and valid, objection. Yet it has not been the only complaint. Ashworth, for instance, once took a Moore-ish approach when he disapproved of 'defining an offence in a way that seems to require no act by the defendant as a basis for liability.'[56] However, as a general objection, this is not valid. There is nothing inherently defective or unjust about an offence that prima facie contains no behaviour element. Such an offence is still capable of satisfying the principles of culpability and ascriptive responsibility introduced in chapter 1.

To see this, *Larsonneur* may be contrasted with the later English case of *Robinson-Pierre*.[57] Early one morning, police officers executed a search warrant at D's house by breaking down the door without warning and charging into the house. D's dog, a pit-bull terrier, was locked inside the house at the time. Unsurprisingly, it went berserk, chasing the officers out of the house and continuing to attack them on the street. D was convicted of an offence of *being* the owner of a dog that caused injury while dangerously out of control in a public place, contrary to section 3 of the Dangerous Dogs Act 1991.

The Court of Appeal upheld D's appeal. Accepting that section 3 created an offence of strict liability, none the less the Court held that the offence 'requires proof by the prosecution of an act or omission of the defendant (with or without fault) that to some (more than minimal) degree caused or permitted the prohibited state of affairs to come about.'[58]

At the level of principle, *Larsonneur* and *Robinson-Pierre* are inconsistent decisions. *Robinson-Pierre* is to be preferred. The result in that case demonstrates that there need be no injustice, and there is nothing intrinsically wrong, in criminalizing states of affairs, so long as the class of potential defendants is clearly identified: *provided that* the defendant could have done something about it. Even where the actus reus is formally stated in situational terms, that need not exclude a voluntariness requirement. It is the failure to observe *this* requirement which is the main problem with *Larsonneur*, and not the failure to require an act by the defendant.

[55] See, e.g., J Hall, *General Principles of Criminal Law* (2nd edn, Bobbs Merrill 1960) 329 n 14 (the 'acme of strict injustice'); Williams, *CLGP*, 11.
[56] Ashworth, *Principles of Criminal Law* (n 38) 105. Ashworth modified his discussion of *Larsonneur* in later editions, withdrawing the phrasing quoted here.
[57] [2013] EWCA Crim 2396.
[58] Ibid, [42].

Larsonneur is problematic in a number of ways. However, the deepest objection to the decision is not that it involved conviction without mens rea, nor that it allowed conviction without action. At least with respect to the defendant,[59] it is most profoundly objectionable because it imposed liability without proof that the actus reus was voluntary. Unless there is a requirement of voluntariness, situational offences are at odds with the principle of moral responsibility.

Contrast a case where the defendant *could* have prevented the actus reus from occurring.[60] In such cases, situational liability is, in effect, a form of liability for voluntary omissions. Moral responsibility for the situation lies on the basis of its avoidability.[61] Although such offences contain no explicit behavioural element, indirectly they involve the defendant being prosecuted for her failure to prevent the actus reus from happening.

We look further at the voluntariness requirements in chapter 8. With all that said, there is nothing wrong with insisting upon a 'voluntary act' in standard cases. The requirement for an *act* by the defendant envisages the central cases of combined moral and ascriptive responsibility, beyond which the criminal law should tread warily. We explore those cases, and their limitations, in the remainder of Part II.

[59] Another line of objection engages the rule of law: that the crime was effectively procured by the authorities.

[60] It is sometimes suggested that this was true of *Larsonneur* itself, in as much as the defendant could have adopted, at an earlier point in time, a pre-emptive strategy by returning to France rather than Ireland. While I am not here concerned with the details of the case, it is worth noting that there is (rightly) no general doctrine of prior fault in the common law. Criminal liability can *sometimes* be grounded in antecedent combinations of actus reus and mens rea elements. However, that possibility is subject to significant constraints: see § 8.5.1.

[61] That is not enough, of course, for ascriptive responsibility. See § 8.4.2.

5
Causation

Causation doctrines govern the connection between D's behaviour and the consequence elements, if any, of an offence.[1] They articulate the paradigm route by which responsibility for those consequences can be ascribed to D. But causation is not specific to the law. It was an earthquake that in February 2011 caused numerous buildings to collapse and lives to be lost in the city of Christchurch. Indeed, in many ways this sort of causal relation might be regarded as a paradigm. Its mechanics can be studied scientifically in order to understand why the buildings collapsed, and to help determine how to stop such consequences from recurring.

For some writers,[2] this type of extra-legal causation, this cement of the universe,[3] is the only type of causation there is. But a mere glance at the textbooks reveals that legal practice is not so simple. The unwelcome nature of a criminal conviction, or an adverse tort judgment, naturally creates pressure to accommodate moral considerations within causation doctrine. If adverse legal consequences, whether punitive or compensatory, follow from ascriptions to D of causal responsibility, those consequences need to be justified. In turn, one might worry, how can the kind of raw physical relationship that an earthquake has to a collapsed building justify, or even support, the imposition of a criminal conviction—unless that relationship itself contains normative ingredients?

A striking example of this type of concern is the UK Supreme Court's decision in *Hughes*.[4] H, who was driving safely, rounded a corner and was hit head-on by V's car, which was travelling on the wrong side of the road. H had no chance of avoiding the collision, in which V died. He was none the less charged with 'causing death by driving' at a time when uninsured:[5] a crime intended

[1] See § 2.3.

[2] e.g. Moore, *Causation and Responsibility*.

[3] Hume's brilliant phrase ('An Abstract of a Book lately Published, entitled, *A Treatise of Human Nature*, &c., Wherein the Chief Argument of that Book is Farther Illustrated and Explained', 1740), taken up in J L Mackie, *The Cement of the Universe* (Clarendon 1980).

[4] [2013] UKSC 56.

[5] Contrary to s 3ZB of the Road Traffic Act 1988 (UK), which makes it an imprisonable crime if D 'causes the death of another person by driving a motor vehicle on a road' should D, at the time of driving, be driving without a licence, or without insurance, or while disqualified. (The predicate wrongs are themselves matters of strict liability.) The statutory phrasing makes it clear that the predicate wrong

Fundamentals of Criminal Law. A P Simester, Oxford University Press (2021). © A P Simester.
DOI: 10.1093/oso/9780198853145.003.0005

by the legislature to be of strict liability. Straining to quash H's conviction, the Court held that, as matter of general—'common sense'[6]—doctrine, causation requires 'at least some act or omission in the control of the car, which *involves some element of fault* . . . and which contributes in some more than minimal way to the death.'[7]

The efforts by the Supreme Court are understandable against the backdrop of an imprisonable strict liability offence. Indeed, in many ways the decision was not revolutionary. The 'moralization' of causation in law was already mainstream. Most legal academics nowadays take the attribution of causation to involve a two-step inquiry. They begin with a 'factual' test, which is generally interpreted as asking whether the alleged cause (C) stands in a 'but-for' or *sine qua non* relationship to the alleged effect (E). From there, the results are refined by also requiring that C stands in a 'proximate' causal relationship with E. This second stage is informed by morally salient considerations, including *novus actus* doctrines. Since both factual and proximate causation must be established, the mainstream approach to legal causation inevitably generates morally loaded conclusions.

Unsurprisingly, many writers therefore see causation findings as little more than a legal conclusion, rather than a real-world input into criminal or tort liability. When lawyers assert that D's conduct 'caused' a harm, they may be doing no more than articulating a judgement that, through his behaviour, D should be held legally answerable for the harm that eventuated. This impression is only reinforced by the amorphous nature of proximate-cause doctrines, which differ across sub-fields of law such as crime and tort. The inference seems unavoidable that causation, at least in law, is a post—and not a pre-legal phenomenon.

I signed up to that last proposition in § 4.2. Yet it suggests a problem. If ascriptions of causal responsibility are legal conclusions, what do they add to the case *for* legal liability? As Clarke worries, 'if causation were not independent of legal or moral liability, it would be a mere tautology to say that someone should be held liable for an injury because they caused it.'[8] At the very least, it seems that we could eliminate the language of 'causation' from our legal liability criteria, in favour of direct reference to the underlying norms. In turn, that would clarify overlaps with other liability elements and, potentially, lead to simplification.

need not be causally salient to V's death; contrast, e.g., *Dalloway* (1847) 2 Cox CC 273, discussed in § 5.4.1.

[6] *Hughes* [2013] UKSC 56, [32] *et passim*. The Court's holding was presented as a 'common sense' causal analysis rather than as a general principle of liability or a glossing of the terms of the statutory offence.

[7] Ibid, [36] (emphasis added).

[8] D M Clarke, 'Causation and Liability in Tort Law' (2014) 5 Jurisprudence 217, 218.

Indeed, 'proximity' might itself disappear. Its dependence on reasonable foreseeability, in particular, brings it into overlap with negligence and duty criteria, to the point that it may have little or no independent role to play.

Notice that this is not to claim that proximate causation rests on *no* pre-legal phenomenon. There need be no circularity about having legal distinctions turn, say, on reasonable foreseeability. The thought here is simply that such work can be done in the law by culpability elements. And if that's right, it raises doubts whether causation has any distinctive normative aspect; and, more importantly, whether there is any distinctive pre-legal, 'natural-world', phenomenon that underpins findings of legal causation.

The task for this chapter is to pick a way through the minefield: to essay an account of causation in the criminal law that points toward some natural-world property that it rests upon, and which shows how that property is capable of bearing the moral freight that causation doctrines must carry. The account seeks, as it must, to reconcile the tension between pre- and post-legal notions of causation, finding a place for the law's morally sensitive causation doctrines. In so doing, it helps to explain what criminal and tortious causation *must* have in common, and where space exists for their causal doctrines to diverge.

The result, seen below, is not a unitary but a multi-part analysis, one that makes room for *novus actus* doctrines as well as omissions, and for variations across different fields of law. To summarize, this chapter will set out three major threads of causation. It begins with *direct* causation. Direct causation is a paradigm form, involving consecutive sequences of events, each of which brings about the next. Resting upon truths about the natural world, it is invariant across the legal system and independent of culpability.

Other threads of causation are interwoven with this paradigm form: indeed, there are few 'pure' direct causation cases of interest to the law. *Indirect* causation operates in contexts where multiple chains of direct causation intersect. It, too, involves truths about the world, as causation must: but here we are in the realm of the so-called *novus actus interveniens*, and we trespass upon the moral domain. Not all interventions break causal chains, or disrupt causal attributions. (Indeed, as we shall see, '*novus actus interveniens*' is a misnomer.) Even where we cannot establish a simple, direct causal chain from cause to effect, establishing indirect causation may be possible. However, the conditions under which indirect causation may legitimately be attributed are informed by moral argument and they vary across crime and tort. Finally, the third major thread of causation concerns omissions and other non-interventions. As will be seen, these are causally significant, and distinctively so, essentially because of their failure to disrupt direct and indirect causal chains. And it is this feature that explains why an omission cannot by itself constitute a so-called *novus actus interveniens*.

The analysis offered here is immediately at odds with unitary, purely mechanical accounts. At the same time, its account of direct causation is opposed to the approach in *Hughes*. Contra the Supreme Court, there is a natural, non-moral form of causation that is properly recognized in law—in crime and tort alike.

5.1 Direct causation: Physical chain reactions, the cement of the universe

The core of 'direct' causation should be, and ordinarily is, familiar and uncontroversial. Suppose that D pulls a trigger, firing a bullet that pierces V's heart, stopping it. D's pulling the trigger causes V's death because we can trace a sequence of physical (including chemical and biological) *reactions* from cause to effect.[9] In tracing that sequence, we discern why the effect occurred even if, for other reasons, it might anyway have happened when it did. This is a central thread of causal ascriptions: it subsists in (continuing[10]) physical chain reactions, of the sort that a forensic scientist might track.

Like the Supreme Court, those with a focus on morally-sensitive tests of causation can easily overlook the truth that legal causation has a core physical thread. A standard example is the well-known case of *Smith*,[11] in which V was stabbed by D with a bayonet. V's lung was pierced, an injury that went unrecognized by those who attended to him. He was dropped twice on the way to the medical station. There the medical officer failed to diagnose the seriousness of the situation and gave the wrong treatment, which very likely increased the risk of death. Perhaps V would not have died but for the mistreatment. Be that as it may, D's conviction of murder was rightly affirmed. The original injury was still, as the Court said, an 'operating' cause of V's death,[12] in that the

[9] Strictly speaking, we can trace a sequence of physical chain reactions from the firing of the bullet to the stopping of V's heart. Death then results because V's blood ceases to circulate and transfer oxygen to the brain tissue. As Gideon Rosen points out, this further link involves a form of 'double-prevention' (G Rosen, 'Causation, Counterfactual Dependence and Culpability: Moral Philosophy in Michael Moore's *Causation and Responsibility*' (2011) 42 Rutgers LJ 405; see also § 5.4.2). I take such links to be causal in nature. Moreover, I take at least some instances of such links, like the one that leads to V's death, to be morally insensitive, and in that sense akin to direct causation. However, there is not space here to develop an account of *which* kinds of double-prevention links are morally (in)sensitive. That task requires another book.

[10] Below, § 5.1.2.

[11] [1959] 2 QB 35.

[12] Ibid, 42–43.

stab wound and consequent haemorrhage were immediate medical factors explaining V's death, albeit alongside other contributions.[13]

The attribution of causation in this case rests not on moral evaluations but on a finding about the physical facts of the matter. If we inquire forensically into the immediate physical cause of V's death, ongoing loss of blood from the stab wound is part of the explanation.[14] That means, *without more*, that D's act of stabbing V was *a* cause of death. We can ignore questions about whether any other actor in the drama was a *novus actus interveniens*: other causes can only be concomitant ones. Moreover, that pre-legal conclusion holds independently of whether, from a legal perspective, we are contemplating a crime or a tort. D's act was a direct cause of death and that's that. Criminal lawyers can move on to mens rea issues.

Contrast another familiar stabbing case, *Jordan*.[15] There, the victim died eight days after being admitted to hospital. However, the original injury played no role in the medical explanation of his death. Indeed, by then it had substantially healed. Death was in fact caused by the 'palpably wrong' treatment he received in hospital (injection of medicine to which the victim was known to be intolerant, causing a massive allergic reaction, and intravenous administration of too much liquid). Here the original injury made no operating contribution to the victim's death. Thus, unless Jordan could be said to have caused death *via* the doctor's intervention,[16] he committed no homicide.

Often, the physical reaction chains underpinning direct causation are helpfully reconstructed backwards. In *White*,[17] for example, W poisoned his mother's glass of lemonade. Before she drank it, however, she died of an unrelated heart attack. W failed to kill his mother. If we ask, 'of what did she die?', the immediate answer is, a heart attack; and, in turn, whatever triggered the heart attack—which was not the poison. Certain hard cases for tort liability dissolve pretty quickly on this analysis, at least for the criminal law. Suppose that D and E, not acting in concert, each culpably shoots at V. There is no-one else in the vicinity. V is injured by a single gunshot wound, but it cannot be proved whether the bullet came from D or E: *Cook v Lewis*.[18] Who is liable for injuring V? In the criminal law, neither—even if both D and E had fired

[13] Compare *People v Lewis* 57 P 470 (1899), 473: 'Drop by drop the life current went out from both wounds, and at the very instant of death the gunshot wound [inflicted by D] was contributing to the event.'

[14] This is not to suggest that being explanatory is a criterion of causation. Causal *explanations* are typically selective, highlighting those causes that are more significant or unusual.

[15] (1956) 40 Cr App R 152; G Williams, 'Causation in Homicide' [1957] Crim LR 429.

[16] Not on these facts: but see, further, § 5.3.4.

[17] [1910] 2 KB 124.

[18] [1951] SCR 830; below, § 5.2–5.2.1.

with murderous intent. We know who physically caused V's death: the person who fired the bullet that wounded him. Unfortunately, we lack sufficient proof that either D or E was that person. But that evidential flaw is only vital because causal responsibility for V's injury rests here on a finding about the presence of a physical causal chain linking discharge of D's or E's gun to V's injury. We cannot establish that either D or E is different from White.

5.1.1 The scalarity of direct causes

While the backward reconstruction from immediate causes of death helps to distinguish *Smith* from *Jordan*, in Smith's case it shows us that other interventions may have played a vital role too. Indeed, there is nothing in a finding of direct causation that requires Smith's own contribution to have been sufficient (or necessary[19]) by itself to cause death, or even that it was the primary cause. For the sake of argument, then, let's concede that Smith's act was not the primary cause of death. The significance to be attached to that possibility is not itself a causal issue. Moreover, it depends also on whether we are in the realm of criminal law or tort. At least in the criminal law, it is sufficient to show that the defendant's behaviour makes *some* causal contribution. Hence, *both* Smith and the medical officer could in principle be guilty of homicide-related offences. Tort law, being concerned primarily with reallocating losses, might approach the liability question differently and contemplate apportionment of liability between defendants, or even between the defendant and a contributorily negligent victim.[20] We need not pursue those controversial issues here—partly because we are principally concerned with causation in the criminal law, but more importantly because they involve a debate concerning tort *liability* rather than causation. There may be no doubt about the proportionate contributions made by two causal agents to the occurrence of some harm. The difficulty lies in deciding what to do about it.

Still, the possibility of multiple causes highlights a point made by Michael Moore: that this type of causation is scalar.[21] Suppose that D and E each stabs V. D inflicts a major wound, causing massive loss of blood; E inflicts a less

[19] Consider, e.g., a cascading domino chain which temporarily splits into two symmetric branches before reuniting. At the point of reunification, neither domino is necessary to continue the chain but both cause the next domino to fall.

[20] Cp. *Hatton v Sutherland* [2002] 2 All ER 1, 20 (Baroness Hale): 'Where the harm suffered has more than one cause, the employer should only pay for that proportion of the harm suffered which is attributable to his wrongdoing unless the harm is truly indivisible.'

[21] Moore, *Causation and Responsibility*, 118.

serious wound, also causing bleeding. If V dies from the combined loss of blood, both D and E cause death. But their causal contributions need not be equal, something that tort liability might (or might not) want to acknowledge.

As we have noted, this distinction does not generally affect the criminal law, since it suffices to show that the conduct of the defendant on trial is *a* cause of death. Indeed, depending on their respective intentions, E may be guilty of a more serious offence than D. But what if E's contribution was trivial? Suppose that Doctor F takes a blood sample from V, who is dying from the stab wounds. The additional loss of blood for the sample may further weaken the patient and hasten death by, say, sixty seconds. Since criminal-law doctrine holds that the contribution made by the doctor (or anyone else) must be more than insignificant or *de minimis*,[22] F's role in V's death would be regarded as causally insignificant.[23] For practical purposes, that may be a useful rule of thumb for the criminal law. But we should be careful not to deny that F's conduct is actually a cause of death. Imagine that F stands to inherit from T's will should T's heir—V—not attain the age of majority, and that V will attain majority at midnight tonight. If F takes the blood sample in order to accelerate death, would we be so complacent about the absence of an actus reus here? Application of the *de minimis* rule to this kind of case is itself morally sensitive.[24] It operates as a boundary rule for the legal system rather than a refutation of causation.[25]

5.1.2 Petering out

Direct causation does not continue forever. Suppose that, when Grandma gives birth to my father, she inaugurates a sequence of events in which, eventually, I kill V. We may accept that there is *some* sort of causal relationship between (C) Grandma's giving birth and (E) my killing V, but we should deny that C is a direct cause of E.[26] Similarly, in terms of legal doctrine, we should deny that C

[22] See, e.g., *Cato* [1976] 1 All ER 260, 265–66.

[23] *Adams* [1957] Crim LR 365. The direction to the jury in that case is reproduced in A Arlidge, 'The Trial of Dr David Moor' [2000] Crim LR 31, 34–35.

[24] Note that it is possible to explain cases like *Adams* without reference to a *de minimis* rule: by conceding that the doctor's intervention is a direct cause of death and (death being no more than obliquely intended: chapter 15), invoking a justificatory claim of necessity. We consider this kind of justification in chapter 18.

[25] Neither should we focus overly upon *acceleration* of death. (Or of anything else: after all, if D blinds V or razes his house, we might say that D has merely brought forward the moment when V no longer has sight or the building no longer stands.) We return to this point in § 5.4.1.

[26] A caveat is in order. Both within and outside the law, we may recognize different kinds of causal relationship (cf. 'occasioning', 'inducing', or 'procuring'). However, I take *causing* to be the central kind of causal relation, and the one that normally matters in criminal law, at least for principal offenders. Secondary parties are discussed in chapter 7 (see, especially, § 7.2).

was an 'operating' cause of E. (For reasons to be discussed in § 5.3, we should also deny that it is an indirect cause of E and, thus, deny that C causes E.)

The 'operating cause' requirement accommodates the fact that causal impact can dissipate over time. Because direct causal linkages are scalar rather than binary, they can *peter out*. Moore's metaphor is a helpful one:[27]

> 'The metaphorical picture is of the ripples emanating from a stone dropped into a quiet pond: gradually they diminish to nothing the further the ripples travel from their source. This attribute of legal causation presupposes that the relation is scalar, because only a more-or-less sort of relation can gradually peter out.'

That is to say: Suppose that we can trace each individual step of a sequence linking C to E as involving localized physical reactions, in which C (perhaps in conjunction with other factors) causes C1; C1 (. . . [28]) causes C2; C2 (. . .) causes C3; and so on, until Cn causes E. The bare existence of such a sequence of localized causes does not establish that C is a cause of E. Direct causation requires also that the links be *continuing* across the entire chain.[29] And the chain as a whole fails to exhibit continuity when the effect of C's intervention has petered out by the time it gets to E.

To give an example: imagine that I drop a ping-pong ball into a turbulent stream. Further down, the stream splits into left and right channels. I can choose which side of the stream to drop the ball; thus, initially, I can influence the location of the ball in the stream. Moreover, the location of the ball at any given moment will be causally affected by its location the moment before. But it may not be the case that I have any control over which channel the ball enters. Over time, my own causal input peters out: it becomes swamped by other, non-sequential causal inputs into the location of the ball. Which side should I choose? It doesn't matter.

This type of phenomenon pervades our world. Physicists helpfully describe it as a form of *deterministic chaos*. Even though it may be possible to control for the initial conditions of an event, over time the link weakens between those initial conditions and the ensuing states of affairs. That is why, for

[27] Moore, *Causation and Responsibility*, 121.

[28] i.e., perhaps in conjunction with other factors.

[29] Some writers insist that causation is inherently transitive, so that if C1 causes C2 and C2 causes C3, it follows that C1 causes C3. (See, e.g., D Lewis, 'Causation as Influence' (2000) 97 Journal of Philosophy 182, 196: hence V's being born causes her death.) On the scalar account presented here, however, causal sequences are not inherently transitive.

example, long-range weather forecasts are less reliable than short-range ones. Ultimately, across a sufficiently lengthy period, the non-linearity of the dynamical systems involved means that one cannot predict or model how an event will unfold. This is not just a point about compounding margins of error, which aggregate across intersecting events to deprive our predictions of reliability. It is not, in other words, merely to say that we cannot explain the importance of the ping-pong ball's initial location with any confidence. Rather, it is that my placement of the ping-pong ball makes an *immeasurably small* contribution to the outcome. Continuity fails. We might loosely say that direct causation has its own (non-moral) 'proximity' constraint. The criminal law implicitly accommodates that constraint via its requirements that direct causes be operating and not *de minimis*.

One may be tempted to quibble about this. What about my act of putting the ping-pong ball in the stream, *simpliciter*? Why is not *initiation* of the sequence that ultimately played out, whatever sequence it was, sufficient to establish causation? Sometimes, it is: but not as an instance of direct causation. As we shall see, that is a problem for indirect causation.[30] If the mere initiation of causal sequences which eventuate in an effect were sufficient to establish causation, both the continuity requirement and scalarity itself would have to be abandoned. And that seems undesirable as well as implausible. Grandma's giving birth to my father may have played an indispensable role in putting into motion a chain of events that culminates in my killing V. But the ping-pong-ball analogy applies here. There are simply too many intervening factors to allow the conclusion that her doing so caused my lethal conduct. Contrast the bayonetting in *Smith*, where we can reliably trace the chain of physical reactions leading to death in a manner that allows us to conclude (indeed, to conclude beyond reasonable doubt) that the injury inflicted by Smith was a cause of that death.

5.2 The moral rawness of direct causation

Notoriously, the difference in outcomes between *Smith* and *Jordan*, like the verdict in *White*, need not reflect anything more laudable about the actors involved. To this extent, causation often seems to generate differences in criminal verdicts that appear morally arbitrary. Suppose that Bob and Charles shoot Arnold, with Charles firing a few seconds after Bob does. Bob's bullet inflicts

[30] See in particular the discussion of *Hart*, below, § 5.3.

severe injuries that would have caused death within minutes. Charles's bullet then passes through the heart, killing Arnold instantly. In both tort and criminal law, as well as extra-legally, Charles kills Arnold and Bob does not. From a moral perspective, they may be equally reprehensible characters. Ascriptively, however, Charles is responsible for Arnold's death. The status of Charles is very different from that of Bob, for causal reasons that need have nothing to do with the merits of their behaviour.

Such distinctions may seem unattractive. Recall the facts of *Cook v Lewis*,[31] in which D1 and D2 each fired negligently at V in circumstances where it could not be established who caused injury (and who missed). There is no conceptual barrier to tort law's reaching a different conclusion from the criminal law about *liability* in such cases. Thus Ernest Weinrib argues that tort liability could indeed be imposed, on the basis that each of D1 and D2 had violated either (i) V's substantive right to physical integrity or (ii) the remedial right derived by V from breach of that substantive right.[32] Whatever the merits of that argument,[33] it clearly illustrates the concern we often have about tying legal consequences too closely to natural phenomena that are, morally speaking, arbitrary: the very concern motivating the UK Supreme Court in *Hughes*.

Yet moral arbitrariness is a conceptual feature of direct causation. Direct causation is both morally insensitive and invariant across criminal law, tort law, and other parts of the legal system. By that same token, however, it is unconstrained by culpability or fault—notwithstanding the discomfort of the Supreme Court. When Brandon Lee died tragically during filming of *The Crow*, after an error in preparing the prop gun, it was actor Michael Massee who pulled the trigger. Massee's doing so was *a* cause of Lee's death despite his lack of fault. We can trace a continuing physical chain reaction between his behaviour and Lee's death, one that is not conditional upon fault. By contrast, applying the 'common sense' principle espoused in *Hughes* would lead us to conclude that Massee did not do an act that caused Lee's death. That conclusion should be rejected.

Similarly, the egg-shell skull 'problem' dissolves as a challenge to causation on the same grounds. Suppose that a doctor, treating a hospitalized patient (P) with recognized symptoms, follows standard medical practice by

[31] Above, § 5.1.

[32] 'Causal Uncertainty' (2016) 36 OJLS 135, §§ 2–3.

[33] And it faces difficulties. Clearly, the difference between D and E is arbitrary. But Weinrib's solution—which depends on the remedial right's being derived from ('the continuation of') V's violated substantive right—suffers also from arbitrariness. Suppose that one of the shots injures V (an injury valued at $1 million), while the other sparks a fire that razes V's million-dollar house. No remedy would lie.

administering the recommended medicine for P condition. Unfortunately and unknowably, P suffers a severe allergic reaction to the medicine and dies.[34] Blamelessly, the doctor has killed him.[35] Direct causation tracks physical reaction sequences that impact upon the world *as it is*, including any pre-existing natural conditions or vulnerabilities in the victim. Thus it is often said that 'you take your victim as you find him.'[36] In a sense, even that is not quite to the point: the maxim articulates the causal upshot rather than the explanation why causation lies in such cases. The underlying point is that direct causal paths are not about the merits. If D's act initiated a sequence of events that would not had occurred had the world been different, from the perspective of direct causation that is neither here nor there. It is neither fair nor unfair to conclude that the doctor caused P's death. It's just true.

5.2.1 Why does direct causation matter?

Direct causal chains are thus a primary vehicle for allocating moral luck. For that very reason, however, we may question whether they can bear normative freight. Why not abandon physical causation altogether, at least within the law, and substitute culpability-sensitive criteria such as foreseeability? Given the unfortunate fact that offences are sometimes enacted without adequate culpability elements, this would not be otiose in the context of criminal law. Doubtless it would lead to significant overlaps in offences that do require proof of culpability. Yet redundancy may seem a small price to pay, compared to having an official blaming system that places substantial weight on criteria like direct causation.

There is not much to be found in the criminal-law literature by way of explanation why direct causation is morally significant. What discussion there is tends to tie its significance to the thought that it is *more culpable* actually to cause some harm than to risk or attempt it.[37] Thus the argument over direct causation becomes one about moral luck.

Views on moral luck differ. It is certainly respectable to maintain that causation makes a difference to culpability. One might argue, for example, that

[34] Compare *Master* [2007] EWCA Crim 142, in which D inflicted a number of stab wounds upon V, aggravating an existing condition of deep-vein thrombosis. In turn, this triggered a pulmonary embolism, from which she died. D was rightly held to have caused V's death.

[35] It is to safeguard against causal miscarriages such as this in strict liability offences that jurisdictions sometimes enact defences of 'accident': see, e.g., Indian Penal Code 1860, s 80.

[36] *Hart and Honoré*, 173, 343; *Blaue* [1975] 3 All ER 446, 450 (below, § 5.4.3).

[37] e.g. Moore, *Causation and Responsibility*, ch 2.

the scalarity of causation should directly affect sentencing, in as much as differences in one's degree of causal responsibility generate differences in one's degree of culpability. That possibility seems plausible as well as important,[38] although I shall reject it in chapter 14. But set that aside for now. There is a more fundamental role for causation, to which I pointed in § 5.2. First and foremost, causation is a ground of ascriptive responsibility. It identifies D as an author of the relevant event. In turn, the primary legal role of causation is *to identify defendants* (and plaintiffs) and, where appropriate, to link defendants to plaintiffs, victims, and wrongs.

Causation performs this function throughout the law. 'Who killed whom?' is a starting point in identifying the appropriate participants in a tort action: D and P are linked in part by the fact that D caused harm to P. Consider too the old common law action for money had and received. Suppose that D receives a payment that P made to her by mistake, having intended to send the money to E. D's enrichment is undeserved, but doubtless there are others in the jurisdiction who recently made windfall gains. Why does the law pick out D? Again, because there is a causal link between P's loss and D's gain.[39] It is causation that connects D to P.

We may retort: what's the point in that? Why does it matter (not least to him) that it was Michael Massee who fired the gun that killed Brandon Lee? Or in tort, even supposing that we can prove who fired the injurious bullet in *Cook v Lewis*,[40] why should we care? Why not distribute the loss equally, if we think the protagonists are equally unmeritorious? For money had and received, why not use a windfall tax or some other redistributive mechanism to compensate those who have suffered unjustified losses?

Like the debate about moral luck, these are important questions. *But identification of defendants is not, in the first instance, a matter of desert.* What is at work here is a more primitive, non-moral ground of ascriptive responsibility.

Notions of ascriptive responsibility are inherent in how we think about the world, in our understanding of ourselves (and other creatures) as individual agents. We are not simply a collective, let alone a moral collective; we engage with the world as distinct agents, each with a transactional history that is part of our self-definition. So it is meaningful, even pre-morally, to ask who caused Brandon Lee's death. Such a question acknowledges that we are separate actors. Norms concerning self-determination and autonomy may rest on that

[38] For a revealing study of folk intuitions, see J T Johnson and J Drobny, 'Proximity biases in the attribution of civil liability' (1985) 48 J Personality and Social Psychology 283.
[39] See A P Simester, 'Correcting Unjust Enrichments' (2010) 30 OJLS 579, 595–97.
[40] Above, § 5.1.

separateness; but the separation exists prior to those norms. And ascriptive responsibility is, to that extent, pre-moral. So, too, with money had and received. Attributing an enrichment to the defendant does not begin with the merits. The merits will come later. It is the transfer itself that first marks out plaintiff and defendant.

Pre-moral causal paths are embedded in the sense we have of our own and others' identities, as individual *agents* in the world.[41] As agents, we are, in part, what we do and bring about: our identity is bound up with our own agency, with our sense of ourselves (and our perceptions of others) as creatures who act in and upon the world. The association between action and effect is thus a natural reflection of the understanding we have of our specific relationships qua distinct human agents with the world, in terms of events, consequences, and their authors. At its most primitive, causation tracks our authorship, as agents, of events. In so doing, it helps to mark the boundaries of our agency. When D moves his finger and V falls dead, establishing a physical reaction chain between these two events gives us an answer to that very basic question, *who did it*? It does not follow that D should be blamed for killing V, nor that others should be exonerated; but it does connect V's death to D's agency. D is not the same agent as E, and this is one of the ways of marking out that difference.

Notice that this is not a claim about the 'separateness of persons',[42] in so far as that concept is deployed in anti-utilitarian arguments. The point here is yet more basic: that acknowledging direct causation is required to preserve even separateness of *agents*, including non-human ones. We cannot maintain separateness of agents without recognizing physical reaction chains.[43]

Even so, further questions remain. It may be natural, but why should the law place normative weight on it? One answer might be that recognizing the separateness of agents is valuable per se. However, we can also point to criminalization reasons.

[41] Cp. A M Honoré, 'Responsibility and Luck' (1988) 104 LQR 530 (1988); for discussion, see S R Perry, 'The Moral Foundations of Tort Law' (1992) 77 Iowa LR 449, 489ff.

[42] Neither is it a claim about 'free, deliberate, and informed' interveners (below, § 5.3.4).

[43] Similarly, *Hart and Honoré* worries (at lxxx–xi) that 'respect for ourselves and others as distinct persons would be much weakened, if not dissolved, if we could not think of ourselves as the separate authors of the changes we make in the world.' Honoré's own thoughts along these lines are sympathetically developed by J Gardner, 'Obligations and Outcomes in the Law of Tort' in P Cane and J Gardner (eds), *Relating to Responsibility* (Hart 2001) 111, 133–34. A counterthought: Couldn't a notion of separate agency be preserved even if we didn't attribute consequences to particular agents? We would still be able to attribute particular bodily movements, as well as particular intentions: couldn't our agency reside in those things, rather in their consequences? Only at the price of a radically impoverished conception of agenthood. Agency is a matter of interaction with the world, not merely something private and to which the world is external. Our lives *as agents* are constituted by those interactions. I cannot be a killer in my mind; I cannot be a killer even if I make appropriate bodily movements in the attempt to be one. I can only be a killer if killing is part of my history.

Some of those reasons are pragmatic. It hardly seems practical to allow P to sue anyone who happens to have been enriched, say by a windfall, at around the time of P's loss. Rule of law values are also relevant, since liability may become too unpredictable if anyone who makes a gain can be coerced into subsidizing the undeserved losers, or if anyone who can prevent harm becomes therefore exposed to criminal conviction.

But perhaps the most important reasons concern liberty. Failing to distinguish causers from, say, mere non-preventers would tend to cast the liability net too wide, in both criminal and civil law. Without that distinction, the occurrence of harm would have potential to involve *anyone* as a possible defendant. The requirement of a causal connection between conduct and harm fosters individual freedom by tending to narrow the range of persons who may come under obligations to intervene whenever such a harm is in play. It is generally[44] undesirable that those with an opportunity to prevent some event should be put to the burden of having to do so unless their connection to that event is sufficiently close. Sometimes, an indirect, non-causal connection to harm ought to be sufficient for criminal or civil liability: physical causation chains merely supply the *primary* way of being involved. We shall explore the arguments for such liability in more detail across the next two chapters, in the context of omissions and complicity theory. Criminalization factors supply good reasons why such liability is ancillary rather than core.

5.3 Indirect causation: Bridging across interventions and the novus actus problem

Let us grant that physical reaction chains exist, and that the criminal law can acknowledge a form of (direct) causation that rests on natural rather than moral properties. How far can that take us?

Some distance. (And much more importantly, some parts of distances.[45]) We can say that C causes E whenever there is a continuing physical reaction chain from C to E. Moreover, doing so allows us to acknowledge a form of causation that is not amenable to being defeated by a *novus actus interveniens*. The criminal law captures this conclusion via the principle outlined earlier: that if

[44] Not invariably. Clearly, not all liberties ought to be promoted. The thought here trades on the systematic nature of law and its potential for invasiveness if uncaused events *generally* were treated as things for which D is accountable. I develop this point further in chapter 6.

[45] As we shall see below, in practice, the most important role for direct causation lies in constituting sub-chains, i.e. component parts of indirect causal chains. See § 5.3.1 (especially n 61).

D's act is an 'operating', direct cause of (say) V's death, other causes are at most concurrent ones—whether deliberate or accidental, whether foreseen or unforeseeable.[46] In such cases, it is irrelevant whether the outcome can be causally attributed to other agents too.[47] Moreover, when multiple causes are concurrently at work, there is no requirement that a defendant's conduct must have been the most important, by itself sufficient, or even necessary to cause V's death.[48] It always suffices for causation that D's own conduct was a direct contributor to bringing about the death.

But can we go further? In particular, can we say that C causes E if *and only if* there is a continuing physical reaction chain from C to E? Let us call someone who holds that view a 'physicalist'. Moore is a self-confessed physicalist. On his account, so-called *novus actus* cases are merely scenarios where direct causation is absent.[49] For Moore, direct causation is all the causation there is.

To test Moore's analysis, we need to think in more detail about the criminal law's major *novus actus* doctrines. First is the familiar 'FDI' rule: that a 'free, deliberate, and informed' intervention by another mature human being 'breaks' the causal chain between D and the relevant outcome, whether or not that intervention is foreseeable. Suppose the following example.

> *South-side*: Following an argument, D assaults V, leaving him unconscious and seriously injured in a dangerous area of the city. V will die of his wounds if left untreated. Before that occurs, however, T comes upon V, who is a member of a rival gang. T deliberately shoots V dead. The risk that this would occur was reasonably foreseeable and indeed foreseen by D.

In the criminal law, it is generally accepted that D does not cause V's death, even if that death was made likely by D's actions.[50] In tort law, by contrast, D *would* typically be held liable for V's death.[51] Thus the FDI rule is context-dependent.

[46] See *Simester and Sullivan*, § 4.2(ii)(c); *Hennigan* [1971] 3 All ER 133.

[47] *Haines* (1847) 2 Car & K 368, 175 ER 152; *People v Lewis* 57 P 470 (1899); *Blaue* [1975] 3 All ER 446.

[48] *Warburton* [2006] EWCA Crim 627, [21]–[23].

[49] Moore, *Causation and Responsibility*, ch 12.

[50] See, e.g., *Dalby* [1982] 1 All ER 916; *Hilton* (1838) 2 Lew CC 214, 168 ER 1132; *Latif* [1996] 1 WLR 104; *Tse Hung-Lit* [1986] AC 876; *People v Campbell* 335 NW 2d 27 (Mich 1983). Canadian law seems to have lost sight of this: *Maybin* [2012] 2 SCR 30.

[51] See, e.g., *Stansbie v Troman* [1948] 2 All ER 48: D was painting P's house. He went out for two hours, leaving the front door unlocked. A thief entered and stole various possessions. D was held liable for P's loss. Compare too *Hines v Garrett* 108 SE 690 (Va 1921); *Richardson v Ham* 285 P 2d 269 (Cal 1955). Contrast *Watson v Kentucky & Indiana Bridge & Railroad Co* 126 SW 146 (Ky 1910); *Reeves v Commissioner of Police of the Metropolis* [2000] 1 AC 360, 367 (Lord Hoffman; albeit liability was upheld on the facts).

The second major *novus actus* doctrine in criminal law is the so-called 'foreseeability' rule: that interventions (human or otherwise) 'break' the causal chain, even though they are not free, deliberate, and informed, if they are, as is sometimes said, 'extraordinary'.[52] Consider the New Zealand case of *Hart*,[53] in which H assaulted V, leaving her lying unconscious on a beach below the high-water mark. V subsequently drowned under the incoming tide. The Court of Appeal held that H had caused the death of the victim. It seems the conclusion would have been different had V been abandoned above the high-water mark, and drowned from a freak tidal wave.[54]

Physicalists like Moore hold that these two *novus actus* doctrines have no place as doctrines of causation. Their justification, if any, in a legal system could only be normative. While they might be relevant to the allocation of legal liability for an outcome, they can have nothing to say about *causal* responsibility for that outcome. In the case of the FDI rule, physicalists would hold this even if it turned out that *no* direct causal path can ever be traced through free, deliberate, and informed intermediaries.[55] Admittedly, were that generalization true, causation could not be ascribed in such a case: but *that* conclusion would follow just from the fact that direct causation was absent, not because of any special rule about free, deliberate, and informed action. So there is no need for an independent FDI rule, except perhaps as a convenient proxy. Moreover, Moore might add, it is not clear why we should concede the generalization. We have yet to see why T's free, deliberate, and informed action can *never* be caused by D.

The 'foreseeability' rule fares even worse: it would be dismissed out of hand by a physicalist, for whom causal explanations are concerned undilutedly with how the world actually works, not with whether we saw it coming. If, like Michael Massee, D's act generated a chain of physical reactions that caused V's death *unforeseeably*, that may affect D's legal liability; but we should not corrupt our metaphysics by pretending that D did not actually cause V's death.

[52] *Environment Agency v Empress Car Co (Abertillery) Ltd* [1999] 2 AC 22, 34–36: below, § 5.3.2. It is worth re-emphasizing that this principle does not apply if direct causation can be established.

[53] [1986] 2 NZLR 408. See also *Hallett* [1969] SASR 141.

[54] Compare R M Perkins, 'The Law of Homicide' (1946) 36 J Crim L & Criminology 391, 393–94; *Green-Wheeler Shoe Co v Chicago RI & P Ry Co* 106 NW 498 (Iowa 1906).

[55] On the possibility of causing another to act, see § 5.3.4.

5.3.1 The incompleteness of direct causation

The clarity and structural simplicity of the physicalist view is attractive. Deceptively so, unless causation is very much rarer than almost anyone thinks. In *Hart*, it seems natural to ascribe causal responsibility for V's death to H. Yet we cannot trace a continuing physical reaction chain from H's punch to V's death. If we ask, 'of what did V die?', the answer is: drowning. The incoming tide killed her, and the incoming tide was *not* something H brought about.

This is not a case of direct causation. Even if V would otherwise have died from the injuries inflicted by H, there is no continuing sequence of physical reactions linking H's punch to V's death. It need not follow that H should be acquitted of manslaughter. In order to sustain a conviction, however, the physicalist would have to create new doctrines of ascriptive responsibility, such as 'opportunity creation'[56] and 'aiding and abetting nature'.[57] But that response seems too free-and-easy. It short-changes the causal picture here.

On Moore's physicalist account, throwing someone in front of a train, or tying them to the track, is not a cause of their death: it merely creates the opportunity for the train, like the tide, to do so. Yet H's relationship to V's drowning seems rightly characterized as causal. Certainly, H's punch was part of the sequence of events that explains why V died.[58] That explanation itself rests upon direct causal chains—but upon a combination of two of them, not just the one. Forensically, we might say, H made the second causal chain relevant. He put V in harm's way. Rather than direct causation, therefore, this is a case of *indirect* causation. A finding of indirect causation addresses D's causal responsibility for consequences of physical reaction chains that D did not originate. It allows us to conclude that the defendant in *Hart* authored his victim's death as much as Michael Massee authored Brandon Lee's. To twist the legal metaphor, D created the setting—and the setting was not merely historical.

Indirect causation is dependent upon, and interwoven with, the same physical reaction chains that constitute direct causation. Both are predicated upon facts about the world and about how D's intervention affected its operation. Moreover, to the extent that findings of causation are morally significant, the two forms have like implications. Proving D's ascriptive responsibility for the result in neither case requires proof of a duty to prevent that result, nor proof

[56] Moore, *Causation and Responsibility*, 144–49.
[57] Ibid, 145.
[58] Notice: as so often, the traditional *sine qua non* test is unhelpful here. Perhaps, if H had not knocked V unconscious, V would have gone to sleep there anyway (in which case the time and place of death would have been unchanged).

of the distinctive mens rea requirements for complicity-based responsibility. Consider too the common-law duty, articulated in *Miller*, 'to take measures that lie within one's power to counteract a danger that one has oneself created'.[59] M, a vagrant, was sleeping in an unoccupied house. He fell asleep while smoking a cigarette, which then set fire to his mattress. Waking to find the mattress smouldering, M simply moved to the next room and went back to sleep. The house caught fire; M was charged with reckless arson. On appeal, the House of Lords held that M's omission to take remedial measures satisfied the actus reus requirement. His inadvertent starting of the fire crystallized a legal duty to prevent risks caused by his earlier, positive behaviour. *Miller* is a direct causation case, but it surely applies also to indirect causal sequences. Had Hart knocked his victim unconscious by accident, perhaps while doing cartwheels excitedly on the sand, the same remedial duty would, and should, have arisen for him too.[60]

Of course, the sequence of events in *Hart* does not involve an 'unbroken' or continuing chain of reactions linking H's punch to V's death. But that's the point. Because of that, the issue for causation becomes: when can we *bridge between* the two direct causal chains operating in this case? This question has moral dimensions.[61] The important point to notice here is that the bridging is chain-*constructive* rather than chain-destructive. Moore describes the law's doctrine of *novus actus* as a doctrine that 'certain interventions break the chain that would otherwise have existed between D's act and some harm to another.'[62] While that reflects a conventional way of thinking about *novus actus*, the truth of the matter is the other way around. Only direct causation is physically unbroken. If we are to acknowledge causal responsibility in cases such as *Hart*, we need indirect causation: not to cut down direct causation, but to augment it.

That is to say: a *novus actus interveniens* does not 'break' the causal chain that otherwise, hypothetically, would link C to E. Indeed, *there is no legal doctrine that severs direct causal chains*. As mentioned earlier, 'operating' causes are always sufficient. *Novus actus* doctrines do not operate as causal trumps. Quite the opposite: in cases like *Hart*, no direct chain exists between H's punch

[59] *Miller* [1983] 2 AC 161, 176 (HL).

[60] The practical importance of the duty in *Miller* is that it generates a second opportunity to satisfy the concurrence requirement in criminal law, i.e. when D—with mens rea—omits to save V from a risk that D has—without mens rea—caused.

[61] Notice, though, that there is no distributive implication here. The direct chains being bridged do not *themselves* become morally loaded. Within their own scope, they remain instances of direct causation. Hence, while in practice few instances of crimes involve a complete chain of direct causation, direct—morally insensitive—causation still has an important role to play in part-constituting chains of indirect causation.

[62] Moore, *Causation and Responsibility*, 229.

and V's death. That 'chain', as it were, is already broken. *Novus actus* doctrines are secondary upon this physical fact. They operate to inform us when we can, and when we cannot, span the gap.

5.3.2 Extraordinariness

We can bridge it, according to standard doctrine, when the intervention of the tide was reasonably foreseeable—ordinary—and not 'something extraordinary'.[63] One way of thinking about the underlying idea here is that the intervention is no mere coincidence. Indeed (assuming the outcome is unwelcome), it is a prospect that supplies a reason we might sensibly give when stating why D should not act as he does. Contrast *Bush v Commonwealth*,[64] in which D shot V, who was taken to hospital and operated upon. V subsequently died of scarlet fever caught from the operating surgeon. On these facts, D's conviction was quashed for lack of causation. Rightly so. Catching scarlet fever was 'the visitation of Providence' and not a consequence of D's act.[65]

This is not a culpability standard. The relevant intervention need not be foreseeable to the defendant.[66] Provided it was foreseeable from the perspective of an ordinary person, it does not count as a mere coincidence. We can extend causation across that intervention, notwithstanding its independent origin.[67]

At this point, though, we have abandoned a purely physicalist account of causation. At least, we have abandoned it unless the criteria of extraordinariness are themselves non-moral: and that seems implausible. Consider the indeterminacy of 'extraordinariness' itself.[68] A tide may be higher than 'normal' without being extraordinary. Partly, the difference is probabilistic, a matter of degree. If, on average, an extreme high tide occurs just once every twenty years, doubtless that would be extraordinary. Once a week, though, would not be. How improbable must the intervention be? The question demands argument rather than stipulation. Moreover, regularity is pertinent. Rather like the

[63] *Environment Agency v Empress Car Co (Abertillery) Ltd* [1999] 2 AC 22, 34–36. Or such as could not 'sensibly have been anticipated': *Girdler* [2009] EWCA Crim 2666, [43].
[64] 78 Ky 268 (1880).
[65] Neither, one might add, was there any evidence that D died from a combination of scarlet fever and the original injury, in which case direct causation would lie.
[66] A point made by Moore, *Causation and Responsibility*, 247. We discuss foreseeability as it relates to culpability in chapters 11–12.
[67] Interestingly, Moore appears to accept this (e.g. at 245–47; 145—restricting his opposition to contrived coincidences; contrast the discussion at 277). To that extent, it seems that Moore is not a pure physicalist.
[68] See on this point *Hart and Honoré*, 165–68; Moore, *Causation and Responsibility*, 246–47.

equinoctial spring tides, a once-a-year 'exceptionally' high tide might not be abnormal if it always occurs on a particular day. This suggests that the 'extraordinariness' standard embedded in indirect causation is tied to reasonable or ordinary expectations. But to adjudicate those, we need to know *whose* (non-omniscient) expectations are to be counted. Suppose that D is a city-dweller who knows nothing about tides, but perpetrates his waterside assault in a fishing village where every inhabitant knows the annual-highest tide is due that evening. Or suppose that D's community has not yet developed to the point where tide patterns are understood. Abnormality in this context is a socialized concept. It is hard to see how a standard of this sort can be morally insensitive.

Neither should it be. In this respect, *Hart* is an extreme example of the ping-pong ball. Indirect causation reflects the insight that, where a person's conduct does not directly cause an event, it can still be apt to regard her as authoring it. Even as they peter out, the direct effects of our actions intersect with a multitude of other causal processes and, in some respects, the world may go differently.[69] Yet the ascription of responsibility for those differences is not automatic. Suppose that Hart had assaulted V *above* the high-tide mark, and a stray dog later dragged V below it. In such a case, we may not be willing to bridge the causal space between Hart's conduct and V's death, despite the fact that his conduct affected the evolution of events. The criteria of indirect causation articulate the extent to which such further effects are to be laid at a person's door—the extent to which her contribution is not merely part of the 'historical setting'. Understood in this way, it becomes easy to see how a test of extraordinariness promotes the values discussed in § 5.2.1. It limits our accountability for the effects of causal processes that do not belong to us.

5.3.3 Intended (or foreseen) extraordinary interventions?

So *Hart* was rightly decided. But what about *contrived* coincidences—extraordinary events that were foreseen or hoped-for by the defendant? Suppose that A strikes B, knocking him out beneath a tree. Half an hour later, the tree topples onto B and kills him. Hart and Honoré argue that it matters causally whether A anticipated that event: 'an extraordinary conjunction of events, if intended or designed, does not negative causal connection.'[70] Moore,

[69] As it did even in *Jordan*: above, § 5.1

[70] *Hart and Honoré*, 170. As the authors remark (at 171), much the same logic applies to foreseen interventions: 'If [D] binds his victim and leaves him on the pavement at a place where he has reason to suppose a heavy tree will fall half an hour later, the victim's death from the fall of the tree is no coincidence.' D's foresight would have to be such that, for him, the intervention is not extraordinary.

however, rejects this possibility. For him, 'it is metaphysics, not legal policy, that tells us when an action *causes* a certain harm.'[71] Judith Thomson holds a similar view:[72]

> '[On Hart and Honoré's account,] the question whether A's hitting B caused his death turns on what A had good reason to believe, or knew, and what his intention was in hitting B. Given one epistemic state and intention, A's hitting B did not cause B's death; given a different epistemic state and intention, A's hitting B did cause B's death. But that *cannot* be right. A's epistemic state and his intention do have a bearing on whether A's hitting B was to blame for B's death. But it cannot be thought that a difference in A's epistemic state and intention fixes that in the one case A's hitting B caused B's death whereas in the other case it did not—for whether A's hitting B caused B's death turns on what the world is like and not on what A does or doesn't believe or want it to be like.'

That's certainly true for direct causation. But we can now see that, in the context of indirect causation, there is no categorical reason to reject the extensional doctrine, since it operates as an exception to a rule that is itself morally informed. Once you've swallowed the camel, there's no point in straining at gnats. To allow bridging on the basis of ordinariness (whatever that is), while rejecting it when a causal path was anticipated, even sought, by the defendant would be arbitrary.

We need to be careful about what is entailed by this. The claim is not that 'intended [or foreseen] consequences are never too remote.'[73] To characterize the exception in that way would be wrong. It would be to elevate a subordinate exception—an exception which itself concerns supplementary, indirect causation—to the level of a primary rule. That is not what is at stake here. To see this, consider a case where D shoots at V on a mountainside, meaning to kill him. She misses, but the noise of her shot triggers an avalanche in which V is killed. D cannot escape causal responsibility for V's death by pointing to the unexpected route of the complete physical reaction chain that she herself initiated. Conversely, recalling *White*,[74] the intention to kill his mother by

[71] Moore, *Causation and Responsibility*, 230. Rather than causation (145), 'one who purposefully utilizes extraordinary natural events to produce harm to others should be liable on an "aiding of nature" ground.'

[72] J J Thomson, 'Some Reflections on Hart and Honoré, *Causation in the Law*' in M Kramer et al (eds), *The Legacy of H.L.A. Hart* (OUP 2008) 143, 162.

[73] See, e.g., *Quinn v Leatham* [1901] AC 495, 537 ('the intention to injure the plaintiff negatives all excuses and disposes of any question of remoteness of damage'); *Hart and Honoré*, 170–72; Williams, *TBCL*, 388–89.

[74] [1910] 2 KB 124; above, § 5.1.

poisoning could not make W causally responsible for her death of an unrelated heart attack. Intentions are irrelevant to direct causation. But the bridging principles governing indirect causation are morally sensitive, and intention and foresight can have a limited place there.

5.3.4 Intervening human beings

Time to return to *South-side*. Famously, the common law of crime knows a rule, and tort law knows no rule,[75] that intervention by a free, deliberate, and informed person (T) 'breaks' the causal chain between D's wrong and the harm that ensues.[76] If D negligently creates an opportunity for T to damage V's property, D may have to pay for it.[77] But D is not himself a vandal.[78] And unlike tort verdicts, convictions are personal.[79]

The *legal* correctness of the FDI rule was endorsed by the House of Lords in *Kennedy (No. 2)*:[80]

> 'The criminal law generally assumes the existence of free will. The law recognises certain exceptions, in the case of the young, those who for any reason are not fully responsible for their actions, and the vulnerable, and it acknowledges situations of duress and necessity, as also of deception and mistake. But, generally speaking, informed adults of sound mind are treated as autonomous beings able to make their own decisions how they will act, and none of the exceptions is relied on as possibly applicable in this case. Thus D is not to be treated as causing V to act in a certain way if V makes a voluntary and informed decision to act in that way rather than another.'

As a proposition of criminal law, the FDI rule is relatively uncontroversial, at least in common-law jurisdictions.[81] Yet it leaves a puzzle. What is the

[75] At least generally: contrast *Watson v Kentucky & Indiana Bridge & Railroad Co* 126 SW 146 (Ky 1910). D spilled gasoline throughout the town. A fire ensued when T dropped his cigar into the petrol. The Court held that, if T's act was of starting the fire were deliberate, it would relieve D of liability for that fire.

[76] *Hart and Honoré*, 136, 326; *Pagett* (1983) 76 Cr App R 279, 288–89; *Latif* [1996] 1 WLR 104, 115 (HL).

[77] See the cases cited above, n 51.

[78] Not just (though also) because vandals cause damage advertently. For *Hart and Honoré*, liability is only 'quasi causal': 194ff.

[79] Cp. § 1. For the importance of this point in a different context, see § 17.4.1.

[80] [2007] UKHL 38, [14]. D prepared a heroin mixture for V in a syringe. V then injected himself with the heroin and subsequently died. The House quashed D's conviction of manslaughter on the ground that D had not caused V's death. The intervention by V was free, deliberate, and informed.

[81] Contrast Scotland, a civil law jurisdiction: *MacAngus and Kane v HM Advocate* [2009] HCJAC 8.

metaphysical basis, if any, for the rule that D's causal contribution to an outcome may be superseded by the free, deliberate, and informed intervention of T?

Moore thinks none. Following Davidson,[82] he points out that reasons too can be causes. It may be tempting to think of free, deliberate, and informed action as somehow self-originated: to view 'the individual's will as the autonomous prime cause of his behaviour.'[83] Criminal lawyers tend to treat the will as 'an uncaused causer'.[84] But deliberate choices are made for reasons, and wills themselves are formed (in part) because of those reasons. As such, for Moore, 'there is no reason whatever to think that willings are uncaused'—even willings that correspond to free, deliberate, and informed choices:[85]

> 'Such functionally specified, physically realized events [as willings] are both causes and effects of earlier causes, like all other events. They cannot, on such an account, be literal fresh causal starts breaking causal chains wherever they intervene.'

Moore is surely right about all this. But what Moore doesn't see is that this fails to solve the puzzle. The important question is not whether T's intervention is caused, but whether T's intervention is *caused by D*. Put differently, the primary question here is whether *South-side* is like *Hart*, in the sense that it is a candidate for indirect rather than direct causation.

Admittedly, T's intervention in *South-side* is reactive; it responds to something D has done. In this sense, the case is not like *Hart*, where D's intervention has no significant effect upon the arrival of the tide.[86] From the perspective of direct causation, however, autonomous actors are, in effect, like units of deterministic chaos. Especially where T has second-order capacities to moderate her own first-order reasoning, there are so many confluent influences, past and present, upon an autonomous actor's values and decision-making processes that mere opportunity-creation does not exercise sufficient control over T's decision to count as having caused it by means of a continuing physical reaction chain. D's contribution is like dropping the ping-pong ball into the turbulent stream. It represents an input into a causal mechanism that is so profoundly complex that D exercises no control over the outcome save by creating

82 Davidson, *EAE* 3; Moore, *Causation and Responsibility*, 266–67.
83 As Glanville Williams puts it: *TBCL*, 391. See too *Hart and Honoré*, 42–43, 51–59, 186–204, 363–88.
84 Moore, *Causation and Responsibility*, 272.
85 Ibid, 273.
86 Insignificant rather than non-existent, in that the gravitational pull exerted by the bodies of D and V upon the tide would be trivial.

the initial opportunity for T to intervene; what happened next was not up (or down) to D.

This is not always the case. For one thing, not all intervening agency is autonomous—think of training animals. It is even possible to condition the responses of moral agents, something parents frequently aim at. Indeed, by the time we reach maturity, most human beings have acquired value-sets that were more or less unchosen, or at least unchosen by them qua autonomous moral agents. On the other hand, having unchosen values implies neither simplicity nor a lack of autonomy.[87] No person is perfectly autonomous; it is enough for moral agency that they are sufficiently so. The matter is one of degree. And that means we cannot always exclude causation of one agent's acts by another. For an agent with sufficiently reduced autonomy or deliberative capacity, especially one incapable of second-order deliberation, it becomes plausible that responses may be directly caused by particular inputs. The responses of Pavlov's dogs may well be the product of direct causation rather than deterministically chaotic.

Scenarios involving moral agents tend to be less straightforward. Ordinarily, virtually all of the factors that underpin T's choice will lie outside the control of D. Yet even as agents become more complex, particular cases might still involve direct causation of responses, as when T's reaction is motivated by a powerful fear that D's threat inspires. This suggests that there is no *tout-court* metaphysical reason why causal ascriptions of another person's acts should be ruled out, or even confined to extreme cases.[88] A choice made by T out of fear may be made rationally yet caused by D's threat—because fear of that threat dominated T's motivation. This time, the ping-pong ball was joined to an engine that cut through the turbulent stream.

Still, conceding this point does not foreclose the issue. The conclusion that D's act supplied a reason why T intervened need not explain why T acted *in the manner that she did*. Suppose that D inflicts a minor wound upon V that requires medical attention. T, the doctor, sees that treatment is required but, owing to incompetence, responds with radically inappropriate treatment that leads to V's death: *Jordan*.[89] Here, we might conclude, the original injury was no

[87] See also §§ 11.5, 14.4.1.

[88] Such as those in which T's own second-order capacities are bypassed by D's threat: a possibility eloquently portrayed in George Orwell's *1984* (Secker & Warburg 1949), where Winston's primal fear of rats effectively subordinated his rational faculties and caused him finally to betray his commitment to Julia.

[89] (1956) 40 Cr App R 152; above, § 5.1.

more than the 'historical setting' for T's mis-intervention, the causes of which swamped D's contribution—like the (unpropelled) ping-pong ball from § 5.1.

We can accommodate most cases of this kind with a test similar to that for *Hart*: whether T's intervention was extraordinary in character. Thus, in *Martin*,[90] D was said not to have caused death after he offered his child a sip of an alcoholic drink, whereupon the child unexpectedly seized and consumed the entire drink. As we suggested in § 5.3.1, the same would be true if, in *Hart*, D had left V above the high-tide mark and a stray dog had later dragged her down the beach. It holds also in tort: as where V is injured by D, but is killed when the ambulance taking him to hospital is hit by a runaway truck.

So, too, for our unpropelled ping-pong ball. Let us suppose that, unbeknown to me, an explosion will occur if the ball ultimately enters the right channel downstream. When I drop the ball in the stream, I put it in harm's way; I create the opportunity for the stream to carry it down the right channel. We have seen that I do not cause it to do so directly. None the less, indirect causation will lie unless it was an extraordinary occurrence for the stream to carry the ball down that channel.

5.3.5 The FDI rule

Hold on a moment, you may say. Aren't even free, deliberate, and informed interveners sometimes predictable? If the intervention in *South-side* was reasonably foreseeable, surely it wouldn't count as extraordinary? Even if we cannot trace direct causation through the complexity of T's dispositions, can we not locate a form of indirect causation here?[91]

They are; it would not; we can. Indeed, there is no reason why the point at which a person becomes so complex that her responses are not directly caused by another must correspond to her being free, deliberate, and informed. Our understanding of the mechanisms that lead moral agents to act remains too limited for us to locate that point unequivocally. Moreover, whether D is sufficiently free, deliberate, and informed to invoke the FDI rule is itself a matter of degree.

Ultimately, the distinctiveness of the FDI rule is not specific to causation. The rule is normative rather than metaphysical. Underpinning the FDI rule

[90] (1827) 3 C & P 211, 172 ER 390.
[91] Compare Moore's persuasive criticisms of Hart and Honoré on this point: *Causation and Responsibility*, 263ff.

is the *principle of personal control* over criminal liability,[92] according to which no one should have the ability deliberately to render another person guilty of a crime. Our liability, like our culpability, flows from what *we* do (or omit to do). It does not, and should not, spring from the choices of others. Hence, by contrast with torts, the common law knows no general doctrine of vicarious criminal liability. This is, in part, because it is normally wrong to blame one person for another's conduct. But it is also for rule of law reasons. To attribute criminal liability in such cases is to empower that other person to put D in contravention of the law, enabling her deliberately to make D guilty of a criminal offence. Outside the adjudicative process, it is undesirable that such a discretionary power should rest in the hands of individuals, whether private citizens or officials.[93]

To be sure, our liability is often *affected* by what others do. D may avoid liability for murder because her attempt to shoot V dead is frustrated by V's taking cover. The example shows that the principle of personal control is asymmetrical: ordinarily, people may intervene to prevent criminal liability from arising, but not to generate liability. Neither is it disputed that others may make unintentional contributions to D's liability.[94] The principle is opposed only to autonomous *deliberate* choices that inculpate D. As such, it finds expression in the FDI rule, which operates to trump a finding of indirect causation.

The principle of personal control can be seen in other contexts. One illustration is the New Zealand case of *Jackson v Attorney-General*,[95] in which the High Court held that a reason for not imposing strict liability in the offence of possessing cannabis in a prison cell was that its imposition would tend to encourage inmates to take retribution against a fellow inmate, by placing cannabis or other drugs in that person's cell. Another example is supplied by the English case of *Porter v Honey*.[96] D, an estate agent, was convicted of displaying a For Sale board on a property at a time when a second board was also displayed. When D erected the board, his was the only one on display. E, a competing

[92] See also § 7.1.

[93] As in the police-generated offences in *Larsonneur* (1933) 24 Cr App R 74 and *Winzar v Chief Constable of Kent* The Times, 28 March 1983; cf. *Martin v State of Alabama* 17 So 2d 427 (1944), where the defendant was (rightly) acquitted.

[94] As in *Roberts* (1971) 56 Cr App R 95, where V injured herself in fleeing D's attack. Neither does the principle foreclose the potential for a third party deliberately to *aggravate* D's liability, in a case where her contribution is merely concurrent with D's.

[95] [2006] 2 NZLR 534, 542. (The offence has since been repealed.) Cp. also *Re Wairarapa Election Petition* [1988] 2 NZLR 74, 117 ll. 36–38 (HC).

[96] [1988] 1 WLR 1420.

estate agent, later erected a second For Sale board on the property. In quashing D's conviction, the House of Lords recognized that:[97]

> 'The courts should surely be slow to impute to Parliament so harsh an intention as to impose criminal liability on a citizen acting lawfully because another citizen, over whom he has no control, acts unlawfully.'

Just so. Obviously, it would be wrong to punish D for the actions of E. But that is not the only objection. In chapter 1, we pointed out that the criminal conviction labels D *personally*, modifying D's status in the community. As such, the potential for conviction should lie in D's hands. Principles of equality before the law demand that others do not have the power to change D's status, by making a criminal out of someone who has, himself, done no wrong. It is the personal nature of criminal convictions, in particular, that gives the principle of personal control its special poignancy. So the principle does not have the same significance for tort law.[98]

In the criminal law, the principle helps to carve our space for a different type of ascriptive bridge-building—for accomplices.[99] It mandates that one who assists or encourages another person to commit a crime must be dealt with by the special rules of complicity liability. Complicity represents the only general exception to the principle of personal control. Its rules differ from the normal liability requirements of the relevant substantive offence, which would otherwise be in play if causation were found. Distinctive complicity rules are required in part because they govern the circumstances in which control over D's liability lies in the untrammelled hands of a fellow citizen.

5.4 Omissions and other non-interventions

Omissions, perhaps needless to say, are different. Causally speaking, they are a species of non-intervention,[100] marked out in part by their very failure to interfere in the world.[101] When Pittwood, the railway gatekeeper, went off for lunch

[97] Ibid, 1426. See also, in other contexts, *Tilley* [2009] EWCA Crim 1426, [37]–[39]; *Robinson-Pierre* [2013] EWCA Crim 2396.

[98] Though it is not without force, in the context of the duty of care: see, e.g., *Michael v Chief Constable of South Wales* [2015] UKSC 2, [97].

[99] See chapter 7.

[100] See § 5.4.2 for a non-intervention example that is not predicated on omissions. We shall focus primarily on non-interventions by omission here.

[101] Contrary, one may add, to a duty or expectation: see § 6.1. The restriction is incidental for present purposes.

without closing the gate,[102] our complaint is not that he initiated, or helped to initiate, a series of physical reactions that led to White's death. Our complaint is not that he changed the world. It is that he failed to change the world, and thereby allowed the accident to happen. We complain, in other words, not about the effects of something Pittwood did, but about what happened when he didn't.

In a sense, omissions are not the cement of anything: more like the absence of solvent.[103] We may conclude that the cart entered the crossing 'because' Pittwood failed to close the gate, but Pittwood did not propel the cart forward. It was pulled by horses, independently driven. This is not to deny that the underlying behaviour constituting an omission can have direct causal effects. Suppose that Victor is drowning. Rather than throw him an old rope she is holding, Diana casts the rope upon the bonfire. Her behaviour causes the destruction of the rope. But not under the description, failing to toss it to Victor. The point here is that the same underlying behaviour can be described in multiple ways, so that it simultaneously constitutes both positive acts and omissions. By tossing the rope on the fire, Diana causes the destruction of the rope, but this fact does not establish that her failure to throw the rope to Victor causes anything at all.

Indeed, Moore would go further. On his account, omissions cannot be causes because they are 'literally nothing at all'.[104] Yet that seems too strong. When we say, D omitted to φ, we do not say 'nothing at all' about what took place. Rather, we aver that there was an event, located in time and space, in which D did not φ.[105] We supply our audience with *some* information about the event itself. Admittedly, it may not amount to much. If we know only that Diana didn't throw the rope to Victor, we don't know a lot about her behaviour on that occasion. Certainly, we know less about it than if told she threw the rope on the fire. But we do know *something*. In particular, we know that her behaviour involved the lack of movements constituting her throwing the rope to Victor. Characteristically, there is an enormous variety

[102] *Pittwood* (1902) 19 TLR 37. D, a gatekeeper on the Somerset and Dorset Railway, was hired to keep the gate shut during the daytime whenever a train was passing. He went off for lunch one afternoon, forgetting that the gate was open. A hay cart subsequently attempted to cross the line and was hit by a train. One passenger (White) was killed.

[103] Indeed, some writers refuse to accord omissions causal status at all: notably Moore, *Causation and Responsibility*, 444–51. In a legal context, compare Fletcher, *Rethinking*, 371, 589ff (although contrast 601–602, in the context of parents who starve their child to death); F H Bohlen, 'The Moral Duty to Aid Others as a Basis of Tort Liability' (1908) 56 U Penn LR 217, 220–21.

[104] Moore, *Act and Crime*, 28. See also ibid, 267ff; Moore, *Placing Blame*, 262ff.

[105] Above, § 4.3.2. While not immediately important here, we aver also there was some reason to expect her to φ: below, § 6.1.

of behaviour that can constitute an omission,[106] which is why we know so little about Diana's underlying behaviour compared to being told that she threw the rope on the fire. (It's also why prohibiting omissions is potentially so burdensome of freedom.[107]) But even if we haven't narrowed the description of D's behaviour very far, we have still narrowed it down. We have not said 'nothing at all' about her conduct.[108] An omission is an *eventful* non-action: the class of D's not-φings is not the same as the class of things that are not D's φings.

5.4.1 Counterfactual outcomes?

Not quite nothings, then. But causes? It is easy to see why that question is controversial. By their nature, non-interventions cannot form links in direct causal chains. When we ask, 'of what did Victor die?', the answer 'Diana's failure to throw him a rope' is not only incongruous but in an important sense wrong. Victor died by drowning. Diana's failure to save Victor is constituted by the *absence* of behaviour on her part that would have prevented what ensued—more specifically, that would have prevented the completion of the causal chain that in fact resulted in his death. In general, omissions do not initiate causal processes; they permit other causal processes to unfold.

The common law approaches such cases with a counterfactual test. It holds that D's omission causes an outcome if, but for that omission, the outcome would not have occurred. In the well-known case of *Dalloway*,[109] for example, D was driving a cart without holding the reins when a young child ran in front of the cart and was struck and killed. The Court ruled that D could be convicted of manslaughter only if it were proved that, had D been using the reins correctly, the child would not have died.

At first glance, this but-for test looks sensible. If the child would have died anyway, it seems safe to conclude that D's omission made no difference, and that causal responsibility does not lie. On closer investigation, though, things are not so simple. For one thing, the foregoing analysis of *Dalloway* is over-simplified. Sooner or later, the child *would* have died—if of nothing else, then

[106] See § 6.1.2.
[107] See § 6.3.1.
[108] Another way of thinking about this is to contrast omissions with nullities. Things that are 'nothing at all' are genuine nullities, like the purported moving of a rook along a diagonal in chess. The 'move' is neither an act nor an omission: it did not happen. Omissions, by contrast, describe real events.
[109] (1847) 2 Cox CC 273.

of old age. Indeed, since we are all going to die at some point, a simplistic but-for test of that kind would never be met, for act or omission. And that cannot be right.

It may seem straightforward to accommodate this concern by tweaking the but-for test. We could merely require that, had D not acted or omitted as she did, the victim would not have died *at the time that he did*. That was more or less the analysis in *Morby*, in which D failed to seek medical treatment for his eight-year-old son, who died of confluent smallpox. His conviction was quashed for lack of proof that D's neglect had 'caused death or accelerated it'.[110] As Coleridge LJ put it, 'to convict of manslaughter it must be shewn that the neglect had the effect of shortening life.'[111] However, there are problems with this kind of approach. For one thing, it risks being massively overinclusive. Any failure, perhaps even any delay, by D becomes homicidal on this test if it accelerates the time of death *at all*. Subject only to the *de minimis* constraint, if his son would have survived an hour longer in hospital, Morby committed manslaughter.[112] Yet it seemingly overstates things to describe him as having caused his child's death. And it would surely be unjust to convict him of manslaughter on that basis.[113]

Moreover, if we construe the proposed but-for test (whether the victim would have died when he did) strictly, the difficulties become even greater. This is because there is nothing in the test that restricts it to *shortening* the victim's life; it would also be satisfied if life were lengthened. Indeed, while an 'acceleration' constraint might be defended as a pragmatic matter, at the level of principle it would be arbitrary. Imagine the following variation upon McLaughlin's famous example:[114]

> *Desert Traveller*: D1 poisons V's water canister just before V embarks on a journey into the desert. The poison she uses would produce instant death. Not knowing this, D2 adds his own poison to V's canister. The later poison blends with the earlier to generate a more slow-acting potion. V dies, as both intended. Both D1 and D2 cause death, even though D2's contribution had the practical effect of extending V's life.

[110] *Morby* (1882) 8 QBD 571, 575 (Stephens J). Cp. *Bradley v State* 84 So 677 (Fla 1920); *Broughton* [2020] EWCA Crim 1093.

[111] (1882) 8 QBD 571, 574. Statutory tests often take a similar approach: in s 299 of the Indian Penal Code 1860, Explanation 1 provides that 'A person who causes bodily injury to another who is labouring under a disorder, disease or bodily infirmity, and thereby accelerates the death of that other, shall be deemed to have caused his death.'

[112] A proposition explicitly accepted by the trial judge: (1882) 8 QBD 571, 572–73.

[113] Tort liability might begin to part company here, in as much as it might place a value upon the extent by which the plaintiff's life would have been lengthened.

[114] J A McLaughlin, 'Proximate Cause' (1925) 39 Harvard LR 149, 155 n 25.

Of what did V die? The compound poison. And that's all we really need to know. Shortening or lengthening is irrelevant. Of course, our McLaughlin variant involves an act. But the same point applies to omissions. Imagine the following case:

> *Camel*: D, neglecting her duties, omits to fill most of V's water bottles. By the time V realizes this, he is a long way out in the desert. V turns around and tries to get back. Alas, V (and the camel) dies of thirst two days later before reaching safety. Had D done as required, V would have continued on his trek and been killed in a sandstorm the following day.[115]

Of what did V die? Thirst. Why? Because D failed to fill his water bottles. The 'acceleration' test is artificial for omissions too.

5.4.2 Interdependence with direct and indirect causation

Even as it illustrates that point, however, the Camel case offers us a way forward. It points toward a more general truth about omissions and other non-interventions as a ground of ascriptive responsibility. Their significance is counterfactual, to be sure, but *not* in virtue of a but-for relationship between omission and outcome. Their causal significance lies in the fact that in the continuing causal sequence, C → C1 → C2 → . . . → Cn → E, that brought about the result, at least one of the internal links was completed only because of D's omission. D's omission, that is to say, is causally significant because it *did not break the causal chain that brought about the result.* If D had intervened between C1 and C2, say, C would not have been a cause of V's death.

One payoff of thinking about matters in this more fine-grained way is that it becomes easier to resist overinclusion. Suppose that, in *Morby*, the father's obtaining medical treatment would have prolonged life by one day. Yet the child would have died of the same smallpox that killed him without the treatment. In this scenario, the causal path from C to E would have been more circuitous had treatment intervened. But it would still have wended its way to E. We should conclude of such a case that the father's omission was not a cause of death.

[115] If death by sandstorm is thought unprovable, remember that the burden of proof rests on the prosecution in causal matters.

Rather than asking a simple but-for question about the outcome's *occurrence*, therefore, our account of non-interventions as causes needs to be tied more closely to how the outcome came about. The causal significance of D's not-φing lies in her failure to prevent the unfolding of chains of events that led causally to the outcome, not in her failure to prevent the outcome as such.[116] More generally, the causal significance of non-interventions depends upon counterfactuals about direct and indirect causal sequences, and upon hypothetical scenarios about what would have happened otherwise.

This makes omission-based causation potentially extremely complicated, since non-interventions can be stacked on top of each other in diverse ways. In *Dalloway*, for example, D's failure to pull on the reins, once the child ran in front of his cart, was a consequence of his antecedent failure to retain a grip upon those same reins. That antecedent failure was negligent; but the subsequent non-intervention made no difference, and so the negligence was non-causative. Non-interventions can even be the product of positive acts:

> *Runaway Train*: An out-of-control train laden with explosives is headed toward an outback town. Because the town is at the end of the railway line, an explosion is inevitable, destroying the town, if the train is not stopped. Officer A fires a missile programmed to blow up the train before it reaches the town. Unfortunately, Officer B, who does not know about the looming disaster, observes the missile on radar and fires a second missile to intercept it. The second missile brings down the first, thereby permitting the train to destroy the town.[117]

In this case, Officer B's act of firing the second missile brings about a non-intervention, since it prevents the first missile from colliding with the train. That non-intervention is, in turn, an omission-based cause of the town's destruction. We may conclude that Officer B's firing of the missile was a cause of the disaster.

It lies outside the scope of this book to analyse all the conceivable variants of non-intervention cases. Inevitably, many of the more complex cases will involve failures to pre-empt indirect causal chains. As such, they will depend on judgements about extraordinariness. The neglectful parent who leaves her

[116] Obviously, this still leaves D constantly failing to prevent the unfolding of causal chains. In terms of ascriptive responsibility, overinclusion is avoided here only by requiring that D also has a *duty* to intervene. Which is as it should be: see chapter 6.

[117] This kind of example is sometimes described as a 'double prevention' case, in that Officer B prevents the first missile from preventing the explosion.

child sleeping on the beach should not be ascribed with causal responsibility for his death by drowning if he was above the high-tide mark, or if he died from an unexpected lightning strike. At least where the complained-of conduct occurs prior to an intercession by other causal agencies, the 'bridging' test is generally the same—whether act or omission. So, for example, our conclusions about Pittwood's causal responsibility for White's death would be unchanged if it turned out that he had negligently opened the gate, and not merely failed to close it. By contrast, in more straightforward scenarios such as *Morby*, the relevant causal sequence is already underway—D's contribution resides specifically in his failure to interrupt it.

5.4.3 Omission as novus actus?

Understanding omissions as non-interventions means their causal significance runs alongside the direct or indirect chains that they fail to prevent. Contra *Hart and Honoré*,[118] it follows that an omission cannot constitute a *novus actus interveniens*, in the sense that it cannot break the relevant causal chain—precisely because it is the failure to break that chain which is our ground of complaint. They can only be *concurrent* causes. To illustrate, consider another example:

> *Antidote*: V is brought to hospital having been poisoned by P. D, the on-duty doctor, correctly diagnoses V's condition but forgets to administer the standard antidote. V dies of the poison. Had the antidote been administered, V would have recovered.

Of what did V die? The poison. However egregious, D's omission does not, indeed cannot, break the direct causal chain leading to V's death. It cannot break it as a conceptual matter, since it is that very failure to interrupt the causal chain which constitutes her omission; one cannot break causal chains by failing to break them.[119] In this case, *both* P and D cause V's death. Their contributions are, in effect, concurrent.

This explanation is key to understanding the controversial case of *Blaue*.[120] In that case, V, a Jehovah's Witness, was brought to hospital after

[118] *Hart and Honoré*, 361.

[119] Admittedly, it is possible for an omission to contribute to breaking a causal chain, but only when combined with a positive intervention: e.g., in a variant of *Pittwood*, when the railway gatekeeper fails to close the gate, causing the ambulance taking V to hospital to be hit by a train. The gatekeeper causes V's death rather than V's original assailant.

[120] [1975] 3 All ER 446; see too *Holland* (1841) 2 Mood & R 351, 174 ER 313.

being stabbed four times by B. Despite having lost a large amount of blood, she refused a blood transfusion on the grounds of her religious beliefs. As she knew she would, V died of blood loss the next day. B appealed his conviction of manslaughter, on the ground that V's refusal to have a blood transfusion was a *novus actus interveniens* that broke the causal chain between the stabbing and V's death. Clearly, the non-transfusion was *a* cause of V's death. Nonetheless, the Court of Appeal ruled that the original wound inflicted by B remained an operating cause of death. Equally clearly, that ruling was correct. We can trace a straightforward, direct causal chain from the stabbing to V's death.

The Court should have left the matter there. Alas, it did not. Counsel for B sought to argue that V's refusal of the blood transfusion was an unreasonable one. In effect, counsel sought to recharacterize the causal path to death as indirect, and thus subject to constraints of foreseeability. Misguidedly, the Court met that submission on its own terms, responding that:[121]

> 'It has long been the policy of the law that those who use violence on other people must take their victims as they find them. This in our judgment means the whole man, not just the physical man. It does not lie in the mouth of the assailant to say that his victim's religious beliefs which inhibited him from accepting certain kinds of treatment were unreasonable.'

That's not right. There is no legal requirement that we must take a victim's *choices* as we find them. As is well established in cases such as *Roberts*,[122] an intervening reaction by V does break the chain of causation where it is extraordinary (or, as was said in *Roberts*, 'daft'). Responses by victims, just like other indirect causal interventions, are subject to reasonable foreseeability criteria. And this means that B does not have to bear responsibility for the consequences of V's choices whatever they may be. He must do so only in so far as V's reaction is a reasonably foreseeable possibility.

The truth of the matter is that *Blaue* did not turn at all on whether V's refusal of the transfusion was 'daft' or unforeseeable, because the failure to transfuse blood was an omission. As such, the case presented a straightforward, unbroken physical chain from stabbing to death. We may wish that the causal chain had been severed. But an omission cannot, by itself, do that. The failure to transfuse, however unreasonable, could only be a concurrent cause of death.

[121] [1975] 3 All ER 446, 450.
[122] (1971) 56 Cr App R 95, 102.

5.5 Conclusion

Blaue returns us naturally to *Hughes*, the case with which we began. The key to both cases is not to lose sight of the core, physical dimension of causation. Direct causation is a real phenomenon, and the physical reaction chains that constitute it lie at the heart of our ascriptions of causal responsibility. Yet its recognition is coming under pressure, especially from those advocate a two-step test of 'factual' plus 'legal' (or 'proximate') causation. Causation is at risk of losing its shape, and Clarke is right to worry whether it can any longer bear legal freight.[123]

Indeed, one payoff of the discussion in this chapter is that criminal lawyers could, without loss, abandon reliance upon the traditional *sine qua non* test for 'factual' causation. A but-for relationship between C and E is neither sufficient nor necessary to establish causation;[124] the test is also a hopeless proxy, since it is massively overinclusive.[125] In short, the test is redundant. Abandoning it would involve no practical loss for our conclusions about causation.[126] A more profitable approach is to focus on *why* E followed C.

In pursuing the latter approach, I have argued that it is important not to lose sight of the underlying, real-world processes involved in causation. Inevitably, the concern here has been with concepts and structure, with core threads rather than comprehensive detail. At the level of case-law, the analysis is broadly consistent with existing decisions. It would, however, generate a different outcome in *Hughes* itself. The momentum of H's car contributed significant energy to the collision in which V was killed.[127] As such, H's driving the car was a direct cause of V's death. Any discomfort about that conclusion should be directed at the legislator.

I suspect that tort law, too, should start with direct causation. As such, the account offered here reduces, but also clarifies, the space for morally sensitive ascriptions of causal responsibility. That still leaves plenty of room for manoeuvre. In principle, the rules of indirect causation can differ across crime

[123] See the quotation in § 5.

[124] This is not to deny the importance of counterfactual analysis generally, e.g. in arguments about extraordinariness, or in the closer analysis of physical reaction chains themselves. What is contested here is the value of the specific counterfactual question: would *E* have occurred if *C* had not?

[125] Overinclusion may not be obvious, in as much as candidate causes are typically pre-filtered for plausibility before applying the but-for test: but that means we are in practice applying a different test, *sotto voce*.

[126] *Pace* those tort cases where there is no difference in the loss suffered by P: as when D starts a fire that razes V's house, but a fire started by E would have burned it down five minutes later. As criminal lawyers have no trouble concluding, D and not E causes the house to be razed. The issue for tort is a different one: that of pricing V's loss.

[127] This point would have been more obvious if, say, V had merely run out in front of D's car.

and tort. Once in the realm of tort law, a different degree of foreseeability might apply; the FDI rule may be eschewed; and tort's concern (*inter alia*) with valuation might support divergent approaches to cases such as *Cook v Lewis*, as well as to overdetermined cases.

Indeed, most of the hard cases for causation arise when we go beyond direct causation—when physical reaction chains intersect, and when other agents are (or should have become) involved in the unfolding of events. Frequently, D's conduct is significant only because of its interaction with other causal processes that D has not initiated. In such cases, ascriptions of indirect causal responsibility allow the law to bridge between the direct physical effects of D's own actions and the way those effects get caught up in, and interact with, the causal maelstrom of the world. Indirect causation articulates judgements about the extent to which D is answerable for outcomes that she does not directly cause, but to which her actions have made a difference. Its principles supplement rather than displace our recognition of direct causation, and it is only once that is recognized that we can properly understand the place of so-called *novus actus* doctrines.

To map this landscape properly, we need to understand the physical aspect of causation, including its limits. Having such a map is essential, for the reasons set out in § 5.2. There is a concept of causation that is capable of bearing normative freight. We should let it do its job. That job includes safeguarding the separateness of agents, by helping to set the boundaries of our agency; and, ultimately, helping to preserve our freedom.

6
Why Not-doings are Special

The criminal law draws a basic distinction between things we do and things we don't.[1] Its default rule is that we are not accountable for failing to prevent something that it would be a crime to bring about by a positive act. There are, of course, exceptions to the default rule. Criminal liability for omissions is becoming increasingly common, especially in regulatory contexts.[2] Structurally, however, it remains exceptional. The default rule is general in nature: the exceptions are specific and thereby confined.

Why? Many writers explain the basic distinction in terms of culpability.[3] Tony Honoré, for example, argues that omissions liability rightly arises only if D falls within the scope of a 'distinct duty'.[4] In addition to the general duties we owe to everyone, for example not to inflict harm, we also owe distinct duties in certain more limited contexts: we owe, for example, duties as parents to our own children.[5] Where a distinct duty holds, breach by omission may well be no better than breach by positive action. But absent a distinct duty, omissions—*per* Honoré—are less culpable. They are mere failures to intervene and thereby improve or rectify things, whereas actions are positive interventions that make things worse. As such, he concludes, the law has good reason to differentiate them.

Others disagree. Jonathan Glover is one of those others.[6] For Glover, failures to prevent harm are, *ceteris paribus*, just as culpable as actions bringing

[1] As does tort law: *Yuen Kun-Yeu v A-G of Hong Kong* [1988] AC 175, 192 (no liability in negligence 'on the part of one who sees another about to walk over a cliff with his head in the air, and forbears to shout a warning'). In contract too, failure to reject an offer does not constitute its acceptance: *Felthouse v Bindley* (1862) 11 CB (NS) 869, 142 ER 1037; *The Leonidas* [1985] 2 All ER 796; *The Santa Clara* [1995] 3 All ER 971.

[2] Albeit not exclusively: cp. s 5(1) of the Domestic Violence, Crime and Victims Act 2004 (UK) (causing or allowing the death of a child or vulnerable adult).

[3] As Andrew Ashworth observes, 'Omissions are often (usually) considered less blameworthy than acts.' A Ashworth, *Positive Obligations in the Criminal Law* (Hart 2013) 31.

[4] A M Honoré, 'Are Omissions Less Culpable?' in P Cane and J Stapleton (eds), *Essays for Patrick Atiyah* (Clarendon 1991) 31 (hereafter Honoré).

[5] On the kinds of distinct duties standardly known to criminal law, see, e.g., *Simester and Sullivan*, § 4.1(i)(b). For insightful discussion of some of the difficulties surrounding the imposition of positive duties to prevent harm, see L Alexander, 'Criminal Liability for Omissions: An Inventory of Issues' in S C Shute and A P Simester (eds), *Criminal Law Theory: Doctrines of the General Part* (OUP 2002) 121.

[6] J Glover, *Causing Death and Saving Lives* (Penguin 1977) ch 7 (hereafter Glover); Another is Jonathan Bennett: *Tanner*; *The Act Itself*.

Fundamentals of Criminal Law. A P Simester, Oxford University Press (2021). © A P Simester.
DOI: 10.1093/oso/9780198853145.003.0006

that harm about. At least where there is a distinct duty, moreover, that conclusion has intuitive appeal. It seems just as bad for a parent deliberately to starve her child to death as for her fatally to poison the same child (say, with a slow-acting poison that reproduces the same degree of suffering as starvation). Yet Honoré's intervention-based distinction seemingly applies to those cases too.

More needs to be said, then, to show why the law should differentiate between parents and strangers who fail to save—and between the latter and strangers who kill. This chapter develops two main arguments. One is institutional. Even if Glover is correct, and I will suggest that he is, in practice the *ceteris paribus* proviso is almost invariably violated. Not-doings are *typically* less culpable, and the law has good reasons to acknowledge this by means of its default rule requiring a positive act.

More importantly, however, the doing/not-doing distinction matters for reasons of ascriptive responsibility. Distinct duties are, first and foremost, conduits to holding the defendant accountable for an event or outcome. Absent such a duty, a not-doer is prima facie not accountable for the consequences of her deed: whereas a doer is.

These arguments will be developed across three sections. I begin by looking at the nature of not-doings and omissions generally: what are the features that distinguish them from actions? This preliminary question matters because, if there are reasons why not-doings are special, those reasons ought to reflect the very characteristics that mark them out. Two such distinguishing *marques* are identified in § 6.1. It then remains to show why those *marques* are morally significant. In § 6.2, I consider whether not-doings really are less culpable, as Honoré contends and others deny. Finally, § 6.3 investigates the argument from ascriptive responsibility for differentiating their treatment.

A cautionary note. The main question for this chapter is the fundamental one: why should we not, *tout court*, treat not-doings and omissions just like actions? As such, the arguments presented here do not conclude any enquiry into whether the law ought to impose particular duties, for example of easy rescue.[7] When another's death is not already my business, the obligations of altruism are yet capable of making it mine. How far those obligations extend is a matter of further, more specific debate. But that debate is of interest only because there are distinctive reasons against criminalizing not-doings and omissions in the first place.

[7] See, e.g., the powerful arguments made by Andrew Ashworth: 'The Scope of Criminal Liability for Omissions' (1989) 105 LQR 424; 'Positive Duties, Regulation and the Criminal Sanction' (2017) 133 LQR 606.

6.1 Doings, not-doings, and omissions

The list of a person's not-doings at any given moment is endless, and very few of its entries are interesting. Normally it boots nothing to say that, as Joseph ate breakfast this morning, he was neither playing rugby nor turning back the tide. Indeed, not-doings like these are typically not characterized as *omissions* at all. We tend to reserve the language of 'omissions' for a subset of our not-doings.[8] Following this practice, I take omissions to be constituted through a particular class of descriptions. A description of Joseph's behaviour names an omission to φ when that description specifies something—φing—that is not done in circumstances where there is some reason or expectation for Joseph to do it: for instance due to custom, duty, a promise or, more generally, standards of reasonable behaviour.[9] Thus to say that there is an 'omission' is to say something more than that there is a description of Joseph's conduct specifying that he did not φ. It is to suggest the need for explanation.[10] Perhaps Joseph can justify his omission. His reasons to act may have been defeasible. Pro tanto, though, 'omission' is a pejorative designation.

This means, of course, that the act/omission distinction comes morally preloaded. Omissions are already special, because they pick out a morally significant kind of not-doing. Hence it is the underlying *doing/not-doing* dichotomy that must bear the moral freight to be argued for here.

6.1.1 Bodily (non-)movements?

What are the characteristics of that more basic distinction?[11] A common move is to tie the distinction to features of the underlying behaviour involved. That seems broadly right. It also has a considerable pedigree. Yet it requires some care. Consider Jeremy Bentham's account:[12]

[8] Honoré remarks (at 36) that all omissions are not-doings of something, but not all not-doings are omissions.

[9] Cp. J Feinberg, *The Moral Limits of the Criminal Law, vol 1: Harm to Others* (OUP 1984) 159–62.

[10] Nothing here turns on the point, but the suggestion seems to be more than that Joseph had a reason to φ. There may have been reasons for me to play tennis this morning (I would have enjoyed it, it would have been good for my health), but I did not omit to do so.

[11] There is agreement, at least, that the presence of a negative proposition in some description of behaviour does not entail that the description specifies a not-doing. See Moore, *Act and Crime*, 23; Honoré, 37.

[12] J Bentham, *An Introduction to the Principles of Morals and Legislation* (1781) 72; ch 7, § VIII.

> 'By positive are meant such as consist in motion or exertion: by negative, such as consist in keeping at rest; that is, in forbearing to move or exert one's self in such and such circumstances. Thus to strike is a positive act: not to strike on a certain occasion, a negative one. Positive acts are styled also acts of commission; negative, acts of omission or forbearance.'

As other writers have pointed out, however, that's too simple. Non-movements can sometimes constitute things done: as when one sits for a portrait.[13] Conversely, we may fail to do something when doing something else instead—as when D walks away rather than answer the telephone, or writes a novel rather than a textbook. Since the same instance of behaviour can simultaneously constitute both things done and things not-done, it seems that the familiar association of quiescence with not-doings is not an intrinsic one.

Michael Moore disagrees.[14] For Moore, sitting for a portrait is a not-doing rather than something done, since it is not constituted by bodily movement. In his account, not-doings (which he terms 'omissions' in a generic sense) are simply absent actions:[15]

> 'An omission by A to save X from drowning at t is just the absence of any willed bodily movements by A at t, which bodily movements would have had the property of causing X to survive the peril he faced from drowning.'

Taken literally, though, this 'absent action' definition is overinclusive.[16] It encompasses cases where one's positive bodily movements *do* cause something, yet those bodily movements are not willed. It seems more than odd to say that if A has an epileptic fit while holding a rope, during which it is flung into the water and B is saved, A *omits* to save B.[17]

Admittedly, my counterexample puts pressure upon just one part of Moore's analysis—specifically, upon his assimilation of the action/omission distinction with that between actions and events.[18] We can drop the 'willed', then, and focus on the bodily movements. Consider the following definition:

[13] See, e.g., E D'Arcy, *Human Acts* (OUP 1963) 41. D'Arcy accepts Bentham's view in part: 'Bentham's criterion is no doubt a negative necessary condition for an omission, but it is not a sufficient one.'

[14] Moore, *Act and Crime*, 31: 'there is no conceptual objection to be made to the movement/non-movement conceptualization of the act/omission distinction.'

[15] Ibid, 28. (On Moore's generic use of 'omissions' to embrace not-doings, see ibid, 28 n 31.)

[16] For criticism, see § 5.4.

[17] M S Moore, 'More on *Act and Crime*' (1994) 142 U Penn LR 1749, 1775–76.

[18] In Moore's account, the action/event, action/omission, and action/inaction distinctions all involve the same concept of action. We explore the action/event distinction in chapter 9.

> An omission by A to save X from drowning at t is just the absence of any bodily movements by A at t, which bodily movements would have had the property of causing X to survive the peril he faced from drowning.

The modified definition points more clearly toward a weaker sense in which non-movements are necessarily involved in not-doings. If I walk away rather than answer the telephone, my not-answering the telephone is constituted by behaviour involving bodily movements; but the bodily movements are irrelevant to the thing not-done (save that they fail to constitute doing that thing). This thought can be developed by refuting an objection. Suppose that A, instead of throwing a rope to B who is drowning, shouts with glee and dances a jig because B is an old enemy. Then, surely, the objection goes,[19]

> 'A's shouting and dancing, the argument goes, are as causally relevant to B's death as are the bodily movements of C in pushing B into the water in the first place; all such bodily movements are equally *necessary* for the death of B to occur.'

Not so, says Moore (rightly). Only A's not-throwing the rope is *necessary* for B's death to occur. Had A failed to shout or dance, it does not follow that B would have been saved. Perhaps we can say that B drowned 'because' A was shouting and dancing: but A's shouting and dancing is causally relevant only in virtue of its being done *instead* of his throwing the rope to B.

Reservations remain. For one thing, this account doesn't dispose of our portrait-sitting example.[20] And a deeper problem is that causal relevance need not turn upon necessity. Throwing the rope may not be a necessary condition of saving B, if I also have a mobile telephone with which I can alert the nearby lifeguard. We need to say something more. Either we augment the causal dimension of the movement/non-movement analysis, or we attack the doing/not-doing distinction at a different point.

Both approaches are precedented, and they are largely complementary. Between them, they yield two key markers of the doing/not-doing distinction.

We pointed to the first marker in § 5.4. Suppose that A's not-throwing the rope to B is a necessary condition of B's drowning. Some writers deny altogether that it *causes* B's drowning: it is merely a failure-to-prevent.[21] That may

[19] Moore, *Act and Crime*, 29–31.

[20] There are other special cases that pose difficulties. See, e.g., B Vermazen, 'Negative Acts' in B Vermazen and M B Hintikka (eds), *Essays on Davidson: Actions and Events* (Clarendon 1985) 93, 95.

[21] Including Moore: *Act and Crime*, 267ff.

sound doubtful to legal ears—and even away from the courtroom, it seems acceptable to say of *Pittwood* that the railway gatekeeper's failure to close the gate before the train came through caused the resulting accident.[22] Yet as we saw in chapter 5, the denial contains an important grain of truth. Even if not-doings can be causes, they involve a different type of causation. Doings characteristically *introduce* changes in the world—they cause *by intervention*. By contrast, not-doings involve failures to intervene in and affect some existing state or causal process, typically such that changes in the world occur in consequence.

The key here is not change per se, but how it came about. One's *doing* might, for example, be what Bruce Vermazen terms a 'resisting',[23] where, through activating appropriate muscles, one prevents one's body from being moved by outside forces. More commonly, however, it is the positive movement constituting a doing which makes that doing count as an intervention: in doing something, we introduce a change in the world by moving our bodies. Similarly, the intervention/non-intervention distinction helps to explain why A's failure to save B is a not-doing despite the presence of bodily movements by A. While there are other things A does, and which are constituted by positive bodily movements, there is no bodily movement such that the salient change is introduced.

6.1.2 Range of alternatives

Jonathan Bennett finds another way of separating doings from not-doings.[24] While it may be that neither throwing nor not-throwing the rope are necessary conditions of B's fate, the variety of ways of saving B (and, indeed, of throwing the rope) is very limited indeed. On the other hand, the ways of not-saving B are many and varied: A might instead shout, dance, read a book, or go for a walk. Suppose we say, then, that (i) B drowned because A was shouting and dancing; and (ii) B drowned because A did not throw him the rope. Both statements may be true, but the first tells us about A's behaviour, and confines the range of bodily movements he might have been making, to a much greater extent than does the second statement, which makes explicit the aspect in virtue of which the first is true.

[22] (1902) 19 TLR 37. Compare *Hart and Honoré*, 31: 'in spite of differences between these cases and the simple paradigms, the very real analogies are enough to justify the extension of causal language to them.'

[23] 'Negative Acts' (n 20) 95.

[24] Bennett, *Tanner*, 55ff; *The Act Itself*, ch 6.

The basic idea here is that when D's behaviour constitutes some deed of φing, φing names a doing rather than a not-doing when only the bodily movements actually involved in D's behaviour, or a small range of similar bodily movements, would have constituted φing. B's failure to throw the rope is, by contrast, a not-doing because it could have been constituted by a wide range of bodily movements.[25]

Most of the time, this 'range of alternatives' account will parallel the causal-intervention analysis, in as much as non-interventions—like not throwing the rope—tend to be unspecific about D's actual behaviour. Not always. Some difficult cases exist, especially those involving immobility (such as sitting for a portrait). Honoré supplies an example:[26]

> 'Take a case in which John is searching for Dick to shoot him. The slightest movement on Bill's part will alert Dick to John's threat, in which case Dick will escape. If Bill remains immobile, and Dick is shot, was Bill's immobility a [doing or not-doing]?'

Bill's stillness does not count as an intervention. However, measured by its range of alternative bodily movements, it is a doing,[27] and that classification seems intuitively right.

It does not follow that we should reject the causal-intervention analysis. Maintaining two characterisations of the doing/not-doing distinction may generate indeterminacy in extreme cases, but it is unnecessary, and not especially desirable, to resolve that. The important point is that these two key characterizations converge, and that they support an account of the doing/not-doing distinction that can be consistently and practicably drawn in almost all cases. What *will* matter are their moral implications, to which we now turn.

6.2 Relative culpability and the neutrality thesis

Cases such as the malicious parent (above, § 6) suggest that, at least sometimes, one can be blameworthy for not-doings.[28] They suggest that criminal

[25] For a response to the worry that there can be infinite minor variations even in the ways that one does something, see Bennett, *The Act Itself*, 93ff. We might loosely capture Bennett's idea by saying there are fewer *kinds* of ways of φing when φing is a doing rather than a not-doing.

[26] Honoré, 40.

[27] Bennett, *Tanner*, 66–69; *The Act Itself*, 96–100, 112–14.

[28] And indeed, guilty of murder: *Gibbins and Proctor* (1918) 13 Cr App R 134.

liability for not-doings need not be ruled out *tout court*. That much seems unproblematic. More controversial is why the criminal law ought to differentiate between doings and not-doings. We have noted that one line of argument centres on the claim that the former are more culpable than the latter. This claim, championed by Honoré, opposes what Bennett calls the *neutrality thesis*: that, *ceteris paribus*, doings and not-doings which have the same outcome are morally equal.

6.2.1 Interventions, non-interventions, and moral neutrality

Honoré's argument builds on the causal discriminant outlined in § 5.4. When *doings* cause an outcome, they do so by intervening in the world such that the outcome is thereby brought about. By contrast, when *not-doings* cause an outcome, they do so by failing to intervene (so far as relevant) in the world, such that the outcome then occurs. For the sake of focussing the argument, assume we are concerned with outcomes that involve harm to the interests of others. Granted all this, Honoré argues that the primary way of causing such harm is when we intervene so as to change things for the worse—which occurs only by our *doing* something. The difference between interventions and failures to intervene is worked out in terms of baselines: the former 'make things worse or create a risk that they will be worse', while the latter merely 'fail to make things better'.[29]

One might count failure to be made better as a species of harm, so why should this difference be so important? Because, Honoré continues, not making someone's position better 'threatens not security so much as the expectation of improvement, which is a different but secondary value, because it presupposes stability.'[30] Harmful interventions, by contrast, have greater significance because they directly threaten the security and stability of our environment.[31]

In effect, Honoré argues for a parallel sequence of causal mappings. Qua interventions, doings make things worse, which undermines our security and stability: qua non-interventions, not-doings fail to make things better, which undermines our expectation of improvement. Thus:

[29] Honoré, 51.
[30] Ibid.
[31] Assuming, as does Honoré (at 50), that 'people and objects on the whole continue as they are unless something intervenes to change them.'

Doings	*Not-doings*
||	||
Interventions	*non-interventions*
↓	↓
make worse	*not make better*
↓	↓
set back *security & stability*	set back *expectation of improvement*

Since security and stability are more important than expectations of improvement, Honoré suggests, we have reason to think that doings which cause a given harm are more serious than not-doings which merely fail to prevent it.

A preliminary worry. Honoré's argument does not explain why we might differentiate between doings and not-doings where an interest that does not presuppose stability is threatened. So it cannot tell us why a doing that causes death should be regarded as worse than a failure to prevent that death.[32] One might expect the core rationale for distinguishing doings from not-doings to be more general.

There is nevertheless something attractive about the reasoning. It is plausible that, even if we don't have very much, being able—at the least—to rely on what we do have is a more fundamental, and more important, need than being able to improve our position. Without that basic level of reliability, without security and stability, it becomes difficult to move one's life forward in any systematic way. This plausibility lends itself to Honoré's claim that there is a moral distinction between making things worse and not making them better, and in particular that (*ceteris paribus*) our obligations to make the world better are less weighty than those not to make it worse.

For the sake of argument, then, let us grant that security and stability are more important than expectations of improvement. How convincingly is that difference connected to the analytical distinction between doings and not-doings? Looking at the diagram, it is hard to see why the causal paths must run in parallel without crossovers. No doubt some doings are interventions

32 Though it surely is: we feel very differently about killers than about non-savers. There may be more than one factor affecting our intuitions here. For one thing, the former are more threatening *de futuro*. Perhaps more importantly, albeit buried by the *ceteris paribus* proviso, omissions are often incidental to the defendant's practical deliberations—they typically disclose a different and lesser fault, of limited imagination or empathy rather than hostility. (See Glover, 111.) This point complements the argument against the *ceteris paribus* proviso in § 6.2.2.

that make things worse, but there can also be interventions that prevent things from becoming better (and thereby forestall an expectation of improvement). Suppose that Peter is trapped in a bay with the tide coming in. If he is not rescued within the next hour, it will be too late; he will be cut off, and eventually will drown. If I intervene and prevent Jim from setting out to save Peter, I no more make things worse for Peter than when (with Jim absent) I myself sit back and watch him drown. Conversely, might not non-interventions often be said to 'make things worse or create a risk that they will be worse'? Peter's lot is worsened, and the risk of his drowning increased (perhaps even from nil), by my non-intervention. Of course, the view one takes of my non-intervention depends in part upon what counts as 'not better' rather than 'worse'. Yet if I take away someone's last chance of rescue—by not-intervening—then is the hapless victim not, *therefore*, worse off for having lost that chance?

It is worth recalling from § 6.1.2 that there was even some doubt about the initial connection between doings and interventions, raised by the unusual cases where only immobility will bring about harm. Although one might classify such instances as doings rather than not-doings, they are presumably cases of non-intervention. (Honoré's example, where Bill remains immobile so that Dick is not warned that John is about to shoot him, does seem to be a case of non-improvement.) Be that as it may, immobility cases also suggest difficulty for the non-intervention/failure-to-benefit link. Consider Bennett's example:[33]

> 'Henry is in a sealed room where there is fine metallic dust suspended in the air. If Henry keeps utterly still for two minutes, some of the dust will settle; and if it does, some is bound to fall in such a position as to close a tiny electric circuit which . . . well, finish the story to suit your taste, but make it something big; and let's call its occurrence S.'

Let's make S bad as well as big. If S obtains then the case looks like one where Henry makes things worse rather than fails to make them better. If that's right, or even if we should take that conclusion seriously, we have further reason to doubt the faithfulness with which the intervention/non-intervention line tracks the worsening/not-making-better divide. For while Bennett's and Honoré's cases are both clearly non-interventions, they are far from similarly placed on the latter scale.

So we should question the generality of the pairings {intervention, making worse} and {non-intervention, not making better}. Similar worries hold for

[33] Bennett, *Tanner*, 66. See Bennett, *The Act Itself*, 96ff.

the pairings {making worse, security and stability} and {not making better, expectation of improvement}. Sometimes a non-intervention that fails to make things better may constitute a failure to safeguard from harm, thereby allowing security to be threatened rather than disappointing an expectation of improvement: as when D fails to close the window during a storm, so that a gust of wind blows her friend's vase off its stand; or when D carelessly fails to lock up her friend's house and thereby provides a thief with the chance to steal the silver.

Honoré does have a further prong on his fork between interventions and non-interventions. Where we cannot dismiss non-interventions as mere failures to improve things, we can alternatively say that they 'constitute failures to react against worsening interventions.'[34] As such, he concludes, they are secondary in character, since they threaten our security interests only indirectly. But this analysis is unconvincing. When D sits back and watches P drown, P's position certainly worsens, but what intervention is D failing to remedy? Similarly, if V falls asleep while driving along a straight road, there is no obvious intervention for her passenger to react to or forestall by wakening her before she crashes at the next corner; although the passenger would thereby prevent a worsening of V's situation.

Conversely, some interventions lead to harm only by allowing a worsening further intervention. Suppose that I *open* the window during a storm, with the consequence that the vase is broken; or that I (carelessly) *un*lock my friend's house, so enabling the thief to enter and decamp with her silver. The wrongful character of these interventions is no less derivative than in the earlier examples they resemble. Whether by intervention or non-intervention (and whether by doing or not-doing), the friend's position is undermined because she is left exposed to the risk of a worsening intervention that threatens her security.

For all these reasons, it is not clear that not-doings have—in virtue of being non-interventions, let alone of being not-doings—the secondary nature that Honoré claims for them. Still less can one conclude that the connections Honoré seeks to draw have systematic moral implications.

6.2.2 Range of alternatives, *ceteris paribus*, and institutional considerations

It doesn't follow that we should embrace the neutrality thesis. As we saw in § 6.1.2, a second difference between doings and not-doings is that there are characteristically fewer ways to do the former than the latter. This being so, the

[34] Honoré, 51.

law prima facie places a greater restraint upon the liberty of its subjects when it proscribes a not-doing than it does when it proscribes a doing. The burden upon a person enjoined not to act is typically borne lighter than that when one is ordered to act, for it involves the sacrifice of fewer options, and is more likely to leave the defendant with a chance of conforming without significant derangement. 'Compare being banished to Liechtenstein with being banished from Liechtenstein.'[35] Or, to coin a more apposite example, compare being prohibited from drowning the other swimmers when sunbathing at a beach to being mandated to save—or, indeed, drown—them.

This thought can usefully be juxtaposed with questions about the appropriate scope of *criminalization*. A criminal legal system that did not distinguish between doings and not-doings would present individuals with far fewer opportunities to avoid liability. It would tend to undermine the rule of law principle that, save exceptionally, citizens should have a general means of steering clear of legal sanctions: by refraining from doing anything. In the absence of such a refuge, negligence-based liability in particular would have the potential to expose citizens to widespread and unexpected legal liability, and to the unanticipated disruption of their lives that criminal proceedings entail.[36]

I turn to the (central) argument about liberty in § 6.3. The range-of-alternatives distinction also has more immediate, practical dimensions. If proscribing not-doings typically constrains more of one's options, it is likely to impinge to a greater degree upon one's interests. This consideration tends to adulterate the *ceteris paribus* proviso.

Most of us accept that people are to some extent entitled to place their own interests, and the interests of those close to them, above the interests of others. A mother who gives her own child pocket money warrants no reproof when she does not do the same for the child next door. Of course, such a view may be no more than a moral mistake. Even so, however, its almost universal acceptance seems unavoidable, an ineluctable flaw of our very human lives. And the mistake can be buttressed. Given that people lack full information, they are typically better-placed to assess and contribute to their own lives, and to the lives of those they know, than to the lives of strangers. Indeed, some of our interests are advanced only if we act ourselves, rather than through another.[37] The parent has reason to look after her own child because doing so is a part

[35] Bennett, *Tanner*, 78.

[36] This point is a contingent one. It would not apply, for example, to those whose omissions occur whilst they are engaged in specialist activities such as driving. See § 3.3.

[37] Cp. Derek Parfit's distinction between action- and outcome-reasons: D Parfit, Is Common Sense Morality Self Defeating?' (1979) 70 J Phil 533; see also his *Reasons and Persons* (OUP 1984).

of her being a good parent, and not just a means to ensure that the child is being looked after. These points help to explain examples where, for instance, someone does not save starving children in Ethiopia: they limit the extent to which the needs of strangers take priority over and mandate the sacrifice of our own projects and commitments. We cannot do everything, and it would be absurd to expect us to try. In deciding what to do we are entitled to acknowledge that the content of our own lives is valuable to us intrinsically, and not merely instrumentally for the sake of the rest of the world.[38]

The argument here is a confined one. It shows that strangers can have *less* claim, but not that they have none. Neither does it show why, *ceteris paribus*, killing a stranger is worse than not-saving her. So it is consistent with the neutrality thesis. But it does have an institutional role, since it aids to justify the law's adoption of the act-omission doctrine as a simple and workable means by which the law can recognize the priority individuals are entitled to accord the various facets of their own lives.

Sometimes, of course, considerations based upon the range of alternatives available are outweighed—especially when there is what Honoré terms a 'distinct duty', such as parents might owe to their children. Honoré gives the example of a nurse who should give her patient a certain medicine but, instead, either gives the wrong medicine or fails to give any medicine at all. In such cases, he concludes,[39]

> '[W]hen a distinct duty exists, the fact that positive acts make greater demands on the person concerned than abstentions does not support the view, as it otherwise would, that an omission is less culpable than a positively harmful act. The argument from distinct duties counteracts the argument from cost.'

However, it is unnecessary to confine the neutrality thesis to distinct duty cases in order to justify the law's doing/not-doing distinction. A different strategy is available. One might accept the distinct duties analysis and yet think—without being a consequentialist—that there is no intrinsic moral difference between doings and not-doings. One might think, for example, that there is an atomistic moral equivalence,[40] to be seen only if the examples are divorced from an

[38] See Bennett, *Tanner*, 78–80; Glover, 105; also J Raz, *The Morality of Freedom* (Clarendon 1986) 280–81.

[39] Honoré, 49.

[40] *Per* Honoré, 50, 'Only if one looks at items of conduct atomistically rather than in their wider setting . . . do acts and omissions appear equivalent.'

everyday context and are instead thoroughly artificial. Indeed, what is striking about the many examples supplied by supporters of the neutrality thesis is just how extraordinary they are. Such might be said, for instance—and whether or not we deem my options morally equal—of the following variant upon Philippa Foot's famous *Trolley* problem:[41]

> Deborah is out walking one day near a railway line when she sees an out-of-control railway trolley. Nearby is a railroad switch. Deborah realizes that she has just two options: she can throw the switch to divert the trolley onto another track, or refrain from doing so. If Deborah throws the switch, James will be hit by the trolley and killed. If she refrains, the trolley will continue on its present track and Victor will be killed.

Suppose that we do find ourselves neutral between the choices to throw and not-throw the switch. We should not belittle the significance of that conclusion. But we should record that it does not straightforwardly answer Honoré's question, are omissions less culpable? *Ceteris paribus*, perhaps the answer is no. But we (and the law) might also and correctly say, virtually always yes: since in order to achieve *ceteris paribus* terms we have to invent fantastic examples, examples the law will rarely encounter; examples where our moral instincts, outwith social conventions, are in any event untrustworthy.

Even if the neutrality thesis is right, the *ceteris paribus* proviso does not normally hold. The law perforce must acknowledge that. Our legal system is so unavoidably rough-grained that it has reason in the first instance to exclude liability for not-doings, and to recognize distinct duties in those areas where a greater refinement is justified and where such a customisation is possible.

6.3 The fundamental rationale: Intervention, ascriptive responsibility, and freedom

Is the neutrality thesis none the less right? The comparison made in § 6, between a parent's starving and poisoning her child, suggests that it is. That thought is reinforced when we look at cases of inadvertent negligence. Suppose

[41] P Foot, 'The Problem of Abortion and the Doctrine of the Double Effect' (1967) Ox Rev 5. The Trolley Problem is famously analysed by J J Thomson, 'Killing, Letting Die, and the Trolley Problem' and 'The Trolley Problem' in J J Thomson, *Rights, Restitution and Risk: Essays in Moral Theory* (Harvard UP 1986) 78 and 94, respectively. In Foot's original statement of the problem, five people are killed if the switch is not thrown; and D is actually on the trolley. I get to the numbers in chapter 18.

that a defendant negligently allows a chestnut tree to remain standing alongside tram lines.[42] During a storm it topples onto a passing tram. Would it make any difference if the defendant, without recognizing the risk, were to fell the tree negligently so that it toppled the wrong way and onto the tram? Alternatively, imagine that Gerard is checking to ensure that a particular safety switch at the factory is set, in order to prevent accidents involving the machinery. Would it matter morally if he were mistakenly (and negligently) to think the switch already set, and so leave it unset, rather than mistakenly (and negligently) to think the switch not set, and so unset it himself? The essential complaint in negligence is one of failure by the defendant to take reasonable care: it does not seem to matter very much whether that failure manifests itself in a doing or a not-doing.

Of course, both of these illustrations involve cases where the defendant might be expected to have a positive duty to intervene. Let us instead, then, take Honoré's example: where a pedestrian (A) fails to pick up a wrapper that someone else has dropped. Had he (B) dropped the wrapper instead of merely failing to pick it up, for Honoré it would have been a worse case, albeit that 'the trouble involved in disposing of a wrapper neatly in a bin or bag is much the same as the trouble involved in picking a wrapper up.'[43] Admittedly, one who picks a wrapper also has to dispose of it, so perhaps the example is not quite *ceteris paribus*. (Although, had the pedestrian dropped the wrapper himself, we might be inclined to discount the effort of uplifting it and adjudge his failure to pick it up to be much the same, morally speaking, as his dropping it.[44]) However, the example is suggestive for another reason. In order to achieve the equivalent upshot, that either way there is one more wrapper on the street than there would otherwise have been, Honoré has to smuggle an extra agent into case (A): the person who originally drops the wrapper our pedestrian later fails to remove. In case (B), only one person is responsible for the wrapper's still littering the street. In case (A), two people are. Prima facie, on this ground, the examples are not *ceteris paribus*.

One line of argument that might be invoked at this point has a quasi-causal character. When I actively drop litter, typically there is a straightforward causal link between my behaviour and the resulting harm. But in case (A), the link to the harm seems to be less straightforward, perhaps bifurcated. That impression becomes all the stronger if (C) there are five pedestrians who fail to pick the

[42] *Berry v Borough of Sugar Notch* 43 Atl 240 (1899).
[43] Honoré, 50.
[44] The *Miller* doctrine is even more demanding: see § 5.3.1.

wrapper up. Now six of us are *morally* responsible for the harm.[45] And if we are *all* responsible for that wrapper's still being there, one might think, perhaps we are not individually as blameworthy as the pedestrian in case (B), who is solely and entirely responsible for what amounts to the same harm?

That line of thought is problematic. Effectively, it builds the intervention/non-intervention distinction into its conclusion. Although in case (C) there is only one harm, it does not follow that there is only one wrong. We may hold that each pedestrian does (or not-does) something wrong in failing to uplift the wrapper, and it is because *each* does something wrong that the harm occurs.

Admittedly, to the extent that the diluted-responsibility argument trades upon distinctions between causal types, it may seem less persuasive because each of the separate wrongs is necessary for the harm to occur. In case (C), they occur, we might say, in series:

Originally . . . Not picked . . . Not picked . . . Wrapper still
dropped up (1) up (2) on street

By contrast, suppose that in Gerard's factory there are actually two switches, both of which must be set in order to prevent accidents, and that Jane has the task of ensuring the other switch is set. Then, should both fail to set their switch, they bring about the harm in parallel:

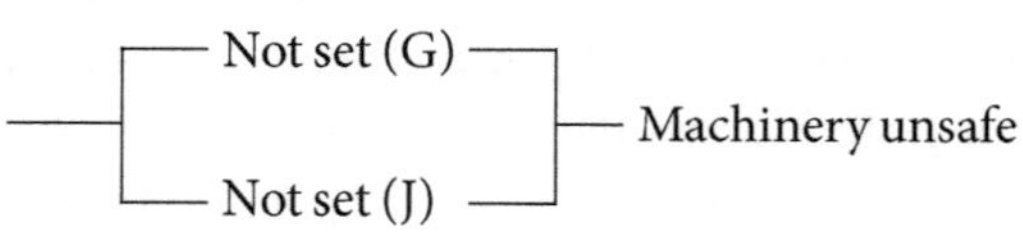

Intuitively, it may be less clear in this case whether blame should be diluted.[46] Strikingly, though, the example does not present a problem specific to not-doings: consider the possibility of judicial executions by firing squad. For that matter, the same question would be raised had both Jane and Gerard accidentally unset their switches.

[45] i.e., eligible for blaming assessments: see § 4.1. I assume that each of us is a moral agent and no one behaves involuntarily.

[46] Compare *Hart and Honoré*, 128: 'Suppose, again, that a house can be built and profitably sold only if *X* delivers bricks and *Y* mortar. If both *X* and *Y* default in delivery so that the projected house cannot be built and sold each can argue, again, that his default was not a *sine qua non* of the loss of profit on the sale of the house, since the default of the other was sufficient to preclude it. Despite this, lawyers and ordinary people would agree in saying . . . that the omission of each is causally relevant to the ensuing harm and that each could in a proper case be held responsible for it.'

According to the engagement view of culpability to be defended in Part III,[47] blame is not diluted in these cases. Suppose we grant that. Doing so raises a further issue. If we are all culpable with respect to the wrapper's being on the street, are we become, and to be judged as, some sort of moral collective? This is the real risk: that a doctrine of general liability for not-doings would result in a system that is largely insensitive to the separateness of agents. Imagine that Stephen stands by and watches instead of intervening, as he could have, when Jeremy stabs John. Only Jeremy inflicts John's injury. Yet without an act/omissions doctrine like the one our legal system presently recognizes, this truth would be valueless.

There is a pragmatic side to the present point. If a swimmer drowns, the law cannot afford to become concerned with the possible prosecution of every person on the beach—let alone of everyone who might have been able to prevent it each time an actus reus occurs. But the point has implications beyond the institutional, implications that were drawn out in § 5.2.1. Simply put, people normally have a sense of their own identity as individual agents in some sort of relationship to the world, a relationship manifested in terms of what they do and don't do. While each pedestrian may be morally responsible, and exposed to reproof, for failing to pick up the wrapper, if we assimilate them with the original litterer we weaken our recognition of the distinctiveness of what the original person *does*, as the primary (even paradigm) author of the littering. And if we so weaken the relationship between a consequence and its author by indiscriminately sharing *ascriptive* responsibility for the authorship of each consequence, our sense of individuality as agents in a specific relationship to the world is much diluted.[48]

The point may be sketched as follows. When Stephen permits Jeremy to stab John, the consequence of his failure to intervene is not only (i) that John is stabbed, but also (ii) that Jeremy stabs him.[49] A failure to distinguish between doings and not-doings would tend to abolish the additional significance of (ii). Indeed, in terms of their moral significance, it would tend to assimilate the facts that (i) and (ii) are consequences of Stephen's behaviour

[47] See esp. chapters 11 and 14.

[48] *Hart and Honoré*, lxxx–xi: 'The idea that individuals are primarily responsible for the harm which their actions are sufficient to produce without the intervention of others or of extraordinary natural events is important . . . to . . . the individual's sense of himself as a separate person whose character is manifested in such actions.'

[49] As John Casey once put it, we could truly, misleadingly, say of both Jeremy and Stephen that 'he so conducted himself with the consequence that John was stabbed': J Casey, 'Actions and Consequences' in J Casey (ed), *Morality and Moral Reasoning* (Methuen 1971) 155, 172ff. See also B A O Williams, 'A Critique of Utilitarianism' in J J C Smart and B A O Williams, *Utilitarianism: For and Against* (CUP 1973) 75, 108.

with a third proposition, (iii) that Stephen stabs John. But Stephen does *not* stab John. Neither does one who leaves the house unlocked herself steal the silver.[50]

Why do these distinctions matter? How do questions of ascriptive responsibility relate to the runaway trolley, or to the difference between killing and not-saving a stranger? The trolley problem is an example where the considerations raised in § 6.2.2, concerning the range of Deborah's alternatives and the priority normally accorded to her own interests, are unhelpful: *ex hypothesi*, the value of anything Deborah might do instead of throwing the switch is trivial relative to the lives at stake.

For Deborah, the choice is stark. She throws a switch or she does not: either way one person dies. Heidi Malm says that she should abstain,[51] and Malm is right. But consider the reason she gives for this conclusion: that people do not have the liberty to change who lives and who dies when other things are equal. It is a plausible reason, as is Malm's suggestion that such a liberty would be at odds with an obligation to respect other people as individual persons, rather than as things that might be interchanged. The limitation of the suggestion, however, is that it applies only when there is a question of *choosing* who of two persons shall die (or, perhaps, be harmed). So it does not dispose of the difference between my not saving a toddler from drowning and my drowning the toddler in circumstances where, morally speaking, the value of any other options is similarly trivial.

What else, then, can be said of the trolley problem? Related to Malm's point is the matter of justification. Deborah cannot justify throwing the switch, and thereby causing James's death, because she does not have a good enough reason for bringing James's death about.[52] Yet if Deborah cannot justify causing a death by behaving in one way (a doing), how can she justify causing a death simply because she behaves in a another way (*videlicet*, a not-doing)? This is the sort of problem posed by the objection, *not to choose is to choose*. If the fact that Victor would otherwise die is not enough to make it permissible that James should die, neither is the obverse. And it will not do here to say that only in one case do we bring the death about rather than permit it, for that would presume the very moral distinction we are contesting.

[50] Or a person who fails to repair a retaining wall himself flood the land beyond: *East Suffolk Catchment Board v Kent* [1941] AC 74. Note that the point here is made solely as a matter of analytical groundwork. In particular, I am not making an argument about the (un)fair labelling of Stephen as a 'stabber': that worry could be met by having duplicate offences in each instance of doing the actus reus and of permitting its occurrence.

[51] H M Malm, 'Killing, Letting Die, and Simple Conflicts' (1989) 18 Phil and Pub Aff 238, 245–50.

[52] Ibid, 246–47; Honoré, 52.

So it seems that Deborah cannot justify making a choice either way, qua choice between who of the two should die. If she points at James's death to explain why she is not at liberty to intervene, it does not follow that she has a liberty *not* to intervene. Deborah must say something else. And she can. Of the decision not to intervene, some remarks can be made in Deborah's defence that are different in kind from those made so far, remarks informed by considerations of the separateness of agents.

The first thing Deborah can say is that the problem posed by the runaway trolley is not hers. She is not the author of Victor's death, or even of the trolley's killing Victor. This being so, we need something more before we can link the tragedy to Deborah. One such way is if she intervenes to divert the trolley. By doing so, Deborah personalizes the event. She can no longer deny ascriptive responsibility for the problem: she has adopted it. The event and its upshot are now connected to her.

Suppose, however, that Deborah does not intervene. Prima facie, she can say: Victor's death had nothing to do with me; I was not involved. And this is ordinarily the first thing that one can say to distinguish not saving a stranger from killing her: that in the former case the death has no connection to me, whereas in the latter I have made it a part of my life, an aspect of my relationship with the world that is distinctive of me and not of anyone else. Moreover, this same point—about Deborah's ascriptive responsibility—explains much of the appeal of Honoré's discussion of distinct duties,[53] where the culpability of harmful not-doings seems more straightforwardly to be on a par with that of doings. The various sorts of duties outlined by Honoré all contemplate a situation where the connection between the defendant and the occurrence of the harm is already in some manner personalized: for instance, when the victim is the defendant's child, who consequently has a distinct duty to feed her which the stranger has not; or where the defendant created the risk of harm himself, a risk he may therefore be required to forestall.[54] Intervention is not the only way of becoming involved.

Deborah is not out of the moral picture. She *is* susceptible to moral evaluation in respect of her failure to save Victor. She is *morally responsible* for Victor's death, in the sense identified in § 4.1. Further, the claim that she was not involved in Victor's death may not be enough to save her from being blamed for

[53] Honoré, 42–47. On the common law, see also *Simester and Sullivan*, § 4.1(i)(b). The same point helps to elucidate Michael Corrado's motionless driver examples: M Corrado, 'Is There an Act Requirement in the Criminal Law' (1994) 142 U Penn LR 1529, 1538–41; discussed by Moore, 'More on *Act and Crime*', 1778–81.

[54] *Miller* [1983] 2 AC 161.

it, on the ground that she should have got involved and adopted the problem of Victor's fate. In the trolley case, that James would have died had she done so counts as an important secondary reason: it underpins Deborah's denial that there was a good enough reason for her to intervene.

More generally, an altruistic reason to get involved *will* sometimes be good enough—as when I can rescue an unknown child from drowning at no risk to myself. Here the consequence is sufficiently severe that my remaining disinterested would be monstrous. Nothing in this chapter rules out the regulation of such cases by the criminal law. But the key point here is that my lack of prima facie connection to the harm underwrites an initial liberty to not intervene which must then be *overridden* by further reasons.

6.3.1 The rationale for a liberty

The moral force of that initial liberty may look small when it comes to particular instances: we may well disregard it when reproaching someone for their failure to intervene in a given case. And it is noticeable that writers tend to treat their examples *in vacuo*, as one-off dilemmas rather than recurrent ones. But *prohibitions* are general in nature. They must attend more closely to the considerations of personal autonomy which make that liberty important. Respect for persons involves respect for individuals as deliberating agents who have the capacity independently to pursue their own goals and values. Against that, untrammelled responsibility for events with which one is prima facie unconnected would, in effect, represent an attack on the idea that one's practical choices should be determined by one's own goals and values. Indeed, a legal system that failed to reflect the difference between doings and not-doings might well end up alienating its subjects from their own lives.[55] Robert Nozick asks,[56]

> 'Why not interfere with someone else's shaping of his own life? . . . I conjecture that the answer is connected with that elusive and difficult notion: the meaning of life. A person's shaping his life in accordance with some overall

[55] Something warned against by Bernard Williams ('A Critique of Utilitarianism', 116), in the context of utilitarianism: its edict 'is to make [the individual] into a channel between the input of everyone's projects, including his own, and an output of optimific decision; but this is to neglect the extent to which *his* actions and *his* decisions have to be seen as the actions and decisions which flow from the projects and attitudes with which he is most closely identified. It is thus, in the most literal sense, an attack on his integrity.'

[56] R Nozick, *Anarchy, State and Utopia* (Basic Books 1974) 50.

plan is his way of giving meaning to his life; only a being with the capacity to so shape his life can have or strive for a meaningful life.'

The conjectured reply is suggestive in two ways. For one thing, the process of shaping one's own life risks being undermined when others assume, or are forced to assume, responsibility for one's conduct. At the same time, self-determination can also be frustrated in a more direct manner. We may say, with Raz, that one's well-being depends upon the successful pursuit of self-chosen, valuable goals;[57] upon the success of the projects and relationships which make one's life meaningful. But the criminal law coerces. It constrains the behavioural choices of individuals by threatening them with criminal liability should they not comply with its demands. In so doing, it impedes people's opportunities for the successful pursuit of their own, constitutive goals. It hinders individuals' loyalty to and engagement with their own commitments: to that extent, it undermines their integrity. Indirectly, the criminal law imposes the legislature's goals upon those individuals.

To some extent, that's part of the law's point. A person might have valueless goals, or goals that don't justify the wrongdoing required to pursue them. The argument here is not that one should always be permitted to ignore the interests of others. But whether or not we concur, with Raz, that well-being depends upon one's goals being valuable,[58] well-being *also* depends upon those (valuable) goals being one's own. When a person's choices are driven by legal injunctions, even if the enjoinder be to do something admirable, she does not live her own life.[59] One can become estranged from one's own worthwhile achievements, an estrangement only too often associated with the recognition that those accomplishments were not attained for one's own sake.

So there is, at least, a prima facie reason against the intrusive use of criminal law. Admittedly, we shouldn't overstate this. It's just a reason, not a trump. In particular, it does not follow that specific prohibitions are wrong. Autonomy neither protects nor requires individual options; it merely requires the availability of an adequate range of options.[60] And its significance cuts both ways. The injunction against murder is justified partly because there are duties to protect and indeed augment the autonomy *of others*,[61] and more generally not

[57] Raz, *The Morality of Freedom* (n 38) 376.
[58] Ibid, 320.
[59] Ibid, 382.
[60] Ibid, 425.
[61] Ibid, 408, 419; S Freeman, 'Criminal Liability and the Duty to Aid the Distressed' (1994) 142 U Penn LR 1455, 1478ff. Such considerations might be sufficient, moreover, to warrant the existence of a limited legal duty to rescue. As cautioned in the introduction to this chapter, the argument here is

to harm them, which override the autonomy-based reasons for permitting such activity.

However, my concern in this chapter is not with specific prohibitions. An injunction such as the one against murder is unlikely to impede citizens' choices in a way that does significant damage to their autonomy. But the same cannot be said of injunctions against not-doings.

And so, at the end, the range-of-alternatives distinction resurfaces, to buttress the causal distinction. One cannot expect to control all aspects of one's life. But in as much as there must be a sufficient range of choices before one can be the author of one's own life, proscribing not-doings is much more restrictive of one's options than is proscribing doings. As such, it is more likely to affect the pursuit of one's more pervasive goals.

It may be tempting to quibble about this conclusion. *Prescribing* a specific option surely would not interfere with the life a defendant has chosen in any substantial, pervasive or long-term sense, since the pervasive goals will normally survive being neglected on such specific occasions? Traces of this quibble can be located in our shared moral intuitions about many of the examples philosophers deploy when talking about omissions—intuitions that tend to neglect the range of alternatives constrained. Yet *were the law to treat doings and not-doings the same*, the consequent instances of specific interference would not merely be sporadic and occasional; they would be systematic and recurrent. Moreover, they would be unpredictable and unavoidable, crystallizing unforeseeably to disrupt the orderly conduct of our lives. Let us return, in closing, to the question posed by *Smith and Hogan*:[62]

> 'Suppose D is sitting at the corner of a corridor with his legs stretched across it. He hears V running down the corridor and deliberately remains still with the intention that V, on turning the corner, shall fall over his legs. Why should this not be a battery? It would be if D had put out his legs with the intention of tripping up V.'

Assuredly, D warrants our moral condemnation. But the main reason why this should not be a battery does not concern culpability. It has to do with criminalization. If D now has a duty to remove his leg, then P is granted a power to put D under that duty, simply by running toward him. The law that facilitates

directed more generally: at why, save exceptionally, the law should be more averse to prohibiting not-doings than to proscribing doings.

[62] D Ormerod and K Laird, *Smith and Hogan's Criminal Law* (14th edn, OUP 2015) 713; above, § 4.3.2.

this becomes a tool by which P may subject D's will to his own. More generally, under a legal system of this sort, D's choices are constrained not merely by his own goals and values but equally by the behaviour of others and by the whims of nature. Rather than an independent person who is primarily responsible for the things brought about by his own behaviour, D is become a member of the society cooperative, driven by its collective need to avert harms occurring; regardless of who in particular brings them about. Without an act-omissions doctrine, we would no longer think primarily about the effects of what we do but, equally, about the effects of what others do.

7
Complicity

Secondary criminal liability is ancient. It finds reference in the writing of Bracton and in the Statute of Westminster.[1] Despite its antiquity, however, complicity remains one of the most uncertain and controversial areas of criminal law. In part, this is because there is a profound oddity about convicting someone of a crime that she did not do. Secondary parties may be labelled as 'murderers', but there is an obvious sense in which they are not murderers. They do not themselves kill. None the less, and leaving aside the question of precisely how we label such persons,[2] we may have good reason to ascribe them with responsibility for the murder. It is the task of complicity doctrine to span that gap.

The controversy is about when to do so. Much of the trouble concerns mens rea. Suppose that S assists or encourages P to commit a burglary,[3] for example by lending him a jemmy.[4] What kind of mens rea concerning P's future actions should be required on the part of S, if she is to be liable for P's crime? And does the answer to that question differ when P's crime occurs pursuant to a conspiracy, or 'joint enterprise', perpetrated with S? Transatlantic and Commonwealth legal systems boast an unsettled range of answers to these questions. In this chapter, I argue that the best approach requires one who aids or abets to act *knowingly or purposively* with respect to the essential matters of P's crime. S need not purpose that P commit the relevant crime: yet recklessness should not suffice. At the same time, this argument preserves space for an advertence-based standard in cases where S's involvement is pursuant to a joint criminal enterprise. Doctrinally speaking, joint enterprise is a quite distinct

[1] H de Bracton, *De Legibus et Consuetudinibus Angliae* (Woodbine edn, 1915) f 142; Statute of Westminster I (1275) 3 Edw 1 cap xiv. Compare A Fitzherbert, *Corone* (1329) f 256b, pl 314; F Pollock and F W Maitland, *The History of English Law before the time of Edward I* (CUP 1895) vol 2, 509.

[2] In most common-law jurisdictions, accessories are convicted as if principals; however, many legal systems have a distinct form of conviction for those who facilitate rather than perpetrate crimes (e.g., s 107 of the Indian Penal Code 1860; § 27 of the German *Strafgesetzbuch*). That strikes me as being, on balance, preferable. Even so, in such jurisdictions the secondary party is not labelled an 'accessory' *in abstracto*, but is convicted (and sentenced) as accessory to a specified crime.

[3] For convenience, I use S and P to designate the secondary party and principal, respectively. Additionally, for clarity of exposition where pronouns are used, I deem S to be female and P to be male.

[4] Or in the US, a jimmy.

Fundamentals of Criminal Law. A P Simester, Oxford University Press (2021). © A P Simester.
DOI: 10.1093/oso/9780198853145.003.0007

source of complicity liability. It will be contended here that the distinction is a morally legitimate one.

7.1 Negotiating criminalization and culpability

Complicity liability is sometimes characterized as 'derivative',[5] in that S is held responsible for P's crime: as such, her liability is dependent upon P's criminal actions as well as her own. Derivative liability is inherently messy. Partly, this is because its duplex character allows for a myriad of scenarios that can be tracked only roughly by liability rules.[6] We should not expect knock-down arguments for the law's optimal response. The nature of the argument made here is that to require knowledge in aiding and abetting, and to differentiate joint enterprise, better reconciles the principles of culpability and ascriptive responsibility in this area of law. Compromise in this matter is a tool of institutional progress.

In many ways, the compromise is a familiar one. As was said in chapter 1, at least in imprisonable crimes the very label, 'criminal', resounds with moral and social nuance. The temptation is natural to extend that label to anyone who deserves substantial blame when serious wrongs occur. At the same time, however, *prohibitions* are not just a matter of judgments about culpability. When the legislature designates conduct as criminal, part of the rationale,[7] and certainly part of the effect, is prevention. The criminal law may be morally loaded, but it is also bluntly coercive. Frequently, such coercion is appropriate, especially when done to prevent persons from harming the interests of others. Yet the criminal law should never be used lightly, even against persons who act culpably. Excessive prohibition can itself be harmful. It stands in the way of freedom. Even if we should use the criminal law to deter, we should be wary of extending its reach. We should not over-deter.[8]

[5] See, e.g., S H Kadish, 'Complicity, Cause, and Blame: A Study in the Interpretation of Doctrine' (1985) 73 California LR 323, 337.

[6] Conceptually speaking, it is possible to have distinct classes of secondary guilt, categorized by degree of involvement and, perhaps, culpability: see, e.g., J Dressler, 'Reforming Complicity Law: Trivial Assistance as a Lesser Offence' (2008) 5 Ohio St J Crim L 427; A F Sarch, 'Condoning the Crime: The Elusive Mens Rea for Complicity' (2015) 47 Loyola U Chicago LJ 131, proposing two-tier schemes of 'full' and 'lesser' complicity. As we know, the criminal law has unavoidably blunt categories even for principals, and one may doubt the practicality of such a scheme. Be that as it may, the concern of this chapter is with derivative liability *in principle*. Hence I disregard further subdivisions here.

[7] See § 1. For a specific defence of this claim, see J R Edwards and A P Simester, 'Prevention with a Moral Voice' in A P Simester, A du Bois-Pedain, and U Neumann (eds), *Liberal Criminal Theory: Essays for Andreas von Hirsch* (Hart 2014) 43.

[8] In his perceptive discussion of complicity, Francis Sayre observes that 'All criminal law is a compromise between two fundamentally conflicting interests. In the first place, there is the social interest in the general well-being and security.... In the second place, there is the individual interest of the particular

We have alluded to these tensions before. They pervade the criminal law. But they are especially poignant for complicity doctrine. The level of involvement required to make S guilty as an accomplice when P commits a crime must weigh the prospect that S may be just as culpable as P (or even more culpable) against the difficulty that secondary liability casts the net of criminalization much wider than usual, beyond the direct perpetration of criminal wrongs, to catch ostensibly innocent conduct that we would not otherwise want to deter: such as lending or selling another person a baseball bat, or a knife, or sometimes even sitting as a passenger in a car.[9]

Fortunately, at such points our resources do not run out. Yet their deployment in the context of complicity is not straightforward. Suppose that it is a legitimately-enacted offence to φ. According to the wrongdoing principle, D can be appropriately convicted of φing only if her φing is an instance of wrongdoing—that is, an unjustified moral wrong. As we noted in § 1.4, part of this principle can be explained in terms of culpability. Any formal judgment of blame, including the finding of guilt on which the conviction is based, must be predicated upon unjustified, norm-violating conduct.[10] Culpability is not a state of nature—it must have an object. We are blamed *for* something, done or not done. One may make moral assessments of a person's character ('Peter is an evil scoundrel, and not a nice man at all,' for example), but those are not judgments of culpability. The criminal conviction, like all true blaming verdicts, expresses moral reproof of a person *in respect of* that person's wrongdoing.[11]

More on the objects of moral assessments in Part III.[12] Complicity doctrines run into difficulty, though, when we try to reconcile them with the wrongdoing principle. For P, the matter is more straightforward. P's conviction can be morally legitimate only if P is ascriptively responsible for the event constituting the crime—φing—with which he is charged. Only then does it constitute *P's* wrong, a breach of duty for which P is accountable. In S's case, though, the wrongdoing principle needs some translation. It requires that S's action—*her μing*—is an instance of wrongdoing *and* that, in virtue of her μing, S is ascriptively

defendant against the restraint of his liberty for offenses for which he was not morally blameworthy.' Sayre observes that conflict clearly. But he misses a key *ex ante* dimension to criminal law: the individual interest of each person against diminutions of liberty through criminalization. F Sayre, 'Criminal Responsibility for the Acts of Another' (1930) 43 Harvard LR 689, 720.

[9] At least when one owns the car: *Du Cros v Lambourne* [1907] 1 KB 40.

[10] More particularly, in the context of criminal law, the norm-violation must be a breach of duty: see § 1.4. The phrasing in the text leaves open the possibility that, sometimes, one may appropriately be blamed merely for acting against first-order moral reasons. See § 11.1.1.

[11] Where, on occasion, the courts have abrogated this principle (cp. *Larsonneur* (1933) 24 Cr App R 74), the conviction may justly be criticized: see §§ 4.3.3, 8.4.2.

[12] See esp. §§ 11.2, 14.2.

responsible for the event constituting P's crime. Notice that S need not be *morally* responsible for P's φing. There is no general requirement that her participation had any causal impact upon P's conduct.[13] Neither does it matter whether S was in any position to prevent P from committing the crime. The wrong that S must be morally responsible for is *her own act of participation* in P's crime. But what makes that act of participation, that μing, a wrong?

Suppose that P means to kill V. Knowing this, S lends P her knife. When P then stabs V fatally, the harm, and the primary wrong, that motivates the criminal law is perpetrated by P. S does not kill V. Moreover, lending someone a knife is, of itself, neither wrong nor harmful, let alone criminal. It does seem appropriate, both morally and legally, to ascribe S with responsibility for the wrong committed by P. Yet there is something a bit fishy about our doing so. One might think that, whenever we reprove a person, the grounds for reproof must originate in the conduct of *that* person. Complicity liability, by contrast, is predicated at least in part upon *P's* wrong.[14]

From a criminalization perspective, complicity doctrines are also in tension with the *principle of personal control* over liability. According to that principle,[15] no one should be enabled deliberately to render another person guilty of a crime. We saw in chapter 5 that the most important expression of the principle is found in the rule that free, deliberate, and informed interventions by third parties are not regarded as having been caused by others. If T freely and knowingly intercedes to bring about an outcome, D's causal responsibility is displaced, at least in the criminal law. On this count, complicity doctrine is egregious. It supplies a general exception to the principle of personal control.[16]

So we have multiple reasons to question the legitimacy of secondary liability as a form of criminal guilt. When, knowing his intentions, S lends P the knife, her liability is now in P's hands. This implication is bound up with the derivative nature of complicity liability.[17] Yet why is it that V's death should

[13] Below, § 7.2.

[14] The oddity is compounded in most common-law jurisdictions by the fact that S is convicted of the substantive offence itself, rather than of complicity in P's offence. She is labelled a 'murderer', not an 'accessory to murder'. See n 2 above.

[15] Discussed in § 5.3.5.

[16] This is not to deny that S too has control over her liability, in as much as she can refrain from lending P the knife. The concern of the principle, though, is with her liability's being controlled by others.

[17] Many jurisdictions also prohibit assistance and/or encouragement as inchoate crimes. (Cp. Part 2 of the Serious Crime Act 2007 (UK); s 107 of the Singapore Penal Code.) As a possible substitute for derivative liability, inchoate liability does not resolve the labelling difficulty identified below in the text. As an *independent* form of liability, one worry about such inchoate offences is the considerable degree to which they extend the reach of criminalization, into scenarios that from P's perspective may not even be preparatory. The justification for punishing S rests ultimately on reference to P's wrong: yet P's wrong need not have started. Criminalization and enforcement in this context is likely to be highly invasive.

be S's lookout, so that S's freedom of action is restricted—especially since S's own action is otherwise and ordinarily lawful? In turn, when, and why, does S's conduct become an instance of wrongdoing, such that she may be blamed for doing it, and held accountable for the further, freely chosen wrong by P?

Sometimes there will be simpler and better alternatives. Conduct that assists or encourages wrongdoing by others might be criminalized directly by specific proscription. Given their potential to facilitate harmful conduct by purchasers, it may be appropriate to prohibit shopkeepers from selling automatic firearms, *tout court*, rather than use complicity law to regulate individual transactions.[18] Prophylactic offences of this sort can offer more definite guidance to citizens about their freedoms and obligations, letting them know where they stand and leaving them personally in control of their criminal liability. Such measures are on occasion preferable to imposing derivative liability. But only on occasion. In other contexts, S's wrongdoing may be inadequately reflected by conviction for a prophylactic offence. If S supplies an automatic weapon to P for the purpose of murdering V, a conviction as accessory to homicide may better represent her criminality than would a conviction for illegal sale. Even more importantly, many varieties of complicity involve conduct that should not, in and of itself, be criminal. Prohibiting sales of automatic machine pistols is one thing: prohibiting the sale of kitchen knives, or baseball bats, is quite another. Complicity doctrines are an important part of the state's criminal-law toolbox. They enable the law to navigate clear of general prohibitions while still attaching liability in particular instances.[19]

The challenge in doing so is to negotiate the shoals of culpability, ascriptive responsibility, and criminalization. And our compass is mens rea. Conventionally, mens rea is thought of as something that helps to establish culpability on the part of the defendant. It certainly plays that role here. But we saw in chapter 3 that it has other functions too, functions that are distinctively in play for complicity. Two in particular are crucial. One is to help establish the morally wrongful character of S's behaviour. The second is to play a mediating role in the criminalization of S's conduct, being part of the *ex ante* trade-off between the protection of potential victims and the preservation of liberties for potential defendants. As we shall see, these further roles demand more

[18] An instance of remote harms criminalization: *Crimes, Harms, and Wrongs*, chs 4–5.

[19] Neither should one neglect the evidential advantages of complicity law, in as much as it facilitates the conviction of a defendant without having to prove whether that person was the principal or a secondary offender: as, for example, in *Du Cros v Lambourne* [1907] 1 KB 40. (D was the owner of a car that had been driven dangerously, but it was not clear whether D or his friend was driving at the time. Nonetheless, D was convicted of dangerous driving, it being irrelevant whether he was the principal or abettor.) There must *be* a principal, but that person need not be identified.

stringent mens rea standards for secondary liability than is needed to satisfy the culpability principle. They help to explain why recklessness on the part of S should be insufficient to support derivative liability for aiding and abetting—and why that conclusion does not extend to joint enterprises.

7.2 Complicity and causation

Mayhap there's an elephant in this room. Surely the grounds for reproving S *do* reside in S's conduct—more specifically, in S's making a contribution to P's crime? A nuanced defence of this line of thought is offered by John Gardner. Gardner accepts that the influence of accomplices is indirect: 'The essential difference between them is that accomplices make their difference through principals, in other words by making a difference to the difference that principals make.'[20] Be that as it may, he says, this difference that accomplices make is a causal one.[21] Even if S does not 'cause' the result of P's act, she makes a 'causal contribution' to it.[22] Hence the nuance: causing something is not the only way of standing in a causal relationship to it. To 'procure' or 'occasion' something, for example, is to *stand in a causal relationship with* that thing, but not necessarily to *cause* it. For Gardner, it is the former that matters in complicity. What counts, as he puts it, is whether the accomplice 'acts with the consequence or result that the principal commits the wrong.'[23]

It is obviously true that S's liability, while derivative, must in part be grounded in S's own conduct. At issue here is how that conduct must engage with P's crime. Gardner is surely right to insist that we change the world by causal means. Equally clearly, however, S's connection to the result of P's action is unlike P's. When S lends P the knife with which he kills V, we may say, and do so fairly, that S played a part in the story of V's death; even that she participated in the causing of V's death. But we should not say that S caused V's death, *simpliciter*, or that S caused P to kill V. We should not say it, and Gardner does not say it, because it is not true.[24] S's action is neither a direct not an indirect cause of V's death, for the reasons set out in chapter 5.

[20] J Gardner, 'Complicity and Causality' (2007) 1 Crim L and Phil 127, 128.

[21] Albeit not one of a type that Moore recognizes: Moore, *Causation and Responsibility*, 293–94. For Moore, there is only one type of causal relation, i.e. causation.

[22] See explicitly on this point J Gardner, 'Moore on Complicity and Causality' (2007) 156 U Penn LR PENNumbra 432, 437ff.

[23] Gardner, 'Complicity and Causality' (n 20) 141.

[24] See, too, *Hart and Honoré*, 377–88.

Admittedly, when S lends P the knife, its use need not be extraordinary or unforeseeable. It may only be the free, deliberate and informed interventions (FDI) rule that prevents us from building a causal bridge from S to P's crime. Yet that's also the point. One of the functions of the FDI rule is to carve out legal space for a different kind of responsibility-ascription, one that respects the separateness of S and P, and recognizes the distinctive way in which accomplices participate in crimes. Without such a distinction, the liability of secondary parties, at least for causation-based offences,[25] would—should—fall simply to be determined under the normal rules for principals, including whatever mens rea requirements apply to the relevant offence.[26] But that would be to elide important differences between S and P, differences that the FDI rule allows the law to accommodate. Gardner's analysis neatly sidesteps these problems, by recognizing that S's contributions may have causal significance without counting as 'causes' for the purposes of satisfying the actus reus of substantive offences within criminal law.

Moore would go rather further. He urges that we abandon the FDI rule itself, worrying that it implies 'we have a moral right to be blind to the intentional wrongdoing of others.'[27] As Moore reads it, an argument along these lines is offered by Antony Duff:[28]

> '[I]t is not my business that what I do makes it easier for P to commit the crime partly because it is P's business whether he commits the crime . . . it is up to P whether he commits the crime or not and—at least sometimes—I am not required to guide my actions by my knowledge of what P will do.'

The response is scathing:[29]

> 'As Heidi Hurd put this justification for the legal doctrines of intervening causation some years before, the doctrines "appear to allow one to navigate

[25] Gardner reinforces his argument with the point that many wrongs are 'nonproxyable', meaning that they can only be done personally and not by means of an intervening actor: thus only P and not S is a killer, even if each is ascriptively responsible for the killing. ('Complicity and Causality' (n 20) 135–37.) The term 'nonproxyable' was first coined by Kadish ('Complicity, Cause, and Blame' (n 5) 373), who had in mind activities such as marrying or torturing; Gardner suggests that the range of nonproxyable wrongs is much wider than that. The point helpfully illustrates our reluctance to assimilate accomplices with principals. For present purposes, however, I set it aside as a supplementary claim. Certainly in the context of harm-based wrongs, the common law has not hesitated to treat D as a principal notwithstanding that death is caused through the agency of another person (who was not a free, deliberate, and informed actor): see, e.g., *Pagett* (1983) 76 Cr App R 279.

[26] Contrast § 7.3–4.

[27] Moore, *Causation and Responsibility*, ch 13.

[28] R A Duff, 'Is Accomplice Liability Superfluous?' (2007) 156 U Penn LR PENNumbra 444, 451.

[29] Moore, *Causation and Responsibility*, 292.

> through life without having to take causal responsibility for the harms that result when murderers, rapists, thieves, and arsonists seize on opportunities for wrongdoing that one's legitimate activities create." The moral principle is that "the justifiable uses of one's time, labor, and property ought not to be thought relative to the unjustifiable uses to which those resources might foreseeably be put by slubberdegullions and shirkers".'[30]

But that's too fast. Duff's suggestion was not that we are *always* entitled to disregard what others may choose to do in light of our actions; merely that this is sometimes the case.[31] As a potential accessory, on other occasions S *must* moderate her actions because of what P will do. This is one of the core achievements of complicity law. It facilitates more nuanced resolutions of problems concerning when S is required to alter her conduct in light of P's. Those problems cannot be resolved simply by assimilating S with P. S is not like P, and her actions are not like P's actions. Taken together with the FDI rule, complicity doctrines allow us to tailor more sensitive rules governing S's liability, rules that allow us to acknowledge more than one type of involvement in crime—whether or not we call each type 'causal'.

Clearly, then, the analogy with indirect causation is at least partially apt. Complicity liability rules govern cases where, in terms of ascriptive responsibility, we can bridge from S's own conduct to P's wrong. Moreover, the remarks in this section are so far consistent with Gardner's analysis. Recall our example from § 5.3:

> *South-side*: Following an argument, D assaults V, leaving him unconscious and seriously injured in a dangerous area of the city. V will die of his wounds if left untreated. Before that occurs, however, T comes upon V, who is a member of a rival gang. T deliberately shoots V dead. The risk that this would occur was reasonably foreseeable and indeed foreseen by D.

In *South-side*, we might say that D 'occasioned' the shooting of V when she left him lying unconscious in a dangerous are of the city. Even if she did not 'cause' it within the terms of a principal's liability. D surely made a difference.

[30] H M Hurd, 'Is it Wrong to do Right when Others do Wrong?' (2001) 7 Legal Theory 307, 314, 308. Note that Hurd's objection was originally articulated in the context of tort law.

[31] Even the combined position of Hurd and Moore admits of exceptions: H M Hurd and M S Moore, 'Untying the Gordian Knot of Mens Rea Requirements for Accomplices' (2016) 32 Soc Phil and Policy 161, 181–82. Admittedly, I disagree with Duff, in that I would draw a line for S at the point where she *knows* what P will do. Contra Hurd, however, I argue in this chapter that foreseeability (and, indeed, advertent recklessness) should not generally suffice for complicity liability.

Yet how far does the analogy go? Can we generalize it in the way Gardner suggests? Must the accomplice act, as he puts it, 'with the consequence or result that the principal commits the wrong.'[32] Not as a doctrinal matter. Constructing our participatory bridge does not depend on whether S's act made a difference to P's. Suppose, for example, that P had been planning to steal S's knife, until S lent it to him; or that, when S opened a window and thereby aided the burglary, P had already arranged for T to open the same window. Or that Ross, the victim, would have ignored the warning telegram that Judge Tally intercepted.[33] Or that Coleman Hawkins was indifferent to Wilcox's presence, and would have gone through with the performance anyway.[34] Or that S, one of many available candidates, was hired as the getaway driver for a robbery that was already fully planned.[35] Or that S acts as lookout but sees nothing untoward.[36] Or that, in a large group bent on violence, S is just one of many and has no personal impact upon P's choices. In all of these cases, S's contribution is sufficient at common law to count as the actus reus of complicity. The encouragement or assistance must be *received*,[37] but S's participation need not *make a difference*.[38]

Or perhaps this is also too fast. It may seem that Gardner's causal-contribution account can be defended against these examples. Even if P would have used that very knife anyway, surely the causal point is that P got the knife *by S's giving it to him*. We might quibble about whether, in Gardner's terms, that makes 'a difference to the difference' made by P,[39] yet it undeniably makes a difference to the causal history behind P's wrong. However, a reply along these lines is problematic.

[32] 'Complicity and Causality' (n 20) 141.

[33] The famous case of *State v Tally* 102 Ala 25, 15 So 722 (1894). Judge Tally, whose brothers-in-law were pursuing and planning to kill Ross, ordered the telegraph operator not to deliver the warning telegram. Ross was found and killed.

[34] *Wilcox v Jeffery* [1951] 1 All ER 464. (Wilcox, a jazz critic, attended a concert given by Hawkins in London. The concert was unlawful because, as Wilcox knew, Hawkins did not have a work permit.) Cp. *Coney* (1882) 8 QBD 534.

[35] Note that S becomes guilty of the robbery at the point when it is committed, not when she commences the getaway.

[36] Compare the unusual case of *Larkins v Police* [1987] 2 NZLR 282. (Persons known to S were engaged in a burglary. Unprompted, S decided to act as lookout in case the police arrived; the burglars were unaware of S's decision to keep watch. As it happened, however, S made no contribution to events, since someone else saw the police arrive and called out a warning.)

[37] Thus, e.g., one who opens the window in order to assist a burglar need not be complicit when the burglar enters by the front door.

[38] See, too, *A-G v Able* [1984] 1 QB 795, 812 ('it does not make any difference that the person [encouraged] would have tried to commit suicide anyway'); *Stringer* [2011] EWCA Crim 1396, [48]. This is not to deny that, when rendered in terms of the Harm Principle, the case for criminalizing the conduct of secondary parties is dependent on the tendency of aiding, abetting, etc., *generally* to conduce toward (harmful) wrongs by P.

[39] A stronger case for Gardner would be where, had S not lent P the knife, P would have borrowed a knife of the same type from Q. In that case, we might more readily agree that S made a causal contribution and Q did not; that S *rather than* Q was the one who made 'a difference to the difference that principals make.'

Suppose that S had refused to lend P the knife when asked. P then stole the knife—or borrowed a similar knife from Q—and used that knife to kill V. Now it is S's *refusal* that forms part of the causal history behind P's wrong. S made a difference to the difference that Q made, which in turn made 'a difference to the difference that principals make.'[40] A causal history analysis proves too much.

Neither should our examples be dismissed as marginalia, as cases where the law foregoes causal nuance for evidential reasons. (Indeed, the common law specifically reserves the term 'procurement' for complicit participation that does make a causal difference.[41]) From a normative perspective, acts of participation of these kinds seem sufficient to warrant the ascription of responsibility to S—provided they are accompanied by an appropriate level of mens rea. S must, of course, stand in a causal relationship to the receipt by P of her aid or encouragement. But the best explanation of complicity liability, at least in the common law, is that S's ascriptive responsibility for P's crime rests upon her act of sufficiently *involving* or *associating* herself with that crime, rather than in her causal impact upon P's wrong.

7.3 Assistance and encouragement ('aiding and abetting')

That participatory act can take different forms: to this extent, of course, the grounds for reproving S do originate in S's conduct. In this chapter, we look at two major categories of participation. Each category requires some preliminary description, owing to the sheer complexity of the relevant doctrines.[42] Moreover, because of significant differences between English and American complicity law, I focus primarily on the former. The two major categories are as follows:

(I) 'Aiding and abetting' liability, predicated upon an act of assistance or encouragement rendered by S to P; and
(II) 'Joint enterprise' liability, predicated upon a conspiracy, formal or informal,[43] acted out with P.

[40] One response to this counterexample might point to the fact that S lacked any intention to assist P by her refusal. However, that response effectively trivializes the actus reus component of complicity. Moreover, it is ad hoc. Consider a case where S shouts encouragement to P, who is perpetrating an assault. S is somewhat far away and P does not hear her. However, Q hears S's words, realizes what is happening, and herself calls out words or encouragement—which P does hear. On a causal history test, S is complicit in P's wrong.

[41] *A-G's Reference (No. 1 of 1975)* [1975] QB 773; *Calhaem* [1985] QB 808; *Millward* [1994] Crim LR 527.

[42] As Hurd and Moore put it ('Untying the gordian Knot' (n 31) 162): 'The difficulty is partly due to the intrinsic complexity of the issues, for there are lots of "moving parts" in this doctrinal matrix; also contributing to the difficulty, however, are the confusions introduced by a history that is far from ideal.'

[43] The traditional English phrasing was 'common unlawful purpose'. See, e.g., Foster, *Crown Law* (1762) Discourse III, ch 1, § 9.

Our concern across §§ 7.3–4 is with category (I), the less controversial form of complicity liability. The essence of aiding and abetting is intentional help or encouragement. Putting it that way, however, is deceptively straightforward, in as much as the mens rea element must relate to two different matters: S's own conduct, in assisting or encouraging P; and P's conduct. While S must intend her own contribution, it does not follow that S must intend or desire that P commit the offence she aids or abets.[44] By way of illustration, consider the following example:[45]

> Stephen is a firearms wholesaler. He sells a firearm to Pamela, a general shopkeeper. Stephen knows that Pamela will re-sell the firearm in her shop, and that Pamela does not have a license to deal in firearms. Stephen does not sell the firearm to Pamela because he wants her to resell it, but rather because he wants the money that Pamela is prepared to pay for it.

Traditionally in England, it will not avail Stephen that he does not mean for Pamela to resell the firearm. That may be characterized as a truth about Stephen's motive, or purpose: which is ultimately to make money. But it is enough, at least under English law, that Stephen intended to provide Pamela with the firearm (which, as he knew, she would resell—an element to which we return below). On the other hand, it does not suffice for secondary liability that S merely thinks it likely P may be assisted. Suppose the following variation:

> Susan is an auctioneer of various goods. She sells an unlabelled box of goods to Peter, a wholesaler. Because the goods are in bond, she is unsure whether the goods are toy pistols or real guns. Susan knows that Peter does not have a license to deal in firearms.

On these facts, Susan lacks the mens rea for secondary participation because she is at most reckless whether Peter is assisted or encouraged.

From S's perspective, these rules float free of the principal's offence.[46] If Peter shoots Victor dead, Peter is guilty of murder at common law only if he intended death or serious injury. But when Sam lends Peter the gun, she need not intend

[44] *Bryce* [2004] EWCA Crim 1231, [61]: 'it is the assistance, not the ultimate crime, that must be intended by the secondary party.'

[45] The example is based on *Cafferata v Wilson* [1936] 3 All ER 149.

[46] More precisely: the mens rea *standard* applicable to S is independent of the mens rea standard for P's offence. The *content* is not independent, in as much as S must know or purpose that P will act with whatever mens rea is required for P to be guilty of the substantive offence. For discussion, see *Simester and Sullivan*, § 7.4(iv)(c).

harm to Victor at all. In most common-law jurisdictions, it is enough that she renders aid *knowing of* Peter's plan. Conversely, where negligence (or less) suffices for Peter's conviction, it does not for Sam's. In the classic case of *Callow v Tillstone*,[47] a butcher was convicted of the strict liability offence of exposing unsound meat for sale. Before he did so, the butcher had asked a veterinary surgeon to examine the meat. The vet performed the examination carelessly, and wrongly certified the meat as sound. Strikingly, the butcher was convicted but the vet's conviction was quashed. Negligence has never sufficed for abetment, even of strict liability offences.

7.3.1 Muddy waters

The seeming incongruity prompts an obvious question. What ought to be the mens rea requirements for secondary liability? Sometimes, S offers assistance or encouragement *in order that* doing so will facilitate some criminal act by P, without being certain what P actually means to do. Of such a case, we can say straightforwardly that S intends to aid or abet P's (potential) crime. However, such a finding is unnecessary. It suffices in England that help or encouragement is rendered *knowing* what it is that P will do. The classic statement of this alternative is in *Johnson v Youden*:[48]

> 'Before a person can be convicted of aiding and abetting the commission of an offence he must at least *know* the essential matters which constitute that offence.'

And for decades, that is where the line was drawn. Recklessness would not do. *Johnson v Youden* excludes the person who lends her jemmy to P suspecting, or thinking it possible, that P means to burgle. Interpreted as a legal standard, to know something, one must (correctly) believe or assume it without significant doubt.[49] In effect, this imports a standard of oblique intention.[50] In order to intend 'to assist P to commit a burglary', S must either act *in order* to assist P to commit a burglary (for example because she has an interest in P's committing

[47] (1900) 64 JP 823.

[48] [1950] 1 KB 544, 546 (Goddard LCJ; emphasis added). On the issue of what count as 'essential' matters that S must know about in a given offence, see *Simester and Sullivan*, § 7.4(iv)(c).

[49] See *Simester and Sullivan*, § 5.4. There seems no persuasive reason why the criminal law should import additional qualifications that are apt to an extra-legal concept of knowledge, e.g. that the belief must be justified as well as correct. Compare Williams, *CLGP* 169; R Charlow, 'Wilful Ignorance and Criminal Culpability' (1992) 70 Texas LR 1351, 1374–75.

[50] See § 15.2.

it), or intend her action in the practical certainty that her conduct *will* assist P to commit a burglary. Will, not may.

Yet there is no consensus. Aligned with *Johnson v Youden*, many common law jurisdictions have continued to insist that recklessness is not enough to establish liability for aiding and abetting.[51] In England, however, some Court of Appeal decisions have ruled that a secondary party may be convicted if she contemplates or foresees P's crime 'as a real or serious risk'.[52] The standing of those decisions is unclear,[53] but they illustrate the point that the normative case for requiring *at least* knowledge of the essential facts of P's crime should not be taken for granted. At the other end of the scale, the law in parts of the United States is even more stringent. In the leading case of *United States v Peoni*,[54] the Second Circuit Court of Appeals held that a 'purposive attitude' to promote criminal conduct was required for accessorial liability. According to Justice Learned Hand, definitions of aiding and abetting:[55]

> '[H]ave nothing whatever to do with the probability that the forbidden result would follow . . . they all demand that he in some sort associate himself with the venture, that he participate in it as in something that he wishes to bring about, that he seek by his action to make it succeed.'

Admittedly, some American courts have ruled that knowledge will suffice,[56] and that possibility remains debated in the United States. Unlike England, however, there is relatively little judicial support for the idea that recklessness is enough.

7.4 On the normative roles of knowledge

One argument invoked by the English Court of Appeal for watering down the requirement of knowledge was conceptual: that it is problematic to require knowledge

[51] See, e.g., *Giorgianni v R* (1985) 156 CLR 473 (HCA); *Dunlop and Sylvester v R* (1979) 47 CCC (2d) 93, 110 (CSC); *Preston* [1949] SCR 156 (CSC); *Crooks* [1981] 2 NZLR 53 (NZCA); *Millar v MOT* [1986] 1 NZLR 660, 674 (NZCA).

[52] See the discussion in *Simester and Sullivan*, § 7.4(iv)(b).

[53] Particularly in light of *Jogee* [2016] UKSC 8; *Ruddock* [2016] UKPC 7.

[54] 100 F 2d 401 (2d Cir 1938).

[55] Ibid, 402.

[56] e.g. *Backun v United States* 112 F 2d 635 (4th Cir, 1940). Useful surveys are found in L Westerfield, 'The *Mens Rea* Requirement of Accomplice Liability in American Criminal Law—Knowledge or Intent' (1980) 51 Mississippi LJ 155; C Corteau, 'The Mental Element Required for Accomplice Liability: A Topic Note' (1998) 59 Louisiana LR 325; B Weiss, 'What Were They Thinking? The Mental States of the Aider and Abettor and the Causer under Federal Law' (2002) 70 Fordham LR 1341.

when P's crime lies in the future.[57] At root here is a notion that one cannot 'know' about future events, rather like the suggestion in *Sunair Holidays Ltd* that one cannot make true or false statements about the future.[58] The notion strikes me as misguided, in as much as it seems possible for one to know about a future event: to know, for instance, that the sun will rise tomorrow.[59] More pertinently, perhaps, there is no convincing reason why the criminal law's concept of knowledge should contain a categorical restriction of this kind. Consider the facts of *Reardon*,[60] one of the English Court's revisionary decisions. Having shot two men in the head and carried them outside, P returned to S, his colleague, saying that one of them was still alive and asking if he could borrow S's knife to 'finish the job'. This was hardly a case where S lacked knowledge of the essential matters of P's crime—but when Reardon lent his knife to P, that crime lay in the future. Reardon correctly believed that P would commit murder even though, when he handed over the knife, his belief was capable of becoming wrong (say, if P had then panicked and run off). What counts legally for knowledge, even of future facts, is the level of conviction: that S believes, correctly and with no significant doubt, what P will do.

Yet what about the merits? Intuitively, there is a desert-based attraction to criminalizing reckless abetment. At least where recklessness is sufficient mens rea for the principal's offence, why should full knowledge be necessary on the part of the accomplice? If knowledge is required, S will escape liability in many cases where she willingly assists P to commit a crime, and has the same mens rea (recklessness) toward that crime as P. One might think that S has crossed the threshold justifying conviction, in terms of exhibiting culpable conduct: S has in fact assisted or encouraged P, and she has done so being aware of the potential to facilitate crime.

The first step in answering this objection is conceptual. It is to acknowledge that doctrines of complicity are separate from those concerning the perpetration of crime. The very basis of secondary liability is different from that of a principal. Although S is held responsible for P's crime, there is no suggestion that she personally commits it. The actus reus for S is quite distinct from that for P: S must aid or abet P, and need not herself satisfy any elements of P's crime. This being so, there seems no reason why the mens rea requirement for participation should be determined by the principal offence.[61] Neither is there

[57] *Bryce* [2004] EWCA Crim 1231, [49].

[58] [1973] 1 WLR 1105; cogently refuted by A White, *Misleading Cases* (Clarendon 1991) ch 9.

[59] See S C Shute, 'Knowledge and Belief in the Criminal Law' and G R Sullivan, 'Knowledge, Belief and Culpability', both in S C Shute and A P Simester (eds), *Criminal Law Theory: Doctrines of the General Part* (2002) 171, 186–87 and 207, 214–15, respectively.

[60] [1999] Crim LR 392 (CA).

[61] For a survey of US cases suggesting that S's mens rea requirement should match P's, and thus vary according to the relevant offence, see Weiss, 'What Were They Thinking' (n 56) 1410–14. The difficulties with this approach would be particularly severe for crimes of negligence.

any need to show a moral equivalence between S and P,[62] although of course S must be *sufficiently* culpable to deserve her conviction.

Indeed, we can put all this rather more strongly. The key question is not whether S is *culpable* in respect of the occurrence of P's crime, but whether S (as well as P) should be *accountable* for that crime. The more important issue, in other words, is not culpability but ascriptive responsibility.

Which takes us back to our discussion of causation in § 5.3. Both within and outwith the law, people are distinctively accountable for the causal consequences of their own actions. Suppose, for example, that some teenager commits a murder. Depending on the circumstances, we may think that his parents have done a bad job of bringing him up, without adequately instilling the values that should have restrained him from killing V. But we are not inclined to treat the parents as murderers, or even as the moral equivalent of murderers. The force of this point, as we have seen, rests in part upon the idea that individuals are separate agents. In a liberal society, the right to be treated as distinct individuals is fundamental. It requires the law to judge persons primarily according to their own actions and not according to what others do. Not exclusively. Sometimes, it is appropriate to ascribe responsibility to D for an event she does not herself bring about, and criminal liability for omissions and complicity does just that. But such occasions are exceptional, and they need careful constraint. Hence the principle that D has a right not to be labelled a criminal unless she is ascriptively responsible for the event constituting the crime of which she is convicted.[63]

As we observed in § 7.1, this means that the mere occurrence of a criminal wrong, together with moral culpability on the part of S, is insufficient to convict S of the corresponding crime. She must be involved in that crime by virtue of some wrong that she *herself* commits. And here we come to the crux of the matter. The most a secondary party does is assist or encourage a crime, not perpetrate it. Since this is much looser connection than is required of the perpetrator, it seems insufficient by itself to warrant holding S accountable for P's crime.[64] S's conduct, by itself, need not be a wrong at all: it may be something that is permitted, such as

[62] Again, this important point is obscured by the fact that in Anglo-American law, S is convicted of the full offence rather than, say, of abetting it. Matters are significantly worsened if the relevant crime involves a mandatory sentence. But I take that last point to be a concern about punishment rules, and ancillary to the core issues here. See also n 2 above.

[63] See §§ 4.2, 13.3.1.

[64] Model Penal Code, § 2.06, commentary at 312 n 42: 'if anything, the culpability level for the accomplice should be higher than that of the principal actor, because there is generally more ambiguity in the overt conduct engaged in by the accomplice, and thus a higher risk of convicting the innocent.' Compare, too, the refusal by the New Zealand Court of Appeal to extend to secondary parties the operation of mens rea presumptions in certain statutory offences: *Samuels* [1985] 1 NZLR 350 (drug possession); *Hill* [2004] 2 NZLR 145 (bankruptcy).

lending P a jemmy—something that we may do innocently in ordinary life.[65] Its criminal character originates from beyond the boundaries of S's own agency.

When computer manufacturers make and sell computers, there is a recognized chance that their customers will use the machines to download and copy music illegally. Yet it seems undesirable to hold those manufacturers criminally responsible for the illegal copying that they facilitate.[66] Or to extend liability to a taxi driver who drops a passenger at a requested location, even though the driver suspects her passenger may be going to take part in a robbery. The same applies for encouragement: the possibility that my conduct may have a side-effect of encouraging or even generating incentives for others to misbehave should not, by itself, bring that conduct within the purview of the criminal law. If I leave my employer's laptop on the seat of my friend's car, aware that a known thief is operating in the neighbourhood, I may deserve reproach but I do not abet its theft; nor vandalism of the car. Simply put: if my action is lawful and not wrong, someone else's crime does not become my lookout—and should not be my responsibility under criminal law—simply because I foresee its possibility. Something more is required.

That 'something more' is supplied by my mens rea: by a requirement either that I act in order to assist or encourage P's crime; or that I act in the knowledge, in the sense of having no significant doubt, that P will commit the relevant crime.[67] It is only then that my helpful, but otherwise lawful, conduct becomes a wrong. We observed in § 3.2 that mens rea quite often plays this type of role. Picking up someone else's property is not the stuff of crime unless it is done with intent to deprive. In the law of theft, mens rea does not operate simply to establish fault, because, in itself, the actus reus does not specify a wrong. Thus it is with complicity. In aiding and abetting, it not S's conduct *simpliciter* to which we object. There is nothing wrong with selling jemmies, for example, or computers. If that is so, it follows that the mens rea requirement does more than simply establish a connection between the eventual harm and S's culpability. It is also part of what makes S's conduct a wrong.

One might query this analysis. In the context of aiding and abetting, why cannot the wrong be supplied by the actus reus—by the fact that P actually

[65] This is not to deny that sometimes S's role (e.g., as criminal mastermind) may be significantly more heinous than P's own contribution. But the scope of complicity is much wider than that.

[66] Various examples of this type of problem are collected by Glanville Williams, 'Complicity, Purpose and the Draft Code—2' [1990] Crim LR 98, 101.

[67] Within these alternatives, a further distinction should be drawn between general and specific knowledge: the latter is needed. As a computer manufacturer, I may know, statistically speaking, that 30 per cent of my customers will use the computer illegally to copy music. In each particular sale, I therefore know there is a substantial possibility that my conduct will facilitate a crime of music piracy. But I do not know whether *this* customer will use the product for such a purpose.

receives aid or encouragement from S?[68] And if that's right, perhaps reckless or even negligence might suffice to establish S's culpability?

Obviously, the wrong constituted by a person's conduct can depend upon its causal effects.[69] This is a familiar normative feature of 'result crimes' like murder. However, as we saw in § 7.2, the link between S's contribution and the effects of P's conduct is not normally one of causation. Indeed, the link need not involve a causal relation at all, let alone the kind of causal relation capable of carrying the moral freight required here. This is not to deny that S must cause P to receive assistance or encouragement. But what is missing is a causal link to *P's wrongdoing*. And the latter is the causal link which, as an actus reus matter, would be required to make S's conduct a wrong.

Absent such a causal link, we need some of the normative work to be done by S's mens rea. A person who sells a jemmy suspecting but not knowing of its intended criminal use, and without its being her purpose to help P, does not identify or ally herself with the crime P then commits. The moral character of her action is innocent: she simply sells a jemmy. Just as many of our projects can miscarry, the jemmy may or may not be put to nefarious use by someone else. But if it is her *purpose* that the jemmy should be so used, then she involves herself in P's crime directly. Similarly, if she *knows* that it will be so used, her conduct is no longer objectively innocent or ambiguous; its moral character of aiding or abetting crime is now unequivocal. She cannot evade the truth that, by her conduct, she is deliberately assisting P's crime. In this way, her mental state is integral to the moral character of her action. Moreover, it goes too far, and curtails S's freedom of action too greatly, to hold it a pro tanto wrong for her to do anything that she realizes *may* lead to crime by another.

The argument here is of a best-generalization kind. It recognizes that the law cannot be infinitely nuanced. By that same token, however, the criminal law should not be extended, willy-nilly, in order to convict the culpable. Its rules are general, which means that punishing a blameworthy S is, in effect, to criminalize the type of conduct that S exhibits. On occasion, someone who sells P the jemmy with which P commits a burglary may deserve moral reproof. But it does not follow that we should prohibit her conduct, by holding her criminally responsible for the burglary.

Admittedly, there are reasons favouring criminalization. Burglary is a serious wrong, and prohibiting others from facilitating it may be expected to help reduce its incidence. In any community, freedom has its limits, and on

[68] Thanks to Antony Duff for suggesting this line of thought.
[69] See esp. §§ 14.2.3, 14.3.

occasion we must each give up valuable liberties for the sake of others. When S passes a tool of crime to P, P is aided and the victim's rights are put at risk, so there is a prima facie reason why the law might demand that S desist.

By requiring knowledge, the law finds middle ground on this issue, utilizing the mediating role that mens rea plays in criminalization.[70] It is a familiar principle that, when contemplating whether to proscribe conduct, one should always take into account the social value of the conduct to be prohibited and the intrusive impact its proscription would have on the freedom of citizens. We noted in § 7.1 that these considerations are especially in point for complicity. Secondary participation widens the scope of the criminal law, so that not only must S not stab people, burgle, and the like; neither may she do anything that helps P to do so, even if that means she must forego her own activities because of P's plans. This widening calls for off-setting protections. Stipulating a more stringent mens rea requirement for complicity means that the prospect of liability will have less impact on the day-to-day lives of law-abiding people. Simply put, they will be required to alter their behaviour on fewer occasions—only when they know, rather than suspect, what P means to do.[71] As such, the invasiveness of complicity doctrine is balanced, appropriately, against the interests of others. The rights of victims not to be burgled, assaulted, *et cetera*, entail that it is sometimes necessary to curtail the liberty of citizens actively to assist criminals.[72] But mens rea requirements can moderate these restrictions. If we reject recklessness as the mens rea standard in complicity, S need not live out her life in fear of what P *may* do; the duty to refrain from assisting arises only when she *knows* that a crime is in view, or where it is her purpose to assist.

A central function of the criminal law is to help safeguard people from harm. But criminal prohibitions are themselves detrimental, in so far as they restrict freedom. Ordinary citizens must not only be shielded from the misconduct of others; they need also to be shielded from the state, which should not impede their ordinary, quotidien activities. Quite apart from its role in establishing a person's culpability, mens rea has an important function to play in keeping citizens outside the scope of criminal prohibitions. We can illustrate this by the extreme example of a strict liability offence: say, of selling adulterated milk. Suppose that D, a milk vendor, is a law-abiding citizen who wants to avoid the risk of criminal liability. The only sure way that he can do so is by getting out of

[70] See, further, § 3.3.1.

[71] Strictly speaking, knowledge about P's intentions is required only for crimes that require proof of intention on P's part. It would normally be sufficient to abet, say, a recklessness-based crime that S knows P will perpetrate the relevant actus reus recklessly.

[72] Addressing the worry expressed by Moore: see § 7.2.

the milk industry. In effect, strict liability makes selling milk a gateway to criminal liability;[73] so, we may say, the debate about strict liability is a debate about criminalization as much as it is about convicting the blameless. The same goes for mens rea. By pitching the standard of mens rea at knowledge rather than some lesser standard, we make it easier for citizens to comply with the law and reduce the range of activities they have to sacrifice in order to avoid the risk of a criminal conviction.

To be sure, none of this is to claim that it should always be permissible to take such risks, especially unreasonable risks, when facilitating or encouraging the conduct of others. But the prohibition of such risk-taking, where appropriate, should be effected by means of more specific offences and other forms of regulation such as licensing regimes.[74] As well as being freedom-enhancing, this is also a rule of law point. Complicity liability is an area where the law needs to give otherwise law-abiding citizens firmer and clearer guidance, without requiring them to make normative guesses about the legal risks involved in pursuing their own lives. Specific offences enable the state to do that.

7.4.1 On the border

Undoubtedly, the stringency of this standard will generate unattractive results. Hard cases often do. Consider the following example:

S illegally sells handguns. P buys a gun from S. He tells S that he will use the weapon to kill V, his partner, if V (despite being warned) continues to steal from their joint business. P says he is confident that V has given up his defalcations, so the need to kill V may not arise. S could not care less what P does with the gun and is interested only in the money she is paid for it. P later uses the gun to kill V.

It is tempting to think that we should hold S guilty of murdering V and not merely guilty of offences under gun control legislation. Surely, we might propose, it suffices that S knows P will be assisted by S's conduct *if* P ultimately does commit crime A? It does not. Much of the temptation is specific to the example. In terms of its more general implications, and subject to one point to be mentioned below, the example is not significantly different from that of

[73] This is the key insight behind Alan Michaels' analysis of constitutional limits upon strict liability: A Michaels, 'Constitutional Innocence' (1999) 112 Harvard LR 828. On strict liability generally, see chapter 13.

[74] It is also worth noting that there is potential liability for such events through tort law. See, e.g., *Stansbie v Troman* [1948] 2 All ER 48; above, § 5.3.

the computer sale, or indeed the laptop theft, both of which would satisfy our proposed test. Some of the normative power in the handgun scenario depends upon the fact that S's conduct is already illegal (and reprehensible). *But that feature can make no difference to aiding/abetting liability*. The only channel of complicity within which S's liability turns on the legality of S's own conduct is joint enterprise, to which we come in § 7.5. Under the core doctrines of liability for assistance and encouragement, it has, rightly, never been relevant whether S's conduct was independently illegal.

Change the guns, then, to baseball bats. (Presumably we don't want to shut down sports goods vendors.) Imagine once more that P tells S why he is buying the bat—'just in case'. Should it be count as aiding and abetting for S to sell P the bat?

We cannot truly say of this case that S *intends* to assist P's killing of V. S acts neither in order to assist P to kill, nor in the practical certainty that P will use the bat to kill. Neither is it a case of conditional intention to assist: it is P whose intention is conditional. Still, the example presents a special case. S knows that the bat will be used to kill *given* a certain contingency, because P has told her. Intuitively, this seems to make it a stronger case for criminalization than the computer sale or laptop theft examples. Even if we concede that, however, if is not at all clear what follows (apart from an argument for some more specific offence). The challenge for complicity law is to ensnare S without criminalizing the computer seller or the lazy laptop leaver; and without introducing a set of practically unworkable mens rea distinctions. For it is the computer seller, the lazy laptop leaver, and their kin about whom we should be concerned here. It is easy to invent examples wherein S's behaviour deserves serious condemnation. That misses the point. Aiding and abetting rules are open-ended, fall-back criminalization provisions. They mop up cases that have not been captured by more specific laws. As such, they address all the everyday things we do that have the potential to encourage or facilitate crime. It is undesirable that generic complicity laws should make ordinary people gamble with their criminal liability by forcing them to estimate whether there is an 'unreasonable' risk some miscreant will exploit what they do.

Admittedly, as Larry Alexander and Kimberly Ferzan have pointed out, adopting recklessness as a mens rea standard for aiding and abetting would, in principle, leave reasonable conduct by S outside the scope of the criminal law.[75] S would not be obliged to cease and desist from helping P *merely* because she realizes that P might commit a crime. Even so, however, a recklessness

[75] L Alexander and K Ferzan, *Reflections on Crime and Culpability* (CUP 2018) 21ff.

standard would significantly impinge upon the liberties of law-abiding persons to pursue their day-to-day activities. It would force them to become legal risk-takers whenever they foresee potential criminality: to second-guess the law's view about what level of risk is permissible. That legal risk is only compounded by the likelihood, should P actually offend with S's aid, that a jury would retrospectively find the risk to have been unreasonable. The potential chilling effects are palpable. Imposing general criminal liability for reckless aiding and abetting, by otherwise lawful conduct, promises to change the character of the world in which we live. It would incentivize us all to adopt an over-cautious, defensive approach to interactions with our fellow citizens.

7.4.2 Shopkeepers and the like?

This kind of concern is particularly evident in the context of regular commercial activities. Consider the facts in the well-known case of *National Coal Board v Gamble*:[76]

> S (the National Coal Board) sold P's employer a large quantity of coal. P, a lorry driver, was despatched to collect some of the coal. Once loaded, the lorry was weighed before leaving the colliery. S's employee, the weighbridge clerk, realized the load exceeded that permitted to be carried on the highway. He drew P's attention to the illegality. P said that he was prepared to take the risk of being caught, whereupon the clerk issued P with a weighbridge ticket. The weighbridge clerk's function in issuing the ticket to P was to record how much coal had been taken, in order that S could then charge the buyer for that amount of coal, and also to pass title in the coal to the buyer.

On these facts, the English Divisional Court ruled that S, through its employee, was an accessory to the offence committed by P. In handing over the ticket and passing title to the coal, S aided P by enabling the lorry to depart from the colliery with the coal (and thereby, as S knew, to commit an offence). The fact that the clerk was motivated only by considerations of accounting was irrelevant to S's liability.

Accordingly, liability for complicity is a real possibility for persons who are merely performing the routines of their jobs or trades. Perhaps, then, even a knowledge requirement is too Draconian? In his great work on *Criminal*

[76] [1959] 1 QB 11. See R A Duff, '"Can I Help You?" Accessorial Liability and the Intention to Assist' (1990) 10 LS 165; G Williams, 'Complicity, Purpose and the Draft Code' [1990] Crim LR 4.

Law: The General Part, Glanville Williams argued that liability should be exempted specifically for shopkeepers and sellers of ordinary commodities:[77]

> 'From the point of view of policy the question is one of some complexity. On the one side are the policy of repressing crime, and the difficulty of distinguishing between the merchant who knowingly assists a crime and the ordinary accessory before the fact. On the other side stand the undesirability of giving too great an extension to the criminal law, and the inconvenience to legitimate trade of requiring a merchant to concern himself with the affairs of his customers. . . . It is submitted that . . . the seller of an ordinary marketable commodity is not his buyer's keeper in criminal law unless he is specifically made so by statute. Any other rule would be too wide an extension of criminal responsibility.'

One worry about this device, which sculpts an actus-reus-based exception for nominated conduct, is that it leaves other valuable, ordinary activities unprotected. An ad hoc fix of this sort becomes less important when the *general* mens rea requirement of abetment is (at least) knowledge. Similarly, a helpful limitation would be to exclude all complicity liability for minor offences. Taken in combination, the latter two constraints offer considerable protection to potential accomplices.

Those points aside, the argument for a 'shopkeepers' exemption is a strong one, even for more serious offences. Williams highlights the inconvenience to shopkeepers if they are required to concern themselves with the affairs of their customers. A similar point may be made regarding ordinary citizens who return the belongings of others.[78] Persons engaging in ordinary activities should generally be able to perform those activities—to live their normal lives—without being harassed by the criminal law; especially if the harassment requires them to modify their own activities because of the plans and conduct of others, and not because of anything they have done themselves. Notice too

[77] *CLGP*, § 124. See also Alexander and Ferzan, *Reflections on Crime and Culpability* (n 75) 40–43; Hurd and Moore, 'Untying the Gordian Knot' (n 31).

[78] Hence one might contemplate a further exception, covering those who return property to its owner, provided that it is not S's purpose to assist the owner to offend and that the contemplated offence is not a serious one: see G Williams, 'Obedience to Law as a Crime' (1990) 53 MLR 445. Arguably, however, the criminal law should take priority over the civil law in this matter. (And it does, in as much as S is not required to return property to an owner if doing so would be a criminal offence: *Garrett v Arthur-Churchill (Glass) Ltd* [1970] 1 QB 92, 99.) Sometimes, where criminal and civil law overlap, the criminal law must perforce follow the civil law, e.g. where it is the civil law that defines the relevant harm. An example is the law of theft—where property rights, the interests being safeguarded by the criminal law, are a creature of civil law. But complicity is not like theft. When S hands P a weapon, P is aided, and the victim's rights are put at risk, equally *whoever* of them owns it.

that the putative duty not to help P arises out of P's intentions, and not from S's own conduct or plans. Thus, Williams objects, in the context of *National Coal Board v Gamble*, that[79]

> 'It seems a strong thing to hold that a man who is simply pursuing his ordinary and lawful vocation, and takes no special steps to assist illegalities, becomes involved as a third party to a crime committed by the customer merely because he realises that his customer will be enabled by what he himself does to commit a crime.'

One should certainly hesitate before allowing the criminal law to reach so far into the ordinary commercial and private activities of citizens. Indeed, this concern seems to offer the strongest ground in favour of the purposive standard found in many US jurisdictions: by narrowing the scope of criminalization, we allow more citizens to get on with their day-to-day lives.

None the less, while Williams's reasoning is powerful, it is not conclusive. These are not cases where S stands by passively and omits to prevent P's crime. S *actively and deliberately helps* P to commit that crime. The rights of victims not to be burgled, assaulted, and so on, mean that it is sometimes necessary to curtail the liberty of citizens to intervene and assist criminals, as well as the liberty of shopkeepers to sell goods to anyone at will. Those rights should prevail here. Moreover, the intrusive implications of this position for the lives of citizens are not as great as they may appear. S's duty is not to refuse aid to those suspected of having, or thought likely to have, a criminal purpose. On the view promoted here, the duty arises only if S knows or purposes that a crime will be committed. Hence the computer seller is not required to reassure herself about P's plans before she peddles her wares. She is simply not free to assist P deliberately when she knows what P plans to do. On balance, that is to say, criminalization of such cases is justified.

7.5 Joint criminal enterprises

An even more controversial ground of secondary liability in Anglo-American criminal law arises pursuant to the acting out of a conspiracy or, as it is variously known, a 'joint (criminal) enterprise' or 'common unlawful purpose'. Here, the actus reus of participation is not an act of assistance or encouragement by S

[79] *TBCL*, 342.

but, rather, participation within a criminal project in pursuance of which P's crime is committed. Joint enterprise is distinct from standard forms of complicity, both doctrinally and normatively. Again, it is necessary first to undertake a doctrinal sketch, focusing primarily on the traditional English form.

Joint enterprise has a distinctive doctrinal structure. Aiding and abetting doctrines involve just one offence: the offence that is directly aided or abetted by S and which ultimately is committed by P. By contrast, joint enterprise liability characteristically involves *two* offences: an offence (A) conspired at by S and P, and the further offence (B) then committed by P alone. Joint enterprise doctrine need have nothing exceptional to say about S's liability for crime A.[80] Its distinctive role concerns the extension of her liability to crime B, the *incident* of the joint enterprise.

The independent existence of joint enterprise liability is often formalized in statutes. New Zealand's complicity provision, for example, uses separate subsections of its Crimes Act to criminalize assistance or encouragement, on the one hand, and joint criminal enterprises on the other:[81]

> 66. Parties to offences
> (1) Every one is a party to and guilty of an offence who—
> (a) actually commits the offence; or
> (b) does or omits an act for the purpose of aiding any person to commit the offence; or
> (c) abets any person in the commission of the offence; or
> (d) incites, counsels, or procures any person to commit the offence.
> (2) Where 2 or more persons form a common intention to prosecute any unlawful purpose, and to assist each other therein, each of them is a party to every offence committed by any one of them in the prosecution of the common purpose if the commission of that offence was known to be a probable consequence of the prosecution of the common purpose.

Like the corresponding provision in Canada,[82] this entrenchment of two basic kinds of secondary liability is drawn directly from Fitzjames Stephen's *Digest of*

[80] Indeed, there need be no requirement that offence A is successfully perpetrated. This is not to deny that a joint enterprise to commit crime A may legitimately ground S's liability for A, should that crime be committed. (The case of a 'plain vanilla' joint enterprise: *Brown and Isaac* [2003] UKPC 10, [13].) However, such cases can typically also be captured via abetment.

[81] Crimes Act 1961 (NZ); also Crimes Act 1908 (NZ), s 90.

[82] Criminal Code 1985 (Canada), s 21(1)–(2); also Canadian Criminal Code, SC 1892, c 29, s 61.

the Criminal Law,[83] where liability for aiding and abetting is similarly distinguished from liability pursuant to a joint enterprise:[84]

> Article 38. Common Purpose.
> When several persons take part in the execution of a common criminal purpose, each is a principal in the second degree, in respect of every crime committed by any one of them in the execution of that purpose.
> If any of the offenders commits a crime foreign to the common criminal purpose, the others are neither principals in the second degree, nor accessories unless they actually instigate or assist in its commission.

While the *Digest* reflected nineteenth-century (and even earlier[85]) common law,[86] joint enterprise doctrine has been a matter of ongoing controversy in uncodified jurisdictions. In *Pinkerton v United States*,[87] the US Supreme Court ruled that partners to a conspiracy are liable as parties to all crimes committed in furtherance of the conspiracy. Similarly, in Australia, the High Court has endorsed joint enterprise as a distinct ground of participatory liability.[88] On the other hand, it was summarily abolished in 2016 by the UK Supreme Court.[89]

7.5.1 Distinct actus reus and mens rea requirements

The US law as stated in *Pinkerton* has rightly been criticized.[90] But it does not follow that we should join with the English Supreme Court and cast out the baby with the bathwater. A properly framed doctrine of joint enterprise liability is a form of participatory liability that is both conceptually distinct and normatively defensible.

Joint enterprise liability cannot be reduced to assistance or encouragement because of its two-crime aspect. For S to be a standard-form accessory to crime

[83] Macmillan 1877. Articles 37 and 39 govern liability for assistance and encouragement.

[84] A parallel separation can be found in ss 34 (common intention) and 107 (abetment) of the Indian Penal Code 1860. Under s 34, participants are convicted, as if principals, of the substantive offence directly; whereas those convicted of ordinary complicity under s 107 are convicted of abetting the substantive offence.

[85] Amongst other sources, see Fitzherbert, *Corone* (1329) f. 256b, pl. 314 (3 Edw 3); Hale 1 PC 463.

[86] See, e.g., *Macklin* (1838) 2 Lew CC 225, 226; 168 ER 1136, 1136 (Alderson B): 'if several persons act together in pursuance of a common intent, every act done in furtherance of such intent by each of them is, in law, done by all.'

[87] 328 US 640, 646–48 (1946); see also *Anderson v Superior Court* P 2d 317 (1947).

[88] *Clayton* [2006] HCA 58; *Miller* [2016] HCA 30. So too has the Court of Final Appeal in Hong Kong: *Chan Kam Shing* [2016] HKCFA 87.

[89] *Jogee* [2016] UKSC 8; *Ruddock* [2016] UKPC 7. And in Singapore: *Daniel Vijay* [2010] SGCA 33.

[90] See, e.g., Moore, *Causation and Responsibility*, 318–19: below, § 7.5.2.

B, she would have actually to aid or abet crime *B* directly (not crime A). Joint enterprise, however, does not require this. Consider the following example:

> P and S agree to commit a burglary. Together they break into V's home. In the course of the burglary, P is challenged by V whom he attacks and injures. S does not assist in the assault, and had specifically discouraged the use of violence at all stages during the planning and execution of the burglary. However, S knew of P's propensity for violence, and realized that P might well assault the occupier of the house were they to be confronted.

On joint enterprise principles, S can be guilty, with P, of assault occasioning actual bodily harm. But she neither aided nor abetted that assault.[91] Nor can we say that S is party to any conspiracy, explicit or tacit, to commit crime B.[92] The agreement is to commit crime A. Yet joint enterprise doctrines are capable of supporting liability for the further crime B. What counts, it will be argued below, is whether the possibility of crime B is *foreseen*. S's liability for crime B rests on the combination of her participation in pursuing the joint criminal enterprise (to commit crime A) and her foresight that the second crime may be perpetrated as an incident of the enterprise. Indeed, the very distinctiveness of joint enterprise doctrine is that it extends liability to certain crimes that occur beyond, albeit pursuant to, the common purpose.

There is a second difficulty about collapsing joint enterprises into mere aiding/abetting. By doing so, we would obviate—and so lose sight of—two key features of the more complex form of liability. The first of those features is that the conspiracy being pursued (to commit crime A) is to do something *unlawful*.[93] It is this element of unlawful concert, moreover, that adds a crucial normative ingredient warranting the extension of liability to crime B even though S merely foresaw that further crime as possible.

[91] Of course, courts might invoke a legal fiction, i.e. that forming a common purpose to commit crime A *ipso facto* encourages crime B. But such a fiction is not merely contradicted by the facts of the example; it is an unhelpful distortion, one that merely obscures the doctrinal and normative differences between joint enterprise liability and aiding and abetting.

[92] This point is seen in *Powell; English* [1999] 1 AC 1, 11 (Lord Mustill), 20 (Lord Hutton).

[93] See, e.g., Foster, *Crown Law* (1762) Discourse III, Chap. 1 § 9, p. 354: 'With regard to assemblies of this kind where the whole party may be involved in the guilt of one or more, I have already supposed that such assemblies were formed for carrying some common purpose *unlawful in itself* into execution. For if the original intention was lawful and prosecuted by lawful means and opposition is made by others, and one of the opposing party is killed in the struggle; in that case the person actually killing may be guilty of murder or manslaughter as circumstances may vary with the case. But the persons engaged with him will not be involved in his guilt, *unless they actually aided or abetted him in the fact*. For they assembled for another purpose, *which was lawful*, and consequently the guilt of the person actually killing cannot by any fiction of law be carried against them beyond their original intention.' (Emphasis in original.)

In ordinary complicity, we saw in § 7.4 that S's otherwise lawful behaviour does not become a wrong unless it is done with intent or knowledge, such that her behaviour constitutes a deliberate act that directly associates S with P's crime. The wrong resides partly in S's mens rea. By contrast, in joint enterprise cases, the wrong lies in the mutual embarkation on a crime. We do not need further knowledge requirements in order to establish the impropriety of S's conduct: her conduct is already a wrong.

Through entering into a joint enterprise, S becomes, by her deliberate choice, a participant in a group action to commit a crime.[94] Moreover, her new status has moral significance: she associates herself with the conduct of the other members of the group in a way that the mere aider or abettor, who remains an independent character throughout the episode, does not.[95] Whereas aiding and abetting doctrines are grounded in S's act of direct participation in another's crime, joint enterprise is grounded in *affiliation*. S voluntarily subscribes to a cooperative endeavour, one that is identified by its shared criminal purpose. As such, joint enterprise doctrines impose a form of collective responsibility, predicated on membership of the unlawful concert.

By her engagement in a joint enterprise, S signs up to its goal. In so doing, and subject to certain conditions (below), she incurs ascriptive responsibility for the wrongs perpetrated in realizing that goal, even though they be done by someone else. Her joining with P in the pursuance of a common purpose means that she is no longer fully in command of *how* the purpose is achieved. Given that P is an autonomous agent, S cannot control the precise manner in which P acts. Yet her commitment to the common purpose implies an acceptance of the foreseen choices and actions that are taken by P in the pursuance of that purpose.

[94] In earlier writing, I stated that S 'changes her normative position' by signing up to joint criminal enterprise. A number of critics misinterpreted that description as an argument. Not so: it was merely a characterization of the normative effects of joining in a criminal enterprise, not an explanation of why those effects arose.

[95] While the point is not central here (since I am concerned primarily with responsibility), there is much to be said for the view that sharing their intentions also makes S and P more culpable: O Blomberg and F Hindriks, 'Collective Responsibility and Acting Together' in S Bazargan-Forward and D Tollefsen (eds), *The Routledge Handbook of Collective Responsibility* (Routledge 2020). The need for a *common*—shared—purpose was emphasized forcefully by the High Court of Australia in *Miller* [2016] HCA 30, [45]. Neglect of this requirement by the English courts had become a real problem by the time of *Jogee* [2016] UKSC 8; *Ruddock* [2016] UKPC 7, in which the Supreme Court abolished the law of joint enterprise. In practice, trial courts had ceased to take this requirement seriously, becoming far too willing to infer a joint enterprise from the mere fact of D's non-accidental presence.

7.5.2 Presence and the mutation problem

Worries lurk, though, about the sheer breadth of any conspiracy-based liability resembling that seen in *Pinkerton*. The case is plausibly castigated by Moore as a mere imposition of vicarious liability.[96] Broadly speaking, *Pinkerton* holds S accountable for any crime committed by a fellow conspirator if that crime lay within the explicit or tacit scope of the conspiracy, was perpetrated in furtherance of the conspiracy, and was a reasonably foreseeable incident thereof. Does the argument here support such a wide doctrine? No. S should not be treated as accepting the risk of wrongs by P that she does not foresee. (We should also embrace the constraint proposed in § 7.4.2, precluding complicity in summary offences.) In addition, S's responsibility for ancillary offences should be limited in further ways that are compatible with *Pinkerton*. S cannot be said to accept risks that are extrinsic to or which depart substantially from their shared enterprise. Imagine that S and P venture out to rob a grocery shop. S knows that P is carrying a gun and might use it to shoot the shopkeeper. During the robbery, V, an old enemy of P's, enters the shop to buy some groceries. P espies V, immediately turns around, and shoots V dead. S is no party to the murder.[97]

Suppose we accept these constraints. The *Pinkerton* doctrine remains troubling, in as much as joining a criminal conspiracy seems to beget open-ended liability—even while S is in prison.[98] Consider, then, a little-remarked feature of the traditional English doctrine. At common law, liability is generally predicated upon the idea of a conspiracy jointly *executed*: that is, where the parties are present and pursuing its commission together.[99] If one conspirator has withdrawn,[100] or been arrested, and is no longer part of the group action, common purpose liability cannot, *and should not*, be extended.

Why not? Recall that joint enterprise liability comes into its own when addressed to ancillary offences, offences that are not themselves conspired at nor directly aided/abetted by S. Such offences emerge not from the *formation* of the shared criminal purpose but evolve dynamically from its pursuance. Aiding and abetting doctrines are poorly suited to evolving scenarios of this kind because those doctrines are fundamentally static. In accordance with standard

[96] Moore, *Causation and Responsibility*, 318–19. As we noted in § 5.3.5, vicarious liability contravenes the principle of personal control; neither does it meet the criteria of ascriptive responsibility articulated in this chapter.

[97] A similar restriction applies at common law to aiding and abetting: *Calhaem* [1985] QB 808, 813.

[98] A feature of *Pinkerton* itself.

[99] Cp. Article 38 of Stephen's draft code: above, § 7.5.

[100] See, e.g., *Hyde* (1672) 1 Hale PC 537; Foster, *Crown Law* 354; *Edmeades* (1828) 3 C & P 390, 392, 172 ER 469, 470.

concurrence principles, they are tied to a particular act of assistance or encouragement, done at a moment in time when S also has the requisite intention to aid/abet the type of offence that P ultimately commits. *Pinkerton* shares something of this static character. It focuses on the formation of a conspiracy as the gateway to S's liability. Yet *Pinkerton* keeps the gateway ajar, on an open-ended basis, as the conspiracy evolves. By contrast, provided S is present, the common-law doctrine of joint enterprise can regulate dynamic scenarios with ongoing reference to S's conduct. As a continuing participant in the execution of their shared purpose, moreover, S retains a measure of control over her liability for what ensues: not only in terms of any potential she has to affect P's conduct but, even more importantly, in her ability to withdraw from the enterprise unfolding before her.[101]

S's presence during the execution of the joint enterprise—including its foreseen attendant risks—can therefore be part of what makes that enterprise a package deal. Just as dynamic risks attend the pursuit of the common purpose, an assumption of those risks flows from S's subscription to, and pursuance of, that purpose. Moreover, those risks are intrinsic in character.[102] Group criminal action tends to encourage and escalate criminality.[103] It presents a threat to public safety that ordinary criminal prohibitions, addressed to individual actors, do not entirely address. As such, joint enterprise doctrine adds a valuable mechanism to the criminal law's regulatory toolbox. It allows the law to respond in more nuanced fashion to fast-moving events, provided they occur in pursuance and within the foreseen scope of a criminal enterprise.

The extension of responsibility to S is supported by evidential rationales. In cases of concerted action, it may be difficult to distinguish between the contributions made by individual actors present, or to establish precisely what part was taken by each member of the combination.[104] But even where the individual contributions of S and P (and any other members) can be identified,

[101] Notice that the normative significance of ongoing presence also explains why the requirements for withdrawal from a joint enterprise differ from those in aiding and abetting: S needs merely to disengage unequivocally from the shared purpose, whereas aid or encouragement must in principle be countermanded: *Simester and Sullivan*, § 7.7.6(vi); cp. the Canadian case of *Whitehouse* [1941] 1 DLR 683, 685.

[102] The idea of intrinsic risk is explored in § 13.5–13.5.1.

[103] See, e.g., P Cromwell, 'Group Effects on Decision-Making by Burglars' (1991) 69 Psychological Reports 579; N K Katyal, 'Conspiracy Theory' (2003) 112 Yale LJ 1307, 1315ff. cp. *Powell; English* [1999] AC 1, 14 (Lord Steyn): 'Experience has shown that joint criminal enterprises only too readily escalate into the commission of greater offences.'

[104] Cp. the special exception to the rule against hearsay for statements made in furtherance of a conspiracy, explicitly preserved by s 118 of the Criminal Justice Act 2003 (UK). With that said, Jeremy Horder has pointed out a disadvantage of having two categories of complicity: that it becomes essential to prove how S became involved in P's crime (i.e., by help/encouragement or by conspiracy). In a trial with multiple defendants, this might generate practical difficulties. For discussion, see J Horder, *Ashworth's Principles of Criminal Law* (9th edn, OUP 2019) ch 12.

there is reason to treat collective wrongdoing of this kind as a special case.[105] Indeed, the threat is not just of an immediately physical nature. A group acting together is a form of society, and a group constituted by a joint unlawful enterprise is a form of society that has set itself against the law and order of society at large.[106] Individuals offending alone do not do this. Concerted wrongdoing thus imports additional and special reasons why the law must intervene.

Neither can S complain that she had an inadequate or unduly limited opportunity to avoid criminal liability. Unlike aiding and abetting, there is no need for more stringent mens rea requirements to negotiate the boundaries of criminalization, since S has a straightforward means of remaining within the law without having to sacrifice valuable activities. She need not join in a criminal enterprise. By offering allegiance to the enterprise, S implicitly endorses its furtherance. It is appropriate, where she does so, to hold her accountable for the crimes that grow out of that wrong, whether or not they are individually aided or abetted.

7.6 Conclusion

Complicity liability is notoriously difficult, both doctrinally and conceptually, in part because its underlying principles are themselves in tension. The pull of judgements about culpability must be reconciled with the demands of criminalization, and with the need for complicity rules to be stated in generalized terms. Frequently, the approach of the courts has been to focus on the defendant's culpability; hence the English Court of Appeal's drift towards recklessness as sufficient mens rea for aiding and abetting. *Ex post*, when the deed is done, this perspective may well be tempting. But it is simplistic. Rather like the law of omissions, culpability is not enough. The better starting point is to distinguish matters of culpability from those of ascriptive responsibility, and to focus on the latter.

Once this is done, it becomes easier to see the centrality of mens rea in ascribing responsibility for another's acts. Quite apart from helping to show culpability, mens rea requirements can also manage the constraints of

105 A striking formalization of one such context is s 396 of the Indian Penal Code 1860, governing murders committed during a dacoity (i.e., a violent robbery perpetrated by an armed gang): 'If any one of five or more persons, who are conjointly committing dacoity, commits murder in so committing dacoity, every one of those persons shall be punished with death ....'

106 Numerous jurisdictions enact offences of membership of a criminal group: M Levi and A Smith, *A Comparative Analysis of Organised Crime Conspiracy Legislation and Practice and their Relevance to England and Wales* (Home Office Online Report 17/02, 2002).

criminalization, helping to balance the *ex ante* liberties of the accessory against the rights and interests of others, and ensuring those who do otherwise innocent actions have sufficient notice that their conduct is potentially criminal. Perhaps more importantly, mens rea can play a key role in establishing that S's actions, otherwise quotidian and unobjectionable, constitute a wrong. On this count, however, aiding and abetting splits from joint enterprise. By forming a joint criminal enterprise, the accessory perpetrates a discrete and independent wrong. What does the normative work, justifying an extension of responsibility for P's crime, is the collusion in pursuing a crime.

8
Moral Responsibility and Voluntariness

Let us return, now and in chapter 9, to matters of moral responsibility. The present chapter has two main aims. It begins by unpacking some of the ways in which moral responsibility for events can be negated through a lack of voluntariness.[1] Later, in § 8.4, we look at how such negations are best accommodated within the criminal law.

8.1 The idea of involuntary behaviour

Chapter 4 claimed that norms of moral responsibility are not negotiable in the same way as they are for ascriptive responsibility. The boundaries of causation, omissions, and complicity liability are a matter of contextual argument, often involving trade-offs with other ascriptive rules and with more specific acts of criminalization. Moral responsibility is in that sense more basic. Whereas ascriptive responsibility is sensitive to a variety of ethical and political considerations, moral responsibility involves a more restricted inquiry into the relationship between agents and events. We might agree that it is generally wrong for one person to apply force to another without justification, and that such events are appropriate matters for criminalization. Suppose, then, that David is standing between Vicky and Tanya. Suddenly, Tanya grasps David's arm and forces it into Vicky's midriff. Tanya is more powerful than David, who has no chance to resist her. From an ascriptive-responsibility perspective, David is *involved* in this event. Should Vicky's injuries be life-threatening, it might be legitimate for the state to require David to help her, for example by calling an ambulance.[2] Yet in the initial scenario at least, David commits no offence because his movements are *involuntary*.[3] He lacks moral responsibility for the

[1] To recall: in this book, D's moral responsibility for an event refers to D's *eligibility* for praising/blaming evaluations in respect of that event. See § 4.1.

[2] Compare *Miller* [1983] 2 AC 161 (HL): see §§ 5.3.1, 17.6.2.

[3] *Farduto* (1912) 10 DLR 669, 673; compare *O'Sullivan v Fisher* [1954] SASR 33, 39–40; *Purdie v Maxwell* [1960] NZLR 599, 606.

Fundamentals of Criminal Law. A P Simester, Oxford University Press (2021). © A P Simester.
DOI: 10.1093/oso/9780198853145.003.0008

actus reus. Indeed, it is Tanya who assaults Vicky, using David's arm, although that distinction is not central from David's perspective.

In the criminal law, these types of case arise in a wide variety of ways. D's arm may strike V as the result of a reflex movement or a muscular spasm.[4] Perhaps a driver fails to stop at a pedestrian crossing because he was stunned by a blow to the head.[5] A sleepwalking woman who gets out of bed and walks to the kitchen 'to peel potatoes', whence she returns with a knife and stabs her sleeping husband, is to be acquitted of unlawful wounding.[6] And so on. Given the range of scenarios, it seems natural to ask whether they share any unifying feature that exempts the individuals involved from moral assessment. Sleepwalking is an instructive case, because the actor's behaviour may well be purposive,[7] and exhibit many outward signs of intentionality. Glanville Williams makes this point vividly:[8]

> 'The sleep-walker does not always proceed as the cartoonists imagine him, with eyes tightly closed and arms outstretched. His eyes may be open and he may appear to be in perfect control. He will open a door and turn a corner, walk downstairs, open a drawer, take out a carving-knife, and return to the bedroom where his wife is asleep. But after waking up he will not remember his deed (except sometimes as a dream). Although his acts have a certain purpose (indeed, he may have an understandable reason for killing his wife), it is the purpose of a dream-state. He is not acting with his normal conscious mind.'

When Lady MacBeth is observed 'washing' her hands at night,[9] her movements are neither random nor uncontrolled. They exude a semblance of purpose; they are not mere reflex movements. But the control that Lady MacBeth has over them is not a conscious one. (Indeed, she is incapable of acting intentionally at all.) In that respect, her movements are not voluntary. She is like David.

Typically, in cases such as these, acquittals need not be predicated on involuntariness. Suppose that Patricia brings about Quentin's death while suffering

[4] *Bratty v A-G for Northern Ireland* [1963] AC 386, 409.

[5] *Hill v Baxter* [1958] 1 QB 277, 282–83, 286; *Burns v Bidder* [1966] 3 All ER 29, 36; *Kay v Butterworth* (1945) 61 TLR 452, 453; *McCone v Police* [1971] NZLR 105, 109.

[6] *Hughes*, reported in *The Times*, 3 May 1978, p. 5. See too *Bratty* [1963] AC 403, 409; *Carter* [1959] VR 105; *Fain v Commonwealth* 39 Am Rep 213 (1879).

[7] Compare *Charlson* [1955] 1 All ER 859.

[8] *TBCL*, 665.

[9] Shakespeare, *MacBeth*, act 5, scene I. See B A O Williams, 'Voluntary Acts and Responsible Agents' (1990) 10 OJLS 1; B A O Williams, 'The Actus Reus of Dr Caligari' (1994) 142 U Pennsylvania LR 1661, 1667ff.

an epileptic seizure, during which her movements cause a heavy object to fall and crush Quentin. Patricia's behaviour is involuntary: she cannot legitimately be convicted of murder. Yet it is unnecessary to base the verdict on that ground. Crimes such as murder require proof of some form of mens rea on the part of the defendant. In most jurisdictions, murder cannot be committed unless the defendant intends (at least) significant injuries to the victim. Thus, even though Patricia's behaviour may have caused death, she lacks the mental element required to be guilty of murder. As criminal lawyers would say, she lacks mens rea.

Involuntariness, however, is not merely a denial of intention, or of other forms of mens rea; it is not specifically a denial of fault. Patricia does not kill Quentin merely *by accident*.[10] Her denial is much more profound. It is a denial that the behaviour which caused Quentin's death belongs to Patricia as a moral agent. Strictly speaking, mens rea questions do not arise.[11] Indeed, sometimes a form of mens rea may be present. Most examples of involuntary behaviour involve an impaired consciousness, but that feature is not indispensable. In the Tanya–David–Vicky example, David may well be aware of events, even welcome them. While it is plausible that all behaviour occurring while unconscious is involuntary, the converse does not hold. It is not awareness per se that marks out voluntary behaviour.

So what is it that makes behaviour (in)voluntary?

8.1.1 Between involuntariness and moral responsibility

When framed in negative terms, the claim that D lacks moral responsibility for involuntary behaviour is relatively uncontroversial.[12] Most criminal theorists endorse an involuntariness constraint in some form. But analysing that constraint is not straightforward. It is revealing, I think, that the air of consensus fades when we try to restate our claim in positive terms. Recalling the discussion in § 4.1, we might say something like the following:

(i) It is a condition of D's being morally responsible for a piece of her behaviour that D's behaviour is *voluntary*, in the sense that it occurs under D's deliberative control.

[10] i.e. non-negligently. 'Accident' is sometimes formalized as a defence: see, e.g., s 80 of the Indian Penal Code 1860 (placing the burden of proof upon the defendant).

[11] One doctrinal payoff of this is that involuntariness can defeat liability for strict liability offences.

[12] Antecedent fault cases apart: below, § 8.5.1.

This formulation is more obviously contentious. There is much less agreement about voluntariness than about involuntariness; and differences too about what it means to be under D's deliberative control.[13]

Up to a point, disagreement is unproblematic, provided we get clear on the terminology. We can all accept that moral responsibility rests on multiple conditions. Indeed, we acknowledged one such condition in § 4.1. Sometimes, D may have the capacities of an agent with respect to his behaviour, and may indeed exercise those capacities by deliberately acting as he does. Yet he may not have the capacities of a *moral* agent: a very young child, for example, may not be someone who responds to moral reasons.[14] Moral responsibility for behaviour requires both voluntariness and what we might call 'moral personhood'.

Many writers, however, go further than that. Focusing, as does this chapter, on the voluntariness requirement, they endorse one or both of the following conditions:

(ii) It is a condition of D's being morally responsible for a piece of her behaviour that D's behaviour is voluntary in the sense of being *an exercise of* D's deliberative control—in particular, of being intentional under at least one description; or

(iii) It is a condition of D's being morally responsible for a piece of her behaviour that D's behaviour constitutes an action rather than an event (i.e., the behaviour occurs as an instance of D's agency).

Consider what David, Lady MacBeth, and Patricia have in common. One shared feature is that they are unable deliberatively to control their behaviour and to prevent that behaviour from occurring. In this sense, the behaviour of each is involuntary. They all fail condition (i). But our three protagonists also fail conditions (ii) and (iii). Their behaviour is neither intentional under any description nor an instance of action. We should ask, then, which of these conditions, if any, matter to moral responsibility.

8.2 Competing conceptions of voluntariness

In order to do so, it is helpful to distinguish two ways of thinking about voluntariness. Some writers see voluntariness as a counterpart to involuntariness,

[13] For a note on ambiguity in the language of 'control', see § 4.3.1.

[14] A matter, in law, for the irresponsibility defences. See § 17.5.

envisaging, as Anthony Kenny puts it, behaviour 'done in the presence of open alternatives'.[15] Others, such as Michael Moore, explain voluntary behaviour in terms of 'volitional' action—behaviour that is intentional under some description; behaviour, one might say, done willingly.[16] But these are not the same phenomena, and we need to avoid their assimilation.

8.2.1 The voluntary as non-involuntary

To mark the distinction, let us characterize behaviour as 'non-involuntary' when it is voluntary in the sense that alternative forms of behaviour are available. This terminology makes it easier to avoid the distracting ambiguity of something's being 'voluntary'. At the same time, it helps to focus our attention on what is missing when D's behaviour is *involuntary*: an approach that lends itself naturally to thinking about moral responsibility in terms of an agent's capacities.

A number of writers conceive of voluntariness in these negative terms, although not always consistently. Glanville Williams, for example, seemingly equates 'voluntary' with 'volitional' when he suggests that behaviour is voluntary if it is 'willed'; yet he considers that a bodily movement is willed, 'generally speaking, when the person in question could have refrained from it if he had so willed; that is, he could have acted otherwise or kept still.'[17] Ultimately, therefore, Williams allows that a bodily movement can be (non-in)voluntary, and may satisfy an actus reus requirement, without being actively willed. Williams's test is capacity-based.[18]

Others analyse involuntariness in terms of the relationship, or lack thereof, between D's behaviour and her practical reasoning. H L A Hart, for example, once proposed that movements are involuntary when they are 'not appropriate,

[15] A J P Kenny, *Will, Freedom and Power* (Basil Blackwell 1975) 52.

[16] Moore, *Act and Crime*, 44–45. Compare Kenny, *Will, Freedom and Power*, 52 ('done because the agent wants to do it').

[17] *TBCL*, 148. Compare P J Fitzgerald, 'Voluntary and Involuntary Acts' in A G Guest (ed), *Oxford Essays in Jurisprudence* (Clarendon 1961) 1, 5: involuntary 'acts' comprise 'the bodily movements outside his control such as reflex actions, heart beats, etc.'

[18] J L Mackie contemplates a similar approach when he identifies a 'weaker' sense of voluntariness, applying to behaviour that is counterfactually 'caused by the lack of any sufficiently strong desire': J L Mackie, 'The Grounds of Responsibility' in P M S Hacker and J Raz (eds), *Law, Morality and Society: Essays in Honour of H.L.A. Hart* (OUP 1977) 175, 180. Mackie evidently has in mind that behaviour is voluntary (in his weaker sense) when, had the agent so desired, she would not have behaved as she did; the causal significance of her lack of desire thus requires that the agent *could* have avoided the behaviour had she so wanted. This suggests, in turn, that what is crucial is the agent's capacity to act in accord with those (absent) desires.

i.e. required for any action (in the ordinary sense of action) which the agent believed himself to be doing.'[19] Hart later came to accept that one might act involuntarily yet advertently, and modified his account to suggest that movements are involuntary when they 'occurred though the agent had no reason for moving his body in that way.'[20] But this too is problematic. A movement can be involuntary even when someone has a reason for making it. Davidson's notorious climber supplies an example:[21]

> 'A climber might want to rid himself of the weight and danger of holding another man on a rope, and he might know that by loosening his hold on the rope he could rid himself of the weight and danger. This belief and want might so unnerve him as to cause him to loosen his hold, and yet it might be the case that he never *chose* to loosen his hold, nor did he do it intentionally.'

Conversely, if Jill scratches her nose inadvertently while preoccupied, and without having any reason so to do, her movement is not involuntary. Indeed, this is so *whether or not* Jill has a reason to scratch her nose (perhaps doing so will remind her friend of something important). What renders a person's movement involuntary is not the existence of reasons for or against the movement. Rather, it turns upon there being a certain kind of disconnect between any such reasons and the movement itself. Hart saw this also:[22]

> 'What is missing in these cases appears to most people as a vital link between mind and body; and both the ordinary man and the lawyer might well insist on this by saying that in these cases there is not "really" a human action at all and certainly nothing for which anyone should be made criminally responsible however 'strict' legal responsibility may be.'

Failures of capacity represent one way of analysing that disconnect. When the doctor tests Jeremy's reflexes by tapping him on the knee, the swinging of Jeremy's leg does not belong to him as a moral agent. It is merely an event in the history of his body, rather like the lurching of passengers standing in a crowded bus. So it is with Patricia's epileptic seizure in § 8.1. Patricia's behaviour is part

[19] *Punishment and Responsibility*, 105.
[20] Ibid, 256.
[21] Davidson, *EAE*, 79. Davidson's example is offered by him as one in which the climber's behaviour is an event rather than an action; that distinction is explored in chapter 9.
[22] *Punishment and Responsibility*, 107.

of her bodily history, but is not traceable to her as a reasoning being, let alone as a moral agent. The same holds for David from § 8.1, and for Lady MacBeth.

From the perspective of moral responsibility, the missing link in these last cases is one of deliberative incapacity. Patricia's behaviour is not responsive to *her*, qua reasoning agent, in the sense that she is incapable avoiding or restraining that behaviour. And this is a necessary feature of *involuntary* behaviour more generally: that D lacks the deliberative capacity to behave differently. Conversely, behaviour is *non-involuntary* when she has that capacity. In this respect, Jill's case differs from Patricia's. Jill's nose-scratching is non-involuntary.

8.2.2 The voluntary as volitional

Another feature of Patricia's case, though, is the absence of any choice by her to behave as she does. Regardless whether she has reasons for or against her behaviour, her behaviour is not motivated by reasons. Acknowledging this, many writers characterize behaviour as voluntary when it is willed or 'volitional'. *Smith and Hogan*, for instance, contemplates a scenario where 'the movement of D's limbs was involuntary in that it did not flow from an exercise by D of his will. The event happened either against, or at least without, his will.'[23] On this approach, an instance of behaviour is volitional *when it is intentional under at least one description*; that is, when it constitutes at least one intentional action.[24] Derivatively, an action can be said to be volitional when constituted by an instance of volitional behaviour, although of course the action need be neither intended nor adverted to (under that description) by the agent. On this conception, Jill is like Patricia. Neither acts volitionally.

As an alternative understanding of voluntariness, that seems fair enough. As well as being etymologically sound,[25] volitional behaviour marks out a familiar category in the philosophy of action. Neither does it seem unnatural to describe an action as 'involuntary' in order to signal that it is in some way

[23] D Ormerod and K Laird, *Smith and Hogan's Criminal Law* (14th edn, OUP 2015) 61.

[24] Brian O'Shaughnessy gives an alternative account of voluntary as volitional (he treats the terms as interchangeable), when he characterizes (B O'Shaughnessy, *The Will: A Dual Aspect Theory*, vol II (CUP 1980) 286) 'the trait of voluntariness [as] nothing but the trait of being . . . a "willing".' At first sight, his account looks somewhat akin to that given here, for he argues also that, 'While no trigger event is a common and peculiar cause predecessor of willings, all willings are the effect and expression of an occurrent act-desire.' But O'Shaughnessy rejects this equation, for (at 248; see also at 244) he includes within the ambit of 'voluntary' both sub-intentional deeds *and* such instances as '[i]dle unnoticed tongue moving during sleep'—willed, it seems, by the unconscious. O'Shaughnessy is concerned here less with voluntariness as an indicator of moral responsibility than with relating conduct to the will. Certainly, such behaviour is not under one's deliberative control.

[25] Compare the latin *volo* (I wish; I want; I am willing).

non-volitional. The common-law category of 'involuntary manslaughter', for example, refers to manslaughter by conduct done without intent to kill or cause serious injury. For clarity, however, I eschew such usages of 'involuntary' here. Indeed, it seems to me that a preferable opposite to 'volitional' might be 'non-voluntary'.[26]

Be that as it may, the important thing is to see that 'volitional' and 'non-involuntary' are not coextensive. As will be explained below, one way to help establish D's moral responsibility is by showing that her behaviour is non-involuntary. By contrast, being volitional is not a criterion of moral responsibility at all.

8.3 A disjunctive account of the voluntary$_{(L)}$[27]

Obviously, the non-involuntary and the volitional overlap. Indeed, it may seem natural to think of the volitional as a subset of the non-involuntary. As they are defined in § 8.2, however, neither is a subset of the other, Consider the following, 'Frankfurt-type' example:[28]

> While talking to a friend, George suddenly realizes his hand has strayed too close to the stove and jerks it away. Had he not done so, the friend—who is not only stronger than George but paying more attention—would have moved George's hand forcibly in precisely the same manner.

George's case illustrates the familiar truth that one can sometimes act volitionally even in the absence of behavioural alternatives. His behaviour is volitional without being non-involuntary. Moreover, it seems clear that this is also a case of moral responsibility, in as much as George is not exempt from evaluations

[26] Cp. Mackie, 'The Grounds of Responsibility' (n 18) 179.

[27] Where necessary, to evade the ambiguities identified in § 8.2, I use 'voluntary$_{(L)}$' to designate behaviour satisfying the law's voluntariness requirement.

[28] Frankfurt, *Importance*, 1ff; cp. J M Fischer, 'Frankfurt-Style Compatibilism' in S Buss and L Overton (eds), *Contours of Agency: Essays on Themes from Harry Frankfurt* (MIT Press 2002) 1, 3. My example is not paradigmatic. George lacks the freedom to *do* otherwise, whereas classic Frankfurtian scenarios deprive the agent of the freedom to *choose* (and by implication do) otherwise. George is in some ways closer to John Locke's example of the man who willingly stays in a locked room; albeit Locke's example involves an omission, which, as will be seen, affects the analysis. (See J Locke, *An Essay Concerning Human Understanding* (Nidditch edn, OUP 1975) Book II, ch xxi, § 10: p 238.) What all these variations share, however, is the suggestion that one can be morally responsible for φing without being free to do otherwise. (To the extent they are acknowledged at all in the criminal law, cases where D lacks responsibility for the choices she makes are typically dealt with via irresponsibility defences and hybrid excuses, rather than under the voluntariness requirement. See §§ 17.5, 19.1.)

of praise or blame for his behaviour. Recall that (in § 8.2.1) we said of Patricia's epileptic seizure that her behaviour is not responsive to *her*, qua reasoning agent, in the sense that she is incapable avoiding or restraining that behaviour. George's behaviour, by contrast, *is* responsive to his reasoning agency—even though he cannot avoid its occurrence.

Cases like George's are admittedly marginal. For the purposes of criminal law, they can readily be accommodated. We should allow that D's conduct satisfies the voluntariness requirement whenever it is intentional under at least one description, as well as whenever D is capable of avoiding or restraining that conduct. None the less, George's case drives an in-principle wedge between voluntariness and the presence of alternatives, and we should not lose sight of the underlying differences between our two conceptions of the voluntary. A mere doctrinal move cannot elide the distinctive feature of George's behaviour that takes it outside a basic, capacity-based account of the non-involuntary.

What *really* matters, though, is that the wedge is bigger than it looks. It is not volition that makes cases like George's special, and which brings his behaviour within the sphere of moral responsibility. Rather, I will suggest in chapter 9 that what counts is that George's conduct *is an instance of his agency*. It involves behaviour that is a form of action rather than event. Suppose the following variation:

> Georgina's case is just like that of George, except that while concentrating on the discussion with her friend, Georgina *absently* moves her hand away from the stove. Georgina is unaware of the movement.

Ex hypothesi, Georgina's conduct is not volitional. Yet it too involves an exercise of (non-volitional) agency. To my mind, Georgina is not relevantly different from Jill the inadvertent nose-scratcher in § 8.2.1. She is morally responsible for her behaviour, notwithstanding that she lacks the capacity to avoid it (because her friend would have moved her arm in exactly the same way). Again, for legal purposes, we should classify Georgina's behaviour as voluntary. The example reveals, however, that the voluntariness requirement contains a more profound disjunction:

> D's behaviour is *voluntary*$_{(L)}$—that is, it satisfies the law's voluntariness requirement—if either that behaviour is non-involuntary (in the sense that D has the deliberative capacity not to behave as she does) *or* that behaviour is an instance of her agency (in the sense explored in chapter 9).[29]

[29] In turn, we can say that D's behaviour is *involuntary* when it is not voluntary$_{(L)}$.

Being $\text{voluntary}_{(L)}$ is a condition of moral responsibility. Intuitively, one might surmise that involuntary behaviour cannot be action, and that seems right. Conversely, all volitional conduct is action. But as chapter 9 will suggest, there is also a category of 'non-volitional action' for which D can be morally responsible.

Perhaps the main payoff of the analysis here is that it reduces some of the pressure created by borderline cases. A simple, one-dimensional test in terms of non-involuntariness could only accommodate Georgina (or George) by appeal to an artificial and highly technical understanding of when someone has the capacity to avoid her behaviour. By embracing a disjunctive approach, we can work with a more natural understanding—and avoid a forced analysis of our examples.

Still, why should we care about such cases? Surely Georgina the absent-minded stove-avoider is not of interest to criminal lawyers? Maybe not, but we should care about the larger conceptual space in which she dwells. That space is where a lot of omissions and situational liability is properly located.[30] Neither is such liability necessarily strict. Negligence, in particular, is capable of being predicated upon behaviour that is not intentional under any description. Admittedly, we don't normally consider people praiseworthy for inadvertent conduct, but that doesn't rule out blame. Give Georgina something hot, move her to a campsite, and perhaps she starts a forest fire. Of course, the culpability of negligence is itself controversial. We revisit that topic in chapters 11–12, where it is argued that negligence can indeed be blameworthy. But to stipulate a volitional-conduct prerequisite of moral responsibility, and in turn of criminal liability, is to pre-empt that conclusion merely by *fiat*.

8.4 Voluntariness and the varieties of actus reus elements

So far, we have focused—rightly, as will be seen—on the voluntariness of D's *behaviour*. In terms of criminal offences, explicit behavioural elements can be either specific or unspecific. They may identify a particular activity (for example, 'sexual intercourse'), or they may be left at large ('an act or omission causing death'). In the context of a specific activity—say, φing—we have suggested that the voluntariness requirement is satisfied either when D can avoid behaving in a manner that constitutes φing, or when her φing is an instance of D's agency. This does not require D to have control over all aspects of the

[30] See, further, § 8.4.1–3.

event that instantiates her φing, or even over all aspects of her own behaviour. Suppose that D is paralysed and her legs are strapped to a wheelchair. She sees V, an old enemy, and swears at him. Her rudeness is voluntary$_{(L)}$ even as the behaviour of her legs is not. What counts is whether D has control over that aspect of her behaviour that constitutes her swearing.

For activity-unspecific behaviour elements, the inquiry is similar but tied more closely to any specified consequence element of the offence, in as much as D's behaviour is identified by reference to that consequence. In general, the prosecution must prove causation by a piece of voluntary$_{(L)}$ behaviour in order to show that D was morally responsible for the occurrence of any consequence element specified in the actus reus. This is not quite the same thing as showing that the consequence itself was unavoidable. As the familiar possibility of causal overdetermination allows, an outcome might be brought about by D's voluntary$_{(L)}$ conduct even though it would have happened anyway.

Of course, some offences contain no consequence elements. Many sexual offences, for example, specify a wrong by reference only to D's activity and its accompanying circumstances (notably, non-consent or age). For such offences, the voluntariness requirement applies only to the specified activity. But all of the foregoing variations are fairly straightforward. The more interesting question is how the demand for moral responsibility relates to other kinds of actus reus elements, especially in crimes that lack reference to specific activities.

8.4.1 Omissions and consequences

Given that they comprise a subset of not-doings, it is unsurprising to find that the voluntariness of omissions works a little differently from that of positive acts. We do not, for instance, talk of a reflex or convulsive omission. Be that as it may, we can still think about omissions in terms of activities and consequences. In general, D's omission is involuntary, and her moral responsibility for the actus reus is negated, when she fails to act—to do some activity and/or bring about some consequence—because it was impossible for her to do so. This analysis was long ago endorsed at common law.[31] In the old case of *Bamber*, a landowner was charged with non-repair of a highway across his land. He was absolved of liability on the ground that repair of the highway was impossible:[32]

[31] A Smart, 'Criminal Responsibility for Failing to Do the Impossible' (1987) 103 LQR 532; Williams, *CLGP*, 746–48.

[32] (1843) 5 QB 279, 287, 114 ER 1254, 1257.

> 'Both the road which the defendant is charged with liability to repair, and the land over which it passes, are washed away by the sea. To restore the road, as he is required to do, he must create a part of the earth anew. . . . But here all the materials of which a road could be made have been swept away by the act of God. Under those circumstances can the defendant be liable for not repairing the road? We want an authority for such a proposition; and none has been found.'

The landowner was not morally responsible for his failure to renew the road.

The foregoing conclusion holds even if the landowner would not have bothered to repair the road had he been able.[33] In such cases, however, it can be important to distinguish between involuntary behaviour and unavoidable *consequences*. Consider the following scenario:

> Edith is sunbathing on the beach when she observes her young son entering the sea and starting to swim in shallow water. Unfortunately, he encounters difficulties and is caught in an outgoing tide. Edith does not know about the riptide. However, she does not lift a finger to help her son, despite his cries to her. She watches as he is swept out to sea and drowned.

Edith can deny ascriptive responsibility for her son's death on the basis of causation. In a prosecution for murder or manslaughter, the prosecution must prove that Edith's failure to intervene was a cause of her son's death. If in fact there was a riptide, and Edith would have been unable to save him anyway, her omission made no difference and cannot ground her conviction.

However, Edith's *behaviour* is not involuntary.[34] As such, she might still be morally responsible, indeed culpable, in respect of any relevant crime wherein causing death is not part of the actus reus: including an attempt. Edith's indolence is in principle capable of constituting the actus reus of an attempted murder. (Whether or not she would be convicted then depends upon questions of mens rea and proximity.)

As the example suggests, the law's voluntariness requirement is tied primarily to the behavioural elements of an actus reus even in the context of omissions. Albeit we can meaningfully speak of voluntariness with respect to consequences, we do so derivatively, with the connection from behaviour to consequence being constructed via causation. This should come as no surprise: as Davidson memorably observed, 'we never do more than move our bodies: the

[33] *Starri v SA Police* (1995) 80 A Crim R 197.

[34] What if Edith was paralysed, unbeknownst to her? I take it that liability in such cases would be ruled out as a form of thoughtcrime.

rest is up to nature.'[35] Ignoring telekinesis, and indeed I do, our capacity to bring about or prevent consequence elements necessarily runs through our behaviour. If the behaviour that causes the consequence is voluntary$_{(L)}$, so is the consequence.

On the other hand, questions about the voluntariness of an omission-to-prevent-a-consequence can usefully be simplified because of the distinctive causal significance of omissions.[36] If no intervention by D could have averted the unwanted consequence, D's omission is causally irrelevant. The same does not hold for positive interventions: this is part of the lesson from § 8.3. Suppose that I realize I am about to sneeze but take no steps to control the forthcoming outburst, with the consequence that the play I am attending is severely disrupted. (I wasn't enjoying it anyway.) Had I not sneezed, the play would have been disrupted in any case by a disaffected, would-be actress who had not been cast—she was about to create a disturbance, but refrained when she saw that I was doing the job for her. I cannot prevent the play's disruption, yet I am ascriptively and morally responsible for it.

8.4.2 Circumstances and states of affairs

In principle, it is one of the defining *marques* of circumstance elements within an actus reus that its existence can lie outwith D's control, without that undermining the legitimacy of the offence. The statutory rapist cannot alter the victim's age, but that doesn't matter. Voluntariness is a requisite of moral responsibility for behavioural elements. In a derivative sense, mediated by causation, we can say that a voluntariness requirement applies to consequences. But circumstance elements do not have to be voluntary. In a legitimate criminal offence, D's voluntary$_{(L)}$ conduct may be objectionable because it occurs *against the backdrop* of those circumstances.[37]

That's the in-principle position. It may appear that what are sometimes called 'situational offences' therefore present a challenge for moral responsibility.[38] Many crimes stipulate no explicit behavioural element at all on the part

[35] Davidson, *EAE*, 59.

[36] Qua failures-to-prevent rather than active interventions: see § 5.4.

[37] Perhaps D does have control over a circumstantial element. The point is that, in terms of voluntariness, this is not required.

[38] See, e.g., P R Glazebrook, 'Situational Liability' in P R Glazebrook (ed), *Reshaping the Criminal Law: Essays in Honour of Glanville Williams* (Stevens 1978) 108; M Dan-Cohen, 'The "actus reus" and Offences of "situation"' (1972) 7 Israel LR 186.

of the defendant, and delineate the actus reus solely by reference to circumstance elements. Prima facie, such offences contain no requirement of voluntariness: they are *purely* circumstantial offences. If that's right, it follows that they admit of liability in contravention of the principle that D must be morally responsible for the occurrence of the actus reus.

At first blush, that thought does seem right. Consider, for example, the offence of being the owner of a dog which attacks another person, contrary to section 57 of the Dog Control Act 1996 (NZ). Seemingly, the actus reus of this offence can be established without the need to prove any act or omission on the part of the defendant.

This is not to claim there are no responsibility requirements *of any kind* in the section 57 offence. It is not legitimate for a defendant to become criminally liable just because something goes wrong—for example, because a dog attacks someone. The defendant must in some way be connected to, and *ascriptively* responsible for, the relevant circumstances. Normally this connection arises through D's having a particular status or relationship with respect to those circumstances. If a dog attacks someone, it is the dog's owner who is picked out for attention by the criminal law and not, for instance, any person living on that street. Situational offences are in this respect similar to offences of omission. Their potential for over-broad criminalization makes accountability constraints vital.

That still leaves us with the problem of establishing moral responsibility. Certainly the behaviour-free language of situational liability offences has sometimes tempted courts to impose criminal liability without proof of voluntariness$_{(L)}$.[39] But legitimate criminal law is only compatible with situational liability provided there is an *implicit* requirement of voluntariness. Otherwise, situational offences are at odds with foundational principles of the criminal law.

Indeed, the worry is not only about moral responsibility. Without such a requirement, situational crimes can indirectly lead to liability for status, generating constitutional as well as ethical concerns.[40] A less familiar issue is that they can also violate the principle of personal control, discussed in § 5.3.5, according to which D's inculpation should lie in her own hands.[41] It is one thing

[39] See *Simester and Sullivan*, § 4.3(ii).

[40] See, e.g., *Robinson v California* 370 US 660 (1962) (being addicted to narcotics); *Papachristou v City of Jacksonville* 405 US 156 (1972) (being a vagrant); C Foote, 'Vagrancy-Type Law and Its Administration' (1956) 104 U Pennsylvania LR 63.

[41] Compare *Strowger v John* [1974] RTR 124, 130, where, on a charge of failing to display a vehicle excise licence (which had fallen off the windscreen), Lord Widgery CJ observed that it might be different if a stranger had broken into the car and removed the licence without D's knowledge.

to say that D failed to prevent harm when she could do nothing about it; it is quite another to say that someone else deliberately made of her a criminal. That possibility should ordinarily be reserved to the law of complicity.[42] Recall the English case of *Porter v Honey*.[43] D, an estate agent, was prosecuted for displaying a 'For Sale' sign on a property at a time when a second such sign was also displayed. D had erected the board at a time when no other board was displayed, and prima facie committed an offence only when (unknown to D) a competing estate agent, E, erected a second 'For Sale' board on the same property. To convict D in such circumstances would be to empower E, a fellow citizen, by a free, deliberate, and informed action to render D guilty of a crime.[44] This is also an objection to the decision in *Larsonneur*,[45] discussed in § 4.3.3, where D was brought into the United Kingdom against her will by the police and thereupon convicted of an immigration offence. To similar effect is *Winzar v Chief Constable of Kent*.[46] D, who had been brought to hospital but found merely to be drunk, was later removed by the police to their car parked on the road outside. He was then arrested and subsequently convicted of 'being found drunk on a highway'. D's crime was procured by the police, not D.

Accommodating an implicit voluntariness requirement is straightforward. It requires us to imply an implicit, unspecific behavioural element into any situational liability offence. Once that implication is allowed—and it is nowadays said to be a common-law interpretive principle[47]—situational liability operates, in effect, much like liability for voluntary$_{(L)}$ omissions.[48] Indirectly, it involves the defendant's being prosecuted for her omission to prevent the actus reus from occurring (or in rarer cases, for bringing it about). As with omissions liability, therefore, moral responsibility is generally denied when it was impossible for the defendant to prevent the state of affairs from arising.

[42] See § 7.1.

[43] [1988] 3 All ER 1045; discussed in § 5.3.5. See too *Leicester v Pearson* [1952] 2 QB 668: in a prosecution for failing to give precedence to a pedestrian on a zebra crossing, D was acquitted because his car had been pushed onto the crossing by another car, which had hit D's car from behind.

[44] The House of Lords avoided this result not, unfortunately, by invoking general principles but by a rather strained exercise of statutory reinterpretation.

[45] (1933) 149 LT 542.

[46] *The Times*, 28 March 1983; cf. *Martin v State of Alabama* 17 So 2d 427 (1944), where on much the same facts D was acquitted.

[47] Albeit one that can be overridden by Parliament: *Robinson-Pierre v R* [2013] EWCA Crim 2396.

[48] Thus, in the well-known case of *Kilbride v Lake* [1962] NZLR 590, D was charged with permitting his car to be on the road without displaying a warrant of fitness. After he had parked and left the car, the warrant somehow became detached. It was conceded that D had no opportunity to rectify this state of affairs, and thus that his omission to do so, and consequently the existence of the actus reus, was involuntary. On this footing, Woodhouse J ruled that D should be acquitted. It is a cardinal principle, his Honour said (at 593), that 'a person cannot be made criminally responsible for an act or omission unless it was done or omitted in circumstances where there was some other course open to him. If this condition is absent, any act or omission must be involuntary....'

Once that interpretive move is made, and a voluntariness requirement then applied, offences of situational liability need not violate the moral responsibility principle. Situational liability is legitimate, however, *only* when that is done. Such offences are legitimate, that is to say, only when they involve an implicit, unspecific behavioural element that stands in a causal relationship with the proscribed circumstance. At the same time, there need not be formal proof of a behavioural element, provided there is proof that the circumstance was either preventable or brought about by D's action.

8.4.3 Possession

Possession is a special case of the situational liability problem. In practice, possession tends to be criminalized as a convenient substitute for the state's true target, such as the *use* or sometimes the *making* (as in indecent photographs) of the thing possessed. Criminalization at the possessory stage both simplifies evidential requirements and makes an offence out of behaviour that otherwise might not even count as an attempt to use. Prophylactic crimes of this sort can allow earlier police intervention without sacrificing the prospect of a criminal conviction.

There are dangers in this kind of pre-emptive criminalization.[49] The more immediate worry, however, is that crimes of possession may have no requirement for an act or omission by the defendant.[50] No doubt D put the crowbar in her car before heading out to commit a burglary, but the offence of 'going equipped for stealing' requires only that she *has* it.[51] So far as proving the actus reus is concerned, it does not matter how that situation came about.

Again, though, the solution to this worry is apparent. Like offences of situational liability, possessory offences can normally be thought of as having an implicit behavioural element, albeit one that the prosecution ordinarily need not prove. In effect, criminalizing D's possession of the crowbar may be treated as

[49] See esp. the writings of Markus Dubber: e.g., 'Policing Possession: The War on Crime and the End of Criminal Law' (2001) 91 J Crim L & Criminology 829.

[50] Compare the Model Penal Code, § 2.01(4), which states that possession is established only 'if the possessor knowingly procured or received the thing possessed or was aware of his control thereof for a sufficient period to have been able to terminate his possession.' According to Gideon Yaffe, 'In Defense of Criminal Possession' (2016) 10 Crim L and Phil 441, 443, criminal law treatises frequently suggest that possession offences contravene the so-called 'voluntary act requirement' (above, § 4.4). That may be true in the United States, but not necessarily elsewhere: the analysis here in § 8.4.2–3 can be found, for instance, in the first edition of *Simester and Sullivan* (2000), §§ 4.1(ii)(b), 4.3(ii).

[51] Theft Act 1968 (UK), s 25.

imposing an indirect liability, either for the act of obtaining the crowbar (that is, acquiring possession) or for the omission by D to dispose of it.[52]

Recognition of this implicit, unspecific, behavioural element helps to explain some of the more difficult cases where the defendant did not obtain the prohibited item by dint of his own efforts. Suppose that D is stopped while in his car, and is found to have with him a package containing cannabis. When questioned, D claims that he had nothing to do with the presence of the package in his car, and that it had been placed there by a friend. While that claim would suggest that D is not responsible for the fact that the cannabis came into his possession, the law may still be justified in imposing criminal liability because of his own failure to dispose of the item.[53] That argument fails, however, when the behavioural element implicitly underpinning D's possession (either by acquisition or non-disposal) is involuntary. Imagine that D acquires possession of controlled drugs but not by means of his own conduct—for example, when it is mistakenly delivered to his house. While D is not morally responsible for acquiring possession, he may become responsible for *being* in possession when he fails to divest himself of the drugs. Suppose further, however, that D realizes the drugs are in his house, yet is unable to dispose of them because he is bed-ridden through illness. For the moment, at least, moral responsibility is missing. His possession is not a consequence of any voluntary$_{(L)}$ behaviour by D.

8.5 Tracking moral responsibility: Two doctrinal challenges

The basic structure of criminal law tracks moral responsibility badly but not ineffectively. At the doctrinal level, a lack of deliberative capacity with respect to the offence-specific actus reus elements is generally recognized through 'defences' of automatism and impossibility.[54] Structurally speaking, however, a

[52] Compare Williams, *CLGP*, 8; D Husak, *Philosophy of the Criminal Law* (Rowman and Littlefield 1987) 12; Moore, *Act and Crime*, 21; *Porter* [2006] EWCA Crim 560 (rendering electronic images irretrievable, at least to D).

[53] What if D was unaware of the package? Doug Husak suggests that the 'voluntary act' requirement should deny liability in such a case: D Husak, 'Does Criminal Liability Require an Act?' in R A Duff (ed), *Philosophy of Criminal Law* (CUP 1998) 60, 71. At the level of principle, however, that claim seems too strong. The reason why D should not be liable is that he lacks mens rea, not that his omission is involuntary. (Alas, English courts have a very mixed record of implying mens rea elements into possession offences. See *Simester and Sullivan*, § 5.6(iv).)

[54] Judges sometimes link automatism specifically to *unconscious* behaviour: e.g., *Sinnasamy* [1956] MLJ 36. At the level of principle, this secondary distinction is unmeritorious. Cf. *Bratty v Attorney-General for Northern Ireland* [1963] AC 386, 409, 'No act is punishable if it is done involuntarily: and an involuntary act in this context—some people nowadays prefer to speak of it as "automatism"—means an act which is done by the muscles without any control of the [conscious] mind, such as a spasm, a reflex action or a convulsion; or an act done by a person who is not conscious of what he is doing, such as an act done whilst suffering from concussion or whilst sleep-walking.'

claim of automatism is not a supervening defence. It is a claim to exemption from, rather than defrayal of, blame,[55] since it denies moral responsibility for the occurrence of the actus reus. In the context of omissions and situational liability, a parallel claim can be made for impossibility. The point of both 'defences' is the same: satisfaction of the actus reus was outside D's deliberative control and, as such, involuntary. D, in turn, is exempted from moral evaluation in respect of that event.

It follows that voluntariness is most naturally understood as an additional, general-part element of the actus reus of all offences. (Similarly, the prosecution ought to bear the onus of proving voluntariness even in jurisdictions that require defendants to prove defences.[56]) Hence the schema set out in chapter 2:

Main offence components

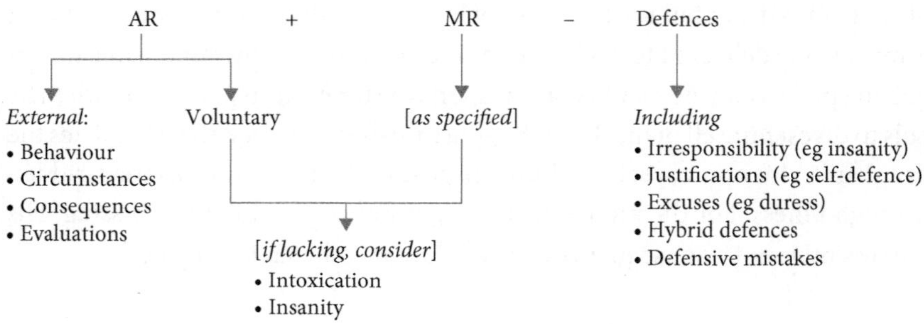

This way of conceptualizing the voluntariness requirement reflects its fundamental nature, its priority over considerations of culpability, justification, or excuse. The conceptualization is not logically essential. Together with other moral irresponsibility 'defences', involuntariness might be categorized formally as a supervening defence, without necessarily compromising moral accuracy. Doctrinally speaking, though, the relocation is risky. Criminal lawyers sometimes lose sight of the fundamental importance of moral responsibility.[57] Indeed, as things stand, the 'defence' of impossibility is only inconsistently recognized as part of the voluntariness requirement, and is sometimes—wrongly—discounted in the context of situational liability.[58] Best not to make things worse.

[55] On the distinction from excuses, see §§ 17.1, 17.5.

[56] Compare the discussion in *PP v Kenneth Fook Mun Lee (No 1)* [2002] 2 MLJ 563.

[57] e.g. in *DPP v H* [1997] 1 WLR 1406, the Court ruled that the insanity 'defence is based on the absence of mens rea, but none is required for the offence of driving with an excess of alcohol. Hence the defence of insanity has no relevance to such a charge as it is an offence of strict liability.' As the later case of *Loake v CPS* [2017] EWHC 2855 (Admin) recognized, this is clearly wrong in principle.

[58] In *Davey v Towle* [1973] RTR 328, for example, the driver of a car was convicted of failing to produce a test certificate, even though it was impossible for him to do so because the car owner was unable or unwilling to produce the certificate.

8.5.1 Antecedence (and concurrence)

There are enough challenges as it is. Exceptionally, involuntariness can be compatible with antecedent guilt.[59] In the well-known case of *Lipman*,[60] L and his friend, V, took a quantity of LSD while in V's flat. During the hallucination that followed, L suffocated V by cramming bed sheet into her mouth, believing when he did so that he was fighting snakes while descending to the centre of the earth. L's behaviour was analogous to sleepwalking. However, his automatism was self-induced. L's claim to be exculpated on the basis of involuntariness was therefore refused, and he was convicted of manslaughter.

Common-law intoxication doctrines can be regarded as a special case of constructive liability.[61] But the possibility of antecedent fault is more general. Suppose that a heavy door begins to swing shut (with disastrous consequences if it closes). John can prevent the door from closing only by staying its movement during the first 15 degrees of its arc; thereafter the door's momentum will be such that he cannot stop it. In such a case, we may characterize John's failure to prevent the door from closing as non-involuntary. Perhaps John did not notice the door begin to swing until it was too late; yet we might still blame him for the door's closure. He should have paid more attention.[62]

These kinds of case are not restricted to inadvertence. We can imagine a further variant in which John is now attempting in vain to reopen the door. Had he gone to a mandatory health-and-safety training session last week, he would have known how to open it. Again, while John's failure to open the door is involuntary today, none the less he might be morally responsible for that failure on the basis that it was brought about by his omission to attend the training. That basis can be generalized. We have argued that the voluntariness requirement can be established by showing non-involuntariness. It follows that, in these types of cases, moral responsibility for the actus reus can turn upon whether we can regard the subsequent event as a *consequence* of the defendant's antecedent, non-involuntary behaviour.

[59] See, e.g., C Finkelstein, 'Involuntary Crimes, Voluntarily Committed' in S C Shute and A P Simester (eds), *Criminal Law Theory: Doctrines of the General Part* (OUP 2000) 143; P H Robinson, 'Causing the Conditions of One's Own Defense: A Study in the Limits of the Criminal Law Doctrine' (1985) 71 Virginia LR 1.

[60] [1970] 1 QB 152. See, e.g., J Horder, 'Pleading Involuntary Lack of Capacity' [1993] CLJ 298, 304ff.

[61] See § 13.5; A P Simester, 'Intoxication is Never a Defence' [2009] Crim LR 3.

[62] See chapter 12.

There is no special doctrine of 'prior fault' here, of the kind sometimes seen in civilian legal systems.[63] Or any need for one.[64] At common law, this is a simple application of the *concurrence doctrine*. If the prosecution cannot prove all the requirements of a crime, including voluntariness, at some time t_1 then, in order to convict, it must show there is another point in time at which those requirements are met. Rather than focusing upon D's involuntary behaviour at t_1, therefore, the prosecution must show that the physical behaviour element of the actus reus occurred, and was voluntary$_{(L)}$, at (say) t_0; and that the required consequence elements (occurring at t_1) were caused by D's behaviour at t_0. Because causation requires time, the concurrence doctrine in criminal law has never required that behaviour and consequence elements occur simultaneously.[65] For the purposes of concurrence, and in particular of identifying the time at which mens rea requirements must be satisfied, the crime occurs *at* t_0. To illustrate this type of analysis, consider the following facts, adopted from the New Zealand case of *Wickliffe*:[66]

> W attempted to rob a jeweller's shop. He threatened those in the shop by pointing a loaded and cocked gun at them with his finger on the trigger. V, the shopkeeper, then sprang at him. W was jolted back against the door, causing his finger to move backward against the trigger, involuntarily depressing it; V was killed when the gun discharged.

W perpetrated a homicide. Even if the immediate cause of death was an involuntary movement, that was not a *novus actus interveniens*; the shopkeeper's aggression was neither an unforeseeable possibility nor free, deliberate, and informed. W's actions *leading up to that point*, in pointing a gun at V and placing his finger on the trigger, were (also) a cause of death. W's earlier conduct, rather than the firing of the gun itself, constituted the behavioural element of the murder.

It is important to emphasize that locating the actus reus at an earlier point in time does not absolve the prosecution of the need to prove, at that earlier time,

[63] Neither, as Moore convincingly shows (*Act and Crime*, 35–37), is there any sleight of hand of the kind alleged by Mark Kelman (see M Kelman, 'Interpretive Construction in the Substantive Criminal Law' (1981) 33 Stanford LR 591, 600–605, 618–20, 637–40).

[64] Indeed, there are rule of law reasons why a general doctrine of prior fault should *not* inform the criminal law, since it would have the potential to render prohibitions activity-unspecific and thereby undermine fair warning constraints. (See § 3.3.) As noted below in the text, the concurrence doctrine is constrained both by causation requirements and by the need to prove mens rea.

[65] See, further, § 14.2.4.

[66] *Wickliffe* [1987] 1 NZLR 55, 60. The approach suggested here was accepted as a possible analysis by the New Zealand Court of Appeal; also by the Australian High Court in *Ryan v R* (1967) 121 CLR 205, 218–19, 231, 233, 239.

the crime's mens rea requirement in respect of the subsequent consequence. For that reason W was rightly convicted only of manslaughter. He lacked the mens rea for murder (under New Zealand law[67]) when he presented the gun.

Needless to say, there are difficult problems of moral luck here, inevitably so when the link from behaviour to consequence depends on factors beyond an agent's control. We look further at those problems in chapter 14. One might have few reservations about a homicide-related conviction in *Wickliffe*. But causation doctrines moderate the role of luck only partially. Recalling our door-closing example, a blaming judgement would only be valid if John's failure to attend the training session was culpable *in virtue of what subsequently occurred*. The consequence must be a matter of intrinsic luck.[68]

8.5.2 The spectrum problem

A more complex structural challenge is posed by capacity *limitations*. Suppose that after the door has moved perhaps 12 or 13 degrees, it may be prevented from shutting only with extreme difficulty. At that point, John's failure to prevent the door's closure is virtually involuntary—it is non-involuntary, but only just.

One worry raised by this kind of case is that, while capacity-responsibility tests generate binary conclusions, the phenomena they measure is scalar. That is compatible with the account presented here only if we accept that capacity-based criteria of responsibility offer negative, threshold conditions of moral evaluation. Thus we require *sufficient* levels of capacity responsibility before moral evaluations are in play. This threshold approach applies not only to deliberative capacity criteria but also to defences such as infancy and insanity.

Consider automatism. The examples given in § 8.1, including sleepwalking and reflex movements, all involve a complete loss of deliberative control. Typically, the greater the degree of consciousness a defendant has, the greater the degree of deliberative control she will have over her actions. But there seems no reason to require a loss of *all* deliberative control over her limbs before foreclosing the possibility of criminal liability. In difficult cases such as hypoglycaemia,[69] the defendant may act in a state of semi-consciousness, with

[67] In particular, New Zealand has no felony-murder rule.

[68] Below, §§ 13.5–13.5.1.

[69] See, e.g., *Quick* [1973] QB 910, 916. The possibility of semi-conscious automatism is also contemplated in cases such as *Stripp* (1978) 69 Cr App R 318, 320–21; *Carter* [1959] VR 105, 108–109. However, English law on this point is unsatisfactory: see *Simester and Sullivan*, § 4.3.1(b).

only a limited awareness of her conduct. Such cases fall short of the threshold required for moral responsibility.

The same holds for irresponsibility 'defences' like infancy. Children have varying degrees of moral maturity. Their capacity for engaging with moral reasons develops across time, so that a nine-year-old typically has a greater ability to moderate his conduct by reference to moral reasoning than does a two-year-old. If that's right, then a nine-year-old is at least somewhat of a moral agent. The point of the law's infancy defence, however, is that neither of them has capacity for moral reasoning *sufficient* to render them eligible for the kind of official blaming judgements that the criminal law involves. Neither child is fully moral responsible; more importantly, each is insufficiently morally responsible.

What looms is a spectrum problem. Beyond its entrance standards, the criminal law's moral responsibility requirements do not distinguish between sufficient and full capacities. The infancy defence operates on an all-or-nothing basis. It has nothing to say to persons one year beyond the cut-off age, even if they typically lack fully developed capacities for reflection and self-restraint.[70] Similarly, where a mature moral agent in fact forms the intention to commit a crime, automatism is excluded even if her awareness is somewhat clouded. Moral responsibility for behaviour is not denied merely because D's deliberative faculties are 'not working in top gear'.[71] An unsettling case of this type is *Kingston*, the facts of which were as follows:[72]

> K, an adult with paedophiliac inclinations but no history of wrongdoing, was invited by P to P's flat for ostensibly innocent purposes. While there, he was given coffee laced with disinhibiting drugs. He was then taken into a bedroom where a 15-year-old boy, also drugged, lay on a bed. K performed sexual acts with the boy. (K's conduct was recorded by P, who had engineered the situation for the sake of later blackmailing K.) K was convicted of an indecent assault, a conviction upheld by the House of Lords.

Seemingly, K would not have acted as he did but for being drugged. But action motivated by a disinhibited intent (or indeed 'irresistible impulse'[73]) is

[70] Such factors may be relevant to sentencing, but not to conviction.

[71] *Isitt* (1977) 67 Cr App R 44, 48; *Coley* [2013] EWCA Crim 223, [22].

[72] [1995] 2 AC 355 (HL); [1994] QB 81 (CA). For insightful discussion of the case, and of the possibility of crafting an excusatory defence, see G R Sullivan, 'Making Excuses' in *Harm and Culpability* 131.

[73] *Bratty v A-G for Northern Ireland* [1963] AC 386, 409; *A-G for South Australia v Brown* [1960] AC 432; see also *Dodd* (1974) 7 SASR 151, 157; *Burr* [1969] NZLR 736, 750.

action for reasons and not automatic.[74] Even impulsive action is conscious and intentional—it is action for a reason, not action uncontrolled by reason.

Let us grant that K was disinhibited but knew what he was doing. We may agree that K is not exempt from moral evaluation in respect of his actions. By the same token, though, we may think that neither is K *fully* responsible for those actions. Surely that is relevant to K's culpability?

Undoubtedly. The point is, though, that these are capacity-related considerations that affect our judgements of *culpability*. We are already in the realm of morally evaluating K with respect to his conduct,[75] and have moved past the stage of excluding him from such assessments. It seems clear that, at least sometimes, we should make allowance for capacity limitations; especially for limitations that are typical, say, of the defendant's age. Part III of this book will offer some thoughts concerning when and how that should be done, taking into account the institutional constraints within which the criminal law operates. It will be argued that allowances for capacity limitations should sometimes be made in the context of mens rea requirements, especially negligence.[76] More commonly, they should be accommodated within certain defences, notably the hybrid excuses.[77] But those are matters for later. For now, it is enough to say that limitations of this kinds take us beyond the basic requirements of moral responsibility and voluntariness.

8.6 Some conclusions

Subject to exigencies of institutional design, moral responsibility forms part of the minimum requirements of criminal liability. Its absence should foreclose conviction, even if the defendant is ascriptively responsible for an actus reus. As a prerequisite of culpability evaluations, it requires us to be satisfied that D is a moral agent whose behaviour—qua implicit or explicit element of the actus reus—is $\text{voluntary}_{(L)}$.

The upshot is that moral responsibility requirements are somewhat piecemeal. They go unmet if D falls short of being a moral agent or if the actus reus occurs involuntarily. This negative approach, which emphasizes what is missing when moral responsibility is denied, focuses practical attention on

[74] Compare *Isitt* (1977) 67 Cr App R 44, 49. A similar analysis applies to provocation; D's provoked intention is still an intention. Thus, notwithstanding the so-called 'loss of self-control' requirement, the provocation belongs in the realm of excuses rather than involuntariness. See § 19.1.

[75] On the objects of culpability evaluations, see §§ 11.1, 14.2.

[76] See, in particular, § 12.3.4–5.

[77] See § 19.1.

the exceptional cases of involuntariness and the irresponsibility defences such as infancy. Yet this negative approach is peculiarly apt to moral responsibility, which contributes preconditions rather than positive elements to the evaluation of D's culpability. Moral responsibility is most salient to our evaluations precisely when it is missing: when D lacks the capacity to subordinate his behaviour to moral reasons; when it is neither produced nor avoidable by any exercise of the capacities which mark D out as a moral agent.

9

(Non-volitional) Action

Never mistake motion for action.[1]

There is a natural distinction, allegedly familiar to dogs,[2] and assuredly to philosophers, between actions and events. On the one hand are *actions*:[3] as Donald Davidson put it, a person's 'deeds and his doings in contrast to mere happenings in his history'.[4] On the other hand are mere behavioural events. If Susan walks to the dairy or waves to a friend, she acts. By contrast, if she suddenly collapses and falls over, or if her leg jerks when the doctor taps her knee with a reflex hammer, her behaviour is (for her) a mere happening; it is no more than an event of which she is not the author. Another way of putting things is that she is an *agent* in respect of walking to the dairy, and not in respect of her falling over. What marks that difference?

One feature that often tracks the distinction is involuntariness. Susan has no control over her reflex leg-kick, no capacity to prevent the movement that her leg—not she—makes. Yet voluntariness and agency do not always run together. Even if a person does not author his own bodily movement, he may be able to prevent it. Imagine the following case:

> Alan takes Bob's hand and smites Charles on the head with it. Bob is capable of resisting Alan but chooses not to do so.

[1] Variously attributed to Hemingway and Benjamin Franklin.

[2] O W Holmes, *The Common Law* (MacMillan 1882) 3: 'even a dog distinguishes between being stumbled over and being kicked.'

[3] A note on terminology. In the context of the action-event distinction, 'action' is generally used in contradistinction to behaviour that is not an instance of agency. Because that usage is so familiar, I maintain it here. According to the conventions set up in § 2.4, however, 'action' refers to behaviour *under a description* that is an instance of agency. Where necessary in this chapter, I shall use 'act' to designate the latter usage. This seems to me unproblematic, in that we do not ordinarily talk of agency with respect to omissions. Sometimes, it may be possible to say that D is an agent with respect to her not-φing if not-φing occurs in virtue of some action, μing, that she does: as when I fail to hold on to the ball by throwing it away. The classification is unhelpful. What counts for moral responsibility in such cases is whether her not-φing is non-involuntary or whether her *μing* is an instance of agency. See, further, §§ 8.3–4.

[4] Davidson, *EAE*, 43.

Fundamentals of Criminal Law. A P Simester, Oxford University Press (2021). © A P Simester.
DOI: 10.1093/oso/9780198853145.003.0009

The event in which Charles's head is struck by Bob's hand is, for Bob, *non-involuntary*.[5] But it is not an instance of Bob's agency.

Despite this, the event is one for which Bob is morally responsible, in the sense outlined in chapter 4. He is eligible for culpability evaluations in virtue of the fact that his behaviour is non-involuntary.[6] And that raises a preliminary question about motivation. If agency is unnecessary for moral responsibility, one might doubt whether lawyers need to worry about it.

There are various reasons why the action–event distinction might matter. One pragmatic consideration is that criminal offences are sometimes framed so as to proscribe specific activities, and a characteristic side-effect of the language used in doing so is to require action rather than mere behaviour by the defendant. Consider, for example, an offence of 'throwing' objects onto a railway.[7] If James trips and lets go of a stone he was holding, wherefore it flies through the air and lands on a railway, we would not ordinarily characterize his behaviour as 'throwing'.[8]

Agency requirements of this kind are ad hoc matters of statutory interpretation. A more general need to investigate the difference between action and event was identified in the previous chapter. Even though action is not a condition of moral responsibility, it can still play a constitutive role. Recall our example from § 8.3:

> Georgina is in the kitchen making dinner. While talking animatedly to her friend, her hand strays close to the stove. Her friend suddenly realizes this. However, just as the friend is about to intervene, Georgina absently moves her hand away from the stove. Had she not done so, the friend—who is not only stronger than Georgina but paying more attention—would have moved her hand forcibly in the same manner. Georgina is unaware of the movement.

Georgina is morally responsible *for moving* her hand. 'It would have happened anyway' denies neither authorship of the movement nor susceptibility to moral

[5] As defined in § 8.2.1: conduct is non-involuntary when D has the deliberative capacity to behave differently.

[6] See § 8.3.

[7] Included in s 32 of the Offences Against the Person Act 1861 (UK). The offence also requires mens rea.

[8] It may be that all examples of this kind also involve involuntary behaviour, although I am inclined to doubt it. It seems to me that we would not describe Bob's case (above in the text) as one where he 'strikes' or 'punches' Charles. For some linguistic worries along these lines in the context of omissions, see *Simester and Sullivan*, § 4.1(i)(c).

assessment for its consequences. And if that's right, it means that a full account of moral responsibility also requires an account of what might be termed *non-volitional action*.

There are at least two ways of going about such an account. One approach is to detach the analysis of (volitional[9]) 'action' from that of 'non-volitional action' and treat the two categories as distinct, perhaps withholding the terminology of 'action' from the latter altogether.[10] Let us call this the standard approach. It is effectively taken by many of the best-known accounts of action, including those developed by Elizabeth Anscombe, Donald Davidson, and Michael Bratman.[11] On the standard approach, a piece of behaviour counts as action if and only if it is intentional under at least one description: and we look to explain action in terms of the intentionality of the actor's behaviour. Cases like Georgina's, then, do not involve action properly so called. Her behaviour lacks intentionality.

My aim here is not to critique the standard approach.[12] Instead, I want to explore another way of thinking about the relationship between volitional action and non-volitional 'action'. Rather than analysing what divides them, it seems to me helpful to consider what they have in common: what separates the both of them from mere events. Doing so has the virtue of focusing attention more directly on what—besides non-involuntariness—underpins moral responsibility for a piece of behaviour and its consequences. This is not to deny that the category of volitional action is important. But it allows that intentionality need not matter to moral responsibility.

For convenience, I'll designate this second approach a 'unifying' one. (And since I am pursuing a unifying approach in this chapter, I shall treat 'non-volitional action' as a form of action.) The approach has other potential payoffs. One might worry, for example, that the standard approach leaves those who take it accounting only for a subset of the cases of agency, albeit a very important subset. Any such account inevitably omits the feature, if there be one, common to all instances of action, including Georgina's, and which distinguishes action from other behaviour. A unified account can avoid that difficulty. In so doing, it opens up a different way of thinking about intentional action. On the standard approach, intentionality has priority over action, in

[9] I take conduct to be volitional when it is intentional under at least one description. See § 8.2.2.

[10] Harry Frankfurt, for example, characterizes the latter as 'being active' rather than action: *Importance*, 58; below, § 9.3.

[11] G E M Anscombe, *Intention* (Basil Blackwell 1957); Davidson, *EAE*, ch 1; M E Bratman, *Intention, Plans, and Practical Reason* (Harvard UP 1987).

[12] For some trenchant remarks, to which I am sympathetic, see J Hyman, *Action Knowledge and Will* (OUP 2015) ch 2.

that the latter is to be understood by reference to the former. On a unified account, by contrast, it becomes possible to develop an explanation of intentional action that appeals to the distinguishing characteristics of action:[13] because intended action is a subset of action.

That last possibility, in turn, permits us to enrich our understanding of intended action by thinking first about the commonalities between volitional and non-volitional action. Plausibly, it seems to me, one shared feature is that the agent's behaviour involves the exercise of certain capacities that *sub-serve* intentional action: capacities that are normally exercised when one acts intentionally. In what follows, I conjecture that it is the exercise of those capacities that changes behaviour from event to action, even when the behaviour is non-volitional.

9.1 Causal explanations?

Both standard and unifying approaches conceive of action in terms of behaviour that is in some sense *made by the agent*. It is Georgina who moves her hand; it is not Bob who moves his. Many theories look to crystallize this insight in causal terms. Davidson offers a well-known *exemplum*:

(i) (Causal-origin thesis) A person's intentional act is caused by the desire–belief pair that rationalizes the act by constituting the reason for which that person behaves as she does;[14] and
(ii) (Volitional-agency thesis) Behaviour is action, as opposed to event, if and only if it is intentional under at least one description.[15]

Davidson's theory is traditional in two respects. It offers a causal account of intentional action, and it adopts the standard approach to action. The conclusion that behaviour is action thus becomes derivative: every instance of action has at least one desire–belief pair which causes it and rationalizes it by providing the reason for which it is performed, and in which respect the action is intentional. For present purposes, however, we should set the volitional-agency thesis aside. The important aspect of Davidson's account here is its depiction of action as behaviour having specific causal origins. Subsequent writers have

[13] As will be seen in chapter 15.
[14] Davidson, *EAE*, 3.
[15] Ibid, 46.

disagreed with Davidson's tracing of those origins to desire–belief pairs,[16] but, at least until recently, there has been widespread endorsement of the idea that action can be explained in terms of causation. Once that was granted, the debate could shift to identifying the agent-related origins.

Unfortunately, whatever the origin, there are known difficulties with a causal analysis. A counterexample is offered by Davidson himself:[17]

> 'A climber might want to rid himself of the weight and danger of holding another man on a rope, and he might know that by loosening his hold on the rope he could rid himself of the weight and danger. This belief and want might so unnerve him as to cause him to loosen his hold, and yet it might be the case that he never *chose* to loosen his hold, nor did he do it intentionally.'

Davidson's account does not exclude deviant causal paths of this kind. And the problem is more general. Can we ever identify action simply as bodily movements with a particular type of causal history? The case of the nervous mountaineer is compatible with the claim that certain mental states must cause or otherwise originate intentional acts. But the example shows that their doing so is insufficient to establish action. The causal-origin thesis requires only that one's body moves as their *effect*, which is what happens to Davidson's climber.

In later writing, Davidson suggested that we might provide sufficient conditions for action in his account by including a proviso that a person's intentional act is caused *in the right way* by the relevant desire–belief pair. But he himself came to the conclusion that further analysis of 'in the right way' is a hopeless task: 'What I despair of spelling out is the way in which attitudes must cause actions if they are to rationalize the action.'[18] There appears good reason for such pessimism, pessimism that many have come to share.[19] Causal accounts tend to omit any requirement for what Harry Frankfurt calls 'the most salient differentiating characteristic of action:'[20]

> 'during the time a person is performing an action he is necessarily in touch with the movements of his body in a certain way, whereas he is necessarily

[16] Bratman, for example, famously explains action in terms of intentions: *Intention, Plans, and Practical Reason*.

[17] Davidson, *EAE*, 79. Irving Thalberg collects a number of similar examples in I Thalberg, 'Do our Intentions Cause our Intentional Actions?' (1984) 21 Am Phil Q 249.

[18] Davidson, *EAE*, 79.

[19] See, e.g., L O'Brien, *Self-Knowing Agents* (OUP 2007) ch 8.

[20] Frankfurt, *Importance*, 71.

> not in touch with them in that way when the movements of his body are occurring without his making them.'

A purely causal explanation, Frankfurt continues, 'must inevitably leave open the possibility that a person, whatever his involvement in the events from which his action arises, loses all connection with the movements of his body at the moment when his action begins.'[21] In other words, analysis limited to causes or origins does not identify the difference between action and mere behavioural effect *as it occurs*. To identify the difference is to identify the feature(s) accompanying such behaviour that mark it out as action. By augmenting the description of the causes and of how they operate, it *may* be possible to generate an account that is functionally isomorphic with one that references concomitant features. But the chances look remote. This is not to agree with Frankfurt that we can ignore the origins of behaviour. But the difficulties of analysing action solely in terms of a causal history look insurmountable. And in this, Davidson's despair seems apt.

There have been multiple attempts in the literature to address the deviant causation problem. I cannot discuss them all here. The difficulty is not resolved simply by amplifying the specified causes in some way: for instance, by requiring, like Dorothy Mitchell, that an originating mental state be virtually concurrent with the behaviour it causes.[22] Merely to specify the temporal concurrence or proximity between cause and effect is to say nothing about the deviance or otherwise of the link between cause and effect. There seems no reason why the climber's desire and belief must vanish while his grip untowardly loosens. Neither need the story be any different if, say, *intention* is the nominated cause. One who intends to loosen his grip and at the same time does so through consequent nervousness need not have deserted his intention when the behaviour suddenly occurs (especially if the behaviour occurs and is over quickly). Compare Frankfurt's own example:[23]

> '[A] man at a party intends to spill what is in his glass because he wants to signal his confederates to begin a robbery and he believes, in virtue of their prearrangements, that spilling what is in his glass will accomplish that; but

[21] Ibid.
[22] D Mitchell, 'Deviant Causal Chains' (1982) 19 Am Phil Q 351. Mitchell's claim is that beyond a certain stage (at which point the intention is virtually simultaneous with the behaviour) any further causal steps cannot be deviant; regardless of how the behaviour is then caused, it will be genuine action. Compare G Keil, 'What Do Deviant Causal Chains Deviate From?' in C Lumer and S Nannini (eds), *Intention, Deliberation and Autonomy* (Ashgate 2007) 69, 77–79.
[23] Frankfurt, *Importance*, 70.

> all this leads the man to be very anxious, his anxiety makes his hand tremble, and so his glass spills.'

We should not concede that, between his anxiety and his trembling, the accomplice abandoned his intention to spill the contents of his glass.

Still, the idea of concurrence seems tantalizingly near the mark. If D abandons an intention before the thitherto-intended behaviour consequently occurs, it seems unlikely that her behaviour will have been caused 'in the right way' by that intention. As Irving Thalberg says of Davidson's climber and similar examples,[24]

> 'My hunch is that . . . a crucial feature is absent. The person's intention only inaugurates a sequence of causally related goings-on which terminate in behaviour; it does not *continue* to shape events, particularly the behaviour. I think a full-blown causal theory prescribes a tighter hookup—what I call 'ongoing', 'continuous' or 'sustained' causation. If someone's behaviour is to count as intentional *X*ing, I believe her or his intention must continuously regulate the *X*ing. He probably does not *dwell* upon his intention frequently or at all while he is engaged in *X*ing. But it remains operative in the sense that if there are impediments to his *X*ing, he takes measures to circumvent them and resume *X*ing—unless of course his plans change.'

The thought here is that not only the intention but also its causal role must be 'concurrent'. In the climber's case, Thalberg therefore diagnoses that 'his current intention did not sustainingly cause his hold to loosen.'

This looks like a positive step, in that we are progressing from considering the origin *simpliciter* toward considering how the behaviour occurs. The nature of 'sustained causation', however, remains opaque. To continuously cause *X*ing is not necessarily to continuously 'regulate' the *X*ing. The latter verb echoes, as Thalberg acknowledges, Frankfurt's proposal that behaviour must be 'guided' if it is to count as action; it suggests a feature distinctive to action as it occurs. That's a promising idea, and one we revisit below. But even granting that guidance, or regulation, is a characteristic of agency, it is doubtful whether that characteristic is captured by Thalberg's suggestion that causation must be 'ongoing' or 'continuous'.

In part, this is because it is unclear what additional ingredients are required in order to render behaviour '*sustainedly* caused' by something. One

[24] Thalberg, 'Do our Intentions cause our Intentional Actions' (n 17) 257.

obvious candidate is temporal concurrence. But that won't solve our problem. The climber's behaviour is sustainedly affected and effected throughout its occurrence—that is, throughout the loosening of his grip—just as if it were intentional. The entire movement is being caused, as it occurs, by his original intention. Neither, as we noted already, is it decisive that the intention itself continues throughout the behaviour's occurrence.

Another possibility is to posit that the causal mechanism linking the origin (say, D's intention) to D's behaviour must have a continuous effect upon that behaviour, or that there is temporal continuity in the operation of the causal mechanism. We might imagine a continuity *of*, and not just *within*, causal mechanisms: in some way the behaviour is guided or regulated by a series of causal mechanisms originating in the intention and bringing about the behaviour as it occurs. But even granting the coherence of such a requirement, our account would not suffice. The anxiety that leads Frankfurt's accomplice to spill his glass may itself be sustained by his intention. Moreover, we remain afoul of the kind of case, inspired by Christopher Peacocke, that John Bishop christens *heteromesial*.[25]

In heteromesial cases, D exhibits the behaviour in question only through the intervention of another agent. Peacocke's own example involves a 'second person, a knowledgeable neurophysiologist who decides on a particular occasion to produce in me exactly the motor impulses needed to realize what he knows, from my neurophysiological states, to be my intentions.'[26] Where Peacocke's knowledgeable neurophysiologist intervenes, I take it, my behaviour is not action.[27]

One weakness of the example itself is that we may be inclined to deny causation, not least on the basis that the neurophysiologist is a free, deliberate, and informed intervener.[28] But we can tweak the example. Suppose the neurophysiologist leaves his control console to get some lunch, and in the meantime leaves the console under the control of a computer which monitors my neurophysiological states and operates the console accordingly. Although he need not have, the neurophysiologist has programmed his computer for 'autopilot'—to

[25] J Bishop, *Natural Agency: An Essay on the Causal Theory of Action* (CUP 1989) 156ff.

[26] C Peacocke, *Holistic Explanation* (OUP 1979) 87.

[27] Cases of this type also present challenges for Markus Schlosser's solution to the puzzle of the nervous mountaineer: 'Basic Deviance Reconsidered' (2007) 67 Analysis 186. For Schlosser, causal theories of action require that 'reason states cause and causally explain actions *in virtue of their intentional contents*' (at 192; emphasis added). Because nervousness does not cause a person's movement in virtue of content, he concludes that it is not a counterexample to causal theories. Schlosser's response to Davidson's case is incompatible with a unifying approach to action, so I merely note it here. Even so, I think that it fails to resolve heteromesial cases, which do seem to involve both causation and causal explanation in virtue of content.

[28] See § 5.3.4–5.

produce 'exactly the motor impulses needed to realize' what it recognizes, from monitoring my neurophysiological states and in the light of its programming, to be my intentions.[29]

In the modified case, there *is* a causal link between the intentions I form and my behaviour. Yet the behaviour is not my action. Even granted that the concept of sustained causation is meaningful, there seems no reason why we should deny its existence in this modified case, where it seems that my intention does continue to 'shape' the behaviour. The continuity of causation is no guarantee that it proceeds 'in the right way'.[30]

9.2 Concomitant characteristics

Kent Bach was right.[31] The difficulty for causal accounts of agency is that they tend to focus upon how a piece of behaviour is initiated rather than upon the manner in which it is executed. It seems unlikely that elucidating the notion of 'causation in the right way' can isolate the difference between action and mere behavioural effect, and ensure that causal paths are not hijacked at the last minute. We need something more.

Here is a suggestion. Following on from the discussion in § 9.1, a richer explanation of the action–event distinction is one that focuses not just on origination but also on how the behaviour is experienced. What seems to be missing in deviant causal chain scenarios is that the actor is, in some sense, no longer 'in touch' with her behaviour as it occurs; no longer actively involved in its occurrence. One promising approach, then, is to explore the nature of this concomitant feature.

The approach I have in mind is modelled upon work by Harry Frankfurt. Rejecting causal explanations of agency, Frankfurt argues that:[32]

> 'What is not merely pertinent but decisive, indeed, is to consider whether or not the movements as they occur are *under the person's guidance*. It is this that determines whether he is performing an action.... Given a bodily movement

[29] To avoid doubt, let us suppose that the autopilot system lacks artificial intelligence: it simply has a very detailed database of pre-programmed instructions.

[30] Bishop's own proposed solution is to augment his causal account with the requirement that feedback, if any, is routed back to the central mental processes of the person exhibiting the behaviour. But there seems no reason why the neurophysiologist must receive the feedback. Perhaps a *very* knowledgeable neurophysiologist might choose to observe, and respond to, her subject's own neurophysiological reactions to the feedback (if any) that the subject's central mental processes receive.

[31] H Frankfurt, 'A Representational Theory of Action' (1978) 34 Phil Studies 361, 363–64. See Bishop, *Natural Agency* (n 25) 123 n 23.

[32] Frankfurt, *Importance*, 72–73.

which occurs under a person's guidance, the person is performing an action regardless of what features of his prior causal history account for the fact that this is occurring. He is performing an action even if its occurrence is due to chance. And he is not performing an action if the movements are not under his guidance as they proceed, even if he himself provided the antecedent causes....'

In Frankfurt's account, behaviour is action when it is guided and when that guidance is attributable to an agent. Frankfurt thereby side-steps the difficulties posed by Davidson's climber, by avoiding reference to the causes or origins of a person's behaviour. Central to this account is his analysis of guidance:[33]

> '[Behaviour is guided] when its course is subject to adjustments which compensate for the effects of forces which would otherwise interfere with the course of the behaviour, and when the occurrence of these adjustments is not explainable by what explains the state of affairs that elicits them. . . . [I]t is not essential . . . that it actually be causally affected by the mechanism under whose guidance the movement proceeds. . . . What counts is that [the mechanism] was prepared to intervene if necessary, and that [it] was in a position to do so more or less effectively.'

Thus Frankfurt asserts that behaviour is guided 'not because it results from causes of a certain kind, but because it would be affected by certain causes if the accomplishment of its course were to be jeopardized.'[34] Although not explicit on the point, it seems that he considers an agent to be acting when she is prepared and able to make the adjustments envisaged.

Two preliminary qualifications. The first is that, while Frankfurt may have a distinctive theory of action, his *approach* to the action–event dichotomy is standard. For Frankfurt, action involves intentional movement. Yet that commitment isn't necessary. It seems possible to develop a modified account of guided behaviour that extends beyond volitional action and is compatible with a unifying approach.

[33] Ibid, 74–75. Thalberg ('Do our Intentions cause our Intentional Actions' (n 17) 257) offers a subtly different account in terms of *regulation*: 'if there are impediments to [the agent's] *X*ing, he takes measures to circumvent them and resume *X*ing—unless of course his plans change.' Thalberg's agent 'circumvents' rather than 'compensates for' impediments, and is more obviously tied to intentionality. See, further, § 9.3.

[34] Frankfurt, *Importance*, 75.

Secondly, it is not clear that guidance is sufficient. Frankfurt envisages his theory as displacing the need for a causal–origins account. Perhaps that's right. But there are reasons for thinking that we cannot ignore the origins of a bodily movement when determining whether it is action, even if we need not particularize its causes. Guidance is best understood as an element that complements reference to behavioural origins, rather than an alternative criterion.

To be clear, I do not think that a causal analysis is wrong: just that it is incomplete. A causal account complemented by guidance may well be the best account of agency. Adopting a unifying approach, however, and tying agency to moral responsibility, I *am* committed to the claim that the origins matter to agency—and those origins are not tied uniquely to intentional action.

9.2.1 Honing guidance

We return to those qualifications below. What counts as being 'guided'? Frankfurt's own answer can be refined. On his account, a guiding mechanism must either (i) be affecting the movement as it occurs, by compensating for actual interfering forces, or (ii) be prepared and able to compensate for some of the effects of forces that may interfere with the course of that movement.[35] But let us take and modify Frankfurt's own example:[36]

> 'A driver whose automobile is coasting downhill in virtue of gravitational forces alone may be entirely satisfied with its speed and direction, and so he may never intervene to adjust it in any way. This would not show that the movement of his automobile did not occur under his guidance. What counts is that he was prepared to intervene if necessary, and that he was in a position to do so more or less effectively.'

In the context of a discussion of agency, we should also claim that the automobile's movement is under the driver's guidance where (iii) he is satisfied with its speed and direction and so never intervenes to adjust it even though something is wrong with the vehicle, so that—although he is able

[35] I interpose 'some' because the guiding mechanism need not be capable of compensating for every effect of every possible force that might interfere. The use of 'may' here, rather than 'would otherwise', reflects Frankfurt's own view (ibid) that 'the causal mechanisms which stand ready to affect the course of a bodily movement may never have occasion to do so; for no negative feedback of the sort that would trigger their compensatory activity may occur.'

[36] Ibid.

to interfere with the automobile's present course—he would be unable to *restore* his desired speed and direction should it be interfered with. In this modified case we see an extension of Frankfurt's criteria: behaviour is also guided where there are no forces interfering with its course and so no compensatory adjustments are being attempted, provided only that a guiding mechanism is prepared to intervene if necessary. Such a mechanism need not be in a position to do so effectively. The inability to ensure that behaviour occurs in the teeth of interfering forces does not mean that the behaviour is not action when no such forces interfere. In non-intervention cases of this kind, it is sufficient that the guidance mechanism adopts the existing behaviour.

9.2.2 Multiple guides?

A more important worry, foreshadowed above, is that it is not sufficient for action that the behaviour occurs 'under the person's guidance'. This is because behaviour can be guided by more than one mechanism. Recall the scenario from the start of this chapter:

> Alan takes Bob's hand and smites Charles on the head with it. Bob is capable of resisting Alan but chooses not to do so.

Suppose further that Bob is prepared to hit Charles himself, were Alan not doing it for him. Then on Frankfurt's analysis, both Alan and Bob smite Charles (with Bob's hand). But that conclusion seems wrong. It is Alan who guides Bob's hand: Bob merely allows his body to be acted upon.[37] To give another example, imagine that Duncan is being taught how to drive in a dual-controlled car. As Duncan slows the car before an intersection, the instructor, Ellen, is prepared to brake should Duncan fail to do so in time. Both Duncan and Ellen guide the braking of the car, but only Duncan brakes the car.

These examples demonstrate that it is possible to guide behaviour without being an agent in respect of it. There is nothing wrong with this in principle, provided we can excise the surplus instances when we attribute the guidance of behaviour *to an agent*, or even to a moral agent. But plainly Alan, Bob, Duncan,

[37] The fact that Bob omits to resist need not, of course, protect him from legitimate criminal liability for the consequences: cp. *Miller* [1983] 2 AC 161 (HL); above, § 5.3.1.

and Ellen are all agents in respect of the guidance they individually have over the relevant behaviour. We cannot use that move to resolve their cases.

Rather, we need to specify further conditions. One obvious modification looms: behaviour can only be action when it is guided by the agent who exhibits that behaviour. Frankfurt probably assumes this requirement, but it does not help us very much, for it leads us to conclude that Bob performs the act of striking Charles, which seems wrong.[38] Thus we need an additional condition: that the behaviour is not caused by guiding forces external to the agent who exhibits it.

All of this shows, contra Frankfurt, that the origin of behaviour *is* important. Behaviour may or may not be action when it is simultaneously guided by an agent who exhibits it and by forces external to that agent. To count as action, it must be uncaused by external guiding mechanisms—while necessarily being guided by the agent. This concession does not, however, commit us to giving a determinate causal account of the origins of action, and to that extent Frankfurt's analysis is preserved.

The foregoing refinements leave open a further possibility. Frankfurt characterizes the distinction he seeks as one between 'events that are actions, in which the higher faculties of human beings come into play, and those movements of a person's body—instances of behaviour other than actions, or mere bodily happenings—that he does not himself make.'[39] It matters, then, what is the source of the *guidance*. When Frankfurt suggests that action is behaviour guided by an agent, he clearly has in mind guidance by a person as distinct from that person's body. The bodily movements involved in natural breathing are not guided by an agent, but rather by the body that exhibits them. Of course, an agent might guide her breathing herself. One might deliberately breathe in a certain manner in order to calm oneself, or when one is asked to do so by a doctor. There is logical space, therefore, for a situation parallel to that of Alan and Bob: where behaviour is simultaneously guided by the agent and by her body. Might there be instances of such behaviour that are caused independently by mechanisms of the agent's body? Tentatively: no. It is difficult to think of any plausible examples of behaviour being guided by an agent but caused by her body, save where the causal bodily mechanism is itself guided by the agent.

[38] Indeed, it can be said that Alan moves Bob's arm, suggesting that the qualification is totally out of place. But for that locution to disclose agency, we need an account of 'Alan moves Bob's arm' that shows Alan to be an agent in respect of his own bodily movements, via which he redeploys Bob's arm.

[39] Frankfurt, *Importance*, 58.

9.3 Does guidance imply intentional movement?

Frankfurt thinks so.[40] He might not buy into Davidson's causal-origin thesis, but he is on board with the volitional-agency thesis. Like so many others.[41] A unifying approach, however, requires us to ask whether bodily movements can constitute action without being intentional under any description. Suppose that I absently and inadvertently scratch my nose while concentrating on a problem. My behaviour cannot be described under any aspect that makes it intentional; none the less, it is a movement that I make and not something that merely happens to me. We acknowledged earlier that one can be morally responsible for non-volitional actions. Indeed, absent-minded or habitual action is sometimes negligent; as when I tap my hand against my knee while concentrating on a discussion, and in doing so spill cigar ash upon the new carpet. Cornman's discussion of this point is particularly useful:[42]

> 'I think there are cases of agency where there is no description, *x*, of the event such that "*P* did *x* intentionally" is true. The clearest class of cases are those of negligence, where a man is the agent of an event, although he intended to do nothing whatsoever.[43] The man who starts a forest fire by absent-mindedly dropping a lighted match or by flipping away a cigarette out of habit often has no intention at the time at all. He may not intend to drop the match, throw it away, or anything else. He just failed to think about or pay attention to what he was doing. He may, of course, sometimes have some intention at the time, but it may be irrelevant to what he did. He may be intending to cut down a tree, for example, and his concentration on that might explain his negligence. In such cases I would claim that the person is the agent of the event of the forest fire beginning, and that there is no description, *x*, of the event such that "*P* did *x* intentionally" is true.'

In general, there are two sorts of cases where unintentional bodily movement is capable of being adjusted by the person who exhibits it. We have already seen examples of each type:

[40] 'Action is intentional movement': ibid, 73.

[41] See, e.g., Williams, *TBCL*, 148; J L Mackie, 'The Grounds of Responsibility' in P M S Hacker and J Raz (eds), *Law, Morality and Society: Essays in Honour of H.L.A. Hart* (OUP 1977) 175, 180; also many of the writers who oppose liability for negligence, noted in chapter 12.

[42] J Cornman, 'Comments on Davidson's "Agency"' in R Brinkley, R Bronaugh, and A Marras (eds), *Agent, Action and Reason* (1971) 26, 32.

[43] Presumably, Cornman did not mean to suggest that one can *never* μ negligently while φing intentionally. But nothing turns on that here.

(1) where I scratch my nose idly and without thinking; and
(2) where I breathe naturally and inadvertently.

Case (1) is an instance of non-volitional action. Case (2) is not action at all.[44] Frankfurt regards the former as an instance of 'being active' rather than action.[45] Suppose then, that we posit three broad categories of behaviour, consonant with the discussion in § 9:

(i) volitional action;
(ii) non-volitional action (or 'being active'), including case (1); and
(iii) mere event, including case (2).

The standard approach places the action–event border between (i) and (ii), whereas a unifying approach puts it between (ii) and (iii). To my mind, there is much to be said for the second location. It looks wrong to regard scratching my nose as a mere happening. As noted earlier, moral responsibility seems to attach for what I do in case (1). Moreover, culpability for my act is assessed in the same manner as it is for acts that I inadvertently do via otherwise intentional movements.[46]

The importance of this last point should be emphasized. If one accepts that D can be culpable for negligent φing, it becomes arbitrary to restrict moral responsibility only to actions that are volitional. It cannot defensibly be a precondition of D's culpability for φing that her conduct also happened to constitute at least one other intentional act of μing. But more on that in chapters 11–12. For now, it suffices to note that the standard approach to 'action' does not accurately distinguish between instances of our agency (for which we are morally responsible whether or not non-involuntary), and mere bodily events (for which we are morally responsible only if non-involuntary).

Some writers have sought to navigate this difficulty by a different route: claiming, as does Bishop, that the actions in type (1) cases *are* intentional,

[44] I might sometimes be morally responsible for such cases qua consequence—as when I forget to hold my breath—but that would be on the ground of non-involuntariness.

[45] Frankfurt, *Importance*, 58.

[46] Cases of this sort cannot be explained away by Peter French's suggestion (P French, 'Fishing the Red Herrings Out of the Sea of Moral Responsibility' in E LePore and B P McLaughlin (eds), *Actions and Events: Perspectives on the Philosophy of Donald Davidson* (OUP 1985) 73, 85) that 'a person may be held morally responsible for a previous event to which that person had unintentionally, even inadvertently, contributed, if he or she subsequently intentionally acts in ways that are likely to cause repetitions of the untoward outcome.' Cornman's negligent fire-starter may take more care in future. At the level of principle, French's attempt to reverse time's arrow is unpersuasive. Subsequent lack of remorse may evidence one's reprehensible character, and a refusal later to adopt precautions may itself be blameworthy, but neither retrospectively alters one's moral responsibility for the event itself.

albeit subconsciously.[47] That analysis should be resisted. Case (1) is not only unintentional but inadvertent under any description. We should not gerrymander the boundaries of intention in action in order to make an awkward truth go away.[48] Davidson himself makes no such claim: he simply does not contemplate non-rationalized action. And they *are* non-rational; as O'Shaughnessy points out, 'no intention finds expression in the act.'[49] Even were we to concede that 'sub-intentional'[50] action can be caused by (say) belief–desire pairs, the latter would not cause such action qua reasons.

There are no convenient, complexity-reducing solutions at hand here. A unifying approach faces pressure points too. The pressure simply arises in a different place: between cases (1) and (2). Within that hinterland, though, lurks at least one heuristic. The behaviour involved in natural breathing is automatic. Although breathing may be controlled, unless an agent guides it intentionally it will necessarily occur as it does. The process of natural breathing is mechanical, and takes place without being guided either intentionally or sub-intentionally. It is, rather, guided by her body. As such, it is not action.

9.3.1 A schema

It may be helpful to summarize the interconnections between chapters 8 and 9 in a table. To that end, let me first restate some examples, drawn from these two chapters:

> (§ 9) Alan takes Bob's hand and smites Charles on the head with it. Bob is capable of resisting Alan but chooses not to do so. (Suppose further that Alan could readily have refrained from acting as he did.)
>
> (§ 8.3) While talking to a friend, George suddenly realizes his hand has strayed too close to the stove and jerks it away. Had he not done so, the friend—who is not only stronger than George but paying more attention—would have moved George's hand forcibly in precisely the same manner.
>
> (§ 8.2.1, § 9.3) Jill scratches her nose inadvertently while preoccupied.
>
> (§ 8.3, § 9) Georgina is in the kitchen making dinner. While talking animatedly to her friend, her hand strays close to the stove. Her friend suddenly realizes this. However, just as the friend is about to intervene, Georgina absently moves her hand away from the stove. Had she not done so, the friend—who is not only

[47] J Bishop, *Natural Agency* (n 25) 181.
[48] On those boundaries, see chapter 15.
[49] B O'Shaughnessy, *The Will: A Dual Aspect Theory*, vol II (CUP 1980) 60.
[50] As O'Shaughnessy terms them.

stronger than Georgina but paying more attention—would have moved her hand forcibly in the same manner. Georgina is unaware of the movement.

(§ 9.3) Keith breathes naturally and inadvertently.

(§ 8.1) David is standing between Vicky and Tanya. Suddenly, Tanya grasps David's arm and forces it into Vicky's midriff. Tanya is more powerful than David, who has no chance to resist her.

Armed with this collection, we can cross-tabulate the possible relationships between categories of agency and of voluntariness, as follows:

	Volitional?	*Non-involuntary?*	*Involuntary?*	*Action/ type?*	*Morally responsible?*
Alan	Y	Y		Volitional Action	Y
George	Y			Volitional Action	Y
Jill		Y		Non-volitional Action	Y
Georgina				Non-volitional Action	Y
Keith		Y		Mere event	Y
David			Y	Mere event	No

As can be seen, action may or may not be volitional, and it may or may not be non-involuntary. But it cannot be involuntary. Be that as it may, the most important point for criminal lawyers is that moral responsibility can attach in all but the last case, David's. The table endorses the claim made in § 8.3 that the law's voluntariness requirement is disjunctive: it is satisfied if and only if D's behaviour is *either* action or non-involuntary. By far the most important category of morally responsible behaviour is, of course, volitional action. Yet D can still be responsible, indeed culpable, in the absence of agency. Conversely, D can be morally responsible for her actions notwithstanding that the behaviour is unavoidable.

9.4 Rounding up: Sources of direction

For convenience, let me consolidate some of the points made in this chapter within a new term. Behaviour is *directed* by an agent when it is guided—in the sense defined by Frankfurt but subject to the qualifications in § 9.2, and without implying that the behaviour is intentional movement—by that agent; and, if that behaviour is guided by any other mechanisms which are either external to the agent or not themselves guided by the agent, it is not caused by those other mechanisms.

The distinction made in § 9.3, between cases (1) and (2), then suggests a possible elaborated account of agency: behaviour is action when it is directed consciously or subconsciously by the person who exhibits it. This is, I think, what we normally have in mind when we say the behaviour is directed *by an agent*—articulating the intuition that action is behaviour that involves a certain kind of connection between body and mind. In both cases, the reason we can say that an agent *makes* the movements has to do with the fact that the behaviour is not simply a mechanistic bodily happening; it is not simply an event that occurs automatically, failing its suppression by the will. To that extent, what Frankfurt calls the 'higher faculties' are in play, even for subconsciously directed behaviour.[51]

There are obvious challenges for pursuing this line of thought into psycho- and physiological detail. Ultimately, an account in terms of the directing mechanisms would require us to specify what counts as an exercise of one's 'higher' faculties, distinguishing subconsciously-directed conduct from, say, automatic behaviour such as breathing or a motor tic. Fortunately, diagnostic *indicia* exist. As was suggested in § 9.2.2, it seems unlikely that a piece of behaviour can be both subconsciously directed and independently caused by the body. Thus we can generally differentiate between cases by reference to defaults. In type (2) cases, since the behaviour is caused independently by bodily mechanisms, it necessarily occurs in the absence of its intentional suppression (which may not even be possible). In other words, the only manner in which automatic

[51] Frankfurt, *Importance*, 58. Elsewhere (esp. 11ff, 69ff), Frankfurt observes that an agent may sometimes fail to identify with (i.e., accept) a desire by which she is motivated. As David Velleman puts it (D Velleman, 'What Happens When Someone Acts?' (1992) 101 Mind 461, 471), on that view, 'what makes the difference between defective and full-blooded actions must be that, in the case of the latter, the agent identifies with the motives that actuate him.' However, we are not concerned here with 'full-blooded' action, or human action 'par excellence' (Velleman, 462). Our concern is with agency *simpliciter*: with the kind of agency that can help to underpin moral responsibility (cp. § 8.3). We are concerned, in other words, with minimum rather than ideal conditions. *Moral* agency may be negated in extreme cases of the kind Frankfurt has in mind, and I note that possibility in §§ 11.4.2 and 14.4.1. But imperfect human agency can still be action—and it can rightly be sanctioned by the criminal law. For a persuasive critique of Velleman's argument along similar lines, see A F Mele, *Motivation and Agency* (OUP 2003) 216.

behaviour might not occur on that occasion is when its non-occurrence is intentionally guided. One cannot *permit* (by abstaining from guiding) that behaviour not to occur. Conversely, in type (1) cases of subconsciously directed behaviour, one cannot permit that behaviour to *occur*.[52]

As might be expected, this kind of approach finds its most difficult cases at the boundaries between subconsciously- and unconsciously-directed behaviour. It would be misleading to characterize sleepwalking, let alone dissociative-state automatism, as behaviour directed merely by a person's body. What is distinctive about such cases for our purposes is that the person who exhibits such behaviour is incapable (on these occasions) of consciously directing her behaviour. While her behaviour may be said to involve an exercise of her higher faculties, those faculties are operating at an unusually low level, one radically different from those of a person seized with deliberative capacities to act. This leads us to a further condition: a person cannot be an agent in respect of a piece of behaviour unless she is conscious.

That last constraint reflects an informing idea behind the account in this chapter. By contrast with writers who interpret agency in terms of volitional conduct, a unifying approach can envisage people as agents not merely through their acting upon (say) beliefs and desires, but through their *exercising the capacities they have* to act upon their beliefs and desires. This is the point foreshadowed in § 9. People have capacities that sub-serve the rational use of their faculties; it is the exercise of those subservient capacities themselves, rather than their deployment in the course of doing things intentionally, that betokens agency and can ground moral responsibility.

Human beings can be deprived of those capacities. They can lose their powers of agency, lose one of the foundations of their humanity. Again, this is not because they fail to act intentionally—that does not diminish their humanity—but because they lose access to the abilities required to do so. We saw in chapter 8 that the loss of such capacities can undermine a person's moral responsibility. The intersections are no coincidence. The conclusion that D's behaviour was involuntary requires that D had no capacity to behave differently. But involuntariness also requires that D did not *exercise* her deliberative capacities, if any, to behave as she did. The capacities, in each case, are those normally exercised when acting intentionally: those which, in virtue of their deployment, mark us out as agents. And those same capacities that underpin agency are crucial, we shall find, to our understanding of blame.

[52] Except, of course, where there is overdetermination due to external forces.

PART III

CULPABILITY AND WRONGDOING

10
Prolegomenon to Part III

10.1 Culpability and wrongdoing, mens rea and defences

In chapter 1, we identified certain key principles for the criminal law. Part II of this book focused on the principles of moral and ascriptive responsibility. It considered why responsibility requirements are important and explored how they are, and how they should be, reflected within our general part doctrines. The task of Part III is to do much the same for the principles of culpability and wrongdoing.

The culpability principle mandates that conviction of a criminal offence, or at least of a stigmatic criminal offence, should not normally occur unless the accused is (morally) culpable with respect to committing that offence. Many criminal theorists endorse the culpability principle, in some form: there are significant variants. Some writers, for example, think that once an offender goes through a 'gateway' of wrongdoing, she may legitimately be held liable for consequences that flow from her initial wrongful action, without being culpable specifically for those further consequences.[1] Similar thinking lies behind the traditional doctrines of felony-murder. One might disagree with that view, and I do.[2] But even those who hold it accept that the offender should in principle be culpable with respect to the initial action. There must, they agree, be *some* culpability, somewhere, to legitimate conviction of a serious criminal offence.

That thought is surely right, even if it was not shared by Hart.[3] We started this book by suggesting that criminal law speaks with a moral voice. When it

[1] See, e.g., Gardner, *Offences and Defences*, ch 2; J Horder, 'A Critique of the Correspondence Principle in Criminal Law' [1995] Crim LR 759. Compare G Rosen, 'Culpability and Ignorance' (2003) 103 Proc Arist Soc 61, 63 n 4 (emphasis omitted): 'When X does A from blameless ignorance, then X is blameless for doing A, provided the act would have been blameless if things had been as the agent blamelessly took them to be.'

[2] See esp. § 13.5–13.5.1. The argument there favours the conclusion that D must be culpable *for the crime of which she is convicted*. As indicated in the text below, however, it also allows that some gateway offences (those imposing what I term 'constructive' liability) are legitimate.

[3] See Hart, *Punishment and Responsibility*, ch 2. Hart argued that the criminal law should require mens rea for rule of law reasons, i.e. in order to ensure that wrongdoers have adequate opportunity to avoid criminal liability. See § 3.3.

Fundamentals of Criminal Law. A P Simester, Oxford University Press (2021). © A P Simester.
DOI: 10.1093/oso/9780198853145.003.0010

does so, it should tell the truth. Especially in the context of serious offences, to label as criminal someone who lacks culpability is to wrong that person. The wrong may be *compounded* by punishment, but it exists even if no sentence is pronounced. Merely to convict the defendant is to label her, publicly, in morally resonant terms. And if the defendant is blameless, it is, morally speaking, to defame her.

Chapter 13 develops this line of argument in the context of strict liability. Yet accepting *that* the culpability principle matters does not take us very far. A more interesting challenge is to show *how* it matters. Meeting the latter challenge is a wider aim for Part III, which explores what the culpability and wrongdoing principles mean for our mens rea and defence doctrines. For example: it is a familiar implication of the culpability principle that all crimes should contain mens rea requirements. Indeed, there are powerful reasons why every actus reus element should, ordinarily, be complemented by a mens rea element.[4] Yet, sometimes, a rigorous correspondence between acts reus and mens rea elements is not required. *Constructive* liability, as I define it,[5] can satisfy the culpability principle.

Albeit they are related, culpability and mens rea are not co-extensive. (Which is part of the point of defences.) For this reason, the term 'mens rea' is used in this book solely in a technical or descriptive sense, referring to such elements as intention, (advertent) recklessness, and (inadvertent) negligence. Suppose that D commits a pro tanto offence but has a rationale-based excuse for doing so.[6] As numerous writers have observed,[7] there is a meaningful sense in which we might deny that D's *mens* is *rea*, in as much as D is not culpable. The courts, too, have sometimes used 'mens rea' in a richer sense, signalling D's culpability and not just her mental state.[8] Modern judicial usage, however, tends to use the language of mens rea in its technical sense, referring simply to the mental elements of the offence,[9] and—if only to avoid confusion—that is the usage adopted here.

[4] See, e.g., A Ashworth, *Principles of Criminal Law* (OUP 1991) § 3.6(g).

[5] See § 13.5.

[6] On rationale-based excuses, see §§ 17.1–2.

[7] See, e.g., G P Fletcher, 'Criminal Theory in the Twentieth Century' (2001) 2 Theoretical Inquiries in Law 265; K Ambos, 'Toward a Universal System of Crime: Comments on George Fletcher's *Grammar of Criminal Law*' (2007) 28 Cardozo LR 2647; M D Dubber, 'Comparative Criminal Law' in M. Reimann and R. Zimmermann (eds), *The Oxford Handbook of Comparative Law* (OUP 2008) 1287.

[8] See, e.g., *Lee v Dangar* (1892) 2 QB 337, 347 (Lord Esher): 'in order to constitute an offence in the nature of a crime, there must be what is called a mens rea; the thing must be done with a bad mind.'

[9] e.g. *Yip Chiu-Cheung* [1995] 1 AC 111 (HL); *Kingston* [1995] 2 AC 355 (HL); *Dodman* [1998] 2 Cr App Rep 338 (C-MAC).

How, then, does mens rea connect to culpability? Across chapters 11 and 12, I argue that D's culpability for a criminal wrong can be grounded *either* in her choice to do or risk that wrong *or* in her failure to take adequate care not to do it. The argument gives us reason to distinguish intention and reckless, on the one hand, from negligence on the other. However, it leaves open a further set of puzzles concerning the relationship between culpability and our most familiar mens rea elements:

(1) Are the Model Penal Code and the UK Law Commission's Draft Criminal Code right to present intention, recklessness, and negligence in terms of a mens rea hierarchy, as ordered 'degrees of fault'?[10]
(2) More specifically, given the argument to be made in chapter 11, that intention and recklessness both support choice-based forms of culpability, is there a meaningful sense in which the former involves a greater degree of choice and, therefore, of culpability?
(3) Analogously, given the argument in chapter 12 that negligence can be culpable without being grounded in choice, how is that difference one of *degree*—and why is a mens rea standard of negligence so rare in serious crimes?
(4) Moreover, why is it that recklessness and negligence contain embedded elements of reasonableness, whereas intention does not?

Amongst the tasks for Part III is to investigate these puzzles. I defend an account of the general part in which establishing culpability plays a lesser role in grounding key mens rea distinctions than most people think. Whereas, for example, it is often suggested that the culpability principle rules out criminal liability for negligence,[11] I argue that the main case against such liability rests in the principle of legitimate enactment: in norms governing legitimate criminalisation.[12] To explain the law's mens rea categories, we must look beyond a simple appeal to culpability differences.

Much the same is true for the intention/recklessness distinction. In order to understand the full significance of that distinction, we need to acknowledge the ways in which it affects a finding of *wrongdoing*. Thus Part III also

[10] See, e.g., Law Com. No. 177, *A Criminal Code for England and Wales* vol 2 (HMSO 1989) § 8.22 (p 195): 'Knowledge or intention is a higher degree of fault than recklessness.'
[11] e.g. L Alexander and K Ferzan, *Crime and Culpability: A Theory of Criminal Law* (CUP 2009) ch 3. A longer list can be found in chapter 12.
[12] To recall from § 1.2, the legitimate enactment principle holds that enacting an offence of φing must be justified, and that this can only be so where the offence is formulated in accordance with the rule of law and meets standard criminalization constraints such as the harm principle. See also § 1.5.

explores how mens rea elements can serve the wrongdoing principle, which holds that D should be convicted of a crime only if D's action was an instance of wrongdoing—that is, an unjustified (or 'wrongful') moral wrong.[13] Proof of mens rea can help to establish that D's action was a wrong. And it can help to establish that it was unjustified.

The wrongdoing and culpability principles are intertwined. Paradigmatically, we don't convict defendants of 'being a criminal'. We convict them of a named wrong. This is not only for rule of law reasons.[14] A similar paradigm holds, it seems to me, in morality. People are not culpable, as it were, in the air. In general, we don't blame them for 'being a bad person'. Rather, we blame them *for doing something wrong*. If the criminal law is to observe the culpability principle, it must also observe the wrongdoing principle. It should not convict D of φing unless φing is an instance of (legitimately criminalized) wrongdoing.

I offer some remarks in defence of these claims, especially with reference to the criminal law, across §§ 11.1 and 14.2. Suppose that we accept them. It follows that culpability judgments are dependent *upon the actus reus*. Chapter 14 will argue that the consequence elements of any crime form a constitutive part of the criminal wrong, because culpability is sensitive to outcome luck. Outcomes change what we are culpable *for*, and they rightly affect what we are convicted *of*. Yet it does not follow that they alter the degree of our culpability, or the quantum of punishment that we deserve. Wrongs are things we do: culpability, however, arises from our engagement with the reasons why we shouldn't have done them.

The dependence of wrongdoing upon mens rea elements is, if anything, even more complex. Chapters 16 and 18, in particular, consider how D's mens rea affects the wrongfulness of her φing. It is a condition of D's being culpable for φing that her action is unjustified. But whether that action is justified itself depends upon D's practical reasoning, and upon the status of any justifying reasons within D's own motivations.[15] Seeing this will help us to address some of the following puzzles, concerning the operation of defences:

(5) There is widespread agreement that, to be justified, a pro tanto wrong must in some sense be *proportionate* to the evil that it averts. The

[13] See § 1.4. Recalling the definitions in § 2.1, I take a 'wrong' to be a breach of duty, which is 'wrongful' when unjustified.

[14] Notably, the need to ensure fair labelling in criminal law. See A Ashworth, 'The Elasticity of Mens Rea' in C Tapper (ed), *Crime, Proof and Punishment* (Butterworth 1981) 45, 53–56; *Simester and Sullivan*, § 2.4; below, § 14.3.

[15] Here I (and the common law) part ways with Paul Robinson: see § 16.4.

criminal law, too, embeds requirements of proportionality or reasonableness in all rationale-based defences.[16] It may be relevant, even crucial, to a claim of justification that only one person's life is lost while five are saved; or that one house is razed when the village is preserved. Yet, for most writers, there are also occasions where the numbers do *not* count, occasions where it is unjustified to sacrifice one life for the sake of five.[17] How is this to be explained? On a simple 'proportionality' test, it seems that such cases cannot readily be distinguished by their outcomes.

(6) Relatedly, it is sometimes asked: given their common element of proportionality, why do we distinguish between *kinds* of justifications? To what extent are justifications like self-defence, lawful arrest, and the like, in truth just special cases of lesser-evils necessity?

(7) And if rationale-based *excuses* also contain a requirement of reasonableness, why should we—if indeed we do—distinguish them from justifications?

As with puzzles (1) through (4), meeting the challenges of (5) through (7) requires us to abandon some familiar tropes. Even though all defences play a role in mediating censure-allocation, the distinction between justifications and excuses is—rather like our mens rea categories—not simply to be drawn in terms of degrees of culpability. Excuses are directly concerned with culpability. Justifications are directly concerned with wrongdoing.

However, not all justifications are alike. Not all justifications align in denying (or conceding[18]) the wrong. The defence of lesser-evils necessity is in this respect distinctive. By contrast with justifications like self-defence, lesser-evils necessity does involve wronging the victim. Moreover, that distinction has implications for the shape of justificatory defences. It alters the range of reasons that an agent can invoke in her own justification. Even if one may intend to kill another in self-defence, for example, one may not do so under conditions of necessity.

Which helps to explain why mens rea is bound up with the structure of justifications. Across the chapters that follow, a number of key claims will be made about puzzles (1) through (4) that help us to resolve puzzles (5) though (7). It will be argued, for example, that perhaps the most important reason to

[16] See chapter 17.

[17] See in particular chapter 18.

[18] As John Gardner has counterclaimed: *Offences and Defences*, ch 4; although see J Gardner, 'In Defence of *Offences and Defences*' (2012) 4 Jerusalem R Legal Studies 110, 113.

distinguish intention from recklessness concerns not relative culpability but wrongfulness. More specifically, the difference is cashed out in terms of which reasons for φing are excluded from D's claim to justification. Sometimes, putative justifications may be disallowed when unintended. Or they may be disallowed when the pro tanto wrong itself is intended. The distinctiveness of negligence is also, partly, a matter of justifications. It is no accident that recklessness and negligence, unlike intention, contain embedded requirements that the risk be unreasonable. The existence of those requirements tracks the distinctive way in which the law, like morality, navigates the wrongfulness of unintended actions.

So a full account of culpability in the criminal law demands an account of the relationship between culpability, wrongdoing, mens rea, and defences: and of how the criminal law reflects that; or at least, of how Anglo-American law would reflect that, were it to satisfy the culpability principle. In what follows, we start that account by looking at the grounds of culpability.

11

A Pluralistic Theory of Culpability

When is a person culpable? When does she deserve the kind of moral indignation that we paradigmatically associate with blaming judgements and, in the criminal law, with pronouncements of guilt?[1] Conventionally, the ascription of blameworthiness in criminal law is thought to rest upon findings of mens rea.[2] And it is certainly true that mens rea elements have a role to play in establishing culpability. Yet how they do so remains obscure. There are many reasons for this. One of the most important is that the grounds of culpability are not unitary.

Suppose that D φs, and that her φing is an unjustified wrong. The gist of the argument in this chapter is that D's culpability for φing does not arise directly from the wrongness of her φing. Rather, it derives from D's *engagement* with the reasons why she should not φ. D is culpable when her engagement with those reasons is defective in a manner that reflects a moral vice on D's part.[3]

Not all vices are moral.[4] Being of low intelligence, for example, is not a ground of blame.[5] *Moral* vices are concerned with an agent's dispositions, attitudes, and the like, and they are vices in as much as those dispositions[6] reflect

[1] Peter Strawson famously associated culpability with reactive attitudes like indignation in P Strawson, 'Freedom and Resentment' (1962) 48 Proc British Acad 1. Without taking a view on the naturalistic dimension of Strawson's project, I adopt R Jay Wallace's suggestion that indignation is a paradigmatic blaming response: R J Wallace, *Responsibility and the Moral Sentiments* (Harvard UP 1994). For a helpful discussion of the criminal law's role in communicating 'moral indignation', see V Tadros, *Criminal Responsibility* (OUP 2004) ch 3. See also above, § 1; below, § 13.3. We should also draw a distinction between blameworthiness and (the action of) blaming. To cast blame, especially through the criminal law, may be unjustified even when the person blamed is actually culpable; and *vice versa*. But those are secondary issues, not pursued here. My concern is with what David Enoch and Andrei Marmor call 'moral blameworthiness' as opposed to 'justified blame-related reactions': D Enoch and A Marmor, 'The Case Against Moral Luck' (2007) 26 Law and Phil 405, 412ff, 432ff.

[2] As noted in § 1.2.3, I use 'culpability' and 'blameworthiness' interchangeably.

[3] The terminology of 'moral vices' is adapted from V Tadros, *Criminal Responsibility* (OUP 2005) ch 3. My usage is broadly aligned with his, albeit not tied to aspects of the agent's character that persist over time. (Cp. § 11.4.)

[4] In particular, I take moral vices to be a narrower category than the *aretaic* vices: see, e.g., G Watson, 'Two Faces of Responsibility' (1996) 24 Phil Topics 227. Unlike Watson, I do not link the distinction between aretaic and moral vices to that between attributability and accountability, for the reasons given in § 4.2.

[5] Or so I argue in § 12.3.3.

[6] Rather like Davidson's well-known term, 'pro-attitudes' (*EAE*, 3–4), I use 'dispositions' here as shorthand for a wide range of desires, inclinations, attitudes, etc. (For a worry about the language of 'pro-attitudes', see § 15.1.1.)

Fundamentals of Criminal Law. A P Simester, Oxford University Press (2021). © A P Simester.
DOI: 10.1093/oso/9780198853145.003.0011

certain shortcomings in the agent's own values: shortcomings, principally, in her concern for the interests of others.[7]

In turn, D becomes culpable for φing when, in her engagement with the reasons she has not to φ, she was insufficiently motivated by—cared insufficiently about—the interests of others. In what follows, I claim that this can happen *both* when D chooses to φ and when D φs inadvertently. Accepting this, however, requires us to accept two distinct accounts of when D is blameworthy. Neither account is reducible to the other.

11.1 Between wrongdoing and culpability

Some preliminaries. I supposed above that D's φing is an unjustified wrong. For the purposes of this chapter, we should also assume that its lack of justification is 'objective': that the guiding reasons for D to φ are defeated, all things considered, by the reasons against.[8] Thus I disregard the complexities of mistaken or unknown justification. Those problems will be addressed in later chapters. For now, our concern is with the central case.

Even outside the criminal law, wrongdoing is the central case for culpability. We don't 'blame' D for doing the right thing. Admittedly, we might blame D for doing something wrong—for φing—even though, at the same time, her conduct also had beneficial effects.[9] But that possibility just requires us to be careful about the description under which D's conduct is being assessed: about which action we are judging D for.[10] Suppose that Pam, a doctor, gives Virgil (an old enemy recently admitted to hospital) drugs in order to kill him. To her chagrin, Virgil proves to have an undiscovered genetic characteristic, and the drugs cure him instead. We can legitimately blame Pam for trying to kill Virgil.

[7] While nothing in this chapter turns on the point, I do not claim that moral vices are solely concerned with the interests of others. It seems to me, for example, that they might also include failures to value one's own interests properly. In *Crimes, Harms, and Wrongs*, 159, we gave the example of a patriotic pop-music fan, who decides to kill herself should her country once again do badly in the next Eurovision Song Contest. Such a person (if she survives) might rightly be censured by her friends for seeking to 'throw away' her life and personal prospects for such trivial reasons.

[8] On the distinction between guiding reasons (which in fact apply to the action) and explanatory reasons (by which the agent is, personally, motivated), see Raz, *Practical Reason and Norms*, 16ff. Note that guiding reasons need not be universal. Their force—and thus the moral assessment of φing—will very often be community-dependent.

[9] Albeit not so as to justify D's φing (our starting point). I have deferred perhaps the most interesting cases of this kind, i.e., where the justification was unknown. I argue later in Part III that such cases are ones where D's φing was *justifiable* but not *justified*.

[10] This seems to be the right response to some of Peter Graham's examples in P Graham, 'A Sketch of a Theory of Moral Blameworthiness' (2012) 88 Phil and Phenomenological Research 38, most notably those in § 3. But there is a considerable literature. We discuss some cases of this kind in § 14.2.4.

We should withhold praise for her action of saving him. But we can't blame her for curing him. If D is to be blamed *for φing*, φing must be something morally undesirable, something that D ought not to have done. Like wrongdoing itself, blame is description-dependent.

There remains quite a lot packed into our central case. It may be useful to highlight a couple of its features. One aspect of linking blame to wrongdoing is that it concentrates attention upon cases in which D *does* something, whether act or omission. I assume without argument that the criminal law is right to focus on such cases.[11] Crimes like 'Compassing the death of the King' violate the principle of legitimate enactment. Outside the criminal law, however, some writers have argued that it can be appropriate to experience indignation at a person—that is, the kind of reactive attitudes we associate with blame—even in the absence of behaviour. This might occur, they suggest, when we realize that D has certain kinds of morally repugnant attitudes or thoughts, albeit those thoughts are not expressed through action.[12]

Perhaps blame-like condemnation is an appropriate reaction to such realizations.[13] For criminalization reasons, they are not a legitimate concern of the criminal law. That ground alone suffices to disregard such cases here. But it is worth registering a doubt about whether another person's thoughts or attitudes really are suitable objects of *blaming* judgements. To be sure, we can make moral evaluations of people, their attitudes, character, thoughts, and the like. And we can make moral evaluations of their actions. We can also make evaluations of how those actions reflect upon the actor, and of whether they disclose a moral vice. Paradigmatic blaming judgements are of the last type.[14] Evaluations of attitudes, however, lack certain features of this paradigm. Most notably, they are not subject to a voluntariness constraint. To conclude that D has reprehensible attitudes is, perhaps, to hold her 'responsible' for such attitudes: but it is also to bypass standard requirements, of the kind explored in Part II, that she be morally responsible for them.[15] That makes moral evaluations of attitudes (and the like) categorically distinct from blaming judgements, notwithstanding what

[11] For cases of situational liability, see §§ 4.3.3 and 8.4.2–3.

[12] e.g. ibid, esp. § 4. I set aside the possibility that some thoughts are voluntary mental acts and might as such be assimilated with (physical) acts: that is not, I take it, Graham's concern.

[13] Although I am sceptical whether our indignant reactions to such attitudes are on all fours with those relating to action. The case of *Kingston*, discussed in § 19.1.3, is instructive. K, who had always suppressed his paedophiliac inclinations, was led to commit an indecent assault through being drugged unawares by another. Many writers have questioned whether K was culpable: yet they would presumably regard his dispositions as abhorrent. If people can be blameworthy for attitudes, it becomes harder to see why we should quibble about whether K was culpable for what he *did*.

[14] I return to these distinctions in § 14.2.1.

[15] Angela Smith sees this clearly: A Smith, 'Responsibility for Attitudes: Activity and Passivity in Mental Life' (2005) 115 Ethics 236, esp. § V.

they have in common. For this reason, too, I exclude such evaluations from the scope of *blaming* judgments in this book.

11.1.1 Legal and moral wrongs

Another feature of our central case is that φing is a *breach of duty*—a wrong—and not merely something we ought not to do. This is paradigmatically true of stigmatic crimes, which are typically moral as well as legal wrongs. Again, however, there are reasons for thinking that breaches of duty are the central case for blameworthiness more generally. Blaming responses like indignation seem inappropriate to a case in which D merely failed to do what he had undefeated reason to do without being under any duty to do it. In part, this is because indignant reactions seem too strong. But they seem also to be of the wrong kind. If D has no moral duty not to φ, blaming reactions would appear to be officious and intrusive, or at least nosy. I don't mean by this to make the more obvious claim that others have no standing to condemn D or otherwise *express* blame, although that may also be true. Rather, the thought is that there is something inappropriate, indeed (without the sexual connotation) almost prurient, about experiencing indignation at D's error. His φing, one might say, is none of our moral business.

Of course, a legal duty *makes* φing the law's business. Still, it may be doubted whether acts of criminalization can transform something that was pre-legally unobjectionable into a moral wrong. One might harbour that doubt even if, as we stipulated in chapter 1, the offence is legitimately enacted. This is a particular concern for offences *mala prohibita*.[16] Frequently, the state declares actions to be unlawful that are not pre-legally wrong. How is it, one may ask, that the mere exercise of legal authority can create the grounds for blame?[17]

Two thoughts will have to suffice here. First, this is not really a problem for the general part doctrines. As I noted in § 1.4, it is a criminalization challenge. At least in the UK, the general part doctrines do not, and are not designed to, empower courts to second-guess the justification of unequivocal legislative

[16] It may have less force in the context of serious, stigmatic crimes, which are the main concern of this book; although that distinction will come under scrutiny in § 13.3.3.

[17] See, e.g., D Husak, *Overcriminalization* (OUP 2007) 103ff; V Tadros, *Wrongs and Crimes* (OUP 2016) ch 11. As Husak and others have noted, not all *mala prohibita* offences raise the same concern. By specifying an age of consent, for example, the state does not so much *create* a wrong of under-age sex as supply that pre-legal, *mala in se* wrong with a legal border.

proscriptions. Given that φing is a pro tanto crime, those doctrines assume it is a pro tanto wrong and proceed from there.

The second thought is more substantial. It builds upon an argument made in *Crimes, Harms, and Wrongs* that, provided the criminalization of φing is justified, a moral duty can arise out of the reasons why that proscription is justified.[18] This is not to suggest that φing becomes (morally) wrong whenever the state says it is. Rather, it is to say that the law characteristically enacts *mala prohibita* crimes for more particular reasons, and those reasons can lend moral weight to the standards it imposes. Many road traffic rules, including speed limits and vehicle-roadworthiness certification requirements, have this character. They implement regimes designed to ensure that drivers use the road safely, or as safely as they can practicably require. In turn, drivers have reason to conform to those rules, grounded indirectly in the purposes they serve.[19]

Granting such rules are justified, however, they are in practice likely to be overinclusive. Perhaps D can, in a particular scenario, exceed the road speed limit without endangering anyone else; perhaps D knows that. Or perhaps D is mechanically trained and knows her vehicle is roadworthy, although it has not been formally tested or certified. Why, then, does D have reason to conform to the (justified) prohibition; reason that could support a finding of blame?

Obviously, the answer is not, or at least not necessarily,[20] because D's nonconformity directly creates or increases any particular risk of harm. Rather, it lies in the value of having the regime itself. Suppose, for example, that vehicle-certification rules are appropriate for standard cases. The constraints imposed by limited state resources and practicalities of enforcement may then entail that individual nuances cannot be evaluated, legally, on an ad hoc basis. Implementing a practicable system for ensuring roadworthiness may depend upon the state's not having to set aside the resources to make personalized claims of difference justiciable. In turn, provided the burden imposed by the regime is not unduly onerous, and the benefits it secures are sufficiently valuable, we may conclude that D ought to conform to its requirements;[21] that there is no sufficient reason why D is entitled to special consideration. In this sort

[18] *Crimes, Harms, and Wrongs*, 25ff.

[19] I assume *arguendo* that the regulations are in fact valuable (and justified), something that depends in part on their being effective.

[20] In some cases, risks might be created by other drivers' relying on D's conformity: see *Crimes, Harms, and Wrongs*, 78–79. But while that point may be relevant for speeding, it remains a contingent matter; in any event, it does not seem to apply in the context of vehicle-roadworthiness certificates. Hence the argument here supplements that in *Crimes, Harms, and Wrongs*.

[21] Compare R A Duff and S E Marshall, '"Remote Harms" and the Two Harm Principles' in A P Simester, A du Bois-Pedain, and U Neumann (eds), *Liberal Criminal Theory: Essays in Honour of Andreas von Hirsch* (Hart 2014) 205, 219–20.

of case, non-conformity is a moral wrong not because of any risk of harm that the regime is designed to prevent. It is a wrong of indirectly undermining the regime, a regime that is itself valuable, which protects against harm, and which deserves to be upheld.[22]

Some may imagine counterexamples. Let us conjecture that mixing a certain group of chemicals is very dangerous; hence it is banned, unless the mixer is specifically licensed for that activity. D, however, is the world's leading expert on these chemicals and, for him, the process is entirely safe.[23] He does not have a license. Surely, it may seem, he has no moral duty to get one before mixing the chemicals?

Not so fast. Clearly there is a public interest in maintaining the licensing regime, which (let us assume) is the most practicable method for ensuring that these kinds of chemicals are mixed safely. There is, in turn, a public interest in enforcing and protecting that regime, derived ultimately from the potential for harm involved in unsafe mixing of the chemicals. Admittedly, D himself poses no risk of such harm. But the creation of a licensing regime introduces the possibility of other harms. In effect, to allow D exceptional treatment *modifies the regime itself*. D can either (a) get the licence or (b) claim to be different. But the latter claim will need to be tested too, via some form of trial or administrative inquiry, the ad hoc cost of which is likely to be much higher than the cost of granting a licence. Moreover, option (b) must then be available in principle to everyone else, since we don't know in advance whether any particular person is such an expert. The result is significantly increased expense, which comes out of the public purse: accommodating D's claim thus deprives others of the resources that are needlessly used up by D. If that's right, it follows that D has moral reasons to pursue option (a) and get the licence; and that the state has good reason to require him to do so.[24] Φing may be a wrong only in virtue of being *malum prohibitum*. For the purposes of the general part doctrines, the prohibition truncates such questions. But it is still a wrong.

[22] We should concede, though, that on this argument D's wrong may be less serious than the wrong of someone who bypasses the regulatory regime and in so doing endangers the safety of others.

[23] The example is based loosely on one discussed by Raz, in the context of authority. See J Raz, *The Morality of Freedom* (Clarendon 1986) 74 ('an expert pharmacologist may not be subject to the authority of government in matters of the safety of drugs'); J Raz, *Ethics in the Public Domain* (OUP 2001) 348 ('if I am the greatest living expert on pharmaceuticals, then the law has no authority over me regarding the safety of pharmaceuticals').

[24] The argument here assumes that a licensing regime is preferable to outright criminalization accompanied by providing a specific defence for persons like D. But that seems plausible. Indeed, it is more than a mere assumption. It is bound up with the claim to legitimacy of the regulatory regime itself, a claim that is undermined when the regime is inefficient.

11.2 The basic challenge

So much for preliminaries. The basic challenge for culpability judgements is to trace our negative evaluation of φing back to D, the person who does it. This is not straightforward because, as intimated already, moral evaluations of an action are not blaming judgements. Their objects of assessment are crucially different. When we blame, we disapprove not of the action by itself, but *of the defendant for doing that action.*[25] The burden for ascribing culpability lies in justifying that evaluative link between action and defendant—that link which allows us to trace judgements of the action back to the agent. I claim in this chapter that there are two ways in which we can sustain that link.

Implicit in this claim is a conceptual unity. My argument is that there are different grounds of culpability, that its material conditions differ between advertent and inadvertent wrongdoing; not that there are distinct concepts of blameworthiness in play. Culpability involves a particular kind of moral evaluation. We can make moral assessments of *people* ('a callous person'), just as we can of actions like φing, or indeed events more generally; but those are not blaming judgements either. To blame someone is to make a moral assessment of that person *in respect of* her action. The challenge for culpability is, one might say, a challenge about how to generate judgements that integrate evaluations of the actor and her action.

For it does not follow from the proposition that D's *action* is morally undesirable that D should be blamed for doing it. Imagine that Pam (from § 11.1), who has not been struck off, this time injects Alex with a painkiller that produces an allergic reaction and causes his death. Pam's killing Alex is undesirable. It is contraindicated by the applicable guiding reasons. It is a matter for regret. But, on these bare facts, it is not a matter for blame. All things considered, Alex should not receive the injection. But if his allergy is unknown, and unknowable, Pam is not culpable for injecting him.

Pam is not culpable and does not merit indignation because, in a sense, the killing does not reflect badly on her. When we trace back from her φing to an explanation of why she φed, the explanation discloses no deficiency of moral virtue; or, more precisely, none falling below what would be expected of a normal person in Pam's position, a so-called 'reasonable' person with decent values and dispositions. In a perfect world, we would always act for undefeated guiding reasons. Pam did not. So there is a sense in which she failed—at least,

[25] See also § 14.2.1.

as it turned out. But not all failures ground culpability. Whence, then, is culpability sourced?

11.3 Choice and inadvertence

For many writers, the crucial positive ingredient in grounding culpability for φing is *choice*. What makes intended or reckless φing culpable is not, as H L A Hart once suggested,[26] the actor's unexercised capacity to refrain from φing. Rather, it is her choice not to exercise that capacity. A well-known example of this kind of account is offered by Michael Moore:[27]

> 'In accommodating responsibility for negligence in this way, Hart, as he recognized, shifted the touchstone of responsibility from choice to capacity. A choice to do a wrongful act then becomes only one way in which the actor's capacity to avoid evil goes unexercised; inadvertence is another. My objection to this shift is a moral one: it relegates choice to a subsidiary role in our responsibility assessments that our judgments won't support. What makes the intentional or reckless wrongdoer so culpable is not unexercised capacity—although that is necessary—but the way such capacity to avoid evil goes unexercised; such wrongdoers are not even trying to get it right. Their capacity goes unexercised because that is what they choose. Choice is essential to their culpability, not one way among others that they could have been seriously culpable.'

(For convenience of discussion, I treat this version of Moore's theory as representative of choice-based accounts more generally.) Moore is right to emphasize a connection between choice and culpability. Choice can help to supply the bridge that allows us to trace judgements about the wrongfulness of φing back to D, underpinning blame. The bridging is not merely permissive but explanatory. When D chooses to act for bad reasons, she accepts and aligns herself with those reasons, and in turn with her wrongdoing. That action, being chosen, expresses her own values and dispositions, her knowing preference for bad reasons over good ones. In the absence of an excuse, it expresses a moral vice. Just as we can criticize her, qua person, for having such preferences, we

[26] See Hart, *Punishment and Responsibility*, 154; below, § 12.3.4.
[27] M S Moore, 'Choice, Character and Excuse' in E F Paul, F D Miller, Jr, and J Paul (eds), *Crime, Culpability and Remedy* (Basil Blackwell 1990) 29, 57. See also Moore, *Placing Blame*, ch 13.

can criticize her for acting upon them—which is to say, we can blame her for that action.

Notice that this account does not tie D's choice to advertence *simpliciter*.[28] An actor may be aware of the risk of φing, while not recognizing the magnitude of that risk. Suppose, for example:[29]

> John is building a campfire. He has cleared a space around the fire, and notices that there is loose dry grass a further distance away. John believes the risk of sparks carrying is very low and decides it is not worth clearing any further. Unfortunately, given the breeze, the risk is higher than he realizes. A spark gives fire to the grass, and the fire spreads to a nearby forest.

John is aware of a fire risk. Yet there is no choice-based fault in choosing to take a risk that, on the facts as perceived, it is reasonable to take. A case of this sort should not be accounted 'reckless', in the subjective sense known to the common law.[30] Trade-offs of this sort are a mainstay of surgeons, health-and-safety regulators, indeed all of us. John's culpability, if any, lies in his failure to recognize the true risk; not in the decision he then made.

Neither can blame for choices persuasively be reduced to a single underlying disposition, such as a desire to humiliate others whenever one assaults them.[31] Moore and Hurd rightly observe that 'someone who renders another unconscious so as to pick his pocket is clearly not motivated by a desire to humiliate; and someone who enjoys embarrassing others is clearly not as culpable as someone who enjoys physically torturing others, even though both may be said to be motivated by a desire to humiliate.'[32] We cannot even say, more generally, that one who chooses to φ is 'indifferent' to the interests of others.[33] Certainly there is acquiescence to the contemplated action. But D may or may not be indifferent. She may choose to risk φing despite wanting strongly not to do so.

[28] Cp. M S Moore and H Hurd, 'Punishing the Awkward, the Stupid, the Weak, and the Selfish: The Culpability of Negligence' (2011) 5 Crim L and Phil 147, 150, criticizing L Alexander and K Ferzan, *Crime and Culpability: A Theory of Criminal Law* (CUP 2009) 69, 78 n 25.

[29] I assume that on the (perceived) risk levels, it would be reasonable to clear no further. The example is based on one developed by W J Winslade, 'Brady on Recklessness' (1972) 33 Analysis 31, 32. In Winslade's version, however, the failure to remove the grass is inadvertent.

[30] 'It is however not the taking of every risk which could properly be classified as reckless. The risk must be one which it is in all the circumstances unreasonable for him to take.' *Stephenson* [1979] 2 All ER 1198, 1203. I return to this point in chapter 12.

[31] Cf., in the context of assaults, J Murphy, 'Bias Crimes: What do Haters Deserve?' (1992) Crim Justice Ethics 20.

[32] Moore and Hurd, 'Punishing the Awkward' (n 28) 172.

[33] Cf. J Brady, 'Indifference and Involuntariness' (1972) 32 Analysis 98, 99: 'indifference distinguishes recklessness from acting purposely.'

Perhaps she drove too fast because she wanted to see her children at home before their bedtime, although she was aware that she might skid and crash in the icy conditions. There is acceptance of the danger even though she very much hopes not to crash. In other scenarios, an actor may positively want to φ—a desire that may or may not motivate her choice to behave as she does.[34] No doubt, in all these cases, we can say the agent does not care *sufficiently*—not indifferent, but insufficiently differing (or worse).[35] However, that weaker claim adds nothing to the point that she chose to φ when she shouldn't have.

We return to the diversity of motivations below. So far, one can broadly agree with Moore, whose discussion is insightful and instructive. But no further. Ultimately, his recipe for culpability has too few ingredients.

A preliminary difficulty is that Moore's account is tied too closely to his theory of excuses.[36] Culpability is presented as the flip side of excuse, which are themselves explained in terms of choice:[37]

> '[According to] what I shall call the choice theory of excuse, ... one is excused for the doing of a wrongful action because and only because at the moment of such action's performance, one did not have sufficient capacity or opportunity to make the choice to do otherwise. Such a choice theory of excuse instantiates a more general theory of responsibility, according to which we are responsible for wrongs we freely choose to do, and not responsible for wrongs we lacked the freedom (capacity and opportunity) to avoid doing.'

Conduct is excused, therefore, in virtue of its not being freely chosen. This move effectively eliminates any middle ground on which to defend a separate account of culpability for inadvertent negligence. If there is a free choice to φ the actor is culpable; *aliter*, she is not. Hence, in Moore's account, all the pressure goes onto the question whether there is a genuinely free choice.

It is worth pausing to bring out an underlying distinction in the quoted passage. If φing is an unjustified wrong, and it is freely chosen by D, then on Moore's account D is culpable for her φing. It is, however, helpful to separate capacity-based and opportunity-based grounds for denying D's culpability.

[34] Suppose that I shoot my fiancée's father out of an intense dislike for him, realizing that this will probably mean the end of my engagement. If I am not motivated to shoot by that realization, then I advertently—without intending it—cause the abandonment of the wedding; even if I secretly find that prospect a source of relief.

[35] I take this point up again in chapters 15–16.

[36] Self-consciously. For Moore ('Choice, Character and Excuse' (n 27) 29), 'the excuses are the royal road to theories of responsibility generally.'

[37] Ibid. (Emphasis omitted.)

Where one φs because of an *incapacity*, say when automatic or paralysed, one is not (what I call) *morally responsible* for φing.[38] That is to say, one is not exposed to moral assessments—good, bad, neutral, or excused—in respect of that φing. Our assessments never get that far.[39]

On my usage, to be morally responsible for an event is to be *eligible* for moral assessment in respect of that event's occurrence.[40] As we noted in chapter 4, that is not the same thing as being culpable or praiseworthy for the event. Rather, moral responsibility is a precondition, one that must be satisfied before we can proceed to those moral judgments: it is a necessary, but not a sufficient, condition of being blameworthy. As such, capacity conditions are generally relevant to moral responsibility; whereas questions of *fair opportunity* generally affect findings of culpability, and arise only after moral responsibility is established.

The distinction matters to 'free'-choice-based accounts of culpability because there is a difference between defences that deny moral responsibility and defences that assert responsibility but deny culpability.[41] Both are sometimes called 'excuses', and Moore combines them here. Admittedly, both affect what Moore calls one's freedom of choice to avoid wrongdoing. But they do so in different ways. The former—*irresponsibility* defences—are pure capacity-based defences. They are not subject to reasonableness constraints. The latter—*rationale-based excuses*—are. An automaton does not have a choice to make, and is not a moral agent in respect of φing. A person acting under duress does, and is. In the latter case, we then inspect the content of that choice, and ask whether his reasons for φing reflect badly on him. So the structure of rationale-based excuses *is* tied closely to culpability assessments, and to the content of the choice that was made. The same is not true, however, of irresponsibility 'excuses'. Irresponsibility defences tell us nothing about blame. They take the defendant out of the realm of moral agency, of agency susceptible of moral evaluation, altogether.

[38] See § 4.1. Moore's terminology is different. For Moore, like most theorists, to be 'morally responsible' for a wrong is to be culpable for that wrong.

[39] This claim needs at least one qualification, to cover cases where D is blameworthy for becoming incapable of controlling his bodily movements, such that D's φing is a consequence of his culpable antecedent μing. See § 7.5.1; *Simester and Sullivan*, § 4.3(iii).

[40] In ordinary language, there is a natural association of moral responsibility with culpability, and my own usage is admittedly technical. Some may prefer to express the distinction in terms of D's being a 'moral agent' in respect of φing, and as such being eligible for moral appraisal (but not necessarily culpable) for φing. I avoid that alternative primarily because, as I argued in chapter 8, one can be morally responsible for an event without being an agent in respect of it. For present purposes, however, we can disregard that possibility. Nothing here turns on it.

[41] See Gardner, *Offences and Defences*, ch 6; below, §§ 17.1, 5.

11.3.1 Inadvertent negligence

Suppose, then, that D φed. She had the capacity not to φ, and we are considering whether D is blameworthy. Must φing be chosen? Many think that it must.[42] Certainly, culpability for inadvertent negligence does not fit easily with a choice theory of blame. [43] An actor cannot be blamed for negligently 'choosing' to φ, since inadvertent actions are not themselves chosen.[44] So it should be no surprise that many writers have denied culpability—and indeed responsibility—for inadvertent actions. As John Mackie elegantly suggests,[45]

> '[I]n so far as I am ignorant of what I am doing or bringing about, the actions which are for this reason unintentional can be seen not as belonging to me as a conscious agent, but to have been foisted upon or obtruded into my course of action by the facts or circumstances of which I was unaware.'

At the level of (what I term) moral responsibility, this seems too strong. Unintentional actions are capable of 'belonging' to me—at least when they are voluntary and I am a conscious agent at the time of doing them. Of course, that conclusion depends on what is the point of an action's 'belonging' to a person. I take it here that moral responsibility, and 'belongingness', serve to mark out those actions that are tied to us qua moral agents: as agents with the rational capacity to act for reasons, to act for them qua reasons, and to deliberate about those reasons. This is why it is a condition of moral responsibility that the actor be a moral agent. As I suggested in § 4.1,[46] she must be the kind of agent who is capable of recognizing and acting upon reasons, who has at least a general capacity to distinguish good reasons from bad, and who can adjudicate between conflicting reasons, by weighing and contrasting them, when deciding what to do.

[42] Compare, e.g., Alexander and Ferzan, *Crime and Culpability* (n 28) chs 2–3. Various other authors are cited in § 12.1.

[43] In line with criminal-law conventions, I use 'negligence' generally to refer to inadvertent wrongdoing, and treat negligence as a species of 'mens rea'. 'Reckless' actions are presumed to be advertent. As was noted in § 11.3, however, there are special cases. D's φing may be negligent rather than reckless even though D has recognized the possibility of her φing: notably, where D has underestimated the likelihood of her φing, and the level of risk that D herself perceives is a reasonable one to run.

[44] See also the criticism of Jean Hampton's account in § 11.5. In case of doubt, this is not to deny that inadvertent actions may be chosen under a different description: as when D deliberately fires a gun while out hunting, but does not notice that her colleague has moved into D's line of fire. Here, D chooses to fire the gun but does not choose to shoot her colleague, even though both actions are constituted by the same piece of behaviour.

[45] Mackie, *Ethics*, 209.

[46] See also § 17.5.

This differs foundationally from the position adopted by Mackie, and originally by Moore.[47] On their view, we are morally responsible actors only when we advertently *exercise* our capacity to act for reasons—it is only then that our actions truly belong to us as moral agents. So responsibility and fault can lie only when we choose to φ. By contrast, on the account offered here, we are moral agents not in virtue of exercising our rational capacities, but in virtue of *having* them. What counts, then, is whether D's φing is susceptible of control by D's rational capacities, not whether it occurs as an exercise of that control.

So far, the difference is primarily formal. Separating the morally responsible from the chosen does not show that the distinction matters, that the gap is populated, that there can be blame without choice. None the less, the gap is significant. When D φs intentionally or recklessly, we can link our judgement about φing back to an evaluation of D for doing it by reference to D's choice to act for the wrong reasons, something that reflects badly on D qua moral agent. The point here is that there may be—and I think there are—other ways in which inadvertent φing can be traced back to D in a manner that reflects badly on her.

Chosen wrongdoing reflects badly on the actor because it shows that he prefers bad reasons to good ones. He would rather stab his opponent than walk away, and so on. By contrast, the complaint when D is negligent is, in a sense, that she fails to act for the right reasons. But this too is a form of defective engagement that can reflect badly upon D qua rational moral agent. It can do so because the capacity for rational deliberation does not merely involve capacities to assess moral reasons (and act for undefeated ones): it also involves capacities to recognize them.

Broadly speaking, reasons for action involve two kinds of proposition: (I) that some outcome or event is valuable; and (II) that some action (φing) will or may facilitate that outcome or event to occur. When we blame D for choosing to φ, the grounds of our blaming judgement arise from conclusions about D's type (I) evaluations; in particular, that D has acted on personal preferences or evaluations at odds with those she should have acted upon. Such conclusions cannot be avoided if we are to have blaming practices at all, since the very idea of blame involves holding actors to a standard at least partially independent of their own values.[48] D's acting upon morally aberrant values reflects directly upon D and is, in itself, a ground of blame.

[47] Moore's views on negligence have evolved since writing 'Choice, Character and Excuse' (n 27): see Moore, *Placing Blame*, 411–19, 588–92; 'Moore and Hurd, 'Punishing the Awkward' (n 28).

[48] See also § 12.2.

By contrast, when we blame D for negligently φing, the grounds for doing so rest upon conclusions about type (II) propositions, concerning the likelihood that the relevant (undesirable) outcome will occur. Explaining this presents a distinct kind of problem from explaining why bad choices are culpable.

For convenience, we might label type (I) failings as *moral-preference errors*, whereas type (II) failings might be called *epistemic failings*. An epistemic failing involves some sort of mistake, some inadvertence or ignorance. Since they are not directly concerned with moral evaluations, it is tempting to see type (II) failings as not being the stuff of blame. But that does not follow. There is no general reason why the explanation of a particular epistemic failing cannot reflect badly on the actor. Suppose, for example, that D is lying on the beach and does not think to check on her children who are playing in the water. The children drift too far out and are drowned. Here, we might blame D, not for choosing to allow the children to drown, but for failing to engage with that risk. In such a case, had D evinced the care she should have shown for her children, *she would have thought* to check on them.

This is not just, although it involves, an evaluation of what happened (that, unfortunately, D did not think of the risk and check on the children, with the result that they drowned). It is also an evaluation of D with respect to what happened. D's failure to think about the situation is blameworthy because it tells us about her; it reflects the fact that she lacks sufficient concern for the well-being of her children. And that is a moral shortcoming in D. It is a moral vice.

We explore such cases further in chapter 12. For now, the example serves to suggest that, depending how they came to be made, epistemic failings too are capable of reflecting badly on the actor and of grounding blame. The underlying analysis, however, is more complex than for choice-based blame, and nowhere near as direct. Most importantly, the connection between inadvertent φing and blame *does not run through choice*, even indirectly; since we cannot infer from a finding of negligence that D would have φed if she had seen the risk.

Negligence, then, demands a more detailed account of what kinds of failure to advert are culpable. That task is for chapter 12. The point here is that it is possible. I do not claim that φing negligently is equally culpable as φing recklessly or intentionally. And chapter 3 explored some powerful reasons why the criminal law should criminalize negligence only rarely. But it is not ruled out *tout court*. Culpability *can* sometimes lie in D's failure to recognize a risk, where the root of that failure is a moral vice on D's part. Like chosen wrongdoing, the explanation of D's φing can reflect badly on her.

In passing, it is worth flagging up here that the distinction between moral-preference and epistemic failings matters in other contexts too. As we shall see in chapter 17, it is particularly important in the context of justifications and excuses; and to the *lawfulness* of certain actions. One of the key implications of the justification-excuse distinction is that chosen official action constituting a prima facie crime can normally only be justified. Individual actors may be excused for choosing to φ, on the grounds that their unjustified φing was blameless. But, qua officials, state actors cannot claim to be excused for an error of moral preference. Their chosen actions must be either justified—lawful—or not. So, I shall claim, official torture is inexcusable, even if—conceptually speaking—it might be justifiable.[49] At the same time, epistemic failing by officials is not foreclosed. Provided the official makes a reasonable mistake, for example when intervening to prevent crime or adjudicating a hearing, the inadvertent error need not undermine the lawfulness of her action.

11.4 Moral characteristics and moral vices

It may seem as if culpability for negligence commits us to a character-oriented theory of blame, or at least to explaining blame in terms of flawed moral characteristics—of what I call moral vices. In one sense, that's true. Any plausible account of culpability for negligence must hold us to blame for our mistakes (only) when the roots of those mistakes lie in certain types of failings. So, for example, inadvertence arising from physical blindness or low intelligence is not normally blameworthy; whereas it may be culpable when arising from the actor's failure to care about his children. Sight and intelligence are not *moral* characteristics.

At one level, reference to moral characteristics should be uncontroversial. It is a natural use of language to speak of 'character' flaws: meaning those types of failings that can ground blame for wrongdoing. Low intelligence may be a deficiency by reference to standards of an 'ordinary' or average person, but it does not involve any deficiency of moral character.[50] So it is not a *moral* vice. Whether we use the language of vices or of character flaws, the underlying distinction is one of substance. A theory of culpability in terms of moral vices presents a genuine alternative to choice- and capacity-based theories. It

[49] I develop these claims further in § 17.4 and §§ 18.2–4.

[50] In ordinary language, accusations of 'stupidity' do sometimes attribute culpability. Typically, in such cases, blame (unless misplaced) is not founded on having low intelligence per se: see § 12.3.3.

is concerned to pick out those kinds of limitations in an actor that *constitute* grounds for ascribing culpability. 'I'm sorry, but I never liked my children,' does not foreclose blame. It founds it.

Suppose that, at the beach, P has been left in charge of a child who then swims too far out to sea and is drowned. Consider three kinds of explanation for P's failure to prevent this disaster:

(1) P fails to rescue the child because he has been paralysed after being attacked suddenly by a swarm of bees.
(2) Owing to P's very low intelligence, he does not realize the risk.
(3) P does not pay attention to the child because his attention is absorbed entirely by a radio broadcast of England's winning a cricket match. (*Mirabile dictu*!)

Case (1) involves no moral responsibility for P's failure to rescue the child. As we saw in Part II,[51] a capacity-based test of involuntariness shows that no moral evaluation of P is possible with respect to his failure to rescue the child. For that purpose, the event does not 'belong' to P.

Cases (2) and (3) are different. In case (2), when assessing P's potential culpability, our evaluation of P's failure to perceive the risk should be relativized to P's personal intellectual capacities. *But not in case (3)*. There, P's failure rests in a moral vice. He falls short of what we expect from a reasonable person, a person who exhibits appropriate—decent—levels of care and concern for those around him. Since this shortfall is of a moral characteristic, culpability follows. In case (3), the failure to meet a non-relativized, impersonal standard reflects badly on P, without more.

11.4.1 Punishment for character? An objection to mainstream character theories

It is important to emphasize that the theory advanced here is not the same as the kind, rightly criticized by many writers, which claims—much more extremely—that blaming judgements are *for* our character traits and dispositions, and only derivatively for the actions that manifest them. As Moore asks,[52]

[51] See esp. chapters 4 and 8.

[52] Moore, 'Choice, Character and Excuse' (n 27) 55–56. It does not matter to the argument, but Molière died before Robespierre was born. Thanks to Nick McBride for the suggestion that the reference may be misremembered from a Jean Anouilh play, *Poor Bitos*.

> '[W]hy not punish people directly for bad character, since that is the locus of their just deserts? Why punish bad character indirectly, only through punishing actions expressive of it? . . . If the character theory were correct, the answer given to Moliere's Robespierre (when the latter asks why he is being condemned to death) should not be jarring: you are being condemned, Robespierre is told, "Because you lack grace." Yet the answer is jarring precisely because no one deserves to be punished for being a poor specimen of humanity. . . . I have yet to see how the character theorist can deny that character-responsibility alone makes it fair to punish, given his notion that character-responsibility is basic and act-responsibility only derivative.'

Quite. One can, of course, make moral evaluations of a person's character. Such a judgement is made here of Robespierre. But those are not blaming judgements. Moreover, blaming judgements do not start there. They start with wrongdoing, and end by tracing that action to a moral vice in the actor. Not the other way around.

Criminal theorists might see an easier reply. There are familiar criminalization objections to punishing for character alone. A theory of culpability should not be mistaken for a theory of liability. All the worries about enacting thoughtcrimes apply to punishment for character too. Those worries are compounded if one thinks that punishment is not the motivating purpose of the criminal law.[53] What comes first is the prohibition: and we certainly should not prohibit people from being who they are. Without wrongdoing of some sort, the state's regulatory role is not engaged. So it is no objection to any character theory of *blame* that the criminal law does not and should not punish for having a bad character.

But those criminalization worries are supplementary. Even outside the law, there is a categorical difference between evaluations of moral-character flaws and blaming judgements for actions.[54] At least paradigmatically, as we observed in § 11.1, blaming judgements take a different kind of object. They are made of the-defendant-in-respect-of-her-action.[55] My claim is not, in Moore's terms (above), 'that character-responsibility is basic and act-responsibility

[53] As I do (unlike Moore): *Crimes, Harms, and Wrongs*, ch 1.

[54] As it happens, I also think that punishment for mere flaws is unjustified. But this second claim, that punishment (like culpability) must be for φing rather than being, is too large to defend here. Part of the thought is that punishment should involve something for which D is answerable (especially, to the persons on whose behalf punishment is imposed)—and that excludes D's moral characteristics, even the flawed ones.

[55] In terms of the distinctions set out in § 14.2.1, blaming judgements are type (iii) evaluations, not type (i).

only derivative.' Blame is *not*, it seems to me, for the choice or character—or indeed the moral vice—that lies behind the action, as some writers seem to think. *Both* the action itself, and the moral flaw(s) by which it is explained, are basic.

Suppose we accept this. Still, Moore and Hurd have an administrative objection to the state's punishing according to character-flaw-based explanations of blame.[56] It is, they say, unworkable. The seriousness of a defendant's moral-character flaws 'varies considerably across actors and circumstances in a way that defeats the ability of legislators to clearly codify them, and the ability of judges to ensure the like treatment of cases that are morally alike.'[57] Amongst other things, they think this generates a fair-warning problem, on the grounds that it becomes impossible to codify the law 'so as to make clear and predictable to citizens when and how much they will be punished if they inadvertently invade others' protected interests.'[58]

No one said it would be easy. Assessments of culpability are often highly nuanced. They reflect not only the specific circumstances and nature of the agent's wrongdoing, but also the complex of her attributes and motivational impulses that led her to φ. The law may be less subtle, but its need at least roughly to track variations in culpability provides one reason why the State normally signals only a broad range of sentences when it prohibits φing, even as it undertakes to impose a more nuanced, desert-based punishment on particular offenders.[59] Provided there is adequate warning of prospective *convictions*, it suffices to lay out a sentencing range based on the general nature of φing, while delegating the more particular assessment *ex post* to a judge. This need not undermine the rule of law, at least not unduly. The criminal law cannot be expected to notify sanctions with exactitude, and its failure to do so hardly leaves potential wrongdoers bereft of notice. A combination of explicit and implicit, desert-based guidance is sufficient for citizens to know broadly where they stand, and how different kinds of φing are likely to be regarded.

Perhaps more importantly, though, much the same worry applies to choice-based wrongdoing. Culpability for choosing to φ is *not* grounded, without more, in the literal choice itself—the moral-preference error made in balancing reasons for and against φing. Even blame for advertent wrongdoing is, and should be, sensitive to the underlying motivations and dispositions that

56 Moore and Hurd, 'Punishing the Awkward' (n 28) 172–73.

57 Ibid, 173.

58 Ibid, 172.

59 *Crimes, Harms, and Wrongs*, § 1.1. This is not to claim that all variations of culpability should be remaindered to sentencing. Sometimes, considerations of fair labelling may demand a more nuanced set of offences (as is often found in homicide law). For a note of some criminalization issues this raises, see ibid, § 11.4.

led D to φ: with *how* D engaged with the reasons he had for and against φing. Someone who does wrong reluctantly (say, because pressured by peers) may not be in the same moral case as another who, in the same circumstances, does exactly the same wrong callously, or even relishing an opportunity to humiliate the victim. One who smothers his terminally ill parent in anguish is not equally culpable as another who, in identical circumstances, seizes the opportunity to inherit. If that's right, the bare choice is not the whole of the story. Nuanced punishment for φing will take account also of D's underlying motivations, and of how his emotions and values informed and structured the choice he made. Maybe the matter isn't quite as complex as it is for inadvertent wrongdoing.[60] But if Moore and Hurd's administrative worry is a serious one, it is hard to see why it doesn't apply to choice-based culpability too.

11.4.2 The 'out-of-character' worry

A more important concern about *character*-based theories, also pressed by Moore,[61] is the problem of 'out of character' wrongdoing. If the grounds for blame originate in a person's character (understood in terms of a more permanent and stable set of values and dispositions), why do we blame persons whose wrongdoing is 'uncharacteristic' or atypical? Moore is right about this too. Isolated instances of wrongdoing, which don't reflect any general tendencies, are not immune from blame. But the 'out-of-character' objection does not apply to the account defended here, because my account does not focus on the actor's non-transient character, long-term or otherwise. Rather, it investigates whether the explanation of her φing reflects badly on her, judged by reference to a generalized, not individualized, standard of moral characteristics—of values, dispositions, and the like. Notice that much the same holds for chosen wrongdoing. Returning to the beach, suppose a new explanation:

(4) Q fails to rescue the child because the child has been disobedient and Q is very angry with her. Q has never done such a thing before, and regrets his failure for the rest of his life.

[60] And perhaps some generalizations are possible. We might, for example, have a distinct category of indifference-based recklessness. It seems unlikely, though, that finer-grained categories of this sort would be especially useful—either too narrow to be important or too heterogeneous to be dispositive.

[61] Moore, 'Choice, Character and Excuse' (n 27) 57.

In case (4), we might accept that Q's choice is out of character; although, more usually, such cases will merely reveal a latent aspect of Q's character in an original context.[62] Either way, however, that choice belongs to Q. Judged by reference to the values and priorities Q ought to have, Q falls short on this occasion. His failure, however aberrant, is culpable.

Ultimately, the theory proffered here is not a 'character' theory of blame in the traditional sense. Granting that, however, one might worry that it is reductivist. Recall our basic challenge for culpability theories; to trace our negative evaluation of φing back to the defendant, D. Something more is required, in addition to the mere wrongness of φing, in order to support that tracing. Moore rejected capacity conditions as doing that work, and he was right to do so. But if the extra ingredient can be ephemeral, what does it amount to—especially since it is identified by a counterfactual test, of whether a person exhibiting decent moral characteristics would have done otherwise? Does this test really tell us anything about D? Does it identify any ground of blame, anything for culpability judgements to grip on? At least in Moore's account, one might think, there is something linking D to her φing, something capable of grounding blame. There is D's choice. What here?

Two thoughts by way of response.[63] The first is that the move to finding culpability is not merely a counterfactual one. On the theory articulated here, it involves a positive conclusion that D exhibited (on this occasion) some moral vice: some flaw of dispositions, values, and the like, that led to his epistemic failing. The failing is not *constituted* by the counterfactual. It is a matter of inference. So it is subject to explanations of how D came to φ that defray blame, and must be supported by evidence of a link between flaw and inadvertence. It requires showing the extent to which failures to advert to risks can be a function of how much we care about them, and about the interests at stake. Establishing such a link may be probabilistic, admitting of varying levels of confidence.

More on that in chapter 12. The second point is to note that the attachment of blameworthiness is event-specific and therefore time-stamped. What counts is whether D exhibited some moral vice *on that occasion*—in that moment of behaving.[64] Again, this point is tied to the insight that blame is *for* φing (and, indeed, for exhibiting some moral shortfall in φing); not for having a poor

[62] See, e.g., R A Duff, 'Choice, Character, and Criminal Liability' (1993) 12 Law and Phil 345.

[63] A different riposte would be to suggest that Moore's account makes too much of 'choice' as a free-standing wellspring of blame, whereas it is better seen as a placeholder for the underlying moral preference errors, for aberrant values and dispositions that might themselves be ephemeral. As cases like *T* (discussed in the text below) suggest, choice only grounds blame to the extent that it too belongs to D. However, that reply doesn't meet the 'counterfactual' worry. It just spreads it around.

[64] This point has ramifications for moral luck. See §§ 14.2–4.

character. This robs culpability of some depth as a concept, but seems inevitable if we are going to accept that basically good people can sometimes rightly be blamed for momentarily doing wrong. That said, any theory of culpability—whether concerned with choice or negligence—will have to leave space for radical disconnection. In *T*, for example,[65] D participated in a violent street robbery. Three days earlier, she had been brutally raped, and was suffering from post-traumatic stress disorder. At least at a superficial level, her conduct was deliberate. She was conscious and responsive to events.[66] Yet something was missing. Her conduct was disengaged from her own values and preferences,[67] and, it seems, unresponsive to any capacity to reason and deliberate about her conduct. Her choices, we may say, did not belong to her.

Distinguish this kind of case from changes in character. Again, this problem is common to both advertent and inadvertent culpability. A well-known example is the case of Patty Hearst, the 18-year-old heiress to William Hearst's publishing empire who was kidnapped by the self-styled Symbionese Liberation Army. While in lengthy captivity, during which she was subjected to a programme of abuse and indoctrination, she unsurprisingly experienced a personality change. Now endorsing her captors' values, she adopted a new name, Tania, and voluntarily joined in perpetrating an armed bank raid. Notice that the difficulty here is choice-based. We cannot blame Patty for being who she became. On the usage identified in § 11.3, we shouldn't even describe her as 'responsible' for being Tania.[68] But she is *answerable* as the moral agent she now is, and open to blame for raiding the bank.

11.5 Reintegrating choice—and capacity?

It emerges from what has been said so far that an account of negligence in terms of moral vices is partially reconcilable with choice theories of blame. Chosen wrongdoing is itself culpable to the extent that the actor's choice falls short of what we would expect from a person exhibiting decent moral characteristics. We can look behind choice as well as inadvertence—neither generates

[65] [1990] Crim LR 256. See J Horder, 'Pleading Involuntary Lack of Capacity' [1993] CLJ 298, 312–15.

[66] The Court allowed D to raise a claim of automatism, a congenial device that involved quite a stretch of legal doctrine.

[67] Potentially, this analysis would allow for cases where D rejects the values by which she is motivated, as in Frankfurt's example of the unwilling drug addict: *Importance*, 17.

[68] Cf. Moore, 'Choice, Character and Excuse' (n 27) 46–47. That qualification apart, Moore's analysis of the case is persuasive. See also the note on constitutive luck in § 14.4.1.

culpability save to the extent it reflects badly on the agent. Consider, then, a final case:

(5) R fails to rescue the child because he is afraid of cold water (or of a tarantula that sits between him and the water, or of the gunmen threatening the rest of his family, or . . .).[69]

In case (5) and its variants, the choice not to rescue the child *does* belong to R. The excusatory power of duress-type scenarios does not rest on the premise that, in such situations, the choice to φ doesn't truly belong to the actor; that φing isn't really 'chosen'.

It is chosen. But we are offered a (potential) rationale-based excuse. Whether R is culpable depends, in turn, on the reasonableness of that excuse: on whether her choice reflects badly on her.[70] At least where a reasonable person—a person of decent values and dispositions—would have responded like R, we cannot make the inference of shortcoming that would otherwise ground blame. In such cases, R's choice to act wrongfully merely discloses an imperfect virtue, not a fault; a limitation characteristic of humans in general, and not particular to R. Thus choice-based and negligence-based culpability share common ground. Each is predicated, in part, upon an agent's being unreasonable.

We develop this claim in chapter 12. Yet we should not push the reconciliation too far. We should not, for example, seek to claim that our moral vices ground blame because they are themselves, in some sense, chosen. Jean Hampton makes a move of this sort when defending a choice-based account of culpability. Hampton argues that culpable negligence is due to a faulty character that D 'knew better than to develop in this way.'[71] So, for example, if D makes a mistake because she is impatient, Hampton would suggest that her culpability resides in an earlier choice to be an impatient sort of person. But this is, surely, rarely true. Most of us don't choose to be bad-tempered, impatient, or otherwise flawed persons. Moreover, a choice-based account requires not merely that the relevant character flaw be chosen, but that *φing* be chosen. D must be aware of the risk. Thus, in order to ground culpability for later actions

[69] This is the kind of case that puts pressure on Moore's account of culpability in terms of 'freedom' (above, § 11.3) and which rationale-based excuses but not irresponsibility defences are equipped to analyse. Contrast the situation where D's fear is literally paralysing: a case of involuntariness, not choice. See § 17.5.

[70] See § 17.1–2.

[71] J Hampton, 'Mens Rea' (1990) 7 Soc Phil and Policy 1, 27. Attempts to explain culpability by reference to antecedent fault are nowadays known as 'tracing strategies'. See Moore and Hurd, 'Punishing the Awkward' (n 28) 176–82.

of negligent φing, D's failure to rectify her character would have to be chosen *in the awareness that* her later φing is the sort of consequence that might ensue if she doesn't. Hampton's analysis is artificial. We blame, rather, because impatience is a dispositional trait that grounds blame directly. It is a moral vice.

More generally, it is implicit in the theory advanced here that one's moral vices need not be chosen. In practice, values, dispositions, and the like do not usually develop self-consciously, except perhaps at the margins. Rather, they tend to emerge as the product of mixed inputs, including environment, upbringing, and genetic inheritance. And they are largely settled by the time we become mature agents. Blaming judgements, at least of the kind we have considered here, are not sensitive to such questions. To blame D for φing is not to ask why D is someone who wants to φ, or someone who does not care about φing.[72] It is enough that, chosen or not, D's values and choices are hers. A blaming judgement assumes that D is a moral agent. It operates just to connect that moral agency, on this occasion, to D's φing.

This analysis makes key the category of *moral* characteristics, whether virtuous or vicious. It makes them the only kind of shortfall that can ground blame. That such a category exists seems obvious, and necessary if culpability exists at all. The explanation, 'I'm just naturally selfish,' warrants rather than excuses blame for φing. But what kinds of characteristics are moral ones? It was suggested earlier that mistakes, even unreasonable ones, seem to be blameless where they arise from a lack of intelligence, and in my view we are not generally entitled to expect non-relativized intellectual capacities from wrongdoers. Neither is deafness a moral vice. Yet more needs to be said about which characteristics, and which incapacities, can ground blame. We turn to that task in chapter 12.

11.6 Backwards and forwards with culpability

None of what has been said in this chapter contradicts Joseph Raz's suggestion that the grounds of blame originate in the guiding reasons not to φ.[73] Indeed,

[72] R Nozick, *Anarchy, State and Utopia* (Basic Books 1974) 225.

[73] Raz, *Practical Reason and Norms*, 186–87: 'Other things being equal, [the guiding reasons for an action] are sufficient grounds for taking the action, and barring reasonable ignorance or other excuses, grounds for finding fault with the actor's conduct, if he fails to take the action.' Cp. R Milo, *Immorality* (Princeton UP 1984) 224. But see more recently J Raz, 'Responsibility and the Negligence Standard' (2010) 30 OJLS 1.

at one level, that proposition seems incontrovertible. We shouldn't choose to φ, and (I would say) we should take care not to φ, *because* φing is a bad thing to do.

Fair enough. Perhaps guiding reasons are primary. However, it is tempting to go further, and think they are primary *simpliciter*. They might, for example, seem to resolve questions of moral luck. After all, we can't be blamed for φing unless we actually φed, and unless φing was something that, objectively speaking, we ought not to have done. Hence Gardner endorses a proportionality principle in punishment 'according to which the sentence should be in proportion to the offender's wrongful action, adjusted for his blameworthiness in respect of it.'[74]

That doesn't follow. There is an important dimension of the idea of 'wrongdoing' that is concealed by the stipulative usage adopted in this book. Recall Pam the doctor, who blamelessly killed Alex. It is true that 'Pam did something wrong' in my stipulative sense. Killing Alex was, all things considered, undesirable. But it would be misleading in ordinary language to say that Pam 'acted wrongfully'.

Part of the distinction might seem to lie in which action we focus upon. Killing Alex may be inherently wrong, at least when unjustified, but it is not inherently wrong to inject Alex with a painkiller when he needs one. However, that insight doesn't carry us very far, because whether it is justified to inject the painkiller can also be said to depend on the (objective) guiding reasons for and against doing so; and, in particular, on the fact that injecting Alex will kill him.

A better way of thinking about the difference is to contrast *ex post* with *ex ante* perspectives. When it comes to blameworthiness, guiding reasons are not the only thing that is primary. Certainly, *ex post*, the raw fact of outcomes, lucky or otherwise, determines what we can be blamed for. Φing—killing Alex—is what Pam did. But that simple truth does not determine why, or to what extent, she is culpable for it. For that, we must look at Pam's situation *ex ante*—up to the moment she φs. We must look forward. We must ask, might a reasonable person, a person exhibiting decent moral characteristics, have made the same choice as Pam?

The point is that culpability does not originate simply in D's doing something that is all-things-considered undesirable, because it is not the case that, *ex ante, D should actually be guided* by the applicable guiding reasons.[75] D is not perfect or omniscient, and is not expected to be. Guiding reasons tell us whether φing is wrongful. But from the perspective of culpability, what counts

[74] Gardner, *Offences and Defences*, 232. See, too, § 14.2.2 below.
[75] Hence, too, the possibility of being vindicated but unjustified.

is how D *engaged* with those reasons. Blaming judgements require us to look at D's *actual* practical reasoning when she φed.[76] (Did she choose badly? Did she fail to consider reasons that she should have?) We must ask: in what way does D's failure to be guided by the applicable guiding reasons reflect badly on D? From the perspective of *culpability*, what is ultimately required is not, as such, to avoid φing per se. D's obligation is to avoid φing through a moral vice; to avoid φing in so far as that is reasonable for someone of her capacities.

I develop this claim further in chapter 14, when exploring its payoff for moral luck.[77] In our example, Pam acted for defeated reasons that we would expect any reasonable person (*ex ante*) to act for. She gave the injection because she wanted to alleviate pain. Perhaps Alex was in extreme pain following a road accident, and it was impossible to test for allergies in the circumstances. Pam administered a standard palliative drug but Alex was one of the very rare persons allergic to it. That Alex died is tragic. Yet it does not follow that Pam should refrain from administering the drug again, when confronted with someone in great pain who needs immediate palliative relief. Indeed, we would want her to make a similar choice in the future. From an *ex ante* perspective, there is a sense in which Pam did not fail. She conducted herself in a manner beyond criticism. And after that, we all must trust to luck.

[76] Importantly, this perspective also allows us to accommodate differentiation in D's reasoning between means, ends, and side-effects. See chapters 16 and 18.

[77] See esp. § 14.2 for the argument that outcome luck affects wrongdoing but not culpability.

12

Being Unreasonable

Reasonableness is in the lifeblood of law. Our legal system does not, indeed cannot, specify with precision what is to be done in every variety of circumstance. Its rules are often stated in terms of what is reasonable, or of what a so-called 'reasonable man' would do. Jurors are enjoined to find the accused guilty of a negligence-based offence only if his conduct has fallen below the standard to be expected of a reasonable person: that standard is left to them without definition. In contract law, objective tests for the formation and interpretation of contracts are elucidated by reference to reasonable understandings: 'The judicial task is not to discover the actual intentions of each party; it is to decide what each was reasonably entitled to conclude from the attitude of the other.'[1] Actions in estoppel are concerned to protect reliance upon reasonable, rather than unreasonable, expectations that the defendant has in some way fostered. And liability in tort generally excludes damage that is not a reasonably foreseeable result of the defendant's conduct.[2]

Very often, in contexts like these, reasonableness operates as part of a balancing exercise between competing legally recognized interests. Especially in private law, it helps to determine whether the plaintiff's interests should take priority over those of the defendant—to determine who should pay when something goes wrong. Sometimes, however, inquiries into reasonableness have an independent moral significance. They do so in the criminal law. As we observed in chapter 1, at least in serious offences, the very judgment against a defendant—the conviction—carries an implication of culpability. That implication extends to recklessness-based crimes, where the risk taken must be an unreasonable one. It informs the rationale-based excuses,[3] which ask whether a reasonable person may have reacted like the defendant, as well as mistake-based defences, which (should) require the defendant's mistake to

[1] *McCutcheon v David MacBrayne Ltd* [1964] 1 WLR 125, 128 (Lord Reid). See also *Smith v Hughes* (1871) LR 6 QB 597, 607; *The Hannah Blumenthal* [1983] 1 AC 854.

[2] *Caparo Industries plc v Dickman* [1990] 2 AC 605 (HL).

[3] See §§ 17.1–3. The paradigm rationale-based excuses is duress. For convenience, in this chapter I refer to rationale-based excuses simply as 'excuses'.

Fundamentals of Criminal Law. A P Simester, Oxford University Press (2021). © A P Simester.
DOI: 10.1093/oso/9780198853145.003.0012

be reasonable.[4] And it reaches even to negligence-based crimes, such as manslaughter and, in many jurisdictions, rape.

Imposing standards of reasonableness in each of these contexts raises a challenge for the criminal law. Are such standards apt to track moral vices? Admittedly, some writers would reject this question altogether in the context of negligence. They would deny that negligence is culpable.[5] But most people tend to think of negligence as something for which a defendant may legitimately be blamed: 'To the plea "I'm so sorry, I just did not think", the answer will often be, not "Oh I see; then you are not to blame", but "That's no excuse; you *should* have thought; a person in such a position has a *duty* to think".'[6] Even if we accept this, however, the question of aptness remains. Regard the standard legal test for negligence, enduringly summarized by Baron Alderson:[7]

> 'Negligence is the omission to do something which a reasonable man, guided upon those considerations which ordinarily regulate the conduct of human affairs, would do, or doing something which a prudent and reasonable man would not do.'

Mutatis mutandis, something similar might be said for recklessness and excuses, to the extent that they rest on findings that the defendant's choice was not one that a reasonable person would have made. But the problem emerges most clearly for negligence. Baron Alderson's test reflects upon a defendant only indirectly. In negligence, whether criminal or civil, there is a sense in which the law is concerned neither with what the defendant did nor with why she did it. Instead, it complains about what she did not do. Prima facie, rather than examine the values and dispositions lying behind the defendant's own actions, the law focuses upon whether her conduct diverged from the standard set by a 'prudent and reasonable man'.

[4] See § 19.2ff.

[5] Below, § 12.1.

[6] E D'Arcy, *Human Acts: An Essay in Their Moral Evaluation* (Clarendon 1963) 114. Compare Hart, *Punishment and Responsibility*, 136: '"I didn't *mean* to do it: I just didn't think." "But you should have thought." . . . [M]ost people would think that, in ordinary circumstances, such a rejection of "I didn't think" as an excuse is quite justified.'

[7] *Blyth v The Company of Proprietors of the Birmingham Waterworks* (1856) 11 Ex 781, 784; 156 ER 1047, 1049.

12.1 Culpability and inadvertence

That approach may be unobjectionable when negligence, or indeed recklessness, is deployed as an actus reus term. In the English crimes of reckless driving and careless driving,[8] for example, the terms 'reckless' and 'careless' qualify the behaviour element of each offence (driving). They refer primarily to the *manner* of D's driving, and in particular to how dangerous it was. Similarly, in ordinary language we might say that 'James waved his hand negligently', without suggesting that his doing so was inadvertent. But that is not how negligence and recklessness elements operate in other crimes, including rape and manslaughter: there, they are mens rea terms. In the latter role, however, if mens rea findings are to support judgements of culpability, there would seem to be a problem about Baron Alderson's approach. Let us concede, for argument's sake, that the standard test sets a *behavioural* standard; it tells us, say, that a reasonable person would φ and, by implication, that the defendant should do so too. Yet we saw in the previous chapter that the fact that D ought to φ doesn't mean she is culpable for not doing so. Recall the example from § 11.6, in which Pam, a doctor, injects Alex with a painkiller that produces an allergic reaction and causes his death. All things considered, Pam ought not to give Alex the painkiller. Her killing Alex is morally undesirable and a matter for regret. But it is not (on those facts) a matter for blame. Assuming his allergy was unknown, and unknowable, Pam is not culpable for injecting him. Expressed in terms of criminal law doctrine, there is the actus reus of a homicide, but no mens rea.

Pam's case illustrates a key point made in chapter 11,[9] that blaming judgements are not moral judgements of action per se. Neither are they judgements of persons. Rather, blame combines person with action. When we blame, we disapprove not of the action *simpliciter*, but of the defendant *for* doing that action. Allegedly, the reasonable person standard responds to that distinction, in as much as it does not require the defendant to act *all things considered*. Pam herself did what a reasonably prudent doctor would do. But that still leaves a problem for the conventional legal test. Given that negligence is assessed by reference to the conduct of a hypothetical figure rather than to the defendant, on what footing can we apply our judgement of that behaviour to *her*? How does the standard of care in negligence tell us anything about the defendant herself?

[8] Road Traffic Act 1972, s 2 (reckless driving); Road Traffic Act 1988, s 3 (careless driving).
[9] See also § 14.2.1.

Variants of this worry apply to recklessness and excuses. According to choice theories,[10] the link between defendant and wrongdoing is constituted when the defendant has chosen to act for bad reasons. She is culpable because she has made a moral-preference error, in aligning herself with the wrong. That explanation still leaves some work to do. Not all choices to risk a pro tanto wrong are unreasonable. Moreover, the possibility of excuses allows that chosen wrongdoing need not express a moral vice. So appeals to reasonableness in recklessness and in the excuses play an important role in grounding blame under choice theories. They help to bridge the space between choice *simpliciter* and culpability.

The gap between choice and inadvertence, on the other hand, is not for bridging. Choice theories lack the moral tools with which to blame an inadvertent-but-negligent wrongdoer, save in special cases.[11] Indeed, choice theorists typically deny that negligence is culpable at all. If choice is *the* ground of blame, they conclude, the attachment of moral judgements to D for unforeseen actions is unwarranted. There is no moral-preference error.

For a choice theorist, advertence is required because of the manner in which morality guides us: by, it is said, giving us a way of evaluating actions.[12] When D is unaware of her prospective action, however, the moral reasons for or against that action cannot guide her *ex ante* assessment of whether she should behave as she does. Suppose, for example, that D walks into a room and flicks on the light switch. We do not expect her to pause before doing so and consider whether the switch is miswired. It seems right to say in such cases that D need not dwell upon apparently irrelevant considerations. Generalizing this thought, failure to select between unknown options doesn't look like something for which one can be blamed. To reiterate John Mackie's suggestion,[13]

> '[I]n so far as I am ignorant of what I am doing or bringing about, the actions which are for this reason unintentional can be seen not as belonging to me as a conscious agent, but to have been foisted upon or obtruded into my course of action by the facts or circumstances of which I was unaware.'

The underlying reasoning is attractive. In various forms it has swayed a number of writers.[14] We cannot blame a defendant for negligently 'choosing' to do a

[10] See § 11.3.
[11] See § 11.5.
[12] See, e.g., Mackie, *Ethics*, 208–10.
[13] Ibid, 209; above, § 11.3.1.
[14] e.g. M S Moore and H Hurd, 'Punishing the Awkward, the Stupid, the Weak, and the Selfish: The Culpability of Negligence' (2011) 5 Crim L and Phil 147; L Alexander and K Ferzan, *Crime and*

morally bad act, since inadvertent options are not themselves chosen. Indeed, an inadvertent defendant might be horrified when she realizes what she has done. The defendant's error lies in her failure to realize that some risk is in play, not in her choice to disregard it.

So it does seem right, as we acknowledged in chapter 11, to decouple the culpability of advertent and inadvertent actions.[15] Yet that just makes the challenge to explain negligence more complex. It is a non-sequitur to conclude that inadvertence cannot be culpable. Choices can indeed ground culpability. But that doesn't make them necessary.

The key insight here is that moral considerations should prompt more than just choices between prospective actions. Suppose that killing James is an unjustifiable wrong. Then, with the choice theorists, we can say that Daisy should choose neither to kill nor to risk killing him. But we can also say that Daisy should *take care* not to kill James. The fact that an action is a moral wrong generates more than one type of reason. *Inter alia*, it generates a reason to take care lest that action be done. Perhaps negligent defendants are not so culpable as persons who choose to kill or risk killing. Be that as it may, inadvertence does not imply blamelessness for V's death.

On the other hand, neither does it follow that negligent inadvertence *is* blameworthy. By denying the exclusivity of the choice thesis, we merely preserve moral space to show that inadvertent behaviour can be culpable. It remains to establish how a finding of culpability can be sustained.

In particular, it is not enough to rely on the (true) proposition that guiding reasons not to φ can exist independently of the defendant's own choices. There is no direct path from such reasons to blame. All things considered, Pam has an overriding reason not to inject Alex with the painkiller that will cause his death. But she is blameless when she acts without considering that reason. Omniscience is not required. And that throws us back upon our earlier question: if, all things considered, D ought not to φ, when does D's φing warrant an adverse moral inference about D? When does her engagement with the reasons she had not to φ reflect a moral vice on D's part? The choice theory addresses one set of cases. Our challenge is to find an alternative basis for blame, one that

Culpability: A Theory of Criminal Law (CUP 2009) ch 3; C Finkelstein, 'Responsibility for Unintended Consequences' (2005) 2 Ohio St J Crim L 579; J Hall, 'Negligent Behaviour Should be Excluded from Criminal Liability' (1963) 63 Columbia LR 632; J W C Turner, 'The Mental Element of Crimes at Common Law' in L Radzinowicz and J W C Turner (eds), *The Modern Approach to Criminal Law* (Macmillan 1948) 195.

[15] Contrast, e.g., J Hampton, 'Mens Rea' (1990) 7 Soc Phil and Policy 1; above, § 11.5.

offers a non-arbitrary distinction between those reasons D should consider (even if she does not) and reasons that D may neglect without censure.[16]

Impliedly, legal doctrine takes the 'reasonable man' test to perform that function. Yet there are obvious reasons to doubt this. Prima facie, it is open to a defendant to claim that if the law employs an 'objective' third-person standard to assess her behaviour, it cannot, without more, use the news that her behaviour is unreasonable to infer that she is culpable. The defendant may answer:

> 'Doubtless the man on the Clapham omnibus would not act as I did. But I am not like that hypothetical "person". Why, therefore, do I deserve blame for not doing what some fictional character would do? Baron Alderson's standard tells us about a reasonable man, or perhaps about Baron Alderson. But how is it a comment on *me*?'[17]

Moreover, sometimes a reply of this sort would be clearly apt. Suppose that D is lying in the sand at a beach, and does not notice when someone else's child falls over in the water and begins to drown. A normal person would have seen the child. Is D negligent? Not if she is blind.[18] To blame, convict, or impose liability on a blind person for failing to see would be both wrong and profoundly unfair.

The case of blindness illustrates the fallacy of thinking that the reasonable person supplies an 'objective' test without reference to the defendant's peculiar characteristics—indeed, the fallacy of anthropomorphizing the reasonable man 'himself'. Rather, the standard is partly objective—imposed—and partly subjective or personalized. In terms of conventional doctrine, if the defendant is blind, or one-legged,[19] or a young child,[20] so too is the reasonable person. The blind defendant is expected to behave like a reasonable blind person, not as if sighted. Similarly, when faced by threats, a young person must show the fortitude expected from someone of her own age.[21]

[16] Some writers have concluded the task is impossible: Alexander and Ferzan, *Crime and Culpability* (n 14) 81ff.

[17] Less compellingly, a similar answer might be proffered in choice-based contexts. 'Perhaps your man from Clapham would have resisted the threat, but how is that a comment on me?' I suggest in § 12.2 that these kinds of cases are more straightforward.

[18] Compare, in tort law, *Bernard v Russell* 164 A 2d 577 (1960); *Keith v Worcester St R.R.* 82 NE 680 (1907); *Balcom v City of Independence* 160 NW 305 (1921).

[19] See *St Louis I.M. & S. Ry v Maddry* 21 SW 472, 474 (1893).

[20] *R (on the application of The Royal Society for the Prevention of Cruelty to Animals) v C* [2006] EWHC 1069 (Admin), [2006] 170 JP 463; also *DPP v Camplin* [1978] AC 705, 718 (provocation). In tort law, see, e.g., *Charbonneau v MacRury* 153 A 457 (1931); *McHale v Watson* (1966) 115 CLR 199; *Yorkton Agricultural Assoc v Morley* (1967) 66 DLR (2d) 37; O S Gray, 'The Standard of Care for Children Revisited' (1980) 45 Mo LR 597.

[21] *Graham* [1982] 1 All ER 801, 806. See also the discussion in § 19.1.

Actually, we need to go further. We need to unpick, even abandon, the so-called 'reasonable person'. We need to stop thinking in terms of the law's fictitious creation and refocus our attention upon the defendant. If reasonableness standards are to warrant attributions of culpability, they ought to set an objective standard in respect of those shortcomings of a defendant that ground blame, while not penalizing subjective characteristics such as blindness. So understood, the 'reasonable person' *is really the defendant, subject only to the imposition of certain objective standards*; the defendant, held up to an objective standard of moral characteristics. The accounting of her behaviour as 'unreasonable' must reflect some shortcoming of the defendant herself; a shortcoming for which morality and the law are justified in saying, the fact that you are unlike a reasonable person is no answer.

12.1.1 Towards a reasonable defendant

Rather than asking what a reasonable person would do, then, we should focus more closely on why the defendant doesn't act reasonably. This way of approaching the problem also allows us to see more clearly what appeals to (un)reasonableness have in common across recklessness, negligence, and the excuses. In all three areas, they supply a basis for inference that D's engagement with the reasons she had for and against φing was defective: defective, moreover, in a manner that discloses a moral vice on D's part. A legal finding of recklessness or negligence, like a finding that D failed to exhibit sufficient fortitude in the face of threats, depends upon the conclusion that D fails to act for adequate reasons—reasons for which our reasonable 'person' would act; reasons for which D herself could be expected to act, were she held to an objective standard of moral characteristics.

Putting the matter this way suggests a more promising road to understanding D's failure, by focusing attention on what is missing: action for adequate reasons. Here the ground is more familiar. One acts for reasons when one's behaviour is motivated by one's dispositions (desires, preferences, *et cetera*[22]) and beliefs.[23] In turn, what grounds culpability findings in these areas is that D fails to act for the reasons that would motivate a 'reasonable' version of herself. In the language of § 11.3.1, she makes either a moral-preference error

[22] As footnoted in § 11, I use 'dispositions' loosely, to include desires, inclinations, attitudes, and the like. One reason for this is to help forestall any suggestion that reasonable persons always *choose* to avoid acting wrongly. Often, we do the right thing without consciously thinking about it.

[23] See also § 15, in the context of intended action.

or an epistemic one (or both). So we should start by investigating how it is that D goes wrong in her dispositions and beliefs.

From here we must wade into detail and make specific arguments, even if only in outline. There is, I think, no other way. What counts in a judgement of blame is not that D failed to act for good reasons, but why. At a very general level, one may adopt an account along the lines proposed by H L A Hart, that D is culpable whenever she has the capacity and a fair opportunity to avoid wrongdoing. That type of account is interesting and revealing. I critique it in § 12.3.4. Ultimately, however, it elucidates by paraphrase. It does not address the need for more detailed analysis of when an opportunity counts as 'fair', such that D's failure to take it reflects badly on her.

12.2 Dispositions and values

Willingness to do something one should not is at the heart of choice-based culpability. In § 11.3, we observed that an agent's moral-preference errors can reflect badly upon her, in as much as she is motivated by the wrong dispositions. They are not the dispositions that, in those circumstances, would have motivated a person with decent moral characteristics—a reasonable person. In turn, the culpability of recklessness can be explained directly in terms of D's choosing to take a risk that is, on the facts as she believes them to be, unreasonable. That choice discloses a moral vice.

The explanation of rationale-based excuses is analogous if more indirect. Suppose that D attacks and injures V because T had threatened otherwise to kill D's family. As I argue in chapter 17, this is a case of excusatory duress. D chooses to act for bad reasons, in as much as his reasons for acting do not justify that action. But D may be excused from blame if it is found that a person of *reasonable* fortitude would have done the same. Such a finding precludes us from holding that D fell short of acting upon decent values and dispositions. The link from deliberate wrongdoing to culpability is foreclosed because D's choice does not disclose a moral vice.[24] Contrast a case in which E attacks V because T had threatened her with something more minor. Here, a finding that E lacked reasonable fortitude can ground blame. In engaging with her reasons for and against attacking V, she cared too little about V's interests and too much about her own.

[24] See further § 17.2.

It is a familiar truth that the law sets constraints upon our dispositions, including their weights. In general, we are entitled to create value for ourselves, by deciding for ourselves what to do and how to live. But only up to a point. I may want Vanessa's Ferrari. Without her permission, however, it is a crime to take it. (Even if I have been threatened, unless a person of reasonable firmness would have done the same.) Whether my actions are reasonable is not up to me.[25]

One reason for this is institutional. Constraints upon a person's reasoning are vital to the authority of a legal system. If its mandates were subject to the whims of individual defendants, the law would have no standards to impose. Whatever one takes to be the ends of law, their achievement requires the coordination of citizens' behaviour through the imposition of norms: by stipulating ('φing is prohibited') rather than asking ('unless you want to'). Individuals cannot be allowed to act beyond the compass of the law merely because they desire it. Both a criminal legal system that aims to prevent or punish wrongs, and a tort system that provides a means of private redress for wrongs, must be able to evaluate behaviour by standards at least partly independent of the defendant.

That is an authoritarian rationale. But the rule of law is complemented here by the rule of morality. In terms of culpability, an objective filter upon dispositions, and the values they reflect, can also be justified outside the legal system. Indeed, the very idea of blame presupposes standards external to the defendant. The moral duty to avoid doing an action is derived from the fact that the action is wrong, not from the defendant's acceptance that it is. A defendant's having and acting upon morally aberrant dispositions ordinarily discloses a moral vice,[26] for which we may blame her action *ipso facto*. To say that a defendant is motivated by bad reasons is not merely to say that what she does is a bad thing. It is to express disapproval of her, for being a person who acts for such reasons: to say that she is bad.

Admittedly, legal values might conflict with general morality.[27] In *Toledo, &c. Railway Co v Pindar*,[28] for instance, the plaintiff was held contributorily negligent for saving some horses rather than a sum of money when both were

[25] Cf. *Scarlett* [1993] 4 All ER 629 (CA), where D's conviction was quashed on the basis that D honestly albeit mistakenly believed the circumstances warranted the degree of force he used. The decision is criticized in *Simester and Sullivan*, § 18.1(v), and is of doubtful authority. See also § 13.4.2.

[26] Subject to excuses and irresponsibility defences. See chapters 17 and 19.

[27] And times may change. John Wilson reminds us that a '"reasonable" man in Calvin's Geneva would have testified to the fact that the sight of female ankles was shocking': J Wilson, *Reason and Morals* (CUP 1961) 35.

[28] *Toledo, Peoria & Warsaw R. Co v Pindar* 53 Ill 447, 5 Am R 57 (1870). See H T Terry, 'Negligence' (1915) 29 Harvard LR 40, 45.

threatened by fire, on the ground that the former were much less valuable than the latter and that the suffering of the horses was of no legal account. Perhaps the decision is defensible in tort, but it is hard to see how it could be defended in the criminal law. If the defendant's action is morally justified, it should not be subject to criminal condemnation or punishment.[29]

We are not concerned in this book with unjustified crimes, so I disregard cases like *Pindar* here. Even so, deep waters remain. The justified content of law frequently involves values over which there is genuine disagreement. This can generate challenges for any account of culpability, whether choice- or negligence-based. Arguments about what to prohibit are often best resolved by democratic processes, and the fact that they are so resolved can lend moral weight to the resulting laws. Concededly, such cases may seem problematic for negligence in as much as findings of negligence are grounded in a duty to take care. An agent might be said to have discharged her duty to 'take care' when, after careful deliberation, she concludes that her contemplated action is morally permissible in circumstances where both law and her wider community would regard it as wrongful. Such a person may be *conscientious*—someone who cares a great deal about her actions and about the values those actions reflect. There are hard questions, questions we cannot resolve here, about the extent to which the state may claim obedience from civic-minded objectors.[30] To be sure, the agent may be less blameworthy, *ceteris paribus*, than one who does not think what she does to be right. But disagreement cannot by itself license disobedience.

12.2.1 Legal and moral ignorance

At the same time, if we grant that divergence of this kind can diminish culpability, a question naturally arises whether the same applies to *ignorance* of moral or legal values. Indeed, some writers have denied that the distinction between factual and moral ignorance has *any* significance for culpability judgements.[31]

[29] The criminal law partially accommodates this challenge by importing moral norms into the evaluative elements of its rationale-based defences: below, chapters 17–18. On the other hand, those defences do not allow a mere claim of reasonableness to undermine specific prohibitions: *Simester and Sullivan*, § 21.3(iii). For discussion in the context of necessity, see chapter 18.

[30] The literature is extensive. A thoughtful criminal-law discussion is R A Duff, 'Relational Reasons and the Criminal Law' in L Green and B Leiter (eds), *Oxford Studies in Philosophy of Law*, vol 2 (OUP 2013) 175, 184–89.

[31] See, e.g., G Rosen, 'Culpability and Ignorance' (2003) 103 Proc Arist Soc 61. Rosen's argument supports exculpation even for wrongs *mala in se*. To take an extreme example (at 64–66), 'until quite late in antiquity it never occurred to anyone to object to slavery on grounds of moral or religious principle. So consider an ordinary Hittite lord. He buys and sells human beings, forces labour without compensation,

There is not the space in this book to explore all the issues raised by ignorance of law and/or morality.[32] It is worth pausing, though, to note a few points. The first is that there are reasons for thinking that a defence of reasonable ignorance of *malum prohibitum* crimes need not extend to crimes *mala in se*.[33] In part, this is because it is hard to imagine cases of reasonable ignorance of the moral norms underpinning *mala in se* crimes, absent some kind of incapacity on the part of the defendant.[34] But that is a contingent matter. The more important point is that crimes *mala prohibita* constitute moral wrongs partly in virtue of their illegality. Typically, they crystallize more general moral values that the relevant law (hopefully) serves. In turn, an exculpatory defence can rest on ignorance of the legal facts. It need not appeal to ignorance of more general morality. Crimes *mala in se* are different. They are independently moral wrongs. Thus ignorance of their *illegality* need not preclude culpability.

This first point allows that the discussion in § 12.3, regarding factual beliefs, has analogous implications for beliefs about the law. In practice, though, the analogy is limited. When one inadvertently causes harm, for example, one's inadvertence need only be synchronic and tied to the particular event. Laws, by contrast, tend to be subsisting;[35] inadvertence to them is generally diachronic. Moreover, much negligence liability relates to specialist activities, and (at least usually) persons undertaking such activities can fairly be expected to familiarize themselves with the relevant laws, provided those laws are reasonably

and separates families to suit his purposes. Needless to say, what he does is wrong. The landlord is not entitled to do these things. But of course he thinks he is. Moreover, we may imagine that if he had thought otherwise, he would have acted differently. In that case he acts from moral ignorance . . . . The example is meant to show that blameless moral ignorance is a possibility. But I should add that in my view it also makes it plausible that insofar as he acts from blameless ignorance, it would be a mistake for us to blame the slaveholder—to feel anger or indignation directed at him for his action.' Intuitions about this kind of example are likely to vary. My own sense is that it would not be a mistake for the slave to feel a moral reactive attitude of indignation or resentment at the landlord's actions; that doing so would be both justified and correct. Perhaps that is a feature of fundamental human rights violations. From the perspective of criminal law, of course, conviction of the Hittite would be precluded by the legality constraint.

[32] For a helpful discussion of the issues involved, see D Husak, *Ignorance of Law: A Philosophical Inquiry* (OUP 2016). Husak is generally sceptical, but ultimately equivocal, about blame for inadvertent actions: Husak, 250–51.

[33] For present purposes, I take crimes *mala in se* to prohibit activities that are (pro tanto) moral wrongs prior to and independent of law. Crimes are *mala prohibita* when their moral wrongfulness is dependent on law. (The dichotomy is serviceable here, but a bit simplistic: see, e.g., R A Duff, 'Crime, Prohibition, and Punishment' (2002) 19 J App Phil 97.)

[34] Husak observes that 'the complete absence of suspicion that a *malum in se* is wrongful is exceptionally rare among sane adults.' *Ignorance of Law* (n 32) 162. There may be marginal cases, but practical considerations make it unlikely that the law should accommodate them by a distinct defence.

[35] Contrast *Lim Chin Aik v R* [1963] AC 160 (PC). D entered Singapore shortly after an order was made (but not published) prohibiting him from doing so. D had no opportunity to know that the order had been made. The Privy Council quashed his conviction.

accessible.[36] Thus what would typically count for an ignorance-of-law defence is whether D had adequate *notice* of the law. This is a fair warning constraint. It puts the emphasis on the legislator, not the defendant—which, in the context of *mala prohibita* crimes, is where it should be. Rather than thinking in terms of blameless ignorance, we might be better to frame the problem in rule-of-law terms, by requiring crimes to be adequately publicized as a condition of their enforcement.

That response would be sympathetic to those who reject differential treatment of crimes *mala in se* and *mala prohibita*. But set *mala prohibita* crimes aside. Consider the broader claim that ignorance of *morality* can affect one's culpability. Douglas Husak, for example, argues that for D to be fully culpable for φing, D must know that φing is morally wrong. Perhaps that's true. It doesn't follow that D is insufficiently culpable to merit blame (and conviction) for φing without such knowledge. Neither does it follow that the law should assimilate ignorance of morality with factual ignorance. This is partly for the authoritarian reason noted in § 12.2. But only partly. There are grounds for thinking that even morality should distinguish between factual and moral ignorance.[37]

To show this, let us grant that D can be culpable for attempting to do something that is *factually* impossible. At the same time, one might doubt whether a mistaken belief that φing is *morally* wrong can make D culpable for attempting to commit the 'wrong of φing'.[38] A parallel doubt finds expression in criminal law, in cases that are said to involve a form of *legal impossibility*.[39] In *Taafe*,[40] for example, the House of Lords ruled that T could not be guilty of attempting to import foreign currency because, contrary to T's belief, the importation of foreign currency was not a crime. The same preclusion of liability need not arise for mistakes of fact.[41] Analogous reasoning holds, I think, in morality. Suppose that it is not morally wrong to φ. D's belief that φing is wrong cannot make him

[36] Cf. the extraordinary case of *Chambers* [2008] EWCA Crim 2467, where, it seems, neither the courts nor the enforcement authorities had to hand the current version of the law.

[37] *Contra* Rosen, 'Culpability and Ignorance' (n 31); also Husak, who sees mistakes of fact and law as symmetrical in principle (see, e.g., *Ignorance of Law* (n 32) 161). Strikingly, however, Husak accepts (in § 4A) that knowledge of φing's wrongfulness need only be latent. Yet for the purposes of recklessness, D's foresight of the risk of φing must normally be advertent.

[38] Or, if D's φing were merely advertent, for an inchoate wrong of reckless endangerment: Husak, *Ignorance of Law* (n 32) 160–61.

[39] 'Legal impossibility' is ambiguous between different kinds of legal mistake in the context of attempts. I use it here in the sense that the 'crime' is imaginary. Suppose that D and E, who are unmarried, have sexual intercourse believing that unmarried sexual intercourse is a crime in the jurisdiction they are visiting. It is legally impossible to commit the crime of having unmarried sexual intercourse if no such crime exists.

[40] [1984] AC 359 (HL).

[41] Indeed, since the enactment of the Criminal Attempts Act 1981, the various forms of 'factual impossibility' no longer preclude liability in the UK: *Simester and Sullivan*, § 9.5(ii).

culpable for φing (or even culpable for attempting 'immorally to φ') when, despite that belief, he goes ahead and φs. He can't be culpable for φing because, quite simply, φing is not wrong.

I love my wife. I know that giving her flowers makes her happy. So I bring her some flowers. I am troubled when I do so, because it is a precept of the faith in which I was raised that giving flowers and similar tokens to others is morally wrong. Despite my belief, the desire to make my wife happy proves too strong. I succumb. And she gets the flowers.

There is no culpability here. Not even a hint of it, because—at least to my mind—an agent's culpability *for* φing depends upon the moral character of her φing, rather than upon the agent's beliefs about φing's moral character. To reiterate a central point made in chapter 11, culpability for φing arises out of the manner in which D engages, or fails to engage, with the guiding reasons for and against φing. D cannot be blamed for doing the right thing, even when she does so for the wrong reasons. Sometimes, her doing so might reflect badly upon D's moral character, and there may be other descriptions of her conduct that identify wrongs for which D is culpable.[42] But when I bring flowers to my wife, not even that much is clear.

Of course, my example points only to an *inculpatory* difference between factual and moral ignorance. It leaves open the possibility that a false belief in the rightness of φing might exculpate. And Husak does not deny that culpability also depends upon the content of moral norms. Even so, there is something odd about grounding culpability in an agent's beliefs about (and dispositions toward) those norms, rather than in their content. I admit that, when D φs wrongfully, the fact that she knows her act is wrong tells us *something* about D. It tells us that she has a defective attitude toward morality. However, that doesn't make D more culpable *for φing*. To hold otherwise makes blaming judgements sensitive to the agent's engagement with morality qua authoritative regime. Yet morality rules us without regard to itself. Unlike law, the authority of moral norms is not contingent upon our generally conforming to them.

There is a strong dose of moral realism to this line of thought, which I assume rather than defend here. Fortunately, ignorance of morality becomes less of a challenge to culpability judgements if one thinks, as I do, that negligence can be culpable. Much of the pressure generated by 'blameless ignorance' of moral (and legal) norms is dispelled if ignorance need not be blameless. We look more closely at that possibility now.

[42] See §§ 11.1, 14.2.4.

12.3 Beliefs

The path to blame for inadvertent actions must negotiate the problem of defective beliefs. It may well be that the defendant cares about the harm she causes and would not have chosen to cause it. Unfortunately, she didn't see the risk. What goes wrong when beliefs are faulty? Either a false belief that the defendant acts upon is (unreasonably) acquired, or some relevant further belief (unreasonably) goes unconsidered. The former possibility is especially poignant in the context of defensive mistakes;[43] for now, we focus primarily on the latter. Either way, though, it is the *process* by which the defendant accumulates and considers beliefs that has failed. What need to be evaluated, therefore, are not the defendant's beliefs as such, but her exercise of the abilities involved in accumulating and considering those beliefs. It is in light of those abilities that one can enquire whether there is anything she should have known, realized, or considered and did not. So, for example, it is not *ipso facto* negligent to miswire an electrical plug if D is certain that the blue—positive—wire is the earth: D's negligence may rest in her misreading of an instruction manual. Had D correctly read a reputable but erroneous manual, a finding of negligence might be defrayed.

Processing beliefs involves complex psychological phenomena that we cannot explore in detail. In the context of inadvertence, it is convenient to group the processes involved in accumulating and considering beliefs into three broad categories:

(i) Paying attention to available information;[44]
(ii) Remembering that which one perceives or infers; and
(iii) Applying intelligent reasoning to that which one perceives and recalls.

For each category, the key question is: to what extent are we entitled to demand an objective or impersonal standard of the defendant? What follows is suggestive rather than conclusive. The point is that some such analysis is necessary if, as will be argued, the demands of reasonableness set an impersonal standard in respect of only *some* aspects of the defendant's practical deliberation. No overarching general theory can displace the need for a closer look at the various ways in which a defendant fails adequately to form her beliefs.

[43] See §§ 19.3–4.
[44] I use 'information' in a loose sense, encompassing beliefs and raw perceptions, as well as that which is available to be perceived (e.g. by looking).

A preliminary note. Models of reasonable belief processing are valuable for the sake of their output. Their usefulness lies in establishing a minimum pool of information that should have informed the defendant's behaviour. Culpability, however, requires us to measure defendants against the union of what they should have believed *and* what they did believe.[45] A defendant who realizes something will explode if dropped is blameworthy unless she acts accordingly, regardless whether an ordinary person would have known the facts. In this the law concurs: 'The defendant is credited with such perception of the surrounding circumstances and such knowledge of other pertinent matters as a reasonable man with the actor's own superior perception and knowledge, if any, would possess.'[46] Rightly so. Suppose that a driver with exceptionally good vision notices an unlit cyclist ahead of her on the road. If she none the less hits him, she should not be permitted to hide behind the incidental fact that drivers with normal vision would not have seen the cyclist in time.

At the same time, approaching reasonable beliefs in terms of processes allows that D may be blamelessly unaware of things she never had the chance to learn.[47] As was said in *Davis v Concord and Montreal Ry*,[48]

> 'If a person of average prudence, put exactly in the place he was, possessed of the same knowledge and *means of knowledge* of the danger and the means of avoiding it, would or might have done as [the actor] did, he was without fault.'

This test remains compatible with the point made in § 12.2.1, that uninformed action of this kind may yet be negligent. An illustrative case is *The Lady Gwendolen*, where brewers who ran a shipping service in order to transport

[45] Subject to any inconsistency. In principle, it is possible to conduct oneself non-negligently because of a reasonable belief, even an erroneous one, which other defendants in the same position may not hold.

[46] C Sappideen and P Vines (eds), *Fleming's Law of Torts* (10th edn, Thomson Reuters 2011) 128. See, e.g., *Clarke v Holmes* (1862) 7 H & N 937; *Argyll v Beueselinck* [1972] 2 Ll Rep 172; in criminal law, *Lamb* [1967] 2 QB 981; *Gossett* (1993) 105 DLR (4th) 681, 694–96; Road Traffic Act 1988 (UK), s 3ZA(3).

[47] And, conversely, that D may be culpable on the basis of greater than normal experience. Fleming's remark, though a claim about the law, seems morally apt: 'An employer, therefore, with greater than average experience of a particular risk may have to respond with more than average precautions; while a parent who permits a child to go to school despite symptoms which a competent doctor would diagnose as scarlet fever, will be judged by whether the defendant is a layman or a medic.' Sappideen and Vines (eds), *Fleming's Law of Torts* (n 46) 128. Compare *Stokes v G.K.N.* [1968] 1 WLR 1776.

[48] (1895) 44 A 388, 391 (emphasis added). Compare *Geier v Kujawa* [1970] 1 Ll Rep 364, where a German girl was excused for failing to use a seat belt whilst in a car in part on the grounds that she had not seen one before; also *Price* [2014] EWCA Crim 229, which held, in the context of a prosecution under the Armed Forces Act 2006 (UK), that D's conduct was to be measured against that of a reasonable serviceman with D's (lack of) training, knowledge, and experience.

stout were held liable for their failure to meet the standard of care required of shipowners. Their claim that they were shipowners only incidentally was robustly dismissed: 'The law must apply a standard which is not relaxed to cater for their factual ignorance of all activities outside brewing: having become owners of ships, they must behave as reasonable shipowners.'[49] In this the law coheres with moral expectations. The fault of the brewers lay not per se in their ignorance of what to do, but in their becoming shipowners without finding out.[50]

12.3.1 Attention

One paradigm of inadvertent action occurs when the defendant simply fails to notice what she is (or is not) doing. Recall the example from § 11.4. When D is lying on the beach and does not think to check on her children who are playing in the water, we may conclude she is to blame when they swim too far out and are drowned. It is not that D has culpably misunderstood some aspect of her conduct or environment. It is that she has (culpably) failed to pay attention. The example shows one role of attention—as a prompt, effectively making connections between perceptions, memories, beliefs, and dispositions. Although the process normally occurs non-reflectively, its upshot, if the relevant concerns are important enough, is to prompt reflective evaluation and advertence to the potential concern. We might say that 'had D shown the care and concern for others that she ought to have, she would have thought of the danger.' In doing so, we are laying the foundations of a blaming judgement. We are not merely criticizing what happened, that she failed to notice the danger. We are criticizing her. Paying attention is the first step in discharging the duty that underpins blame for negligence—the duty to take care not to φ. D's failure in the example to think about the situation is blameworthy because it reflects upon her; it reflects an insufficient concern for the welfare of her children. And this is a shortcoming in D. It is a moral vice.

Obviously, D's failure to notice the danger need not be chosen. Given that noticing such matters is typically a non-reflective process, one might worry that it is something that merely happens to D, a mental event in respect of

[49] [1965] P 294, 305.

[50] So, too, the driver who suddenly collapses may be excused blame for losing control of her vehicle (*Robinson v Glover* [1952] NZLR 669; *Waugh v Allan* [1964] SC 102), *unless* she has done so before: *Gordon v Wallace* (1973) 42 DLR 3d 342; *Boomer v Penn* (1965) 52 DLR (2d) 673.

which D is passive. This might suggest, in turn, that it is inappropriate to attribute moral responsibility to D for the occurrence or non-occurrence of that mental event.

I think this worry is overstated. We saw in § 4.3 that moral responsibility can be founded on voluntariness—more specifically, on non-involuntariness.[51] Indeed, that is why liability for mere events or states of affairs is sometimes justified.[52] So the important question for moral responsibility here is not whether D chose (not) to attend, but whether D could avoid her failure. And normally she can.

In most cases, the defendant can rectify the source of her inattention. Where a person is careless, she can seek to improve her character, to become the sort of person who cares more, and correspondingly alter or condition her cares and concerns, including those which prompt attention. Alternatively, an agent's failure to attend may be traceable to particular factors, such as her impulsiveness, preoccupation, or distraction, the appropriateness of which must then be examined. Perhaps I was so excited by the offer of an ice cream that I forgot to complete a vital task undertaken earlier. Of course, reasonable defendants are not bereft of emotions. But I may be blameworthy for failing to control my emotions, or for failing to learn how to do so: 'we need to take care not to be blinded or distracted by anger, greed, lust, ambition, etc . . . we hold people responsible not only for exercising such capacities of self-control; we hold them responsible for acquiring them, so that lack of such capacities does not excuse.'[53] This holds true even if we are unaware of a weakness. Our duty to take care, which requires us to exercise self-restraint, obligates us also to develop the capacities so to do. In effect, we may be expected to ascertain our faults and to remedy them.

Or at least to compensate. Just as someone who knows of her blindness is expected to take the care that a blind person should, so too with non-physical limitations: if, for example, D has a tendency to forgetfulness, we may expect her to allow for that by taking additional precautions when the matter is important. Similarly, a person who does not care about some risk can still make herself pay attention, and choose to consider whether that risk exists. Tracing strategies like these go some way toward explaining why negligence can be culpable.[54]

[51] See §§ 8.2–3.

[52] See § 8.4.2.

[53] R Milo, *Immorality* (Princeton UP 1984) 87–88. See too G Watson, 'Skepticism About Weakness of Will' (1977) 86 Phil Rev 316, 331–32.

[54] Multiple strategies are possible. One approach looks to ground culpability in antecedent choices to be a careless or inattentive person: as we noted in § 11.5, however, that is not the same thing as choosing

But tracing strategies are incomplete. More directly, a person may also be culpable for her shortcomings, *simpliciter*. That one fails to care enough about something, or is distracted by anger, is something that can normally ground blame without more. Even if someone cannot alter her dispositions, we may fairly hold her culpable for acting on them.[55] And to the extent that inattention is due to such dispositional traits, it can ground blame too. Conversely, where that conclusion is unavailable, we should exculpate. Inattention caused by extraneous factors, for example when a patient is injected with morphine to suppress pain, warrants no reproof. Similarly, we should—and do—excuse failures of attention when D is understandably distracted by news of her sister's illness.[56]

One possible reservation about this argument is that it seems to ignore the time-frame over which activities occur, and thereby risks imposing a standard of attention that is impossibly strict. The law's reasonable 'person' is presumably consistent, maintaining its standard of care without even momentary variation. In the context of attention, this seemingly requires a defendant *continuously* to pay vigilant attention to her environment. Yet it is natural for attention to wander, especially during prolonged and concentrated periods of activity. Sometimes we should take a break. But that may not always be practicable. In such cases, to expect unwavering concentration appears to impose a standard of strict liability rather than of culpability.[57]

A tentative response: the law need not be so inflexible. It should demand only invariably *reasonable*, imperfect attention. Reasonable fluctuations are not excluded. Moreover, there seems no reason why the standard cannot accommodate circumstances. After spending twenty-four hours on duty during

to φ, the action now complained of. Another approach treats failures to develop emotional control as a gateway to constructive liability, of the kind explored in § 13.5. I take Rosen's strategy ('Culpability and Ignorance' (n 31) 63) to be of the latter kind: 'If I recklessly shirk that obligation and wind up ignorant as a result, *the ignorance itself is culpable*, and in that case it's no excuse.' (Husak adopts a similar analysis in *Ignorance of Law* (n 32) ch 3.) Like all constructive liability, however, Rosen's claim should be subject, *inter alia*, to a constraint of intrinsic luck.

[55] See §§ 11.4.2–11.5. Cp. also the sort of case contemplated by Frankfurt, *Importance*, 64: 'Surely it is possible for a person to recognize that a certain passion is unequivocally attributable to him, even when he regrets this fact and wishes that the passion did not occur in him or move him at all. Perhaps after long struggle and disillusion with himself, a person may become resigned to being someone of whom he himself does not altogether approve.' Even here we may expect the reluctantly accepting defendant to take precautions that compensate for his inattention. Moreover, where no such precautions are taken, we may reasonably dismiss any suggestion (going beyond Frankfurt's case) that the defendant's failure to care is external to her, a value that she resists.

[56] *West Ky. Tel. Co v Pharis* 25 Ky LR 1838 (1904). (Cp. excused mistakes: § 19.3.) See also *Pigg v Bloom* 177 NW 2d 441, 446 (1970); *Wand v Shelbina* 420 SW 2d 348, 350 (1967).

[57] Many writers also worry at this point about the disproportionate role of moral luck. See, e.g., N Lacey, *State Punishment: Political Principles and Community Values* (Routledge 1988) 64. The distinction between intrinsic and extrinsic luck helps to moderate this problem: below, § 13.5–13.5.1.

an emergency, a doctor may be excused a mistake that would be culpable had she been fresh.[58] But the driver who can no longer maintain concentration should stop and rest.

12.3.2 Memory

In law, the defendant is generally considered negligent if she forgets something that normally one would not.[59] Warren Seavey once doubted whether that is apt:[60]

> 'Memory seems to be a purely mechanical process existing independently of the will . . . . Not only do we forget much that we will to remember, but we remember many things we would like to forget. Thus the mental processes connected with memory approximate the purely physical processes. In view of this it would seem that liability should not be based upon a standardized memory.'

We do not attribute negligence when D's shortcoming is, say, poor sight; why should we do so when it is poor memory? One reason is that there are steps one can take to remember something. Indeed, it is for this reason that we tend to regard 'I forgot' as only a mitigating excuse—often we reject such a plea, provided D has the general capacity to remember,[61] because we think it betokens mental sloth. It is normally possible to improve a weak memory.[62] Alternatively, where a person realizes the significance of an item of information, she may be expected to make a concentrated effort to remember it, or to take additional measures to remind herself.[63]

[58] See, e.g., N S Robins, *The Girl who Died Twice. Every Patient's Nightmare: The Libby Zion case and the Hidden Hazards of Hospitals* (Delacorte 1995).

[59] *Froom v Butcher* [1976] QB 286, 295; *Reynolds v Los Angeles Gas & Elec. Co* 122 P 962 (1912); *City of Charlottesville v Jones* 97 SE 316 (1918). Note that these are all tort cases.

[60] W Seavey, 'Negligence—Subjective or Objective?' (1927) 41 Harvard LR 1, 20.

[61] I have in mind cases such as those where D's biochemical ability to write memories into the brain by rearranging neurons is lost. See, e.g., S M Taubenfeld et al, 'A Molecular Correlate of Memory and Amnesia in the Hippocampus' (1999) 2 Nature Neuroscience 309.

[62] For an example of a program designed to do so, see C L McEvoy and J R Moon, 'Assessment and Treatment of Everyday Memory Problems in the Elderly' in M M Gruneberg, P E Morris, and R N Sykes (eds), *Practical Aspects of Memory: Current Research and Issues*, vol 2 (John Wiley 1988) 155.

[63] See, e.g., the measures discussed in D J Herrman and M Palmisano, 'The Facilitation of Memory Performance' in M M Gruneberg and P E Morris (eds), *Aspects of Memory*, vol 1 (2nd edn, Methuen 1992) 147.

Again, though, there seems to be a more direct connection. Even if memory is mechanical in the way Seavey envisages, none the less we can expect to have a better memory for things more important to us; things in which we are more interested. Suppose that I forget my appointment for a haircut. Doing so is less a cause for surprise—and for an adverse inference about my cares and concerns—than if I forget to attend my own wedding. Antony Duff gets this exactly right. For the bridegroom to forget his wedding,[64]

> '[I]tself manifests an utter lack of concern for his bride and their marriage. Had he cared at all for her, he *could* not have forgotten their wedding. The fact that he forgot it shows that he did not care; and that lack of concern, as manifested in his conduct, is the fault for which she rightly condemns him.'

At least sometimes, then, forgetting discloses a moral vice. In this respect, lapses of memory can be analogized to inattention: they may be culpable in virtue of reflecting D's failure to care sufficiently. Support for this linkage can also be found in the psychological literature. Psychologists have long recognized that our working memory responds to incentives.[65] Our recollection of things is better when we care more about them.[66]

Not always. Any finding of culpability in such cases must be sensitive to the explanation of *how* it was that D came to forget the matter at issue. Had D been playing football and suffered a concussion, for example, the inference to culpability should not be drawn. Thus, one way of thinking about the argument here is that it favours a rebuttable presumption. At a pragmatic level, too, the law has evidential reasons to treat an abnormal memory lapse as presumptively unreasonable. A claim that 'I forgot' is all too easy for a defendant to make and difficult for the prosecution to disprove.[67] Rather more should be required for such lapses to exculpate.

[64] Duff, *IACL* 163 (albeit Duff ties the example to an account of criminal recklessness). Cp. A Smith, 'Responsibility for Attitudes: Activity and Passivity in Mental Life' (2005) 115 Ethics 236.

[65] See, e.g., Y Cho et al, 'Incentives to Perform: The Effects of Reward on Working Memory' (2017) 81 Biological Psychiatry S389; J A Meacham and J Singer, 'Incentive Effects in Prospective Memory' (1977) 97 J Psych 191.

[66] And pay them more attention: A D Baddeley et al, 'Attention and Retrieval from Long-Term Memory' (1984) 113 J Experimental Psych: General 518; B B Murdock, 'Effects of a Subsidiary Task on Short-Term Memory' (1965) 56 British J Psych 413. *Per* A D Baddeley, *Human Memory: Theory and Practice* (Lawrence Erlbaum Associates 1990) 148: 'It is almost certainly the case that motivation will influence the subject's willingness to attend to the material to be learnt.'

[67] As was once said in the context of automatism, '"blackout", to use one of the titles, is one of the first refuges of a guilty conscience': *Cooper v McKenna, ex parte Cooper* [1960] Qd R 406, 419.

12.3.3 Intelligent reasoning

Not all failures to recognize a risk are due to inattention or forgetfulness. Sometimes, the defendant exhibits poor levels of reasoning. She fails, one might say, to put two and two together. Or she does so and gets five.

Of course, we all make mistakes when forming or failing to form beliefs. What counts, as I suggested in § 12.3, is not so much the content of our beliefs as the process by which we got to them. Those processes can go awry in all sorts of ways. Some mistakes are impeccable. Perhaps a jury finds D guilty on the basis of the available evidence. Its finding is rationally grounded on that evidence. Actually, though, D is innocent. The jury has made a mistake—a justified one. In other scenarios, an agent's mistake may be clearly *inexcusable*. One alleged example of this was the well-known 2012 shooting of Trayvon Martin by George Zimmerman, Zimmerman apparently believed that Martin posed an unlawful threat. Suppose, as was argued by the prosecution but not proved, that Zimmerman's belief was false and that it was predicated on racist assumptions. Such a belief would disclose a moral vice. It would help to establish rather than preclude Zimmerman's culpability for shooting Martin. Legally speaking, it would support the conclusion that any claim of self-defence rested on an unreasonable mistake and should be disallowed.[68]

Perhaps the hardest cases, however, are those where D's flawed belief formation owes itself to a deficiency in the *operation* of D's reasoning processes. Inferences that are unwarranted by the evidence need not be morally vicious. Nobody is perfectly intelligent. But in what sense, if any, must D be *reasonably* intelligent? Legally speaking, the answer is uncertain. Tort unequivocally saddles the defendant with a reasonable intelligence: 'It is not enough that the defendant did the best he knew how.'[69] In criminal law, however, the position is much more controversial.[70] Consider the facts of *Elliot v C*,[71] where C, a fourteen-year-old girl in a remedial class at school,[72] set fire to a shed by igniting white spirit. On a charge of arson it was found, *inter alia:*[73]

> 'That the [defendant] had given no thought at the time that she started the fire to the possibility of there being a risk that the shed and contents would be destroyed by her

[68] See §§ 19.3–4.

[69] *Vaughan v Menlove* (1837) 3 Bing NC 468, 471.

[70] Contrast *Creighton* [1993] 105 DLR (4th) 632, *Hardie* [1985] 1 WLR 64, and *Hudson* [1966] 1 QB 448 with *Lavender* [2005] HCA 37, [128], *R, Stephen* (1984) 79 Cr App R 334, *Elliott v C* [1983] 1 WLR 939, and *Stone and Dobinson* [1977] QB 354.

[71] [1983] 1 WLR 939.

[72] At first instance ([1983] 1 WLR 939, 942), 'The justices were of opinion that the defendant was of very low intelligence for her age of 14 years'.

[73] [1983] 1 WLR 939, 945.

actions [and] in the circumstances this risk would not have been obvious to her or appreciated by her if she had given thought to the matter.'

How should we approach such cases?[74] The evidential difficulties associated with establishing low intelligence do not seem prohibitive. We do have means with which to evaluate a person's intelligence, at least approximately, and the first instance justices in *Elliott v C* made findings of this very type. Further, and crucially, low intelligence neither reflects one's moral characteristics nor is it within one's control. Indeed, it is in many ways akin to age: which, as we noted in § 12.1, is something that reasonableness standards generally accommodate, especially in the context of excuses.

There is a distinction between the mistake that is understandably made by a person of low intelligence (Andrew), and the mistake that is stupidly made by one not stupid (Beryl). We may criticize Beryl's stupidity in making her mistake, because Beryl could and should have done better than she did. Implicit in such criticism is that Beryl's failure reasonably to exercise her intelligence manifests a culpable failure to be sufficiently careful. By contrast, Andrew's mistake does not reflect upon his moral worth. It may be deplored but not criticized.[75] Like physical limitations such as blindness, stupidity is a condition that cannot much be altered by someone who suffers from it. Moreover, a person of low intelligence is likely to be poorly placed to take precautions against the harmful consequences of his own stupidity. Neither can low intelligence be attributed to the defendant's failure to care sufficiently—to a moral vice that grounds blame *simpliciter*.

Prima facie, therefore, the arguments favouring standardized expectations of memory do not apply to the intellect. Similarly, low intelligence is distinguishable from cases of unreasonable inattention, inattention that could have been avoided were the defendant a more caring and concerned person. So there is good reason, at least in the criminal law, not to expect reasonable intelligence of the defendant but, rather, to expect *that she reasonably use the intelligence she has*.[76] Beryl, and not Andrew, may be accounted culpable.

[74] What the Divisional Court *did* was, following *Caldwell* [1982] AC 341 and *Lawrence* [1982] AC 510, to convict her of *reckless* destruction of property. (Moreover, leave to appeal was refused by the House of Lords: [1983] 1 WLR 939, 951n.) The judgment is perhaps the nadir of modern English criminal law. Happily, none of these decisions is any longer authoritative, and recklessness once again requires foresight with respect to the actus reus. See *Simester and Sullivan*, § 5.2.

[75] John Gardner disagrees. For him, stupidity is a vice: *Offences and Defences*, 26. He may be right about that. But it is not a *moral* vice—a distinction Gardner does not draw. See below, § 12.4; also § 19.1.2.

[76] And by the same token, those with above-average intelligence may be expected to meet a higher standard of care. Perhaps the criminal law ought to limit what may be asked of persons with superior abilities. But not for lack of culpability.

12.3.4 Hart's capacity conditions

This conclusion should prompt us to re-examine H L A Hart's well-known 'capacity and fair opportunity' analysis. In the context of punishing criminal negligence, Hart proposes the following liability conditions:[77]

> '(i) Did the accused fail to take those precautions which any reasonable man with normal capacities would in the circumstances have taken?
> (ii) Could the accused, given his mental and physical capacities, have taken those precautions?'

Satisfaction of condition (i) is taken by Hart to establish, objectively, a fair opportunity to avoid the relevant wrong, while condition (ii) reflects a personalized requirement of capacity. To illustrate how the test can work, suppose that in *Elliott v C* (§ 12.3.3), the defendant C was incapable of foreseeing the conflagration that might follow her actions. Condition (ii) suggests that she ought not to be convicted, since her incapacity pre-empts the attribution of blame.

Taken by itself, that result seems correct. Indeed, the same test would appropriately preclude blame for a failure of perception due to blindness, or for a failure of memory due to clinical amnesia. However, the analysis of these cases is plausible only because it turns exclusively on the application of condition (ii). Difficulties arise when the two conditions are conjoined. Condition (ii) is purely negative: it excludes blame and cannot ground it. In Hart's account, culpability implies capacity; incapacity implies blamelessness. The implication is unidirectional. Rightly, a failure to satisfy condition (ii) exculpates the defendant in *Elliott v C*. But the converse is not true. It does not follow, if C has personal capacity, that she is blameworthy. Once condition (ii) is satisfied, it has nothing more to say. It supplies no reason to think that D is culpable.

The positive task, to establish when criminal punishment is warranted, falls to condition (i). And at first glance, that condition appears to do the work we need. On closer inspection, though, it doesn't. This is because the 'fair opportunity' criterion is impersonal. Hart intends it to be applied objectively, independent of the accused's own capacities and limitations. D is to be adjudged negligent when there was a fair opportunity for a 'reasonable person' to avoid φing. Now, if D actually has ordinary powers of intellect, self-restraint, and the like, condition (i) might be a suitable test. But what if D has lower than average

[77] Hart, *Punishment and Responsibility*, 154.

intelligence? Prima facie, we ought to blame people for unreasonably deploying the intelligence they have, not for failing to be reasonably intelligent. On Hart's analysis, though, D is expected to exhibit reasonable intelligence; *not* to use reasonably the intelligence she has. Like Baron Alderson's test (§ 12), culpability becomes assessed by comparison to a hypothetical figure. It is difficult to see how such an approach can track culpability. It looks only at the existence of an opportunity to avoid harm, and not at why the defendant missed that chance.

The difficulty is not resolved by applying Hart's conditions in tandem. To see this, an example may help. Suppose that in *Elliott v C* the risk was not obvious to C, but that she was (just) capable of recognizing it, had she thought very hard about the matter for some time—whereas a person of reasonable intelligence would have recognized the risk straightforwardly. Applying Hart's test would suggest that C is culpable for burning down the shed. In my view, however, C is *not* culpable unless it was reasonable, and not merely possible, for one of *her* limited intelligence and experience to comprehend the risk. (Similar analysis, requiring defendants reasonably to exercise the capacities they have, applies in some hybrid defences.[78]) In the absence of further arguments, along the lines of those made earlier regarding attention and memory, the fact that a hypothetical 'normal' person would have avoided φing says nothing about whether the defendant had a fair opportunity to do so.

12.4 Criminalizing the unreasonable

The connection between epistemic failings and moral vices is a matter of inference.[79] We have seen already that the inference is not inevitable, even when D falls short of what we normally expect of someone in D's position. It depends on the manner in which D falls short. Consider Victor Tadros's discussion of two well-known English cases, *Adomako* and *Misra*.[80] In *Adomako*,[81] D was the anaesthetist attending an operation when the tube supplying oxygen to the patient became dislodged. D realized something was wrong and made increasingly desperate efforts to fix the situation. But in all those efforts he failed to notice the basic problem: that the tube had become disconnected. Some nine minutes later, the patient suffered cardiac arrest and died. D was convicted of manslaughter, on the footing that his failure to diagnose such an obvious

[78] See § 19.1.2.
[79] A point noted in § 11.4.2.
[80] *Criminal Responsibility* (OUP 2005) 84–85.
[81] [1995] 1 AC 171.

problem was a gross dereliction of the standard of care that may reasonably be expected from a competent anaesthetist.

Tadros queries whether we can blame D. Doubtless he fell well short of being a competent anaesthetist. For John Gardner, that's enough: 'The question of whether and how one's actions reflect upon one *just is* the question of whether they point to one's fitness or unfitness for whatever role one is occupying, for whatever life one is leading.'[82] That may indeed be enough to warrant tort liability, especially for someone occupying a specialist role. As Tadros points out, however, D's obvious unfitness as an anaesthetist does not by itself establish that he exhibited a *moral* vice:[83]

> 'At the moment when he realised that something was wrong, it may well be that he did everything that he could to ensure that the patient survived. Admittedly his judgement about what was required was wildly wrong. But in doing everything that he *thought* was required, he showed himself properly to be motivated by the patient's interests in survival, at least at the time of the operation.'

To emphasize the point, Tadros contrasts the facts of *Adomako* with those of *Misra*.[84] In the latter case, two senior house doctors were convicted of gross negligence manslaughter following the death of a post-operative patient under their care. The patient developed a serious infection in the operation wound, which they failed to diagnose despite obvious symptoms. Ultimately, the patient died as a result of the untreated infection. By contrast with *Adomako*, the defendants were lackadaisical. They failed to order blood cultures to be taken, even though they were advised to do this by the sister on duty, and failed to look at the results of a blood test ordered by another doctor. Tadros concludes:[85]

> 'All of this strikes one as a lack of motivation on the part of the defendants to care for their patient in the proper way. It is true that the defendants in *Misra* were not aware of the specific infection that there was to the patient, just as Adomako was not aware of the specific cause of the death of the patient. But it is difficult to see the actions of the defendants in *Misra* as displaying anything but insufficient interest in the well-being of the patient, and that is not true of Adomako.'

Fair enough. The defendants in *Misra* exhibited exactly the kind of culpable inattention outlined in § 12.3.1. They simply did not care enough about their

[82] *Offences and Defences*, 131 (see also at 129).
[83] Tadros, *Criminal Responsibility* (n 80) 84.
[84] *Misra and Srivastava* [2004] EWCA Crim 2375.
[85] *Criminal Responsibility* (n 80) 85.

patient's welfare. Indeed, the contrast between these two cases to my mind *reinforces* the core claim made in § 11.3.1, that unchosen wrongs can be culpable. But it also illustrates the point that the connection between unchosen wrongs and culpability may be less robust than it is for chosen wrongs. This is not to concur with Tadros that Adomako was blameless for causing his patient's death. As the defendant himself confessed, 'after things went wrong I think I did panic a bit.'[86] Just when it mattered, he fell apart. To my mind, that discloses a moral vice. Yet Tadros is right to think the case is nowhere near as clear cut as *Misra*. Indeed, this is one reason why we should normally demand a standard of *gross* rather than ordinary negligence in the criminal law: the point is not so much that a grossly negligent defendant is more culpable, but that we can be more confident that she is culpable at all.

12.4.1 A puzzle

Suppose, then, that we were to restrict inadvertence-based criminal liability to gross negligence. That would still leave unresolved one of the puzzles identified in the Prolegomenon. Why is (gross) negligence so rare among the stigmatic offences? Once we have accepted negligence as a culpability standard, why not make it the *default* mens rea element?

One way of responding to these questions might be to deny their validity. We might contest the thought that recklessness is the default mens rea requirement for crimes, although it certainly is at common law.[87] Numerous statutory offences stipulate negligence as their mens rea element, or impose strict liability but allow a no-negligence defence.[88] And some very serious, *mala in se* crimes can be committed negligently. Still, in a sense that just emphasizes our puzzle. If inadvertence-based culpability may suffice for rape and manslaughter, why not for other serious offences? What makes advertence- or choice-based culpability so special?

An alternative response might be to point to systematic differences in culpability between advertent and inadvertent (albeit negligent) wrongdoing. I have accepted already that the grounds of culpability differ. It seems plausible that, other things equal, negligent wrongdoing is less culpable than its reckless or intentional counterparts. Yet the question is not whether negligence is *equally*

[86] [1995] 1 AC 171, 182.
[87] *Sweet v Parsley* [1970] AC 132.
[88] Often with the burden of proof reversed: indeed, this is the default common-law position in much of the Commonwealth. See *R v City of Sault Ste Marie* (1978) 85 DLR (3d) 161; *Millar v MOT* [1986] 1 NZLR 660; cp. below, § 13.2.2(ii).

blameworthy as choice-based culpability. Rather, it is whether negligence is *sufficiently* culpable to count as the mens rea for other serious crimes. And if it is sufficiently culpable to warrant convictions for rape and manslaughter, presumably it is sufficiently culpable for at least some other, serious offences too.

The puzzle is important in its own right. But it is also part of the larger argument to which we pointed in chapter 3, about the significance of culpability and its relationship to mens rea requirements. The state *should* be reluctant to inflict serious criminal sanctions upon persons who have merely been negligent. However, the primary reasons for that reluctance need not arise from the domain of culpability. There is reason to think that they arise from the other functions of mens rea: most importantly, from the roles that mens rea plays in giving defendants fair warning and in negotiating the boundaries of criminalization.

The analysis in this chapter has suggested that, even without using tracing strategies, it is possible to defend appeals to (un)reasonableness in terms of a defendant's blameworthiness. Sometimes the defendant's failure to meet an objective standard does reflect a moral vice on her part: on those occasions, we are right to think her culpable. As was said earlier, the function of the so-called 'reasonable person' in this context is really to hold the defendant up to an external standard of moral characteristics. Conversely, if it is to comprise a standard of culpability, the 'reasonable person' ought to be personalized to the extent that the defendant's shortcomings do not disclose moral vices. In particular, and alongside physical limitations, that includes shortcomings of intelligence.

It should be no surprise that 'the reasonable person' sets a mixed standard, part personal and part imposed. Without external standards of comparison, judgement is impossible. Without reference to the defendant, judgement cannot lead to blame. The device of the reasonable person is, in a sense, one means by which the law seeks to reconcile the impersonal with the humane. In a wider sense, reconciliation is at the core of reasonableness. To be reasonable is, in a sense, inhuman. For reasonableness is not so much a state as an approach, a tool that articulates the shared understandings, principles, and expectations of a society; a framework for discussion, argument, disagreement, and even agreement—not only over issues of culpability, but also about such questions as our obligations in society and our values as human beings. It provides not answers, but an opportunity to get near them. As such, the reasonable person is no more than a conduit for shared human judgements. Yet that is no small thing. Ultimately, we are irredeemably human. So we cannot always know what is right. Sometimes, all we can do is form judgements, and aspire that they be reasonable.

13

Strict and Constructive Liability

One reason why the debate about negligence is so important is that it is also a debate about the minimum standards of mens rea. The next option 'down' is strict liability, which is widely thought by scholars to be unjustified in the criminal law. There is, moreover, a broad consensus about why strict liability is wrong. It violates the culpability principle. It leads to conviction of persons who are, morally speaking, innocent. Convicting and punishing those who do not deserve it perpetrates a serious wrong. Thus strict liability is a misuse of the criminal law—an institution which, because of its moral significance and grave implications for the lives of convicted defendants, should be reserved only for the regulation of serious wrongs done by culpable wrongdoers.

There is much that is right about this view. We *should* object to the enactment of a strict liability homicide offence of, say, causing death by one's action. Such an offence would expose blameless persons to criminal liability in a way that is profoundly objectionable. This is the central conclusion of § 13.3 below: where strict liability leads to conviction of the blameless, its enactment in stigmatic crimes is morally illegitimate.[1]

Clear enough, one might think. Yet the path to that conclusion is more complex than may at first appear. Not all types of strict liability offences are indefensible. In particular, there are at least some (broadly instrumental) arguments that can be offered in favour of strict liability. We explore those arguments in § 13.2. Ultimately, in the context of stigmatic crimes, they are defeated by intrinsic objections to strict liability. Still, they retain some force, and it may be that strict liability is occasionally legitimate in what I shall call 'non-stigmatic', or 'quasi-criminal' offences.

As we noted in chapter 1, this book is concerned with stigmatic offences, so that last possibility will be left open here.[2] More interestingly, however, there

[1] Perhaps there are extreme cases where some existential crisis necessitates, on a lesser-evils basis, the creation of a strict liability crime. I cannot explore that conjecture here. However, even if justified, it strikes me that to convict the blameless of such a crime would still be to wrong them, for reasons discussed in § 18.3.

[2] But see § 13.3.3 for a doubt whether there is a sufficiently distinct boundary between stigmatic and non-stigmatic offences.

Fundamentals of Criminal Law. A P Simester, Oxford University Press (2021). © A P Simester.
DOI: 10.1093/oso/9780198853145.003.0013

are also cases where the imposition of strict liability regarding some element of the actus reus need not lead to systematic conviction of the blameless. In these cases, the intrinsic objections to strict liability fall away, so that its use might sometimes be legitimate even in stigmatic offences. Consider the following example:

> Deborah is driving through a village at a speed twenty miles per hour in excess of the speed limit. Rounding a corner, she loses control of her car, mounts the pavement, and kills Allan, who had been walking quietly toward the local shop in order to buy a newspaper.

Let's stipulate that driving through the village at such a speed is dangerous. Suppose, further, that there is an offence of dangerous driving causing death, which offence requires no mens rea element to be proved in respect of the death.[3] A key element in the actus reus of that offence therefore involves strict liability. Yet it seems to me there is nothing wrong with convicting Deborah of that offence. Not only is Deborah culpably guilty of 'dangerous driving', she is also culpably guilty of 'dangerous driving causing death'—because, as will be argued in § 13.5, she is also culpable with respect to the death.

Of course, one example of a legitimate conviction does not a legitimate offence make. The offence may still be objectionable because of its application to some class of cases within which Deborah does not fall. None the less, the example usefully suggests the possibility that offences with substantial strict liability elements may be enacted without their being objectionable in the manner that strict liability offences so often are.

13.1 Two definitions; two claims

For present purposes, I take an offence *formally* to impose 'strict liability' if it contains at least one *material* element[4] of the actus reus without a corresponding mens rea element.[5] This definition accommodates the fact that strict liability offences characteristically do contain mens rea elements. They are

[3] See, e.g., s 1 of the Road Traffic Act 1988 (UK).

[4] I adopt the definition in § 1.13(10) of the Model Penal Code: an element is material where it 'does not relate exclusively to the statute of limitations, jurisdiction, venue or to any other matter similarly unconnected with (i) the harm or evil, incident to conduct, sought to be prevented by the law defining the offense, or (ii) the existence of a justification or excuse for such conduct.'

[5] In line with chapters 11 and 12, I count negligence as a mens rea element.

strict because of what they lack: a mens rea requirement in respect of one or more elements of the actus reus. A good example of this is the notorious case of *Prince*,[6] in which D was convicted of an offence against the Offences Against the Person Act 1861 (UK). Section 55 provided that 'whosoever shall unlawfully take . . . any unmarried girl, being under the age of sixteen years, out of the possession and against the will of her father or mother . . . shall be guilty of a misdemeanour.' D did as proscribed, whereupon he was convicted notwithstanding that he reasonably believed the girl's age was eighteen. The prohibition was, in that respect, absolute. Yet it is clear that the offence involved mens rea regarding other elements of the actus reus. Had D thought that the girl was in no one's possession or that he was authorized by her father to accompany her, D could not have been convicted.

Formal can be differentiated from *substantive* strict liability.[7] According to this distinction, an offence imposes substantive strict liability when it contemplates the conviction of persons who are blameless for committing that offence. For clarity, 'strict liability' *simpliciter* refers in this chapter to formal strict liability. But one way of reading this chapter is to see it as a two-part investigation: into the possibility that substantive strict liability might sometimes be justified; and into the possibility that formal strict liability does not always impose liability that is substantively strict.

Notice that, on this definition, substantive strict liability contemplates the conviction of persons who are blameless *in respect of the offence for which they are convicted*—even if they are culpable for some other wrong or offence.[8] As will be seen, the argument against formal strict liability in stigmatic crimes extends to such persons. In part, this is because of the communicative and labelling functions of the criminal law.[9] But it also reflects a more general point about blaming judgements. Even if D acts culpably, it does not follow that she is culpable for every morally undesirable action that her behaviour happens to constitute.[10] In turn, a conviction is not warranted by the prosecution's proving that D was culpable for *something* when the actus reus occurred. Thus, one payoff of the discussion here is an implicit rejection of any (putative) transferred mens rea doctrines that would cut across different offence-types.[11]

[6] (1875) 2 CCR 154.

[7] See esp. S P Green, 'Six Senses of Strict Liability: A Plea for Formalism' in *Appraising Strict Liability* 1.

[8] A concern also highlighted by A Harel and A Porat, 'Aggregating Probabilities Across Cases: Criminal Responsibility for Unspecified Offences' (2009) 94 Minnesota LR 261. See, further, §§ 13.5.1, 14.3.

[9] To which we come in §§ 13.3.1 and 14.3.

[10] See in particular the discussion of intrinsic luck in § 13.5–13.5.1.

[11] The argument in this chapter thus aligns with the modern doctrine of transferred malice at common law, in as much as that doctrine is generally confined to immaterial variations within

13.1.1 Stigmatic crimes and quasi-criminal regulations

We should also recall the distinction drawn in § 1.1.1 between 'regulatory' offences and 'true', stigmatic, crimes.[12] As we observed there, it is a *marque* of the criminal law that its verdict, the conviction, operates as a condemnatory statement on behalf of society. By labelling the defendant a 'criminal', the conviction asserts publicly that she is a reprehensible wrongdoer. 'The disgrace of criminality'[13] is merely reinforced—not constituted—by the censorious nature of any punishment that may additionally be imposed. Yet it is a familiar notion that not every offence involves the sort of public condemnation that is implicit in convictions for a serious crime. A parking offence, for instance, involves little or no stigma. There are a large number of offences prohibiting 'acts not criminal in any real sense, but . . . which in the public interest are prohibited under a penalty.'[14] These, too, are 'criminal' offences, in so far as their commission may be followed by prosecutions that are criminal in nature and subject to rules of criminal (not civil) evidence and procedure. But in substance, it would be more accurate to describe such offences as 'quasi-criminal'.[15] They fall within the rubric and forms of the criminal law, but they lack a key underlying feature that sets the criminal law apart from the civil: the declaration of reprehensible wrongdoing that is implicit in the verdict against, and punishment of, the accused. Hence it was intelligible in *Wings Ltd v Ellis* for Lord Scarman to say that the Trade Descriptions Act 1968 (UK) 'operates by prohibiting false descriptions under the pain of penalties enforced through the criminal courts. But it is not a truly criminal statute. Its purpose is not the enforcement of the criminal law but the maintenance of trading standards. Trading standards, not criminal behaviour, are its concern.'[16]

Suppose we accept that it is appropriate to describe such crimes, in a familiar judicial idiom, as 'not truly criminal in character'.[17] The phrase 'quasi-criminal regulations' can then be used to designate crimes that do not import any significant element of stigma—in contradistinction to what will be termed 'stigmatic crimes'. Notwithstanding its blurred boundary, the dichotomy seems

offence definitions; it does not support transferring 'guilt' between different offences. See *Simester and Sullivan*, § 5.7.

[12] *Sweet v Parsley* [1970] AC 132, 149 (Lord Reid), 163 (Lord Diplock); *Alphacell Ltd v Woodward* [1972] AC 824, 839 (Viscount Dilhorne), 848 (Lord Salmon); *Gammon (Hong Kong) Ltd v A-G for Hong Kong* [1985] AC 1, 12–14.

[13] *Warner v Metropolitan Police Comr* [1969] 2 AC 256, 272 (Lord Reid).

[14] *Sherras v De Rutzen* [1895] 1 QB 918, 922 (Wright J).

[15] As in *Pearks, Gunston & Tee Ltd v Ward* [1902] 2 KB 1, 11.

[16] [1985] AC 272, 293.

[17] *London Borough of Harrow v Shah* [2000] 1 WLR 83, 88 (Mitchell J).

a meaningful one: most parking offenders worry about the cost of the fine rather than about any element of censure. Even so, in § 13.3.3 I raise a question whether the boundary is so blurred that it should not be drawn *within* the criminal law.

The category of quasi-criminal regulations need not be identical to what are sometimes termed 'regulatory' or 'public welfare' offences in criminal law texts, albeit there is a significant overlap.[18] Still less does it track the distinction between crimes *mala in se* and those *mala prohibita*. Some crimes *mala prohibita*, such as those regulating trades in financial markets, can import a significant element of censure.[19] Wherever they do so, they count for present purposes as stigmatic crimes rather than quasi-criminal regulations.

13.1.2 Two claims

With these definitions in mind, we can formulate two main claims for this chapter:

(i) Substantive strict liability is always wrong in stigmatic crimes.
(ii) In some circumstances, formal strict liability may not be wrong in stigmatic crimes.

The following discussion approaches these claims indirectly. It begins in § 13.2 by elaborating what I (loosely) call the 'instrumental' arguments for and against using strict liability in criminal law. In § 13.3, the core moral objections to strict liability are then considered. It will be argued that those objections defeat the instrumental reasons in favour of strict liability for stigmatic offences: this is claim (i). However, provided a clear distinction can be maintained between stigmatic crimes and quasi-criminal regulations, the same objections do not necessarily defeat the instrumental considerations, set out in § 13.2, when it comes to quasi-criminal regulations. Finally, §§ 13.4–5 consider whether there are any types of formally strict-liability offences, even stigmatic ones, to which the intrinsic objections in § 13.3 do not apply; that is, offences where formal strict liability does not generate substantive strict liability. The possibility and

[18] 'Public welfare offences' is often used to refer to offences that regulate and control excesses in an otherwise acceptable trade or practice.

[19] A point made by Peter Alldridge: 'Making Criminal Law Known' in S C Shute and A P Simester (eds), *Criminal Law Theory: Doctrines of the General Part* (OUP 2002) 103, 106ff.

justification of such offences will be identified, and the boundaries explored of their legitimate deployment.

13.2 Instrumental arguments

Instrumental reasons exist both for and against using strict liability. I begin with arguments in favour, before turning to counterarguments.

13.2.1 For

Suppose that the state has good reason for wanting to reduce the incidence of φing by citizens, and that its prohibiting φing would be consistent with the harm principle, in virtue of reducing either direct or remote harm to others. Suppose, too, that φing is the type of activity that can be defined without reference to a mental element.[20] Prima facie, there are instrumental reasons to frame the prohibition as a strict liability offence. It is arguable that the use of strict liability increases the efficiency and the effectiveness of law enforcement administration, especially in respect of corporate defendants. Strict liability may also increase the deterrent effect of the prohibition, leading to fewer instances of φing, because (it may be contended) the use of strict liability tends to encourage potential defendants to take greater precautions. Alternatively, strict liability may be an efficient mechanism for allocating the costs of risk-creating activities.

These claims are both contingent and vulnerable to countervailing arguments. Let us examine them more closely.

(i) Cost

From an administrative perspective, the costs involved before and during trial are likely to be considerably decreased if φing is made a strict liability offence, since the number of elements required to be proved at trial, and thus the number of potential issues, is reduced.[21] This consideration matters because criminal justice is very expensive. It is plausible that, if every one of a nation's offences required proof of mens rea with respect to all elements of the actus

[20] Contrast, e.g., theft or blackmail. (See § 3.2.) In the criminal law, this point is more likely to affect stigmatic crimes than quasi-criminal regulations.

[21] Against this would need to be weighed any increased costs (after deducting additional revenue from fines) that may be incurred should strict liability lead to a greater number of trials.

reus, administration of the criminal law would be not merely cumbersome but unaffordable. As such, the state essentially has two options: first, to reduce the number of criminal offences by eliminating some of them; secondly, to simplify some proscriptions by dispensing with certain of their elements (especially, some of their mens rea elements). It may, of course, do both. But if we assume that all the existing offences are consonant with the harm principle, the second option presents a *via media* by which harms may feasibly be proscribed. If it is impossible fully to protect victims from harm while maintaining a Rolls-Royce system of criminal justice, the conflicting interests of defendants and other community members, including victims, may be mediated in part by simplifying the mens rea elements of certain offences.

Once this possibility is accepted, the use of strict liability becomes an issue of priorities. The range of harms that call for prevention exceeds the range of offences for which the state can, in practice, administer a criminal justice system where every offence contains mens rea requirements corresponding to every element of the actus reus. Thus, it may be concluded, the state should consider *which* offences to 'skimp' on. If the choice is either cutting corners or abandoning the prohibition altogether, a pared-down regulation (say, with reduced sanctions attached) may well be preferable. Grave instances of φing might, at the same time, be addressed by enacting a supplementary, more serious, version of the crime, one that involves proof of mens rea and greater penalties.

(ii) Accuracy

Reducing the number of potential issues, by removing one or more mens rea elements from the definition of an offence, is also likely to promote accuracy in criminal adjudication (that is, the reliability of the court's verdict that the elements of the offence did, or did not, occur). Having fewer substantive issues at trial decreases the points at which the court's finding may err; and, moreover, decreases them by removing elements of a type—mens rea—that is characteristically more difficult to ascertain. To prove and know the content of a person's mind is typically harder, because more a matter of inference, than to prove and know the occurrence of physical events.

Admittedly, forensic accuracy is not the exclusive aim of the trial process. It is constrained by a panoply of rights and duties, notably including the right to be acquitted unless each element of the offence is proved beyond reasonable doubt: we prefer that inaccurate verdicts favour the defendant and not the prosecution. But a right of this sort takes forensic error as a given; it is not compromised by measures that increase the accuracy of verdicts. Neither does it suppose that inaccuracy per se is desirable, even where that error falls to benefit the defendant.[22]

For all that, fault elements normally can be excised from the offence definition only if they are reintroduced at the sentencing stage. The judge cannot pass sentence without considering whether the offence was committed knowingly, negligently, or blamelessly[23] and, if such matters are disputed, a further hearing may be required to determine them.[24] In light of this, one might suppose that the evidence may as well be heard straightforwardly before conviction.[25] Yet that conclusion would be too hasty. Error at the point of sentence is different from, and less important than, error at the point of conviction. The court's principal options at trial are stark: to convict or acquit. By contrast, the sentencing decision involves selection from a *continuum* of options, ranging upwards from an absolute discharge.[26] Unlike the (binary) conviction decision, imprecision is thus relatively tolerable within a sentencing decision, and there is less reason to protect the defendant against error.[27] Hence, *overall* accuracy of disposition may be improved by incorporating questions of culpability into the sentencing decision.[28]

(iii) Regulating corporate activity

Both efficiency and accuracy seem especially in point for corporate defendants. The proof of mens rea presents especial difficulty in prosecutions of corporate bodies, since there may be no one person whose conduct can be attributed to the corporation and with whom the corporate mind can be identified. Strict liability, by contrast, is much more easily applied to corporations since it can be administered without reference to the defendant's mental state.

[22] The same is true of other types of rights, such as constraints on methods of gathering evidence, which are not motivated by the need to protect against the costs of inaccuracy but by concerns for human dignity, the need to fetter state power, and the like.

[23] See, e.g., *Smedleys Ltd v Breed* [1974] AC 839, 857 (Viscount Dilhorne); *Lester* (1975) 63 Cr App R 144.

[24] *Newton* (1983) 77 Cr App R 13. Similarly, in *Blakely v Washington* 124 S Ct 2531 (2004), the US Supreme Court ruled that where a finding of fact is required in order to increase a criminal sentence, that fact must be proved before a jury beyond a reasonable doubt.

[25] As was suggested in *R v City of Sault Ste. Marie* (1978) 85 DLR (3d) 161, 172 (SC).

[26] Within the terms of this argument, the power to discharge absolutely supplies an important safeguard against inaccuracy (and injustice), since it provides a means by which convictions can be annulled.

[27] For example, where a hearing is required to decide contested facts that were not settled by conviction and which are relevant to sentence, it is arguable that proof should be required only to the balance of probabilities. Indeed, to require the higher standard may result in worse rather than better justice, since it is likely to lead to defendants' consistently being punished less than they deserve. Contrast, however, *Ahmed* (1984) 80 Cr App R 295 (CA).

[28] Notice that this argument is undermined if the conviction decision is itself non-neutral; which is partly why the argument loses its force in the context of stigmatic crimes (below, § 13.3).

The significance of this consideration is augmented to the extent that corporate activity frequently occurs on a large scale, with the potential to create widespread risks of harm. Further, where offences regulate the specialist commercial behaviour of corporations the prosecutor is likely to be poorly placed to understand the nature of the defendant's own specialist activity. This forensic disadvantage compounds the challenge of proving the conduct of particular individuals within large and complex organizations.

Commercial activity needs to be regulated in a cost-efficient manner, especially where the offences involved are minor and, taken individually, pose no risk of serious harm. Moreover, effective regulation of trivial infractions can protect against cumulative harms that may be very substantial indeed. From an economic perspective, the costs of regulating a commercial activity are part of the costs of carrying on that activity. It is therefore arguable that the burden of criminal penalties should be borne as a form of production expense by those who voluntarily undertake risk-creating activities.[29]

(iv) Deterrence

It is also arguable that strict liability increases the deterrent effect of a prohibition. That is to say, there are likely to be fewer instances of the actus reus when φing is prohibited on a strict-liability basis, because (it may be thought) the use of strict liability tends to encourage a higher level of precautions by potential defendants.[30]

The proposition that strict liability increases deterrence is implicit in one of the most common arguments given for abandoning a full mens rea requirement: that protection of the public sometimes requires a high standard of care on the part of those who undertake risk-creating activities. This rationale is consistent with the thought that strict liability offences are often enacted in order to protect the public from risks created by industrial and other specialist activities. Extra care, the argument goes, needs to be taken by such persons; without strict liability, the careless will have insufficient incentive to reduce or eliminate those risks. The threat of liability thus supplies a motive for persons in risk-generating activities to adopt precautions which might not otherwise be taken, in order to guard even against unforeseeable mishaps and errors.[31]

[29] See § 13.2.1(v).

[30] *Per* Lord Salmon: strict liability 'encourages riparian factory owners not only to take reasonable steps to prevent pollution but to do everything possible to ensure that they do not cause it.' *Alphacell Ltd v Woodward* [1972] AC 824, 848–49. According to Donovan J, in *St Margaret's Trust Ltd* [1958] 1 WLR 522, 527, 'There would be little point in enacting that no one should breach the defences against a flood, and at the same time excusing anyone who did it innocently.' But see § 13.2.2(i) below.

[31] *R v City of Sault Ste. Marie* (1978) 85 DLR (3d) 161, 171. For an extreme version of this type of argument, see B Wootton, *Crime and the Criminal Law: Reflections of a Magistrate and a Social Scientist* (2nd edn, Sweet & Maxwell 1981) 47ff.

Particularly where the harmful impact of the actus reus is severe and widespread, the law has pressing reason to provide incentives through criminalization for persons not only to refrain from advertent wrongdoing, but to go beyond that by taking maximal care against such harm.

(v) Cost allocation

Alternatively, strict liability need not be justified in terms of deterrence but could be analogized to a statutory tort. Normally, the legal implications of risk without fault lie within the realms of insurance and tort liability, but there is no reason why, especially in quasi-criminal regulations, they could not also be a concern of the criminal law. This is the force of the idea that criminal penalties may be viewed as part of the production costs incurred by those who initiate risk-creating activities. As Lord Salmon observed, in *Alphacell Ltd v Woodward*,[32]

> 'In the case of a minor pollution . . . a comparatively nominal fine will no doubt be imposed. This may be regarded as a not unfair hazard of carrying on a business which may cause pollution on the banks of a river.'

On a cost-allocation model, one may expect the regime of fines to be calibrated according to the harmful costs imposed by the regulated activity. A system of strict liability offences serving this function could, moreover, systematically be complemented by a regimen of more serious crimes requiring proof of mens rea and carrying more severe, punitive, sanctions.

The rejoinder is obvious: no doubt harmful activities *could* be criminalized on this basis, but why should they be? Why not control them with other legal mechanisms? One answer might lie in the fact that there are certain advantages to using the criminal law. Amongst those advantages is the symbolic significance of declaring that φing is prohibited. Criminalization can be a tool for communicating more strongly to the public that the prohibited activity is a legal wrong that *must* not be done—rather than signalling that it must be paid for if done, for example through taxation or a licensing system. Where the imperative voice is desirable, there is reason to favour a criminalization response.

When contrasted with tort law, there are also practical benefits. Tort law, for example, generally requires a victim. But certain activities, like some forms of environmental pollution, may wrong no identifiable victim with standing to sue. Alternatively, even where there are particular victims, the aggregate harm

[32] [1972] AC 824, 848.

to individually wronged plaintiffs may be less than the overall cost to society that the activity imposes. Relying exclusively on tort law is likely, in these cases, to result in under-enforcement. Moreover, given that the state pays the costs of detecting, prosecuting, and punishing offences, it may be better placed to regulate φing than private individuals through the law of tort. If the sums involved are not large, it may be impractical to pursue wrongdoers through the law of tort—especially where those wrongdoers have far greater resources with which to defend themselves. But a criminal prosecution shifts many of those costs onto the state. Hence the use of criminal regulation has the potential to advance the rule of law, by enhancing the consistency with which legal rights are enforced.[33]

13.2.2 Against

The force of prima facie arguments favouring strict liability may be disputed. Absent empirical evidence, it is not clear that the criminal justice process will operate more efficiently if fault must still be established prior to the imposition of an appropriate sanction. It also seems doubtful that strict liability is an effective deterrent spurring potential defendants to increased precautions.[34]

(i) Deterrence

Indeed, it is conceivable that strict liability will lead to *reduced* precautions being taken, by comparison with a negligence-based standard of liability. A negligence standard has the virtue of signalling to actors, *ex ante*, what level of precautions will, if taken, secure immunity from conviction. By guaranteeing non-conviction in this way, the criminal law creates a powerful incentive for actors to take reasonable precautions. Where that guarantee is removed, however, actors are left with no guidance from the criminal law about what level of *ex ante* precaution is optimal. In that case, a rational actor will commit herself to taking additional precautions up to the point at which the marginal cost of taking those additional precautions exceeds the reduction in expected liability costs, adjusted for her personal risk preferences. This could occur at any point on the continuum from zero to the maximum-possible precautions. As such, and depending on how the scale of sanctions is structured, strict liability could

[33] The *potential*. It might also generate worries about discretionary enforcement: below, § 13.2.2(iii).

[34] See B S Jackson, '*Storkwain*: A Case Study in Strict Liability and Self-Regulation' [1991] Crim LR 892; G Richardson, 'Strict Liability for Regulatory Crime: The Empirical Research' [1987] Crim LR 295; R Baldwin, 'Why Rules Don't Work' (1990) 53 MLR 321.

well result in fewer-than-reasonable, rather than enhanced, precautions being taken by the actor.[35]

Proponents of strict liability in the criminal law tend to assume that its prospect will lead people to maximize precautions against the occurrence of the offence. But there is no reason to think that is true. Typically, there will be a point at which it becomes, in effect, unfeasibly expensive to take further precautions for little payoff. In a strict liability system, there is no magic number: no level of precautions that will guarantee immunity from committing the offence. The optimal amount of precautions an actor should take becomes a function of how much risk she is willing to bear.[36]

Contrast the situation in which it is known that a certain level of precautions (call it P_{RC}) constitutes reasonable care and pre-empts legal liability. Here we have a new factor. Anyone who would otherwise choose to take fewer precautions than P_{RC} now acquires an incentive to uprate those safeguards, since there are now extra savings to be made in terms of future liability costs (which at P_{RC} reduce abruptly to zero). Of course, moving to a negligence standard might, for some strongly risk-averse actors, mean that they can safely reduce the level of precautions below what they would otherwise have taken. However, we cannot conclude a priori that overall levels of precaution would reduce if strict liability were displaced by negligence. They may go up. Hence strict liability has the potential to result in less than reasonable care being taken.

In order to avoid this underdeterrence, one could look to manipulate the incentives created through strict liability by introducing a finer-tuned, more differentially geared, structure of sanctions. On that approach, those who take more, albeit vain, precautions can expect to suffer correspondingly lesser penalties. However, a system of this sort would tend to sacrifice any advantages in efficiency that strict liability might otherwise offer. Alternatively, the sanctions could simply be increased to the point where no rational actor would contemplate taking fewer than reasonable precautions. Yet (even in instrumental terms) that, too, seems undesirable, since it runs the risk of deterring the underlying activity altogether.

Of course, this is an inherent feature of strict liability: the actor must either desist from the risk-creating activity *tout court*, or persist and accept that she must run all remaining risks, however esoteric and unlikely, that the actus reus

[35] We can take 'costs' of precautions to include such outlays as time and effort; liability costs may include consequential losses, including any losses attendant upon the conviction itself.

[36] For a suggestion that strict liability, especially in the corporate sphere, can encourage precisely the wrong people into risk-creating ventures, see C S Lerner and M A Yahya, '"Left Behind" after Sarbanes-Oxley' (2007) 44 Am Crim LR 1383.

will occur.[37] Assuming that the first option is not intended, the deterrent function of regulatory laws is intelligible only as an attempt to discourage people from entering into an activity (or from executing it in a manner) which creates *unreasonable* risks of the unwanted harm occurring. But *that* aim can be achieved by negligence liability. Moreover, imposing a negligence standard does not lead to underdeterrence. What suffices as reasonable care depends, in part, on the seriousness of the harm involved. Thus, where the risks created by D's activity are of, say, a severe and widespread harm, a correspondingly higher standard of precautions will be demanded of D. Strict liability lacks this element of tailoring. Instead, it forces the blameless defendant to become an unrewarded risk-taker in respect of non-negligent misfortunes, subject to a criminal legal lottery over which she has no reasonable control.

(ii) Regulating corporate activity

The need for effective regulation and prosecution of corporate defendants could also be met by a negligence-based standard. Proof of negligence can be established without reference to the company's mental state (in particular, without proving the state of mind of a controlling officer), since negligence is typically proved by reference to conduct. It is, of course, true that negligence obliges the prosecution to establish relevant conduct that is attributable to the company. But the same constraint applies to strict liability.

Alternatively, proof difficulties in respect of specialist commercial activities might be met by reversing the burden of proof. That step has been taken successfully in a number of Commonwealth jurisdictions,[38] where 'strict liability' offences require the prosecution to prove only the actus reus beyond reasonable doubt—whereupon the defendant may exculpate itself by proving absence of fault (that is, a 'no-negligence' defence) on the balance of probabilities. In essence, these approximate fault-based offences of negligence with a reverse burden of proof.

An obvious question arises. Compared to the normal requirements for proving mens rea, which burden the prosecution to establish guilt 'beyond reasonable doubt', is it legitimate for the state to lower the standard of proof demanded and therefore to take an increased risk of wrongly convicting D?

[37] The clumsiness of strict liability as a deterrent has been noted by others: see, e.g., L Alexander, 'Is There a Case for Strict Liability?' (2018) 12 Crim L and Phil 531, 533–34; J Hasnas, 'Reflections on *Prince*, Public Welfare Offenses, *American Cyanamid*, and the Wisdom of the Common Law' (2018) 12 Crim L and Phil 427, § 4.

[38] *R v City of Sault Ste Marie* (1978) 85 DLR (3d) 161; *Millar v MOT* [1986] 1 NZLR 660. As Andrew Ashworth observes, they are becoming increasingly popular in the UK: A Ashworth, 'A New Generation of Omission Offences' [2018] Crim LR 354.

As will be noted in § 13.3, we already accept a certain level of systemic risk in criminal trials, by demanding only proof beyond reasonable doubt. Is there a peremptory argument against reducing that demand to, say, a 'balance of probabilities' standard?

Arguably, allocating the burden of proof is part of balancing the costs and risks of an activity between actors and potential victims.[39] At least in quasi-criminal regulations, it is not clear that D has a right that trumps this balancing process. Indeed, where D's activity is a specialist one that imposes risks upon others, it is appropriate for the state, when licensing that activity, to specify how the activity is to be done. (For example, the state may legitimately regulate driving by permitting it yet demanding that it be done in accordance with prevailing traffic regulations—on a particular side of the road, subject to certain maximum speeds, and so forth.) In principle, that specification could embrace a requirement both that D conduct the activity in a prescribed manner and that she be able to prove that she has done so. Hence D's being able to document her conduct may be a legitimate condition of the overall regime by which that conduct is permitted and facilitated.[40] Moreover, given the advantage the defendant may have of familiarity with a specialist activity, the shift in evidential burdens has the potential to result in more efficient and better justice. Very often, it may be more difficult for the prosecution to prove mens rea where the defendant's activity is a specialist one, not readily understood by others, than it is for the defendant to prove lack of fault.

(iii) Discretionary enforcement

A further concern is that regimes of strict liability offences are administered by enforcement agencies which, in practice, tend to use the prospect of strict liability as a bargaining tool in securing compliance by potential defendants.[41] Typically, prosecutions are brought only in cases where the accused was actually at fault.[42] Indeed, they should be brought only where doing so is in the public interest.[43] It may frequently be difficult to see how a prosecution of

[39] See, e.g., D Hamer, 'The Presumption of Innocence and Reverse Burdens: A Balancing Act' (2007) 66 CLJ 142.

[40] For an elegant argument along these lines, see R A Duff, 'Strict Liability, Legal Presumptions, and the Presumption of Innocence' in *Appraising Strict Liability* 125, 137ff; also *Oliver* [1944] KB 68; *John v Humphreys* [1955] 1 WLR 325.

[41] See, e.g., K Hawkins, *Environment and Enforcement: Regulation and the Social Definition of Pollution* (OUP 1984); B Hutter, *The Reasonable Arm of the Law: Law Enforcement Procedures of Environmental Health Officers* (OUP 1988). Prosecution is typically a last resort: K Hawkins, *Law as Last Resort: Prosecution Decision-Making in a Regulatory Agency* (OUP 2002).

[42] G Richardson, A Ogus, and P Burrows, *Policing Prosecution: A Study of Regulation and Enforcement* (Clarendon 1982).

[43] *Smedleys Ltd v Breed* [1974] AC 839, 856 (Viscount Dilhorne).

blameless offending satisfies that criterion.[44] As Parker J observed, in *James & Son v Smee*, 'Where legislation, as here, throws a wide net it is important that only those should be charged who either deserve punishment or in whose case it can be said that punishment would tend to induce them to keep themselves and their organization up to the mark....'[45]

Unfortunately, the lack of public interest in a prosecution is not, as such, a defence. Consequently, defendants are on occasion found guilty of offences even though, in the view of the court, a prosecution should not have been brought.[46] Given that strict liability offences are characteristically used as an ad hoc negotiating tool, this reliance on dispensations by the enforcement agency puts at risk the rule of law, in so far as it leaves the prospect of criminal conviction to the discretion of enforcement officers.

13.2.3 A case for strict liability?

Despite these powerful counterarguments, the instrumental case for strict liability is not entirely defeated. Strict liability might be more efficient. Depending on the nature and structure of each particular offence, it might lead rational actors to take more than reasonable precautions. It may also be justified as a tool for allocating the costs of specialist, risk-creating, activities. In this last role, its advantage over taxing such activities is that it allocates the cost to the harmful *outcome* of the activity, not to the risk-creating activity more generally. Hence, the criminal mechanism offers incentives to take precautions which a generic tax would not. In doing so, moreover, it identifies and communicates more clearly the precise harm at which the prohibition is directed.

13.3 Intrinsic objections

It is, in short, arguable that there are valuable benefits to be gained from the device of strict liability, although their scope and extent is uncertain. However, assuming they exist, those benefits must be measured against the intrinsic moral objection to strict liability set out below. In the context of stigmatic crimes, it seems to me that this objection is decisive.

44 Of course, instrumental reasons may exist, e.g. of general deterrence or cost allocation. The question is whether such reasons would be sufficient.
45 [1955] 1 QB 78, 93.
46 e.g. *Smedleys Ltd v Breed* [1974] AC 839; *Hart v Bex* [1957] Crim LR 622; compare *James & Son v Smee* [1955] 1 QB 78.

13.3.1 Wrongful censure

Suppose that the state were to create a crime of 'homicide', defined as a strict liability offence of causing death. Objections to crimes of this type depend, in turn, on the nature of the criminal law. Without dwelling on the familiar analysis,[47] there are various paradigm features associated with the criminalization of μing. *Ex ante*, μing is declared to be a prohibited wrong: citizens are not merely requested but instructed not to μ, on pain of punishment. *Ex post*, where D is found to have transgressed, she is convicted of μing and liable to sanctions which may be substantial, perhaps including imprisonment. The conviction and the sanctions also express censure,[48] to D, to V, and to the public at large. As well as suffering hard treatment, D is labelled as a particular sort of criminal (a 'μer'), a labelling that conveys a public implication of culpable wrongdoing.

The main objection to making μing a strict liability crime, at least where strict liability leads to conviction of blameless defendants,[49] arises directly from these paradigm features; and it lies at the heart of the culpability principle. Morally speaking, it is wrong to convict those who are not blameworthy. If a person does not deserve to be convicted, she has a right not to be; and her conviction cannot be justified by consequential considerations like deterrence.

Since both are censorious, this objection applies to both conviction and punishment. The imposition of punishment is, qua punishment, justified only when D deserves it in virtue of culpably having done wrong. Indeed, the imposition of hard treatment cannot count as punishment unless it conveys this message. But in the context of strict liability, the state does not rely on the proposition that D is culpable as a precondition of imposing punishment. So the state cannot claim to be punishing D in accordance with D's desert; it is simply responding to the fact that μing occurred.

This criticism may be evaded, in part. Even if μing is a strict liability offence, the quantum of punishment imposed for transgressions might still be related to desert in a criminal legal system that required *sentencing* to reflect D's level of culpability, with fault thereby becoming a post-conviction matter. However, the same get-out is not available with regard to the conviction itself.[50] As we noted in chapter 1, conviction for μing has the effect of naming D a criminal (in respect of that particular offence), a branding which is communicated to society as well

[47] See chapter 1; also *Crimes, Harms, and Wrongs*, § 1.1.

[48] In the context of punishment, see, e.g., A von Hirsch, *Censure and Sanctions* (Clarendon 1993).

[49] For exceptions, see §§ 13.4–5.

[50] A special case might be where the sentencing options include an absolute discharge (i.e. without conviction) and the courts were willing to treat this form of disposal as commonplace.

as to D. Assuming that, if imposed on a strict liability basis, the label 'criminal-μ' continues to retain its stigmatic quality, this amounts to a systematic moral defamation by the state.[51] Given the public understanding of that designation, when it labels her a criminal the state is no longer telling the public the truth about D. People have a right not to be censured falsely as criminals, a right that is violated when one is convicted and punished for a stigmatic crime without proof of culpable wrongdoing.

That falsehood is no ordinary lie. There is something especially troubling when wrongful censure is imposed by the state. In ordinary defamation cases, the attack is characteristically private; it may affect D, and even harm D's interests, but it lacks the authoritative voice of the state and normally does not undermine his membership of the community. An act of defamation may bring D into conflict with P, but it normally does not alienate D from society.[52] By contrast, convictions are official. They condemn D on behalf of society as a whole. To say that D has a criminal record is to say that he has been labelled as a reprehensible wrongdoer; that the state has made a formal adverse statement about *him*. Moreover, the statement marks D out in such a way that it becomes appropriate, within the community, for the regard in which he is held to be affected. Certain exclusions, both social and professional, may legitimately follow. Depending on the crime for which D is convicted, he may be ostracized by his peers, disenfranchised (for life in some jurisdictions), excluded from certain professions, disqualified as a company director, prevented from working with children, refused insurance coverage (if a fraudster), and so on.[53] As such, the criminal record becomes part of the material that frames D's engagement with his community, with adverse implications for D's ability to live his life—a life that is, in part, defined in terms of D's interactions within, and membership of, his society. The conviction (and indeed the punishment) tends not only to censure D for the particular act that is proscribed, but also to undermine D's participation in the society itself.

Putting it this way pluralizes the objection. One reason why the state ought not falsely to censure D for a serious crime is supplied by the consequences for D's life. But the two do not always go together, and D has a right to be neither

[51] 'Morally defamed', as opposed to defamed in law, since the state is a privileged wrongdoer in such cases. (Contrast the private citizen in *Carver v Pierce*, an action for slander based on the words, 'Thou art a thief, for thou hast stollen my dung' (1648) Sty 66, 82 ER 534.) The phrase 'morally defamed' is used here to convey the sense of an untrue and adverse labelling by the state, in that the defendant is labelled with a stigmatic criminal conviction where the implicit social meaning of that label is unjustified.

[52] Save in special cases, e.g. where the sentiments are pervasively held, or where P has representative standing in the community.

[53] See, e.g., the various studies by Gabriel Chin and Zach Hoskins, footnoted in § 1 of this book.

falsely censured *nor* falsely stigmatized. Even if D suffers no stigma,[54] the state should not purport to censure her without believing her to be culpable. Telling lies is wrong in itself and not merely because of the consequences.

One might hesitate at this point. Since both the state and D know that fault has not been proved, surely the state is not *really* censuring D when it convicts him of a strict liability offence? The problem with this 'private colloquy' reasoning is that it is not a private colloquy. The state is not communicating merely with D. It is also speaking to the community. When labelling D guilty of a stigmatic crime, therefore, the state is not entitled to disregard the public meaning of the words it uses. Hence, for example, Parliament cannot legitimately enact an offence of 'paedophilia', defined as 'parking for more than one hour on a central London street'.[55] It cannot do so because that is not what paedophilia means.[56]

Defamation, of course, happens. Some error in the criminal justice system is unavoidable. When the state convicts a person of a stigmatic offence, it generally requires that guilt be proved beyond reasonable doubt. Inevitably, this leaves open the possibility that a particular defendant, properly convicted on that standard of proof, is not in fact guilty. The defamation and wrongful punishment of such persons is none the less justified. Moreover, it is justified by consequential reasons: in particular, by the need to set an achievable standard of proof if society is to have a practicable criminal justice system *at all*. It might be thought that an analogy can be drawn between these instrumental considerations, which permit wrongful convictions whenever the criminal proof standard is met, and those set out in § 13.2, which support convictions on the basis of strict liability.

But the analogy does not go through. Where guilt is proved beyond reasonable doubt in stigmatic crimes, the state convicts in good faith—D is

[54] In some circumstances, particular convictions may even become a badge of honour, e.g. in the context of a gang membership or, notoriously, a conviction for contempt of Congress following refusal to testify before the House Un-American Activities Committee during the McCarthy era.

[55] For the sake of illustration, this example is deliberately extreme. But it may be less far-fetched to imagine anti-terrorism legislation that enacted an offence, so defined, of 'Endangering the Safety of the Realm'. Notice, too, that the constraint identified here also binds individuals. E should not call D a paedophile when D overstays his parking permit.

[56] Treating a conviction for 'paedophilia' as highly stigmatic is, of course, a reasonable public response. A more difficult case would arise if the reaction of the public, in terms of stigmatizing D, is unreasonable and far exceeds what is deserved in light of the state's censure: John Stanton-Ife helpfully describes this as a case of 'psychological' rather than 'normative' stigma. (J Stanton-Ife, 'Strict Liability: Stigma and Regret' (2007) 27 OJLS 151, 156ff.) Suppose that, in the public mind, parking offenders, labelled as such, came to be regarded like paedophiles. In that event, a strict liability parking conviction, although not intended as censorious, would be highly psychologically stigmatic. The argument in this section does not extend to such cases, and I am not concerned with them here. With that said, at least where the psychological stigma is predictable, that fact would plausibly generate additional constraints for the state.

believed to be culpable. Moreover, although error is inevitable, its distribution is in principle random.[57] By contrast, where strict liability is employed in a stigmatic crime, the state consistently labels D as a culpable wrongdoer without believing this to be true. Moreover, defamation is no longer distributed randomly: defendants are especially likely to be censured and punished wrongly for these offences. As such, while institutional arguments may sometimes be relied upon to justify systemic risks of good-faith erroneous convictions, arguments of that type are inadequate to justify strict liability for stigmatic crimes.

13.3.2 Other rights?

I conclude that the right not to be wrongly censured defeats any instrumental case for strict liability in stigmatic crimes. But there is a catch. When it comes to non-stigmatic offences, that right is not engaged. For such offences, therefore, it seems that the arguments canvassed in § 13.2 are not ruled out. They may yet be capable of justifying strict liability. Perhaps, then, we can invoke some other right as a ground of objection? What we need is a right that does not depend upon there being an implication from conviction to censure. As it happens, I doubt that we can find a suitable candidate. Still, it is worth examining a couple of alternatives.

One possibility is a right not to suffer undeserved *hard treatment*. Punishment for stigmatic offences involves, in addition to censure, the imposition of hard treatment—typically, onerous deprivations of assets or liberties. This is also a feature of sanctions, characteristically fines, attached to quasi-criminal regulations. The infliction of hard treatment itself stands in need of justification. Ordinarily in the criminal law, the hard treatment is justified in virtue of the fact that D deserves it. But that justification is normally unavailable where the offence is one of (substantive) strict liability.

How pressing is this concern? Not very. Hard treatment or deprivation may legitimately be imposed for a variety of reasons. Tort law frequently deprives D of assets for reasons grounded primarily in the interests of P. Similarly, deprivations through the taxation system are imposed for all sorts of purposes. Unlike punishment, hard treatment need not be justified in terms of D's desert. Thus, fines for strict liability offences, understood as

[57] In principle. The legitimacy of a criminal legal system may yet be undermined by systematic discrimination. See, e.g., M Alexander, *The New Jim Crow: Mass Incarceration in the Age of Colorblindness* (New Press 2012).

mere hard treatment and not punishment,[58] may in principle be warranted by considerations of deterrence. Or they may be part of a regime distributing the costs of an activity, voluntarily undertaken, that benefits D; especially when the activity imposes risks on others who didn't volunteer for exposure to those risks.

On the other hand, the matter would be very different if parking tickets were to attract a sanction of imprisonment, for at least two reasons. First, if the imposition of a sanction is to be morally legitimate, its level and nature should be warranted *within* the terms of the rationale by which the offence is justified. It seems clear that imprisonment cannot be accommodated, for example, within a cost-allocation model of non-stigmatic offences. More generally, it is arguable that imprisonment is inherently a punitive sanction; as such, its imposition is always illegitimate unless deserved. Indeed, there may very well be a human right not to be imprisoned save in accordance with justified punishment.[59] Such a right would straightforwardly interdict imprisonment for parking offences.

One can concede all this, however, without foreclosing the possibility of strict liability offences. No doubt it is wrong to imprison a person without proof of fault. But that is a matter of sentencing rather than conviction. Thus it appears to involve a different right, namely the right not to suffer disproportionate punishment.[60] The state might avoid abrogating this right, for example, by enacting dual—strict liability and mens rea—regimes of offences, the former incurring fines and the latter imprisonable. Indeed, strictly speaking, the injunction against disproportionate punishment does not even foreclose the possibility of strict liability offences carrying terms of imprisonment, provided that sentences of imprisonment were not actually imposed without proof of fault. Doubtless such offences are more likely to be regarded by the public as stigmatic crimes rather than quasi-criminal regulations. But that is a concern for undeserved censure.

A different objection might invoke the rule of law. Prima facie, strict liability also contravenes the requirement for fair warning, since citizens may have no way of knowing or predicting when they might be about to incur criminal liability. No doubt the public needs to be protected from the harms that

[58] I do not deny that, in practice, the message may be ineluctably mixed: see § 13.3.3.

[59] Compare the right not to suffer inhuman or degrading treatment, *per* Art 3 of the European Convention on Human Rights. For discussion, see G R Sullivan, 'Strict Liability for Criminal Offences in England and Wales Following Incorporation into English Law of the European Convention on Human Rights' in *Appraising Strict Liability* 195; cp. *References re Section 94(2) of Motor Vehicle Act (BC)* (1985) 24 DLR (4th) 536.

[60] D van Z Smit and A Ashworth, 'Disproportionate Sentences as Human Rights Violations' (2004) 67 MLR 541.

non-stigmatic offences are designed to prevent. Yet the public also needs to be protected from random liability. It is a rule of law value that D should have fair opportunity to evade criminal labels and sanctions. Arguably, criminal liability without fault breaches rule of law requirements, because it undermines the confidence one can have of staying on the right side of the law.

We need to be careful here. It is true that the criminal law is there not solely to tell police and judges what to do after someone offends. It should also offer *ex ante* guidance to citizens. However, the claim that strict criminal liability violates rule of law requirements is not incontrovertible. Typically, strict liability rules are activity-specific and *do* offer advance guidance. Provided that such offences are clearly drafted in sufficiently precise terms ('when driving, do not exceed 70 miles per hour on the highway'), they are capable of putting citizens who engage in the relevant activity on notice that precautions must be taken to avoid perpetrating an actus reus. Indeed, this potential is implicit in the very use of strict liability offences for deterrent purposes.

Admittedly, there may be strict liability offences, especially situational offences, where the prohibition is context-insensitive and D cannot be said, in virtue of her conduct, to have advance notice that the offence is about to occur. But this is not an inherent feature of strict liability offences (which, in practice, tend to regulate voluntary specialist activities). Neither is the objection restricted to strict liability offences. Negligence-based offences, especially those involving omissions, present the same difficulty. At root, this concern seems to be no more than a special case of the worries about moral luck and liability for inadvertent conduct more generally.[61]

A distinction can be drawn between fair warning and avoidability. In *Smedleys Ltd v Breed*,[62] the defendants were convicted of an offence against section 2(1) of the Food and Drugs Act 1955 after supplying to a retail store a tin of peas which was found to contain a caterpillar. The defendants, whose factory canned 3.5 million tins of peas during the picking season, were found to have taken all reasonable precautions during the canning process to prevent the presence of the caterpillar in the tin; its presence was, in practice, unavoidable.[63] Yet there is fair warning in such cases: those who can peas will, sooner or later, commit an offence against the Food and Drugs Act 1955.

The warning is, of course, generic to the underlying activity of canning peas and not to the specific occasion on which the offence is committed.

[61] For more on fair warning, see § 3.3. Moral luck is discussed in chapter 14.

[62] [1974] AC 839.

[63] The caterpillar was similar in colour, size, density, and weight to the peas in the tin, was sterile and would not have constituted a danger to health if consumed.

Nevertheless, in the case of non-censorious hard treatment, this level of advance notice seems sufficient. In other areas of law, especially tort, generic warnings are frequently the only form of advance notice available. The facts of *Smedleys Ltd v Breed* are analogous to cases of product liability, where remedies are awarded against defendants who voluntarily assumed the risks that their activities generate without knowing, *ex ante*, when or how those risks may crystallize. Similarly, in *Rylands v Fletcher*,[64] the rule that the defendant should compensate the plaintiff can be justified by reference to the defendant's voluntary creation of a potential hazard, rather than by any finding that the defendant was wrong to create that hazard or that the incident which caused loss was specifically predictable. Even though the crystallization of risk in these cases is unknown, as in *Smedleys Ltd v Breed*, it can—and should—be planned for, and the financial costs smoothed, by taking out insurance and making financial provisions through reserves.[65]

13.3.3 Segmenting the marketplace, or diluting the brand?

So it seems that the objection to strict liability does hinge on the right not to be wrongly censured. That makes it importantly contingent. The case against strict liability in stigmatic crimes assumes that crimes can be stigmatic even though strict. Conversely, any case *for* strict liability in non-stigmatic offences assumes that the normal criminal-law connection between hard treatment and punishment can be severed, so that quasi-criminal regulations attract convictions and sanctions that are not perceived as censorious. Each of these assumptions stipulates a category that is conceptually possible. But it is a further question whether those categories are populated.

There is room here to offer just a few observations. So far as the first category is concerned, the presumption that, if imposed on a strict liability basis, the label 'criminal-μ' continues to retain its stigmatic quality is plausible but non-trivial, and need not readily be accepted. It is characteristic in many offences for the public to look behind the fact of a conviction where such

64 (1868) LR 3 HL 330.

65 Bob Sullivan argues that 'A company like Smedleys can absorb these uncertainties, and the costs of appellate litigation, into its risk assessments and financial contingencies. Yet the proprietor of a small business in similar circumstances might well not be able to sustain such costs and pressures.' ('Strict Liability' (n 59) 215.) But if we disregard the costs of appellate litigation (surely rare in this context), and assuming the offence is committed in the same proportion, it is not clear how a smaller business is in different case. It will commit the offence fewer times, and *ex ante* should make the same proportionate provisions. If it cannot afford to do so then, assuming the hard treatment is justified (e.g. as a form of cost allocation), it should not be in the business.

convictions are routinely imposed on a strict-liability basis, although whether this will actually occur may depend on the scale of the associated sanctions and other factors. If, for example, a crime potentially attracts sentences of imprisonment, it may well be regarded as stigmatic even if liability is strict. So too where the same label, μ, is standardly used for different types of offences, in which case the class of strict liability convictions is less likely to be distinguished in the public mind from convictions for μing that rest on proof of culpability.[66]

The conceptual category of quasi-criminal regulations is certainly problematic. Using the 'criminal' law in non-stigmatic offences inevitably links such transgressions to the paradigm of censure and sanctions by which crimes are distinguished from other forms of legal wrong. It is no surprise that the line between quasi-criminal regulations and 'true' stigmatic crimes is not easy to draw. If a clear distinction between 'quasi-criminal' and 'truly criminal' offences cannot be drawn, or if that distinction fails to secure public recognition,[67] then the core objection to strict liability carries over to quasi-criminal regulations, trumping for both models the instrumental arguments set out in § 13.2. Strict liability convictions are likely then to generate both over- and understatement: they risk being understood as communications, in some cases, that D is a culpable wrongdoer when she is in truth blameless and, on other occasions, that D may not be a culpable wrongdoer (since convicted only of a strict liability offence) when she is in truth culpable and deserving of public censure.

Moreover, it is not at all obvious that extending criminal liability to non-stigmatic offences is good for the criminal law. To do so potentially undermines the moral authority of the criminal law generally, through weakening the paradigm association of criminal laws with culpable wrongdoing. Thor's hammer was not meant for driving nails. Blurring the condemnatory messages that are part of the institution's defining marque leaves the criminal law more closely aligned to civil law. It threatens superfluous duplication and diminishes a distinct, valuable, tool for social control and doing justice.

All the more so when strict liability is deployed in stigmatic crimes. Francis Sayre was right: 'When it becomes respectable to be convicted, the vitality of

[66] An example of this might be the strict liability offence of homicide reviewed in *New Jersey v Rodriguez* 645 A 2d 1165 (1994). (For discussion, see D Husak, 'Strict Liability, Justice, and Proportionality' in *Appraising Strict Liability* 81.) The opprobrium attached to other forms of culpable homicide may be expected to inform, rather than be undermined by, public perceptions of the offence in *Rodriguez*.

[67] One piece of anecdotal evidence is the story of Sir Peter Berger, noted in § 1.1.1 and recounted in *Appraising Strict Liability*, vii.

the criminal law has been sapped.'[68] If the public begins to discount the importance of criminal prohibitions and convictions, we jeopardize the criminal law not only as a distinctive labelling device but also as a tool of education; a means by which conduct, perhaps not widely recognized as untoward, can be marked out and condemned as a serious wrong. Using strict liability in serious crimes is not just intrinsically wrong. It risks gunking up the state's most important censuring machine.[69] In the long run, strict liability promises to muffle the distinctive moral voice of the criminal law.

All this suggests that a clear line between quasi-criminal regulations and stigmatic crimes cannot, and should not, be drawn within the existing system of *criminal* justice. To the extent that quasi-criminal regulations are, or are perceived to be, 'criminal' at all, they invoke the intrinsic objections made earlier in this section, which rule out strict liability. And if they are not stigmatic at all, then they should not be even 'quasi' criminal.

Yet the force of the instrumental reasons for strict liability, set out in § 13.2, remains. One way forward might be for the state to modify the existing system, entrenching more deeply the distinction between stigmatic crimes and non-stigmatic offences, by instituting a second regime—say of administrative *violations*—covering minor offences, punishable only by small fines, where strict liability might legitimately be deployed.[70] Violations, so labelled, need not generate a criminal record and, by their formal categorization, would be clearly marked off from the criminal law. We can always hope. (Perhaps, though, we should not be optimistic.)

13.4 Defending formal strict liability (sometimes) in stigmatic crimes

Let us turn now to the second claim made in § 13.1.2. Sometimes, formal strict liability is not in substance strict. This occurs where the fault element contained in the rest of the offence, disregarding the strict liability elements, is sufficient

[68] F B Sayre, 'The Present Significance of *Mens Rea* in the Criminal Law' in R Pound (ed), *Harvard Legal Essays* (Harvard UP 1934) 399, 409.

[69] A point made in P H Robinson, 'Strict Liability's Criminogenic Effect' (2018) 12 Crim L and Phil 411.

[70] Compare the proposals in R Macrory, *Regulatory Justice: Sanctioning in a Post-Hampton World* (Cabinet Office 2006). The Macrory Review recommended introducing a complementary regime of Monetary Administrative Penalties, using strict liability to enforce regulatory breaches outside the criminal law. On the character of parallel formal regimes in France and Germany, see J R Spencer and A Pedain, 'Approaches to Strict and Constructive Liability in Continental Criminal Law' in *Appraising Strict Liability* 237.

to underpin an attribution of culpability for the offence in its entirety. There are a number of ways in which this can occur, although not all are important or controversial.

13.4.1 Strict liability going to a non-material element

I mention this case only for completeness. Trivially, strict liability is likely to be appropriate when it is imposed with respect to a non-material element, such as a limitation of time or jurisdiction.[71] That death occurs within a year and a day of D's homicidal act is a common-law element of the actus reus of murder.[72] However, it lacks a corresponding mens rea requirement. Rightly so: it is a condition that does not affect D's culpability with regard to the homicide as a whole.

13.4.2 Strict liability going to an evaluative element of the offence

Evaluative elements can present a distinctive type of actus reus component.[73] An illustration is the New Zealand case of *Police v Starkey*,[74] which involved an offence against section 55 of the Local Elections and Polls Act 1976 (NZ). The section prohibits (a) publication of a document containing (b) an untrue, (c) and defamatory, statement (d) which was calculated to influence the vote of any elector. In respect of element (c), the court held that no mens rea element was required.

Formally speaking, section 55 therefore imposes strict liability. Yet the decision seems unobjectionable. The question whether the statement was defamatory is for the court to decide, since it involves the application of an evaluative standard, the setting of which falls within the *demesne* of law. Hence it is no answer for D to say, 'I did not think it was defamatory,' or, 'in my view, this was fair comment.' D must know the facts of the matter—including the content of the statement he publishes—but he need neither know nor concur with the normative evaluation of those facts that the law makes.

[71] See the Model Penal Code definition in n 4 above. Strictly speaking, the possibility of this case was foreclosed by the definition of 'strict liability' adopted in § 13.1.

[72] Now repealed in Britain: Law Reform (Year and a Day Rule) Act 1996 (UK).

[73] See § 2.3.2.

[74] [1989] 2 NZLR 373.

Similarly, whether conduct is 'dangerous', 'indecent', or, say, 'obscene' is primarily a matter for the jury, something to be measured by a standard independent of the defendant. D's deliberate conduct either is or is not dangerous (obscene, *et cetera*), regardless of D's own view about the matter.[75] If D puts his hand up V's skirt while dancing in a nightclub, the assault (if it be one) is indecent,[76] regardless whether D thinks it is appropriate behaviour in that context. In effect, evaluative actus reus elements integrate fact with law. They introduce normative standards, requiring an evaluation which may well be at variance with D's own assessment of her conduct.[77]

There are authoritarian reasons favouring the imposition of formal strict liability for evaluative elements.[78] The rule of law requires not only that criminal laws be not discretionary in the hands of individual officials, but also that they be fixed in the hands of citizens. Part of the point of a law regulating, say, obscene conduct is to coordinate social interaction by imposing a common standard of acceptable behaviour, displacing the potentially divergent standards that persons have for themselves. Such coordination would be unachievable if people were exempted from the scope of that law simply because they had different personal values. Even in stigmatic crimes, what counts as wrongful behaviour must be determined by a standard independent of the particular defendant.

Suppose, then, that for a valuable purpose the legislature enacts a stigmatic crime imposing some common evaluative standard, in respect of which liability is formally strict. Does the crime thereby impose substantive strict liability? Not necessarily. D's very mis-assessment of the situation can be constitutive of her culpability. That D *thinks* her conduct is not dangerous may be unproblematic because D is simply wrong, and culpably so. The adjudication whether, say, a particular instance of D's driving is dangerous is not arbitrary: the considerations affecting that judgment are, in turn, considerations that we can expect individuals such as D to take account of, and we can blame D for failing sufficiently to acknowledge them when acting. If D knowingly

[75] Notice that, in principle, D must have mens rea regarding the underlying facts. For example, if the defendant in *Police v Starkey* had no reason to know the content of the statement being published, his perpetration of the actus reus ought not to be accounted culpable. The evaluative standard in any given offence should be applied to the facts that (depending on the offence's other mens rea requirements) D knew or ought to have known.

[76] Or now, in the UK, 'sexual': Sexual Offences Act 2003, s 3.

[77] The same holds when evaluative elements occur in defences, as when D uses unreasonable force in self-defence. It is for the court to determine whether the force used was reasonable, and it is no defence that D herself thought her response proportionate. (Compare, on this point, *Owino* [1996] 2 Cr App R 128, contradicting *Scarlett* [1993] 4 All ER 629; *Simester and Sullivan*, § 18.1(v).) For cases where D is mistaken about the underlying facts, see chapter 19.

[78] See also § 12.2.

takes a blind corner at 80 miles per hour, she not only drives dangerously; we can reprove her for thinking it an acceptable manoeuvre. Moreover, evaluative terms, at least those in common parlance, need not make liability unpredictable or unavoidable. We understand them and know how to apply the implicit judgements they import; especially where there is a high degree of social consensus about what counts as appropriate behaviour in the relevant context. In matters of road safety, for instance, a proscription of 'careless' or 'dangerous' driving may tell drivers all they really need to know.

13.5 Constructive liability

Perhaps the most important type of legitimate, formally strict liability crimes impose not substantive strict liability but *constructive liability*.[79]

Suppose that a stigmatic crime is enacted of the form, it is an offence to do X in circumstance Y or with consequence Y. Further, suppose that the actus reus elements of X all have corresponding mens rea elements, that Y is a matter of strict liability, and that Y is a material element. (Let us call this type of crime an 'X+Y' crime.) Provided certain conditions are met, strict liability crimes of this type need not involve the conviction of persons who are blameless in respect of the occurrence of Y. Consider the example set out at the beginning of this chapter:

> Deborah is driving through a village at a speed twenty miles per hour in excess of the speed limit. Unexpectedly she loses control of her car, mounts the pavement, and kills Allan, who had been walking quietly toward the corner shop in order to buy a newspaper.

This scenario is often proscribed by an X+Y offence, where X specifies dangerous driving and Y specifies the causing of death. Such an offence is one that, formally, imposes strict liability. Yet it does not invoke the objections raised in § 13.3. (Although it does raise the question, to be taken up in chapter 14, whether it is fair to punish Deborah *more* because Allan is killed.) Certainly it is, in one sense, unchosen and outwith Deborah's control that Allan is killed. But the possibility of that outcome is not random or unrelated to the wrong

[79] In what follows, I restrict 'constructive liability' to morally *legitimate* 'X+Y' crimes. My usage therefore differs from that of Andrew Ashworth and Kenneth Campbell, who take constructive liability to involve any form of aggravating 'X+Y' crime, where Y is a strict-liability element. See their note, A Ashworth and K Campbell, 'Recklessness in Assault—And in General?' (1991) 107 LQR 187.

that Deborah does in driving dangerously. The risk of causing death forms part of the very reason why dangerous driving is a pro tanto wrong and, indeed, is typically criminalized in its own right.[80]

What moral constraints apply to X+Y offences? The most important restriction concerns the relationship between X and Y. To illustrate, consider an alternative scenario:

> Denise bears a grudge against Joshua. She throws a stone at him while in an open field, intending to injure him. Joshua ducks and she misses. The stone damages Ken's binoculars, which were lying concealed in the long grass.

An X+Y offence covering this case, of assault causing property damage, would not be appropriate. To impose strict liability here would be illegitimate because there is insufficient connection between Denise's culpability and the harm she has done. Vandalism is a very different type of offence from assault, and the prospect of property damage does not supply reasons why, *ex ante*, assault is a pro tanto wrong. Strict liability is objectionable in this case because it makes a stigmatic conviction turn on luck rather than desert.

The difference is not simply a matter of foreseeability. It rests on the distinction between two types of risk: intrinsic and extrinsic.[81] That distinction is further explored in § 13.5.1 below. But the basic idea is that Denise should not be held criminally liable for damaging Ken's property because that risk was extrinsic to the grounds of her culpability.[82] Such risks can affect the outcome, and in turn affect our retrospective judgments about what D did, but they are not factors that make a difference to the question, in advance of acting, of what D should do. And as we saw in § 11.6, blame for φing requires more than that D should not have φed: it requires also that, from an *ex ante* perspective, D should have chosen, or taken reasonable care, not to φ.

By contrast, in the dangerous driving example, the risk of death *was* intrinsic to Deborah's culpability: it formed part of the reason why, even *ex ante*, such behaviour is a wrong. It is Deborah's commission of X that brings the risk of Y into play. Where that risk is intrinsic, there seems no difficulty about holding a defendant culpable for Y. In failing to engage adequately with the reasons why

[80] See, e.g., s 1 of the Road Traffic Act 1988 (UK).

[81] The distinction is similar to that drawn by Bernard Williams in the context of luck: B A O Williams, 'Moral Luck' in B A O Williams, *Moral Luck: Philosophical Papers 1973–1980* (CUP 1981) 20, 25–26.

[82] Ken Simons disagrees: below, § 13.5.1.

she ought not to do X, she fails to engage adequately with the reasons why she should not do Y.[83]

Moreover, constructive liability is consistent with the rule of law. Where the connection is predicated on intrinsic risk, X+Y crimes do not defeat the desire to give fair warning in criminal law. D is sufficiently forewarned of her potential criminal liability since she can only be convicted if she has committed the preliminary wrong specified in X (for example, dangerous driving) with mens rea;[84] and the risk of Y forms part of the rationale for blaming D and regarding X as a wrong.[85] Thus liability for the full constructive crime is both predictable and something D has a fair opportunity to avoid. At the same time, prohibitions of this form have the advantage of publicly highlighting the seriousness of the wrong (killing) involved in D's conduct, with an emphasis that cannot be achieved by enacting a generic offence of dangerous driving.

Constructive liability crimes are also capable of advancing the goal of fair labelling in the law. It would be incomplete and thereby misleading simply to describe Deborah's conduct as dangerous driving. Even where the mens rea for two offences is the same, representative labelling in the criminal law is responsive to harm. Inchoate crimes, such as reckless endangerment by dangerous driving, attempts to kill, and the like, are wrongs not because they involve any direct harm to the victim, but because D manipulates, subordinates, or attacks V's interests and autonomy. By contrast, when an attempt succeeds, when dangerous driving kills, the harm is rather different. V is dead. Only by acknowledging that fact can the criminal law communicate what D has done.[86]

Not all X+Y crimes impose constructive liability, because not all of them meet the constraint set out here. Perhaps the best-known X+Y offence in English criminal law is manslaughter by an unlawful act. If D commits a crime which creates a foreseeable risk of *some* (not necessarily serious) harm to V, D becomes guilty of manslaughter should his preliminary crime in fact cause V's death—there is no mens rea requirement concerning the crucial actus reus element, death. The problem with this form of manslaughter is that the range of offences capable of constituting the predicate unlawful act is too wide for

[83] This way of putting things leaves open the possibility that, at least in some X+Y contexts, one may engage adequately with the reasons why one ought not to do Y while engaging inadequately with other reasons why one shouldn't do X. I don't think that possibility applies to Deborah, but will offer some remarks touching upon it in § 13.5.1.

[84] I take dangerous driving to be a mens rea offence of (gross) negligence. Compare s 2A(1) of the Road Traffic Act 1988 (UK), which defines a person's driving as dangerous if '(a) the way he drives falls far below what would be expected of a competent and careful driver, and (b) it would be obvious to a competent and careful driver that driving in that way would be dangerous.'

[85] See also § 3.3, on the possibility of fair warning without advertence.

[86] More on this in § 14.3.

death to be an intrinsic risk.[87] The offence therefore imposes a form of *substantive* strict liability, since defendants are at risk of being convicted of a homicide offence without proof of culpability *with respect to V's death*.[88] Although the offence is sometimes called 'constructive manslaughter', in truth it is no more than a simulacrum of constructive liability. It bypasses what should be the minimum culpability requirements for a homicide conviction, and it fails to give defendants fair warning.

Implicit in the discussion so far is a second constraint: that X must be a pro tanto wrong. Absent that, an attribution of culpability for Y cannot be made out. Many legitimate activities create at least remote risks of harm. Turning on a light switch may, if there is miswiring or a short circuit, cause injury. Even careful driving risks death. Yet these activities are not in themselves wrongs. Purporting to impose constructive liability in such cases would, therefore, be illegitimate. It would lead to conviction and punishment of the blameless.

13.5.1 Intrinsicalness

Ken Simons has doubts about Denise. Partly, this is a matter of divergent intuitions about whether damaging the binoculars really is an extrinsic risk,[89] a question to which we return below. More comprehensively, however, Simons rejects the intrinsic-luck criterion entirely, preferring a test of 'minimal foreseeability':[90]

> '[E]ven though the risk of property damage is ordinarily not a reason that we should expect an actor throwing a projectile at another to consider as counting against performing such an act, that risk is nevertheless what I shall call "minimally foreseeable"; and, in my view, posing a risk of even this modest magnitude justifies treating the actor as criminally culpable with respect to the harm that is so risked.'

For Simons, the category of 'minimally foreseeable risks' includes risks that a conscientiously law-abiding defendant need not treat as significant when

[87] See, e.g., *Mallet* [1972] Crim LR 260. D punched V who fell awkwardly, striking his head and sustaining fatal brain injuries. D received only a suspended sentence of imprisonment.
[88] An analogous objection applies to the law of felony-murder in the United States.
[89] K Simons, 'Is Strict Criminal Liability in the Grading of Offences Consistent with Retributive Desert?' (2012) 32 OJLS 445, 456.
[90] Ibid, 456–57.

deciding what to do.[91] Once the defendant has gone through the gateway of perpetrating a culpable criminal act, those additional risks also 'count on [the] defendant's moral ledger, and thus do justify greater punishment when they culminate in a harm or wrong.'[92]

Structurally, Simons' analysis bears some resemblance to felony-murder doctrines, because it relies upon the fact that the defendant has 'crossed the line', as it were, to ground culpability for those additional risks. It relies, that is to say, on the wrongness of the gateway action, X, to support an extension of culpability (and liability) to Y, *regardless of how the former relates to the latter.* Simons himself acknowledges that there is nothing in the 'minimal foreseeability' criterion that makes it culpable in its own right for Denise to damage the binoculars.[93] Thus if the binoculars had been similarly damaged while Denise and Jay were skimming stones on a river, Denise would not be culpable for damaging them.

One challenge to Simons' analysis is posed by Holly Smith's lazy secretary:[94]

> '[T]he daughter of a business executive has been assigned a science project of investigating the distribution of blood-types within the population. To assist her, the executive asks his secretary to survey the office staff and prepare a report on their blood-types by noon. Instead of carrying out this request, the secretary reads a spy novel. At 11:45 a co-worker suffers massive bleeding as a result of an office accident. Paramedics arrive, and could start a transfusion immediately if the workers' blood-type were known. Unfortunately he is unconscious, cannot provide this information, and so dies before the transfusion can be started. Had the secretary followed her boss's orders, she would have known the worker's blood-type and his life would have been saved. Her failure to obtain this information is both objectively wrong *and* culpable, and it led to her inability to save her co-worker's life. But [there is] no inclination to say that the secretary is to blame for the co-worker's death.'

[91] According to Simons, a risk is minimally foreseeable if '(a) the risk is more than trivial, ie, more than extraordinarily unlikely, and (b) the defendant's act significantly increased the probability of that risk': ibid, 457. As Simons helpfully elaborates, 'The category of minimally foreseeable risk captures a wider swath of risks than "intrinsic" risk, because it includes risks that are quite unlikely—specifically, sufficiently unlikely that a conscientiously law-abiding defendant need not count them as a reason not to engage in the conduct that created the risk.'

[92] Ibid, 457.

[93] Ibid, 456: 'To be sure, [the risk of property damage] it is not the main reason, nor is it a sufficient reason by itself. And in the actual hypothetical, it has virtually no bearing on the justifiability of [Denise's] act or on the sanction she justly deserves.'

[94] H Smith, 'Culpable Ignorance' (1983) 92 Phil Rev 543, 550. For the sake of argument, assume that the secretary's contract of employment explicitly includes duties of this sort.

Presumably, it is a minimally foreseeable risk in Smith's example that not having a record of blood types may impair emergency treatment in exactly the manner that it did. Simons' account makes the lazy secretary's culpability with respect to the co-worker's death either a clear case or at least a borderline one.[95] By contrast, on the intrinsic/extrinsic test, the example is a clear case of *non-*culpability. And to my mind, the lazy secretary *is* a clear case of non-culpability with respect to death. That intuition counsels against Simons' approach, which puts the pressure on the wrong places: on the wrongness of the gateway action and, separately, on the foreseeability of the further consequence.[96] The point of Smith's example is that the risk of a co-worker's dying for want of a medical record is not what makes the secretary's failure culpable. Her failure *is* culpable; but not for that reason.

Part of the payoff of the intrinsic/extrinsic distinction is that it blocks a generic doctrine of transferred guilt.[97] Given D's culpability for some criminal offence (φing), satisfying the actus reus of a further crime (μing) is insufficient by itself to support conviction of that further crime. D must be culpable with respect to *μing*. Recalling the discussion in chapter 11 (and to which we return in § 14.2), what that means, in this context, is that there must be something deficient—something that reflects a moral vice on D's part—about D's engagement with the reasons why she should not do that further crime. There must be something deficient, in other words, about D's engagement with the reasons why she should not μ.

In principle, culpability for Denise's damaging the binoculars can arise in two ways. It may arise directly, out of a deficient engagement *simpliciter* with the guiding reasons Denise has to avoid damaging the binoculars. Certainly, she has such reasons. Whether aiming at Jay or skimming stones with him, however, she exhibits no deficiency in engaging with those reasons. Even allowing that the risk was minimally foreseeable, Denise isn't negligent with respect to it. It is not the case that she should have foreseen the risk and therefore refrained from behaving as she did.

[95] It may count as borderline on the question of minimal foreseeability.

[96] The work done by the gateway wrong can also be seen in the following example, for which thanks are due to Mike Dowdle. Suppose that D lights up and smokes a marijuana joint in his friend's house. (Assume *arguendo* that D's smoking the joint is illegal and demonstrates what Simons calls 'criminal culpability'.) Unfortunately, there is a gas leak in the house and it burns down. Provided the risk of gas leaks is at least minimally foreseeable, on Simons' analysis this case is starkly different from one in which D lights up a cigarette with the same incendiary result.

[97] See, e.g., Coke, 3 Inst 56: homicide in the course of an unlawful act is murder. This rule, later restricted by Foster to felony-murders, is decried in J F Stephens, *A History of the Criminal Law of England* vol 3 (Macmillan 1883) 57.

Alternatively, culpability may arise *indirectly*, through a gateway wrong. In such cases, D's culpability for φing helps to explain why she is culpable for μing. The significance of the intrinsic/extrinsic distinction in this context is that it tracks the cases where D's reasons not to μ are embedded within her reasons not to φ. In turn, D's deficient engagement with the latter implies a deficient engagement with the former. That's what makes Deborah, our dangerous driver from § 13.5, different. Her choice to drive dangerously implies a deficient engagement with the reasons she has not to kill. In Smith's case of the lazy secretary, by contrast, failing to avert the death of a co-worker does not explain why the secretary has a duty to prepare the report. The reason it supplies is not embedded. It is ancillary.

What makes a reason ancillary? I don't have a full answer to that question. The basic idea is one of superfluity: it is not the reason, or one of the reasons, that does the work. The secretary has two sources of guiding reasons for preparing the report. The first (R1) is that she is contractually obliged to do so, since her employer has requested it. The second (R2) is that a co-worker's life will thereby be saved. R1 is both necessary and sufficient to make her failure a wrong. R2 is neither necessary nor sufficient. In turn, it is the secretary's choice to act against R1 that makes her culpable. R2 is ancillary.

One might think to strip this down to a simple test of necessity: R1 is necessary to make the secretary's inaction a wrong; R2 is not. However, more complicated cases can arise, especially for overdetermined wrongs. In Deborah's case, for example, the duty she has not to drive dangerously rests upon multiple grounds: (R1) the prospect of causing property damage, and (R2) the prospect of causing harm to persons. Either suffices to make dangerous driving a wrong. Strictly speaking, therefore, neither is necessary. But that presents no difficulty here. Neither R1 nor R2 is ancillary. When Deborah culpably drives dangerously, she exhibits deficient engagement with *both* sets of guiding reasons, assuming both are in play.

A similar analysis holds where one of two complementary reasons is embedded inside the other. Murder, for example, is a constructive liability crime in as much as intentionally inflicting grievous bodily harm (the gateway wrong) becomes murder should the victim die. In principle,[98] the risk of death is intrinsic to the gateway wrong. The duty not to inflict grievous bodily harm intentionally is justified both because doing so is wrong in itself *and* because it is likely to cause death. Each ground suffices to make it a wrong.

[98] I assume here that a sufficiently high threshold is required for the bodily harm to count as *grievous*. As it happens, that may not be true of English law. See *Simester and Sullivan*, § 10.6(ii).

It is worth emphasizing that the remarks here are merely elucidatory. Even if they are unpersuasive, the underlying intrinsic/extrinsic distinction does not stand or fall with them. It remains meaningful (if vague). And useful. It gives lawmakers a legitimate means to specify via X+Y crimes that the prospect of Y is a reason why it is wrong to do X, and in turn that culpably doing X constitutes culpability for Y, without the need for prosecutors to prove independently that Y was reasonably foreseeable. Notice, moreover, that there is no moral short-changing here. On the indirect route, the defendant may be culpable for Y even though, on this occasion, Y was *not* reasonably foreseeable.[99] Imagine the following variant on Deborah's case:

> Edith is driving in the countryside at a speed well in excess of the limit. There is no other person or car within the visible distance. Rounding a corner, she loses control of her car, which spins onto a field of maize. Unfortunately, her car lands on Bert, a runaway prisoner who was sleeping concealed in the maize.

It is morally legitimate in this case to blame (and convict) Edith for dangerous driving causing death. Part of the point of crystallizing duties is that, absent emergencies, defendants are not entitled to adjudicate the underlying risks for themselves. Provided those risks are intrinsic to the gateway duty, it suffices for culpability that they are in fact in play. A defendant fails to respect those risks by failing to respect the duty that protects against them. *Simpliciter*.

Where, though, does that leave Denise, who throws a stone at Joshua and damages Ken's binoculars? On the account developed here, hers is a case of extrinsic luck. Why is it a wrong to throw stones? The short answer: it isn't! The gateway wrong in play here is one of attempted battery, a wrong that rests upon the interests we have in physical integrity. The risk of damaging property may contribute *something* to the case for making battery a wrong, but its contribution is neither necessary nor sufficient. It is ancillary.

What turns Denise's stone-throwing into a wrong is that she is trying to hit Joshua. Her duty not to do that defeats (indeed, excludes) the satisfaction she derives from hitting him as a reason to do so. In turn, Denise is culpable because she has chosen to pursue defeated reasons. She has *also* failed to conform to the guiding reasons she has not to damage the binoculars. But so far as the

[99] Which is not to deny that foreseeability may affect an agent's *degree* of culpability.

latter are concerned, she has not exhibited any culpability-grounding failure to engage with them.

13.5.2 Semi-constructive liability

One typical feature of constructive liability crimes is that X constitutes an offence in its own right. Paradigmatically, the occurrence of Y operates as an aggravating element, constituting a second, more serious, crime. Is this a necessary feature of legitimate X+Y criminalization?

Seemingly not. Perhaps the easiest case is where X is not itself a criminal offence, but where it would be legitimate to make it one. In this case, the strict liability element can operate as a form of dispensation: the gravamen of the crime is X, yet there is a fortuitous exemption from criminal liability where Y does not eventuate. Even if there were no offence of dangerous driving, say, it would still be legitimate to enact an offence of dangerous driving causing death, for the same reasons that justify constructive liability.

That possibility gives us a distinction between two types of case. In the first, X may or may not be criminalized, but Y operates as an aggravating factor. In the second, Y (or more precisely, the absence of Y) operates purely as a dispensing element. In the first type of case, the occurrence of Y makes the X+Y crime of which D is convicted more serious than would have been a crime of X alone; it may also—and typically does—lead to the imposition of greater punishments. On the analysis in § 13.5, where the relationship between X and Y is one of intrinsic risk, such crimes impose constructive rather than substantive strict liability. The culpability element in X extends also to element Y, so that X+Y is not a crime of substantive strict liability.

In the second case, X alone is not criminalized (although it might have been); Y need not aggravate the seriousness of the crime. If Y does not modify the wrong in X, its presence may reflect institutional considerations. In such cases, there seems no reason why the relationship between X and Y need be one of intrinsic risk, provided it is not arbitrary.

This form of dispensation can bring rule of law benefits, in as much as it confines what otherwise might be wider-ranging powers of arrest and prosecution. Suppose, for example, that the legislature wishes to criminalize a failure to disclose one's HIV-positive status to one's sexual partner. The risk of malicious or discriminatory prosecutions may be reduced by including a strict liability requirement that one's partner consequently becomes infected.[100] That requirement may also have practical advantages in terms of reducing the costs of policing: Y must occur before the criminal justice system, with all its intrusion and expense, is in play.

However, payoffs of this sort do not warrant adding *any* filtering element to the offence. The element should not be arbitrary. Suppose that there were no offence of dangerous driving, but that the state were to enact an offence of dangerous driving within one mile of any building painted yellow (with the latter element being of strict liability). The strict liability element here has no impact on the proscribed wrong. It is normatively immaterial, so that defendants who are culpable in respect of driving dangerously cannot claim to lack culpability for the full offence. None the less, arbitrary dispensations of this sort violate constraints of fairness in the distribution of convictions and punishment. It is unfair to single out one person rather than another for punishment, when both are equally deserving, unless there are good reasons—which may in part be institutional—for distributing such burdens unevenly. Arbitrary rules violate this constraint.

13.5.3 Making things worse?

It is one thing to say that D can be culpable for Y. It is quite another to say that Y makes things worse. Yet constructive and semi-constructive liability crimes suggest that it does. Is it right to treat strict liability elements as aggravating or compounding the seriousness of the wrong done? It may be appropriate to label Deborah's conduct as dangerous driving causing death, but should death increase her punishment? And in terms of prohibitions, should Y's occurrence change things so much as to warrant criminalization where, absent Y, they do not?

These are familiar problems of moral luck. Indeed, they are not specific to strict liability.[101] Notoriously, the common law does not criminalize grossly negligent or reckless endangerment of life even though, if death occurs, the case becomes one of manslaughter. Rather like constructive liability offences, what makes the difference is the addition of just one actus reus element. But this chapter is long enough. We must defer these issues to chapter 14.

[100] Lacking empirical evidence on the matter, my claim is only that this plausible. It might be, too, that other strategies would do a better job of reducing the risks of enforcement abuse. I express no view on that here.

[101] But see, in the strict liability context, K Simons, 'When is Strict Criminal Liability Just' (1997) 87 J Crim L & Criminology 1075, § V.

13.6 Conclusion

Tom Nagel once remarked that strict liability 'may have its legal uses, but seems irrational as a moral position.'[102] At the core, Nagel was right. The moral condemnation and punishment of blameless actions is wrong. Moreover, it is wrong even when a person is in some other way culpable. None the less, it should come as no surprise that this core objection to strict liability is surrounded by a complex penumbra. Perhaps most importantly, the difference between two criminal wrongs can be a matter of formal strict liability—indeed, of moral luck—without that foreclosing the attribution of blame for the more complex, constructive, wrong. Substantive strict liability may be irrational as a moral position: formal strict liability need not be.

Once this is seen, imposing legitimate strict liability through constructive stigmatic crimes becomes an issue of criminalization. Strict liability for the consequence (Y) of a particular activity (X) turns the underlying activity, X, into a gateway. Consequential risk is not normally something over which we have full control, so that the prospect of a criminal conviction is avoidable only by sacrificing the underlying activity. It may be that Y is the harm the offence is designed to address. But its proscription via constructive liability is legitimate only where X is a wrong from which we may legitimately oblige citizens to desist.

[102] T Nagel, *Mortal Questions* (CUP 1979) 31.

14
Outcome and Other Luck

In § 13.5, we considered the possibility of constructive liability offences. A constructive liability offence involves the (legitimate) criminalization of, say, doing X with consequence Y, where the occurrence of Y is a matter of strict liability. Such 'X+Y' offences can sometimes be morally legitimate to enact, at least where the risk of Y's occurrence is intrinsic to the culpability of one who does X—that is, where that risk forms part of the reason why X is a wrong. Provided the risk is intrinsic, it may be appropriate to hold D culpable for Y.

But should the occurrence of Y make things worse for D? In practice, most constructive liability crimes treat the occurrence of Y as aggravating or compounding the seriousness of the wrong done by D. Even if it can be distinguished from strict liability, therefore, constructive liability may none the less be thought problematic. Like strict liability, it has the effect of making liability depend on luck.

The problem is well known. Suppose that D shoots at V and misses. She commits attempted murder. If V is hit and dies, though, D's liability is converted to murder; a different conviction with very different penal consequences. Yet, once D has pulled the trigger, the result lies outwith her control. 'We never do more than move our bodies: the rest is up to nature.'[1] Scenarios like these raise familiar problems of moral—*outcome*—luck: the luck of how things turned out. They present challenges for both criminalization and punishment. In general, citizens are free to act rashly with respect to others' lives, but if death occurs they commit manslaughter. Attempted killings are themselves criminal, but even completed attempts tend to be punished more severely if they succeed. And so on. Without any difference in D's raw conduct, or her mens rea, differential treatment may follow just because of the outcome.

In this chapter, I defend a distinction between being culpable for more, once the outcome is taken into account, and being more culpable. To accept the legitimacy of constructive liability is to accept that D may be culpable for something worse. But that doesn't make D more culpable.

[1] Davidson, *EAE*, 59.

Fundamentals of Criminal Law. A P Simester, Oxford University Press (2021). © A P Simester.
DOI: 10.1093/oso/9780198853145.003.0014

14.1 Control and responsibility

More than one kind of worry can be raised about the role of outcome luck in criminal law. At a foundational level, it is arguable that the dependence of outcomes on luck means that we should not be held morally *responsible* for such outcomes. As Thomas Nagel puts it:[2]

> 'Prior to reflection it is intuitively plausible that people cannot be morally assessed for what is not their fault, or for what is due to factors beyond their control. . . . Without being able to explain exactly why, we feel that the appropriateness of moral assessment is easily undermined by the discovery that the act or attribute, no matter how good or bad, is not under the person's control.'

Luck, it may be thought, is something over which we have no control. Its operation is, for us, involuntary. And that undermines our susceptibility to moral evaluation for its effects. So, Nagel continues:[3]

> 'Whether we succeed or fail in what we try to do nearly always depends to some extent on factors beyond our control. This is true of murder, altruism, revolution, the sacrifice of certain interests for the sake of others—almost any morally important act. What has been done, and what is morally judged, is partly determined by other factors. However jewel-like[4] the good will may be in its own right, there is a morally significant difference between rescuing someone from a burning building and dropping him from a twelfth-storey window while trying to rescue him. Similarly, there is a morally significant difference between reckless driving and manslaughter. But whether a reckless driver hits a pedestrian depends on the presence of the pedestrian at the point where he recklessly passes a red light. . . . [T]he broad range of external influences here identified seems on close examination to undermine moral assessment as surely as does the narrower range of excusing conditions. If the *condition of control* is consistently applied, it threatens to erode most of the moral assessments we find it natural to make.'

[2] T Nagel, 'Moral Luck' in *Mortal Questions* (CUP 1979) 24, 25. The essay is a revised version of his reply to Bernard Williams in (1976) 50 Proc Arist Soc, Supp Vol 137. Quotations here are from the later version.

[3] 'Moral Luck' (n 2) 25–26. (Emphasis added.)

[4] A reference to I Kant, *Foundations of the Metaphysics of Morals* (1785) § 1.

Nagel's challenge also confronts other forms of luck, as we see in § 14.4. It is helpful, though, to start by focusing on outcome luck. We saw in Part II of this book that D cannot be morally responsible—hence should not be held criminally liable—for the consequences of her behaviour if that behaviour is involuntary. Nagel's 'condition of control' echoes that constraint. As a first pass, the constraint can be formulated as follows:

> *Control*: An agent can be morally responsible (i.e. *eligible* for praise or blame[5]) only for outcomes that are under the agent's control.

For Nagel, the puzzle generated by outcome luck crystallizes with recognition that, in practice, we do not control the outcomes of our acts, because of the 'broad range of external influences' upon which those outcomes depend.

14.1.1 All or nothing?

There are grounds for thinking that Nagel overstates the challenge. Consider the two propositions, that (i) 'whether we succeed or fail in what we try to do nearly always depends to some extent on factors beyond our control,' and that (ii) 'if the condition of control is consistently applied, it threatens to erode most of the moral assessments we find it natural to make.' We can accept (i) without embracing (ii). Many factors affecting an outcome are beyond our control. But that doesn't mean the outcome itself is beyond our control. It is only *given* our behaviour that the outcome is—thereafter—beyond our control. As agents, we typically do have control over the outcomes of our actions; we exercise control over that outcome *through* the behaviour that constitutes those actions. It is D's reckless driving, or her pulling the trigger, that brings the uncontrolled factors into play, and makes outcome luck relevant. Thus consistent application of Nagel's condition of control, requiring that the outcome must not be 'beyond' D's control, need not erode D's moral responsibility for an outcome. To that extent, there is no paradox about moral luck.

[5] See § 4.1. (To recall, 'moral responsibility' in this book refers to an agent's *eligibility* for moral evaluations in respect of some event. It is thus a precondition of culpability.)

Part of the puzzle here concerns the best way to formulate the condition of control and, behind that, what purpose it serves. Consider the following variants:

> *Sufficient-control*: An agent can be morally responsible (i.e. eligible for praise or blame) only for outcomes that are sufficiently under the agent's control.
>
> *Full-control*: An agent can be morally responsible (i.e. eligible for praise or blame) only for outcomes that are fully under that agent's control: that is, only if each and every factor that determines whether the outcome occurs is under D's control.

Full-control tends, as Nagel sees, to undermine virtually any blaming judgement we find it natural to make. If Diane lights a match by scraping it on the side of a matchbox, she may know that oxygen is present.[6] But Diane does not control its presence. Neither, when Eric pulls the trigger of a handgun, does he control any of the other factors that combine to cause Vera's death once Eric has moved his finger.[7] According to *Full-control*, Diane is not morally responsible for lighting the match-stick; neither is Eric morally responsible for killing Vera. By contrast, *Sufficient-control* allows that moral responsibility may lie in those cases.

Sufficient-control accords more closely with fundamental criminal-law doctrine. It would be natural for criminal lawyers to see Eric as eligible for blaming evaluations (subject to questions of mens rea and defences) so long as his finger-movement was sufficiently voluntary.[8] Recalling the analysis from Part II, the voluntariness requirement operates as a negative, capacity-based condition of moral responsibility: D is in eligible for praise or blame regarding an outcome whenever that outcome is, vis-à-vis D, *in*voluntary. The condition of control is analogous. In general, what counts is whether Eric had the capacity to behave differently, so as to avoid setting in motion the events that led to Vera's death; so as not to leave the rest up to nature.[9] Preferring *Sufficient-control* over *Full-control* as a criterion of moral responsibility thus goes some way toward reconciling the condition of control with our intuitions about

[6] Oxygen is not necessary to burn the chemicals on the head of the match (which contain their own oxidizer), but it is necessary for the matchstick to burn.

[7] See, e.g., the discussion in A Ashworth, 'Taking the Consequences' in S Shute, J Gardner, and J Horder (eds), *Action and Value in Criminal Law* (OUP 1993) 107. On the distinction between full and sufficient control, see also Moore, *Placing Blame*, 211–18.

[8] See in particular § 8.3. Voluntariness can itself come in degrees: § 8.5.2.

[9] Alternatively, Eric may have *exercised* control through his own agency: § 8.3.

moral assessments. Moreover, it is compatible with a narrower and more intuitive objection to outcome luck:

> *No-difference*: While not denying moral responsibility for outcomes altogether, luck should have no impact upon our blaming judgments; nor upon the criminal law's response to wrongdoing.

We turn to that thesis now.

14.2 Making a difference to culpability? The objects of moral assessment

No-difference extends even to constructive liability. It suggests that the occurrence of the strict liability element should have no effect on D's liability—since it makes no difference to D's culpability. We may be culpable for the entirety of the X+Y crime, and X+Y may be a different wrong than is X alone. However, it remains to be shown whether we should distinguish between them in our response.

Andrew Ashworth,[10] amongst others,[11] has raised this type of concern when opposing the differential treatment of attempts. Where the difference is merely down to luck, he argues, a failed attempt to kill ought to be treated just as severely as if it succeeded. On Ashworth's analysis, the criminal law should not concern itself with results. Properly understood, common-law murder is a kind of constructive liability offence: the gateway crime committed by D is an *attempt* to kill or do grievous bodily harm, and what elevates D's crime to murder is merely the additional actus reus element of causing death. But, says Ashworth, even as a matter of intrinsic luck, the happenstance of whether death occurs does not modify D's culpability. And it should not, more pointedly, change D's punishment.

None of this means that Ashworth is soft on crime. In his account, the attempted murderer deserves as much as if she succeeded. So, if Ashworth believed in the death sentence, he would presumably hang 'em all. But he would define their criminality in the inchoate mode.[12]

[10] See A Ashworth, 'Taking the Consequences' (n 7); also his 'Criminal Attempts and the Role of Resulting Harm' (1988) 19 Rutgers LJ 725 and 'Belief, Intent, and Criminal Liability' in J Eekelaar and J Bell (eds), *Oxford Essays in Jurisprudence* (3rd Series, OUP 1987) 1. The argument is restricted to 'complete' rather than 'incomplete' attempts: R A Duff, 'Subjectivism, Objectivism and Criminal Attempts' in *Harm and Culpability* 19, 22–23.

[11] e.g. L Alexander and K K Ferzan, *Crime and Culpability: A Theory of Criminal Law* (CUP 2009) ch 5.

[12] Ashworth, 'Taking the Consequences' (n 7) 124.

It is important to separate two claims here. One is concerned with definition and labelling: that crimes should be defined without reference to outcomes. The second concerns culpability and punishment: that D's level of culpability is unchanged by outcome luck, and therefore any desert-based sentence should be unaffected by outcomes.[13] In what follows, I shall argue that Ashworth's first claim is mistaken. But he is right about the second.

14.2.1 The type mismatch problem

Ashworth's conclusions are notoriously counterintuitive. For most of us, outcome luck looms as a brute fact in our moral judgements. Where 'one negligently leaves the bath running with the baby in it, one will realize, as one bounds up the stairs toward the bathroom, that if the baby has drowned one has done something awful, whereas if it has not one has merely been careless.'[14] To put a name to Nagel's example, there is a morally significant difference between Joseph's drowning the baby and his 'merely' running that risk. Of the two potential descriptions of Joseph's behaviour, one is a morally worse thing to do than the other.

What follows from this? In terms of relative culpability, not much. Specifically, it does not follow from the fact that I am culpable for having done something morally worse that I am more culpable. It is important to recall the point made in chapter 11, that there are distinctions between various kinds of objects in our moral assessments.[15] Amongst others, we can make evaluations of:

(i) moral agents;
(ii) their actions;[16] and
(iii) moral agents with respect to their actions.

The morally significant difference in Nagel's example involves type (ii) evaluations of actions. By contrast, blaming judgements are type (iii) evaluations.

[13] I leave aside here the possibility that sentences may justly be varied from that which is deserved. My concern in Part III is with blameworthiness rather than justified blame-related reactions such as punishment. As David Enoch and Andrei Marmor put it, 'Questions of blameworthiness are about the truth or falsehood of attributions of blame': D Enoch and A Marmor, 'The Case Against Moral Luck' (2007) 26 Law and Phil 405, 413; see chapter 11 n 1.
[14] Nagel, 'Moral Luck' (n 2) 30–31.
[15] See § 11.2.
[16] See § 2.4.

When we blame, we disapprove not of the action by itself, nor of the defendant by herself, but *of the defendant for doing that action*. To be sure, blaming judgements involve tracing a negative evaluation of a person's action back to the person who does it. They involve, and their ingredients overlap with, type (i) and type (ii) evaluations. However, it doesn't follow that blaming judgements are a simple function of those other types.[17] So we cannot simply conclude that variations in outcome are tracked by variations in culpability.

Much the same point can be seen in the context of praising judgements, which are also type (iii) assessments. Suppose that Diane intends to help Peter in some charitable endeavour by gifting him a painting, which she thinks is worth $5,000. The painting turns out to be worth $100,000, enabling Peter to achieve many more of his charitable goals. A better outcome, assuredly: but Diane may be no more praiseworthy for its promotion.

Thus far, the point is a preliminary one, of the non-sequitur variety. Since they are distinct types of evaluations, it cannot be assumed that variations in type (ii) evaluations imply corresponding variations in type (iii) evaluations. Further argument is required. As Nagel himself remarks, 'when we blame someone for his actions we are not merely saying it is bad that they happened, or bad that he exists: we are judging *him*, saying he is bad . . . .'[18] Yet it seems that outcome luck should make no difference to our type (i) moral judgements of *agents*. Granted that Joseph's negligent behaviour is the same in both scenarios, the fact that the baby drowns does not establish that he is a morally worse person than if the baby survives. And if it reflects no worse on the agent,[19] why should we think that agent more culpable?

14.2.2 The structural argument

Further argument is on offer. The most promising approach looks to understand outcome luck by reference to the structure of culpability evaluations. This is the approach adopted by John Gardner, who accepts that blaming judgements combine agent with action:[20]

[17] As Simons observes, 'We cannot simply rank all harms and wrongs in one scale of significance, then rank all mens rea or culpability criteria in a second scale, then multiply the values to arrive at a composite measure of the actor's just deserts.' K Simons, 'Understanding the Topography of Moral and Criminal Law Norms' in R A Duff and S P Green (eds), *Philosophical Foundations of Criminal Law* (OUP 2011) 228, 241.

[18] Nagel, 'Moral Luck' (n 2) 25.

[19] Although it may affect evaluations of the agent's *life*: J Gardner, 'Wrongs and Faults' in *Appraising Strict Liability* 51.

[20] Gardner, *Offences and Defences*, 231.

> 'There is no automatic and comprehensive opposition between assessing the gravity of a crime in terms of the offender's blameworthiness and assessing the gravity of a crime according to the way it impacts upon its victim. That is because, to assess the offender's blameworthiness we must begin by asking "blameworthiness in respect of which action?"'

Agreed. To blame someone is to make an adverse moral assessment of that person in respect of their action. In turn, Gardner notes, blaming judgements are necessarily dependent upon what the agent has done:[21]

> 'Since on any plausible account of human agency there can be actions which are, like killing and wounding, defined at least partly in terms of their actual impact upon other people independently of the way things seemed *ex ante* to the perpetrator, it follows that an inquiry into the perpetrator's blameworthiness cannot be made independently of this impact.'

So far so good. What we blame an agent *for* depends on what that agent has done. That's an important point, to which we return below. But Gardner extends the reasoning. He thinks *how much* the agent is blameworthy also depends upon the actual impact of the agent's behaviour. For Gardner, the dependence of culpability upon actions means that we should reject a proportionality principle that makes sentences 'proportionate to the offender's blameworthiness or culpability in committing the crime,'[22] and replace it with a principle 'according to which the sentence should be in proportion to the offender's wrongful action, adjusted for his blameworthiness in respect of it.'[23] The wrong, the thing actually done, is primary; it supplies our starting point. And outcome luck really is brute fact.[24]

Gardner's conclusion follows, in part, from his thought that the grounds of blame originate in the guiding reasons we have not to act as we do.[25] We shouldn't choose to φ, and we should take care not to φ, *because* φing is a bad thing to do; because we ought not to do it: a type (ii) judgement. Our culpability, and the case for deserved punishment, derives directly from our failure to act in accordance with those reasons, defrayed only by any justification, excuse, or irresponsibility defence we may have.[26] If we did something worse,

[21] Ibid, 231.
[22] Ibid, 226.
[23] Ibid, 232; above, § 11.6.
[24] Or, rather, semi-brute—given the normative complexity of causation.
[25] See also Raz, *Practical Reason and Norms*, 186–87.
[26] Gardner, *Offences and Defences*, 227.

those guiding reasons are stronger, and so in turn is our culpability. And that's why what we actually did—how things turned out—makes a difference to the deserved sentence.

Yet as we saw in § 11.6, that gets things the wrong way around. Guiding reasons against φing do not reflect badly on D's moral characteristics *directly*. Famously, strict liability wrongs may tell us nothing about D's culpability at all. What makes the difference, when moving to blaming judgements, is how D *engages* with those reasons. Was there some deficiency in her practical reasoning, something that reflects a moral vice on her part; something that explains why she came to behave as she did (and thereby to φ)? This inquiry does not depend upon the actual consequences of that behaviour. D's engagement with guiding reasons crystallizes at the very moment when she behaves as she does, and thereby actuates the outcome-risk of φing. Deficient or otherwise, it is unaffected by what happens next.[27] Outcome luck may determine what D agent is culpable for, but it has nothing to say about *why* D is culpable for it.

This is a key payoff for culpability theories. In the process of explaining why D is culpable, a successful theory ought to provide some guidance about the extent of D's culpability. According to the account given in chapter 11, the grounds of culpability depend upon D's engagement with the guiding reasons she had for and against behaving as she did. How well did she choose? To what extent did she pay sufficient attention to the risks? And so on. Those questions must be answered with reference to *the moment of D's behaviour*; not once the consequences are known. Gardner does not show why outcome luck changes the answers to those questions. And he can't. Because it doesn't.

14.2.3 Changing the wrong, and risking it

As it happens, I still think we should reject the *No-difference* thesis.[28] Even though it doesn't affect the degree of blameworthiness, outcome luck has an impact upon the *content* of blaming judgements. We cannot blame Joseph for drowning the baby unless the baby in fact drowns. Thus the evaluation differs when the relevant outcome actually occurs. Lucky Joseph is culpable for risking his baby's life. Unlucky Joseph is also culpable for causing the baby's

[27] In terms of blame for outcomes, this proposition is subject to qualification where D has a subsequent opportunity to intervene: as in *Miller* [1983] 2 AC 161. In such cases, though, the outcome is not (at least, not yet) outwith D's control.

[28] See § 14.1.1.

death. Since outcome luck is embedded in the actions one does,[29] it is also embedded in type (iii) judgements regarding those actions.

The same goes for the wrongs those actions constitute. Wrongs are event-dependent. One can only breach a duty by actually doing whatever the duty interdicts. Hence Joseph does a different wrong when he causes the baby's death than when he merely, carelessly, risks it. To risk a wrong is not to perpetrate that wrong, although it may be to do a related wrong. Moreover, the secondary duties arising from those wrongs can also differ. Depending on the circumstances, one who causes harm may have a duty to compensate, whereas one who merely risks that harm need only apologize, perhaps take more precautions in future, and so on.

I say more about distinguishing such wrongs in § 14.3. Even if we accept that, however, changing what Joseph is culpable *for* doesn't mean that Joseph is more (or less) culpable. The conclusion that Joseph's action is a wrong is a type (ii) evaluation.[30] His culpability, on the other hand, is a property of Joseph's relationship to that wrong. It is an implication of the account developed in chapter 11 that guiding reasons do not determine *why* an agent is culpable for her action. *That* is a function of the agent's failure to conform to the reasons by which *she should be guided*, at the moment of acting. This means, in turn, that the starting point for agent-regarding culpability evaluations must involve reference to potential descriptions of the agent's behaviour, not merely the descriptions that turn out to apply.

To see this, notice that the existence of guiding reasons does not depend upon what is actually done. It cannot be the case that Dave has reason not to kill Victor only if he actually kills Victor. The reason exists generally. Most of the time, though, that reason has no practical relevance to an agent's behaviour. As he sits drinking a beer with his friend, killing Victor is the last thing on Dave's mind.

Things change, however, when one's conduct involves a risk of causing death. In the context of outcome luck, what generally gives a guiding reason its bite on our practical deliberation is not the value it expresses but the prospective engagement of our behaviour with that value: an epistemic matter. Let us restate, more formally, one of the examples from chapter 11:

> Alex presents at hospital with recognized symptoms and no prior medical history. Pam, a doctor, injects Alex with a painkiller that is the most appropriate

[29] At least, to the extent that those actions involve consequence elements.
[30] See § 14.2.1.

treatment for his condition. Unfortunately, the injection produces an unforeseeable allergic reaction and causes Alex's death.

Pam has a decisive guiding reason not to kill Alex. Doubtless she knows that. She also has a decisive guiding reason not to administer the painkiller. But Pam does not know that, and she has no reason to know that. Indeed, there is an important sense in which Pam *should* administer the painkiller to Alex. Based on all the available information, it is the optimal treatment. Suppose that Pam were to give Alex an experimental drug, not recommended for patients in his condition. She would be guilty of culpable medical malpractice, malpractice that happens to save his life.

The difficulty here is posed by the epistemic limb of reasons: specifically, by Pam's failure to realize that her undoubted reason not to kill gives her reason not to act as she does.[31] In turn, culpability in Pam's case depends not on whether that reason exists, or even on whether it was decisive in this case; it depends on *whether she ought to have treated it as decisive*. It depends, for Pam, on whether she ought to have brought the reason she had not to kill to bear upon her own behaviour. An agent's culpability may be value-based. It may lie in her failure to give enough weight to the risks. Or it may lie in her underestimating those risks. But it does not lie in her failure to get the outcome right.

This disconnect between guiding reasons and 'those reasons by which an agent should be guided' is compounded by the all-or-nothing character of type (ii) evaluations. D's behaviour did-or-did-not cause death. From the *ex ante* perspective of someone about to act, however, that link tends to be probabilistic in character. Like the rest of us, Pam lacks omniscience about what will happen if she behaves as she does. Hence she lacks omniscience about which guiding reasons actually are engaged by that behaviour. Pam makes the right decision, measured in terms of *ex ante* expectations and the reasons by which she ought to be motivated. She makes the wrong decision, measured in terms of outcomes and guiding reasons. But the gap does not reflect badly on her.

14.2.4 Coherence and concurrence

One point in favour of the foregoing account is that it goes for praise too.[32] Suppose that, in a bid to cheer him up, Jane sends Keith some roses.

[31] This is not merely a question for inadvertent negligence: perhaps the drug is known to cause allergic reactions in very rare cases.

[32] Moreover, as we see in § 14.4, it is compatible with constitutive and circumstantial luck.

Unfortunately, through no fault of Jane's, the florist delivers the flowers to the wrong address. On the account offered here, Jane deserves just as much praise for trying to cheer Keith up as she would for having succeeded. Her efforts reflect equally morally well upon her: 'it's the thought [behind the action] that counts.' Analogous to cases deserving blame, the admirable motivation behind her action is crystallized at the point of her behaviour.

The same goes for unexpectedly positive outcomes. Consider the example in § 14.2.1, wherein Diane supports a charitable endeavour by gifting a painting that she thinks is worth $5,000. Unexpectedly, the painting proves to be much more valuable, facilitating additional charitable activities. Diane may take the 'credit' for those additional benefits, in as much as they lie, ascriptively, at her door. But they shine no favourable light upon her moral virtues, and they do not increase the degree of her praiseworthiness.

In a more complex case, imagine that David visits his sick grandmother and gives her pills that he thinks will kill her, hoping thereby to accelerate his inheritance. As it happens, David has mixed up the pills, and the ones he gives to his grandmother have the unforeseen result of curing her instead. David has done two actions, one wrong (attempted murder) and one right (curing his grandmother). But the *degree* of his blame- or praise-worthiness is, once again, determined by his motivation for administering the pills. He chose to do so in order, unjustifiably, to kill. His actions disclose a moral vice. They reflect badly upon him regardless of the outcome.

Notice, too, that this analysis helps to explain the criminal law's doctrine of *concurrence*, which in broad terms mandates that the actus reus and mens rea of a crime must coincide in time.[33] That broad formulation, however, obscures a crucial distinction. More precisely, it is only the *behavioural* and generally the *circumstantial* elements of the actus reus that must concur with D's mens rea. Consider the following example:

> One evening, while driving home, D collides with a cyclist who has suddenly cut in front of her car. Upon getting out of the car, D recognizes that the cyclist is V, her enemy. Having no opportunity to save him, she rejoices while he dies of his injuries.

[33] *Fowler v Padget* (1798) 7 Term Rep 509, 101 ER 1103; *Simester and Sullivan*, § 5.8. The concurrence doctrine is subject to some well-known exceptions, including the 'single transaction' principle espoused in *Thabo Meli v R* [1954] 1 All ER 373 (PC). My concern here is with the central cases.

Perhaps D is guilty of a homicide offence, but she has not murdered V—even if, while rejoicing, she was willing V to die. Conversely, if D deliberately poisons V, and V takes some hours to die, the fact that D repents in the meantime will not absolve her of murder.[34]

Because behaviour can be temporally separated from its outcomes, it seems natural to ask whether the concurrence doctrine should apply to *all* kinds of actus reus element, requiring a continuity of mens rea over time; or just to some of them. In practice, concurrence is required of D's behaviour *rather than* of the consequence. Why? On the argument in this chapter, the reason becomes clear: concurrence is tied to behaviour because that is when D's culpability is fixed with respect to bringing about the consequence. We need to know about D's mens rea at the moment of her behaviour in order to evaluate her culpability for what she did.

14.3 Naming the wrong, and proscribing it

In § 14.2, I argued in favour of Ashworth's claim that, to the extent they are matters of luck, variations of outcome make no difference to the degree of an agent's culpability. At the same time, I conceded that outcome luck has a role to play in constituting the wrong(s) an agent does. The concession brings us to the second of Ashworth's claims, that criminality should generally be defined in the inchoate mode. On Ashworth's approach, both the attempted and the successful murderer would be convicted of attempted murder. And Joseph, whether lucky or unlucky, would be up on a careless endangerment charge, assuming such an offence were to hand.[35]

What's in a label? It certainly matters outside the law. If David kills Victor, we don't merely (i) disapprove of the attack, and separately (ii) regret its success. We also (iii) reprove the murder—what David *did*. As a communicative institution, the criminal law has reason to do the same, by articulating its conclusions in conventional formats. It would be odd to criticize David for attempting to kill Victor, while separately lamenting the 'tragedy' that Victor is dead.

The point, though, is not merely conventional. Criminal justice needs to be done *visibly*, which implies a degree of precision when identifying what

[34] *Jakeman* (1982) 76 Cr App R 223. Notice also the coherence of this view with the discussion of constitutive luck in § 14.4.1. Perhaps D becomes a better person. But blaming judgements are concerned with the relationship between D's action and D—the person she is—at the time of acting.

[35] *Sheppard* [1981] AC 394. We return to the proviso below.

misconduct the accused is found to have perpetrated.[36] It will not do, for example, to label offenders unspecifically as 'criminals'. That would effectively equate the convictions of rapists with those of pickpockets. The state has multiple obligations to communicate its verdict clearly. It owes it to the defendant, in order that D may know what he has been found guilty of and why he is being punished—so that his punishment is meaningful to him and not arbitrary. The state owes a parallel obligation to the victim, if any, as part of vindicating V's status as a member of the community whose rights have been violated. Justice is delivered *to V*, in part, by a formal verdict that V was wronged, and in what way. Beyond D and V, too, the conviction is not merely part of a private dialogue. The public also has an interest in understanding the nature of D's transgression. For this reason too, the conviction should accurately record D's wrong. As was said in § 13.3.1, Parliament cannot legitimately enact an offence of 'paedophilia', defined as 'parking for more than one hour on a central London street', because that is not what paedophilia means. Even if all the participants in a subsequent trial, including D, recognize that the label is merely a technical usage, those participants are not the whole of the audience. The State may not disregard the fact that the conviction is a public statement, nor the effect that it will have on D's life. The public record matters. An employer may have few qualms about hiring a convicted insider-trader as an orderly in a children's hospital. But it would be entirely different to contemplate employing someone guilty of a child sex offence.

It is therefore vital that offences should be defined and labelled so as to capture the moral gist of the prohibited conduct, in a record that is not misleading or over-general. Differences between offences should reflect meaningful distinctions in the public mind between types of culpable wrongdoing. This requirement mandates that offences be drawn up in such a way that they capture significant differences in the harmfulness, wrongfulness, and/or culpability of prohibited actions. Which brings us, in turn, to the question of inchoate formulations, of the type Ashworth advocates. Is too much of significance lost when we criminalize murder and attempted murder within the same rubric?[37]

[36] The principle of 'fair labelling'. See, e.g., A Ashworth, 'The Elasticity of *Mens Rea*' in C Tapper (ed), *Crime, Proof and Punishment* (Butterworth 1981) 45, 53–56; G Williams, 'Convictions and Fair Labelling' [1983] CLJ 85; B Mitchell, 'Multiple Wrongdoing and Offence Structure: A Plea for Consistency and Fair Labelling' (2001) 64 MLR 395, 398–400; J Chalmers and F Leverick, 'Fair Labelling in Criminal Law' (2008) 71 MLR 217. The discussion here draws in part from *Crimes, Harms, and Wrongs*, § 11.4.

[37] Note that the mens rea requirements for murder often differ from their inchoate counterpart. That is not a conceptual necessity. Compare, e.g., s 307 of the Singapore Penal Code: 'Whoever does any act with such intention or knowledge and under such circumstances that if he by that act caused death he would be guilty of murder' commits attempted murder. One may, of course, quibble about labelling something done without an intention to kill as 'attempted' murder, but *that* worry would not extend to an offence of, say, 'inchoate murder'. (None the less, we should hesitate before criminalizing endangerment: see § 14.3.1.)

Yes. The distinction between murder and attempted murder is significant because the wrongs (and indeed the harms) at stake are quite different; and the moral resonance of those differences is sufficient to warrant their distinct recognition by the criminal law. Attempted murderers do not kill, and merging their conviction with that of murderers neglects that point. It leaves open, publicly, the possibility that they may have committed the more serious wrong. Defendants who do not kill may reasonably complain that they are being labelled under an inchoate-liability system *as if* they are murderers—when they are not. At the same time, such a system pays inadequate attention to the interests of victims, for whom the distinction between an inchoate and a 'consummated' wrong matters greatly. An inchoate system focuses primarily on the defendant. In doing so, its verdicts refuse to acknowledge what was actually done to the victim. This constitutes a failure of the criminal law's role as official fact-finder. It is not enough for the state to vindicate the victim's standing and interests by acknowledging that *a* wrong was perpetrated: part of the verdict's point is to articulate *in what way* she was wronged. Refusal to do so diminishes the victim as a participant in the criminal justice system and, indirectly, in the community.

14.3.1 Proscriptions

Let us grant that attempts and successes ought to be separately proscribed. Snuffling at the back of the room is yet another elephant. Most harm-based crimes, such as causing physical injury or property damage, can be committed recklessly. If outcome-luck makes no difference to an agent's degree of culpability, why not criminalize recklessly endangering such injury or damage? As with attempts liability, reckless endangerment constitutes a different wrong from recklessly injuring another: but that counsels in favour of separate proscription, not permission.

One response to this challenge might be to flip it around. 'So much the worse,' one might retort, 'for recklessness offences generally (let alone negligence). If risk taking is not serious enough to warrant criminal liability, mere accidents of causation cannot change that.'

Two thoughts contraindicate. Intuitively, the deliberate choice to expose V's person or property to unreasonable risks of harm *does* seem sufficiently blameworthy to meet the threshold for criminal condemnation. More importantly, that intuition is supported by the account of culpability developed in chapter 11. On that account, there is no deep distinction between intention and advertent recklessness qua grounds of blame. As we saw in § 11.3, both advertent recklessness and intentional wrongdoing reflect badly upon the agent in virtue of her preferring bad reasons to good ones. The failing in each case discloses a moral vice. Crucially, that ground applies likewise to intention and recklessness. To anticipate the discussion of Terror and Strategic Bombers in § 16.1, chosen wrongdoing discloses advertent deficiencies in practical wisdom; advertent failures to give sufficient weight to morally appropriate goals. *Regardless whether the wrongdoing is chosen as means or side-effect*, both kinds of actors fall within the framework of choice-based fault.[38] In turn, that suggests we should not erect any fundamental barrier for criminal liability between reckless and intended wrongdoing.

Why, then, draw a line between reckless endangerment and reckless 'consummation', as the common law so clearly does?[39] Admittedly, the line is generic rather than universal. Sometimes we prohibit endangerment via context-specific, 'substantive-inchoate' crimes.[40] Discharging my firearm in a public space, for example, might appropriately be prohibited as a wrong in its own right. Substantive-inchoate crimes of this type can usefully clarify the duties of citizens, giving them firmer guidance about their potential liability. However, they also raise familiar criminalization problems.[41] In particular, the risk-generating activity may not in itself be suitable for prohibition. Driving a car is intrinsically risky, yet that doesn't warrant its proscription *tout court*. Substantive-inchoate offences alleviate some of the problems posed by endangerment. But they do not resolve them all.

Ultimately, the argument for permitting reckless endangerment is also criminalization-based. Generic non-liability for unconsummated endangerment is best understood as a form of dispensation: conversely, liability for consummated endangerment wrongs is a form of *semi-constructive liability*.[42] Thus a crime of 'reckless criminal damage' can be thought of as an X+Y offence,

[38] This is not to claim that all chosen wrongdoing is equally blameworthy. D's practical attitudes toward the deaths may be complex and nuanced (see §§ 11.3, 11.4.1). Across chapters 16–18, I also claim that the intention–foresight distinction systematically affects D's access to justifications.

[39] The common law contains no general offence of reckless endangerment. Neither does the Model Penal Code, although § 211.2 makes it a crime to 'recklessly engage in conduct which places or may place another person in danger of death or serious bodily injury.' The crime is imprisonable for up to one year. Not unreasonably, Vincent Chaio sees this as 'disproportionately lenient': V Chaio, 'Intention and Attempt' (2010) 4 Crim L and Phil 37, 49.

[40] Cp. P Roberts, 'The Presumption of Innocence Brought Home? Kebilene Deconstructed' (2002) 44 LQR 48, 55–56.

[41] See the discussion of remote harms in *Crimes, Harms, and Wrongs*, chs 4–5.

[42] See § 13.5.2.

where the gateway wrong—X—is the defendant's act of recklessly endangering another person's property; while Y is a pure actus reus component, requiring actual causation of damage. Y is a matter of luck. Rather than operating as an aggravating factor, though, its non-occurrence alleviates D's—otherwise deserved—criminal liability. The damage requirement effectively acts as a liability filter.

One argument for having such a filter is that enacting general inchoate-endangerment offences has the potential considerably to expand the criminalization net. Inevitably, in a finitely resourced system, enforcement tends to be selective. The liability of defendants is thereby remaindered to the decisions of officials, in turn creating the risk of uneven or even discriminatory prosecutions.[43] Moreover, in the absence of crystallized damage, the evidence-gathering process is likely to become significantly more invasive, not to mention dependent upon the whims of complainants.[44] Retaining an actual-damage requirement helps to safeguard against those hazards.

Neither is the consummation requirement uncorrelated to culpability. In practice, whether D's act of reckless endangerment goes on to cause damage is not *entirely* a matter of outcome luck. Its likelihood varies with the manner and dangerousness of D's behaviour. 'Recklessness' merely sets a threshold. It requires only that the foreseen risk was unreasonable. But the greater the risk taken, the more probable it is that damage will occur. Thus a requirement of actual damage can be a rough proxy for the riskiness of the agent's behaviour.[45] We may conclude that it is neither arbitrary nor unfair to single out for liability those who actually cause damage, rather than those who merely risk it. There are reasons to differentiate them.

[43] The risks are real. Overinclusive ASBO legislation famously became a tool for use against prostitutes and beggars in particular: E Burney, '"No Spitting": Regulation of Offensive Behaviour in England and Wales' in A von Hirsch and A P Simester (eds), *Incivilities: Regulating Offensive Behaviour* (Hart 2006) 195, 206. Similarly, prosecutions for under-age sex where both parties are below the age of consent are almost always brought against the male: e.g. *C* (2009) 173 CL & JW 303.

[44] This is one of the complaints made by Alec Walen against Alexander and Ferzan's attempt to strip outcome luck from the criminal law in *Crime and Culpability*: A Walen, 'Crime, Culpability and Moral Luck' (2010) 29 Law and Phil 373, 381.

[45] As Enoch and Marmor observe, 'actual results often have considerable evidential value': 'The Case Against Moral Luck' (n 13) 415. (See also the citations noted by Enoch and Marmor, ibid, 415 n 17; contrast A Cornford, 'Resultant Luck and Criminal Liability' in R A Duff et al (eds), *The Structures of the Criminal Law* (OUP 2011) 36, 42.) There is a more general aspect to this point. Plausibly, the difference between endangerments and consummations is correlated also to the actor's willingness to embrace greater risk. That might, in turn, be a factor helping to explain our intuitions that successes and consummations are more culpable than their inchoate counterparts.

14.4 Other forms of luck

The challenges posed by moral luck are not restricted to outcomes. In *Lynch*,[46] the defendant was ordered by the IRA to act as driver for an IRA hit squad. Knowing that he would be killed if he refused, Lynch drove his passengers to a location where they shot and killed a policeman. Lynch assisted a murder.[47] Yet he was a victim too—a victim, one might say, of 'circumstantial' (or 'situational') luck. Our actions are very often the product of circumstances in which we find ourselves and over which we have no control. As the saying goes, 'There but for the grace of God, go I.'[48] Doubtless Lynch would never have agreed to help the IRA but for his being under threat of death. Others, who would have done the same in like circumstances, are never called to account for their untested willingness.

Characteristically, both the criminal law and ordinary blaming judgements accommodate circumstantial luck by means of justifications and excuses; not by irresponsibility defences.[49] In so doing, they disavow the thought that circumstantial luck undermines moral responsibility. Admittedly, if the circumstances are, from D's perspective, involuntary, D cannot be blamed for their occurrence. But that is beside the point. D may not deserve to be in the situation he finds himself,[50] but he is not being blamed for that. What D is morally responsible for is his *response* to those circumstances—for what he did next. Our blaming (and praising) evaluations assess that response *in light of* D's situation, taking account of the guiding reasons created by that situation as well as D's own motivations. Lynch had a guiding reason to drive the car, in virtue of the fact that otherwise he would be shot. That reason may have been inadequate to justify what he did. At least arguably, it was sufficient to excuse. Like all culpability judgements, whether D was excused (morally speaking) depends on whether his actions, taken in those circumstances, disclosed a moral vice. Far from pre-empting a blaming evaluation, D's situation is one of its ingredients.

One might conceive of Lynch's case differently. It is tempting to think that responsibility for an agent's behaviour lies with the circumstances that induced it rather than with the agent. Even if (under duress) Lynch had himself pulled

[46] *DPP v Lynch* [1975] AC 653 (HL).

[47] In the case itself, the House of Lords allowed a defence of duress to secondary participants (but not principals) in murder; an allowance later retracted in *Howe* [1987] AC 417 (HL).

[48] Cp. Nagel, 'Moral Luck' (n 2) 33–34.

[49] See chapter 17.

[50] I assume in this section that the circumstances are genuinely unlucky rather than deliberately engineered. See P H Robinson, 'Causing the Conditions of One's Own Defense: A Study in the Limits of Theory in Criminal Law Doctrine' (1985) 71 Virginia LR 1.

the trigger, we might be inclined to hold that responsibility for the policeman's death really lay with the IRA, not Lynch.[51]

The main difficulty with this view is that it fails to respect Lynch's moral agency. Lynch was no mere cipher. He lacked control over the source of his reasons for action, but he did have control over what he did next; and blaming judgements evaluate him for the latter. Lynch was morally responsible for driving the car (and would have been responsible for pulling the trigger). The driving was not involuntary: he chose to drive. His choices were limited, to be sure, and unattractive. That is exactly what a responsibility-*affirming* excuse like duress accommodates.

We look in more detail at the distinction between excuses and irresponsibility defences in chapter 17. If circumstantial luck were to make an agent genuinely non-responsible, it would not matter what was the nature of his action taken in response to those circumstances. Neither would it matter *what reasons those circumstances generated for the agent*. Suppose the following example:

> D comes upon V's wallet, lying on the pavement, which he then steals. If V's wallet had not been lying there, D would not have stolen it. However, D had no control over the fact that V had just dropped his wallet.

If Nagel's worry is taken at its highest, D would lack moral responsibility for stealing the wallet. But D is in that respect no different from Lynch. Both chose their actions, and both acted non-involuntarily. The true difference lies in their culpability.

This analysis helps us to address an objection raised by Michael Moore, who argues that rejecting outcome luck is incompatible with endorsing other kinds of luck.[52] Nagel's own discussion cuts across varieties of luck.[53] Moore, however, makes the point explicit. He contends that there is no principled line between outcome luck—which the argument in § 14.2 sought to limit—and other kinds of luck. If we accept circumstantial luck, for example, we ought to accept outcome luck too.

[51] I leave aside the obvious rejoinder that more than one agent can be morally responsible for an action or event: see chapters 5 and 7.

[52] Moore, *Placing Blame*, ch 5. Unlike Nagel, Moore straightforwardly endorses the place of luck in our blaming judgements.

[53] See, e.g., Nagel, 'Moral Luck' (n 2) 35: 'The area of agency, and therefore of legitimate moral judgment, seems to shrink under this scrutiny to an extensionless point. Everything seems to result from the combined influence of factors, antecedent and posterior to action, that are not within the agent's control. Since he cannot be responsible for them, he cannot be responsible for their results . . . .'

That doesn't follow. Provided we understand clearly what kind of evaluation a blaming judgement involves, the distinction between circumstances and outcomes is both defensible and important. Circumstantial luck does not render meaningless the question, what now should we do? In most scenarios, the reasons for action that we ought to act upon are situation-dependent. We should loose the arrow if it is pointing safely at an archery target. We should not loose the arrow if it is pointing at a person. Unless that person is attacking us. And so on. The fact that the situation lies outside D's control does not make those reasons suddenly disappear, becoming irrelevant to D's practical deliberations. Rather, they (continue to) exist, and form the backdrop to our evaluation of D's response. Since blaming judgements are grounded in D's failure to act for the reasons she ought, they take the situation *as a datum*. Unluckiness is neither here nor there.

Timing matters. Circumstantial luck occurs prior to D's behaviour. As we noted in § 14.2.2, D's engagement with the applicable guiding reasons crystallizes at the moment of his response. Circumstantial luck *informs* that evaluation because and to the extent that it helps to constitute those guiding reasons. By contrast, outcome luck occurs afterwards—which is why it cannot affect the question, were there any deficiencies in D's practical reasoning when she behaved as she did?

14.4.1 Constitutive luck

So we should accept circumstantial luck, even if we ought (partly) to reject outcome luck. For somewhat analogous reasons, we should also accept *constitutive* luck—the luck that goes into making us the kind of person we are.[54] That Barbara is naturally courageous might be no more up to her than whether she gets the chance to show it. Our dispositions, values, and the like that constitute our moral character vary with our genetic make-up, schooling, family and social environments, and other formative ingredients that are all beyond our control. By the time we mature as moral agents, those moral characteristics are very difficult for us to alter. This is not to deny that we have *any* control over them. We can work on improving our attitudes and values. But the potential for success is usually marginal. Most culpable actions are likely to be the product

[54] Nagel identifies a fourth kind of luck, being the 'causal' luck in 'how one is determined by antecedent circumstances'. I disregard it here. For present purposes, the issues it raises are similar to those raised by constitutive and circumstantial luck.

of character flaws that exist, for the agent, involuntarily. Like circumstantial luck, however, that need not undermine her culpability.

Assessments of character—Barbara is a courageous person, Kent a selfish one—involve type (i) evaluations.[55] They say nothing of whether Barbara *deserves* to be courageous, or whether Kent deserves to be selfish. Type (i) evaluations are simply not predicated upon desert, and they do not require that the agent's moral character be self-chosen or voluntarily formed.

The same goes, in turn, for type (iii) judgements. Culpability and praiseworthiness assessments are predicated upon the relationship between an agent and her action. Blame is deserved in virtue of the fact that D's wrongful action reflects a moral vice: not in virtue of how she came to have it. It is enough that the vice is *hers*. This still leaves open the possibility that such evaluations can be undermined. Perhaps Kent rejects his instinctive selfishness and has struggled all his life to be a generous person. Under pressure, however, he finds his second-order desires overwhelmed by the very first-order preferences that he rejects.[56] In an extreme case, he may be like Harry Frankfurt's unwilling drug addict, 'hopelessly violated by his own desires'.[57] These kinds of cases present distinctive problems not of desert but of *identity*. Perhaps we cannot say that the moral-character flaw explaining why an agent chose to φ truly belongs to that agent, in which case blaming judgements are undermined. Type (iii) evaluations, though, take the agent's moral characteristics as *datum*. As we observed in § 11.5, 'I can't help being selfish' is not exculpatory. It concedes a ground of blame. Thus constitution is like situation, and unlike outcome. It is an ingredient of behaviour, not its product.

The tenor of this analysis is compatibilist. Much of our moral character is shaped and determined by factors outwith our control. Famously, a person's character may even be deliberately reshaped by others.[58] Blaming judgements are unaffected by that. They do not require us to be responsible for being who we are. To that extent, and despite their complexity, they lack profundity. They can tell us whether a moral agent, qua the person she is, deserves punishment. But they cannot tell us whether she deserves to be the person who deserves that punishment.

[55] Above, § 14.2.1.

[56] See also § 17.5.

[57] Frankfurt, *Importance*, 76. Or she may be someone temporarily dissociated from her ongoing character, as in the case of *T*: above, § 11.4.2.

[58] As in Patty Hearst's case, discussed in § 11.4.2.

14.5 A sense of perspective

Douglas Adams had many clever ideas. One of them was the *Total Perspective Vortex*, a chamber supposedly built as an application of the theory of atomic interactivity. The idea was that, if every atom of the universe is affected by every other atom of the universe, it is theoretically possible to extrapolate a model of the whole universe using any single piece of matter—such as a slice of fairy cake—as its starting point. Wrongdoers were sent into the Vortex, where they were shown a complete picture of the entire universe. The picture included a microscopic pointer with the words, 'You are here.' The sense of perspective destroyed their minds.[59]

In the scale of the universe, individual human agency is a small thing. Our contributions are microscopically small when measured against the story of the cosmos; and they—like us—are very much influenced by what has gone before. But none of that means they—or we—count for nothing. We still have *a* place in the universe, and so do our actions. However much our actions are the product of their, and our, antecedents, those actions belong to us. Like Lynch, we are no ciphers. Respect for human beings as moral agents requires that we be treated as morally responsible for the contributions that we do have control over: for our voluntary behaviour and its consequences.

[59] According to *The Restaurant at the End of the Universe* (Pan 1980) ch 12, 'The man who invented the Total Perspective Vortex did so, basically, in order to annoy his wife. Trin Tragula, for that was his name, was a dreamer, a speculative thinker, or, as his wife would have it, an idiot. . . . "Have some sense of proportion!" she would say, thirty-eight times a day. And so he built the Total Perspective Vortex—just to show her. And in one end he plugged the whole of reality, as extrapolated from a fairy cake, and in the other end he plugged his wife: so that when he turned it on she saw in one instant the whole infinity of creation and herself in relation to it. To Trin Tragula's horror, the shock annihilated her brain. But to his satisfaction, he realised he had conclusively proved that if life is going to exist in a universe this size, the one thing it cannot afford to have is a sense of proportion.'

15
Distinguishing Intended from Advertent Action

In chapter 11, we identified two paths to culpability, running through choice and carelessness. Both paths share the insight that D's engagement with the reasons not to act as she does can reflect a moral vice on her part. But they are also very different. The road through carelessness is long and winding. That through choice is more direct and more robust.

Action can only be chosen when it is sufficiently advertent—as lawyers sometimes say, when it is foreseen.[1] We can generally say that an action is 'chosen' when D is aware of a risk of doing it by behaving as she does. Such action has three main features:

(i) D's behaviour occurs under her direction;[2]
(ii) That behaviour constitutes the action in question;[3] and
(iii) D believes it is possible for her behaviour to constitute that action.

[1] I admit that the line between advertence and inadvertence is not sharp. (Cp. F Stark, *Culpable Carelessness: Recklessness and Negligence in the Criminal Law* (CUP 2016) 111ff; M S Moore and H Hurd, 'Punishing the Awkward, the Stupid, the Weak, and the Selfish: The Culpability of Negligence' (2011) 5 Crim L and Phil 147, 152ff; K K Ferzan, 'Opaque Recklessness' (2001) 91 J Crim L and Criminology 597.) What level of consciousness should findings of advertence require? Doug Husak observes that 'a given belief must be able to play a role in the practical reasoning of a wrongdoer if it is to provide a basis for holding her culpable according to a subjectivist reason-responsive theory.' (D Husak, *Ignorance of Law: A Philosophical Inquiry* (OUP 2016) 201.) I agree with that. Moreover, it seems right to say that one need not focus consciously on a belief in order for that belief to inform intentional action and to meet Husak's test. One can be guided by what are sometimes called 'preconscious' beliefs: experienced drivers, for example, draw upon such beliefs to change gears without focusing on what they do. We generally think of such actions as intentional. They are done, albeit with a limited awareness, in the service of some overarching intentional activity. However, some care is required here. In the context of unintended-yet-advertent wrongdoing (especially, recklessness), the relevant belief is not explanatory but one *despite which* D acts. So its place in D's practical reasoning is different. When formulating judgements of culpability, especially in the criminal law, to say that D *chose* to risk φing, that D φed advertently, is to say something more than that D had a preconscious belief that she might φ by her conduct. These are difficult issues, which we cannot explore at length. For the purposes of this chapter they are incidental, in as much as they put pressure on the advertence–inadvertence boundary rather than on the distinction between intended and otherwise advertent action.

[2] The action/event distinction: see chapter 9. For omissions, it suffices that the behaviour is non-involuntary: see § 8.4.1.

[3] The terminology comes from § 2.4. An 'action' is tied to a particular description of D's underlying behaviour, which it describes and by which it is constituted.

Fundamentals of Criminal Law. A P Simester, Oxford University Press (2021). © A P Simester.
DOI: 10.1093/oso/9780198853145.003.0015

Morally speaking, this doesn't take us very far. Suppose that D chooses to φ and that, all things considered, she ought not to φ. It doesn't follow that D exhibits choice-based culpability. Her φing may be justified or excused. It is even possible for D's choice to be a good one in terms of the *perceived* risks, in circumstances where she has, perhaps culpably, misperceived those risks.[4] Our three features do no more than mark out a domain within which choice-based culpability operates.

Moreover, that's about all they do. They offer no guidance about how to differentiate intended actions from (subjectively) reckless ones; nothing to distinguish between those who, say, want to harm others and those who are merely willing to bring such harm about. If advertence were all there is to choice-based culpability for actions, that would suggest culpability is simply a function of the seriousness of the relevant wrongful action and the degree to which its likelihood was foreseen. Yet virtually everyone, judges and academics too, thinks there is a significant division between actions that are intended and those that are merely advertent.

Interrogating that last thought is a challenge for the next two chapters. In chapter 16, I argue that the principle of wrongdoing requires us to subdivide intended from otherwise advertent action. In particular,[5] whether D's action is justified depends in part on whether D intended that action. This alone gives us reason to explore the criteria of intended action, which is the main task of chapter 15.

Even the intended/advertent division is too blunt. The niceties of justification make it important also to distinguish, *within* intended actions, between actions done as ends and those done as means. Further, in delineating the boundaries of the intended, we need to consider two special categories, of *obliquely*-intended and *inseparably*-intended actions. It may be appropriate to treat obliquely-intended actions as if intended when assessing D's mens rea, but they should not be similarly assimilated when evaluating justifications.[6] Cases of inseparability, on the other hand, are rightly categorized as intended.

These subdivisions can generate a tension between law and ordinary language, because 'oblique' intention is a legal notion. Obviously there are rule of

[4] See § 11.3.

[5] Though not exclusively. We encountered another way in which intention can matter to wrongdoing in § 3.2: when it is D's intention that makes D's action the particular kind of wrong that it is. Common-law murder, for example, requires an intention to kill or inflict grievous bodily harm; recklessness will not suffice.

[6] See esp. chapters 16 and 18. Doctrinally speaking, it may be that oblique intention remains distinct from recklessness in as much as it rules out a general justification of reasonable risk: a directly intended actus reus must be justified within the terms of a recognized legal defence. Given the discretionary aspect of oblique intent findings (see § 15.2), nothing of substance turns on this refinement.

law reasons why the legal definition of intention should be rooted in ordinary usages. Indeed, typically the courts proceed without invoking formal definitions, and an elaborate jury instruction may do more harm than good.[7] Still, elaboration is sometimes required. So we should begin with a clarification. At common law, the legal territory of intention comprises two alternative categories. D may be found to have intended her action if:

(I) *Direct intention*: D intended that action in the ordinary, core sense of intention; or
(II) *Oblique intention*: D believed that the action was 'virtually', 'practically', or 'morally' certain to be constituted by her behaviour.

The first case, direct intention, is the standard variety. In this paradigm case, we might say that D was trying or seeking to φ. She had a reason of some kind (not necessarily a good reason) to φ, and that is why she behaved as she did. By contrast, in the oblique intent case, D did not act in order to φ; that is not what she was trying to do. Her direct intention was to μ. Yet she knew that, if she μed, she was virtually certain to φ. It was, she recognized, a practically inevitable concomitant.

Oblique intention is not, properly so called, a form of intention.[8] On the other hand, cases of 'inseparable' intent are different again. They sit at the border between direct and oblique intent. I argue in § 15.3 that they are legitimately analysed as a variety of direct intent.

15.1 'Direct' intention

Before heading to the frontiers, though, we should be familiar with the heartland. Choice and intentionality can be commingled in ordinary language. Indeed, there is a meaningful sense in which my advertent actions can be said to 'fall within the scope of my intentions', or even be characterized as 'intentional'.[9] Taken too far, that might be thought to suggest that all 'chosen' actions

[7] *Moloney* [1985] AC 905, 926 (Lord Bridge): 'The golden rule should be that . . . the judge should avoid any elaboration or paraphrase of what is meant by intent, and leave it to the jury's good sense to decide whether the accused acted with the necessary intent.' As Lord Scarman noted in *Hancock* [1986] AC 455, 468, 'there is always the danger that the inevitable generality of guidelines intended to cover a class of case may be inapplicable or misleading in some cases.'
[8] A point made convincingly by John Finnis, 'Intention and Side-effects' in R G Frey and C W Morris (eds), *Liability and Responsibility: Essays in Law and Morals* (CUP 1991) 32. However, Finnis omits the special case to be discussed in § 15.3.
[9] Duff, *IACL*, 79–80.

are intended. It is helpful, therefore, to start by outlining the characteristic similarities and differences between intended and other chosen actions. Doing so will help to explain why our intuitions about the distinction are sometimes clouded, as well as generating some yardsticks with which to measure the boundary cases.

A familiar way of paraphrasing (direct) intention is to say that D generally intends the result of an action if it is something that she acts *in order* to bring about; if she acts with the aim, purpose,[10] or object of bringing it about. Unlike the extensional category of oblique intention, it is irrelevant in such cases whether D thinks the result is virtually certain, probable, or merely possible. Consider the following example:

> *Incompetent Assassin*: D has agreed to kill V in exchange for a substantial payment. However, she wishes to minimize the risk of being caught. Hence she takes up a hidden position a long way away from D's car. When D approaches the car, V lines up her rifle on him and fires, with the object of killing D. As D knows, however, she is a poor shot; she is so far away that V is nearly out of range; and her overall probability of success is very low.

Should D succeed, however improbably, the killing is intended—in virtue of the fact that she acts in order to kill.[11]

An account of this sort characterizes intention by reference to D's motivations. As such, it can usefully be expressed in terms of means, ends, and side-effects. Things done as means or ends are intended; side-effects are not.[12] Consider the well-known case of *Hyam*.[13] Hyam and Booth were rivals in love. Hoping to frighten B into leaving town, H poured petrol through the letter box of B's house and set fire to the petrol. While her aim was only to frighten, H realized that her conduct risked causing death.[14] Tragically, and criminally, two children in the house were killed. Since H had set fire to the house as a means of frightening B, both setting fire to the house and frightening B were intended. But it was no part of H's aim or purpose to kill. The ensuing fatalities were neither a means nor an end. They were side-effects of her conduct and, as such, unintended.

[10] *Burke* [1991] 1 AC 135, 147 (HL).

[11] *Gollins v Gollins* [1964] AC 644, 663 (Lord Reid); *DPP v Smith* [1961] AC 290, 327 (Viscount Kilmuir LC); *Hyam v DPP* [1975] AC 55, 79 (Lord Hailsham).

[12] Finnis, 'Intention and Side-effects' (n 8); cp. G Williams, 'Oblique Intention' (1987) 46 CLJ 417, 421.

[13] [1975] AC 55. See also § 15.2.

[14] In England, the letter box is often set into the front door of the house itself.

The example points us toward an elucidation. The purposes or ends for which one acts supply the motivating reasons *why* one acts. Direct intention, however, embraces both these and the intermediate objects—the means—that one aims at in order to achieve those ends.[15] So there are two central cases of intention. D's action is intended as an end if:[16]

(a) D's behaviour occurs under her direction;
(b) That behaviour constitutes the action in question;
(c) D believes it is possible for her behaviour to constitute that action;
(d) D wants to do that action (for its own sake); and
(e) D behaves as she does because of her belief and desire in (c) and (d).[17]

Of course, not all desires motivate.[18] Often people want things they never set out to achieve. If D stands to inherit from his mother's will, he may have a reason for wanting her death. He may wish for her death. But he need not intend it. Distinguishing between desire and intention here is (e), that D behaves as he does because of that desire. His desire must also explain *why* D does the action. It must be a motivating desire.

On the other hand, desiring an action for its own sake is not a condition of intending it.[19] Often, we bring things about not because we want them, but because they are a *means* to something else (that we do want). The parent who punishes a child for misbehaving may do so regretfully, believing it to be her only option and wishing very much that there were something else she could do; yet she intends to punish him all the same. Perhaps she wants to deter her child from behaving that way again, and she punishes him in order to achieve that aim. But she does not desire his punishment, at least not for its own sake. This sort of case, where the action is done as a means to an end, is captured as follows:

(a′) D's behaviour occurs under her direction;
(b′) That behaviour constitutes the action in question;

[15] *Hyam* [1975] AC 55, 74 (Lord Hailsham): intention includes 'the means as well as the end'; Williams, *CLGP* § 16.

[16] In keeping with § 15, and indeed the spirit of this book, my aim here is not to develop a set of necessary and sufficient conditions of intended action, but to explore its structure and, in turn, its moral significance.

[17] Or, at least, in part because. D may have multiple ends.

[18] I use 'want' and 'desire', interchangeably, here in order to convey the positive nature of D's disposition (for reasons that should become clearer in § 15.1.1).

[19] Cp. *Mohan* [1976] QB 1, 11 (James LJ): intention is 'a decision to bring about, in so far as it lies within the accused's power, the commission of the offence . . . no matter whether the accused desired that consequence of his act or not.'

(c′) D believes it is possible for her behaviour to constitute that action, *and* believes that the action is a viable means to some further action (μ);
(d′) D wants to do that further action (μ); and
(e′) D behaves as she does because of her beliefs and desire in (c′) and (d′).

Hyam believed that by setting fire to the house she would be able to frighten Booth. Since that was why she acted as she did, we can conclude that she intended her act of arson. By the same token, she lacked an intention to kill, as either means or end.

15.1.1 Desires and pro-attitudes

So far, so familiar. While some writers seek to unify the two, I take the case of a means to be structurally, and morally,[20] different from that of an end. Moreover, it is not obvious that an illuminating unified account exists. Most such accounts are forced to attenuate their 'desire' element to the vanishing point of a 'pro-attitude',[21] a point at which the element is no longer explanatory of intention but might itself be inferred from the conclusion that the relevant action was intended. Of course, even ends may be wanted in different ways, more or less strongly, and with a variety of attitudes. But the point about an end is that D's positive attitude toward its occurrence is what supplies the motivation behind her behaviour. By contrast, a means need not be wanted for its own sake *at all*. Its occurrence may be regarded with loathing or horror by the agent. In such a case, the prospect of bringing about the means has no motivating force. Consider Jonathan Bennett's famous bomber cases:[22]

> 'Terror Bomber and Strategic Bomber both have as their goal promoting the war effort against Enemy. Both intend to pursue their goal by dropping bombs. Terror Bomber's plan is to bomb the school in Enemy's territory, thereby killing children of Enemy [whose deaths are intended as a means], terrorizing Enemy's population, and forcing Enemy to surrender. Strategic

[20] See chapters 16 and 18.

[21] Davidson, *EAE*, 3–4. Admittedly, 'pro-attitude' is a useful shorthand for the variety of inclinations and dispositions, preferences, and desires that can motivate our behavioural choices. In many ways it is a better catch-all term than 'wants' or 'desires'. The attenuation only becomes problematic when the term is used in the extrinsic sense objected to below in the text.

[22] Restated here as they are summarized by M E Bratman, 'What is Intention?' in P R Cohen, J Morgan, and M Pollack (eds), *Intentions in Communication* (MIT Press 1990) 15, 23. See Bennett, *Tanner*, 95; Bennett, *The Act Itself*, ch 11. The parenthetical insertions are mine.

Bomber's plan is to bomb Enemy's munitions plant, thereby undermining Enemy's war effort. However, Strategic Bomber also knows that next to the munitions plant is a school, and that when he bombs the plant he will also kill the children inside the school [whose deaths are obliquely intended].'

In terms of *attitude* toward the children's deaths, there seems to be nothing to distinguish Terror from Strategic Bomber. Both want their ultimate goal sufficiently strongly to override whatever aversion they may have to killing the children. Each chooses to kill the children, we may say, because he is insufficiently averse to that prospect—not because he wants or has any kind of positive attitude (let alone positively-motivating attitude) toward their deaths. Each *accepts* the deaths, even if finding them abhorrent.

Against that thought, one might suggest that a means must be wanted at least in some extrinsic sense, and this sense is captured by the wider idea of a pro-attitude. Doubtless a means need not be wanted for its own sake, yet it 'inherits' some of the motivational attraction of the end to which it is a means. Hence, one may say, its prospect *makes a difference* to the agent.

It is not clear what this extrinsic sense adds. Consider Antony Duff's 'test of failure', a useful rule-of-thumb indicator of intention. Duff's test asks a hypothetical question of the actor: 'if an expected effect is not produced, then will the action be regarded (by the actor) as a failure?'[23] If the answer to that question is yes, this suggests the actor intends the effect; *aliter*, the effect is merely foreseen. According to Duff, 'the test of failure identifies those effects whose occurrence is necessary for the success of the agent's action; and it is only those effects which she acts with the intention of bringing about.'[24] Of course, since one cannot determine what is a success and what is a failure except by reference to D's reasons for acting, the test is diagnostic rather than explanatory. However, its reliability depends in part upon D's belief that the means is a *necessary* route to D's end. Consider the following example:

Suppose that I act as I do in order to bring about X and Y, either of which I believe may bring about Z. Z is the thing that I really want out of my action, and I do not want either X or Y in themselves. (Or if I do, that incidental desire has nothing to do with my acting.)

[23] Note that the test is to be applied in the light of the agent's beliefs at the time of the action (cp. § 14.2.4).
[24] Duff, *IACL*, 62. See also R A Duff, *Criminal Attempts* (OUP 1996) ch 1.

In this case, we would determine whether my action was a success or failure according to whether it brings about Z, and whether Z occurs may be independent of whether X or Y individually occurs.[25] The example suggests that success—and in turn, the motivational power of pro-attitudes—derives from ends rather than means.[26]

There are other characteristic differences between means and side-effects. Michael Bratman has noted that the fact that Strategic Bomber does not act in order to kill the children means that—unlike Terror Bomber—his (proposed) course of conduct will not be affected by facts which affect the behaviour required to bring about the children's deaths.[27] If it is learned that the munitions are due to be transported elsewhere on a particular date, the knowledge will affect the planned behaviour of Strategic Bomber but not Terror Bomber; whereas if the children are to finish schooling by that date, this will affect the plans of Terror Bomber but not Strategic Bomber. That seems broadly right. (Suppose that we observe D pointing a gun in the direction of V, who then moves ten paces to the right. If D intends to shoot V, she would be expected to alter her aim correspondingly.) But Bratman's point also looks diagnostic. In general, we would expect each Bomber to be influenced by facts that affect the prospects for success in achieving his *motivating end*; it is only derivatively that facts affecting the prospect of achieving a means matter. Suppose that, after forming their plans, it is discovered that on the other side of the school is a large reservoir containing most of the country's water supply. If the reservoir is bombed, Enemy will be forced to surrender immediately; bombing the reservoir is therefore a much more efficient route to winning the war than either Bomber's strategy thitherto. We may expect the behaviour of *both* Bombers to be affected by this new information.

All of this tends to undermine the case for assimilating our accounts of means and ends by invoking a unifying pro-attitude criterion. A unified account of D's intended φing would have to allow that D's attitude toward φing

[25] If neither X nor Y are brought about, then my action *will* be considered a failure. All that tells us, however, is that I intend at least 'X or Y'. Conforming with that answer to the test of failure, I may intend only (say) X. This could occur if I do A in order to bring about X while recognizing that it might instead bring about Y. Either X or Y might bring about Z, which is my motivating end: but I intend to bring about X rather than Y because I perceive that X has a higher probability than Y of bringing Z about.

[26] Suppose that I bring about X and/or Y but not Z. Could we say that my behaviour was a partial success (and a partial failure)? Not usefully. If that thought were accepted, then we are reduced to saying that my actions were a failure with respect to Z, and a success with respect to X and/or Y. But as soon as we have done this we have lost. For one can always say that behaviour is a failure or success with regard to some outcome, whether or not the prospect of that outcome motivated the actor.

[27] M E Bratman, *Intention, Plans and Practical Reason* (Harvard UP 1987) 141–42.

itself has no motivational power, which makes it hard to see how such an attitude could satisfy a condition like (e).

An alternative response is possible. One might grasp the nettle by eliminating reference to (d), the desires condition:[28]

> 'We can explain what it is to act with the intention of bringing a result about by referring only to those beliefs about the likely results of what she does which determine the agent's actions; no reference to her wants or desires is necessary.'

The thought here is that if desires become attenuated to the point of pro-attitudes with no intrinsic motivating power, they lose their explanatory value. We can simply infer them from the fact that D behaves as she does because she believes it is possible thereby to φ. Consider the case where an unintended outcome is foreseen as a possible consequence of D's behaviour. The key feature that distinguishes this type of case is that D does not behave as she does *because* of that possible consequence. It does not seem to matter, in such a case, whether D desires the consequence, either intrinsically or extrinsically.

There is something beguiling about the idea that desire is a fifth wheel on the intention coach. Even so, I think the nettle is not for grasping. Sometimes reference to desires *is* necessary, and we do need to understand which of our desires—or, we might say, *intrinsic* pro-attitudes—are doing the motivational work. Consider D, whose job it is to service electrical appliances. D passes a charge through a circuit board in order to evaluate its condition, hoping as she does so that the board will not fail because she will then be put to the trouble of repairing it. D acts as she does because D believes that the circuit board might fail, but D does not desire that outcome, and does not intend it.[29]

Perhaps more importantly, assimilating the two varieties of direct intention is artificial. One reason for this is that the distinction has moral significance, as will be seen in chapter 16. But it is also because reference to desires (in an intrinsic sense) has practical significance. It is standard law that evidence of desire is admissible in a criminal trial, *inter alia* in order to support the inference that a defendant committed the actus reus intentionally. 'To prove

[28] Duff, *IACL*, 67.

[29] Contrast a terrorist, T, who is trying to wire a bomb and has misplaced the instruction manual. She connects the yellow wire to the blue one because she believes it is possible this will activate the bomb. The activation is intended: what makes the difference in T's case is that this is what she wants. A variant case, of conditional intent, might be where D is employed as a tester and is motivated by a desire for the circuit board to fail if it is defective. As we see in chapter 16, this variation would affect the scope of justifications available to D.

the intention, you may show the motive, and this is a link in the chain of evidence.'[30] That approach does not fit well with an account of intention in which one assesses the other criteria first, and thence infers a pro-attitude. As sources of motivation, our intrinsic desires matter. Their significance is lost within a unitary account rendered in terms of pro-attitudes.

15.1.2 Belief and influence

Conversely, neither should we dispense with reference to belief. Intended φing is a *sub*category of the advertent: one cannot intend to do something without foreseeing the possibility of doing it. Suppose that I want to kill Victor. I pull the trigger of a gun I am aiming at him. If I am sure that the gun is unloaded I cannot intend thereby to kill Victor.[31] This is one of the points at which trying and intending can come apart. Suppose that I want to show (as I believe) that I *cannot* φ. I pull on a lever with all my might in order to show that it is hopelessly stuck. To my complete surprise, I succeed in my attempt. But I do not intend to open the lever: condition (c′) in § 15.1 does not hold.

In general, if D does not believe at all that she can bring about some consequence, then D can do no more than wish for it, and make vain, signal gestures toward bringing it about. D's wish is not even a hope. One cannot entertain a hope that one's behaviour will have an effect without believing that there is at least *some* chance that it will. A hopeless wish to φ cannot be motivating, save for some action other than φing. It cannot be motivating in the sense of satisfying condition (e) or (e′) above.

As our Incompetent Assassin from § 15.1 illustrates, D's belief need not be held with certainty or even confidence. The action need only be seen as possible. However, it is worth noting a further wrinkle to the belief requirements. Consider the following passage from *Cunliffe v Goodman*, where it was said that X cannot, 'with any due regard to the English language,' be said to intend a result the occurrence of which,[32]

[30] *Heeson* (1878) 14 Cox CC 40, 44 (Lush J).

[31] See, e.g., D Pears, 'Intention and Belief' in B Vermazen and M B Hintikka (eds), *Essays on Davidson: Actions and Events* (Clarendon 1985) 75, 80. The same holds even for purely behavioural elements of an actus reus. If D tries to raise his arm, and at the same time is certain that it is immobile (perhaps because of a mechanical restraint), D does not intend to move his arm.

[32] [1950] 2 KB 237, 253. As Antony Duff puts it (*IACL*, 56), 'I cannot intend to bring about a result if I believe that its occurrence depends upon too many factors beyond my control.'

> '[T]hough it may not be wholly uninfluenced by X's will, is dependent on so many other influences, accidents and cross-currents of circumstance that, not merely is it quite likely not to be achieved at all, but, if it is achieved, X's volition will have been no more than a minor agency collaborating with, or not thwarted by, the factors which predominantly determine its occurrence.'

To tease this out, compare an unskilled dart thrower aiming at the triple twenty with a dice player aiming to throw a double six. The dice throw depends on factors which the player does not control, and it seems right to say the player cannot *intend* to throw a double six: the most he can intend is to throw the dice, and hope for a double six. Conversely, the unskilled dart thrower who happens to throw a triple twenty can intend her doing so.[33] She is not remaindered to the domain of hope.

Why? Notice that these cases are not differentiated by the belief conditions articulated earlier. Both agents believe that their throws *may* bring about the result sought. Neither do the cases turn on perceived levels of probability. One can believe one will probably miss, but still intend to hit the target; indeed, the dart thrower may have a lower chance of success than her dice playing counterpart. Suppose, then, that the thrower does hit a triple twenty. It may be natural for us to hesitate in our description of the case. We commonly say that a fortunate outcome is not so much intended as lucky, in circumstances where a *misdeed*, such as the Incompetent Assassin's, would readily be said to be intended. It seems, then, that our hesitation may be prompted by the favourable nature of the outcome. Beginners' luck is compatible with intention: the fortunate outcome remains intended rather than unintended.

By contrast, the dice player is incontestably lucky when he throws a double six. Part of the difference is reflected in the thought that ordinarily it is meaningless to ask whether someone is 'skilled' at rolling dice: the outcome is random. Our dart-thrower believes that the manner in which she throws the dart will influence the outcome: she exercises her limited influence to best effect by aiming at her desired target with the maximum accuracy she has, throwing her dart in the direction of the triple twenty. The dice player does not believe that the manner in which he rolls will influence the outcome, and cannot try to make his roll a double six.[34] It is because of *how* the dice player thinks his behaviour may produce a double six that he cannot intend to do so.

[33] The two cases are equated, I think mistakenly, in Duff, *IACL*, 56–57. (It is possible that Duff's unskilled dart thrower believes, unusually, that her throw is like a dice roll.)

[34] Of course, one may be aware that a particular set of movements, if exactly repeated, should result in the same outcome; but (I assume) such knowledge cannot be exploited, and the conscious manner of one's rolling does not discriminate between possible outcomes. It would be a different case where a

So it seems that one can intend a triple twenty, albeit not a double six. Our belief conditions need to be supplemented by a proviso: it is not the case that D believes her attempt to the action is solely an invocation of chance. But there is a further wrinkle to the double six case. Suppose that I am faced by a vicious criminal who is also something of a gambler. I must enter a wager, and if I throw a double six he will spare Pat's life. No other roll will do. When I roll the dice, motivated to do so by my desire to try to save Pat, it seems that we would say (i) I intend to save Pat's life, even though (ii) I cannot intend to roll a double six.

The difference is, in part, means-dependent. If I attempt to bring about a double six by rolling dice, the link from means to end depends only on chance. But the link from rolling a double six to saving Pat is not merely random. Reflecting this, we can say that (i) I can [attempt to] roll a double six with intent thereby to save Pat's life. But we cannot say that (ii) I can [attempt to[35]] roll the dice with intent thereby to get a double six. Under description (i) I have some control over what I do: a particular way in which I can try to save Pat. In this case it is by making a wager. In the dart throwing case, the control is of a different sort, but the dart thrower also has a particular way in which to try to bring about her desired outcome (*videlicet*, by aiming her throw at the triple twenty). When one's aim is to roll a double six, however, the description of the result pre-empts even the choice to roll. The specification of the result, 'roll a double six', implies that one rolls the dice. By contrast, the result, 'save Pat's life', contains no such implication about how one will attempt to bring it about.

15.1.3 Types of actus reus elements

We saw in § 2.3 that the criminal law has a predilection for deconstructing its wrongs into component building blocks, often with diverse mens rea requirements.[36] This can sometimes generate translational challenges, especially in the

player believes, rightly or wrongly, that rolling the dice in a certain way increases the probability of a double six: in this last case, he can intend to do so.

35 I may have a muscular disease making it difficult to grasp and roll dice. The possibility is noted here in order to illustrate the point that nothing turns on the apparent asymmetry when 'attempt to' is omitted.

36 Compare the New Zealand case of *Police v Starkey* [1989] 2 NZLR 373 (noted in § 13.4.2), which considered an offence against section 55 of the Local Elections and Polls Act 1976. The section prohibits (a) publication of a document containing (b) an untrue, (c) and defamatory, statement (d) which was calculated to influence the vote of any elector. The Court held that its mens rea requirements were, as to (a) intention; (b) strict liability; (c) none, since it was a question of law; and (d) knowledge of likelihood to influence.

context of circumstance elements. Things are more straightforward for 'result crimes', wherein the gist of the criminal-law wrong lies in the bringing about of a proscribed consequence. For such crimes, it is the consequence in particular that must be intended, either as an end or means. So, for example, in terms of the account stated in § 15.1, the wrong is done as an end when:

(a) D's behaviour occurs under her direction;
(b) That behaviour brings about the consequence in question;
(c) D believes it is possible for her behaviour to bring about that consequence;
(d) D wants to bring about that consequence (for its own sake); and
(e) D behaves as she does because of her belief and desire in (c) and (d).

And *mutatis mutandis* for the account of intending a consequence as a means.

Very often, when the focus is on consequences, the behaviour element is unspecific. But it need not be. Suppose a crime exists of 'throwing an object upon a railway line,'[37] for which the mens rea requirement is intention. Now, by contrast, D must not only intend to bring it about that the object is on a railway line: she must intend to do that by throwing. If she deliberately kicks a stone onto the tracks, the crime is not committed.[38]

Circumstance elements, as we noted in § 2.3.1, are different. Imagine this time a crime of assault, defined as 'touching another person without consent'. again intention-based. D's mens rea regarding V's non-consent can satisfy the law's demands of intention in more than one way. The most stringent sense in which we can say that D intends {to act in a given circumstance} depends upon D's being able to bring the circumstance about by her behaviour, even though doing so is not required by the offence definition.[39] D might for example, intend to touch V in such a way that her behaviour also causes V not to consent. In that case, we can say unequivocally that D intends {to touch V without consent}.

That stringent sense is legally recondite. In what we might call the 'plain' sense of intention with respect to circumstances, we can also say that D2 intends {to touch V without consent} when D2 is motivated to behave as she

[37] Cp. s 32 of the Offences Against the Person Act 1861 (UK). Unsurprisingly, the crime defined in s 32 can be committed in other ways too.

[38] At least where the gravamen of the crime lies in its consequence elements, the courts have an understandable tendency to read out the colour added by behaviour-specific elements. Cp. the language of 'infliction' in s 20 of the Offences Against the Person Act 1861 (UK): above, § 2.3.

[39] See § 3.4.

does by her desire, not merely to touch V, but *to do so without V's consent*. Duff's test of failure illustrates the plain sense clearly:[40] D2 would regard herself as having 'failed' if V did in fact consent to the touching.

In practice, however, even the plain case is rare. Much more commonly, intention will be established for the purposes of the criminal law when the defendant realizes that her victim does not consent, without caring about it. In this situation, D3 intends to 'touch V without consent,' because she intends {to touch V} *believing* {that V does not consent}.[41] At this point, direct intention begins to shade into the oblique.[42] Like oblique intention with respect to consequences, the equation of belief-based intention with the plain sense of intention is legal and moral, not psychological. Because D3's belief need have no motivational force,[43] belief-based intention trespasses upon the domain of advertent recklessness. The common law keeps them apart by requiring that, in the context of intention, D3 must believe positively—with no significant doubt—that the circumstance exists; whereas recklessness demands only that the defendant is aware the circumstance *may* be present.[44]

Perhaps the most notable translational difficulties for intention arise in the context of attempts, especially with respect to ulterior mens rea elements.[45] Even for actus reus elements, though, nice questions can arise. Let us extend a line of examples developed by Gideon Yaffe:[46]

> Suppose that there is an aggravated offence of shooting a State Governor. Sylvester shoots with intent to kill at Arnold Schwarzenegger, who is at

[40] Above, § 15.1.1.

[41] Notice that the plain sense of intention (D2) is not simply a special case of belief-based intention (D3). Rather like the Incompetent Assassin in § 15.1, in the plain case D2 may think the likelihood that V does not consent is low. None the less, provided he believes it is non-zero, D2 can intend the assault.

[42] See § 15.2. Curiously, oblique intention with respect to consequence elements is a much more controversial legal category. This may be because consequence elements play a more complex role in claims of justification—to which the intention/foresight distinction is crucial, as we see in chapter 16.

[43] *Pace* Gideon Yaffe, for whom the 'insalience' of such a belief 'blocks' the conclusion that the circumstance falls within D's intention: G Yaffe, *Attempts: In the Philosophy of Action and the Criminal Law* (OUP 2010) 151. But it seems that the 'salience' in Yaffe's analysis may be incidental: something D welcomes but which is entirely ancillary to her choice to behave as she does. It is not clear, morally speaking, why salience of this kind should make a significant normative difference (and engage the kinds of distinctions canvassed in chapter 16). It certainly doesn't with respect to consequences.

[44] *G* [2003] UKHL 50, [41] (Lord Bingham): a person is reckless with respect to a circumstance 'when he is aware of a risk that it exists or will exist.' (The perceived risk must, of course, also be unreasonable: § 16.3.) The lower boundaries of recklessness are themselves controversial. It is arguable that D should be held reckless about a circumstantial element *unless* D positively believes that the circumstance is absent. On this view, when D touches V, it may be a reckless assault if D has given no thought to the matter, provided D lacks a genuine belief that V consents: *B (a minor) v DPP* [2000] 2 AC 428, 459 (Lord Mackay), 466 (Lord Nicholls).

[45] See § 3.4.1.

[46] Yaffe, *Attempts* (n 43) ch 5; see also M S Moore, 'Yaffe's *Attempts*' (2013) 19 Legal Theory 136, § III.6.

the time Governor of California. Sylvester knows but does not care about Arnold's gubernatorial status. He just hates bad movies.

Suppose that Sly's shot hits Arnie. Does he commit the aggravated offence? It depends, in part, on the best interpretation of the legislation. There are multiple criminalization options here. One can imagine a statute in which it is sufficient to intend {to shoot a person}, being reckless whether that person is a State Governor. Sly more than meets *that* test. But perhaps the offence definition requires us to show that he acts 'with intent to shoot a State Governor'. What, then, must Sly have been thinking? Must Arnie's elevated status have played a motivational role in Sly's practical deliberation? In the criminal law, I take this, too, to be a matter of interpretive choice. Of course, which answer is preferable depends upon the rationale underpinning the crime itself. Usually, however, the better approach will be the more expansive. Recalling our railway-throwing example, consider two cases:

(i) D1 throws a rock, intending that it land upon the railway line; and
(ii) D2 throws a rock, intending that it land upon something that, as D knows, is a railway line.

D2 should be convicted too. Doing so advances both the preventive aims of the statute and the demands of justice.

15.2 Obliquely intended consequences (at common law)

The pivotal element of any account of intention is (e)/(e′), that D behaves as she does because of some desire–belief combination. If D foresees a consequence, and indeed welcomes it, but that prospect plays no part in her decision to act, she does not intend it.[47] The consequence is, for D, incidental. A judge who awards compensatory damages to the plaintiff may realize that doing so will bankrupt the defendant; ordinarily, however, that has nothing to do with why she awards the damages. The bankruptcy is no more than a foreseen side-effect.

English law has not always been clear on this point. In *Hyam*,[48] which we discussed in § 15.1, the defendant was convicted of murder, a conviction that

[47] Cp. A J P Kenny, 'Intention and Purpose in Law' in R S Summers (ed), *Essays in Legal Philosophy* (Blackwell 1968) 146, 155.
[48] [1975] AC 55, 86.

required (and still requires) proof of an intent to kill or cause grievous bodily harm. Numerous cases from around that time assimilated foresight of a probability with intention.[49] Indeed, Lord Diplock felt able, following *Hyam*, to hold that the law was now 'well-settled':[50]

> 'Where intention to produce a particular result was a necessary element of an offence, no distinction was to be drawn in law between the state of mind of one who did an act because he desired it to produce that particular result and the state of mind of one who, when he did the act, was aware that it was likely to produce that result but was prepared to take the risk that it might do so.'

That proposition is no longer good law, and on the same facts Hyam would not be convicted of murder today. Yet her conviction in 1974 reflects, in part, the moral pull of those facts. One might readily think that she *deserved* to be convicted of murder; that her conduct ought to be labelled as murder. Plausibly, one might even deny that it was the moral *equivalent* of murder, preferring to say that it was an instance of murder, whatever the law might say. Either way, though, there is attraction in the idea that some forms of advertent wrongdoing are as bad as their intended counterparts. The common law seeks to capture this idea with the supplementary category of 'oblique intention', although its authoritative statement is deliberately imprecise:[51]

> '[I]n the rare cases where the [standard] direction that it is for the jury simply to decide whether the defendant intended to kill or to do serious bodily harm is not enough, the jury should be directed that they are not entitled to find the necessary intention, unless they feel sure that death or serious bodily harm was a virtual certainty (barring some unforeseen intervention) as a result of the defendant's actions and that the defendant appreciated that such was the case.'

Oblique intention thus embraces consequence elements that, as D recognizes,[52] are so closely bound to other intended actions that they are 'virtually certain' to occur alongside. Its endorsement by the courts gives the

[49] e.g. *Hardy v Motor Insurers' Bureau* [1964] 2 QB 745, 764 (Pearson LJ): the accused 'must have foreseen, when he did the act, that it would in all probability injure the other person. Therefore he had the intent to injure the other person.' See also at 758 (Lord Denning MR).

[50] *Lemon* [1979] AC 617, 638; a similar dictum is expressed in *Hyam* [1975] AC 55, 86.

[51] *Woollin* [1999] 1 AC 82, 96.

[52] One oddity about the *Woollin* direction is its expressed requirement, untested in later cases, that the relevant consequence must also *be* virtually certain. In part, this may be a constraint upon over-expansion of oblique intention as a legal category (which already extends well beyond the special cases of inseparability discussed in § 15.3).

prosecution an alternative way to argue that a consequence is intended, at least in law. Someone who acts in the virtual certainty that another will be killed or grievously injured can, if that other dies, be convicted of murder without the need for proof that death or serious injury was directly intended.

Acknowledging a category of oblique intention enables the law to make certain findings of intention that are morally rather than conceptually driven. Strikingly, however, the model direction (above) is expressed in negative terms: 'the jury should be directed that they are not entitled to find the necessary intention, unless they feel sure that death or serious bodily harm was a virtual certainty.' Foresight of a virtual certainty is necessary before oblique intention is established, but it is not sufficient.[53] Where there is virtual certainty, the jury is permitted to conclude that the defendant intended the consequence and, absent any special considerations, the jury should normally so conclude;[54] but it is entitled not to find intention should there be such considerations. Suppose, for example, that D takes a virtually certain risk of killing or injuring his children by defenestrating them during a house fire, because that is the only chance—however slight—of saving them.[55] D's intention is to save rather than to take life.

We can accommodate that type of example by a negative condition: that the finding of oblique intention be compatible with D's direct intentions.[56] More problematic cases are those involving 'double effects'. For example, a doctor may know that by injecting a terminally ill patient with the morphine necessary to dull pain, it is virtually certain that she will shorten the patient's life. The doctor does not aim to shorten the patient's life, and does not directly intend his death. In such a case, notwithstanding that it is a virtually certain side-effect, the jury is entitled to conclude that she does not intend his death, even obliquely. The common law thus confers an element of discretion upon the jury,[57] enabling it to refrain from calling such cases murder. By this informal

[53] Cp. *Matthews* [2003] EWCA Crim 192, [43]: 'the law has not yet reached a definition of intent in murder in terms of appreciation of a virtual certainty.'

[54] Ibid, [46]: 'If the jury were sure that the appellants appreciated the virtual certainty of Jonathan's death when they threw him from the bridge and also that they then had no intention of saving him from such death, it is impossible to see how the jury could not have found that the appellants intended Jonathan to die.'

[55] The example, invented by Lord Goff, is discussed by the Law Commission in LCCP No. 177, *A New Homicide Act for England and Wales?* (Home Office 2006) § 4.21. For a real case along these lines, see *Emperor v Dhirajia* AIR 1940 All 486, where D jumped down a well with her baby in order to escape her violent husband.

[56] Strictly speaking, a finding of oblique intention would be precluded only if it were incompatible with the directly intended action that the relevant side-effect is virtually certain to accompany. In cases where D acts with multiple intentions, a finding of oblique intention would not be precluded merely because D has an another intention incompatible with the obliquely intended action.

[57] A result that has found favour with the Law Commission: Law Com No. 304, *Murder, Manslaughter and Infanticide* (Home Office 2006) § 3.20–3.26. For critical discussion, see V Tadros, 'The Homicide Ladder' (2006) 69 MLR 601.

means, a fudge is achieved. Justifications may be accommodated that, in the context of necessity, would be unavailable to directly intended wrongs.[58]

15.3 Inseparable actions

Set legal artifice aside, for now. Sometimes, an action is not done as a means or end, but there is so close a connection between that action and another directly-intended action that we nevertheless hesitate. As Philippa Foot once put it,[59]

> 'A certain event may be desired under one of its descriptions, unwanted under another, but we cannot treat these as two different events, one of which is aimed at and the other not. And even if it be argued that there are here two different events—the crushing of the child's skull and its death—the two are obviously much too close for an application of the doctrine of the double effect.'

This is the problem of 'inseparable' actions. The criminal-law literature abounds with examples to test our intuitions about such cases, many of them due to Glanville Williams:[60]

> 'D, an eccentric and amoral surgeon, wishes to remove P's heart completely from P's body in order to experiment upon it. D does not desire P's death (being perfectly content that P shall go on living if he can do so without his heart), but recognizes that in fact his death is inevitable from the operation to be performed.'

Suppose that D will somehow save two other patients by carrying out this operation. Then, we may ask, is his patient's death a case of bad means to a good end, or of a bad side-effect of the means to a good end? Another of Williams's examples has received judicial attention:[61]

> '[S]uppose that a villain of the deepest dye blows up an aircraft in flight with a time-bomb, merely for the purpose of collecting on insurance. It is not his

[58] See, in particular, § 18.5.

[59] 'The Problem of Abortion and the Doctrine of the Double Effect' (1967) 5 Ox Rev 5, 6–7.

[60] *TBCL*, § 18. With one eye to its vintage, we should assume in the example that no life-sustaining machinery exists that is capable of keeping P alive following the operation. (I cast doubt on the currency of the example in § 15.3.2.)

[61] 'Oblique Intention' (n 12) 423; compare his earlier *The Mental Element in Crime* (Magnes 1965) 34–35.

> aim to cause the people on board to perish, but he knows that success in his scheme will inevitably involve their deaths as a side-effect.'[62]

One might see a case here for denying that the deaths are a mere side-effect. For Lord Hailsham, 'if any passengers are killed he is guilty of murder, as their death will be a moral certainty if he carries out his intention. There is no difference between blowing up the aircraft and intending the death of some or all of the passengers.'[63] Similarly, Lord Bridge accepted in *Moloney* that there may be cases where things which are seemingly not sought as ends or means should be analysed as cases of intention:[64]

> 'A man who, at London Airport, boards a plane which he knows to be bound for Manchester, clearly intends to travel to Manchester, even though Manchester is the last place he wants to be and his motive for boarding the plane is simply to escape pursuit. . . . By boarding the Manchester plane, the man conclusively demonstrates his intention to go there, because it is a moral certainty that that is where he will arrive.'

Many writers accept that there are actions which—while not themselves sought—are so intimately connected to a directly intended action that they must also be regarded as intended.[65] The idea certainly has intuitive appeal. But it remains controversial which actions are inseparable and why. We lack criteria, and a rationale for those criteria, which describe when a side-effect, not directly intended according to the discussion in § 15.1, is to be treated not merely as obliquely intended but as *inseparable* from another, intended, action.

Mere certainty will not do it. A rugby player may be sure that tackling his opponent will be painful, but he does not act with masochistic intent.[66] Neither is logical entailment the answer: the connection between Williams's airplane explosion and the passengers' deaths is not a logical one. What then? H L A Hart's view is suggestive:[67]

[62] *Pace* the extraordinary story of Vesna Vulović, who in 1972 apparently fell from 33,000 feet after an explosion on JAT Yugoslav Airlines Flight 367. Everyone else died.

[63] *Hyam* [1975] AC 55, 74.

[64] [1985] AC 905, 926.

[65] See, e.g., Kenny, 'Intention and Purpose in Law' (n 47) 156: 'most plain men, as well as lawyers, would agree that the eccentric surgeon described by Glanville Williams intended the death of the patient whose heart he removed.' See too, amongst many, Hart, *Punishment and Responsibility*, 120; Duff, *IACL*, 89ff. Contrast Finnis, 'Intention and Side-effects' (n 8).

[66] See, e.g., G Harman, Practical Reasoning' in his *Reasoning, Meaning, and Mind* (OUP 1999) 46, 48; Duff, *IACL*, 89–90.

[67] Hart, *Punishment and Responsibility*, 120.

> 'The neighbour who for the pleasure of the music plays her gramophone at 6 a.m., well knowing from my frequent complaints that it will wake me from sleep, as it does, would not normally be said to have intentionally woken me up or woken me up intentionally . . . . The exceptions to this usage of "intentionally" are cases where a foreseen outcome is so immediately and invariably connected with the action done that the suggestion that the action might not have that outcome would by ordinary standards be regarded as absurd, or such as only a mentally abnormal person would seriously entertain: the connexion between action and outcome seems therefore to be not merely contingent but rather to be conceptual.'

Reference to absurdity can be found, too, in both Bennett and Michael Moore.[68] The point is not that immediacy and invariance are determinative, albeit they are surely relevant. In part, this is a probabilistic matter. Where there is a temporal gap or a lengthy causal chain between an action and some further event, we may think that event less certain to follow the action. Certainty is, I take it, part of the idea of inseparability. Equally, though, it is not the whole. We do not consider the suggestion 'that the action might not have that outcome' to be absurd *merely* because we are certain the outcome will occur. Neither did Hart. Hart imagined a connection that was 'not merely contingent but rather . . . conceptual'. Ideas of immediacy and invariance are best understood as being *bound up* with that kind of connection, rather than as its constituents.

'Not merely contingent' seems right. Where Hart's proposal goes awry, though, is in characterizing the connection as conceptual.[69] A more promising approach is to think about inseparability in terms of the agent's *conceptions*. At work here is the thought that some action, φing, is inseparable from μing if, although there may exist worlds in which it is possible to φ without μing, the world as the agent understands it admits of no such possibility. In cases of inseparability, we might say, the agent's practical conception of what it is for her to φ shall include μing: she cannot conceive of φing alone. This is simply a preliminary suggestion, and the second part of it is no corollary of the first. But Lord Bridge may well have had something like this in mind in *Moloney*:[70]

> 'The fact that, when the appellant fired the gun, the gun was pointing directly at his stepfather's head at a range of about six feet was not, and could not be, disputed. The sole issue was whether, when he pressed the trigger, this fact and its inevitable

[68] Bennett, *The Act Itself*, 213; Moore, 'Yaffe's *Attempts*' (n 46) 164.
[69] Neither Bennett nor Moore makes this mistake (see n 68).
[70] [1985] AC 905, 920.

> consequence were present in the appellant's mind. If they were, the inference was inescapable, using words in their ordinary, everyday meaning, that he intended to kill his stepfather.'

Potentially, there are resources here that can help us to respond to Moore—who takes an attractive, sceptical stance when he analyses the debate about inseparability in terms of the individuation of actions. In Moore's account, the idea of inseparability becomes an empty one: just like 'separable' actions, so-called 'inseparable' actions are nevertheless conceptually distinct. Since they are distinct, the intentions to do those actions must also be distinct:[71]

> 'Asymmetric causal relations exist between: heart-removals, and deaths; blowing up a plane in flight, and the deaths of any passengers on it; getting drunk, and being hung over. . . . In each of such cases, there are distinct types of events, and an intent to bring about the first is not, accordingly, an intent to bring about the second.'

In turn, Moore claims, if we are to equate two distinct intentions, whether 'separable' or otherwise, we may only do so pursuant to a moral argument. Moreover, he continues, moral arguments along the lines that an agent's knowingly blowing up the passengers is just as bad as her intentionally blowing up the plane do not look like arguments that depend upon the idea of inseparability. The idea of inseparability, then, adds nothing.

We come to the moral debates in chapter 16. For now, we can agree with Moore that 'inseparable' actions are distinct. His argument effectively disposes of Hart's idea that the link between two such actions is conceptual. Contra Moore, however, that is not an end to the matter. The treatment of intended actions as inseparable is not merely a matter of moral argument. More specifically, there are grounds for concluding that such actions are *not* merely done as side-effects that happen to be inseparable. This is not to say they are an ordinary part of the defendant's means or ends. Rather, it is to recognize that there is a third way in which an action may be intended. While the action may be done for its own sake, or as a means to an end, it may also be done as a practical *instance* of an end.

Herein lies the explanation of Lord Bridge's hypothetical airline passenger: he goes to Manchester as an instance of going somewhere out of London. A similar relationship often holds for circumstance-dependent wrongs, in as much

[71] Moore, *Placing Blame*, 467.

as it is not required that the defendant intend a morally-relevant circumstance in order to intend the wrong. In a crime of rape, for example, the defendant may simply want to have sexual intercourse, being quite content to satisfy that desire should his victim also consent. However, where such a defendant knows that his victim has not consented, it remains the case that his behaviour is motivated by desire for the end (having sexual intercourse) that having non-consensual intercourse instantiates. The unusual feature of his motivation is that it is not means-end: he rapes his victim not in order to have sexual intercourse (*simpliciter*) but as an instance thereof.

Below, we explore the two main grounds for treating actions as inseparable. Both grounds distinguish those actions from ordinary side-effects by invoking the idea of instantiation. I do not claim that instantiation always goes hand-in-hand with inseparability. In particular, inseparability differs from an instantiating link involving accompanying circumstances in the following way. Subject to what was said in § 15.1.3, normally it suffices to prove that D intends the proscribed action (say, rape) by showing that D intends the more general action (sexual intercourse) and that D knows of the relevant circumstance (non-consent). In contrast, for the two varieties of inseparability discussed below, it is the more specific action that we must first show is intended.

15.3.1 Definitions

Charles Fried once remarked that[72]

> '[I]t is inadmissable to say that one intends to put a bullet through a man, stab him, crush him, or blow him to atoms but does not intend to harm him. All of these things just *are* harming him.'

The 'is' relationship claimed by Fried between stabbing and harming is not one of identity. Rather, it involves a form of generalization: all stabbings are harmings, because stabbing is a *species* of harming. Even then, however, the claim is problematic. Bennett counters:[73]

> '[I]t is too obviously false that crushing and stabbing *conceptually* or *essentially* involve harming or killing. So [Fried's] claim must be a contingent one

[72] C Fried, *Right and Wrong* (Harvard UP 1978) 44. (Emphasis in original.)
[73] Bennett, *Tanner*, 108; cp. Bennett, *The Act Itself*, 207–08.

> about the nature of particular actions: this head-crushing (the claim must be) is a killing, this stabbing is a harming.'

Seemingly, Fried has in mind something more than a contingent connection between particular actions. Rather like Hart, he appears to be pointing toward a conceptual link between activities. To that extent, Bennett's riposte is apt. One might argue that the concept of harming is to be explicated by appeal to paradigm cases, including crushing and stabbing. But that argument quickly runs into difficulty. One can imagine a crushing that, with some resilient material, does not result in harm; likewise with a stabbing.[74] So Fried's examples do not convince. However, it is possible to defend a version of his more general thought. Suppose that I want to move my finger, in order to bid at an auction, and so crook it. My crooking my finger, we might think, is not a means of moving it but an *instance* of doing so, because crooking 'just *is*' a certain kind of movement. The two actions are inseparable in virtue of a *definitional* instantiation.

Definitional instantiation does not involve any false equation of the sort repudiated by Moore. Clearly, moving one's finger and crooking it are not identical. It follows that intentions to do those things are not identical, and (as Moore observes) to talk of 'the same intention' would be wrong. Admittedly, sometimes we may correctly speak of 'the same intention' to φ and to μ when φing and μing are understood to be semantically identical:[75]

> 'For most persons we know, "bachelor" and "unmarried male" are synonymous ways of picking out the same class of individuals. For such persons an intention to remain unmarried and an intention to remain a bachelor are [provided the person is male] one and the same intention.'

But inseparability does not require this. One who tries to kill a bachelor may rightly be held to have intended the death of *a person*. The law characteristically uses more general descriptions of this kind when framing prohibitions, for

[74] Hamleys sells a 'Magic Plastic Balloon' made of resin that does not burst when punctured by a sharp instrument—the balloon surface can simply be pinched together to reseal.

[75] Moore, *Placing Blame*, 468. Care is required here. To those who do not recognize that 'bachelor' and 'unmarried male' are synonyms, 'an intention to remain a bachelor' and 'an intention to remain an unmarried male' are not the same. None the less, an intention to remain a bachelor and an intention to remain an unmarried male are one and the same intention. Suppose there is a specific law constraining people from intending to kill persons who are bachelors. If Alex seeks to kill someone whom he knows is an unmarried male, then he cannot claim that he did not intend to kill a bachelor; even though he does not correctly understand the meaning of 'bachelor'. Alex might argue that he misunderstood the law, but that would be (if anything) a separate defence. Compare the Model Penal Code, § 2.02(9).

example of murder. Bringing particular cases within generic definitions is what lawyers do. However, links of this kind tend to be canonical. Recall our example from § 15.1.3:[76]

> Suppose that there is an aggravated offence of shooting a State Governor. Sylvester shoots with intent to kill at Arnold Schwarzenegger, who is at the time Governor of California. Sylvester knows but does not care about Arnold's gubernatorial status. He just hates bad movies.

Does Sylvester intend by his behaviour {to shoot a State Governor}? No.[77] We cannot dispose of this case via instantiation, for the thing intended is not the more specific.

15.3.2 Instantiation and practical conceptions

Certain more controversial cases raise the issue whether *practically* inseparable actions can be distinguished from mere side-effects by reference to ideas of instantiation, and thereby assimilated for moral purposes to actions that are intended as a means. We might put the idea as follows. The terrorist who blows up a plane has a practical conception of what it is he intends to do: it is a part of that conception that he kills the passengers, given that he seeks to blow up the plane in mid-air with passengers on board.

Before we get off the ground with this, though, Bennett offers a preliminary worry. Preliminary, yet profound. In his *Tanner Lectures*, Bennett questioned the very distinction between actions done as side-effects and those done as a means, arguing that there is no account of 'intended as a means' which yields acceptable results when applied in particular cases.[78] Consider the following example:[79]

[76] See Yaffe, *Attempts* (n 43) ch 5. In Yaffe's own analysis, inseparability is not a species of intention. Morally speaking, he acknowledges (at 123) that 'Sometimes knowing what will happen if one acts is just as bad as intending it; usually it is not.' But he does not give an account of how to distinguish those cases.

[77] Hence, as we saw in § 15.1.3, if Sylvester is to be convicted of an intention-based offence here, the law must incorporate a belief-based test for intention with respect to circumstances.

[78] Bennett, *Tanner*, 113. The worry does not reappear in *The Act Itself*, in part because his analysis of inseparability cases evolved in the interim, becoming much closer to the position argued for here. See too Moore, 'Yaffe's *Attempts*' (n 46) 165 (concurring with Bennett's modified position).

[79] *Tanner*, 110; cp. *The Act Itself*, 210.

> 'A political leader takes action against a trade union, intending to bring about a month-long state of disintegration in which the various locals break off from the parent body and severally fall into further disunity. This is his intended means to the end of the union's being unable to call a strike during December. He is rightly sure that if the union falls apart for that long it will never be reconstituted, but all he cares about or intends is the one-month dissolution: if he were sure that the union would recover during January and flourish for many years, that would not reduce his motivation for moving against it.'

We might conclude of such a case that the one-month dissolution is intended (as a means), but not the permanent dissolution. Yet if so, surely we may say of Terror Bomber that 'All that was intended was that the people's bodies should be inoperative for long enough to cause a general belief that they were dead, this belief lasting long enough to speed the end of the war . . . .'[80] Or, of an arsonist, that she 'does not intend the building to be permanently destroyed, just that it be reduced to cinders for long enough for the insurance company to pay up . . . .'[81]

Bennett's concern is a large one. It demands a response even if we reject inseparability, so long as we still want to distinguish morally between Terror Bomber and Strategic Bomber. The key point, I take it, is that one may want and intend to φ because of a certain feature of φing, rather than because of φing in all its aspects. So Terror Bomber kills the civilians because one feature of their being dead (namely, their lengthy inoperativeness) is wanted by him as a means to win the war. But granted this interpretation is possible, why do we prefer it in Terror Bomber's case to one where the deaths are a side-effect or further consequence. Why do we prefer it to the sort of interpretation we accept for Bennett's political leader?

A useful starting point here is a suggestion attributed to Gilbert Harman:[82]

> 'Suppose that someone expects his behaviour to produce an F and a G, and that his only thought about this is a coarse-grained one about F-and-G-in-a-lump, with nothing in his mind corresponding to the notion of "producing F and not producing G"—that being a mental refinement which he has not achieved. . . . [I]f his actual state of mind involves nothing of the form "F and not G", we ought not to say that he intends to produce F and does not intend to produce G.'

80 *Tanner*, 111.
81 Ibid, 111.
82 Reported by Bennett: ibid, 111–12.

Assume that Harman's agent paradigmatically-intends to bring about F. His conception of F includes G because he cannot practically conceive of bringing about F alone: they are, as Foot would say, 'much too close'.[83] In such a case, it seems right to say that he intends to bring about that which he conceives of when he conceives of F. He sets out to beget 'F and G' because he wants F, a feature of 'F and G'.

The idea of a practical, instantiated conception explains the distinction Bennett queries, both in general and in the inseparable cases where that distinction cannot be drawn. Not, however, without elaboration. For Bennett isn't finished. Presumably, he suggests, it is sufficient for a distinction to be in a person's mind,[84]

> '[T]hat the person should consciously, episodically think of the distinction—e.g., that the arsonist should play with the idea of the world's running normally to the point where the insurance company pays off, and then events in the vicinity of the building running in reverse like a film played backwards. He need not think of it as naturally possible, let alone probable. All he needs is some thought of it, sparked by fancy or whimsy . . . .'

It is not sufficient. Practical instantiation is concerned with an agent's conception of her action in the world as she understands it, and not in some logically possible world existing only as her conjecture. Whatever his occasional whimsies, the arsonist understands himself to be about to permanently destroy the building—this is, we may say, his own practical conception of what he is about to do. His practical conception is of the 'F-and-G-in-a-lump' type, and this distinguishes the arsonist (and Terror Bomber) from the politician. The politician is able to practically conceive of the union's temporary disunity without, as part of doing so, comprehending its permanent dissolution. The arsonist cannot.

The point is not that the arsonist has a limited imagination, but rather that any such conjecture would be recognized by him as merely fanciful. Of course, Bennett's politician regards the union as not having a credible chance of survival. But it is not merely whimsical for the politician to conceive of unions surviving a temporary disunity, and his ability to do so means that his practical conception of the particular union's disunity is not of the 'F-and-G-in-a-lump' type. It is conceivable that instances of bringing about the *type* of effect he seeks may not bring about the 'inseparable' effect because the conditions under

[83] Foot, 'The Problem of Abortion and the Doctrine of the Double Effect' (n 59) 7; above, § 15.3.
[84] Bennett, *Tanner*, 112.

which the two effects would not concur are much less extraordinary than are those for the arsonist's case.

My 'whimsy' test does not generate clear-cut boundaries. But that is as it should be, because the underlying idea is vague too. A helpful way of thinking about the test is in terms of possible worlds:[85] if F is produced then so too is G, and this correspondence sustains across a long sequence of the nearest possible worlds. (Hence it is not enough that G is certain to accompany F on this occasion, or even on every occasion that F is produced in this world.) In turn, the ascription of intention to an agent depends, in part, upon the agent's understandings about how the world works—especially, that a world in which we can produce F without G is *very far* from the actual world. The indeterminacy of such an account is, I think, appropriate to the idea of inseparableness within our conceptions of what we do.

This way of thinking also helps to bring out why it matters that G is, as Hart put it, 'invariably and immediately' connected to F. Where the connection between them is variable, our conceptions of F and G are pretty much bound to be separable. Similarly, where the connection is not immediate, such that there is a significant causal or temporal gap between F and G, it becomes easier for an agent to disengage producing F from producing G in her own conception of her action. And that's what counts.

All of which makes Glanville Williams's surgeon a hard case. To see this, contrast it with another well-known scenario:[86]

> A party of potholers is led by a fat man who gets stuck, trapping the others beneath him. Flood waters are rising within the cave. The only means of clearing the blockage is to blast the fat man from where he is using a stick of dynamite. In doing so, the others realize, they will kill him.

The connection between blowing up the fat man and killing him is so temporally and causally tight that their conceptional separation requires whimsies in the order of Bennett's arsonist. Partly because of advances in medical science, however, the same is not demanded of Williams's surgeon. Even if he knows

[85] I make no claim about the existence of such worlds. The suggestion is merely that this is an illuminating way of thinking about inseparability.

[86] Described in Foot, 'The Problem of Abortion and the Doctrine of the Double Effect' (n 59) 7. J G Hanink ('Some Light on Double Effect' (1975) 35 Analysis 147) suggests that the others may blow him up with a convenient stick of dynamite without intending his death, since descriptions exist which do not mention his death and under which their conduct is intended. So too L Geddes, 'On the Intrinsic Wrongness of Killing Innocent People' (1973) 33 Analysis 93: *contra* R A Duff, 'Intentionally Killing the Innocent' (1973) 34 Analysis 16; J Finnis, 'The Rights and Wrongs of Abortion: a Reply to Judith Jarvis Thomson' (1973) 2 Phil and Pub Aff 117, 135–36.

the patient will die, it is no longer the stuff of fantasy for the surgeon to conceive of removing a heart without death's being an aspect of the action that he understands himself to be doing. It is—of course—murder. But not because of inseparability.

15.4 How would inseparability matter?

We have elucidated two possible bases for assimilating 'inseparable' actions to actions that are directly intended. On the account here, the extension of direct intention to embrace inseparable actions is not arbitrary. But why would such an extension matter—and would it be morally arbitrary?

The answers to those questions depend upon a more general inquiry: whether it matters that an action is intended rather than merely foreseen. We begin that inquiry in the next chapter. But let us suppose, as I shall argue, that the difference between intention and foresight does matter, and that the distinctions between ends, means, and side-effects are morally and legally significant.[87] It is then meaningful to ask, where amongst those distinctions ought inseparability to fall? On the analysis proposed here, the problem of how to treat such actions is relatively straightforward. Cases of instantiation are analogous to cases of means, since the proscribed action is intended though not for its own sake. A clear illustration of this is Lord Bridge's fugitive, who flies to Manchester not as a means but as a practical instance of escaping London. Just as Terror Bomber wants to win the war, and so he sets out to kill the children, the fugitive wants to leave London, and so he catches the plane to Manchester. He values being in Manchester as an instance of being out of London, even though he may not want to go there in particular.

Notice, though, that the fugitive is not a case of inseparability, of the kind described in § 15.3. One could leave London without going to Manchester. Rather, Lord Bridge's fugitive illustrates the fallacy of assuming that all intended actions are done as either end or means. We need to avoid that mistake if we are to resolve the problem of inseparability. A true inseparability case would be the Londoner who flies to Manchester on business. Our commercial traveller inseparably leaves London, even though she may not want her behaviour under that description; for she cannot conceive of her travelling to Manchester while remaining where she is.

[87] See, in addition to chapter 16, §§ 18.2–3.

Contrast cases of oblique intention, which do not involve instantiation of the kinds described in § 15.3. There is little ground outside the law for treating such cases as intended, and indeed to do so would seem merely arbitrary. Obliquely intended actions are not done as ends, means, or instantiation. Such actions play the sort of role in the practical deliberation of an agent that the children's deaths do for Strategic Bomber. The deaths are contemplated, but constitute no part of the sequence of actions Strategic Bomber sets himself to do. They are incidental to the events he is motivated to bring about. At least for the purpose of justification, they are side-effects.

16
On the Moral Distinction between Intention and Advertence

Excepting the special category of oblique intention, the criminal law broadly embraces the distinction outlined in previous chapter, between intended actions and those merely foreseen. That embrace calls for normative defence. One way of defending it is to appeal to what I shall call the standard view, that intended wrongdoing is, *ceteris paribus*, inherently more culpable than advertently-risked wrongdoing.[1] Perhaps that's right. We might still wonder why the law applies a condition of unreasonableness before concluding that advertent φing is reckless,[2] whereas intended φing must rely on a supervening defence.[3] But there are reasons to doubt the standard view. In this chapter, I offer a different, albeit compatible, explanation. On my account, the most systematic difference between intended and foreseen wrongdoing is not measured in degrees of culpability, Rather, it is worked out in terms of what actions may legitimately be invoked to justify pro tanto wrongdoing. In general, foreseen actions do not lend any favourable weight to the justification of intended ones. Thus one cannot justify intended φing by appeal to the overall reasonableness of one's conduct (and, especially, by appeal to its advertent side-effects). Yet one can make appeals of that kind to justify advertent φing.

16.1 Preliminaries

In chapter 15, we distinguished between chosen actions primarily in terms of whether such actions are done as means, ends, or side-effects. Recall Jonathan Bennett's famous example, helpfully summarized by Michael Bratman:[4]

[1] See, e.g., Duff, *IACL*, 113.
[2] See, e.g., Model Penal Code, § 2.02(c).
[3] See also chapter 18. On supervening defences generally, see chapter 17.
[4] See § 15.1.1: Bennett, *Tanner*, 95; Bennett, *The Act Itself*, ch 11; M E Bratman, 'What is Intention?' in P R Cohen, J Morgan, and M Pollack (eds), *Intentions in Communication* (MIT Press 1990) 15, 23.

Fundamentals of Criminal Law. A P Simester, Oxford University Press (2021). © A P Simester.
DOI: 10.1093/oso/9780198853145.003.0016

> 'Terror Bomber and Strategic Bomber both have as their goal promoting the war effort against Enemy. Both intend to pursue their goal by dropping bombs. Terror Bomber's plan is to bomb the school in Enemy's territory, thereby killing children of Enemy, terrorizing Enemy's population, and forcing Enemy to surrender. Strategic Bomber's plan is to bomb Enemy's munitions plant, thereby undermining Enemy's war effort. However, Strategic Bomber also knows that next to the munitions plant is a school, and that when he bombs the plant he will also kill the children inside the school.'

Terror Bomber intends the deaths, but Strategic Bomber does not. Diagrammatically, the differences can be illustrated as follows:

Terror Bomber: C_{TB} ———➤ Kill Children ———➤ Win War

Strategic Bomber: C_{SB} ———➤ Blow Up Plant ———➤ Win War
|
Kill Children

In the case of Strategic Bomber, the prospect of the children's deaths does not provide him, at least so far as he is concerned, with a reason for his conduct.[5] Neither does it explain his conduct. Even if he is incidentally happy to kill the children, he does not bomb the plant in order to do so. For Strategic Bomber the deaths are neither a means nor an end, but rather a side-effect: his belief that they may occur does not connect to his motivation.

The main question for this chapter is why that distinction in the structure of an agent's practical deliberation should matter. One answer might be that side-effects are less in need of deterrence. I set that possibility aside. In part, my doing so reflects a conclusion reached elsewhere, that deterrence is relevant primarily to criminal *prohibitions* rather than to punishment.[6] The quantum of punishment we should impose for criminal wrongs varies according to desert, not deterrence. Even in terms of deterrence, though, it is not obvious that we should incentivize the choice to risk a bad action differently from seeking it as a means.[7] No doubt we ought to incentivize less dangerous *conduct*, but the law

[5] In Bratman's restatement ('What is Intention?' (n 4)), 'Strategic Bomber has worried a lot about this bad effect. But he has concluded that this cost is outweighed by the contribution that would be made to the war effort by the destruction of the munitions plant.'

[6] J R Edwards and A P Simester, 'Prevention with a Moral Voice' in A P Simester, A du Bois-Pedain, and U Neumann (eds), *Liberal Criminal Theory: Essays for Andreas von Hirsch* (Hart 2014) 43.

[7] One argument in favour of doing so was seen in § 3.3.1: that criminalizing reckless φing (in addition to intended φing) further restricts freedom. In general, however, that argument is more likely to be decisive in the context of negligence.

already does that. Moreover, the dangerousness of a particular piece of conduct is not dependent on whether the damage it may cause is intended rather than foreseen. It is dependent on how D actually behaves.[8] Deterrence-based arguments would also need to be offset against other instrumental considerations, such as potential gains in simplification of the criminal law (especially for proof) were it sufficient to establish mens rea by showing mere advertence to the actus reus. So the argument from deterrence seems at best equivocal.

16.1.1 A matter of degree?

Turn, then, to intrinsic moral differences. According to the standard view, the distinction between intention and advertence translates as a matter of degree. *Ceteris paribus*, it is simply more culpable to do a wrong intentionally than to do it advertently. Put so baldly, however, that view seems overstated. It allies too quickly the means with the end. In the Bomber cases, for example, it is not obvious that we should distinguish morally between the deaths of the children as a bad means and that same outcome as a bad side-effect. We cannot, for instance, use the fact that death is intended by Terror Bomber as a clue to his having a moral-character flaw in a way that merely foreseeing and 'accepting' death is not. Indeed, as we noted in § 15.1.1, the agents' *attitudes* towards the harm itself can be indistinguishable.[9] There is no reason to suppose that either bomber would behave in the same fashion were he to have an alternative means to his ultimate end.[10] Neither of them desires, or is motivated to seek, the deaths for their own sake.[11] Rather, each wants to win the war, and is insufficiently concerned by the means/side-effect involved to override that desire.

This last proposition is crucial to the potential blameworthiness of each agent, and it counsels against rather than for distinguishing them. If we fault the agents, we do so because they prefer doing the actus reus to not doing it (and thereby failing to achieve their motivating end), and because they deliberately implement that preference. Each case involves advertent failures to give sufficient weight to morally appropriate goals. Each case thus falls within the framework of choice-based fault outlined in chapter 11, in as much as each

[8] For a fuller discussion of this point, see A P Simester, 'Why Distinguish Intention From Foresight?' in *Harm and Culpability* 71, 73ff.

[9] See too Bennett, *Tanner*, 99ff; Bennett, *The Act Itself*, 215ff.

[10] The usage is adopted from A J P Kenny, 'Intention and Purpose in Law' in R S Summers (ed), *Essays in Legal Philosophy* (Blackwell 1968) 146, 160: 'When an agent wants it to be the case that *q* and not in order to make anything else the case, we may say that *q* is his ultimate end.'

[11] Or, if he does, then he does not behave as he does because of that desire.

agent *chooses* to conduct himself in such a way that the deaths are caused. This is not, of course, to argue that all choices are equally blameworthy.[12] But they are not differentiated, culpability-wise, by the intention/foresight divide *simpliciter*.[13]

16.1.2 Wrongness?

A different line of thought might be that the moral character of one's conduct is determined primarily by one's intentions. We noted in § 3.2 that this is at least sometimes true. Certain wrongs, like attempts and exploitation, are in part constituted by the intentions with which D acts. Moreover, the reasons for this can be somewhat generalized. To take the example of economic wrongs, the intention/foresight divide plays a crucial role in marking out legitimate market activity that has deleterious effects on the interests of others from illegitimate attacks upon those same interests. We need such a dividing line because other-affecting conduct is ubiquitous. The potential effects of D's conduct can be so multifarious that we cannot fairly expect D to refrain from risking them all. Hence, while it may be a pro tanto wrong to *seek* economic harm to others, the need to limit such harms as side-effects is secondary.

However, not all wrongs are constituted by intentions in this way. If I burn my house down to collect the insurance, knowing that a disabled person is asleep inside with no chance of escape, my conduct is monstrous.[14] Its moral character is shaped not by my end, but by the foreseen side-effect. Moreover, the basic wrongness of my conduct derives from the same source as if I were to kill that person for the sake of inheriting: from my moral obligation not to kill. This is to concur, at least in part, with Bennett:[15]

[12] This point was noted in § 11.3, in as much as D's attitudes toward the deaths may be complex and nuanced. Neither should we ignore the possibilities of justification or excuse.

[13] Indeed, that's why oblique intention is treated as a supplementary category of intention for mens rea purposes: see § 15.2. It may be that intended wrongdoing is *typically* accompanied by attitudes that deserve greater condemnation than those that typically accompany advertent wrongdoing, in which case the intention/foresight distinction may be a useful legal proxy for relative culpability. I cannot explore that possibility here.

[14] The case is from T Baldwin, 'Foresight and Responsibility' (1979) 54 Philosophy 347, 352. Interestingly, in *Immorality* (Princeton UP 1984) 247–48, Ronald Milo takes the view that indifference is actually morally worse than deliberate 'wickedness', a possibility that Baldwin (at 353) at least expresses sympathy for. However, that possibility is not tied to the means/side-effect distinction, in as much as one may intrinsically desire, regret, or be indifferent to means and side-effects alike.

[15] Bennett, *Tanner*, 97.

> 'The morality I consult as a guide to my conduct does also guide my intentions, but not by telling me what I may or may not intend. It speaks to me of what I may or may not do, and of what are or are not good reasons for various kinds of action; and in that way it guides my intentions without speaking to me about them.'

We may doubt that morality speaks to us *only* regarding what to do.[16] Bennett himself allows that morality can speak to ends.[17] That seems both right and important. Yet morality surely also speaks about what to do. Indeed, that manner of speaking is a natural formulation for many moral norms ('do not φ'), from which obligations not to seek or choose to φ, and to take care not to φ, may be derived. Our intended actions are not the only way in which we relate to the world as moral agents. Advertent actions—even, I have argued, inadvertent actions—constitute ways in which we interact with the world. From the perspective of culpability, such actions are capable of reflecting badly upon us as moral agents. Morality, then, is not concerned merely with what to intend. It is concerned, *inter alia*, with what ends to seek *and* with how to behave in order to fulfil those ends. If there is no way of behaving so as to satisfy an end without incurring harmful side-effects, an agent may be required morally to abandon her pursuit of that end. Failure to give adequate weight to such side-effects can, in turn, be a ground of blame.[18]

The example of economic wrongs has force. But its force does not go to culpability *directly*. It does not go to the question about how an instance of wrongdoing can reflect badly upon the agent. Rather, it goes to the question whether D's action comprises wrongdoing in the first place. *That* is not a difference of degree. It is a structural difference.

16.2 Justification and the importance of motive

One feature of that difference is that it tracks distinctions in D's practical deliberation. It seems to me that something similar can be said of the

[16] So, in Raz's example (*Practical Reason and Norms*, 181–82), 'love of one's children is an appropriate motive for performing parental duties towards them. Those who conform with those duties, but for reasons other than love for their children, are at fault: they do not manifest the required moral attitudes which parents ought to possess and to be motivated by.'

[17] Bennett, *Tanner*, 99; *The Act Itself*, 215.

[18] Compare John Mackie's suggestion that 'The function of morality is primarily to counteract this limitation of men's sympathies': *Ethics*, 108. When our sympathies are limited, we tend to bring about bad consequences via side-effects in particular.

relationship between pro tanto wrongs and wrongdoing. Motivational distinctions—especially, distinctions between means, ends, and side-effects—are integrated with the availability of justifications. To explore this idea, let me start with some cases.

16.2.1 Four cases

Suppose that Nurse Charlie (NC) is in possession of a placebo and of a poison which induces considerable pain. The two drugs are indistinguishable to the eye and have in some way been mixed up in the medicine cabinet so that he cannot tell them apart. Charlie wishes to find out which one of the commixed drugs is which. Ordinarily it would be unjustified to ascertain the first drug's nature by trial and error. But conjecture also that his patient has a disease of the sort proposed by Shelly Kagan:[19]

> 'Imagine a disease which has no painful symptoms for an initial period, but which—if left untreated—eventually erupts, regularly causing the patient excruciating pain, with no chance of remission or treatment. Luckily the disease can be cured, if treated during the initial, dormant stage. Treatment, however, requires inflicting a significant amount of pain upon the unfortunate patient: causing pain to the patient's body stimulates it to release certain hormones and antibodies (which cannot be otherwise produced) that destroy the disease-causing virus.'

As with Bennett's Bombers, we may illustrate the difference with diagrams representing the chain of actual or possible actions contemplated by Charlie:

Experiment:
NC ———➢ Neutral End[20] [Ascertain Drug Identity]
|
Bad Side-effect [Pain] ———➢ Good Side-effect [Cure]

[19] S Kagan, *The Limits of Morality* (OUP 1989) 168. The example is credited to Parfit.

[20] Strictly speaking, this is a trivially good end rather than a neutral one. I treat it as neutral because, on the account of justifications to be defended here, Nurse Charlie's end is insignificant by comparison with the other actions her conduct constitutes; it is not what is doing the justificatory work. (John Gardner disagrees: I explore his account in § 16.5.) In case it be suspected that the trivial goodness of Charlie's end introduces an important asymmetry, we can replicate ascertainment of the drug identity as a neutral (or trivially good) side-effect in the other three cases set up in this section, without affecting the analysis.

By hypothesis, were the drug known to be a poison then it might justifiably be injected in order to bring about the patient's cure.[21] This would be a straightforward case of doing something bad as a means to a good end:[22]

Treatment:
NC ———➢ Bad Means [Pain] ———➢ Good End [Cure]

In *Experiment*, the promise of a cure makes the risk of causing pain to his patient a reasonable one to take. He knows that even if the drug he tests proves to be pain-inducing, there would be a good reason to use it on the patient. While we might disapprove of Charlie as a person, it seems that he can justify causing pain to the patient.[23] At the same time, however, I doubt that we would tolerate Charlie's action were he sadistically to inject the patient *in order* to bring pain about, knowing of but not wanting (perhaps even regretting) the beneficial consequences:

Sadistic:
NC ———➢ Bad End [Pain]
|
Good Side-effect [Cure]

Of course, the Sadistic Nurse does not cause pain as a means. In order to draw a closer analogy with *Treatment*, suppose this time that Nurse Charlie causes pain because of a bribe:

Bribery:
NC ——➢ Bad Means [Pain] ——➢ Neutral End [Money Receipt]
|
Good Side-effect [Cure]

[21] Kagan continues: 'Since the pain necessary for treatment, although significant, is far less than that caused by the disease itself, we may have good reason to deliberately induce pain in one who has recently contracted the disease.'

[22] One may query whether this case really does involve a bad means: there is an important sense in which the pain caused, however unpleasant, is not a harm but rather treatment, since it is just what the patient needs. If that's right, it might be better to use an example where a protected interest of the victim is more obviously invaded. My own feeling, though, is that a different example isn't needed. Nurse Charlie *does* inflict pain, and deliberately. It is hard to see how doing so stands other than in need of justification; or, were this not so, how we could condemn Charlie in the *Sadistic* and *Bribery* cases (to follow). The unusual feature of the case would be that in *Treatment*, causing pain is intended not as a means but as an instance of treatment (see § 15.3). Yet it is still intended.

[23] Admittedly, there remains a use-wrong, which Charlie commits by experimenting on the patient. My primary concern here is with his action of causing pain; but see the qualification in § 16.2.3.

Here is a central asymmetry. Though what happens in *Treatment* is morally acceptable, and although Charlie's actual conduct is the same for both cases, *Bribery* is not.

These examples illustrate some important moral differences between means, ends and side-effects. In what follows, I sketch those distinctions a little further before defending them.

16.2.2 Justifying ends: *Treatment* and *Sadistic*

Begin with *Treatment* and *Sadistic*. I assume that *Treatment* is a standard example of an intrinsically[24] bad means that is justified by the good end to which it leads. Such cases exist because we can say that where an agent's conduct constitutes both a bad action and a good action, and those actions stand respectively in a means-end relationship in the agent's motivation, doing the bad action may sometimes thereby be justified.[25] In effect, justification may be claimed for an intended action if the choice to do that action is motivated by the further action that justifies it.

From the perspective of traditional formulations of the doctrine of double effect, this conclusion is itself important. Compare *Treatment* with the following variant:

> *Medical-side-effect*: The patient has the same disease as in Shelly Kagan's example. There is only one known treatment. This time, however, the pain arises as an inevitable by-product of the treatment and plays no curative role. (Assume that the pain is significant but not of the order arising should the disease be left untreated.)

If *Medical-side-effect* is justified, and I think it is, it is hard to see why *Treatment* is not. Yet that is the very conclusion reached in classic double effect formulations:[26]

[24] The usage is conventional. Roughly speaking, I take it that doing an action is intrinsically good (neutral, bad) when its doing is good (neutral, bad) after discounting the instrumental value, whether good or bad, that the action has in virtue of its consequences.

[25] Sometimes. Justification is subject to various further constraints, including an appropriateness—non-exclusion—requirement (see §§ 18.1–3), as well as various proportionality constraints, notably that the end be sufficiently grave to warrant the means; that no sufficiently better alternative is available (cp. in Kagan's example, 'requires'); and that the side-effects are also proportionate.

[26] J Mangan, 'An Historical Analysis of the Principle of Double Effect' (1949) 10 *Theological Studies* 41, 43.

'A person may licitly perform an action that he knows will produce a good effect and a bad effect provided that four conditions are verified . . .

(1) That the action itself from its very object be good or at least indifferent;
(2) that the good effect and not the evil effect be intended;
(3) that the good effect be not produced *by means* of the evil effect;
(4) that there be a proportionally grave reason for permitting the evil effect.'

I take it to be a generic feature of double effect doctrines that it matters morally whether a bad action is done as a means or as a side-effect. The analysis in this chapter supports that proposition. It is compatible with various modern versions of double effect. However, it contradicts condition (3) of this classic formulation. Perhaps there are some actions that can never be justified when done as a means. At any rate, I argue in chapter 18 that a range of such actions cannot be justified by reference to necessity. But it goes too far to deny that one can ever do harm as a means. At least, it goes too far to deny that for the criminal law, and it seems to me that it goes too far to deny it for morality too. Like *Medical-side-effect*, *Treatment* is compatible with the agent's having virtuous desires and very much regretting the pain that he causes. Moreover, prohibiting the treatment in *Treatment* would deprive the patient altogether of a legitimate cure—a result that seems arbitrary and driven by nothing more than an accident of causal paths.

Significantly, though, the justification in *Treatment* derives from Nurse Charlie's *end*. Contrast *Sadistic*, where the two actions stand in an end/side-effect relationship. On the account presented here, the agent in *Sadistic* is not justified in doing the bad action merely by the fact that his conduct also involves a good action. Desiring a bad action is morally vicious: correspondingly, it seems morally unacceptable to do a bad action for its own sake, since to do so is to act motivated by such a desire. As Bennett puts it, there 'is moral significance in what an agent intends as an end'; in what he is motivated to seek by an intrinsic desire therefor. 'It would be a bad man who wanted civilian deaths for their own sakes.'[27] And it would be a bad thing for him to kill them for that reason.

An obvious lesson of the difference between *Treatment* and *Sadistic* is that the question, 'was it the right action?', cannot be answered by the simple enquiry, 'did it have the best consequences?' The limited potential for intended bad actions to be justified in these cases neatly disposes of that equation

[27] Bennett, *Tanner*, 99.

through an asymmetry, for while an end might sometimes justify a means or side-effect, no means or side-effect can justify an end. That asymmetry, in turn, explains why it was important to distinguish means from ends when analysing direct intention in § 15.1.

It is also worth noting that the distinctiveness of ends carries over into evaluations of moral credit or praise—for which neither means nor side-effects qualify. I do not warrant approval if my carelessness saves a life. Neither do I deserve (moral[28]) praise for saving your life if I did so only because my inheritance depended upon it, a contingency but for which I would have let you die.[29]

16.2.3 Means and side-effects: *Treatment, Bribery,* and *Experiment*

So there is moral asymmetry between ends, on the one hand, and means or side-effects on the other. Bad ends cannot be justified, and only good ends merit praise. Compare now *Treatment* and *Bribery*. In each instance the same good and bad actions are done. And if the agent's raw *conduct* is morally acceptable in *Treatment* then, qua conduct, it must be morally acceptable in *Bribery*. Yet *ceteris paribus* we think less of Nurse Charlie as a person in *Bribery* than we do in *Treatment*. His engagement with the reasons he has not to inject the patient is defective in a manner that reflects a moral vice on his part. Moreover, it seems to me that Charlie's *action* of inflicting pain for the sake of a bribe is unjustified. I defend this claim in § 16.3. If I am right about this, it suggests a restriction upon the generalization drawn above from *Treatment*. If it is ever morally acceptable to do an intended bad action, this ought to be the case only if, though not whenever, that action is done by the agent *because* it is a means to a further, good action. It should not assist such an agent that his conduct happens also to constitute some other good but unsought action. (We return to this restriction below.)

Treatment and Bribery turn on the justification of actions that are intended qua means. By contrast, *Experiment* raises the problem of justifying merely

[28] By 'moral praise', I mean praise of the kind that references moral virtue. Perhaps I warrant (non-moral) praise for the skills I display in saving you.

[29] Similarly, E D'Arcy, *Human Acts: An Essay in Their Moral Evaluation* (Clarendon 1963) 126: 'Suppose that A, who in his undergraduate days had belonged to some Fascist or Communist organization, which he has long since quit, is about to be appointed to high office; B happens to know of A's past association, but refrains from making it known, with the result that A is appointed. This may be to B's credit; but not if his reason was the prospect of blackmailing A once he was in office.' See also at 161–62, and at 166 for an example involving a morally neutral end.

advertent actions, actions that are done qua side-effects. The case involves two side-effects, one bad (pain) and one good (cure). Because of the accompanying cure, it seems to me that we should describe the bad side-effect as foreseen *yet not reckless*. It is not reckless because, in the circumstances, the risk of causing pain is a reasonable one to take.

At first glance, this might look a bit odd. Implicit in the discussion of *Sadistic* and *Bribery* is that one cannot always justify an action by appealing to the overall reasonableness of one's conduct and its effects. Unlike those two cases, however, in *Experiment* we are unavoidably in the realm of trade-offs. Again, this is not a difference in degrees of culpability. It is too much to ask of agents that they tailor ends-based justifications to every foreseen effect of their conduct. In this respect, recklessness has a family resemblance to negligence. As a general rule, one is justified in causing or risking an intrinsically bad side-effect *provided* it is reasonable in the foreseen [for negligence, foreseeable] circumstances to do so. When making that evaluation, the various means and other advertent side-effects, as well as ends, may all be relevant to the assessment. Whether it is reckless for D to behave in a given fashion, and thereby risk the [foreseen] side-effect at issue, thus depends *inter alia* upon the other [foreseen] actions that D's behaviour has the potential to constitute, whether good or bad, and whether or not intended by the defendant.[30] More on this, too, below.

My claim is a generalization. We have noted already the lesson of *Bribery* and *Sadistic*, that beneficial effects may be excluded from the justification of a bad means or end. The same can sometimes hold for the justification of a bad side-effect, especially in the context of lesser-evils necessity. Consider the following example, due to Victor Tadros:[31]

> *Lever*: A trolley is heading down a track toward five people who will be killed if nothing is done. V is standing on a side track. By the side of the track there is a jammed lever. Shifting the lever will turn the trolley away from the five to the track on which V stands. D can shift the lever only by toppling V onto it. Toppling V onto the lever will not directly harm V. However, the trolley will kill V if this is done.

[30] A parenthetical extension. For negligence, we can substitute [reasonably foreseeable] for [foreseen] into a parallel account. Analogous to the intention/foresight distinction argued for here, one should not be able to invoke an *unforeseen* benefit of one's conduct to render an otherwise reckless, advertent action reasonable. By contrast, the assessment of negligence for an unforeseen but reasonably foreseeable side-effect may take into account any reasonably foreseeable benefits of D's action, even if those benefits were unforeseen by D. Luck is no less intrinsic to wrongdoing in negligence than it is to the rest of the law.

[31] 'Wrongful Intentions without Closeness' (2015) 43 Phil and Pub Aff 52, 61.

V's death is a side-effect, yet Tadros thinks V's killing is 'clearly wrong'. That seems correct. I argue in chapter 18 that certain wrongs, including killings, cannot be justified by appeal to necessity when done as a means. Tadros's example suggests that the exclusions defended in chapter 18 extend beyond that. In particular, they extend to cases in which those wrongs are done as side-effects of another necessitous wrong to the victim. But such cases are exceptional, and they are specific to claims of lesser-evils necessity.[32] I set them aside here.

16.2.4 A preliminary summary

Let us briefly summarize. An upshot of the foregoing sketch, and one that explains the case *exempla*, is a structural asymmetry between intention and foresight. The central moral distinction between intended actions and those merely foreseen is not simply a matter of degree, but rather that the foreseen do not lend any favourable weight to the justification of the intended. They can lend favourable moral weight only to offset other, bad side-effects (as, for instance, in *Experiment*). By contrast, *Treatment* and *Medical-side-effect* illustrate that good *ends* may sometimes be invoked to justify an intrinsically bad means or side-effect.

Flipping the matter around, our examples suggest that the key difference between *means* and *side-effects* is that (as with ends) one cannot justify a bad means by appeal to good side-effects; whereas one can generally make such an appeal in order to help to justify a bad side-effect. A bad means can only be justified by reference to its ends.

16.3 Defending the asymmetry

More remains to be said. If the facts are such that some intended pro tanto wrong is, as one might say, *justifiable* as a means to another albeit unintended consequence, why hold it unjustified?[33] Here is a pivotal case for morality and

[32] No such exclusion applies to Nurse Charlie's actions in *Experiment*, in part because a justification of best-interests medical treatment is in principle available. Curing the patient is not an excluded reason to cause pain.

[33] 'Justifiable' is somewhat closer in spirit to what T M Scanlon calls 'permissible': *Moral Dimensions: Permissibility, Meaning, Blame* (Harvard UP 2008). As I argue in this and the next two chapters, the criminal law should ask whether D's action is justified. (Even granting this distinction, however, chapter 18 explores intention-based restrictions on necessity that are incompatible with Scanlon's account.)

law. On the analysis sketched above, the defendant is culpable for perpetrating the wrong, and may not justify her doing so by reference to that other, unintended consequence. In effect, being intended knocks out of consideration, rather than outweighs, the good side-effects.

That need not be so when D causes harm (φs) as a foreseen side-effect. As we have noted already, to proscribe advertent harming outright would be intolerable—paralysing—because we cannot always avoid affecting the interests of others and because the side-effects of our actions are so often incalculable. Hence, we generally take the foreseen side-effects as a package deal, and refrain from holding D a wrongdoer in such cases unless she φs recklessly; unless her choice to φ is unreasonable. In order for D's φing to count as reckless, it must be the case that, on the facts as D understands them, the prospect of φing supplies decisive reasons why D should not behave as she does. Those reasons are generally not contingent upon D's own intentions. They are guiding rather than explanatory.[34] By the same token, however, in order to count as decisive those guiding reasons must help to defeat any guiding reasons weighing in favour of D's behaviour, including any (unexcluded) guiding reasons supplied by its other foreseen effects. Thus, in *Experiment*, Nurse Charlie's causing pain can be justified, albeit he did not intend the cure that makes it such. He has not inflicted pain recklessly, even though his own (explanatory) reason for doing so was an inadequate warrant. Subject to the qualification noted in § 16.2.3, ordinarily it is morally acceptable to choose to incur a risk that, on the facts as the agent understands them,[35] it is reasonable to run.

Things are otherwise when another defendant, E, intends the pro tanto wrong (φing), in as much as we are looking at the justification of her action more narrowly, not as part of an overall risk-management exercise. The problem case arises when the question, did E act wrongfully, is asked in a situation where φing would have been a justifiable way for her to achieve some further end, but where she did not φ for the sake of that end. It seems to me that we *should* regard E's φing as an instance of wrongdoing in such a case, and that we may validly blame E *for φing*. Her choice to φ reflects a moral vice on her part.[36] Moreover, provided φing is a pro tanto offence, the law ought to convict her.

[34] Raz's terminology: *Practical Reason and Norms*, 16–20.

[35] The proviso operates in two directions. If Nurse Charlie were unaware of the drug's curative power, his experiment would be unjustified. Conversely, an agent's choice may be reasonable in terms of the perceived risks—not reckless—yet negligent. My concern here is with choice-based culpability. See § 11.3ff.

[36] I claim it as a strength of the argument made here that it coheres with the accounts of culpability and moral luck articulated in chapters 11 and 14.

As English law currently does. In *Thain*,[37] T shot and killed someone escaping from an army foot-patrol, in circumstances where (arguably) he was permitted to do so qua lawful arrest. Although he was apparently aware of those circumstances, T admitted that he was not seeking to arrest the victim, and consequently was convicted of murder. Analogously, in *Dadson*,[38] a policeman shot and wounded a thief. The thief was, unbeknown to the defendant, a felon, and the policeman would have been justified in shooting to prevent the escape of a felon. The policeman was convicted of unlawful wounding. Rightly so. *Dadson* differs from *Thain* in that the justificatory factor went unrecognized by the defendant.[39] The cases are alike, however, in as much as both defendants meet the criteria of culpability defended in chapter 11. Both chose to cause harm in a manner that reflected badly upon them by disclosing a moral vice. In law, like morality, justifications are not of conduct at large, but of conduct *under a description*: the actus reus when done with mens rea. It is only when the scope of a proscription is restricted by a qualifier such as 'recklessly' that we consider the reasonableness of D's conduct with reference to other, unintended actions. Otherwise, there seems no reason to do so.

The same, it may be added, goes for some other areas of law. US constitutional law requires government legislation and other actions limiting fundamental rights to survive 'strict scrutiny'. According to that standard, the legislation must be necessary and proportionate to achieving an essential government purpose; *and* that purpose must be the reason for which the government acted. Other legislation need only have a 'rational basis', being rationally related to a conceivable legitimate governmental purpose, regardless whether that was the actual purpose of the legislation.[40] We can make a similar argument for international law. The 2003 invasion of Iraq, purportedly to implement UN Security Council Resolutions 678 and 1441, should not be accounted justified by reference to the ancillary humanitarian benefits that were said to have followed, but which did not explain why Australia and the United Kingdom invaded.[41]

The denial of blame in *Sadistic* and *Bribery* rests, if anywhere, upon the truth that Nurse Charlie's action of inflicting pain is justifi*able* as a means to cure his patient: hence, one may say, it is not (in this context) a bad thing to do. We

[37] [1985] NI 457. See the discussion by G R Sullivan, 'Bad Thoughts and Bad Acts' [1990] Crim LR 558.

[38] (1850) 2 Den 35, 169 ER 407.

[39] Only *Dadson* would be good law under the Model Penal Code (§§ 3.02–3.07), which requires merely that the defendant believes the justifying circumstances exist. On that test, the defendant in *Thain* would be allowed to claim lawful arrest.

[40] *Federal Communications Commission v Beach Communication* 113 S Ct 2096 (1993).

[41] For application of the present arguments in that context, see R Cryer and A P Simester, 'Iraq and the Use of Force: Do the Side-Effects Justify the Means?' (2005) 7 Theoretical Inquiries in Law 9.

should make no mistake, however: it remains, in itself, a bad thing to do. This is why, *ceteris paribus*, it is morally and may be legally proscribed. No doubt it is not proscribed absolutely (compare *Experiment* and *Treatment*). However, since it is a pro tanto wrong, both the law and morality have grounds to restrict the basis upon which it is allowed. And the restriction ought to be: unless Charlie's choice to do it was made for good reasons.

We look further at the justification of intended pro tanto wrongs in chapters 17 and 18. There, it is argued that the best interpretation of situations where a justificatory defence operates is that the circumstances underlying the justification partially liberate the defendant from her legal (and moral) duty not to commit the pro tanto offence.[42] But they only do so *in virtue of* the pro tanto wrong's being a means to the justificatory end. The guiding role of reasons is not served by granting that liberty to *Sadistic* alongside *Treatment*. Given that inflicting unwanted pain on another is intrinsically bad, the licence ought not to be extended beyond that which is necessary. We should not allow a defendant hypocritically to avail herself of a convenient outcome by which she was not motivated. And the overall reasonableness of her conduct should absolve neither a repugnant intention nor the action it spawns.

16.4 Robinson's 'deeds' theory

Famously, Paul Robinson opposes the rule in *Dadson*.[43] For Robinson, what counts for justification should be the *existence* of undefeated guiding reasons favouring D's action, not whether D acted for those reasons or was even aware of them. In effect, this is to make D's lack of justification part of the actus reus of each offence. A defendant who deliberately kills another when 'unknowingly justified' should, instead of murder, therefore be convicted of *attempted* murder. She has tried, and failed, to do what was prohibited.

A number of jurisdictions are aligned with that view. In Sweden, for example, the criminal law is not structured in terms of the actus reus/mens rea division, but by reference to a division between the 'unlawful' (prohibited) act and personal culpability elements. The main difference this makes is to bring the absence of justification within the parameters of the proscribed wrong. In

[42] See § 17.6. In particular, defences like self-defence and necessity do not cancel the defendant's criminal-law duties. Rather, they acknowledge exceptions to them or allow them to be overridden.

[43] P H Robinson, 'Competing Theories of Justification: Deeds vs. Reasons' in *Harm and Culpability* 45; a follow-up to P H Robinson, 'A Theory of Justification: Societal Harm as a Prerequisite to Criminal Liability' (1975) 23 UCLA LR 266.

common with cases where D shoots at D but misses, justificatory moral luck is thereby remaindered to the realm of attempts.

This approach doesn't seem to be incoherent. Is it better? Unfortunately, Robinson's own defence of his 'deeds' theory is prejudiced by the fact that he considers its only serious rival to be a 'reasons'-based account of justification: according to which D is considered justified whenever, on the facts as she believed them to be, a justification would be available. But that is not a plausible account of justification. Admittedly, the law sometimes allows defences to be claimed on the basis of D's erroneous beliefs about the facts: more on that in chapter 19. Yet when it does so, it extends the relevant legal defence beyond its justificatory paradigm. The defence in such cases rests on the *mistake*, not on the purported justification to which the mistake relates. Morally speaking, D's explanation for choosing to do the actus reus is excusatory.[44]

The more serious opponents for Robinson are what he terms 'dual requirement' theories, according to which D must have *both* guiding and explanatory reasons in her favour. What is offered in this chapter is a dual requirement theory. For Robinson, however, a dual requirement theory exhibits the same flaw as the reasons theory:[45]

> '[It] denies the significance of the analogy between the unknowingly justified actor and the impossible attempter. That is, by denying a defence to the unknowingly justified actor, it treats him as indistinguishable from the actor with a similar culpable state of mind who is not objectively justified. This view understandably appeals to those theorists who oppose giving significance to resulting harm, but it seems clear that this view does not reflect our shared intuitions in assessing blameworthiness nor does it reflect current law's treatment of resulting harm. Every known criminal law system gives significance in grading to whether a resulting harm or evil occurs. There is no apparent reason why the significance of resulting harm or evil should be denied in the context of the unknowingly justified actor.'

This objection needs a clarification. By 'resulting harm', Robinson means *net* harm in a consequentialist sense. Robinson's thought is that, if D kills V in otherwise-justifiable-but-unknown self-defence, there is no net harm: no harm of the kind that the criminal law should be concerned to prohibit. Like

[44] If that. Sometimes, it is no more than mitigation or partial excuse, especially if the mistake is unreasonable. See, further, § 19.3–4.

[45] Robinson, 'Competing Theories of Justification' (n 43) 68–69.

Sweden, what the law should be criminalizing is *unjustified* killings. Seen in those terms, the unknowingly justified actor merely attempts to do a proscribed wrong. Hence Robinson challenges dual requirement theories with the question: 'Is the absence of a net harm significant or not?'[46]

Pretty obviously, the view taken here is that things are not so simple. What is significant, to put it in Robinson's terms, is the absence of resulting harm per se—intrinsic, not net.[47] That harm *does* occur. V is dead, and a conviction acknowledges it. D did not merely attempt to kill: she succeeded. Robinson's claim that a deeds-based approach better discharges the law's communicative function is undermined here, in as much as it is misleading to convict an unknowingly justified killer of 'attempted murder'.[48] That one has a supervening defence does not mean that the pro tanto wrong involved a different harm than usual. Suppose that David seriously injures Victor in (justified) self-defence. David may not wrong Victor.[49] Perhaps Robinson is right to deny there is any net harm. But David most definitely harms Victor. Indeed, there is precisely the kind of harm that crimes of causing grievous bodily harm address.[50]

Admittedly, in David's case the availability of self-defence offsets the guidance that is otherwise offered by such crimes. David is entitled to take account of the fact that his act is legally permitted.[51] But the same does not apply to *Dadson*. Even were we to accept Robinson's thought that there is no 'net' harm in such cases, the law's guiding function cannot engage with that fact. Given his ignorance of the justificatory circumstances, D ought to choose *not* to behave as he does. Robinson's argument here echoes that of Thomas Macaulay, more than a century earlier:[52]

> 'When an act is of such a description that it would be better that it should not be done, it is quite proper to look at the motives and intentions of the doer, for the purpose of deciding whether he shall be punished or not. But when

[46] Ibid, 68.

[47] Moreover, comparing harms to decide whether there is an overall 'net' harm risks buying into a bad theory of necessity: below, § 18.2.

[48] A point made in § 14.3, in the context of moral luck. There are other difficulties with the communication argument. Robinson argues that the reasons theory fails to distinguish between verdicts predicated on true moral justification and those founded on excuse, citing the fallout from the notorious trial of police officers filmed beating Rodney King ('Competing Theories of Justification', 64–67). However, common-law verdicts do not differentiate between justifications and excuses; neither is that distinction tracked by recognized legal defences. Hence, even if it be acknowledged that 'mistaken justification' is a mere excuse, acquittals would in principle remain ambiguous.

[49] See §§ 17.6, 18.3–18.3.1.

[50] See, e.g., Offences Against the Person Act 1861 (UK), ss 18, 20.

[51] See § 17.4.

[52] *A Penal Code Prepared by the Indian Law Commissioners* (1837) 100. Cp. G Williams, 'Offences and Defences' (1982) 2 Legal Studies 233, 250.

an act which is really useful to society, an act of a sort which it is desirable to encourage, has been done, it is absurd to inquire into the motives of the doer for the purpose of punishing him if it shall appear that his motives were bad.'

Macaulay argues that the conduct of such a defendant is to be encouraged because it is useful to society. But it does not seem 'useful' to society that X should murder Y rather than Y murder X a few moments later, and it is certainly not clear that conduct of the type in *Dadson* is to be encouraged. The only way of doing so is by encouraging the commission of pro tanto offences in the hope that they might fortuitously be defensible; but to do *that* is to subvert a central function of the criminal law, which is to *dis*courage pro tanto offences that do not fortuitously prove defensible.

Neither does an appeal to the position of bystanders help. In claiming that the deeds theory better tracks relevant moral and legal distinctions, Robinson observes that it is guiding reasons that tell us whether a third party can intervene or not, and on whose side.[53] In order to know the answers to those questions, we have to know the actual facts. That's true, and it helps to dispose of the reasons theory as a theory of justification. It shows that guiding reasons count. But it doesn't show that they count *exclusively*. In particular, a dual requirement theory would expect the third party *also* to know the relevant facts and be motivated by them. It is no accident that references to third-party interveners in order to diagnose the justification/excuse distinction typically assume that the third party has full information.[54]

The problem is revealed by Robinson's own example.[55] If D goes to shoot V, who (unknown to D) is about to shoot D, Robinson claims that T, a bystander, should not intervene to resist D because D is in fact justified. But why is it better that D should shoot V than that V should shoot D? On Robinson's analysis, the law merely rewards with a justification the person who shoots and kills the other first. The better view is that neither is justified.

16.5 Gardner's dual requirement theory

Not all dual requirement theories are alike. For John Gardner, it is crucial in *Experiment* that what I call a 'neutral' end is actually a good end, albeit trivially

[53] Robinson, 'Competing Theories of Justification' (n 43) 51ff and 59ff.
[54] See § 17.3.2.
[55] Robinson, 'Competing Theories of Justification' (n 43) 59–60.

good.[56] This is because, in Gardner's account, justification requires that the agent acts upon an undefeated reason. 'No action or belief is justified,' he says, 'unless it is true *both* that there was an applicable (guiding) reason for so acting or so believing *and* that this corresponded with the (explanatory) reason why the action was performed or the belief held.'[57] At first glance, this looks like a fairly straightforward defence of the requirements in *Dadson* and *Thain*. Justificatory reasons are available only if they both actually ('objectively') apply and they are ('subjectively') one's reason for action. Thus, according to Gardner, 'one justifies one's own arms dealing by pointing to the arms dealing of others thereby avoided only if one deals in arms *in order to* avoid arms dealing by others.' 'Justifying one's wrongs,' he continues, 'isn't cancelling them; it is showing that one committed them for a sufficient reason, that one was not unreasonable in committing them.'[58]

However, a closer inspection of Gardner's logic undermines this way of presenting the matter. When we come to the detailed account, it turns out that one's reason need not itself be 'sufficient':[59]

> 'For it is a basic principle of practical rationality, which is at the root of the whole pros/cons asymmetry, that one should always act for *some* undefeated reason, i.e. that at least one of the (guiding) reasons in favour of doing as one did should have been one's (explanatory) reason for doing it.'

This isn't the same as saying that one justifies arms dealing 'only' if one acts in order to avoid arms dealing by others. There is nothing here to require that one act for the very reason that does the work in justifying one's action; that is, for *sufficient* reason. One need only act for an *undefeated* reason:[60]

> 'And the principle that we should always act for some undefeated reason is a principle which identifies what we should be looking for, in the way of motivation, if we are to maximize our prospects of acting as reason demands. We should look for an undefeated reason to act as we do. There is no point in going further and looking for *all* the undefeated reasons to act in that way. That would be ridiculous overkill. The very fact that the reason for which one

[56] Above, § 16.2.1; Gardner, *Offences and Defences*, 103 n 22.
[57] Gardner, *Offences and Defences*, 94.
[58] Ibid, 73 (emphasis in original); see, too, at 149. For (partial) disagreement with the claim that justifications do not cancel wrongs, see § 18.3.1.
[59] Gardner, *Offences and Defences*, 100 (emphasis added).
[60] Ibid, 101 (emphasis in original).

acts is undefeated is enough by itself to guarantee that, all things considered, it is on the winning side in the whole overarching conflict of reasons. Thus the basic principle of rationality which I cited, although modest, is as strong a principle as we need to ensure that our explanatory reasons for action reliably push us towards an action that ought, all things considered, to be performed.'

Provided they aren't cancelled or excluded, it doesn't matter which of the guiding reasons favouring a justified action motivates the agent. So long as it is one of them. As it is in *Experiment*.

Gardner derives support for his analysis from its inherent plausibility, especially from how it coheres with his account of practical reasoning. It may be helpful to think about Gardner's approach in the following way. Having started with the wrong, he then looks at the (guiding) reasons in favour of doing that wrong. If those reasons are defeated, the wrong is unjustified. If they are undefeated, the wrong is in principle justifi*able*. It then becomes justified if, and only if, the wrongdoer subjectively acts for one of those undefeated reasons.

The account in this chapter adopts a different approach. It looks first at the wrongdoer's *actual* practical reasoning, at the (explanatory) reasons why she acted, and then asks whether those reasons were objectively sufficient. Doing so has the advantage of focusing attention on the structure of the actor's reasoning. It emphasizes the differences between means, ends, and side-effects, foreseen and unforeseen. If those distinctions matter to justification,[61] the question whether undefeated reasons existed *in abstracto* for one's act or wrongdoing becomes a less obvious starting point.

Perhaps there is no deeper principle of rationality to resolve disagreements of this sort. But here are some intuitive moral considerations. Suppose there are two unexcluded reasons in favour of φing, R1 and R2. R1 is necessary and sufficient; R2 is neither. On Gardner's analysis, there is no reason why one need even be *aware* of R1, let alone act for it. Since R2 is undefeated, one is justified even when acting on R2 alone.

Let me elaborate. A reason for φing can be defeated in various ways, two of which matter here. It may be applicable but on balance *outweighed*, or it may be inapplicable because *excluded* from consideration. To illustrate the difference, suppose that Jim attacks me with potentially lethal force and I respond by shooting him. In so doing, I preserve my own life and, incidentally, stand to inherit a considerable fortune under Jim's will. Here, I have only one undefeated

[61] And not everyone thinks they do: cf. D Enoch, 'Intending, Foreseeing, and the State' (2007) 13 Legal Theory 69, 73ff.

reason to shoot Jim: self-defence. This reason is both undefeated and sufficient. The other reason, by contrast, is excluded. It cannot help to justify my shooting Jim.[62]

In the situation I have set up, however, R2 is not excluded. It is just minor. In this case, both reasons are undefeated.[63] This is so even though it is R1 that does all the work; indeed, if R1 did not exist, R2 would be outweighed. Here, then, R2 is an undefeated but insufficient reason to φ. Yet in Gardner's account, one is justified when acting on it.

Imagine, for example, that V attacks D, intending to push D aside and to kill E, who is standing behind D. Unaware of the threat to E,[64] D responds with lethal force, force that would be excessive against the threat to D by itself. Gardner's account would hold D justified.[65] Yet, if we allow justification in this case, why not go the whole hog and agree with Robinson? So far as the culpability of the actor is concerned, the difference between this case and one such as *Dadson* looks arbitrary. It seems to me that D's action here is a wrongful one, and that the law should convict her for it. We have no grounds for departing from Gardner's own stipulation that the justification of intentional action operates as a species of exculpatory *explanation*. If an incidental outcome does not explain why D sought to inflict harm, then it cannot justify her doing so. One must act for the reasons that do the work.

The denial of culpable wrongdoing rests, in D's case, upon the fact that E's life was saved; hence, again, D's response was justifi*able*. Yet, for D, that was a fluke. Moreover, killing V remains, in itself, harmful and undesirable: for Gardner, it is a basic wrong. We have acknowledged that self-defence partially liberates D from her pro tanto duty not to commit such wrongs. But, as I argued in § 16.3, it does so only in virtue of the pro tanto wrong's being a *means* to the justificatory end. An extension to cover side-effects, as here, would be gratuitous. We should not allow D to avail herself of a convenient defence by which she was not motivated. Once again, in terms of the account of culpability given in chapter 11, D's action discloses a moral vice; her engagement with the reasons for and against that action reflects badly upon her. Moreover, as I suggested earlier, it seems desirable to convict persons who deliberately perpetrate an

[62] Raz, *Practical Reason and Norms* § 1.2.

[63] As Gardner notes, wherever the unexcluded reasons for φing outweigh the reasons against, all of them are undefeated: *Offences and Defences*, 102.

[64] Or even, on the account in this chapter, 'aware of but uninterested in the threat to E.'

[65] I assume that self-defence here is a by-itself-outweighed but not excluded reason to use force against V. The degree of force in the example could easily be varied to accommodate disagreement on that issue.

actus reus without doing so for sufficient cause. Their choices to act stem from deficiencies of practical reasoning for which they may properly be faulted.

Consider, too, an obverse case, where I take a reasonable risk of causing harm. This time, Gardner seems too harsh. He requires that my actual reason for acting as I do be undefeated; whereas, it may be thought, what counts is whether the risk was a reasonable one.

To illustrate, let's vary *Bribery*. Suppose that D, a doctor, is bribed by T to administer a drug to D's patient, P. T's motivations are unknown. The drug is appropriate and recommended treatment for P's condition, but in these cash-strapped days there is a shortage and P might not otherwise receive it. Like *Medical-side-effect*, this treatment will cause P a great deal of pain in the course of curing P's condition. D does not care about her patient's need, but wants the money so administers it to P. In Gardner's account, everything turns on whether the bribe is a good reason to administer the drug (and it isn't, because excluded); as opposed to the appropriateness of the drug, the suitability of the treatment, and D's knowledge of that appropriateness. So, in Gardner's account, D's action of inducing pain is unjustified because D failed to act for an undefeated reason. Yet it seems to me that the true wrong in this case is taking the bribe.

The point here is that, in terms of D's practical reasoning, inducing pain is a side-effect. Where this is so, what counts is whether the (foreseen) reasons for or against that action are undefeated. We noted in § 16.3 that the existence of those reasons need not be contingent upon the agent's own intentions. As such, even when foreseen benefits are unsought, they can supply reasons why her incidental choices are reasonable or unreasonable. It is impracticable to expect one's actions never to have side-effects; in general, it is enough that incurring those side-effects be reasonable. All of which helps to explain why the mens rea standard of recklessness, unlike intention, contains an embedded normative element.

In both of these cases, Gardner's account places undue weight on whether the explanatory reason for which D acts is undefeated. Consequently, too much turns on whether that reason is excluded (the first case would be straightforward, for example, had D killed V for V's money). This diverts the emphasis from the reasons doing the heavy lifting. Because he doesn't distinguish acting for sufficient reasons from having sufficient reasons and acting for one of them, Gardner makes justification turn only partially on the actor's actual, practical reasoning. Yet, if that reasoning is significant at all, we should take its structure more seriously.

16.6 Legal implications

For the criminal law, two main implications arise from the bifurcated view of justification presented here. The first is that defences which seek to justify directly-intended φing (a pro tanto offence) should require that there be a nexus between the facts giving rise to the defence and the agent's choosing to φ, such that the justification actually lies in the ends toward which the agent sought to φ as means.[66] Both *Thain* and *Dadson* were correctly decided. The second is that the law ought to distinguish intention from advertence, in order that a general requirement of 'unreasonableness' may apply to the latter.[67]

Admittedly, the law may have evidential grounds for adopting the position in the Model Penal Code and endorsing *Dadson* but not *Thain*. There are instrumental reasons for acquitting where the justificatory side-effect is foreseen, given the desirability of simplifying the elements required to prove an offence. However, those gains do not appear to be substantial, and it is not clear that they provide sufficient reason to acquit a defendant in cases like *Thain*.

The analysis in this chapter also offers some support for the common law's default rule that recklessness is sufficient mens rea for serious crimes. If φing as a means is not intrinsically more culpable than φing as a foreseen side-effect, we have reason for thinking that advertence to an unreasonable risk of φing ought generally to suffice for criminal culpability.

This is not to suggest that the definition of, say, murder should be realigned to include lethal acts done with foresight of the possibility of death.[68] Terms such as 'murder' are not transparent. When the law states, 'do not murder', people should be entitled to assume that by this it means, do not murder. Ordinary language here respects a different distinction. Murder and manslaughter are both actions that are wrong, but they are different actions and different wrongs—and the difference owes itself to the killer's intentions. Murder is a distinctive, and particularly serious, kind of killing, marked by the fact that the killer does so by means of an intentional infliction of serious violence. Hence, for example, the causing of death through deliberately dangerous driving is not regarded as murder. *This* is why reckless killing is not murder; not because recklessness is systematically less culpable than intention.

[66] The same applies to cases of inseparability, discussed in § 15.3; but not to ordinary cases of oblique intent.

[67] For some further reasons why a general defence of 'reasonableness' should be denied to intended actions, see also § 2.1.1 and, more generally, chapter 18.

[68] Favoured by some of the judges in *Hyam* [1975] AC 55; above, § 15.1, 15.2.

17

Distinguishing Defences (from Offences, and from Each Other)

Substantively and evidentially, the criminal law draws a distinction between offences and defences.[1] If a person satisfies the specified actus reus and mens rea elements of an offence, prima facie she commits the offence. None the less, there is no crime if she has a supervening defence: that is, a defence which denies neither actus reus nor mens rea but, rather, seeks to avoid liability by reference to accompanying considerations not contemplated in the offence definition. A person commits no assault, for example, when she uses reasonable force to protect herself against her attacker. She may commit the pro tanto offence, but criminal liability does not follow.[2]

That legal distinction, between offence and defence, often tracks a corresponding moral distinction. Suppose that D has a duty not to φ. If D φs, she commits a pro tanto wrong. Yet, even if she φs intentionally, it may not follow that D is culpable for φing. Additional factors can preclude that conclusion.

Not always. Within the criminal law, certain supervening defences have no implications for an agent's culpability. Claims of statutory limitation or diplomatic immunity,[3] for example, oust the defendant from the realm of the pertinent court, without further moral evaluation. Defences of that sort are procedural rather than substantive. But the mainstream, substantive criminal defences are not like that. They speak, rather, to grounds for withholding blame from a defendant who φs. This chapter begins our exploration of how they do so.

[1] See § 2.1ff.

[2] Admittedly, there is a line of authority in the common law to the effect that she does not even commit a pro tanto offence, purportedly on the grounds that the actus reus of assault requires 'unlawful' force. For criticism of that approach, see §§ 19.2–3.

[3] On 'non-exculpatory' defences, see, e.g., P H Robinson, *Structure and Function in Criminal Law* (OUP 1997) 71ff. Many such 'defences' operate as procedural bars to trial rather than as defences in their own right: see, e.g., A Ashworth, 'Testing Fidelity to Legal Values: Official Involvement and Criminal Justice' in S C Shute and A P Simester (eds), *Criminal Law Theory: Doctrines of the General Part* (OUP 2002) 299.

Fundamentals of Criminal Law. A P Simester, Oxford University Press (2021). © A P Simester.
DOI: 10.1093/oso/9780198853145.003.0017

17.1 A taxonomy

The substantive defences are united by the culpability principle. They all play a role in preventing convictions of blameless defendants who satisfy the actus reus and mens rea of a crime. Like the rest of the general part, however, that need not be their exclusive concern. The availability of a justificatory defence, for example, typically also has criminalization implications.[4] By recognizing self-defence, the state enhances the freedom of persons who find themselves under attack. And when articulating the boundaries of that defence, the state makes normative trade-offs between the duties, liberties, *et cetera*, of participants in a dangerous situation. Does it matter that one's self-defensive action takes place in one's own home?[5] Or consider the 'defence of property' defence. Can one shoot the thief who is stealing one's apple,[6] or a log of wood?[7] Debates about these matters are not merely debates about culpability. They are debates about the kind of society we want to live in.

Moreover, even when debates about criminal-law defences *are* framed in terms of the culpability, the relationship is not always direct. Traditionally, theorists have acknowledged this by dividing the substantive defences into two categories: justifications and excuses. That division is helpful, in as much as excuses directly engage findings of culpability whereas justifications are primarily concerned with wrongdoing. But it is also misleading. There is another class of defences that deny culpability indirectly—those that deny moral responsibility. The dichotomy should be a *tri*chotomy:

(1) Irresponsibility defences (which deny moral responsibility;[8]
(2) Justifications (which deny wrongdoing); and
(3) Excuses (which deny culpability for wrongdoing).

Some defences, that is to say, deny culpability by denying moral responsibility. Others admit moral responsibility but deny wrongdoing. Still others admit wrongdoing yet deny culpability. This makes the category of excuses residual. And somewhat hodge-podge. For practical purposes in what follows, we can subdivide the excuses into three subcategories:

[4] Cp. the guiding role of justifications, noted in § 17.4.
[5] See, e.g., Criminal Justice and Immigration Act (UK), s 76; *Simester and Sullivan*, § 21.2(iv)(a).
[6] Cp. Judgment of the Supreme Court, September 20, 1920, 55 RGSt 82: yes.
[7] Cf. *Dadson* (1850) 4 Cox CC 358: no.
[8] Such as insanity and infancy. On the question whether irresponsibility 'defences' are properly so-called, see §§ 17.5–6.

(3a) Rationale-based excuses;[9]
(3b) Hybrid and partial irresponsibility defences; and
(3c) Defensive mistakes.

Hybrids and mistakes will be considered in chapter 19. With respect to excuses, the focus in this chapter is on rationale-based excuses. The chapter will pursue two main inquiries. First, what are the basic similarities and differences between justifications, excuses, and irresponsibility defences? Secondly, in light of that, what makes them substantive *defences*? What underlying moral distinction, in other words, does the offence-defence partition reflect?

17.1.1 Do we need a trichotomy?

A preliminary question. I do not claim that the division between irresponsibility, justification, and excuse always has legal significance. With the exception of insanity-based verdicts, the availability of a defence normally leads to an undifferentiated acquittal. That convergence of outcomes allows the legal definitions of defences such as self-defence and duress to overlap and, indeed, cut across the underlying moral categories of justification and excuse. This presents no difficulty for the criminal law because those defences need not be exclusive. But it does raise a question: why distinguish between them?

Doubts of this sort have been expressed before. For Chris Clarkson, there is no fundamental difference between the justificatory and excusatory defences known to criminal law. He argues in favour of collapsing traditional distinctions and absorbing them within a single defence of *necessary action*:[10]

> 'A new defence of necessary action would have the advantage of simplicity and, most importantly, would enable the focus to be on the true issue that unites the present defences: whether, given the pressure/crisis, etc., facing the defendant, the response, taking into account the context and all the circumstances, was a reasonable and proportionate reaction to that danger.'

Clarkson rightly points out that defences such as self-defence, duress,[11] and lesser-evils necessity share key elements. Each requires that the defendant's

[9] Paradigmatically duress, but arguably also entrapment and provocation (see §§ 19–19.1).

[10] C Clarkson, 'Necessary Action: A New Defence' [2004] Crim LR 81, 95. Compare too L Alexander, 'A Unified Excuse of Preemptive Self-protection' (1999) 74 Notre Dame LR 1475.

[11] Formally, English common law distinguishes between 'duress by threats' and 'duress of circumstances': see *Simester and Sullivan*, § 20.1. Both varieties have essentially the same criteria, and

response be evaluated relative to the circumstances. Thus it will not do to shoot the person who threatens to spit on me. My doing so is unreasonable in virtue of being disproportionate, and the same would be true were I to shoot an innocent third party because someone else had threatened otherwise to spit on me. Of course, the traditional defences also contain differences. For Clarkson, however, those doctrinal distinctions are mere accidents of history; they lack a normative rationale. If he is right about this, a unified defence may indeed be possible. But is Clarkson right?

No. One might take the easy road here and point to irresponsibility defences, which we discuss in § 17.5. Those are certainly distinctive, but they were not Clarkson's concern. His challenge should be understood as a challenge primarily to the distinction between (2) and (3a); one that perhaps extends to (3b) and (3c). And there is force in the challenge. It will be argued below that, compared to the irresponsibility defences, justifications and rationale-based excuses are in many ways fundamentally similar. Some writers claim that justifications are 'about the act' and excuses 'about the actor'.[12] But, at least in the context of rationale-based excuses, that's wrong. Each is about both. *Irresponsibility* defences are about the actor. By contrast, rationale-based excuses and justifications are similarly personal, and impersonal, to the defendant. *Both* are rationale-based. Both subject the defendant's reasons for acting to objective evaluations, and this is a key part of what distinguishes them from other kinds of defences.

None the less, despite what they have in common, they are also fundamentally *dis*similar. The difference between them tracks a categorical moral distinction concerning the normative status of an agent's conduct—whether it is wrongful; and in that much, justification has priority over excuse. In practice, the main driver of that distinction is whether the agent's reason for acting was, or was not, what Raz calls 'excluded'.[13] If not excluded, a justification may well lie. Yet, whether or not excluded, *it may ground a rationale-based excuse*. Excuses acknowledge this possibility by asking whether, in doing so, the agent exhibited a moral vice. That culpability-based inquiry is structurally different from the question whether her action was justified.

I will treat them here together as if they comprise a single defence. I also take duress to have, morally speaking, the same scope as what is sometimes called 'excusing necessity'. The American categories are more complex: see P Westen and J Mangiafico, 'The Criminal Defense of Duress: A Justification, Not an Excuse—And Why It Matters' (2003) 6 Buffalo Crim LR 833.

[12] See § 17.3.2.

[13] Raz, *Practical Reason and Norms*, § 1.2.

So there are key differences in how, morally speaking, the defendant's rationale is relevant to her exculpation. In order to track those differences, the internal workings of justification, excuse, and irresponsibility defences must also differ. Superficially common requirements of 'reasonableness' and urgency work differently within justifications than they do within excuses, because they serve distinct functions. Moreover, the distinction between justification and excuse is itself legally significant. Admittedly, either type of defence leads to blameless acquittal, at least for individual defendants. Justified action is, however, lawful: which matters in particular to actions by the state. State action may be justifiable, but it cannot be defended with a rationale-based excuse.

17.2 Distinguishing justification from rationale-based excuse

A justifiable action is a morally appropriate response to the circumstances and is, for that reason, permissible. In turn, D has a justification when his reasons for φing are sufficient to defeat those that militate against φing, so that φing is morally permitted. Permitted, not tolerated. Douglas Husak suggests that 'an act is permissible when it is tolerated.'[14] That may be true—legally speaking. Not morally. One can tolerate something that one considers to be wrongful.[15] Justified φing is not like that. It may be harmful in some way. It may generate reasons for regret. But if it is morally justified, φing is not, all things considered, wrongful. Where a pro tanto wrong is legally and not morally permitted, it would be more accurate to say the defendant's action is *condoned* rather than justified—a paradigm case of toleration. But nothing here turns on this distinction: condoned actions are, like justified actions, lawful.

Notice that this approach to justification takes account of D's own reasons. In putting it this way, I am embracing the conclusion of chapter 16: that justification depends upon D's actual or 'subjective' reasons for φing, and not solely upon any guiding—'objective'—reasons that are in fact available to justify φing.[16] It is not sufficient that φing be justifi*able* in the

[14] D Husak, 'On the Supposed Priority of Justification to Excuse' in D Husak (ed), *The Philosophy of Criminal Law: Selected Essays* (OUP 2010) 287, 296–97.

[15] Indeed, some writers have suggested that one can *only* tolerate something that one considers to be wrongful. On that view, something that is morally permissible does not call for toleration at all, because there is nothing wrong with it. See, e.g., P King, *Toleration* (St Martin's 1976) 44–54; J Raz, 'Autonomy, Toleration, and the Harm Principle' in R Gavison (ed), *Issues in Contemporary Legal Philosophy* (OUP 1987) 313. Contrast Gardner, *Offences and Defences*, 97.

[16] I adopt the distinction drawn by Joseph Raz between guiding (objective, applicable-in-fact) and explanatory (subjective, motivating) reasons: Raz, *Practical Reasons and Norms*, 16–20.

circumstances.[17] D's own reasons must themselves be valid, and sufficient, for D's action of φing to be justifi*ed*.

For convenience, let us call this the *motivational thesis*. The motivational thesis concerns the range of reasons eligible to justify D's φing. For present purposes, the important point to start with is that, whatever reasons are treated as eligible, justification requires those reasons to be sufficient. They must pass an evaluative, objective,[18] test of whether, taken as a whole, they supply D with good reasons to φ. Overall, they must defeat, or at least match, the reasons D has not to φ. They must make it morally okay—or as Kent Greenawalt puts it, 'warranted'—to φ.[19]

No such requirement exists for excuses. That said, there is a tendency to relegate excuses to a catch-all dustbin. Expressed most generally, D can be said to have an excuse if the explanation why he φs are such that he is not culpable for doing so. Unfortunately, while that definition is appealingly simple, it can be applied more-or-less to any of the kinds of exculpatory defences we identified in § 17.1, including justifications. No surprise, then, that writers often add a proviso that excused conduct is unjustified,[20] or that they sometimes conflate irresponsibility defences with rationale-based excuses.[21]

Rationale-based excuses differ from irresponsibility defences in that they address D's own reasons for action, not her capacity for reasoning. D's φing is excusable if, in choosing to φ, she exhibits no shortcoming of a kind that grounds blame—no shortfall of the moral characteristics that we should expect of an ordinary, decent person; no moral vice of the kind discussed in chapter 11. D need not be perfect. We all have limitations, even decent folk. Exculpation requires only that the limitations explaining why D φed be normal ones, ones that do not reflect badly on D. Perhaps supererogation was possible. Perhaps D could have exhibited abnormal levels of altruism, *et cetera*, and refrained from φing. But blame does not turn on D's failure to merit praise. It requires that he

[17] Cp. what TM Scanlon calls the 'permissible': *Moral Dimensions: Permissibility, Meaning, Blame* (Harvard UP 2008). On my account, φing may be both permissible and unjustified. However, I cannot think of a context in which that possibility would be independently important to the criminal law. (Some may consider that it matters to the normative position of third parties who are in a position to intervene: for a note on this, see § 17.3.2.)

[18] This should not be read to mean that the validity and weight of reasons—and thus the range of what is morally permitted—is universal rather than society-independent; or even that it is independent of law. The point here is simply that the evaluation of D's reasons is not up to D. In criminal law, it is a matter for the court.

[19] K Greenawalt, 'The Perplexing Borders of Justification and Excuse' (1984) 84 Columbia LR 1897, 1903. (Greenawalt, however, does not distinguish between warranted and entitled: see esp. the discussion at 1904–905.)

[20] e.g. M McBride, 'Justifications and Excuses: Mutually Exclusive?' (2011) J Ethics & Social Phil (discussion note).

[21] See § 17.5.

fall short, not of standards of perfection, but of standards of decency. And excuses require only that his failings be, so to speak, reasonable ones.[22]

Like justifications, and unlike the irresponsibility defences, all rationale-based excuses therefore require that D's reasons for φing be subjected to evaluative assessment: an assessment that is not relativized to any personal limitations of virtue that the defendant might have. The difference lies in the conclusion of that assessment. When justified, there is no moral error—it is morally okay for D to φ. In the case of excuse, D is not culpable for φing even though φing may not be okay. Any moral error by D is, we might say, *understandable*: it is the kind of error that a decent person might well make.

17.2.1 The priority thesis

Put this way, justifications and excuses can overlap. Legally speaking, as we noted earlier, that presents no problem. Redundancy is possible in the law's scheme of rationale-based defences. Suppose that Frances shoots and injures George, her attacker. Frances may qualify for overlapping defences of self-defence, necessity, and duress. Under the legal heading of 'duress',[23] we may acquit her because she acted in response to a threat of death. At the same time, Frances may avail herself of a lesser-evils necessity defence: it is better that injury be suffered than that death result. Even more aptly, her action may be a legitimate use of force in self-defence.

This kind of doctrinal overlap shows only that the legal categories are somewhat rough-and-ready. There is nothing wrong with that. Allowing multiple defences in a particular situation is an instance of complementariness rather than contradiction, partly because the verdict is the same either way: acquittal, provided at least one defence is made out. In practice, if the same facts are relied on to establish a justification and an excuse, the former is normally treated in court as supervening over the latter. We should ask, however, whether that practice tracks the underlying moral categories. Duress is paradigmatically (though not necessarily) excusatory,[24] self-defence justificatory. Can one really be simultaneously justified and excused? Or is there supervenience in

[22] See chapter 12.

[23] As mentioned earlier in n 11, and in line with common law developments in recent decades, I use 'duress' as an umbrella term to include 'duress by threat' (from another person) and 'duress of circumstances' (where the danger arises from other sources). See *Simester and Sullivan*, § 20.1.

[24] As is implicit in the case of Frances and George, the criteria of duress can include scenarios where D's response is justified.

morality too? Should we accept the widely held *priority thesis* (or more properly, *theses*): that (i) justifications and excuses are mutually exclusive, with (ii) the former taking priority over the latter?[25]

In principle, one's being attacked can generate both justificatory and excusatory grounds for exculpation. The fear of death may make D's response blameless whether or not permitted. Normally, where his response is also justified, there will be a convergence, so that the very reasons that tend to excuse will simultaneously support D's justification. But consider Doug Husak's example, where the two remain separate:[26]

> *Coincidence*: 'Suppose, for example, that a defendant is threatened with serious bodily harm unless he inflicts a somewhat greater harm on the next person to walk into his office. By chance, this next person happens to be a personal enemy who begins to attack the defendant. In this example, the defendant has two independent, sufficient reasons to inflict personal injury, each of which constitutes a defense from liability. His first reason, duress, is generally categorized as an excuse; his second reason, self-defense, is almost always categorized as a justification.'

Assuming the defendant acts for both reasons, he is at once justified and excused.

Husak intends this as a counterexample to the priority thesis. Specifically, his example undermines the claim of mutual exclusivity. Notice, however, that in Husak's scenario the excuse and the justification are predicated on concurrent but independent reasons. It is, in that sense, a special case. It shows that justifications and excuses are not just action-specific but rationale-dependent. If D acts for multiple rationales, some of those rationales may (individually or collectively) be sufficient to justify the action, while others may excuse without justifying. By contrast, those who claim that justifications and excuses are mutually exclusive are usually concerned with defences that arise out of the very same rationale. Let us vary the hypothetical:

> *Unitary*: E is threatened with serious bodily harm by F, a personal enemy, and realizes that the only way to save himself will be by inflicting a somewhat greater harm on F. When F walks into E's office and begins to attack E, E has

[25] See Husak, 'On the Supposed Priority' (n 14) 287–90 for a large collection of priority thesis supporters.

[26] Ibid, 298–99 (footnotes omitted).

> one sufficient reason to inflict personal injury, which constitutes a defence from liability.

The excusatory force of *Unitary* seems no less than in *Coincidence*. Yet most theorists would straightforwardly regard E as being justified *rather than* excused. The very reason why E acts is sufficient to make her conduct permissible, and not (merely) non-culpable.

Perhaps there is no harm in saying, with Husak, that E is both justified and excused in *Unitary*. But to the extent that 'excused' means something more than 'not culpable', it is misleading to describe E's defence as an excuse. Excuses do distinctive moral work only when they relate to an unjustified action. Suppose, this time:

> *Pure Duress*: T credibly threatens to kill G's family unless G inflicts a substantial harm on the next person to walk into his office. G attacks and seriously injures that person, V.

This case *is* one of excuse. Despite his rationale, G's conduct remains wrongful. Yet we should be reluctant to fault him. Notwithstanding that G's reason for acting was (objectively speaking) inadequate, it is understandable that G should have acted for that reason. Even a decent person might, like G, have attacked V out of fear for his family's lives. As such, we cannot make the inference of culpability that would normally entitle us to blame G for her actions. Hence, an excuse.

All this suggests that we need to refine the definition of rationale-based excuses with which we began. D's rationale for φing is—distinctively—excusatory when it establishes that he is not culpable for φing, without sufficing (either alone or in tandem with any other reasons why the agent φed) to justify his φing. In the same vein, a partial excuse ameliorates D's culpability for φing while falling short of full exculpation.[27] This reformulation survives Husak's counterexample in *Coincidence*. Moreover, it maintains the priority of justification over excuse.

As a practical matter, the most important reason why justifications have priority over excuses lies in their implications for the lawfulness of a defendant's action.[28] Even if a defendant's action could be both justified and excused, its

[27] Thus, the law's distinction between substantive partial excuses and post-conviction, culpability-related mitigation is primarily operational. It does not reflect a fundamental moral distinction.

[28] Below, § 17.4.

lawfulness would turn on whether the defendant was justified. But the priority thesis also has rational appeal. Within the realm of rationale-based defences, most of us would rather be justified than (merely) excused in our actions. Better not to make the moral error at all than to do so understandably, and blamelessly. Yet this aspect of the priority thesis is also denied by Husak, who sees 'no general reason why a defendant should prefer to be acquitted on the ground that his behaviour is [permitted] than because he is excused.'[29] He offers two intuitive counterexamples. Here is the first:[30]

> 'Smith and Jones deliberately inflict a fairly serious but not life-threatening injury on White. Imagine that the story is embellished in either of two ways. In the first scenario, Smith's behaviour is barely tolerable, although no one would regard it as commendable. Suppose White is a deranged thief who is escaping with Smith's television set. Smith's act, I assume, is permissible and thereby justified. In the second scenario, Jones is well below the age of criminal responsibility, and injures White in a schoolyard brawl. Even if Jones has not acted in self-defense, I assume he is excused. From a moral point of view, why should we conclude that Smith's defense is superior to that of Jones?'

Quite. But notice that Jones's defence is one of irresponsibility, not rationale-based. Irresponsibility defences are logically prior to rationale-based defences, to *both* justifications and excuses. Whether or not a defendant might prefer them, they come first.[31] Only responsible actors can claim rationale—or mistake-based defences. By the same token, however, Husak's first example cannot establish that justifications lack priority over rationale-based excuses. Neither can his second hypothetical:[32]

> 'Perhaps I am permitted to push someone from a plank to save myself.[33] Suppose further that mistakes about justifications, even when reasonable, give rise to an excuse rather than a justification. Perhaps I am excused when I falsely but reasonably believe that I must push a single individual from a lifeboat to save two others. Again, why think that the justification casts the agent in a better moral light than the excuse?'

[29] Husak, 'On the Supposed Priority' (n 14) 297.
[30] Ibid.
[31] In law too: see, e.g., *Oye* [2013] EWCA Crim 1725 (insanity taking priority over mistaken self-defence).
[32] Husak, 'On the Supposed Priority' (n 14) 297.
[33] For simplicity, I assume that Husak envisages repulsion rather than expulsion.

Again, the comparison is with a different category of supervening defence. Moreover, the difference matters, especially to the lawfulness of official action.[34] Mistakes cannot be assimilated with rationale-based excuses. It is telling, I think, that Husak does not offer an intuitive example comparing a justification with a genuine rationale-based excuse. And it remains hard to see, within the realm of rationale-based defences, why one wouldn't prefer to be justified than excused: to not be in the wrong at all.[35]

17.3 Operational implications

Why else would it matter whether one is justified or excused? Partly, because justifications and excuses have differing internal structures. Hence, even as an agent may be excused without being justified, she may be justified without being excused. In cases like *Coincidence*, she may be both. The border-lines of justification and excuse are not simply fuzzy. They are not even contiguous. To see all this, however, we need to expose two common myths.

17.3.1 The difference is one of degree?

It is sometimes envisaged that justifications and excuses lie on an exculpatory spectrum, or continuum, of explanation, where the difference is one of degree. According to Clarkson, for example,[36]

> 'in reality there is a continuum of pressurised conduct with it being impossible to distinguish clearly . . . . It becomes a question of judgment as to when understandable reasons become sufficient ones.'

On this view, justification is essentially *more* exculpatory: the reasons D has to φ are stronger than they are when D is excused, so much so that their conduct crosses not merely a first threshold of being non-culpable but a second, higher one of being genuinely okay. Conversely, one might say, of a person who offers a very bad reason for φing, that the person is 'not excused let alone justified'.

[34] Below, § 17.4.1.

[35] Notice that I have side-stepped Husak's question: 'why think that the justification casts the agent in a better moral light than the excuse?' In terms of the priority thesis, that question is not in point. *Ex hypothesi*, neither form of rationale-based defence reflects badly on the agent.

[36] C Clarkson, 'Necessary Action' (n 10) 85.

This way of thinking about the difference is problematic because the exculpatory force of reasons works differently for justifications than it does for excuses; and the difference is one of kind rather than degree. What counts for justification is whether D's reasons were good ones, reasons that went undefeated by those militating against her φing. Determining that is an evaluative matter, involving the logic of practical reasons. It is also an all-or-nothing matter: either φing is permitted or it is not. The status of being justified is a binary. It does not come in degrees.[37]

By contrast, when considering whether D is excused, we do not assess *whether* D acted wrongfully, but why. Our concern lies not with the objective, practical quality of D's reasons, but with why D came to act upon them and what moral vices, if any, he displayed in doing so. Sometimes there may be a connection. Wrongful acts can be more excusable when they came very close to being justified.[38] Indeed, this is one reason why the law should not test the proportionality of a self-defensive action 'on jeweller's scales':[39] because some misjudgement, especially in emergencies, is likely anyway to be excusable. So the objective force of a guiding reason to φ will sometimes be relevant to the question whether D fell short in acting on it.

Typically, however, excuses do not track the force of guiding reasons in this way. In the case of provocation, D has *no* unexcluded reason to kill his victim.[40] Yet he is understandably—even rightly—angry. We recognize how it was that he came to attack the victim, overreacting in a manner that even a reasonable person might have done.[41] D's response remains wrongful, indeed culpable, but the explanation diminishes his culpability.

Notice that there is no element of justification about the killing here *at all*. When writers such as Andrew Ashworth state that provocation rests on a 'partial justification',[42] we should not take them to be denying this. Perhaps some other aggressive but less serious response by D would have been justified; and the reasons for that are relevant to the excusatory power of the case. But to

[37] *Contra* Husak 'On the Supposed Priority' (n 14) 302–03. But Husak does not show how an action can be partially permitted.

[38] Not always; especially when the counter-considerations are authoritatively excluded (itself, perhaps, a finely balanced matter). One familiar example is the legal status of euthanasia.

[39] *Reed v Wastie* [1972] Crim LR 221 (DC). By not requiring 'jeweller's scales' (or 'golden scales': *Jai Dev v State of Punjab* AIR 1963 SC 612, 617), the law side-steps having to consider a general excuse of borderline moral error; instead piggybacking such cases on the relevant justification. *Morally* speaking, a case of (say) excessive self-defence would be at most excusatory: cp. the partial defence to murder of 'exceeding private defence' in the Indian Penal Code 1860, s 300.

[40] Raz, *Practical Reason and Norms*, § 1.2: 'excluded' reasons should be given no weight in one's practical deliberation.

[41] *Might*: but see § 19.1.

[42] A Ashworth, 'The Doctrine of Provocation' [1976] CLJ 292, 307. See § 19.1.

accept that is not to admit that D has any kind of 'partial reason' to kill; neither that he has a partial justification for doing so.

The same can hold even for full excuses. Suppose that a terrorist, Trevor, bursts into Edgar's house and threatens to shoot Edgar's family unless he assists to murder Victor, a policeman.[43] In terms of justification, it is irrelevant here that V is elderly and, say, in the early stages of a terminal illness. It is irrelevant because Trevor's threat supplies Edgar with *no unexcluded reason at all* to kill Victor. This is implicit in Victor's having a right to life. That right pre-emptively defeats certain kinds of reasons. It excludes from consideration many factors that might otherwise seem to favour killing Victor,[44] such as the benefit to Edgar's family. The existence of those benefits adds no weight to any justificatory case for killing Victor. They cannot be stacked up against Victor's life when deciding what is permissible.

Edgar has no claim to justification, not even the beginnings of one. Morally speaking,[45] however, he has an excuse. Even though Edgar has no sufficient grounds for preferring the lives of his family to those of policemen, it is understandable that he should act as if he does. It is understandable that the reason was good enough for him. That same rationale, irrelevant to his justification, is central to his excuse. In being motivated to comply with the terrorists' threat, Edgar does not fall short of the qualities we expect in a decent person. Indeed, in caring about his family's welfare so much, he demonstrates a virtue rather than vice.[46]

We can readily see why the realm of excuse is no mere penumbra of justification—and why it is a mistake to think that there is an underlying relationship between excusing duress and justifying necessity.[47] Edgar is nowhere near being justified. Establishing an excuse involves a quite separate kind of inquiry, into culpability rather than justification: an inquiry into what moral vices, if any, were displayed in acting *wrongfully*. Moreover, as the provocation example shows, excuses can come in degrees. They may diminish culpability even when they do not cancel it. Thus one's degree of excuse may be

[43] A variant on *DPP for Northern Ireland v Lynch* [1975] AC 653.

[44] Though not all: it may be an unexcluded reason to shoot V that doing so will protect D's family from attack *by V*. Implicit in this analysis is the crucial importance of 'excluded' reasons for understanding the difference between justifying and excusatory rationales; and for understanding justifications generally. More on this in chapter 18.

[45] Not legally, as the common law stands: *Howe* [1987] AC 417. Contrast Germany: StGB § 35.

[46] The example shows that excuses, as well as justifications, can be role-related. Compare *Hasan* [2005] UKHL 22, [21(3)], restricting the scope of duress to threats directed at those close to the defendant; below, § 17.4.2.

[47] Compare the so-called 'duress of circumstances' cases in English law, many of which (e.g. *Pommell* [1995] 2 Cr App R 607 (CA)) straddle the divide rather awkwardly. See *Simester and Sullivan*, § 20.1(ii).

independent of the force of one's claim to justification. Unjustified actions, by contrast, are unjustified *tout court*.

Still more tellingly, it is possible for actions to be justified without being excusable at all. That occurred in *Re A (Children)*,[48] in which the Court of Appeal ruled that it would be lawful for surgeons to separate conjoined twins, even though the known consequence was that one twin would die within minutes.[49] Here, the question for the Court turned on whether such an operation would be justified: does the case for protecting one life warrant an intervention that kills the other? Otherwise, however, the surgeons have no possibility of an excuse. There is no factor here, apart from the very claim to justification, available to exculpate their killing the twin. This is not a scenario where morally erroneous action occurs in an emergency, under pressure of circumstances, threats, or other motivating factors which might make wrongdoing understandable. To operate would be to take morality into one's own hands, as it were. Like the rule of law, the rule of morality requires that doing so be justified, not excused. The reasons supporting a justification, therefore, have no necessary implication for the question whether one is excused. The two overlap but do not dovetail.

17.3.2 Justifications are repeatable, and about the act; excuses are ad hoc, and personal to the actor?

Let us turn now to the second myth. It is often said that justifications are about the act, and excuses about the actor.[50] Justifications apply to actions that others in like circumstances could legitimately perform, whereas we would hope or even expect that others refrain from repeating a person's excused act.[51]

That distinction works well when applied to irresponsibility defences, which are paradigmatically personal. Insanity, infancy, and the like accommodate incapacities that are particular to the defendant. They do not purport to say

[48] [2001] Fam 147.

[49] See, further, § 18.5. The 'weaker' twin's own heart and lungs were inadequate to sustain her life, and would fail within minutes upon separation. She was incapable of independent existence. Unfortunately, the heart of other twin was not strong enough to sustain both lives: inevitably, both would die within a few months if left conjoined.

[50] See, e.g., J Dressler, *Understanding Criminal Law* (3rd edn, Lexis 2001) 202–203; Fletcher, *Rethinking*, 761–62; D Husak, 'Justifications and the Criminal Liability of Accessories' (1989) 80 J Crim L and Criminology 494, 496–97; P H Robinson, *Criminal Law Defenses*, vol 1 (West 1984) 100–101.

[51] e.g. Greenawalt, 'The Perplexing Borders' (n 19) 1915: 'Justifications typically arise out of the nature of the actor's situation, excuses out of the actor's personal characteristics.' Greenawalt himself recognizes difficulties with this 'basic distinction', although his analysis is affected by a failure to segregate irresponsibility defences from rationale-based excuses.

anything more generally about the defendant's conduct. But the same distinction does not hold for the rationale-based defences.

Even so, there is a grain of truth in it. Not a bushel. The truth resides in the fact that, to justify her φing, D's reasons for acting must be sufficient objectively, qua guiding reasons. But it does not follow that those reasons are independent of D or of D's circumstances. It is *D's action of φing* that must be justified, not φing in general. For those who embrace the motivational thesis of justification, this requires that D acts *for* the reasons that make her φing permissible. Moreover, there are other ways in which the applicability of justifying reasons can depend in part on the actor. A mother may have reasons to discipline her child that others do not. Alternatively, suppose that P launches a violent attack on E, in circumstances where E can easily fend P off. E may not be entitled to use pre-emptive force that F, who is less mobile or strong, would have been permitted to use. Justifications are personal too.

To accommodate these points, one might clarify the claim that justification is about acts by allowing that it is φing in the same circumstances (including D's role, physical capacities, and the like) that is repeatable.

Yet, once the claim is clarified, we can see that it applies also to rationale-based excuses. Such excuses are themselves subject to restrictions that are external to the agent; and to that extent, they are susceptible of generalization. In other words, rationale-based excuses are impersonal too. To say that D is excused in this context is to say that *anyone* in the same circumstances (including D's role, physical capacities, and the like) would be excused—because they have not fallen short of the standards of decency in action that undergird blame. It is *not* to say anything distinctive about D. Neither is D claiming any special dispensation. The 'concession', if it be one, is to human beings as a whole, not to idiosyncratic frailties of the agent.[52] This helps to explain why it goes too far to say, as does Mitchell Berman, that 'a justified action is not criminal, whereas an excused defendant has committed a crime but is not punishable.'[53] The excused defendant's action is wrongful. More than that: it is *unlawful*.[54] But as we observed in § 2.1.1, it is not *criminal*, and an excused defendant is not a criminal either. It becomes criminal only when it is also culpable.

Of course, this analysis of the exculpatory nature of rationale-based excuses depends on D's motivation. But according to the motivational thesis, that is

[52] See the discussion in *Howe* [1987] 1 AC 417, 432–35. On the possibility of hybrid defences, see § 19.1.
[53] M Berman, 'Justification and Excuse, Law and Morality' (2003) 53 Duke LJ 1, 4 (emphases omitted); above, § 2.1.2.
[54] See § 17.4.

equally true of justifications. Both justification and excuse start by asking why D φed, and subject D's reasons and circumstances to critical evaluation. If made out, both exculpate D. The difference lies only in the basis of exculpation.

Much the same goes for third party interventions. Famously, one key distinction is said to be that, when D's φing is justified, bystanders may help her and should not interfere with her doing so. By contrast, if her φing is merely excused, others should not assist. Indeed, they may intervene to resist.[55]

That analysis makes the mistake of over-abstraction, of objectifying justifications. Like excuses, justifications are, in part, personal. Suppose that T is a bystander when P attacks Q. Whether T is justified in interfering to protect Q must be assessed *with respect to T*; it is not determined merely by asking whether Q is permitted to shoot back at P.[56] Here, it is *T's action of shooting P* (say) that must be justified. To be sure, the required analysis for each party overlaps, and the considerations that warrant Q's self-defensive response will also support T's intervention. But that only shows that the existence of undefeated guiding reasons is *necessary* for anyone to be justified. It does not show that their existence is sufficient.

Two examples by way of illustration. The first is a simple one, and trades on the fact that the motivational thesis applies to third parties too. Suppose that T doesn't know that P is attacking Q; he is an old enemy of P's and has sworn to shoot P on sight. T is not justified in shooting P even though Q may be. Even if T has full information, however, his normative position may still diverge from Q's. Suppose, instead, that while Q is justified in shooting P (who is much stronger than Q), T is a martial arts expert and can easily resolve the conflict without causing serious injury to anyone.[57] T should not, I take it, assist Q to shoot P. Rather, T would be justified in preventing each of them from harming the other.

17.4 Lawfulness

Still, at least one practical consequence does attend the justification-excuse distinction. Because rationale-based excuses address the culpability of an agent's

[55] See, e.g., P H Robinson, 'Competing Theories of Justification: Deeds vs. Reasons' in *Harm and Culpability* 45, 59: 'Whether the deed is or is not actually justified is central to whether the law should allow it to be resisted.' Similarly, see G P Fletcher, 'The Right and the Reasonable' (1985) 98 Harvard LR 949, 971ff.

[56] This point is made in § 16.4.

[57] The example is loosely based on one discussed by Greenawalt, 'The Perplexing Borders' (n 19) 1924–25.

choice to act wrongfully, they generally exclude reliance on the fact that φing can itself be excusable. D had better not choose to φ *because* she thinks she has an excuse. Agents who act under duress are exculpated because they act directly out of pressure; not because they think it is blameless, let alone lawful, to do so. Someone who says, 'I chose to φ because I knew that φing would be excusable in such fearsome circumstances' simply fails to engage the conditions of the defence. Excuses supply rules of adjudication, not rules of guidance for conduct.[58] They constitute grounds of exculpation; in the criminal law, of acquittal. They do not constitute reasons to φ. Justificatory reasons do.[59] Hence, by contrast with excuses, the lawfulness of a justification is something the defendant is morally, and legally, permitted to consider.

This distinction affects other parts of the legal system, especially public law. The divide between justification and excuse helps to shape the lawfulness of one's action. In general, action constituting a pro tanto crime can only be lawful because justified or condoned, not because excused. Where φing is justified, it is lawful. There is good (sufficient) reason to do it. Otherwise, the action is unlawful. There is no middle ground.

17.4.1 Officials

All this matters greatly to officials. It is sometimes suggested otherwise. David Dyzenhaus, for example, contemplates that officials in an emergency who act outside the law may sometimes invoke a rationale-based excuse.[60] They may not. It is not open for the state, or any individual acting qua official, to claim an excuse of that type. Official action constituting a pro tanto crime can only be defended by showing it is permitted—lawful.[61] Even in emergencies, wrongs such as official torture are inexcusable. And they would remain so even were we to concede that they might (*possibly*) be justifiable.[62]

[58] The classic article is M Dan-Cohen, 'Decisions Rules and Conduct Rules: On Acoustic Separation in Criminal Law' (1984) 97 Harvard LR 625, 638.

[59] Which is why justifications have the *ex ante*, criminalization dimension noted in § 17.1. One might doubt whether this is true of condonations (see § 17.2). But it seems especially in point that D can be guided by, indeed rely on, the law's permission to act for condoned reasons that otherwise would be excluded.

[60] D Dyzenhaus, 'The State of Emergency in Legal Theory' in V V Ramraj, M Hor, and K Roach (eds), *Global Anti-Terrorism Law and Policy* (CUP 2005) 65, 84.

[61] This point was crucial to the granting of a court order in *Re A (Children)* [2001] Fam 147. See §§ 18.4–5.

[62] More on this in chapter 18.

Notice that the generalization here applies to rationale-based defences and not to mistake-based defences. Actions by officials can be lawful, even law-creating, notwithstanding that they are predicated on mistakes. A policeman who arrests the wrong person can still effect a valid arrest; and the arrestee may have no right of resistance. To a large extent this is a pragmatic matter, predicated on the need for officials to have decision-making powers that are authoritative. If we allow the validity of those decisions to be second-guessed whenever the official is mistaken, we undermine their very authority. So we cannot always require officials to be right. That does not mean their decisions are, or should be, unimpeachable. Perhaps we can require their mistakes to be reasonable. Either way, however, we should deny that officials may *choose* to act impermissibly.

The point here is not merely about the lawfulness of actions, official and private.[63] It is also that the state cannot be *exculpated* by rationale-based excuses. Official choices to act wrongfully are conceptually inexcusable even in a criminal proceeding.

We need to be careful about what this 'non-exculpation thesis' entails. In the context of mistakes, Ashworth has argued that, under the right-to-life provisions in Article 2 of the European Convention on Human Rights, state agents such as police officers should not be entitled to rely on unreasonable factual mistakes to found a successful claim of mistaken self-defence.[64] His argument is not that unreasonable mistakes should be disallowed for *all* agents when they generate perceived scenarios of self-defence.[65] It is that they should be disallowed specifically for police officers, soldiers, and the like. However, the non-exculpation thesis does not support conclusions of this kind. When a policeman, like anyone else, is tried for a crime, she is tried as an individual, qua subject-citizen, not qua state official. The conviction is personal, not official. There are, to be sure, some crimes that can only be committed by a state official (for example, some forms of corruption), just as there are some crimes that can only be committed by factory owners: but in such cases the role is partly constitutive of the wrong. Mistaken self-defence contexts are not ones where the agent's official role is constitutive of the wrong. As such, officials are entitled to

[63] See, too, the thoughtful essay by François Tanguay-Renaud, 'Puzzling about State Excuses as an Instance of Group Excuses' in R A Duff, L Farmer, S Marshall and V Tadros (eds), *The Constitution of Criminal Law* (OUP 2012).

[64] A Ashworth, *Principles of Criminal Law* (6th edn, OUP 2009) 124–25; see also F Leverick, *Killing in Self-Defence* (OUP 2006) ch 10.

[65] *That* argument is made here, in chapter 19.

claim the same range of excuses as anyone else—provided, as with any excuse, it applies to them personally.[66]

Still, the state itself can be a defendant. When it is, the non-exculpation claim would allow justifications and deny it any rationale-based excuse. This claim may seem counterintuitive. Surely one can be excused when acting on behalf of others? It is uncontroversial law that duress can sometimes be levied through a third party: we saw that in § 17.3.1, when Trevor's threat was directed at Edgar's child. It seems entirely understandable for Edgar to be moved by concern for his family into committing the wrong that Trevor demands. Yet if Edgar may claim an excuse, then perhaps the state may, analogously, succeed to an excuse when acting on behalf of those threatened by a predicted attack? If it would be excusable for D to μ, why can't the state μ in D's place?

17.4.2 No vicarious excuses

There are two lines of argument for the non-exculpation thesis. First, the analogy to third-party threats does not defeat the point that a rationale-based excuse like duress must apply personally to D. Duress is not vicarious: what counts is the effective pressure that the threat exerts *upon D*. Thus, in Edgar's case, it makes a difference that the threat is to his own child. Edgar acts neither impersonally, nor impartially, but because the threat directly engages his most cherished values. He acts not from sympathetic concern for the child's predicament, but out of personally experienced emotions. Recognizing this aspect of duress helps us to make sense of the common-law restriction that the threat must be directed against either the defendant himself or someone close to him.[67] Each and every life is valuable and, as human life, valuable equally. Without more, a stranger cannot adjudicate between them. But we can quite understand, indeed hope, that a father does not think that way. A father who sacrifices another's interests to save the life of his child may be a wrongdoer. Yet in doing wrong he exhibits the very human quality of being a good father.[68]

[66] A proviso: role-related duties may sometimes restrict the availability of excuses, so that officials may be required on occasion to resist a danger, or to take greater care, than would a private citizen. This point is not specific to officials; similar role-related duties may apply to doctors et al too.

[67] *Hasan* [2005] UKHL 22, [2005] 2 AC 467. Make sense of, but not necessarily justify. One can imagine scenarios in which a person's concern for the welfare of others is sufficient, depending on the nature of threat, to lead that person into compliance even though the threat is against a stranger. (Cp. J Horder, 'Self-Defence, Necessity and Duress: Understanding the Relationship' (1998) 11 Canadian J Law and Juris 143, 163; also s 94 of the Singaporean Penal Code, excusing for threats of death 'to that person or any other person'.)

[68] The example illustrates a more general point: that even one who acts blamelessly may be damaged, morally speaking, by the position in which he finds himself.

Individual persons like Edgar, then, may be excused for acting unlawfully. But excuses, which reflect profoundly human characteristics, are prima facie inapplicable to artificial actors such as the state. Suppose that we accept a theory of group agency whereby corporate organizations, including the state, are moral agents in their own right, whose choices and intentions are not reducible to those of individual, constituent human members.[69] The intentions, beliefs, and decisions of the organization are the upshot of an internal constitutional framework that co-ordinates the inputs of its various members in such a manner that the results distinctively belong to the organization rather than to the individual members. On that account, the organization may be a moral agent; but it is not a human being. Indeed, it is not even quasi-human, in as much as the irreducible upshots that mark out the organization are essentially cognitive rather than affective. They do not seem to include the kinds of human 'frailties', such as the ability to experience and be motivated by fear, that underpin excuses. Rationale-based excuses are personal—one cannot experience them vicariously.

Needless to say, that line of thought rests on a controversial theory of corporate agency. It is circumnavigated by abandoning the idea that corporate organizations are autonomous moral agents. Instead, one might analyse corporate agency via some theory of identification with the acts and intentions of senior members. In that case, the attribution of an individual official's excuse might plausibly be thought to run alongside the attribution of her acts and intentions. Similarly at international law, doctrines of identification are required to recognize the state as an agent, and in principle such doctrines could also impute excuses. More generally, there seems no reason to exclude the possibility of excuses within any legal system where the state is itself a subject. We allow the official an excuse qua individual: why not pass that on to the state in whose name she acts?

17.4.3 Authority

The second line of argument is, therefore, apt to domestic rather than international law. Besides being artificial, the state is a special type of actor. The relationship of a state to its citizens is nothing like that of Edgar to his children, or indeed any form of inter-human relation, because the state is a

[69] See, e.g., C List and P Pettit, *Group Agency: The Possibility, Design, and Status of Corporate Agents* (OUP 2011).

purely instrumental creation, without personal values. That lack of personal preferences—that impartiality—is no accident. In accordance with the state's claim to authority, its relationship to citizens is constituted by rules, including those rules which grant powers to the state and its officials. The requirement of lawfulness binds the state to act according to those rules. This is a central requirement of the rule of law. Part of the very point of being an official is impersonality. It is not open for the state, or its officials, to prefer the interests of one person to another, since the state is not entitled to be closer to one person than another. It is not like Edgar. It is equidistant, impartial to all.

So must it be. The state's duty of impartiality rests on its claim to legitimate authority over its citizens. It is widely accepted that the state has moral constraints upon its ends. (Most formulations of the Harm Principle, for example, rule out enforcing morality for its own sake.) Beyond that, however, the state also has constraints upon the means by which it goes about its ends. One key constraint is that it should act within the law. At the heart of the state's relationship with its citizens, and central to its claim of authority, is respect for the complex web of rules by which the legal system is constituted and by which the society is governed. Not only must the state act lawfully, *it must seek to do so*. If that's right, then it is not open for the state to defend its conduct by reference to a rationale-based excuse. Such excuses involve deliberate wrongdoing, deliberately unlawful conduct. If admitted, they would threaten to dissolve the glue that legitimates recognition of the state itself.

Suppose that we accept these lines of thought. It follows that even emergency action by state officials, such as shooting down the hijacked aeroplane flying toward an office building,[70] is inexcusable. For my money, that's a payoff. Cases such as these are profoundly difficult. But the difficulty is not about whether shooting the plane down involves a confession of human frailty, normal or abnormal. References to excuse just obscure the true question here, which is whether shooting down the aeroplane is morally *permitted*; whether it is okay to shoot down the plane. The real issue is one of justification.

17.4.4 Borderline cases?

For all that, doubt may persist. Surely, one may ask, the state is entitled to be moved by the plight of its citizens? Consider, for example, the controversial

[70] There is a considerable literature. See, e.g., T Hörnle, 'Shooting Down a Hijacked Plane—The German Discussion and Beyond' (2009) 3 Crim L and Phil 111, together with other papers in that issue.

case of Wolfgang Daschner, vice-president of Frankfurt-am-Main police. Daschner led investigations into the kidnap of eleven-year-old Jakob von Metzler, son of a prominent banker. The kidnapper, Mangus Gaefgen, was arrested after collecting the ransom payment but refused to disclose Metzler's whereabouts despite lengthy questioning. Hoping to save the boy, Daschner eventually instructed that Gaefgen should be threatened with torture, at which point Gaefgen confessed that Metzler was already dead and revealed the location of his body. Daschner was subsequently found guilty of coercion. Yet the charge was a misdemeanour—more serious charges were not pressed—and the conviction suspended,[71] reflecting the considerable support that his case attracted. It seems that many regarded Daschner as a 'moral hero', one who chose to disobey the law for the sake of a moral imperative.

Perhaps this is a borderline case. Undoubtedly, it has a complex moral pull. But it is a mistake to think the pull is *excusatory*. 'Moral heroes' are not excused. They are heroes because, despite the impediments, they do what is morally right. If there is hesitation over the assessment of Daschner's case, it is because of uncertainty about whether his conduct was *justified*: morally speaking, might it have been permissible? Or did he act for an excluded reason, like so many—perhaps all—putative reasons for threatening or perpetrating torture?

More on that last question in § 18.2.1. For the moment, what counts is that an uncertain justification is not in itself a ground to find an excuse. As we noted in § 17.3.1, whether someone is justified in perpetrating a wrong is an all-or-nothing question. Justification doesn't come in degrees. If, all things considered, there is sufficient reason to φ, one crosses the threshold into permissible action; otherwise, one remains outside, consigned to the world of acting badly. Determining that question may involve borderline judgements about the balance and eligibility of reasons, but the conclusion is discrete: between the competing reasons, it is winner-takes-all. If justified, the actor needs no excuse; but if unjustified, whatever reasons there were in favour of φing are defeated and have nothing more to offer. Thus, the possibility of justification

[71] This may need explanation for common lawyers unfamiliar with the German penal system. (Thanks to Antje du Bois-Pedain for her help with this.) Although found guilty, Daschner was not sentenced but rather 'warned' that a fine of €10,800 would be imposed should he reoffend within one year. Under German law, the effect is that the finding of guilty does not count as a criminal conviction. This disposition of a criminal case is highly unusual and should be distinguished from a 'suspended sentence', in which execution of the sentence is merely held pending. A trial court can only dispose of a case with a 'warning' instead of punishment if (1) the court expects that the defendant will not reoffend; (2) special circumstances of the case exceptionally make the imposition of punishment unnecessary; and (3) non-imposition of punishment in the case does not undermine the rule of law.

supplies no direct foundation for excuse.[72] The case for each must be built separately.

17.5 Contrasting irresponsibility

Criminal law textbooks diverge regarding what kinds of irresponsibility conditions count as defences at common law, but perhaps the most generally accepted examples are infancy and insanity.[73] Defences of this kind are predicated on a denial of the defendant's moral responsibility for φing.[74] They recognize her inadequacy as an agent capable of moral deliberation, one able to process and apply moral reasoning to her φing. Rather than undertaking any exculpatory evaluation of the defendant's rationale for φing, defences such as insanity and infancy take the defendant out of the realm of moral agents.[75] It follows that, unlike justifications and excuses, these kinds of defences are *context-insensitive*. Their availability is independent of the moral character of the defendant's action, its appropriateness, and its proportionality to the occasion. Irresponsibility defences are capacity-based. As such, they contain no requirement of proportionality or reasonableness, no evaluation of the defendant with respect to her action. They do not speak to culpability assessments: they pre-empt them. They do not defray blame: they exempt from it.

Irresponsibility defences may explain how it was that something came to be done, but there is an important sense in which they do not address *why* it was done. A rationale-based defence, by contrast—whether justification or excuse—affirms D's responsibility for her action and articulates the reasons why she did it. 'Yes, I did it,' she says, '*and here's why*.' The rationale-based defences are choice-based explanations of pro tanto wrongdoing. They are predicated upon the reasons for which D deliberately acted as she did, and they hold D up to moral evaluation for the choices she made.

Which is why calling irresponsibility defences 'excuses' tends to mislead.[76] Rationale-based excuses are, in this respect, quite unlike irresponsibility

[72] As we noted in § 17.3.1, this is not to deny that the *underlying* reasons in favour of an action can—whether or not defeated—be pertinent to an excuse, in so far as it is understandable why D treated those reasons as sufficient.

[73] The old common-law defence of marital coercion was another (controversial and uncertain) candidate. Some writers categorize automatism as a defence, although in principle it denies voluntariness. For a note on the place of irresponsibility 'defences' within the structure of criminal law, see § 2.2.

[74] See § 4.1.

[75] Admittedly, legal doctrine does not always capture well the underlying moral phenomenon. Notoriously, under the *M'Naghten Rules*, D may be quite mad yet fail to qualify as legally insane, and vice versa. For critical discussion, see *Simester and Sullivan*, §§ 19.1, 22.2(i) and references there cited.

[76] The leading articulation of this point is Gardner, *Offenses and Defences*, ch 6.

defences. The point is often missed. John Austin, for example, characterized justification as an acceptance of responsibility alongside a denial that the action was bad; whereas, he said, excuses 'admit that it was bad but don't accept full, or even any, responsibility.'[77] Similarly, George Fletcher states that claims of justification 'challenge whether the act is wrongful; claims of excuse concede that the act was wrongful, but seek to avoid the attribution of the act to the actor.'[78] Not so. *Irresponsibility defences* do indeed speak to whether the actor is sufficiently morally responsible for her act. Excuses, including rationale-based excuses don't. They speak to culpability. Thus the most basic distinction within defences is between irresponsibility and the other defences, rather than between justifications and excuses. Unlike irresponsibility defences, both justifications and excuses are context-dependent, in that their exculpatory power depends on the nature and seriousness of D's action, as well as upon the circumstances in which it was done. Because of this, all true justifications and excuses contain some form of proportionality or reasonableness condition, some element that imposes an objective constraint upon D's claim to exculpation. Irresponsibility defences don't.

A parallel source of confusion here is the tendency of lawyers to characterize duress in terms of an 'overborne will'.[79] In ordinary duress, however, the will is not overborne. Threats *might* do that. But such cases would be of a different kind—let us call them *coercion*. Consider the threatened use of a rat by O'Brien, the torturer in George Orwell's *1984*.[80] Faced, literally, with that prospect, Winston's primal fear of rats effectively bypassed his rational faculties[81] and caused him to betray his commitment to his partner, Julia—something he had steadfastly refused to do. From the perspective of blaming judgements, there is a meaningful sense in which Winston was not morally responsible for doing so. He was, Frankfurt might say, violated by his own phobia.[82]

We must be astute, though, to ring-fence this kind of case. In a paradigm case of excusatory duress, T presents D with an unwelcome range of alternatives. Yet D has the capacity to choose between them—and does so. She makes

[77] J L Austin, 'A Plea for Excuses' (1956) 57 Proc Arist Soc 1, 3.
[78] *Rethinking*, 759. See, more fully, at 798ff.
[79] Famously decried in P Atiyah, 'Economic Duress and the Overborne Will' (1982) 98 LQR 197.
[80] G Orwell, *Nineteen Eighty-Four* (Secker & Warburg 1949).
[81] I take it *arguendo* that this is what happened.
[82] Like Frankfurt's unwilling drug addict (*Importance*, 17): '[He] hates his addiction and always struggles desperately, although to no avail, against its thrust. He tries everything that he thinks might enable him to overcome his desires for the drug. But these desires are too powerful for him to withstand, and invariably, in the end, they conquer him. He is an unwilling addict, hopelessly violated by his own desires.' The unwilling addict is motivated by desires that are, in an important sense, external to him. See also § 14.4.1.

a choice under duress because she thinks that choice is her best option. D may not, of course, desire that option for its own sake. But she chooses it as a means, and she forms the will that she desires. Unlike Winston, D is morally responsible for what she does; the problem is, rather, that she has an unreasonable range of options. Denials of moral responsibility, including Winston's, involve more fundamental disabilities to recognize or be motivated by reasons.

Like other defences, irresponsibility defences in the common law are generally event-specific. Winston may have failed, but he was in many ways a decent person. Similarly, a condition of insanity is exculpating only in so far as the defendant's condition affects his moral responsibility for the relevant event.[83] Even a radically psychotic killer may be fully competent to buy groceries or obey the traffic laws.[84] Irresponsibility can also come in degrees, something implicitly acknowledged by the modern defence of diminished responsibility.[85] More general defences, such as infancy, draw only very rough lines, marking a boundary where, typically, actors are thought to have *sufficient* capacities for moral reasoning to be counted as morally responsible agents, so that formal assessments of culpability are appropriate. In effect, they operate as threshold conditions for proceeding with a determination of the defendant's culpability (and guilt).

It lies outside the scope of this book to analyse specific irresponsibility defences in detail. What they have in common, however, is that they all involve capacity failures occurring at the level of moral agenthood. The agent's behaviour may be volitional, but it is insufficiently responsive to normative reasons. D acts as she does because she lacks sufficient capacity to be motivated by those reasons for which she ought to act. Failings of this sort take D outside the realm of moral responsibility.

17.6 Revisiting the offence–defence distinction

Morally speaking, an exemption does not look at all like a 'defence'—because it isn't. Since moral responsibility is a precondition of culpability evaluations,

[83] See § 2.2. This is not true of all legal jurisdictions: cf. M Moore, 'The Quest for a Responsible Responsibility Test: The Norwegian Insanity Law after Breivik' (2015) 9 Crim L and Phil 645.

[84] Perhaps not always: contrast Frankfurt's *wanton*, an agent who 'does not care about his will. His desires move him to do certain things, without its being true of him either that he wants to be moved by those desires or that he prefers to be moved by other desires.' *Importance*, 16. Amongst human beings, very young children may fall within this category. Amongst adults, however, such cases are surely exceptional.

[85] See, also, § 19.1ff. The difficult case of *Kingston* [1995] 2 AC 355 (see § 8.5.2) presents another variety of partial irresponsibility; unfortunately, one that the House of Lords considered legally intractable.

it might reasonably be thought that determinations about irresponsibility conditions like infancy and insanity should arise prior rather than subsequent to proof of wrongdoing; rather like the requirement of voluntariness. As we noted in § 2.2, however, there are pragmatic reasons for the law to treat irresponsibility conditions as defences. This is particularly true of insanity, which generates a distinctive verdict and authorizes institutionalization—provided there is an actus reus. Acquittal for lack of actus reus is a very different outcome from acquittal on grounds of insanity. Moreover, an insanity verdict is compatible with either the presence or absence of mens rea on D's part (and, indeed, with either the presence or absence of voluntariness). Yet the difference matters. In the absence of voluntariness or mens rea, a finding of insanity works *against* the defendant—since its effect is to deprive D of an outright acquittal. The same holds if the defendant would otherwise be entitled to an excusatory defence such as mistake, but where the mistake arises from a condition of insanity.[86] By treating such conditions as 'defences', the law retains nuances that a blanket exemption-based approach cannot accommodate.

That legal nicety does not, of course, indicate that the offence–defence line tracks any significant moral distinction. So let us set irresponsibility aside, and focus on justification and excuse, our topics for the next two chapters. In chapter 2,[87] we outlined a variety of institutional reasons, especially communicative and evidential ones, why the criminal law distinguishes as it does between offence and defence elements. As a prelude to chapters 18 and 19, though, we should ask whether there is any inherent moral substance to that distinction. Or is it largely instrumental?

Part of the answer is straightforward. Excuses sit in the moral space between wrongdoing and culpability. Since wrongdoing is both normatively and legally significant, it is meaningful to engage with excusatory defences separately.[88] The more controversial, and difficult, question is why we should carve off justifications. Suppose that φing is a pro tanto crime. If D φs with a (legally recognized) justification, D does no prohibited act. One might reasonably think, therefore, that justification elements ought in principle to be grouped together with the actus reus and mens rea.

That thought would resonate with criminal lawyers in Sweden.[89] According to the conventional structure of Swedish criminal law, justifications are treated as part of the offence definition. Common lawyers, too, occasionally suggest

[86] As in *Oye* [2013] EWCA Crim 1725.
[87] See § 2.1ff.
[88] This point has a practical implication for justifications: see § 17.6.4.
[89] See § 16.4.

that such defences are merely elements of every actus reus which, because of their generality, are not always specified.

It is important to notice that this reconfiguration is not substantively neutral. For one thing, it would foreclose the possibility of unknown-justification cases like *Dadson*,[90] discussed in the previous chapter. Dadson, a policeman, shot and wounded a thief who was stealing wood. The thief was in fact a felon; in principle, therefore, a lawful-arrest justification was available of preventing the felon's escape. Nevertheless the policeman was convicted of unlawful wounding, since he had not known of the circumstances that made his actions justifi*able*. But: if the absence of justifying circumstances were become part of the actus reus, actors like Dadson could not be so convicted, since they would not satisfy the actus reus.

It would also determine cases of *mistaken* justification such as *Beckford*,[91] which we consider in chapter 19. Beckford, also a policeman, had been chasing a suspected criminal. By the time Beckford caught up with him, the victim, who was unarmed, had his hands raised and was begging his pursuer not to shoot him. None the less, and apparently believing—unreasonably—that the victim was about to open fire, Beckford shot him dead. Again: if the absence of justifying circumstances were become part of the actus reus, actors like Beckford should not be convicted, since they would lack mens rea. (Which was more or less the conclusion of the Court.)

Maybe actors like Dadson and Beckford *should* be acquitted? Well, not according to the arguments found in chapters 16 and 19 respectively. What counts for present purposes, though, is the conceptual space that those arguments require. Both sets of arguments depend for their purchase upon there being a normatively significant distinction between offences and defences. More specifically, they depend upon there being a significant distinction between (i) the pro tanto wrong, designated by an actus reus–mens rea combination, and (ii) the wrong *simpliciter* that is perpetrated when, additionally, no justification is available.

We noted in chapter 2 that it can be open for the criminal law to *introduce* such a distinction, in a way that is meaningful within the terms of the legal system. Suppose that the state is in the process of establishing a new regulatory regime, as part of which it is desirable to prohibit advertent φing except when circumstance X is present. Now the state gets an option. It might choose to

[90] (1850) 4 Cox CC 358; see § 16.3.
[91] *Beckford* [1988] 1 AC 130 (PC).

make not-X an element of the actus reus;[92] or it might make the presence of X a defence. Perhaps it may label the former crime 'φing without X', the latter just 'φing'. Endorsement of *Dadson* and rejection of *Beckford* can make options of this kind valuable. By electing to place X on one side or the other of the offence–defence divide, the state can alter both the burden of proof with respect to X (as it does in many jurisdictions[93]) and the substantive conditions required to make X an exonerating factor. On the offence side, X would pre-empt liability for the crime regardless whether the defendant was aware of it;[94] as a matter of defences, the defendant's belief that X would exculpate only if reasonable. Distinctions of this kind can add useful flexibility to the criminal law. But that is an ad hoc matter. In the context of stigmatic crimes such as murder, arguments about the merits of *Dadson*, *Beckford*, and the like assume that the analysis of at least some wrongs (and at least some of their justifications) involves a structural distinction that rests on something deeper than convenience.

Intuitively, that seems right, if only because we are not always indifferent about the classification of offence elements. Indeed, at least for some crimes, the debate is clearly asymmetric. It concerns whether to bring justifications within the offence elements, not the other way around. Few would suggest that we should frame a crime of 'murder' in terms that make the lack of death a defence element.[95] In the absence of something that makes for a wrong, at least provisionally, we lack anything for justifications to grip upon. Death is an essential constituent of the wrong of murder. Hence it should be an offence element. Yet it does not follow that justifications should *not* be offence elements. No doubt the existence of justifications as a distinct category depends on there being a separate category of offence elements. But the question here is whether justifications *are* a distinct category—in particular, whether there are any elements going to the permissibility of an action that are, properly, not part of the pro tanto offence.

To anticipate what follows, I argue in the rest of this chapter that the offence–defence distinction can be defended by reference to a meaningful difference between actions that do not call for justification and actions—pro tanto wrongs—that do. That difference helps to underwrite the motivational

[92] Sometimes called an 'offence modifier': see § 2.1.2. *Dadson* and *Beckford* might be contrasted with the offence-modifying exception that some jurisdictions have for judicial executions. Perhaps a hangman takes the job because he enjoys killing people. Legally speaking, that doesn't matter.

[93] Including the UK, in certain contexts: *Hunt* [1987] AC 352 (HL); more generally, compare s 107 of the Evidence Act 1997 (Singapore). The merits of altering the burden of proof lie outside the scope of this book. For a note of the issues, see *Simester and Sullivan*, § 3.2.

[94] Although inchoate liability might be possible: see § 16.4.

[95] Some might propose an inchoate crime of, say, 'murderous conduct' in which death is not an offence element. But that does not capture the wrong of murder: see § 14.3.

thesis defended in chapter 16. It also supports the claim in chapter 19 that defensive mistakes are a distinct category of excuse. At the same time, the analysis below foreshadows a further subdivision: between justifications that deny the wrong and justifications that concede it. The existence of that subdivision, which I defend in chapter 18, supplies additional reason to think that justifications are rightly distinguished from the pro tanto wrongs they justify.

17.6.1 Infringements and violations

One way of approaching the divide between offences and defences is by looking at a parallel debate in the philosophy of rights, over whether there is a meaningful category of 'infringed' but not violated rights. Doug Husak's summary is helpful: 'When an action implicates our rights justifiably, I will say that our rights are *infringed*. When an action implicates our rights *un*justifiably, I will say that our rights are *violated*.'[96] Infringement, thus, is posited as something intermediate between observance and violation. The parallel thought for the criminal law is that while D's pro tanto wrong may not violate the relevant criminal-law duty, there is a meaningful sense in which D at least infringes it—a sense in which D's action is *at odds* with that duty. By giving substance to that thought, we can give substance to the distinction between offence elements and justifications.

Care is required here, because there is more than one sense in which a right can be infringed. Consider Joel Feinberg's well-known *Cabin* example:[97]

> *Cabin*: Suppose that Denise is on a backpacking trip in the high mountain country when an unanticipated blizzard strikes the area with such ferocity that her life is imperiled. Fortunately, she stumbles onto an unoccupied cabin, locked and boarded up for the winter, clearly somebody else's private property. She smashes a window, enters, and huddles in a corner for three days until the storm abates. During this period she helps herself to her unknown benefactor's food supply and burns his wooden furniture in the fireplace to keep warm.

[96] D Husak, *Overcriminalization* (OUP 2007) 96.

[97] J Feinberg, 'Voluntary Euthanasia and the Inalienable Right to Life' (1978) 7 Phil and Pub Aff 93, 102. For convenience, I have named the protagonist.

For Feinberg, while Denise's actions are permissible, none the less she has 'infringed the clear rights of another person.'[98] Feinberg's underlying thinking is clear enough. The cabin owner has, *inter alia*, a right that Denise not break into the cabin; because her action is permissible, that right is not *violated*; even so, the owner's right is in some sense *contravened* (as Husak would say, 'implicated'), a point evidenced by Denise's ensuing obligation to pay compensation; and to capture that sense Feinberg characterizes it as *infringed*.

There are various ways of contesting this analysis. One possibility is to foreclose a distinct category of infringement by assimilating it with permissibility—in particular, by denying in *Cabin* that compensation is owed at all.[99] This is the line taken by John Oberdiek, who otherwise disputes whether there is a normatively significant gap between what Feinberg sees as 'infringements' and full-blown violations. In particular, Oberdiek argues that recognizing—and compensating for—a category of infringements effectively makes violations unimportant. Consider a case in which trespass to the cabin is *im*permissible:[100]

> *Lazy*: As in *Cabin*, except that the backpacker broke into the cabin on a sunny day, merely because she wanted to rest indoors.

Clearly, *Lazy* involves an impermissible wrong, a *violation* of the cabin-owner's rights. Yet if Denise the trespasser has to pay compensation in *Cabin*, Oberdiek suggests, her case becomes no different from *Lazy*.

That conclusion does not follow. Even granting that compensation is owed in both *Cabin* and *Lazy*, there are significant normative differences. Because Denise's actions in *Cabin* are permissible, the owner is not (either morally or legally) entitled to resist them, and a third party knowing the facts of the matter would be entitled to assist her to break in. That isn't true in *Lazy*. Hence 'permissibly violated' is not an oxymoron.

Notice, however, that once the debate is formulated in these terms it becomes specific to necessity—which is, for reasons set out in chapter 18, a special case. Exceptionally, justifying necessity involves a *permissible wrong*,[101] in as much as the cabin owner's property rights are *overridden* without regard to the right-holder's agency. In such cases, we could indeed use the language of

[98] Ibid.

[99] See, e.g., J Oberdiek, 'Lost in Moral Space: On the Infringing/Violating Distinction and Its Place in the Theory of Rights' (2004) 23 Law and Phil 325, 336–37; J Oberdiek, 'What's Wrong with Infringements (Insofar as Infringements are not Wrong): A Reply' (2008) 27 Law and Phil 293, 302–305.

[100] Oberdiek, 'Lost in Moral Space' (n 99) 326, 335.

[101] For a related category of permissible wrongs, see also Judith Thomson's discussion of conflicting claim-rights: J Thomson, *The Realm of Rights* (Harvard UP 1990) 159.

'infringement' rather than 'violation' to capture the distinctive nature of a permissible wrong: for clarity, call this 'infringement$_{(PW)}$'. But this is not the sense of infringement articulated by Husak. Neither is it the sense of infringement that we need in the wider context of the criminal law's offence–defence distinction, a context that ranges across justifications as a whole and is not specific to necessity. Our challenge here is locate a more general infringement–violation dichotomy—that is, a dichotomy unspecific to necessity. Any more general distinction of this nature should not be reserved to cases, like *Cabin*, in which compensation is owed: because it must apply to self-defence cases too.

So let us introduce another example:

> *Samurai*: Jealous of Dimitri's successful career, Vladimir charges at Dimitri wielding a katana. Correctly realizing that Vladimir means to kill him, having no other weapon to hand, and being much smaller (*et cetera*) than Vladimir, Dimitri pulls out his Smith and Wesson and shoots Dimitri in the chest, killing him.

For the sake of argument, stipulate that killing Vladimir in such circumstances is a proportionate response. As such, this is a standard case of justified self-defence. Yet we can have a similar, albeit not identical, debate about infringement *a là* Feinberg. Vladimir has, *inter alia*, a right not to be killed (by anyone, including Dimitri). Yet, because Dimitri's action is permissible, that right is not *violated*; even so, as Husak would say, Vladimir's right is 'implicated'; and to capture that sense we might characterize it as *infringed*.

What if anything goes awry in this line of thought?

17.6.2 Conditional rights and moral residues

One demurrer might be that Vladimir's right not to be killed *is* violated. Even if killing in self-defence is sometimes permissible, one might argue that it is always a wrong.[102] On this view, Vladimir's right not to be killed is breached even in *Samurai*. Breaches may be permissible or impermissible, and we acknowledge this by labelling them infringements and violations, respectively. When we do so, we treat Dimitri's response in *Samurai* as a justified wrong. It is no different from *Cabin*.

[102] Compare Gardner, *Offences and Defences*, ch 4: but see J Gardner, 'In Defence of Offences and Defences' (2012) 4 Jerusalem R Legal Studies 110, 113; below, §§ 18.3–4.

In many ways, this reasoning is attractive. There is surely *something* problematic about killing a human being, even in self-defence. Killing Vladimir is not morally analogous to killing a plant or insect. Ultimately, however, it is misleading to characterize Dimitri's action as wronging Vladimir. Not only is Dimitri's action permissible, eligible for assistance from third parties, and not open to resistance from Vladimir, but (as is claimed in chapter 18) no moral duty to compensate or apologize arises.[103] In short, it lacks any of the ramifications that we normally associate with a wrong. Rather, it is Vladimir who wrongs Dimitri. This is not to deny the possibility that two such protagonists could each wrong the other—notably, where neither knows about the other's attack.[104] In the context of *Samurai*, however, it seems more apt to characterize Dimitri's response as responding to—preventing—a wrong; not adding a new one. In turn, this suggests that Vladimir lacks a right not to be killed by someone acting in proportionate self-defence.[105] To be sure, Vladimir has a right not to be killed, even by Dimitri. But the right is a qualified one.[106]

Right-qualifications can be either external or internal to the right they qualify. One external condition of Vladimir's right not to be killed, for example, is that Vladimir is a human being.[107] An external condition, if unmet, *cancels* the right. Qua external constraint, therefore, we might characterize Vladimir's right {not to be killed} as suspended while Vladimir is attacking Dimitri: as is sometimes said, Vladimir effectively 'forfeits' his right not to be killed while he is attacking Dimitri.[108] Alternatively, one might treat the limitation as being

[103] See esp. § 18.3.1. As noted there, this is not to deny the appropriateness of feeling (or even showing) regret.

[104] See §§ 16.3–5.

[105] Obviously, the truth of this proposition also depends upon what one means by a 'right': see § 17.6.3.

[106] Up to a point, this this possibility is compatible with what Oberdiek calls a 'moral space' conception of rights ('Lost in Moral Space' (n 99) 326), whereby—drawing upon Nozick's analysis—the scope of a right is 'determined exclusively by facts about the right-holder.' As Oberdiek observes (at 326), the conception is shared by Thomson and Feinberg: 'Of course, where Nozick thinks that the moral space surrounding a right-holder and her holdings is, to extend the metaphor, impenetrable, Thomson and Feinberg clearly do not. After all, to say as Thomson and Feinberg do that infringing (but not violating) a right is possible is just to say that it can be justifiable to penetrate a right-holder's moral space. But, to repeat, Thomson and Feinberg do maintain, with Nozick, that a right-holder enjoys an unchanging moral space—specifically, one that is not affected by circumstances of necessity.' In the context of self-defence, the scope of the limitation upon the right-holder's holdings remains dependent upon facts about the right-holder. Self-defence responds to the right-holder's agency: it is the threat posed by the right-holder that supplies Dimitri's justification in *Samurai*. This, in turn, helps to explain why Dimitri's response is not merely justified: it is not a wrong. (See § 18.3.1.) With that said, however, whether the response is proportionate also depends upon facts about the *respondent*: if Dimitri is much larger and able easily to disarm Vladimir, shooting him may be impermissible. Ultimately, therefore, conditional accounts are incompatible with a moral space conception.

[107] If animals too have such a right, this condition requires modification but remains external.

[108] I take the language of 'forfeiture' here merely to characterize the manner in which Vladimir's pro tanto right is defeated in self-defence contexts. As Massimo Renzo points out, it does not explain *why* that right should be defeated: M Renzo, 'Rights Forfeiture and Liability to Harm' (2017) 25 J Pol Phil 324

internal to the right: Vladimir's right is {not to be killed except in proportionate self-defence}.

There are known difficulties with an external-condition account of self-defence. It suggests what is sometimes called an 'outlaw' status: that for the relevant period, Vladimir's life stands outside the protection of the law and/or morality, as the case may be.[109] Anyone can kill Vladimir—even if unaware of the attack—without wronging him. Even if some of those difficulties can be negotiated by tweaking the external condition,[110] there remains a structural oddity. Intuitively, it seems plausible that Vladimir *never* holds a right not to be killed in proportionate self-defence. But on an external-condition account, he does hold such a right (as part of his general right not to be killed) until he begins to attack Dimitri. To my mind, that analysis has the wrong shape. It fails to track the way in which the primary justifications (like self-defence) carve out *exceptions* to the rights they qualify, rather than temporarily *cancel* them.

For our immediate purposes, however, this is a side-issue. Regardless whether the qualification be internal or external, treating Vladimir's pro tanto right not to be killed as conditional fits with the thought that, in self-defence contexts (and unlike necessity), that right is not merely overridden.[111] Yet for that very reason, both condition-based accounts face the same challenge. The challenge is to identify a sense in which Vladimir's right not to be killed *continues to speak* even in circumstances of self-defence, such that it is meaningful to describe the right as infringed.

How can we show that Vladimir's right continues to speak in such cases? One promising approach would be to point to some *moral residue* that follows its infringement.[112] To the extent that Dimitri has infringed Vladimir's right, we might expect that a derivative duty falls upon him to do something to repair the damage; where the grounds of that duty arise from Vladimir's original, infringed, right—the residue of which continues to make demands of its infringer, on a next-best basis, for partial conformity.[113] But it is not easy to

[109] A point made in G P Fletcher, 'The Right to Life' (1979) 13 Georgia LR 1371, 1381.

[110] See, e.g., K K Ferzan, 'Forfeiture and Self-defense' in C Coons and M Weber (eds), *The Ethics of Self-Defense* (OUP 2016) 233.

[111] See chapter 18 for the claim that necessity is a case of overriding (and thus of infringement$_{(PW)}$); also for the distinction between primary and residual justifications.

[112] See, e.g., Thomson, *The Realm of Rights* (n 101) 84ff.

[113] John Gardner makes a similar point about reasons, in what he later named the 'continuity thesis': 'If one does not fully conform to a reason—if one does not do exactly what it is a reason to do—the reason does not evaporate. It does not evaporate even though one was justified in not conforming to it. It does not evaporate even though it is now too late fully to conform to it. Instead it now counts as a reason for doing the next-best thing.' See J Gardner, 'Wrongs and Faults' in *Appraising Strict Liability* 51, 57; and, for the christening, J Gardner, 'What is Tort Law For? Part 1. The Place of Corrective Justice' (2011) 30 Law and Phil 1.

locate any such residue. Indeed, the absence of a derivative duty for Dimitri to compensate or apologize suggests there is none: which counsels against the possibility of a distinct category of infringement, at least for the primary justifications.

Perhaps, though, we just need to try harder? Consider the following example:

> *Disablement*: As in *Samurai*, except that when Dimitri shoots Vladimir, he inflicts serious injuries but does not immediately cause death. Now disabled and prone, Vladimir is slowly bleeding to death. Dimitri has a mobile telephone and can summon medical aid that will save Vladimir's life.

It is plausible that, once his assailant is disabled, Dimitri acquires a (moral and legal) duty to do what he reasonably can to avert Vladimir's death. His normative position is not the same as that of a bystander.[114] Moreover, the duty is seemingly derivative. Suppose that Diane is CEO of a business in competition with Edgar. Diane's superior marketing skills rapidly win over Edgar's customers and drive Edgar out of business. Diane is under no duty to mitigate the losses her marketing campaign may cause to Edgar, because she does not wrong him in the first place. Given that Dimitri was under no duty not to kill Vladimir while being attacked, *Disablement* challenges us to explain why Dimitri's position is unlike that of Diane or indeed a bystander.

That challenge can be met, however, without invoking a moral residue. Recall the case of *Miller*,[115] discussed in § 5.3.1:

> Miller, a vagrant, was sleeping in an unoccupied house. He fell asleep while smoking a cigarette, which then set fire to his mattress. Waking to find the mattress smouldering, Miller simply moved to the next room and went back to sleep. The house caught fire; Miller was charged with its reckless arson. On appeal, the House of Lords held that his omission to take remedial measures satisfied the actus reus requirement. His inadvertent starting of the fire crystallized a legal duty to prevent risks caused by his earlier, positive behaviour.

The grounds of Dimitri's duty in *Disablement* are analogous to those in *Miller*. When he shoots Vladimir, Dimitri breaches no duty. When the mattress

[114] I take it that, if the bystander owes a duty at all to rescue Vladimir, that duty has a different stringency from the one owed by Dimitri. (At any rate, this is true in all legal systems with which I am familiar.)

[115] [1983] 2 AC 161 (HL); see § 5.3.1.

catches fire, Miller breaches no duty either.[116] Yet in both cases the defendant thereby becomes causally involved in the ensuing chain of events, sufficiently so to make each of them accountable for what follows. The duties arising in both *Miller* and *Disablement*, that is to say, turn not upon the moral residue of antecedently broken duties but upon questions explored in Part II, of *ascriptive responsibility*. As such, the relevant normative question is whether the defendant is accountable for the death or the house fire. If he is so accountable, the defendant has a duty to prevent it from happening.

Ascriptive responsibility can arise in a variety of ways, as we saw in chapters 5 through 7. Even a passer-by would have a duty to intervene in *Disablement*, were Vladimir her dependent child. But the important point for now is that ascriptive responsibility is not wrong-dependent. Consider, too, a variant of Jeff McMahon's well-known example of an innocent threat, to which we return in chapter 18:[117]

> *Cell-phone**: A villain has secretly tampered with Veronica's cell phone in such a way that if she presses the 'call' button, she will detonate a bomb to which David has been tied by this same villain. Pressing the call button does not immediately detonate the bomb: rather, it starts a countdown timer that will trigger detonation in a few minutes. Veronica types in a number and presses the call button. Just after doing so, however, Veronica learns the facts. She also realizes there is a way of disabling the bomb.

Normatively speaking, I take it that *Cell-phone** resembles *Disablement* and *Miller*. It seems plausible that, analogous to those other cases, Veronica would come under a duty to stop the timer before it triggers detonation.

Viewed together, the examples suggest that Dimitri's duty in *Disablement* to save Vladimir is not derivative—it does not arise from the moral residue of a prior wrong. The duty now owed by each of the foregoing protagonists is a primary one, not to cause death by omission; where the ascriptive responsibility each bears for the looming fatality rests *simpliciter* upon their earlier, causal contribution to its occurrence. Alas, therefore, *Disablement* does not yield a solution to our moral residue problem.

[116] Nothing turns for present purposes on who owns the mattress: I assume that it (but not the house) belongs to Miller. Even *aliter*, Miller would breach no criminal-law duty: his duty is not to avoid causing damage, but to avoid causing damage *recklessly*. This important point, which affects Miller's—and our—range of freedoms, was explored in § 3.3.1. In any event, in the case itself, causing the fire was treated as an accident; rightly, the *Miller* principle does not turn on whether the initial causative act was negligent.

[117] J McMahon, 'The Basis of Moral Liability to Defensive Killing' (2005) 15 Phil Issues 386, 397.

17.6.3 Rights, duties, and rationales

We have found little evidence so far that Vladimir's right not to be killed by Dimitri continues to speak in *Samurai*. If anything, the opposite is indicated. Vladimir's right seems to have nothing to say about Dimitri's actions—and to generate no moral residue—because the conditions, whether external or internal, of that right are unmet.

Suppose we concede that. When we do so, however, we should draw two distinctions. What does continue to speak in *Samurai*, if not the right itself, is the rationale behind it.[118] And that is not a trivial matter. Moreover, it doesn't follow that no rights of any kind are in play. As Judith Thomson might put it,[119] one type of right that preserves its voice in *Samurai* is the *cluster-right* to life that Vladimir has—and which he retains even while attacking Dimitri. Cluster-rights are 'rights that contain other rights':[120] more specifically, claim-rights, privileges, powers, and immunities. A cluster-right protects something of value (in Vladimir's case, his life) by means of the more specific claim-rights, *et cetera*, that the cluster-right both contains and explains.

Cluster-rights can themselves be subject to external conditions. (Vladimir's cluster-right to life, for example, is contingent upon his being a human being.) Provided any such external conditions are met, a cluster-right may be contravened even when it is unsupported by, say, a claim-right. Herein lies an explanation of how one might *infringe* a claim-right without wronging the right-holder. We can meaningfully say that an underlying cluster-right is contravened, and that the interests protected by it and a contained claim-right are set back, even though the claim-right itself is not violated because one of its conditions goes unmet. The rationale supplied by the cluster-right subsists, even if it does not support a claim-right not to be killed on this occasion; that rationale continues to explain other rights within the cluster.

This analysis also supports the distinction between *making an exception* to a claim-right and *cancelling* it. Suppose that John owns a book. His ownership-right contains a claim-right that others, including Mark, not take the book. But if John transfers the book to Mark, that claim-right against Mark is cancelled. John's act of transference does not operate like a justification at all. It does not generate positive reasons for Mark to take the book, reasons that defeat the grounds of John's

[118] Unfortunately, there is ambiguity in the language of rights. One might take the underlying rationale to be embedded within the 'right' itself (as in Raz, *The Morality of Freedom*, 255). For the sake of exegesis, I assume that is not true of claim-rights.

[119] *The Realm of Rights* (n 101) 55–57.

[120] Ibid, 55.

claim-right. Rather, John's claim-right ceases to exist; and, crucially, so does the cluster-right that contained it.

By contrast, even if Vladimir lacks a claim-right in *Samurai* not to be killed by Dimitri in proportionate self-defence, his underlying right to life remains. Thus the *rationale* for holding that Vladimir has a claim-right against Dimitri remains applicable in *Samurai*. The cluster-right continues to speak, and to inform the requirement of proportionality governing Dimitri's response.

The payoff for criminal law emerges clearly from a parallel analysis of Dimitri's duties. Dimitri has a duty, let us concede, not to kill Vladimir or any other human being. The reasons in favour of imposing that duty continue to apply in *Samurai*. None the less, Dimitri does not breach the duty. His conduct is lawful. Why? For Dimitri to have such a duty means that he has a first-order reason not to kill Vladimir; and that he has a second-order reason excluding various reasons that might otherwise count in favour of killing. What is *not* excluded, however, is a first-order reason not to be killed by Vladimir, which is the same kind of reason that grounds the duty itself and which the exclusionary reason protects.[121] Ultimately, this unexcluded reason is what makes killing Vladimir permissible all things considered.

At the same time, two constraints subsist. First, the countervailing first-order reason not to kill Vladimir remains in play, and still needs to be defeated.[122] Dimitri's unexcluded first-order reason(s) for action must be sufficient to justify killing Vladimir—the requirement of proportionality.[123] Secondly, the second-order reason also remains in play.[124] It is not cancelled either. The original reasons why Dimitri is under a duty not to kill Vladimir continue to justify the existence of that duty—the operation of which continues to exclude bad reasons for killing Vladimir, just as before. It is simply that the exclusion doesn't apply to Dimitri's reason in *Samurai*: it never applied to reasons of that type. This is part of the explanation of the motivational thesis. It helps to explain why, as I argued in the previous chapter, it is only if Dimitri acts *for* unexcluded reasons that his action can be justified. Yet once we concede these

[121] I do not claim that an exact match of reason-kinds is necessary. It seems likely, for example, that one may sometimes be justified in killing in order to prevent an aggressor from inflicting extremely serious injuries.

[122] I assume that, in *Samurai*, it is indeed defeated. More particularly, the fact that Vladimir is trying to kill him gives Dimitri an exclusionary permission to disregard that countervailing reason: cp. J. Raz, 'Permission and Supererogation' (1975) Am Phil Q 161. But this is not a feature of justifications per se; it arises from the fact that Vladimir is violating Dimitri's own right not to be killed.

[123] Suppose that Vladimir was merely prodding Dimitri angrily with a finger. Even if there were no other means available to prevent that assault, Dimitri would not be justified in killing him. Cp. § 17.1.1.

[124] The point is incidental here, but this seems to me a weakness of external-condition accounts of self-defence.

two constraints, we cannot say that Vladimir's right not to be killed by Dimitri has ceased to exist. It merely admits of exceptions. The case for exceptions arises out of the ineluctable need to trade off freedoms and interests within a society of interacting, sometimes conflicting, human beings. Ultimately, Dimitri's interests have priority over Vladimir's in *Samurai*—in part because it is Vladimir's actions that have put them in tension.

17.6.4 Offence, defence

The cancellation/exception dichotomy translates naturally to the law's offence/justification distinction, and thus to its offence/defence distinction. As a preliminary matter, notice that there is a pragmatic institutional reason for assimilating justifications with the other defences. We saw in chapter two that there is a meaningful distinction between the *unlawful* wrong, constituted by the pro tanto offence when done without justification, and the *crime* that results when no other defence is available either.[125] At the level of principle, excuses do not deny the defendant's wrong. Rather, they address her culpability for that wrong. As such, they can and should be distinguished from offence elements: a point made in § 17.6. This point may be straightforward, but it has knock-on implications for justifications. When translated into common-law practice, the theoretical distinction between justification and excuse cuts across the doctrinal boundaries of recognized defences. Some defendants qualifying for a legal defence such as duress may in principle be justified while others are merely excused. As a matter of doctrinal structure, therefore, justifications are inevitably classified alongside excuses on the defence side of the offence–defence distinction.

Happily, the grounds for doing so are not merely pragmatic. The example of John and Mark (§ 17.6.3) illustrates how the distinction between cancellations and exceptions or overridings can be tracked by offence and defence elements. At the point when Mark takes the book, both the first—and second-order reasons for him not to take the book—the reasons that otherwise would derive from John's ownership-right[126]—have ceased to exist. Mark has no duty at all to refrain from taking the book. Move along, as the police might say: there's nothing to see here.

Contrast *Samurai*. Treating the conditions of self-defence as part of the pro tanto offence—specifically, as part of the actus reus—would amount to treating

[125] See §§ 2.1–2.

[126] Of course, there may be other reasons for Mark not to take the book. Perhaps John would otherwise give it to Kay, who has greater need for it. But those reasons do not derive from John's ownership-right.

Vladimir's legal right to life as cancelled, and his interest therein as outside the protection of the criminal law. But that gets things exactly wrong. We recognize self-defence on the basis that it is acceptable for a defendant *in such circumstances* to set back the victim's interests. The grounds for doing so are not predicated upon there being anything different about the victim's right to life, or about the injury he suffers. Sometimes, exceptionally, it is permissible to do the very type of thing that we have a criminal-law duty not to do, where the circumstances are such that the duty itself is not cancelled and what we do remains a pro tanto wrong. By marking such circumstances as justificatory rather than offence modifiers, the law signals more clearly the values being protected and the duties that protect them. Doing so allows the pro tanto offence to articulate the outer boundary of the criminal-law wrong; justifications carve out exceptions to that wrong while preserving its basic shape and communicating its underlying character. Andrew Ashworth once suggested that 'someone who makes a murderous attack on another must forfeit his right to life if this appears to be the only way in which the victim's life can be preserved.'[127] But the criminal law need not, should not, be quite so blunt. By segregating defences, it restricts itself to allowing that Vladimir's conduct partially liberates Dimitri from his duty not to harm Vladimir, but not from all the duties contained in Vladimir's cluster-right to life. And so it respects Vladimir as well as Dimitri.

Notice that the role of exonerating factors therefore depends upon what wrong it is that the legislator wants to prohibit, and why. It depends, in other words, upon the legislator's *ex ante* grounds of criminalization.[128] For this reason, even consent can sometimes operate as a ground of exception rather than cancellation. Consider an argument that was judicially endorsed in the notorious case of *Brown*.[129] According to that (paternalistic) argument, it should not be legally possible to consent to the mutual infliction of serious injuries,[130] because the underlying, valuable interests that both parties have in their own health and physical integrity are set back regardless of their consent. One possible response to an argument of this kind might concede the premise but claim that norms of privacy and free expression none the less defeat the case for criminalization. Such a rejoinder would, in effect, argue for a

[127] A Ashworth, 'Self-Defence and the Right to Life' [1975] CLJ 282, 288.

[128] See the discussion in § 2.1.2.

[129] [1994] 1 AC 212; see *Simester and Sullivan*, § 21.1. The defendants voluntarily engaged in sadomasochistic sexual acts on an organized basis. However, their consent was ruled legally irrelevant on charges of occasioning actual bodily harm and unlawful wounding.

[130] The argument in the text assumes more serious injuries than were caused in the case itself, none of which required medical treatment.

consent-dependent exception.[131] And it would be consistent with the rule in *Brown* that consent to such injuries is a defence element.[132]

17.7 In closing

The criminal law rightly differentiates between offences and defences. The distinction is intrinsically meaningful as well as instrumentally valuable, Even so, there are limits to how far we can generalize about the ingredients of blaming judgements. As this chapter has suggested, justifications and rationale-based excuses have much in common, not least in their implications for criminal-law verdicts. On the other hand, the distinction in morality between rationale-based and irresponsibility defences has fundamental implications for the structure of their corresponding defences in law. The analogy that Fletcher drew between duress and 'normative' involuntariness, for instance, turns out to be profoundly mistaken.[133] Involuntariness is context-insensitive: duress is not. The rules of the criminal law reflect that distinction. And so they should.

131 Specifically, a condonation: above, § 17.2.

132 A similar analysis holds in the context of medical necessity, which is conditional (where relevant) upon the patient's consent. In such cases, consent operates as a defence element.

133 Cp. Fletcher, *Rethinking*, 802–807.

18

Unpacking Justifications

Emergencies are isolating. Faced with the need to φ, D is on her own. She needs to take urgent action that cannot be authorized in advance by officials—but that action is prohibited. Through no fault of her own,[1] she is caught in a legal and moral dilemma: it is wrong to φ, but grave consequences await if she doesn't. At the crucial moment when nuanced guidance is most needed, she is cut off.

A daunting picture. And an exaggerated one. Certainly, when we face the prospect of illegality and prosecution, we need guidance as well as understanding. But when emergency comes, and official help is unavailable, the law does not run out. Action, if taken, need not be extra-legal. The common law knows a range of rationale-based defences, according to which otherwise pro tanto wrongs may become permitted, or at least exculpated. By articulating defences like self-defence and necessity, the legal system adds the interstitial nuance that its prohibitions require.

In order to do so, however, the law must appeal to broader ideas such as proportionality and reasonableness. And that raises a worry. Surely its doing so undermines the rule of law? Doesn't it render the law unpredictable and discretionary? Concerns of this variety have been expressed before. Indeed, they led to the rejection of lesser-evils necessity,[2] in particular, as a justification in Canada:[3]

> 'The Criminal Code has specified a number of identifiable situations in which an actor is justified in committing what would otherwise be a criminal offence. To go beyond that and hold that ostensibly illegal acts can be validated on the basis of their expediency, would import an undue subjectivity into the criminal law. It would invite the courts to second-guess the legislature and to assess the relative merits of social

[1] Or, at least, outwith certain types of fault: see, e.g., P H Robinson, 'Causing the Conditions of One's Own Defense: A Study in the Limits of Theory in Criminal Law Doctrine' (1985) 71 Virginia LR 1.

[2] Necessity as a legal defence has a number of distinct threads, especially in medical contexts, but my focus in this chapter is primarily upon the 'lesser-evils' version; and, within that, upon cases in which necessity comes into its own as a residual defence, not overlapping with other justifications like self-defence.

[3] *Perka v The Queen* [1985] 13 DLR (4th) 1, 14 (SCC) *per* Dickson J.

Fundamentals of Criminal Law. A P Simester, Oxford University Press (2021). © A P Simester.
DOI: 10.1093/oso/9780198853145.003.0018

policies underlying criminal prohibitions. Neither is a role which fits well with the judicial function.'

The Canadian Supreme Court went too far. Necessity is not a rationale-based excuse,[4] because it involves permitted—lawful—action. And the difference matters.[5] Yet one can readily appreciate the Court's concern. Unlike other justifications, necessity is unconfined by reference to specific activities, such as protecting oneself from attack or executing an arrest. Its field of application is amorphous and open-ended. That sheer breadth gives weight to the Supreme Court's worry.

Even so, the worry was overstated. It is not true that necessity is based on expediency. Neither does necessity have an untrammelled structure—either morally or, properly understood, legally. To see this, though, we need to see why necessity differs from other, primary,[6] justifications. For necessity is certainly *different*, and the differences are profound. It is unlike the primary justifications in both its normative significance and its internal structure. The category of justifications is not so unitary as many think.

Defending these claims requires a closer consideration of justifications more generally. Suppose that D's act of φing is a pro tanto wrong. Across §§ 18.2 and 18.3, I begin by developing two theses, which can be summarized as follows:

(i) *Wrong-dependence*: Whether D's φing is justified depends on the type of (pro tanto) wrong that φing is.
(ii) *Justification-dependence*: Whether D's φing is a wrong *simpliciter* depends on the type of justification that D has.

Justification-dependence engages what is sometimes called the 'closure' view of wrongdoing, according to which D's φing cannot be a wrong (*simpliciter*) unless it is done wrongfully—unless, that is, it is done without justification.[7] On that analysis, if D's φing is justified, it is no more than a pro tanto wrong. Many criminal theorists endorse the closure view;[8] it has been described by Mitch

[4] Although it can overlap with other defences, including excuses: see § 17.2.1. German law helpfully disambiguates: justifying necessity is permitted in StGB § 34; excusing necessity is exculpated in StGB § 35.

[5] See, in particular, §§ 18.4–5.

[6] Including self-defence, defence of property, and prevention of crime. See esp. § 18.3.3.

[7] Cp. Gardner, *Offences and Defences*, 77: according to the closure view, 'no action is wrong unless it is wrong all things considered.'

[8] *Inter alia* G Fletcher, 'The Nature of Justification' in S C Shute, J Gardner, and J Horder (eds), *Action and Value in Criminal Law* (OUP 1993) 175; Moore, *Placing Blame* 673; A Norrie, *Punishment, Responsibility, and Justice: A Relational Critique* (OUP 2000) 153.

Berman as 'standard'.[9] For John Gardner, on the other hand, 'by pleading a justification [D] does not *deny* but rather *concedes* criminal wrongdoing, which is the very thing that he then tries to justify.'[10] Justified φing, according to Gardner, is a wrong *simpliciter*.

Justification-dependence holds that neither of these views is right. Whether justified φing is a wrong depends on what kind of justification is in play. The primary justifications do indeed negate the wrong. But necessity does not.[11]

That difference may not matter very much when it comes to criminal-law verdicts. Either way, a justified actor is not a wrongdoer.[12] She is in principle blameless and eligible for acquittal. However, it matters for the law more generally, since it explains why D's φing under necessity can generate an obligation to compensate. Such obligations are derivative: they arise from the normative residue of D's wrong. And they do not arise when D's φing is pursuant to a primary justification.

The difference also affects the criteria of justifications *within* the criminal law. Where D commits a pro tanto wrong and claims necessity rather than one of the primary justifications, she loses access to some potentially justifying reasons that would not otherwise be excluded from consideration. Sometimes, those reasons are ruled out entirely; on other occasions, they may be disallowed when they stand in a means–end relationship with the pro tanto wrong. Either way, it follows that the criminal law ought to differentiate between types of justification and, specifically, that it ought to recognize a justification of necessity. Moreover, the Canadian Supreme Court need not have been so troubled by that prospect. Once we dispel certain misconceptions about the defence, a principled account of necessity can be given, in which its existence is both legitimate and exceptional.

18.1 Corralling justifications generally

Suppose that V is a terrorist who is about to detonate an explosive in a crowded shopping mall. D, a police officer, recognizes what V is about to do and shoots him dead. D has committed a pro tanto crime, but she has a supervening,

[9] M Berman, 'Justification and Excuse, Law and Morality' (2003) Duke LJ 1, 7–9.

[10] Gardner, *Offences and Defences*, 79. Gardner himself came to doubt this claim: see § 18.3.3.

[11] Cp. J McMahon, *Killing in War* (Clarendon 2009) ch 4; J Quong, 'Killing in Self-Defence' (2009) 119 Ethics 507.

[12] i.e., someone who does an unjustified wrong: see § 1.3.2.

rationale-based defence. In her case, the claim is one of justification. We might say—and criminal theorists often do say—that her action was a proportionate and necessary response to the emergency situation. More accurately, though, we can say that D's action was an *appropriate* response and, for that reason, permitted.

The tweak may seem minor. But it points towards an important feature of justifications within morality and law. Many formulations of necessity run along the lines that conduct is justified whenever, after weighing up all the alternatives, φing is a 'proportionate' evil, a 'lesser' evil than not-φing. According to § 3.02(1) of the Model Penal Code,

> 'Conduct that the actor believes to be necessary to avoid a harm or evil to himself or to another is justifiable, provided that: (a) the harm or evil sought to be avoided by such conduct is greater than that sought to be prevented by the law defining the offense charged.'

A similar, common-law version has found favour in the English Court of Appeal:[13]

> 'The claim is that [D's] conduct was not harmful because on a choice of two evils the choice of avoiding the greater harm was justified . . . . According to Sir James Stephen there are three necessary requirements for the application of the doctrine of necessity: (i) the act is needed to avoid inevitable and irreparable evil; (ii) no more should be done than is reasonably necessary for the purpose to be achieved; (iii) the evil inflicted must not be disproportionate to the evil avoided.'

A key question, of course, is how to evaluate when harms are proportionate or 'lesser'. One might naturally think that the harms involved need to be measured against each other in order to determine which harm, or which set of harms, is the weightier.[14] (Let us call this a *ranking* approach.) D can break into a cabin during a snow-storm because saving a life is more important than respecting property rights. Fire-fighters can raze V's house to create a fire break

[13] *Re A (Children)* [2001] Fam 147, 236, 240 (Brooke LJ). The reference is to J F Stephen, *Digest of the Criminal Law* (4th edn, MacMillan 1887) 24–25.

[14] Nuanced approaches are possible. Peter Westen and James Mangiafico, for example, offer an analysis in which the weight of each harm can be tweaked: P Westen and J Mangiafico, 'The Criminal Defense of Duress: A Justification, Not an Excuse—And Why It Matters' (2003) 6 Buffalo Crim LR 833, 888ff. Westen and Mangiafico suggest (at 835–36) that 'an evil which is greater than another when inflicted upon a bystander can become less than, or equal to, the other evil when inflicted upon an aggressor; and an evil which is greater than another when it is initiated by an actor can become less than, or equal to, the other evil when it is simply redirected by an actor.' The authors remain, however, committed to a ranking approach.

because losing the village outweighs the evil of losing one home. In the notorious Trolley Problem,[15] D can throw a switch to divert the trolley because five deaths constitute a proportionately greater harm than just one. And so on.

Now if that really were the right way to decide when a harm is proportionate, necessity would threaten to swallow not only the other justifications but also the rule of law. A general 'lesser-evils' defence of this kind would be enormously elastic. Especially during a crisis, it could too easily garb extra-legal measures with cloaks of legitimacy. Even in ordinary times, necessity would risk undermining legislative prohibitions. In effect, such a defence might threaten to revise every pro tanto offence into an ad hoc exhortation, not to inflict harm save proportionately. Determining what actions were permissible would then become a matter of case-by-case discretion, notwithstanding legislative efforts to lay down general rules.[16] No wonder the Canadian Supreme Court was sceptical. It seems clearly inappropriate for individuals or even courts to substitute their ad hoc judgements of the balance of interests, Robin-Hood like, for the general determination of social priorities that is properly made by Parliament:[17]

> 'The law regards with the deepest suspicion any remedies of self-help, and permits these remedies to be resorted to only in very special circumstances. The reason for such circumspection is clear—necessity can very easily become simply a mask for anarchy.'

However, there are a number of factors that mean necessity, properly understood, does not do this. The first is the emergency itself. Unilateral action is permissible only when an individual is faced with having to act in situations where recourse to the state is unavailable. In such cases, the individual does not usurp the determinative role of the legal system. Conversely, if the situation is

[15] To recap: D is the driver of a runaway rail trolley that is about to strike and kill five workmen on the track ahead. If he diverts the trolley to a siding, the five will be saved but the trolley will instead strike and kill a lone worker who is on the siding. See P Foot: 'The Problem of Abortion and the Doctrine of the Double Effect' (1967) Ox Rev 5; J J Thomson, 'The Trolley Problem' (1985) 94 Yale LJ 1395.

[16] In practice, this risk can be ameliorated where a statute enumerates the permissible exceptions with sufficient specificity to exclude a justification based on the facts at hand: compare the Model Penal Code, § 3.02(1)(b)–(c); *Quayle* [2005] EWCA Crim 1415 (permissibility of privately using cannabis for pain relief held to be excluded by the comprehensive nature of the legislative scheme). Inevitably, though, explicit provision of this kind is not the norm.

[17] *Southwark London Borough Council v Williams* [1971] Ch 734, 745–46 (Edmund Davies LJ). Hence, in a tort action for trespass, the Court denied Williams a defence of necessity. Appropriately so: the use of vacant council properties, as in Southwark, is best resolved by political decision-making processes, implemented by consistent administration, rather than by self-help actions like squatting. However, to anticipate the text below, Williams could justifiably have sheltered in that same council house if, in an emergency, he needed to do so in order to survive a dangerous storm.

not urgent, so that resolution by the state is possible, that same individual may not take the situation into her own hands.

This first point applies to justifications generally,[18] and it is institutional. It does not resolve the question whether authorization, if available, *should* be forthcoming. Consider *Re A (Children)*.[19] In that case, the Court of Appeal was asked to rule whether a medical operation to separate conjoined twins would be lawful. Emergency was not in play; necessity was. What other factors, then, can we point to? What else constrains the generic proportionality criterion that all justifications must satisfy?

One important consideration was identified in chapter 17. It is that justifications are not simply a matter of weighing up the strength of the reasons not to cause various harms.[20] For a reason to justify committing a pro tanto wrong, not only must it possess the requisite strength, but it must also stand in an eligible relationship to that wrong. This constraint begins, though it does not end,[21] with the truth that some reasons for committing the wrong may be excluded,[22] under certain or even all circumstances, from consideration. And it tends to be overlooked in standard formulations of necessity, because the possibility of excluded reasons is not addressed by generic criteria of a proportionate or 'lesser' evil.[23] A justification cannot be established merely by piling up the assorted desirable features of an action and balancing them against all the various disadvantages. The matter is not simply a weighting exercise. Justificatory reasons are a matter of category as well as degree.

18.2 Wrong-dependence

The range of excluded reasons for doing an action is not fixed. It depends upon what action is being done. Consequently, the scope of available justifications *varies with the wrong that falls to be justified*. Safeguarding property is an excluded reason to kill, but it may be grounds for creating a fire-break on another's land. Or suppose that Donald is about to be killed by an assassin. Donald is justified in pulling a table in front of him to use as a shield. He is not

[18] Compare s 99 of the Indian Penal Code 1860: 'There is no right of private defence in cases in which there is time to have recourse to protection of the public authorities.'

[19] *In re A (Children) (Conjoined Twins: Surgical Separation)* [2001] Fam 147: below, § 18.5.

[20] Or even the adjusted strengths, as Westen and Mangiafico suggest: see n 14 above.

[21] Below, § 18.3.

[22] Raz, *Practical Reason and Norms*, § 1.2. For elucidation, see §§ 18.2–3.

[23] Cf. StGB § 34, requiring the court not only to weigh up the conflicting interests, including the degree of risk to them, but in addition requiring that the necessitous action be an 'appropriate' means to avert the danger.

justified in dragging Virgil, an innocent bystander, in front of the bullet. The wrong of damaging property is more easily justified than the wrong of killing.

At first glance, this might seem a simple matter of proportionality. If nothing else, however, it isn't simple. Saving life is sometimes an excluded reason, sometimes not. It may, for example, be available to justify killing one's attacker even as it is disallowed as a ground for doing other (pro tanto) wrongs, such as torture.[24] Indeed, it is arguable that a wrong like torture is never justifiable: that torture is an *absolute* wrong, in as much as all possible reasons to torture are excluded. I take this last claim to be at the heart of the controversy whether, morally speaking, torture is ever legalizable.[25] Doubtless there are compelling practical and institutional arguments why the legal system should prohibit torture absolutely, without possibility of derogation;[26] but those arguments become less important if torture is never morally permissible. We should start, therefore, with the intersection of specific wrongs and their justification. And we should start by recognizing that at least one familiar approach to that intersection is profoundly mistaken.

The mistake is made when one views the justification of wrongs such as torture through the lens of necessity, and it is compounded by applying a ranking-based metric of lesser-evils. Since torture is abhorrent, something pretty extreme is required to justify it and, in practice, such cases may be unlikely. Yet implicit in this way of thinking is that, in principle, it is just a matter of finding a sufficiently serious case. Unless evils are treated as infinite, the moral prohibition is not, indeed cannot be, absolute:[27]

> 'The use of torture is so profound a violation of a human right that almost nothing can redeem it—almost, because one cannot rule out a case in which the lives of many innocent persons will surely be saved by its use against a single person.'

[24] Unavoidably, this chapter involves some first-order ethical discussion, especially of the conditions under which torture and killing may be permissible. Discussion of these *exempla* is not my direct concern. It is included only to help tease out more general theses about necessity and self-defence (in particular).

[25] See, e.g., D Dyzenhaus, 'The State of Emergency in Legal Theory' in V V Ramraj, M Hor, and K Roach (eds), *Global Anti-Terrorism Law and Policy* (CUP 2005) 65, 84.

[26] For instance, there is a risk that officials might stretch the boundaries of legal torture, exploiting its selective permission to brutalize and abuse the powerless: see, e.g., O Gross, 'Are Torture Warrants Warranted? Pragmatic Absolutism and Official Disobedience' (2004) 88 Minnesota LR 1481, § I; S F Kreimer, 'Too Close to the Rack and the Screw: Constitutional Constraints on Torture in the War on Terror' (2003) 6 U Pennsylvania J Const L 278, 322. A more profound objection, that authorizing torture strikes at the heart of any decent legal system, can be found in J Waldron's inspiring essay, 'Torture and Positive Law: Jurisprudence for the White House' (2005) 105 Columbia LR 1681, 1726ff.

[27] S H Kadish, 'Torture, the State and the Individual' (1989) 23 Israel LR 345, 346. In a footnote, Kadish seeks to safeguard his position by suggesting that the imbalance in the weighting of evils must be 'extremely great'.

The difficulty with this analysis is that, provided the stakes are high enough, potentially anything goes.[28] For those who argue that official torture is capable of justification, an extreme case can be generated as a kind of high-water mark. Once a single case is accepted on the weight of numbers, algebra can take over. Indeed, there is no principled ground to limit official torture to the infliction of harmless but unbearable pain.[29] Why not mutilate the suspect—or the suspect's family—to get her to talk? (If that's worse, its justification merely requires that more lives depend on it.) The conclusion of this approach is that, at the very point when its bite is most needed, the 'right' not to be tortured loses its teeth. It becomes a right not to be tortured *until we really need to*. The game is lost: not so much because we have underestimated the evil of torture, but because we have misunderstood its justification.

In other contexts, the courts have been astute to avoid this approach. Recall the facts of *Dudley and Stephens*:[30]

> The defendant sailors, survivors of a shipwreck, were adrift in an open boat in the South Atlantic. They killed and consumed without his consent the cabin-boy, Parker, who was the youngest and weakest member of their party. But for this act, Dudley and his companions would probably have died prior to rescue.

For present purposes, let us assume that death was practically certain. It was said in *Dudley and Stephens* that, although their lives were at stake, the ship-wrecked mariners were not entitled to kill and eat Parker. Rightly, necessity did not justify his murder. But perhaps we can generate a high-water mark? Would it make a difference if a hundred, or a thousand, lives depended on the homicide? No. Dudley had no unexcluded reason in the circumstances to kill Parker, because the need to save his life, or the lives of the others, was incapable of generating one. Multiply the numbers, and you still get zero. So it is with torture. For a parallel example, imagine the state is confronted with an ultimatum:

> *Ultimatum*: Officials in a particular city receive a credible threat from terrorists that, unless V—a randomly selected, innocent person who happens to

[28] As Kreimer observes: 'Too Close to the Rack and the Screw', 306.

[29] Alan Dershowitz advocates judicial torture warrants with such a restriction: *Why Terrorism Works: Understanding the Threat, Responding to the Challenge* (Yale UP 2003) ch 4. He does, however, recognize the ad hoc nature of the limitation at 146. (Dershowitz's argument rests on institutional values of transparency and accountability, given his prediction that officials will practice torture even if prohibited.)

[30] (1884) 14 QBD 273.

be of a different religion—is tortured publicly, the terrorists will detonate a bomb in the city and thereby kill a thousand people.

On these facts, the officials are not morally entitled to torture V.[31] We can reach that conclusion, moreover, without invoking wider instrumental reasons not to bow to terrorist threats. The officials cannot justify torturing V by reference to the ultimatum because the putative reasons it generates are excluded.

18.2.1 Wrinkles

So far, we have augmented the claim that justifications are wrong-dependent with the suggestion that this is not just a matter of weight. One can't get to permissibility merely by increasing the number of lives saved. Pro tanto wrongs exclude *types* of reason—and excluded reasons cannot justify wrongdoing, however weighty they might otherwise be. In Donald's case, for example, dragging the innocent Virgil in front of a bullet is impermissible *however* many lives are thereby saved: those payoffs are simply incapable of justifying that wrong.

Yet that leaves a puzzle. If it makes no difference when excluded reasons multiply, why do some cases seem more difficult, more borderline, than others? An excluded-reasons analysis seemingly admits of no middle ground and, therefore, of no hard cases. And if there are genuinely hard cases for the justification of a pro tanto wrong like torture, that would seem a reason for doubting the validity of an excluded-reasons analysis.

Part of the explanation is that the question, whether a particular reason for φing is excluded, may itself be borderline. Once a given reason is excluded, multiplying the numbers may make no difference;[32] but are we always convinced of its exclusion? That depends, in part, on how important the underlying interests are and on why we value them. In the case of torture, our interests as human beings in dignity and integrity are profound, and (to my mind) they straightforwardly exclude general reasons of necessity. Some may think the matter a closer call: for them, that could help explain why certain cases are perceived as hard. But the truly borderline cases, where a potential

[31] Neither can they be excused: § 17.4.1.

[32] Admittedly, there may be special cases where multiplying the numbers changes the character of the relevant action. Perhaps preventing mass extermination, for example, is in different case from preventing multiple individual murders. I cannot explore that possibility here.

justification may not be excluded, lie elsewhere. Their appeal arises because they go beyond a claim of necessity.

The better view is that torture can never be justified by necessity. But that doesn't imply torture can never be justified. Consider again the case of Wolfgang Daschner:[33]

> Wolfgang Daschner was vice-president of the Frankfurt-am-Main police. He led investigations into the kidnap of 11-year-old Jakob von Metzler, son of a prominent banker. The kidnapper, Mangus Gaefgen, was arrested after collecting the ransom payment but refused to disclose Metzler's whereabouts despite lengthy questioning. Hoping to save the boy, Daschner eventually instructed that Gaefgen should be threatened with torture, at which point Gaefgen confessed that Metzler was already dead and revealed the location of his body.

Even though only one life is at stake, this seems a more plausible case for justification than many multi-person hypotheticals. Cases like Daschner's involve a key feature that differentiates them from *Ultimatum*. They involve torturing the would-be wrongdoers themselves—those responsible for planting the bomb, hijacking the plane, abducting the child, and so forth—in order to forestall *their* wrong.

Morally speaking, this additional ingredient starts to reorient the justification away from necessity and towards self-defence.[34] We can see this, too, in the analogy to homicide. *Dudley and Stephens* illustrates an exclusionary rule that one may not take V's life in order to preserve one's own life or the life of others. Yet, notwithstanding the interdiction, one may do that very thing when acting in self-defence: *when V is the source of the threat*. This is a crucial difference between self-defence and necessity, the additional feature that prevents self-defence from collapsing into the general, residual justification of necessity. In self-defence, one responds to a threat from V by attacking V, the source of that threat.[35] In necessity, one responds to a threat by attacking someone else.

Here, then, is a second wrinkle to the claim that justifications are wrong-dependent. The wrong we commit doesn't just affect the types of reason we can rely on. It also affects the types of justification we can rely on. Imagine, this

[33] See § 17.4.4.

[34] (On behalf of another.) Legally speaking, in England the relevant defence would be prevention of crime. See, however, s 134 of the Criminal Justice Act 1988 (prohibiting torture).

[35] I assume here that the threat is an unjust one. For lengthy exploration of this type of condition, see S Uniacke, *Permissible Killing: The Self-Defence Justification of Homicide* (CUP 1994).

time, that Virgil hired the assassin, whom he could call off at any time. Can Donald drag Virgil in front of him? I take it that the answer is, yes. Now that Virgil is not an innocent bystander, we are relying on a different justification. He may be harmed by way of self-defence.

The possibility of self-defence shows that even fundamental rights can have limits. V's right to life does not exclude self-protection as a reason for action, even lethal action, on behalf of those whose lives V threatens. But the response must be addressed to V. Otherwise, one is on the wrong side of Thomas Nagel's distinction between fighting 'clean' and fighting 'dirty': 'To fight dirty is to direct one's hostility or aggression not at its proper object, but at a peripheral target which may be more vulnerable, and through which the proper object can be attacked indirectly.'[36] V is 'the proper target' because it is V who is making the threat. One cannot target a peripheral victim, T, because T's right to life disallows that move. Vis-à-vis T, the justification is one of necessity, and excluded.

Tentatively, that conclusion can be generalized for fundamental rights. It may be that directly-intended violations of a fundamental right can never be justified; and this is part of what it means for a right to be fundamental. (If that's correct, the corollary is that necessity is always unavailable in such cases, because, as claimed below, necessity is the residual defence of a justified wrong.) But fundamental does not mean exhaustive. The underlying interest may not be protected comprehensively by the right. In turn, this is why, *unlike* necessity, the primary justifications—including self-defence, defence of property, and prevention of crime—can operate to justify harmful actions by showing that the action was not a wrong. Let us turn to these claims now.

18.3 The basic distinction

In supplementing the role of exclusions with distinctions between types of justifications, we can make further progress in fleshing out the notion that justifications involve 'appropriate' responses. Self-defence, for example, is applicable where D acts against V in order to ward off a threat that V himself poses. In these cases the driving normative force behind the defence is D's right to protect herself (or another person) against unlawful attacks; a right grounded in the interests that each of us has in personal autonomy and physical integrity.

[36] T Nagel, 'War and Massacre' in *Mortal Questions* (CUP 1979) 53, 65. Nagel uses the example (at 69) of distracting, and thereby capturing, an enemy throwing hand grenades at you by machine-gunning his nearby wife and children.

That right, which allows for limited self-preference, defeats V's interests and carves a partial liberty out of D's obligations not to cause harm to others: and, I take it, gives D what Joseph Raz calls an *exclusionary permission* to prefer her own life even to those of multiple attackers.[37] As with all justifications, the extent of the liberty remains dependent on norms of proportionality,[38] and its recognition by the legal system is constrained by rule of law considerations—in particular, the requirement of urgency.[39] But the moral and legal character of D's conduct here is distinctively *righteous*.[40] D acts to preserve a moral, and legal, entitlement; and her reason for harming V is, in principle, an admissible reason for acting and not excluded *tout court*. It is no accident that self-defence overlaps with prevention of crime defences.[41] D has a right not to be attacked. In situations where it is impracticable for the state to assert that right on her behalf, she upholds that right by acting in self-defence. Even against five attackers.

In other cases of justified action, by contrast, D's conduct may not be fully consonant with either morality or law. Yet the wrong is morally and legally permitted: as when D breaks into V's house in order to call an ambulance on behalf of E, a person urgently in need of medical treatment. Here, 'lesser-evils' necessity comes into its own. Its advantage—and its weakness, as well as its challenge to the rule of law—lies in the fact that the defence lacks the kind of narrow, right-upholding focus found in self-defence. Even though neither D nor E is wronged, D can cite her life-saving reason in order to defeat the duty she owes not to violate V's property rights. She can do so because a reason of this sort is *not* excluded by V's proprietary rights.[42] It can be stacked up against the reasons not to damage V's property when determining whether, all things considered, it is permissible for one to act as does D. This does not mean the wrong goes away: there may, for example, be a duty to compensate for V's loss.[43] Yet it is a justified wrong. All things considered, D does not act for defeated reasons. Her reasons for acting are sufficient (admissible and proportionate) to render her conduct morally permitted and, in turn, lawful.

[37] J Raz, 'Permission and Supererogation' (1975) Am Phil Q 161.

[38] Like any justification, D's unexcluded reasons for acting as she does must be undefeated.

[39] See § 18.4.

[40] i.e., right-upholding. Distinctively, but not uniquely: cp. defence of property.

[41] Such as s 3 of the Criminal Law Act 1967 (UK), which also prescribes that the force used must be 'reasonable in the circumstances'.

[42] In the Razian terminology adopted by Gardner (below, § 18.3.1), the fact that V has a property right supplies a *protected reason*: a first-order reason to respect V's property coupled with a second order, exclusionary reason to disregard certain sorts of reasons for overriding that first-order reason. Self-aggrandizement is excluded as a reason for overriding V's property right, whereas preservation of life is not.

[43] As in *Vincent v Lake Erie Transportation Co* 124 NW 221 (1910). See, further, § 18.3.1.

That conclusion does not always follow. The open-ended scenarios in which necessity may arise do not beget open-ended permissions. D's reasons not to violate V's person, for example, are not like those concerning V's property. They exclude a much wider range of counter-considerations. Thus, in the absence of V's consent, it adds *no weight at all* to the case for removing one of V's kidneys that transplanting the kidney into T's body will save T's life. That reason is excluded from consideration; indeed, its exclusion is part-and-parcel of the very significance of our rights to personal autonomy and physical integrity—that they are not amenable to this kind of algebra. T's need for the kidney cannot be stacked up against the reasons not to harm V when deciding, all things considered, what to do. Absent some further non-excluded reason, we can conclude that, all things considered, the surgeon should not remove V's kidney. Were she to proceed with the operation, she would both wrong V and, in so doing, act without justification. Her reasons for acting are insufficient (because excluded) to render her conduct justified.

It may be tempting to read these examples as showing no more than that the exclusion of reasons is a matter of hierarchy,[44] so that necessity is available only where the interest saved is of a higher order than the victim's. Not so. In the Trolley Problem, notwithstanding that the interests at stake are of similar order, diverting the trolley to save five at the expense of one is, I take it, justified. By contrast, it would clearly be unjustified for a surgeon to harvest one patient's organs in order to make life-saving transplants into five other patients. Compare, too, *Dudley and Stephens*.[45] Had the shipwrecked mariners not killed and consumed Parker, doubtless they would have died; but they were convicted of murder and their claim of necessity was—rightly—refused.

We can see here that the exclusion of reasons is itself contextual. It turns in part on the relationship of the reasons, excluded and excluding, within an agent's practical deliberation. Sometimes reasons are excluded when they stand in an *ends–means* relationship, without always being excluded in other roles. In the Trolley Problem, it matters crucially that the victim's death is a side-effect of the driver's intended action. By contrast, the (unjustified) wrong to her patient is directly intended by the surgeon as a means to an end. In *Dudley and Stephens*, violation of Parker's bodily integrity was similarly intended as a means to an (excluded) end and was, as such, unjustified.

[44] Compare A Brudner, 'A Theory of Necessity' (1987) 7 OJLS 339, 365: 'The justification afforded by necessity is based on a hierarchy of qualitative values whose order is governed by agency, not on a balancing of quantitative harms in pursuit of an indeterminate welfare.'

[45] (1884) 14 QBD 273; above, § 18.2.

18.3.1 Why necessity is special

The examples show us something else too, something to which we have pointed already. They reveal that permissibility is not simply a matter of which reasons are excluded. Lying underneath is a more basic distinction. That basic distinction is between types of *justifications*, not types of wrongs. It is between necessity and the other, primary, justifications. At the intersection between pro tanto wrongs and their justification, it is not enough to be astute to the character of the wrong. We must be astute to the distinctive character of necessity.

Necessity is the special case of a permissible wrong. It is special because the permissibility of D's action is grounded in considerations that are extraneous to V. In particular, the reason for (pro tanto) wronging V *does not respond to V's agency and does not address V as a subject.*[46] It responds to the needs of others. This makes the defence potentially open-ended, which is why the courts rightly treat it with caution. The primary justifications are different. When D shoots V dead in legitimate self-defence, D does not wrong V at all. A claim of self-defence, for example, denies that V's right to life was violated,[47] because V's right does not exclude self-protection as a reason for action, even lethal action, on behalf of those whom V threatens.

This analysis faces objectors on both hands.[48] On the one hand, Gardner has argued that justified pro tanto wrongs are wrongs *generally*, not just in the case of necessity.[49] Admittedly, *any* killing may constitute a permanent blemish on the killer's life.[50] Yet that truth is not dependent on the killer's violating a duty. If I kill my attacker, V, in legitimate self-defence, I have powerful ground for regret—my underlying reason not to kill—which continues to exist even when the need for self-defence arises. That reason is merely defeated, not cancelled. I shall have to live with having acted against it. Contra Gardner, however, it doesn't follow that I *wrong* V. I have a general duty not to take lives; a protected reason not to kill that excludes all sorts of reasons in favour of killing. But it doesn't exclude this one. I *don't* have a general duty not to kill in self-defence. And I don't have to compensate V in such cases. I don't even have a duty to show regret, though I have reason to feel it. Not all justifications deny

[46] The conjunction allows for best-interests interventions like medical treatment, which may respond to V's predicament rather than to her agency. For simplicity's sake, I focus on agency in what follows.
[47] For a sense in which it may be described as *infringed*, see § 17.6.1.
[48] Cp. the introduction to this chapter.
[49] *Offences and Defences*, esp. 77–82, 253–56; but see the recantation below, § 18.3.3.
[50] Gardner makes this point vividly: 'Wrongs and Faults' in *Appraising Strict Liability* 51.

the wrong, as necessity shows. But self-defence does. And so do all the other primary justifications.

The seeds of this account were planted in chapter 17.[51] Although Gardner treats justifications as cancelling permissions, which 'cancel the second-order protective reasons not to act for certain countervailing reasons,'[52] the better view, it seems to me, is that the second-order protection is not cancelled when self-defence arises. It continues to exclude other reasons for action, just as before. Neither the first-order reason nor its protection disappears. Rather, legitimate self-defence is an *exception* to that protection. The protected reason continues to constitute a duty capable of being breached in other scenarios—which is also why, as I argued in chapter 16, the need for self-defence must be *my* reason for action. If I don't know about the attack when I lethally pre-empt it, I wrong V.

At the other extreme, many writers deny that *any* justified pro tanto wrong is a wrong. Yet the case of necessity is disanalogous to the primary justifications. When killing in self-defence, I acknowledge V as a responsible, autonomous human being; my action responds to and addresses V's conduct, recognizing V as the author of a wrong and treating V with the respect due to an autonomous moral agent behaving like V.[53] In this sense, one person can harm another person respectfully, without using them or denying their shared humanity. When I act in self-defence, it matters to the justification that it is *V's* interest that is set back. If I am to respect V's rights to life and bodily integrity, my actions must be astute to V's conduct and normative position; there must be, if you like, no mere *use* of V. Necessity, by contrast, involves the *overriding* of V's rights without addressing V and without acknowledging V's distinctive claim to respect. A parallel analysis holds can be articulated for duties. In cases of necessity, D contravenes a duty that applies without qualification to the case at hand: the duty is neither cancelled nor subject to a relevant exception. D is justified only because the protected reason constituting that duty is overridden. Hence the wrong.[54] And the normative residue.

[51] See esp. § 17.6.2–3. The present analysis fits naturally with an internal-condition analysis of my victim's right not to be killed.

[52] *Offences and Defences*, 107.

[53] For this reason, self-defence against the insane may seem a borderline case, in so far as insane aggressors are not morally responsible for their actions. The point here, though, is that, by responding to the victim's actions, one still treats the victim as a subject, i.e. respectfully and without violating the victim's claim to human dignity.

[54] Hence, too, the distinctive sense of 'infringement' ($\text{infringement}_{(PW)}$) contemplated by Feinberg: see § 17.6.1.

18.3.2 Internalism, duties to retreat, and the like

The difference is not solely a matter of how D treats V. In as much as the primary justifications respond to V's own conduct, the permissibility of D's pro tanto wrong *lies in V's hands*. Thus the primary justifications admit of a trade-off, a trade-off in which V's autonomy is respected and plays a constituent role. By contrast, the circumstances giving rise to necessity are not under the control of V. V is a mere victim. She may be required to sacrifice her interests because of an event, or state of affairs, for which she was not ascriptively responsible.

The importance of this point is sometimes neglected by philosophers who argue that even the primary justifications are unavailable unless the defensive response is *necessary* as well as proportionate. Suppose for example, the following two cases:

> *Parachute*: Pat, an unjustified aggressor, attacks David by chasing after him and shooting at him. She chases David to the edge of a cliff. As it happens, David has both a gun and a parachute. He can thus save his own life by either (a) jumping to safety, using no force against Pat, or (b) shooting and killing Pat. David is an experienced parachutist, and jumping is not dangerous for him.[55]

> *Home Invasion*: Petra, an unjustified aggressor, enters Duncan's house and starts shooting at him. Duncan has a gun. He can save his own life by either (a) shooting and killing Petra, or (b) by jumping out of a window at the back of the house and making his way to safety at a nearby air-raid shelter. The jump holds some danger and he may well break a rib; more serious injuries are not likely.

According to (what are sometimes called) 'internalist' accounts of justifications like self-defence, they do not extend to harmful actions that are unnecessary for averting a threat.[56] The same used to hold in the common law, in as much as the law imposed a duty to retreat;[57] it remains true of Scots law.[58] David, therefore, should jump rather than fire back. And if we understand internalism

[55] The example is based on one developed by Helen Frowe: *Defensive Killing* (OUP 2014) 88.
[56] See, e.g., J McMahan, *Killing in War* (OUP 2009) 8–9.
[57] No longer: *Julien* [1969] 1 WLR 839 (CA), now codified in s 76(6A) of the Criminal Justice and Immigration Act 2008 (UK).
[58] *HM Advocate v Doherty* 1954 JC 1.

to require taking 'the least harmful means available' to avert a threat,[59] even shooting Petra is an impermissible wrong.[60]

The literature on defensive force is vast, and it is impracticable to engage with it all here. One generic worry, though, is that because of its preoccupation with the pro tanto wrong—the use of force—it sometimes fails to attend to the basic distinction drawn in 18.3.1. And so it can lose sight of what makes self-defence a primary justification: that it responds to V's agency and treats her as a subject.[61] Imposing a distinct 'necessity' requirement upon the primary justifications denies them any priority over necessity in virtue of the fact that they respond to V's agency. It neglects what makes necessity special.

This matters because the scope of justifications affects our autonomy. *Pace* the internalist, there seems to be at least something of significance about the fact that escaping the threat requires Duncan to flee his own house or to risk injury. Yet if, under an internalist analysis, we just weigh up the alternatives and ask whether someone can avert the threat at lesser cost, those interests go unprotected. Neither can we evade the difficulty by stipulating some constraint such as 'at no significant cost', or that 'your home is your castle'. Such moves are ad hoc. Even being required to run away involves a significant infringement of one's rights and interests. There are no free escapes.

Proportionality-type reasons tend to be assessed *ex post*—that is, in light of the actual situation. P is attacking D: what should D do *now*? But that perspective neglects the *ex ante* dimension of justifications, something to which we pointed in § 17.1. If it is impermissible for D to respond to P with otherwise proportionate force, this means that (*ex ante*) P has certain normative capacities to modify D's autonomy and his range of permissible options. Indeed, P can exploit this. Notwithstanding that P herself acts wrongfully, she can create a moral obligation for D to leave the house, jump off the cliff with the parachute, *et cetera*. The existence of such capacities is an implication of the internalist view. But it is also a reason for thinking the internalist view is wrong.

Consider the famous case of *Beatty v Gillbanks*.[62] Local magistrates had ruled it unlawful for the Salvation Army to march (otherwise lawfully) in the town of Weston-super-Mare, on the ground that they were likely to be attacked by a collection of rowdies styling themselves 'The Skeleton Army'. (The latter

[59] H Frowe, 'The Role of Necessity in Liability to Defensive Harm' in C Coons and M Weber (eds), *The Ethics of Self-Defence* (OUP 2016) 152, 153.

[60] Ibid, 163 (holding that one should accept the price of a broken leg in escaping rather than kill one's unjust attacker).

[61] The same could be said of Clarkson's proposal to merge the rationale-based defences into a single defence of 'necessary action'; see § 17.1.1.

[62] (1882) 9 QBD 308.

had developed a practice of disrupting the Salvation Army's marches against alcohol by raising a riot, which had resulted in a number of deaths and numerous injuries to the Salvationists.) Rightly, the Divisional Court quashed the magistrates' ruling. To hold otherwise would make the law a tool for oppression, an instrument for achieving the very purpose of the Salvationist's miscreant opponents. It would create a contingent duty not to appear in public places, the triggering of which lay in the hands of fellow citizens and wrongdoers.

As with law, so with morality. To hold with internalism would be to disconnect *ex post* normative positions from their *ex ante* origins. This is not to claim that right need never yield to wrong, as once was said in German criminal law.[63] (Suppose that Michael charges at Dan with intent, as Dan knows, to slap Dan about the face with a soggy lettuce leaf. Michael is bigger and quicker than Dan, and the only way Dan can avert the battery is by shooting Michael. Dan is not permitted to shoot. The proportionality constraint is not satisfied.[64]) But it is to claim, *inter alia*, that it matters how things come about. It matters, in other words, who starts things.[65] Rights don't cease to exist once violated, and the wrong of their violation doesn't disappear once perpetrated. It continues to inform the question of what D should do now. We acknowledge that wrong by refusing to apply a 'least harmful means available' requirement to the primary justifications. It is sufficient that D acts for undefeated (proportionate, non-excluded) reasons: the demands of appropriateness are met in virtue of the fact that the primary justifications address and respond to their victims' conduct. For such justifications, therefore, the existence of alternatives should merely be another consideration in evaluations of proportionality—of whether D had undefeated reason to act as she did. By contrast, imposing a supplementary 'least harmful means available' requirement *is* apt to the residual defence of necessity itself, because V is not the source of D's predicament.

18.3.3 Primary and residual

One might question whether the labels, 'primary' and 'residual', are apt. The Model Penal Code, for example, treats lesser-evils necessity as a paradigmatic

[63] Judgment of the Supreme Court, September 20, 1920, 55 RGSt 82 (killing a thief who was absconding with fruit held to be justified).

[64] This is part of the difficulty for so-called 'your home is your castle' and 'stand your ground' doctrines: they tend to neglect the proportionality constraint.

[65] The argument here also lends support to a 'causing the conditions of one's own defence' doctrine, whereby justifications and excuses might (under certain conditions) be excluded because D has brought about the situation in which her use of force against P would otherwise be justified.

general justification.[66] In much the same vein is Gardner's striking reassessment of his earlier writing:[67]

> 'These days I tend to agree . . . that acts of necessary and proportionate self-defence against a guilty attacker do not violate the rights of the attacker. The guilt of the attacker neutralises at least some of the reasons not to kill or injure her in the attack. If it neutralises enough of them (or the right ones) then . . . the wrong involved in killing the aggressor is negated by self-defence. And if that is the correct conclusion, then probably one of my prime examples of a justified offence in *Offences and Defences*—the one in which a terrorist is killed to prevent his imminently detonating a large bomb that will kill many—is a bad choice of example, for it is most naturally read as a case in which at least some objections to killing are neutralised, lessening or eliminating the need for justification.'

It seems that Gardner came to accept that action taken in self-defence is not a wrong. By that same token, however, he suggests that self-defence is not paradigmatic. The less we have to justify, one might think, the less central a case of justification we're dealing with. So if self-defence is a justification at all, it is at best a residual or peripheral one.

That modified analysis resonates with the English decisions in *Williams* and *Beckford*,[68] which purported to assimilate self-defence with wrong-denial (specifically, denial of the actus reus). I argue in chapter 19 that those decisions are misguided. But they too raise the question of why we should view the distinction between wrong-denying and wrong-conceding justifications as mapping onto a distinction between primary and residual.

Justifications like self-defence are primary in the sense that they have *priority*. Just as it is better to be justified than to be rationally excused, it is better to have a primary justification than a residual one: because it is better not to not be in the wrong at all than to do a justified wrong. Between self-defence and necessity, self-defence comes first.

The payoffs are real. Primary justifications leave no normative residue, moral or legal.[69] The defendant incurs no derivative duty to make next-best efforts of

[66] A view endorsed by Larry Alexander: 'Lesser Evils: A Closer Look at the Paradigmatic Justification' (2005) 24 Law and Phil 611. See the Model Penal Code, § 3.02 ('Justification Generally: Choice of Evils'). While I do think of necessity as residual rather than paradigm, the more important point in this section is that it lacks priority.

[67] J Gardner, 'In Defence of Offences and Defences' (2012) 4 Jerusalem R Legal Studies 110, 113.

[68] *Williams* [1987] 3 All ER 411; *Beckford v R* [1988] AC 130.

[69] See the discussion in § 17.6.2. My claim is only that they leave no normative residue qua infringements of duty. The underlying first-order reasons may continue to supply grounds for regret (cp. § 18.3.1).

conformity to the original duty, for example by apologizing or paying compensation to the victim. Necessity, by contrast, does leave derivative duties of this kind. Indeed, one might characterize the 'least harmful means' requirement, discussed in the preceding section, as being grounded in that residue. That requirement makes the proportionality element of necessity a more stringent test than in the primary justifications. In practical terms, therefore, necessity is very much a fallback defence. It is a less good option for actors who cannot avail themselves of a more specific, primary justification.

Which is as it should be. Grant me an increasingly idealistic fantasy, that we are all members of a basically egalitarian community, in which our various interests are safeguarded by a framework of rights and duties.[70] Those rights and duties help to set the rules of engagement for situations in which our interests might otherwise collide. They are also reciprocal. I am free, as the metaphor goes, to wave my arm around. But my freedom runs out at the end of your nose.[71] And your freedom runs out at the end of mine.

Justifications, both primary and residual, are part of that allocative framework. They help to fine-tune it by compromising the rights and duties it contains. In so doing, they operate as a kind of mediator in human interaction, enabling us to negotiate the mutual enterprise of human co-existence. Justifications help to construct the dialogue, the give-and-take, of conflict and reconciliation.[72] The compromises they articulate are a matter of fairness and trade-off. When you attack me, I am entitled to take reasonable measures in self-protection, even if those measures endanger you, because it is fair that my interests should take precedence over yours. This, too, is reciprocal. You benefit by the same allowance should anyone attack you. Similarly, it is fair to require Victor to accept limits upon his proprietary dominion, for example, if a trespass is necessary to save life. Victor himself may take advantage of similar limits on the property rights of others, should that be needed.

In much of this, lesser-evils necessity is no different. Like other justificatory rules, it can—should—be articulated *ex ante*, so that each of us may benefit from its guidance. The difference, however, is that primary justifications are not merely reciprocal. They are also *interactional*. This is why the primary

70 And the like: I use 'rights and duties' as shorthand.

71 As J B Finch put it: 'The Defence Reviewed' in *The People versus The Liquor Traffic: The Great Speeches of Hon. John B. Finch* (Citizen 1887) 89, 105.

72 This gives us one reason to doubt whether torture is *ever* morally permissible, even in self-defence. Torturing someone doesn't seem to fit within any *shared* human enterprise. There is no social dialogue in torture, no give-and-take. It is incompatible with respect. As such, torture is plausibly beyond the reconciling power of self-defence. Even the strongest cases seem irredeemably borderline.

justifications speak, in the first instance, *to the victim*. In effect, they warn her about the normative implications of her conduct. By the same token, they create a normative space in which she is at least partly insulated from the conduct of others. That normative space is protected by a gateway. If the victim doesn't want to compromise her normative position, she has a means of achieving that. Just don't do anything that puts another person's interests at risk.[73] Don't, in other words, go through the gateway.

In a sense, therefore, primary justifications are the opposite of necessity. We observed in § 18.3.2 that their operation is a matter within the victim's control. Paradigmatically, such cases are *unnecessary*. They are triggered by the victim. And, unlike necessity, they involve *responses* to her conduct.

These differences matter. Victor has no way to insulate himself from the predations of necessity. Lesser-evils lacks a protective gateway because it is a justification that does not engage with his conduct. And to that extent, necessity is defective: not *dis*respectful, to be sure, but also not fully respectful. It may be a proportionate use, but it is a use all the same. Victor has tipped over from subject to object.

18.4 On the importance of being urgent

As we saw in chapter 17, not all rationale-based defences are justifications. In cases where D commits a pro tanto crime without justification, normally the secondary possibility will arise that D has a rationale-based excuse. Suppose, for example, that D attacks and injures V because *T* threatens otherwise to kill her. Notwithstanding that it was impermissible for D to act as she did, in the sense that there were insufficient unexcluded reasons for her conduct, we may be reluctant to fault D. Our reluctance is because, although D's reason for acting was (objectively speaking) inadequate, we can quite understand that it was good enough *for D*. She feared for her life. Assuming that any reasonable person might have been impelled by such a fear,[74] we cannot make the inference of culpability that would normally entitle us to blame D for her actions. In such cases, therefore, we should allow an excuse: for the sake of clarity, I have called this excuse *duress*.

[73] To simplify the discussion, I leave aside wrongdoing that is not other-affecting, yet which can give rise to justifications such as prevention of crime and judicial punishment. (I suspect the analysis of such cases is similar, but cannot explore that thought here.)

[74] Compare *Graham* [1982] 1 All ER 801, 806 (CA), requiring that the threat be such as to overcome the resistance of a 'sober person of reasonable firmness'.

Some writers have argued for the assimilation of duress and necessity;[75] some have argued for the assimilation of duress and self-defence.[76] One unifying feature of all three defences is said to be that the defendants in such cases all act 'under extreme pressure'.[77] Yet even if we admit that feature is shared,[78] the role of the pressure differs. In self-defence, for example, the emergency is important for rule-of-law reasons. It explains why D is not usurping the proper role of the state.[79] In duress, by contrast, the pressure directly explains D's motivation. D is right to fear for her life: her only mistake is to treat that as a reason for injuring V.[80] As pointed out in § 17.2, however, that mistake merely discloses an imperfect virtue—a limitation—not a fault. We do not count, among the qualities reasonably expected of D, the levels of self-control and altruism that would be needed for D to refrain from acting. In this sense, it is apt to describe the defence as a 'concession to human frailty'.[81] It reflects an imperfection characteristic of humans in general, and not one peculiar to D.

The role of 'pressure' in necessity is not excusatory. As we noted in § 18.1, it too is a rule-of-law constraint. One cannot raze V's house in order to create a fire break, and thereby preserve the village, without official authority unless the fire is at hand.[82] Thus necessity is like self-defence rather than duress, in that D's motivation constitutes, objectively speaking, an undefeated reason for acting. Necessity involves a *permissible* wrong, not merely an understandable one. Correspondingly, the scope for necessity to arise is wider than duress. (Albeit the range of actions it justifies is reassuringly narrow.[83]) What makes duress exculpatory is the understandable difficulty of resisting the threat to D, so it is no surprise that qualifying threats must be severe; and there may be institutional

[75] C Clarkson, 'Necessary Action: A New Defence' [2004] Crim LR 81; above, § 17.1.1.

[76] L Alexander, 'A Unified Excuse of Preemptive Self-protection' (1999) 74 Notre Dame LR 1475.

[77] Clarkson, 'Necessary Action' (n 75) 82. Cp. Gardner, *Offences and Defences*, 113: 'in general no excuse is accepted into the criminal law which is not also a partial justification, and no justification is accepted which is not also a partial excuse.'

[78] And it was not true of the surgeons in *Re A (Children)*, discussed below.

[79] Hence an objection to *Kelly* [1989] NI 341, where D was held justified in fatally shooting someone believed by D to be a terrorist who, if allowed to escape, would go on to commit terrorist offences at some point in the future. In the absence of urgency, it should not be open to D to bypass normal state mechanisms for regulating potential wrongdoing by others.

[80] That is to say, her only—and understandable—mistake is to treat the reason as non-excluded; since, but for its exclusion, it may well have sufficed to justify her action.

[81] *Howe* [1987] 1 AC 417, 432–35.

[82] A crucial point in *Shayler* [2001] 1 WLR 2206. D, a civil servant employed in MI5, was held to be in breach of the Official Secrets Act 1989 (UK) after he shared secret information with a newspaper, notwithstanding that he believed MI5's actions threatened rather than enhanced public security. D was not attempting to avert some crystallized, imminent catastrophe—there was no forthcoming incident his actions were intended to avert, merely a fear that the covert operations of MI5 threatened public security generally.

[83] It follows from the analysis in this chapter that permissible responses are restricted mainly to (pro tanto) property offences and 'victimless' crimes. I take this to be a benefit. Perhaps the Canadian Supreme Court would agree.

reasons for formalizing this, as in the old common-law rule that the threat must be of death or serious injury.[84] By contrast, necessity exculpates because D has, all things considered, sufficient reasons to act as she does—she does not act badly overall. Thus there is no structural reason for similarly restricting the seriousness of reasons that may be considered when deciding whether D's action was permitted. We have seen that, depending on the wrong committed, some reasons may be excluded. Others may be inadequate to defeat the reasons militating against D's conduct, so that the response is disproportionate. But that is a case-by-case matter. The preservation of property may warrant a fire engine's driving through a red light,[85] but not its ploughing through a crowd to get to the blaze.

The role of urgency therefore tracks an even more basic division than the distinction between necessity and the primary justifications. It tracks the division between justifications and rationale-based excuses. What that means, in turn, is that urgency is not always required. Provided the matter is within the relevant court's (or other official's) jurisdiction,[86] authorization may be issued on the basis that the action is justified. This is one of the lessons of *Re A (Children)*, to which we now turn. The twins' predicament was not an emergency. Yet a court order was in principle available (and, I will suggest below, rightly issued). That court order could not have been issued if the operation was unlawful.[87] More specifically, the order *could not have been issued if the operation was excused rather than justified*. This alone supplies reason to doubt the Canadian classification of necessity as an excuse.[88] Officials may not choose to authorize the impermissible.

18.5 *Re A (Children)*

When we talk about self-defence, duress, and necessity, then, we talk not about one defence but three. Each has a distinct rationale and, correspondingly, a different structure. The reasons for admitting a defence operate, and interrelate, differently. But we should still ask, what's the payoff? In particular, given that

[84] *Hudson* [1971] 2 QB 202 (CA); *Graham* [1982] 1 All ER 801 (CA); *Conway* [1989] QB 290 (CA). Cf. the Indian Penal Code, s 94, where only the threat of death suffices.

[85] As Lord Denning thought it should in *Buckoke v Greater London Council* [1971] 1 Ch 655, 668.

[86] Obviously, this is not a simple issue. In *Re A (Children)*, to be discussed below, the jurisdiction of the Court of Appeal was a matter of family law; which allowed the Court to act as decision-maker, effectively *in loco parentis*, rather than decision-reviewer (as in administrative law).

[87] See, too, § 17.4.

[88] *Perka v The Queen* [1984] 2 SCR 232.

the legal categories of various justifications can overlap, does it really matter whether we keep them distinct?

It does. In *Re A (Children)*,[89] the Court of Appeal was asked to rule whether it would be lawful for surgeons to undertake an operation to separate conjoined twins. The implications of separation were that one twin, Mary, would certainly die within minutes and that the other, Jodie, would most probably live (as indeed she did). If the operation were not performed, both twins were expected to die within a matter of months. M's own heart and lungs were inadequate to sustain M's life, so that her survival depended on J; in particular, on J's heart continuing to pump the blood oxygenated by J through both twins' bodies. Unfortunately, sustaining both lives was imposing an excessive strain on J's heart. It was common ground that J's heart would fail within a few months, and that M's death would inevitably follow J's. Under these circumstances, was the Court right to hold that killing M was defensible? In principle, the analysis in this chapter ought to help us address such difficult cases.[90]

Categorization of the case was crucial. Part of the problem was the rule laid down in *Dudley and Stephens*[91] that, like duress,[92] necessity is not available as a defence to murder. Prima facie, the surgery would be murder of M, since both the actus reus and mens rea elements of murder would be present. Thus the challenge for the Court of Appeal was to circumnavigate, without undermining, the rule in *Dudley and Stephens*.

18.5.1 When is a justification primary?

One way to distinguish *Dudley and Stephens* would be by analysing the situation in *Re A* as a case of self-defence (or its third-party equivalent, defence of another). If V puts D's life in danger without justification, D is entitled to assert her right to life. The hard case is, of course, where that right can only be asserted at the price of V's life. There, it is only because V's actions have caused the threat that D has priority. Notwithstanding that D and V have rights to life of equal standing, it is V, albeit perhaps blamelessly, who has generated the conflict. D should be under no obligation to surrender her life for the benefit of V.

[89] *In re A (Children) (Conjoined Twins: Surgical Separation)* [2001] Fam 147.

[90] The remarks made here are not intended to be an exhaustive analysis of either the facts or decision in *Re A* itself. It is discussed here as an illustrative case study.

[91] (1884) 14 QBD 273; above, § 18.2.

[92] *Howe* [1987] AC 417.

Various boundary questions arise. Is the victim's agency necessary or merely paradigmatic? It is clearly objectionable to harm innocent persons, such as the family members of a defector or a suicide bomber, in order to deter wrongdoing. That is punishing 'dirty'. Conversely, it is part of the appeal of Wolfgang Daschner's case that the policeman's threat to torture Gaefgen is made in order to prevent wrongdoing *by Gaefgen himself*; to uphold the child's right to life against the unjust threat that Gaefgen has posed. Arguably, though, what counts is whether D's pro tanto wrong is perpetrated in response to an event *for which the victim is ascriptively responsible*. As we saw in the chapter on complicity, sometimes people may be collectively responsible for wrongs they do not themselves perpetrate. Indeed, the kinds of cases that motivate proponents of official torture typically differ in this respect from Daschner's.[93] Officials have, say, captured one member of a terrorist group while the remaining members, having eluded arrest, are now embarked on the group's mission to destroy an occupied building. It is permissible, some argue, for the officials to use a degree of torture against the complicitous wrongdoer in order to identify and then evacuate the target.

Collective responsibility can be a natural source of borderline cases.[94] Fortunately, *that* difficulty is not raised by *Re A*. The problem lies near the other end of the spectrum. Is the victim's agency *sufficient* to bring a case within the realm of self-defence? Some would set the bar for primary justifications rather higher. Consider the following example of an innocent threat, proposed by Jeff McMahon:[95]

> *Cell-phone*: A villain has secretly tampered with Veronica's cell phone in such a way that if she presses the 'call' button, she will detonate a bomb to which David has been tied by this same villain. The villain has trussed David up so that he cannot escape or alert Veronica to his plight. But the villain has given David a weapon with which he can kill her. Veronica has typed in a number and is about to press the call button.

[93] See, e.g., Dershowitz, *Why Terrorism Works* (n 29) 143–44.

[94] A similar issue arises in contexts like homicide. For instance, any proposal that the bombing of Hiroshima was a justified act of self-defence involves, implicitly, a claim that the citizens of that city were responsible for the aggressive actions of their Government—and to that extent the bombing was not entirely 'dirty'. Whether or not that claim is plausible (and it has been rejected in international law), the broadening of responsibility doctrines in this way is clearly problematic for justification in general.

[95] J McMahon, 'The Basis of Moral Liability to Defensive Killing' (2005) 15 Phil Issues 386, 397. I have tweaked the description for clarity. I take it that nothing in his example turns upon the fact that the bomb will kill David rather than various equally innocent persons.

McMahon concedes that David might be justified in killing Veronica, but insists that she is not 'liable' to be killed in self-defence,[96] because the threat she poses was unforeseeable. In effect, McMahon assimilates *Cell-phone* with necessity rather than self-defence. On the account developed in this chapter, by contrast, what matters for the core justifications is not foreseeability on the victim's part, but addressing her agency. To anticipate Lord Justice Ward's observations in *Re A* (below), if a six-year-old picks up an automatic weapon and starts killing everyone in the playground, it seems reasonable to think that neither compensation nor apology is owed should someone kill him in their defence. The same reasoning applies to Veronica.

Yet does the rationale underpinning self-defence actually apply to *Re A*? Ward LJ thought so. In his Lordship's judgment, the crux of the case was that, albeit blamelessly, M was killing J. Therefore, J (or someone intervening on her behalf) would be justified when acting in order to negate that threat, even though doing so would kill the person who was the source of that threat. The difficulty with this analysis is that M cannot be described as an aggressor. Even when we set the bar for primary justifications lower than McMahon would favour (and, in law, we do), M still seems to get nowhere near it. Admittedly, as Ward LJ pointed out, there is no requirement in self-defence that the attack be a criminal offence:[97]

> 'The six-year-old boy indiscriminately shooting all and sundry in the school playground is not acting unlawfully for he is too young for his acts to be so classified. . . . [H]owever, . . . *in law* killing that six-year old in self-defence of others would be fully justified and the killing would not be unlawful. I see no difference in essence between that resort to legitimate self-defence and the doctors coming to Jodie's defence and removing the threat of fatal harm to her presented by Mary's draining her life blood.'

Killing the six-year-old boy is capable of being justified morally as well as legally. But the analogy does not carry over to M. There is no violation of J's right to life by M because there is no *act*, lawful or otherwise. It is not that M wrongs J innocently, like the six-year-old. M does not wrong J at all. The threat to M's

[96] Ibid, 397–98. Killing Veronica, in other words, would be an infringement$_{(PW)}$ of her right to life (above, § 17.6.1). The language of 'liability' is philosophical rather than legal. McMahon's suggestion is that, in cases of self-defence, V is 'liable' to be harmed in as much as V lacks a right not to be harmed. (Hence a liable V is not wronged.) By contrast, in cases of lesser evils necessity, V is not 'liable' to be harmed—she is wronged, albeit permissibly, when she is harmed in such a case.

[97] [2001] Fam 147, 203–204.

life, like the threat to J's, is a state of affairs; M has not generated the conflict but, like J, is a victim of circumstance. By contrast with the six-year-old, *Re A* falls on the other side of the basic distinction.

It is worth observing that in *Re A* itself, Ward LJ sought to buttress his self-defence analysis by noting that, if one weighs up the respective best interests of J and M, the scales were tipped heavily in J's favour because she was the only child with any prospect of life extending beyond the following few months. Yet this consideration merely illustrates the importance of defence categorization. It matters, if at all, only when the case is viewed as one of necessity. In the context of self-defence, it is irrelevant. Consider, for example, a case where P attacks D when D has only a few hours to live and P is healthy. D is still entitled, if need be, to kill P in self-defence.

18.5.2 Necessity?

An alternative analysis is to characterize the scenario in *Re A* as one of lesser-evils necessity, a move made by Brooke LJ:[98]

> 'The claim is that [D's] conduct was not harmful because on a choice of two evils the choice of avoiding the greater harm was justified.'

As mentioned in § 18.1, his Lordship set out three criteria for the defence, according to which the intervention in *Re A* would be permissible:[99]

(i) The act is needed to avoid inevitable and irreparable evil;
(ii) No more should be done than is reasonably necessary for the purpose to be achieved; and
(iii) The evil inflicted must not be disproportionate to the evil avoided.

The limitation of these criteria is that, without more, they would also exculpate the defendants in *Dudley and Stephens*. Moreover, it will not avail to point out that 'Mary is, sadly, self-designated for a very early death.'[100] So was the

[98] Ibid, 236. By contrast with Ward LJ, Brooke LJ (at 240) explicitly eschewed reliance on the proposition that M was an 'unjust aggressor': 'None of the formulations of the doctrine of necessity which I have noted in this judgment make any such requirement: in this respect it is different from the doctrine of private defence.'

[99] Ibid, 236.

[100] Ibid, 239.

cabin-boy in *Dudley and Stephens*, whose condition was far more acute than that of the others. Similarly, the same doctors who operated in *Re A* would not have been free to accelerate M's death in order, say, to facilitate the early transplant of one of her working organs into P, some otherwise healthy patient. These are, once again, excluded reasons for violating M's autonomy and personal integrity.

What is not excluded, however, is the need to protect J. Although Brooke LJ did not rely on this point, it mattered that, by contrast with *Dudley and Stephens*, the doctors were not seeking *to kill M in order to* save J. Rather, the *separation* was undertaken in order to save J's life,[101] by protecting J from the threat to her life, even though that operation would have the effect of accelerating M's death.[102]

This distinction engages one of the key differences that we have identified between self-defence and lesser-evils necessity: one may (sometimes) directly intend to kill in self-defence, but not in necessity.[103] In *Dudley and Stephens*, the cabin boy's death was intended as a means: the defendants killed him in order then to eat him. In *Re A*, M's death was no part of the doctors' aim or purpose, although it was an inevitable consequence of what they sought to achieve. It is only by supplementing Brooke LJ's analysis with these considerations that the rule in *Dudley and Stephens* can safely be evaded.

Although lawyers tend to run them together, we should distinguish lesser-evils necessity *stricto sensu* from cases, like *Re A*, which are necessitous only in a broader sense. In the latter type of case, even though D's intervention is not made in response to V's agency, D does not *use* V or treat V as an object. This is part of the reason why, when justifying side-effects, a reasonableness standard is embedded in the mens rea elements of recklessness and negligence. That standard helps to delineate our duties not to harm others. Paradigmatically, the specific justificatory defences (including self-defence and necessity) have distinctive application in the context of intended action, action done as a means to a justifying end: whereas, I argued in § 16.3, foreseen side-effects are generally a package deal.[104] We do not blame D for causing harm in such cases unless she

[101] Subject, of course, to their satisfying the other criteria of necessity (notably, those identified by Brooke LJ).

[102] It is here (and, more generally, in decisions about which life to save) that the matter of M's life expectancy may be a consideration going to the proportionality criterion.

[103] See chapters 15–16. In the case at hand, it seems clear that the doctors did not directly intend to kill. M's death was neither sought for its own sake, nor sought as a means to or instance of an end. (And it was not, I think, the kind of inseparability case discussed in § 15.3.) M's death supplied no part of the reasons why the doctors were operating; it was not an aim of the operation; the doctors would not have regarded themselves as having 'failed' in any sense if M had somehow survived.

[104] Subject to special cases like Victor Tadros's *Lever* example, noted in § 16.2.3.

does so recklessly—in particular, unless her choice to do so is unreasonable. That standard coalesces the specific justifications. It realigns them all with a broader sense of necessity.

18.6 Concluding remarks

No one, least of all the Court of Appeal, would suggest that *Re A* is a case of duress.[105] *That* would make the intervention unlawful. No court order would be available to authorize it in advance. So far as the surgery was concerned, it was justification or nothing. Admittedly, the case is tremendously difficult. I have sought to show why such cases are hard rather than to give a fully generalized account. Yet what emerges from discussing *Re A* is the importance of distinguishing, and not conflating, the different rationales at work when one claims a justification. Had the doctors sought to save J *by* killing M (a case of direct intention), it seems most unlikely that their intervention would have been regarded as lawful—because the case is not truly one of self-defence. Nonetheless, it appears that conduct undertaken in the awareness that death will be accelerated may be justified in certain cases of lesser-evils necessity.

It turns out that we can acknowledge this without inviting chaos. If properly understood and applied, necessity is no malleable tool with which to negotiate the rule of law. To the contrary: it offers a mechanism by which the conduct of persons in extreme situations none the less falls to be normatively regulated, by the courts, *within* the legal system.

Re A illustrates a more general point running through this chapter. All the rationale-based defences have common requirements of proportionality. That an element is common, however, does not make it unifying. And so it proves. Doctrinal distinctions amongst the defences track important differences in their underpinning rationales. Those rationales involve profound distinctions concerning the reasons why D should be exculpated when he does a prima facie offence: about how they operate, about the range of reasons for action that are admissible, and about how those how reasons stand in relation to each other.

[105] See, e.g., [2001] Fam 147, 235–36 (Brooke LJ).

19

Unpacking Excuses: Hybrids and Mistakes

In § 17.1, we subdivided the excuses into three categories:

(a) Rationale-based excuses;
(b) Hybrid and partial irresponsibility defences; and
(c) Defensive mistakes.

What unites these categories is that each involves some form of excusatory explanation. Broadly speaking, the domain of excusatory explanations ranges over all unjustified acts for which blame is defrayed rather than exempted.[1] When D asserts an excuse, she concedes moral responsibility for wrongdoing, and claims none the less that the explanation why she came to φ does not disclose a moral vice on her part.

That shared raiment cloaks a considerable diversity in the ways that the excuses operate. The rationale-based excuses are in many respects a paradigm for excusatory explanations. Yet they are a relatively small category, with duress supplying the only straightforward examples.[2] Admittedly, duress may not be the *only* form of rationale-based excuse. Provocation is generally thought to be a rationale-based partial excuse: more on that below. It is sometimes suggested that entrapment can be explained in similar terms.[3] Even if we grant all that, however, the range of purely rationale-based, fully exculpatory excuses remains narrow. By comparison, there is a much wider variety of hybrid and mistake-based defences. In this closing chapter, we sketch the latter two categories.

[1] On exemptions, see § 17.5.
[2] This is not a claim about the legal category of duress, which can overlap with justifications (in particular, with necessity): see § 17.2.1. I have in mind those cases of duress that do not generate a moral justification.
[3] At least partially: e.g., Fletcher, *Rethinking*, § 7.3.

Fundamentals of Criminal Law. A P Simester, Oxford University Press (2021). © A P Simester.
DOI: 10.1093/oso/9780198853145.003.0019

19.1 Hybrid and other defences: between irresponsibility and rationale-based excuses

Sometimes, an exculpatory explanation straddles the line between irresponsibility and rationale-based excuse. Within the common law of provocation,[4] this possibility was embraced by the short-lived decision of the House of Lords in *Smith (Morgan)*.[5] In that case, it was held that the key question, whether the provocation to D was enough to make 'a reasonable man' lose self-control, should be evaluated *inter alia* by reference to D's own peculiarities, such as depression, which bear on the degree of self-restraint fairly to be expected of him. The decision has been heavily criticized.[6] Such cases, it is said, really depend upon a claim of diminished capacity, of partial irresponsibility.[7] Provocation does not. As John Gardner says, the provocation defence 'depends on the reasonableness of the provoked person's reaction to the provocation.'[8] Andrew Ashworth makes a similar point: 'Where an individual who is congenitally incapable of exercising reasonable self-control is provoked by a petty affront, his loss of self-control must surely be ascribed to his own personality rather than to the provocation he received.'[9] These characterizations place provocation squarely within the realm of rationale-based defences. Persons who claim rationale-based defences do not rely on abnormal capacities of self-restraint and the like: they live up to the standard of a reasonable human being. By contrast, it is through the irresponsibility defences that we allow for persons, like Morgan Smith, who fail in some way to be full moral agents.[10] A rationale-based excuse is compatible with there being no diminution of the defendant, no undermining of 'their standing as fully responsible human beings, and hence their self-respect.'[11] For Gardner, an irresponsibility defence is not, or at least not entirely.[12]

[4] Now displaced in the UK by a statutory defence of 'loss of control', pursuant to the Coroners and Justice Act 2009, ss 54–56.

[5] [2001] 1 AC 146; abandoned in *A-G for Jersey v Holley* [2005] UKPC 23 and not revived by the Coroners and Justice Act 2009.

[6] e.g. J Gardner and T Macklem, 'Compassion without Respect? Nine Fallacies in *R* v. *Smith*' [2001] Crim LR 623.

[7] Doctrinally speaking, the appropriate defence was therefore diminished responsibility: Homicide Act 1957 (UK), s 2.

[8] Gardner, *Offences and Defences*, 134.

[9] A Ashworth, 'The Doctrine of Provocation' [1976] CLJ 292, 312.

[10] Note that nothing in this section is meant to suggest that agents with an irresponsibility condition cannot respond reasonably to, say, a provocation. (The point that irresponsibility need not be a status defence is touched upon in §§ 2.2 and 17.5.) The same holds for agents with a partial irresponsibility condition such as diminished responsibility.

[11] Gardner and Macklem, 'Compassion without Respect?' (n 6) 630.

[12] Gardner, *Offences and Defences*, 181–82. I take it that, in referring to self-respect, Gardner does not mean to suggest that others should *treat* the defendant with less respect. For a persuasive discussion of the relationship between respectful treatment and equality, building on the work of John Rawls, see I Carter, 'Respect and the Basis of Equality' (2011) 121 Ethics 538.

This way of putting things needs a preliminary qualification. To my mind, it would be an exaggeration to say that the provocation defence envisages a defendant who fully lives up to our expectations. If D's reaction were truly that of a reasonable person, we should not be putting D in gaol. And ordinarily we *should* be putting D in gaol. Decent people don't react to provocation by killing. Assuming that's right, it means that provocation is at best a rationale-based *partial* excuse.

For present purposes, however, we can set this aside. D overreacted. At least in paradigm cases, though, D had good reason to be angry. The key point being made by Ashworth and Gardner is that the mainstream law on provocation does not require appeal to a defendant's abnormal capacities. So the decision in *Smith* was doctrinally misguided.

Doubtless that's right. Yet it is easy to see the attraction of such cases. The pull is strongest in scenarios akin to that in *Ahluwalia*,[13] where the provocation involved a long history of abuse. One feature of 'battered woman syndrome' is the effect of that history on the defendant's ability to make rational decisions. In a sense, it explains why the defendant's moral responsibility was itself diminished. And it can do so without demeaning the defendant, at least in cases where the impairment is temporary. As such, it has some genuine excusatory force. Suppose that any decent person, when exposed to the defendant's history, would have exhibited diminished powers of self-restraint at the time of her action. In that case, the defendant did not fall short of our expectations. And to that extent, she is morally entitled to an excuse. Certainly this is not a paradigm rationale-based excuse. Neither, however, is it a simple case of partial irresponsibility. It is a hybrid excuse. Irresponsibility defences do not measure D's response against any criteria; they do not ask whether D fell short on any dimension of the reasonable person. Excuses do. Even in *Ahluwalia*.

19.1.1 Unreasonable but understandable

This thought can be expanded. Even after we carve off the irresponsibility defences, there remains an enormous domain for excusatory explanations to cover. Within that domain, the point of *rationale-based* excuses is that we understand the actor's reasons for acting: we accept that her having and acting for those reasons

[13] [1992] 4 All ER 889. (After waiting for her abusive husband to fall asleep, D got a can of petrol, poured it over his bed, and set the bed on fire.) Note that, on the facts of *Ahluwalia* itself, there was no finding that D actually suffered a 'sudden and temporary loss of control', as the legal test then required. For the purposes of this discussion, however, I assume that she did. The assumption permits a distinction to be drawn between *Ahluwalia* (the hypothetical version) and another difficult case, *Kingston* [1995] 2 AC 355 (HL). See § 19.1.3.

discloses only an imperfect virtue—a limitation, not a vice. We do not require, among the qualities expected of D, the levels of self-restraint, altruism, and the like that would have been needed for D to avoid her wrongdoing. The imperfections on show are characteristic of humans in general, or at least of humans in D's situation. They are not peculiar to D.

Granting that, however, and deferring for now mistake-based defences, we should ask whether excuses of that type *exhaust* the domain of excusatory explanations. (Gardner thinks they do: in what follows, I use his arguments as a foil.) Certainly, excusatory duress is rationale-based. But is the same true of a defence like provocation? Or, if it is, might there be a variant—let's call it 'understandable loss of self-control'—which isn't?[14] Consider the following three explanations of wrongdoing:

> *Escape*: 'I can see why she did it; she did it because she could see no other escape . . . [or] for the sake of her children, whom she thought would be the next target.'[15]
>
> *Jealousy*: 'He did it because he was so angry at the thought of his former girlfriend's being with another man.'
>
> *Doughty*:[16] 'He did it because he was so frustrated and stressed by the baby's incessant crying, because he had reached the end of his tether and could no longer cope.'

Citing *Escape*, the 'whole point' of the provocation defence, Gardner says, 'is that it depends on the *reasonableness* of the provoked person's reaction to the provocation.'[17] One can see in this the quasi-justificatory drift of Gardner's own account of excuses,[18] since the explanation looks very like a claim of self-defence. Indeed, assuming the response was 'reasonable', as Gardner puts it, and there was no mistake, self-defence would presumably be available: an odd paradigm on which to base the familiar claim to provocation.

[14] Or perhaps we should call it, 'understandable loss of temper'. Stephen Morse has expressed deep scepticism about 'lack of control' tests, arguing that excuses of this kind are better explained in terms of impaired rationality. See, e.g., S Morse, 'Against Control Tests for Criminal Responsibility' in P H Robinson, S P Garvey, and K K Ferzan (eds), *Criminal Law Conversations* (OUP 2009) 449. I am sympathetic to Morse's argument, but cannot pursue the matter here.

[15] Gardner, *Offences and Defences*, 134.

[16] *Doughty* (1986) 83 Cr App R 319.

[17] *Offences and Defences*, 134.

[18] Gardner sees excuse is a simulacrum of justification: the agent justifies not the action itself, but rather her own belief that the action was justified or the emotion that motivated it: e.g. ibid, 110, 178. For disagreement on this point, see § 19.3.

Contrast *Jealousy*. Here, the motivation is barbaric. If explanations like these qualify as provocation, it's no wonder some legislatures have moved to abolish the defence.[19] But of course they don't qualify. As Gardner points out, a reason-based version of provocation requires evaluating the explanation on offer:[20]

> 'In making an excuse one relies on the fact that one's unjustified action was taken on the strength of a justified belief or attitude or emotion, etc. An excuse for an angry action, *qua* angry, depends on the justification of the anger itself. Even in the realm of excuse, therefore, the analysis is moral and not merely causal, for the question of the justification of the anger (and hence the excuse of the angry action) is a moral question.'

Depending on the facts, then, the ex-boyfriend loses the defence. There being no betrayal, no breach of duty, his anger was unjustified. The husband coming home to find his spouse with another might be assessed differently.[21]

This analysis can admit an excuse in *Escape*. It rules *out* the explanation in *Doughty*, and so does Gardner.[22] But even if we don't call it provocation, the third case seems rather more sympathetic than the second. If D's loss of self-control was understandable in the circumstances, in that even a person with reasonable powers of self-restraint, when placed in D's situation, might have lost self-control, then it is hard to see how there is not a claim to exculpation; a claim, moreover, that need not involve the diminution of D.

Gardner demurs:[23]

> 'The question at this stage is not one of mere explanation. The question here is one of justification—that is, justification of one's becoming so angry as to lose self-control and kill, thereby excusing one's killing. It is not a matter of *why* one lost one's temper, but a matter of why one *should* have lost it. That "should" is built into the very idea of the reasonable person as a standard.'

If this is true of the rationale-based defences, it seems that understandable loss of self-control is not a rationale-based excuse. But it *is* an excusatory explanation, or a partially excusatory explanation, albeit one with some affinity to the irresponsibility defences. Built into the excuses is weakness as well as

[19] Not just the UK: also New Zealand.
[20] *Offences and Defences*, 161 (chapter co-authored with Timothy Macklem).
[21] Though see now s 55(6) of the Coroners and Justice Act 2009 (UK), which specifically rejects 'sexual infidelity' as a ground of provocation.
[22] *Offences and Defences*, 157–62.
[23] Ibid, 168.

strength. Sometimes, what a defendant does is *un*reasonable. But it may be understandable, none the less. And to that extent, the defendant's culpability may be defrayed.

Suppose that D does an unjustified wrong. Her culpability is then negatived only if she was irresponsible or had an excusatory explanation for doing that wrong. We have noted that irresponsibility defences do not measure D's response against objective criteria; they do not ask whether D fell short when measured against our expectations of a reasonable person in D's position. In terms of the irresponsibility-justification-excuse trichotomy from § 17.1, it follows that *all* explanations of unjustified wrongdoing that defray blame, and which depend at least in part on a non-relativized standard, are excusatory.[24] Rationale-based or not.

19.1.2 Relative capacities

Apart from mistake-based defences, this logical space is most likely to be populated at the boundaries of morally responsible agency; in places, one might say, where moral responsibility comes in degrees. Sometimes, we can explain why responsibility itself was diminished. *Ahluwalia*, discussed earlier, points us to one such case. Capacities can themselves be affected by events, and part of the point of that case is that even a reasonable person, exposed to the defendant's history, might exhibit diminished powers of, say, self-restraint at the time of her action. At least where such effects are temporary, to accept this is to acknowledge that the defendant's then-diminished capacities did not fall short of our expectations. And so it is to accept an excusatory explanation. Gardner may reply that persons making such a claim demean themselves, just as they do when they assert diminished responsibility.[25] Perhaps they do demean themselves. *But not in the same way.*

Scenarios like *Ahluwalia* can be excusatory, then, because and to the extent that the actor lives up to our expectations. But what are our expectations? What kinds of shortfall *can* ground blame? Obviously, our expectations are not always relativized to the capacities of each particular defendant. The explanation, 'I'm just not very brave,' discloses rather than defrays culpability for perpetrating a wrong. On the other hand, I argued in § 12.3.4 that the same does not

[24] This is not to deny that 'pure' partial irresponsibility defences are also excusatory, even though they do not depend on a non-relativized standard. See § 19.1.3.

[25] *Offences and Defences*, 181.

hold for the intellectual capacities of wrongdoers. If that's right, at least some capacities are relativized.

It seems to me that a natural way of distinguishing these two kinds of shortfall would be to deny (as I did in chapter 12) that intelligence is a *moral* characteristic, any more than blindness. But not everyone concurs. Gardner, for example, thinks that 'stupidity is a vice, not an excuse.'[26] This is not just an ad hoc matter. For Gardner, role is key. One must exhibit the qualities appropriate to one's role. Failure to do so *necessarily* shows one in a bad light:[27]

> 'The question of whether and how one's actions reflect upon one *just is* the question of whether they point to one's fitness or unfitness for whatever role one is occupying, for whatever life one is leading. So valid excuses, which prevent one's wrong actions from reflecting badly upon one, cannot conceivably invoke standards of character (or for that matter standards of skill or taste or physical or intellectual fitness[28]) which fall short of the standards of fitness for the role in which, by doing the wrong thing, one failed. In particular, those standards cannot be capped according to the capacities (be they past, present, or even future) of the person to whom the excuse is supposed to apply. For such incapacity, far from militating against unfitness, is a mode of unfitness in its own right.'

It reflects badly on me qua athlete, then, that I have a torn hamstring. But that isn't the concern of culpability judgements, which measure us *as human beings*. Of course, the law can play a constitutive role in setting minimum standards of fitness,[29] and thereby help to establish what, in our various roles, we owe to each other. Yet standards of fitness are not standards of culpability. Indeed, standards of fitness *cannot* supply an account of which incapacities are inexcusable, since the minimum conditions of fitness qua human being necessarily include the rational capacities for responsible action. Gardner himself thinks that failure to evince such capacities reflects badly on that person qua human being. One degrades oneself, he says, when claiming an irresponsibility defence.[30] Maybe so. Many things 'reflect badly' upon us, it might be said, including being stupid. But not all of them are constitutive of culpability. If that's

[26] Ibid, 26.

[27] Ibid, 131; note too, at 129, the 'automatic correlation between being unfit for the role one occupies and being shown in a bad light.'

[28] Here and elsewhere (e.g. ibid, 136), Gardner suggests that excuses require that one live up to standards that are not merely standards of moral character.

[29] Ibid, 136–37.

[30] See, e.g., at 181 (diminished responsibility).

right, the excuses—understood as the defrayers of culpability—should be relativized to at least some capacities. They should be relativized to capacities, like intelligence, where shortfalls do not constitute a moral vice.

We can't *blame* an athlete for running badly with a torn hamstring, even if we conclude she isn't much of an athlete. And suppose that D, in her role as a pool attendant, fails to observe a drowning swimmer. We may find an unjustified wrong of failing to save the swimmer. But is D culpable for that wrong? Suppose, in an unexpected allergic reaction, that she is temporarily blinded. She has failed in her role as a pool attendant, failed to exhibit the capacities the role demands. It reflects badly on her qua pool attendant. It is a blemish on her life. But it is no fault of hers.

19.1.3 Gathering and scattering: the hybrid and the partially irresponsible

Let me sum up these brief remarks. What capacities can we expect of a defendant in order to qualify for an excuse? According to Gardner, we can expect those capacities that are appropriate to D's role, including D's role as a human being (if that is aptly described as a role). For my money, though, we should relativize our expectations to D's capacities when those capacities do not undermine D's moral character; when they do not reflect a moral vice. So we should differentiate between stupidity and cowardice.[31]

A cautionary note. When we descend into detail, variations proliferate. Consider again *Doughty* and *Ahluwalia*. Doughty was not wronged by his baby. The incessant crying may have *caused* D to lose his temper and react aggressively, but it did not constitute a reason for him to do so. Doughty's excusatory explanation was not rationale-based. Ahluwalia's claim to provocation, by contrast, *was* rationale-based, albeit requiring that she be judged by reference to her own impaired capacity, rather than the capacities of an ordinary person.

I cannot explore all these refinements here. But I can add to them. Both types of cases admit of further variations. In the well-known case of *Camplin*,[32] C killed his assailant immediately after being raped. C was fifteen at the time. On appeal, the House of Lords ruled that C's age was relevant to the capacity for self-restraint that could reasonably be expected of him. The same

[31] I am grateful to Grant Lamond for suggesting this way of capturing the discussion.
[32] [1978] AC 705.

reasoning would extend to similarly-aged defendants in cases like *Doughty* and *Ahluwalia*.[33]

Being aged fifteen is not, of course, an abnormality. A more troubling case is *Kingston*.[34] K, who had paedophiliac inclinations, was invited to T's flat, apparently to discuss some business matters. Once there, K was given coffee that T had laced with disinhibiting drugs.[35] T then led K to a bedroom where a fifteen-year-old boy, also drugged, lay unconscious on the bed. K performed non-penetrative sexual acts on the boy.[36] He had no previous record of such behaviour; it was accepted that, save for being drugged unawares, he would not have acted as he did. On these facts, the House of Lords upheld K's conviction of indecent assault. His case fell outside the scope of any legally recognized defence.

K's self-restraint was impaired by his involuntary intoxication, which bears on the level of restraint that can fairly be expected of him. In this respect, *Kingston* is analogous to *Ahluwalia*. But the two cases are also very different, in that an ordinary person would presumably not have chosen to do what K did even if similarly disinhibited—whereas the appeal of Ahluwalia's case rests, in part, on the moral wrongness of the abuse to which she was responding. Any claim to exculpation in *Kingston* rests on K's understandably reduced capacities rather than on a non-relativized standard. As such, it does not involve a *hybrid* (partially rationale-based) defence. It takes us instead into the realms of a temporary, partial irresponsibility. Had *Kingston* been a prosecution for murder, the plea of diminished responsibility would have been straightforward. Yet their Lordships were rightly wary of crafting a more general, and potentially amorphous, 'involuntary disinhibition' excuse. Legally speaking, corralling such a defence would not be at all easy.[37] Fencing in provocation has been challenging enough.

Ultimately, the criminal law must remainder some of these difficulties to sentencing. My aim in this section has not been to resolve them but to highlight their existence; and, more generally, to draw attention to a category of excuses that is not purely rationale-based. Within this rather broad category,[38] culpability can be defrayed on a variety of grounds. Some of those grounds overlap with the rationale-based excuses. But they are also distinctive, in as much as

[33] And what if a defendant has greater than normal powers of self-restraint? But perhaps a legal system should forego such niceties on pragmatic grounds.

[34] [1995] 2 AC 355 (HL). See also § 8.5.2; G R Sullivan, 'Making Excuses' in *Harm and Culpability* 131.

[35] Apparently D was slipped three different kinds of drug, which were likely to affect judgment, consciousness, and memory.

[36] The facts came to light because T filmed K's actions in the bedroom and subsequently sought to blackmail him, whereupon K went to the police.

[37] *Kingston* [1995] 2 AC 355, 375–77.

[38] Further subdivision seems possible, but lies beyond the scope of this book.

they are sensitive to certain of the defendant's own limitations. And in that aspect, they are allied to defences of partial irresponsibility. What unites this category is the thought that not all of our personal failings are the stuff of blame, let alone punishment: even when they are abnormal. Recognizing that is not so much a matter of respect as it is a demand of humanity.

19.2 Mistakes in criminal-law defences

The final category of defences identified in § 17.1 is mistake-based. In this book, I have used the terminology of 'mistake' loosely, to include other forms of epistemic error. At least in the context of defences, though, the scope of mistakes is not *entirely* open-ended. Suppose that I am in a jungle, where I see what I think is a dangerous animal about to attack.[39] I shoot and injure the creature. Unfortunately, the 'creature' turns out to be a human being, stumbling about lost. In such a case, there is no defence of mistake. I am not guilty of assault or malicious wounding, simply because I lack mens rea.

As with law, so with morality. Mistaken φing rules out choice-based culpability. It falls to be considered under negligence. It may or may not be culpable. But whether it is culpable is not a question for the exculpatory defences. By contrast, mistake-based *defences* are parasitic. They involve mistakes that concern the rationale-based elements of another defence:[40] where, if the mistaken belief were true, the defendant's *choice* to φ would have been justified or excused.

Or so things used to be. A funny thing happened on the way to the twenty-first century. In 1976, *Halsbury's Laws of England* had this to say of mistake as a defence:[41]

> '[W]here the defendant intended the prohibited act and asserts that he was mistaken as to facts which, had they existed, would afford justification or excuse, the general rule is that his mistake affords him a defence only if it was honestly made and there were reasonable grounds for making it.'

By 1988, however, the classic statement of the fourth edition was tersely disclaimed:[42]

[39] See, e.g., *State Government of Madhya Pradesh v Rangaswami* AIR 1952 Nag 268, 1951 Cri LJ 1191 (tiger); *Waryam Singh v Emperor* AIR 1926 Lah 554 (ghost).

[40] That is to say, they concern the elements of a rationale-based defence or the rationale-based elements of a hybrid defence.

[41] 11 Halsbury's Laws (4th ed) para 21.

[42] 1988 Cumulative Supplement (vol 11, para 21).

'The reasonableness of the defendant's belief is material to the question of whether the belief was held by him at all; if it was in fact held, its unreasonableness is irrelevant....'

The revision in *Halsbury's* was predicated on two appellate decisions, *Williams* and *Beckford*.[43] Those decisions are specific to the common law. Yet they raise important structural issues concerning the role of mistakes in criminal law more generally. Here are three ways of thinking about mistakes:

(i) that mistakes deny mens rea;
(ii) that mistakes can part-constitute rationale-based defences (and their hybrid counterparts); and
(iii) that mistakes going to rationale-based defences are a distinct ground of defence.

In what follows, it is contended that mistakes going to rationale-based defences represent a distinct type of defence. They are different in kind from the denials of mens rea with which they were assimilated in *Williams* and *Beckford*. Neither are they, morally speaking, to be assimilated with the underlying defence that each mistake concerns. Given that they are a distinct ground of exculpation, moreover, it will be argued (contra *Williams* and *Beckford*) that there are persuasive reasons why defensive mistakes should be subject to an additional constraint of reasonableness.

19.2.1 A little bit of history

At common law, it used to be routinely accepted that mistakes of fact could have either of two different effects, depending on whether the mistake related to an actus reus or defence element. That distinction relied, in turn, upon the basic division, drawn in § 2.1 and defended in § 17.6, between offences and defences.[44] We noted above that some mistakes deny mens rea. This possibility was at the heart of the contentious 1975 decision in *DPP v Morgan*,[45]

[43] *Williams* (1983) [1987] 3 All ER 411 (CA); *Beckford v R* [1988] 1 AC 130 (PC).

[44] In practice, lawyers tend to call any ground of acquittal a 'defence', so care is required here. The 'defence' of alibi, for example, denies that the defendant satisfied the physical elements of the actus reus at all. In terms of substantive criminal law doctrine, it is not a defence. By contrast, supervening defences—notably, for current purposes, the rationale-based and hybrid defences—deny neither actus reus nor mens rea. Rather, they seek to avoid liability by reference to additional facts, facts extraneous to the actus reus.

[45] [1976] AC 182, 214.

concerning the law of rape. The actus reus of rape required, *inter alia*, sexual intercourse with a person who does not consent.[46] As the House of Lords ruled, the mens rea requirements of that offence must therefore be satisfied with respect to the circumstances constituting non-consent, and not merely to sexual intercourse:[47]

> 'Once one has accepted, what seems to me abundantly clear, that the prohibited act in rape is non-consensual sexual intercourse, and that the guilty state of mind is an intention to commit it, it seems to me to follow as a matter of inexorable logic that there is no room either for a "defence" of honest belief or mistake . . . . Either the prosecution proves that the accused had the requisite intent, or it does not.'

Suppose, in other words, that the mens rea standard for rape were intention.[48] An intentional offender must believe that consent is absent.[49] In such a context, there is no 'defence' of mistake about consent. Rather, D's mistake is a simple denial of mens rea.[50] It leads, in other words, to inadvertent performance of the actus reus. In the context of choice-based mens rea standards, it entails acquittal regardless whether D's mistake is reasonable—it need only be genuine.

Contrast mistakes that purport to found a supervening defence; that is, mistakes which generate a defence without denying any requirement of mens rea. Historically, the common law required that the latter be reasonable.[51] This was clearly understood in *Morgan* itself. Notwithstanding that their Lordships held (rightly) that the element of non-consent was part of the actus reus of rape,[52] they expressly left undisturbed the requirement that mistakes going to supervening defences, such as self-defence, must be reasonable.[53]

[46] Or who has withdrawn it if given: *Kaitamaki v R* [1985] AC 147 (PC).

[47] *Morgan* [1976] AC 182, 214.

[48] Which it was not, even in 1976: advertent recklessness sufficed with respect to the victim's non-consent. *Morgan* was itself displaced by the Sexual Offences Act 2003 (UK), which effectively imposes a mens rea requirement for rape of negligence. For discussion of why that may be appropriate in the context of sexual offences, see § 3.3.

[49] On the translational mens rea requirements for circumstances, see §§ 3.4, 15.1.3; also *Simester and Sullivan*, §§ 5.1(v), 5.2(iii).

[50] At the time, this point had been made explicitly in *Smith* [1974] 1 QB 354, 360.

[51] Early judicial pronouncements to this effect abound: 'As a general rule an honest and reasonable belief in a state of facts which, if they existed, would make the defendant's acts innocent affords an excuse for doing what would otherwise be an offence' (*Proudman v Dayman* (1941) 67 CLR 536, 540–41); see also the numerous cases collected in *Albert v Lavin* [1982] AC 546.

[52] Overruling the Court of Appeal on this point: below, § 19.4.2.

[53] Lord Hailsham explicitly acknowledged (*Morgan* [1976] AC 182, at 214) a distinction between 'cases where there is a special "defence" like self-defence or provocation, and cases where the issue relates to the primary intention . . . .' See also at 238 (Lord Fraser), 202–203 (Lord Cross). (The defendant's conviction was in any event upheld, on the ground that his claim of mistake was not plausible.)

Thus *Halsbury*'s pronouncement in 1976 was accurate. Even in the wake of *Morgan*, the common law continued to distinguish between mistakes concerning the actus reus elements of an offence and those going to supervening defences.[54]

But not for long. In *Beckford*, the victim, who was unarmed, was shot when he had his hands in the air and was begging the defendant, a policeman, not to shoot him. Constable Beckford apparently believed that the victim was firing upon him: at issue on appeal was whether an action taken in self-defence could be exculpated where it arose from an unreasonable mistake. The Privy Council advised that it could, and that the accused's conviction should be quashed. The Judicial Committee began by accepting that mistakes raising a supervening defence were traditionally required to be reasonably made:[55]

> 'There can be no doubt that prior to the decision of the House of Lords in *DPP v Morgan* the whole weight of authority supported the view that it was an essential element of self-defence not only that the accused believed that he was being attacked or in imminent danger of being attacked but also that such belief was based on reasonable grounds.'

Rather than being consistent with extant law, however, *Morgan* was thought to have altered it fundamentally.[56] The Privy Council cited in particular the 1983 decision in *Williams*, a case in which the defendant purported to come to the defence of another person whom he wrongly believed was under attack. In fact, the 'attacker' was a citizen effecting a lawful arrest. Yet in *Williams*, the Court of Appeal had brought D's mistake within the ambit of *Morgan* by redefining the actus reus of assault:[57]

> '"Assault" . . . is an act by which the defendant, intentionally or recklessly, applies *unlawful* force to the complainant . . . . The mental element necessary to constitute guilt is the intent to apply unlawful force to the victim. We do not believe that the mental element can be substantiated by simply showing an intent to apply force and no more.'

[54] *Albert v Lavin* [1982] AC 546, 639; G Williams, 'Offences and Defences' (1982) 2 Legal Studies 233, 249.

[55] *Beckford* [1988] 1 AC 130, 141.

[56] [1988] 1 AC 130, 143, 145.

[57] *Williams* (1983) [1987] 3 All ER 411, 413–14 (emphasis added).

On that basis, D's mistake, going to a justification, resulted in his actions being perceived to be lawful and, in turn, his acquittal *for lack of mens rea*. *Beckford* adopted that reasoning—and extended it beyond assault:[58]

> '[I]t is an essential element of all crimes of violence that the violence or threat of violence should be unlawful . . . . If then a genuine belief, albeit without reasonable grounds, is a defence to rape because it negatives the necessary intention, so also must a genuine belief in facts which if true would justify self-defence be a defence to a crime of personal violence because the belief negatives the intent to act unlawfully.'

By drawing a parallel with consent in rape, the Privy Council concluded that the common-law test for self-defence is now whether D uses proportionate force in such circumstances as D honestly (even if unreasonably) believes exist.[59] And so we ended the twentieth century other than where we began.

19.3 What *type* of defence?

One could read a decision like *Beckford* as speaking only to the law of self-defence. Doing so would align self-defence doctrine with the law of various other common-law jurisdictions,[60] while leaving open the question whether mistakes going to other supervening defences must be reasonable. But that reading would not be true to the logic of the decision, which extends to all mistaken justifications.[61] Neither would it be faithful to the decision's underlying rationale, or to the structural issues *Beckford* raises. In § 17.2.1 we made the point that the doctrinal defence categories cut across their underlying normative counterparts. Nowhere is this more true than in the context

[58] [1988] 1 AC 130, 144.

[59] [1988] 1 AC 130, 144–45.

[60] See, e.g., s 48 of the Crimes Act 1961 (NZ) (below in the text); contrast, e.g., Indian Penal Code 1860, s 79 (read together with s 52).

[61] As it happens, the 1988 Halsbury's revision went too far in holding that mistakes going to *all* supervening defences (or at least, all rationale-based defences) need not be reasonable. Because *Beckford* was restricted to mistakes going to the lawfulness of the defendant's actions, it has no application to mistakes relating to a rationale-based excuse such as duress. Suppose that D mistakenly believes that T has threatened to kill him unless he, D, seriously injures V. Even if D's belief were true, it would not point to facts making D's action lawful. At common law, mistakes in duress must be reasonable: *Hasan* [2005] 2 AC 467 (HL); confirming *Graham* [1982] 1 All ER 801 (CA).

of mistakes. Consider, for example, section 48 of the Crimes Act 1961 (New Zealand):[62]

> **48 Self-defence and defence of another**
> Everyone is justified in using, in the defence of himself or another, such force as, in the circumstances as he believes them to be, it is reasonable to use.

Constable Beckford's mistake falls squarely within the terms of the section 48 defence. But morally speaking, his claim is *not* one of justified self-defence. It is a claim of mistake. More specifically, it is a claim that, if we deem his belief about the circumstances to be true, he *would have been* acting in justified self-defence. In fact, he was not. This is not a case where the mistake brought him within a right to self-defence, notwithstanding that the wording of section 48 might give this impression. Rather, the putative right of self-defence is parasitic upon his mistake.[63] And because of that, there is no justification—and no right—of self-defence in play here. Beckford's victim is entitled to fight back; third parties knowing the truth of the matter should side with his victim too. In terms of the underlying rationales, what should be at issue here is not the law of self-defence but the law of mistakes—in particular, the law of mistaken justifications.[64] This is so even in cases where a defendant's mistake is reasonably induced by the victim's own conduct, so that civil liability may not follow.[65] Albeit that D's *mistake* may be a justified, his *action* is not. It may be resisted by the victim and better-informed bystanders. D acts for all-things-considered defeated reasons.

Kent Greenawalt disagrees.[66] He points to the case of *People v Young*,[67] the facts of which were very similar to those in *Williams*:[68]

[62] Cp. Criminal Justice and Immigration Act 2008 (UK), s 76(3): 'The question whether the degree of force used by D was reasonable in the circumstances is to be decided by reference to the circumstances as D believed them to be . . . .'

[63] Which is why it must also be shown that, assuming the believed circumstances actually existed, Beckford's response was proportionate.

[64] A point seen clearly in s 79 of the Indian Penal Code 1860, and in the original 1837 draft.

[65] See, e.g., *Courvoisier v Raymond* 47 P 284 (Colo. 1896). An analogy might be drawn here with the distinction between self-defence and necessity, discussed in § 18.3: reasonable mistakes of this kind are astute to the victim's agency. While they do not justify D's response, it may be fair that the victim should bear their cost.

[66] So too does Victor Tadros: *Criminal Responsibility* (OUP 2005) § 10.4.

[67] 183 NE 2d 319 (NY 1962).

[68] K Greenawalt, 'The Perplexing Borders of Justification and Excuse' (1984) 84 Columbia LR 1897, 1919.

> 'Young came upon two middle-aged men beating and struggling with a youth. Reasonably believing the youth was being unlawfully assaulted, Young went to his rescue, pulling on or punching at the seeming assailants. They turned out to be plain clothes detectives trying to make an arrest for disorderly conduct.'

In Greenawalt's view,[69]

> 'Young is to be praised, not blamed, for what he did, and members of society would wish that others faced with similar situations requiring instant judgment would act as Young did. A moral assessment of Young's act would treat it as justified.'

That assessment, in turn, casts doubt on the link between D's being justified and the rights of others to assist or resist D. But Greenawalt's characterization of Young's 'act' conflates two different descriptions of Young's conduct. Young is to be praised for what he *tried* to do: he tried to resist an assault; but not for what he *did*, which was to resist a lawful arrest. His mistake was justified, being (let us concede) a reasonable inference from the available evidence. But that merely goes to his culpability. It does not establish that he did the right thing.

To my mind, Gardner gets this broadly right when he asserts that 'whether the agent was excused by her mistakes depends on whether her mistakes were justified . . . .'[70] Yet even that is too strong, in as much as mistakes themselves can sometimes be excused. D's mistake is *justified* whenever it is rationally grounded in the evidence to hand, including any reasonably available evidence to which D should have adverted. When D's mistake is not so grounded, however, it need not reflect badly upon her; it need not arise from a moral vice. A mistake might, for instance, be explained by D's being (understandably) distracted following news of a family tragedy. Or it may be reasonable to overlook something when under considerable stress.[71] This is to disagree with Gardner's more general account:[72]

[69] Ibid, 1919–20.
[70] *Offences and Defences*, 228.
[71] See § 12.3.1.
[72] *Offences and Defences*, 110. For a different type of counterexample, suppose that A is a sophisticated legal academic. She is threatened with the murder of her children unless she participates in an attack upon a policeman. Because she has been thinking about such problems, A realizes that her participation would be unjustified. It would be extraordinary if that realization were to cost her any claim to excuse.

> '[T]he structure of excuse [including mistake-based defences] derives from the structure of justification. To excuse an action is not, of course, to justify that action. Rather, one justifies one's belief that the action was justified.'

Not necessarily. Sometimes one's erroneous belief is merely excused.[73]

We should not see excuses as a simulacrum of justifications. But we *should* see mistake-based defences as a simulacrum of the rationale-based defences that they subserve.[74] Sometimes they are made for good reasons. Even when unjustified, however, they too can involve the defendant in offering up her explanation for evaluative assessment, claiming that she exhibited no shortfall of moral characteristics, no deficiency of moral virtue, below what we would expect of an ordinary, decent person in like circumstances.[75]

19.4 On the merits

Whether justified or excused, defensive mistakes are not to be assimilated with the rationale-based defences themselves.[76] Neither are they like primary mistakes that lead a defendant to φ inadvertently. That makes them a distinct type of defence. But it does not resolve the key question that *Beckford* raises. *Should* defensive mistakes be held to a standard of reasonableness, especially in offences for which negligence does not satisfy the mens rea requirement? We turn to that question now.

19.4.1 Emergencies and emotions

One argument for allowing defences like self-defence to be predicated upon unreasonable mistakes is developed by Jeremy Horder.[77] As Horder points out, justifications and excuses often arise in highly charged environments involving considerable pressure, like the scenario faced by Constable Beckford.[78] For Horder, the inference from negligence to culpability in such cases is

[73] And, of course, sometimes it is not even excused—as when it is unreasonable. Cp. *Beckford* itself. See also the discussion in § 12.3.3.

[74] And, to the extent that they involve rationale-based exculpation, the hybrid defences too.

[75] See, more generally, § 12.3.

[76] See esp. § 17.4.1.

[77] J Horder, 'Cognition, Emotion and Criminal Responsibility' (1990) 106 LQR 469.

[78] This is not a defining feature of justifications (cp. the facts of *Re A (Children)*): §§ 18.4–5.

unwarranted, because it fails to allow for the heightened emotions that the situation itself generates:[79]

> '[Negligence] is not culpable where the urgent desire in question was of a kind which ethically well-disposed agents might themselves have experienced as dictating that immediate priority be given to the kind of action in satisfaction of the desire that the defendants took, and not to action based on rational considerations.'

Horder suggests that emotions such as fear and compassion are insufficiently accommodated by orthodox standards of negligence. Especially in emergencies, such emotions should at least sometimes be permitted to displace an actor's rational considerations without leading to a finding of guilt.

One might worry about the rule of law here. It seems undesirable, even in highly pressurized situations, that the law should allow emotions a free rein in conduct. In cases of provocation we put the 'reasonable man' in gaol. And that, as I said before, is where he should be.[80] Compassion does not entitle one to kill another, even if that other consents.[81] Maybe the legislators have got that last one wrong. But resolving controversies about what kinds of reasons a killer is permitted to act upon is part of *their* job.[82] It is not something delegable to the vagaries of individual preference.[83]

We need not dwell upon that concern, however, because it does not go to the core of Horder's thesis. Nothing in his argument requires that the defendant's motivations should render her conduct justified: the main focus is on when a defendant may properly be regarded as *culpable*. And on that count, the difficulty is that Horder has failed to do justice to negligence itself. He analyses orthodox, 'objective' approaches to negligence as asking whether,[84]

> 'Even if defendants did not know that there was a risk of wrongdoing occurring as a result of their conduct, were there facts from which they could reasonably have inferred that the risk was present?'

[79] Horder, 'Cognition, Emotion' (n 77) 482.
[80] Above, § 19.1.
[81] *Rutherford* [1947] JC 1, 5–6.
[82] See § 2.1ff.
[83] See, too, §§ 12.2, 13.4.2.
[84] Horder, 'Cognition, Emotion' (n 77) 481.

This burdens the negligence standard with too little sophistication. The 'objectivist' asks other questions too, including whether it was reasonable to run the risk. We usually exculpate a prima facie 'negligent' mistake because it was not unreasonable in the circumstances: because the defendant's mistake was justified by the available evidence, or because the mistake (albeit unjustified) does not reflect a moral vice on her part. As we saw in chapter 12, when we examine negligence we evaluate a defendant's conduct in the light of certain expectations about her dispositions and beliefs. Those dispositions *include* compassion and self-preservation. It is perfectly reasonable to feel fear, and doing so need not reflect badly on the defendant. Even more to the point, our expectations about the defendant's beliefs are also sensitive to the circumstances. This is why, as Bernard Williams once remarked, it is sometimes reasonable to react precipitously.[85] When in peril, one may be justified in truncating further enquiries. That isn't legal news. In *Cordas v Peerless Transportation Co.*, for example, D was confronted with the immediate prospect that he 'would suffer the loss of his brains'—a future that appropriately pre-empted further consideration.[86] Contrary to Horder's surmise, the legal test of reasonableness is not 'judged from the rational perspective of the cold light of day.' When Horder suggests that the negligence in the passage quoted earlier 'is not culpable', he misses the point that it is not negligence at all.

19.4.2 Incongruity

Glanville Williams mounts a different attack. In his view, it is 'intellectually incongruous' to require defensive mistakes to be reasonable when we do not require the same of mistakes going to offence elements.[87] Williams suggests that there is no sensible distinction between Jim, who shoots his wife believing her to be a rabbit, and Bob, who shoots his wife thinking she is a burglar about to attack:[88]

[85] B A O Williams, *Ethics and the Limits of Philosophy* (Harvard UP 1985) 185; cp. Horder, 'Cognition, Emotion' (n 77) 481.

[86] 27 NYS 2d 198, 199 (1941). (D, a taxi driver, leapt from his vehicle when an uninvited passenger boarded the taxi and 'immediately advised him "to stand not upon the order of his going but go at once," and added finality to his command by an appropriate gesture with a pistol addressed to his sacroiliac.' The taxi ran on and injured a pedestrian. D was held not to be negligent.) Holmes J once commented that 'detached reflection cannot be demanded in the presence of an uplifted knife': *Brown v United States* 256 US 335, 343 (1921). More prosaically, compare *Wood v Richards* (1977) 65 Cr App Rep 300; Williams, *TBCL*, 90.

[87] Williams, 'Offences and Defences' (n 54) 242.

[88] Williams, *TBCL*, 138.

> 'An acquaintance of mine shot his wife in the shrubbery, believing she was a rabbit.[89] (Fortunately he only shot her in the leg.) This was a mistake as to a definitional fact (since the offences against the person are confined to action against a human being), and he could not have been convicted of any offence, even if gross negligence had been established. But if he had shot his wife in the dark in the woodshed, thinking she was a robber about to attack, he could, theoretically, be convicted of anything from murder downwards according to circumstances, if his mistake had been accounted unreasonable. Is this distinction sensible?'

We saw in § 17.6, however, that a meaningful distinction *can* be drawn between these types of cases. Bob's deliberately shooting another person is a pro tanto wrong, and he is on notice that he needs good reasons for doing so. The case is fundamentally, structurally different from that of Jim. What Jim understands himself to be doing involves no pro tanto wrong. Jim needs no further reasons for doing it. On this ground alone, Williams's assimilation of the two cases is unconvincing.

For much the same reason, defensive mistakes are not exposed to the traditional academic objection to negligence, that punishment is morally unjustified unless a defendant 'has in his mind the idea of harm to someone.'[90] One of the many tasks of this book has been to contradict that proposition. But even if we were to grant it, it is irrelevant to mistakes supporting defences. Bob has precisely that idea in his mind, and his case is thus disanalogous to that of Jim.

There is some irony here. In time, *Morgan* has led to a more lenient law of defensive mistakes, but it was really a decision about the mens rea of rape—and a controversial one. The decision was subject to stringent academic criticism, on the basis that it allowed unreasonable mistakes about the victim's consent to deny criminal liability for rape:[91] thereby tilting English law too far in favour of defendants, and failing to protect victims in the manner it should. However, in terms of legal doctrine, their Lordships' options were limited. Negligence has never been available as a mens rea option at common law.[92] The Court's choice was therefore between (i) finding that offenders must be subjectively reckless

[89] Comparable cases are a staple of the Indian treatises: e.g. *State Government of Madhya Pradesh v Rangaswami* AIR 1952 Nag 268, 1951 Cri LJ 1191 (tiger).

[90] J W C Turner, 'The Mental Element in Crimes at Common Law' in *The Modern Approach to Criminal Law* (1945) 195, 205ff; the formulation (which Hart criticizes) is by Hart, *Punishment and Responsibility*, 145ff.

[91] See, e.g., J Temkin, *Rape and the Legal Process* (Sweet & Maxwell 1987) 76ff.

[92] *Sweet v Parsley* [1970] AC 132, 162–65 (HL). For extra-judicial discussion, see P Devlin, *Samples of Lawmaking* (OUP 1962) 67–82.

with respect to their victim's non-consent, and (ii) denying that non-consent was an element of the pro tanto offence at all: that is, holding that consent was instead a *defence* element, wherefore a negligence standard would apply. The latter path was the one taken by the Court of Appeal.[93] But the House was correct to reject it. There is no general duty not to have consensual sex. Consent is, thus, not a ground for making an exception: in circumstances where consent is present, there is simply no pro tanto wrong to justify or defend.[94]

On the other hand, the legislative reform of 2003 was certainly welcome.[95] In terms of criminalization, the mens rea requirement for non-consent elements in sexual offences *should* be negligence. This is not to deny the need for criminal law to ensure that actors receive fair warning about their potential criminal liability. Negligence is rarely an appropriate mens rea standard for serious offences. People ought to be given sufficient *ex ante* notice about the risk of criminality, and that notice is prima facie lacking when they act inadvertently. However, requirements of notice within the criminal law can be met in different ways. In the context of other-regarding sexual activity, that notice is inherent. Adequate warning that consent is implicated arises, in itself, from the choice to engage in such activity.[96] Sometimes, negligence is the right call.

19.4.3 Middle ground?

Williams is not done yet. Even if negligence is a sufficiently sensitive moral standard, one that can intelligibly be demanded of mistakes going to defences and not offences, he asks why should we make such a demand?[97]

[93] *R v Morgan* [1976] AC 185 (CA). The Court of Appeal analogized the case to that of *Tolson* (1889) 23 QBD 168 (CCR), where, on a charge of bigamy, the Court held that the defendant's reasonable belief that her first husband was dead is a defence to bigamy. As in *Morgan*, this should have been treated as a denial of mens rea (and, as in *Morgan*, a mens rea standard of negligence might be appropriate).

[94] At any rate, none recognizable to the general law. Michelle Madden Dempsey and Jonathan Herring have argued that even consensual acts of sexual penetration call for justification, in virtue of the fact that they constitute forceful entry into the body of another person, thereby generating non-trivial risks of harm to the penetrated person: M Madden Dempsey and J Herring, 'Why Sexual Penetration Requires Justification' (2007) 27 OJLS 467. Accepting that such risks exist, their argument shows there is a *reason* not to do such acts. But it does not show there is a *duty* not to do them. And even if it did, this would not be the same duty as the one articulated by legislators in the modern prohibition of rape under the Sexual Offences Act 2003. (Indeed, the authors are careful not to claim that sexual penetration is a pro tanto rape.)

[95] Sexual Offences Act 2003, s 1, which effectively imposes a mens rea standard of negligence. Manslaughter by (gross) negligence is the isolated exception.

[96] See § 3.3.

[97] *TBCL*, 137–38.

> '[I]t is not murder to shoot and kill another by negligence, however gross. But if a person kills another in the convinced but mistaken and unreasonable belief that he himself is about to be killed by the other, he is theoretically guilty of murder, even though on the facts as he believed them to be he would not have been guilty of any crime. Is this not a harsh rule?'

In other words, granted that there is a logical distinction, is there a suitable moral one?

Unpicking Williams's question, we find two points. The implicit point is that there is a moral difference between intentional commission of the actus reus *simpliciter*—without defence—and intentional commission of the actus reus accompanied by a negligent defensive mistake. That difference counts against requiring defences to be reasonably perceived. Indeed, had we a highly nuanced criminal legal system, it is a difference we might well accommodate. And as it happens, a nuanced possibility of this kind is available specifically within the law of homicide. We could recognize a partial defence to murder, reducing the conviction to manslaughter and a discretionary sentence. There is much to be said for doing just that. However, this possibility is ad hoc. Unlike homicide offences, most forms of wrongdoing in the common law are not regulated by a hierarchy of variously severe offences, and it is not realistic to argue that they should be. For the majority of crimes, unreasonable mistakes in defence must either be irrelevant or support a complete defence.

So we return to Williams's question. Which path should we take? In my view, negligent mistakes denying a mens rea requirement of (say) recklessness *are* in morally different case from those claimed in defence, and the difference is sufficient to warrant conviction in the latter instance but not the former. This is plainly to disagree with Williams, whose tolerance for the latter seems indulgent:[98]

> 'If the defendant, believing that he has to act urgently in self-defence, kills or wounds a person who is completely innocent, this must be accounted a tragic accident, and it is pointless to punish for it.'

Indeed, Williams views this case even more benignly than he does negligence *simpliciter*:[99]

[98] G Williams, *Textbook of Criminal Law* (1st edn, Stevens 1978) 452.
[99] Williams, 'Offences and Defences' (n 54) 243.

> 'It would be perfectly possible, and would indeed be rational and proper, to say that even if negligently hitting someone is an offence, a person who believes he is being attacked is entitled to act on that belief, whether the belief is negligent or not.'

Morally different, of course, does not mean morally worse. But it strikes me that morality militates in the direction opposite to that suggested by Williams. The reason is grounded in the structural distinction defended in this book between offences and defences. A defendant who relies upon a supervening defence chooses to commit a pro tanto offence. As Lord Diplock put it, and unlike the case where the actus reus is perpetrated inadvertently, 'There is nothing unreasonable in requiring a citizen to take reasonable care to ascertain the facts relevant to his avoiding doing a prohibited act.'[100] By contrast with Jim,[101] who is inadvertently negligent, Bob recognizes that he is inflicting harm, and so is on notice that his action requires justification. This distinction underlies our requirement of Bob, but not of Jim,[102] that his mistakes be reasonable. Effectively (and unlike Jim), Bob is asserting a liberty, in the circumstances, to inflict harm *deliberately*: it does not seem too much to ask for reasonable ascertainment of those circumstances.

19.4.4 Taking sides?

One might think that the foregoing argument is stronger in the context of necessity, where the defendant is not responding to the agency of her victim, than it is in self-defence, where paradigmatically it is the victim who has put the defendant in danger. But that thought overlooks the fact that mistaken self-defence is *not*, morally speaking, a claim of self-defence, or indeed of justified action at all. Bob's wife has not put him in danger. Bob only thinks she has. From the perspective of criminal-law trial verdicts, there may be no harm in assimilating reasonably mistaken self-defence with self-defence properly-so-called; but as we remarked in § 19.3, criminal-law theorists should not be misled by

[100] *Sweet v Parsley* [1970] AC 132, 165; cited in *Morgan* [1976] AC 182, 203 (Lord Cross), 221 (Lord Simon), 233 (Lord Edmund-Davies).

[101] Above, § 19.4.2.

[102] Having argued in chapters 11–12 that one can be culpable for negligence, I accept that Jim may deserve blame for shooting his wife. But we have seen that there are good reasons why we should hesitate before criminalizing such cases: notably, the need for fair warning (see § 3.3) and its impact upon freedom (§ 3.3.1; see also §§ 12.4.1, 14.3.1). Even if Jim's action warrants punishment, that does not establish the case for general offences of negligently harming others.

that assimilation into thinking that cases of the former involve claims of justified action.[103]

Or indeed claims of *justified* mistake. An important payoff of unpicking the relationship between defensive mistakes and the substantive defences to which they pertain is that Bob may still be exculpated if his mistake is merely excused, as it might be when induced by a powerful emotion like fear; or if it is caused by involuntary intoxication. Like negligence more generally, adjudicating a plea of defensive mistake requires us to evaluate the grounds of the defendant's mistake. That was the lesson of chapter 12. Bob's unjustified mistake may be excused when, in making that mistake, Bob exhibited no moral vice. And just like the result in *Cordas*, mistakes passing that test, including mistakes induced by fear, should be accounted reasonable.

Yet we should extend latitude to the defendant no further than that. If one rationale for legislative displacement of *Morgan* was to strike a better balance between the interests of attacker and victim, it is even more relevant where the attacker is aware of the mischief. We noted in § 19.4.2 that the argument for criminalizing negligent rape rests,[104] in part, on the thought that what the negligent rapist does *advertently* gives him good reason to be on his guard; hence the law should acquit for only reasonable mistakes about the victim's consent. The pro tanto offender, likewise, has good reason to guard against mistakes. If anything, he has better reason than the negligent rapist, in as much as his advertent action looks closer to an offence than sexual intercourse *simpliciter*. The words of Lord Simon in 1976 remain just as apposite now:[105]

> 'It would hardly seem just to fob off a victim of a savage assault with such comfort as he could derive from knowing that his injury was caused by a belief, however absurd, that he was about to attack the accused.'

In *Beckford*, the victim was an unarmed man who had his hands in the air and was pleading for his life. He was deliberately shot three times. The defendant then claimed a belief that he was being fired upon—a belief that was found by the jury to be unreasonable—and walked from his appeal a free man. It is wrong to regard this as a 'tragic accident'. It was a culpable killing.

[103] Albeit they involve counterfactual claims about the justification of D's action had her beliefs been correct.
[104] Compare Horder, 'Cognition, Emotion' (n 77) 475–77.
[105] *Morgan* [1976] AC 182, 221.

19.5 At last

Beckford nicely illustrates the help that decent theory can offer to the criminal law. The case was not simply one of mistaken and inadvertent commission of an offence, and to approach it as did the Privy Council was inappropriate. The central question in *Beckford* was not whether *Morgan* warranted the killer's acquittal, because it did not. Rather, at issue was whether the law *should* permit rationale-based defences like self-defence to be mounted on the back of unreasonable mistakes. But the Court never got to first base on that question. It is easy to lose sight of the underlying issues when your structures are wrong.

And that is what this book has been about: the fundamental shape and structure of the criminal law; together with the shape and structure of the moral judgements it reflects. As a blaming institution, the criminal law works better when its foundations tracks those of morality. Inevitably, it lacks the same nuance. We cannot, should not, expect moral precision. But we can, and should, try to get its basic distinctions morally right.

Index

Figures are indicated by *f* following the page number